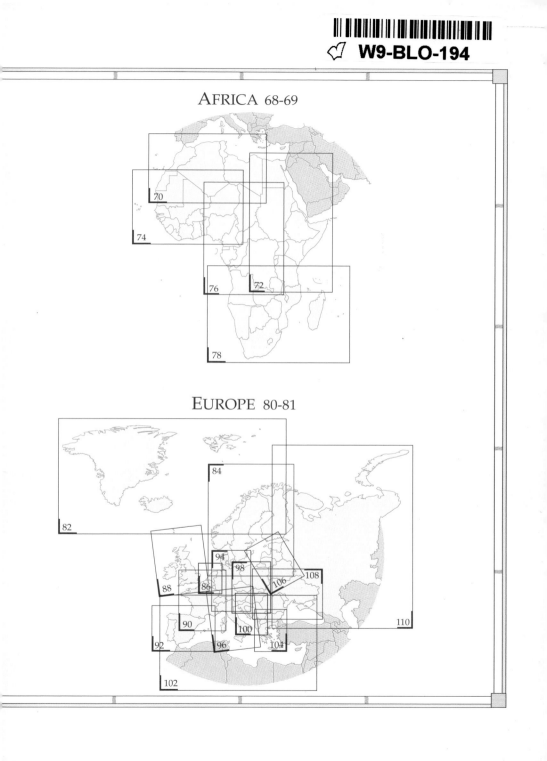

AFRICA 68-69

EUROPE 80-81

ESSENTIAL
WORLD
ATLAS

LONDON, NEW YORK, DELHI, PARIS,
MUNICH AND JOHANNESBURG

LONDON, NEW YORK, DELHI, PARIS,
MUNICH AND JOHANNESBURG

FOR THE SECOND EDITION
EDITOR-IN-CHIEF Andrew Heritage
SENIOR MANAGING ART EDITOR Philip Lord
SENIOR CARTOGRAPHIC MANAGER David Roberts
MANAGING EDITOR Punita Singh
SENIOR CARTOGRAPHIC EDITOR Simon Mumford
PROJECT CARTOGRAPHERS James Anderson, Alok Pathak
PROJECT LEADER Uma Bhattacharya
PROJECT EDITOR Razia Grover
PROJECT DESIGNERS Rachana Bhattacharya, Karen Gregory, Sabyasachi Kundu
SYSTEMS COORDINATOR Phil Rowles
PRODUCTION Michelle Thomas

DORLING KINDERSLEY CARTOGRAPHY

PROJECT CARTOGRAPHY AND DESIGN
Julia Lunn, Julie Turner

CARTOGRAPHERS
James Anderson, Roger Bullen, Martin Darlison,
Simon Mumford, John Plumer, Peter Winfield

DESIGN
Katy Wall

INDEX-GAZETTEER
Natalie Clarkson, Ruth Duxbury, Margaret Hynes, Margaret Stevenson

PRODUCTION
Hilary Stephens, David Proffit

EDITORIAL DIRECTION
Andrew Heritage

ART DIRECTION
Chez Picthall

First American edition 1997. Reprinted with revisions 1998. Second Edition 2001
Previously published as the Concise World Atlas

Published in the United States by Dorling Kindersley Publishing, Inc., 95 Madison Avenue,
New York, New York 10016
Copyright © 1997, 1998, 2001 Dorling Kindersley Limited

see our complete catalog at
www.dk.com

A CIP catalog record for this book is available from the Library of Congress

ISBN 0-7894-7989-3

Reproduced by GRB, Italy
Printed and bound in Spain by Artes Gráficas Toledo

D.L. TO: 343 - 2001

This book is supported by a website. For the most up-to-date information, visit
www.dk.com/world-desk-reference

KEY TO MAP SYMBOLS

PHYSICAL FEATURES

Elevation

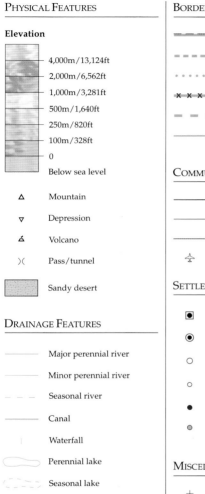

4,000m/13,124ft

2,000m/6,562ft

1,000m/3,281ft

500m/1,640ft

250m/820ft

100m/328ft

0

Below sea level

△ Mountain

▽ Depression

⌂ Volcano

)(Pass/tunnel

Sandy desert

DRAINAGE FEATURES

Major perennial river

Minor perennial river

Seasonal river

Canal

Waterfall

Perennial lake

Seasonal lake

Wetland

ICE FEATURES

Permanent ice cap/ice shelf

Winter limit of pack ice

Summer limit of pack ice

BORDERS

Full international border

Disputed *de facto* border

Territorial claim border

×—×—× Cease-fire line

Undefined boundary

Internal administrative boundary

COMMUNICATIONS

Major road

Minor road

Rail

✈ International airport

SETTLEMENTS

◉ Over 500,000

◎ 100,000 - 500,000

○ 50,000 - 100,000

○ Less than 50,000

● National capital

◉ Internal administrative capital

MISCELLANEOUS FEATURES

+ Site of interest

∿∿∿ Ancient wall

GRATICULE FEATURES

Line of latitude/longitude/Equator

Tropic/Polar circle

25° Degree of latitude/longitude

NAMES

Physical features

Andes

Sahara   Landscape features

Ardennes

Land's End   Headland

Mont Blanc 4,807m   Elevation/volcano/pass

Blue Nile   River/canal/waterfall

Ross Ice Shelf   Ice feature

PACIFIC OCEAN

Sulu Sea   Sea features

Palk Strait

Chile Rise   Undersea feature

Regions

FRANCE   Country

JERSEY (to UK)   Dependent territory

KANSAS   Administrative region

Dordogne   Cultural region

Settlements

PARIS   Capital city

SAN JUAN   Dependent territory capital city

Chicago

Kettering   Other settlements

Burke

INSET MAP SYMBOLS

Urban area

City

Park

▪ Place of interest

□ Suburb/district

CONTENTS

THE WORLD TODAY

Flags of the World 6-7
The Political World 8-9
The Physical World 10-11
Time Zones 12-13
Geology & Structure 14-15
World Climate 16-17
Ocean Currents 18-19
Life Zones 20-21
Population 22-23
Languages 24-25
Religion 26-27
The Global Economy 28-29
Global Conflict 30-31

THE WORLD'S REGIONS

NORTH & CENTRAL AMERICA

North & Central America 34-35
Western Canada & Alaska 36-37
Eastern Canada 38-39
USA: The Northeast 40-41
USA: The Southeast 42-43
  Bermuda
USA: Central States 44-45
USA: The West 46-47
  Los Angeles & Hawaii

USA: The Southwest 48-49
Mexico 50-51
Central America 52-53
The Caribbean 54-55
  Jamaica, St. Lucia, & Barbados

SOUTH AMERICA

South America 56-57
Northern South America 58-59
Western South America 60-61
  Galapagos Islands
Brazil 62-63
Southern South America 64-65
The Atlantic Ocean 66-67

AFRICA

Africa 68-69
Northwest Africa 70-71
Northeast Africa 72-73
West Africa 74-75
Central Africa 76-77
  Sao Tome & Principe
Southern Africa 78-79

EUROPE

Europe .80-81
The North Atlantic 82-83
Scandinavia & Finland 84-85
The Low Countries 86-87
The British Isles 88-89
  London

continued....

EUROPE *continued*

France, Andorra, & Monaco 90-91
  Paris, Andorra, & Monaco
Spain & Portugal 92-93
  Azores & Gibraltar
Germany & the Alpine States . . .94-95
  Liechtenstein
Italy 96-97
  San Marino & Vatican City
Central Europe 98-99
Southeast Europe 100-101
  Bosnia & Herzegovina
The Mediterranean 102-103
  Malta & Cyprus
Bulgaria & Greece 104-105
The Baltic States & Belarus 106-107
Ukraine, Moldova,
  & Romania 108-109
European Russia 110-111

NORTH & WEST ASIA

North & West Asia 112-113
Russia & Kazakhstan 114-115
Turkey & the Caucasus 116-117
The Near East 118-119
  West Bank
The Middle East 120-121
Central Asia 122-123

SOUTH & EAST ASIA

South & East Asia 124-125
Western China & Mongolia . . .126-127

Eastern China & Korea 128-129
  Hong Kong (Xianggang)
Japan .130-131
  Tōkyō & Nansei-Shotō
South India & Sri Lanka 132-133
North India, Pakistan,
  & Bangladesh 134-135
Mainland Southeast Asia 136-137
Maritime Southeast Asia 138-139
  Singapore
The Indian Ocean 140-141

AUSTRALASIA & OCEANIA

Australasia & Oceania 142-143
The Southwest Pacific 144-145
Western Australia 146-147
Eastern Australia 148-149
  Sydney
New Zealand 150-151
The Pacific Ocean 152-153
Antarctica 154
The Arctic Ocean 155

INDEX – GAZETTEER

Overseas Territories
  & Dependencies 156-159
Glossary of Geographical
  Terms 160-161
Continental Factfiles 162-163
Geographical Comparisons . . .164-166
Index-Gazetteer of Places
  & Countries 167-256

FLAGS OF THE WORLD

NORTH & CENTRAL AMERICA

ANTIGUA & BARBUDA
PAGES 54-55

BAHAMAS
PAGES 54-55

BARBADOS
PAGES 54-55

BELIZE
PAGES 52-53

CANADA
PAGES 36-39

COSTA RICA
PAGES 52-53

CUBA
PAGES 54-55

DOMINICA
PAGES 54-55

SOUTH AMERICA

NICARAGUA
PAGES 52-53

PANAMA
PAGES 52-53

ST. KITTS & NEVIS
PAGES 54-55

ST. LUCIA
PAGES 54-55

ST.VINCENT & THE GRENADINES
PAGES 54-55

TRINIDAD & TOBAGO
PAGES 54-55

UNITED STATES OF AMERICA
PAGES 40-49

ARGENTINA
PAGES 64-65

AFRICA

SURINAME
PAGES 58-59

URUGUAY
PAGES 64-65

VENEZUELA
PAGES 58-59

ALGERIA
PAGES 70-71

ANGOLA
PAGES 78-79

BENIN
PAGES 74-75

BOTSWANA
PAGES 78-79

BURKINA FASO
PAGES 74-75

DEM. REP. CONGO (ZAIRE)
PAGES 76-77

DJIBOUTI
PAGES 72-73

EGYPT
PAGES 72-73

EQUATORIAL GUINEA
PAGES 76-77

ERITREA
PAGES 72-73

ETHIOPIA
PAGES 72-73

GABON
PAGES 76-77

GAMBIA
PAGES 74-75

MALAWI
PAGES 78-79

MALI
PAGES 74-75

MAURITANIA
PAGES 74-75

MAURITIUS
PAGES 78-79

MOROCCO
PAGES 70-71

MOZAMBIQUE
PAGES 78-79

NAMIBIA
PAGES 78-79

NIGER
PAGES 74-75

SUDAN
PAGES 72-73

SWAZILAND
PAGES 78-79

TANZANIA
PAGES 72-73

TOGO
PAGES 74-75

TUNISIA
PAGES 70-71

UGANDA
PAGES 72-73

ZAMBIA
PAGES 78-79

ZIMBABWE
PAGES 78-79

CYPRUS
PAGES 102-103

CZECH REPUBLIC
PAGES 98-99

DENMARK
PAGES 84-85

ESTONIA
PAGES 106-107

FINLAND
PAGES 84-85

FRANCE
PAGES 90-91

GERMANY
PAGES 94-95

GREECE
PAGES 104-105

MALTA
PAGES 96-97

MOLDOVA
PAGES 108-109

MONACO
PAGES 90-91

NETHERLANDS
PAGES 86-87

NORWAY
PAGES 84-85

POLAND
PAGES 98-99

PORTUGAL
PAGES 92-93

REPUBLIC OF IRELAND
PAGES 88-89

ASIA

UKRAINE
PAGES 108-109

UNITED KINGDOM
PAGES 88-89

VATICAN CITY
PAGES 96-97

YUGOSLAVIA
PAGES 100-101

AFGHANISTAN
PAGES 122-123

ARMENIA
PAGES 116-117

AZERBAIJAN
PAGES 116-117

BAHRAIN
PAGES 120-121

IRAN
PAGES 120-121

IRAQ
PAGES 120-121

ISRAEL
PAGES 118-119

JAPAN
PAGES 130-131

JORDAN
PAGES 118-119

KAZAKHSTAN
PAGES 114-115

KUWAIT
PAGES 120-121

KYRGYZSTAN
PAGES 122-123

OMAN
PAGES 120-121

PAKISTAN
PAGES 134-135

PHILIPPINES
PAGES 138-139

QATAR
PAGES 120-121

SAUDI ARABIA
PAGES 120-121

SINGAPORE
PAGES 138-139

SOUTH KOREA
PAGES 128-129

SRI LANKA
PAGES 132-133

AUSTRALIA & OCEANIA

VIETNAM
PAGES 136-137

YEMEN
PAGES 120-121

AUSTRALIA
PAGES 146-149

FIJI
PAGES 144-145

KIRIBATI
PAGES 144-145

MARSHALL ISLANDS
PAGES 144-145

MICRONESIA
PAGES 144-145

NAURU
PAGES 144-145

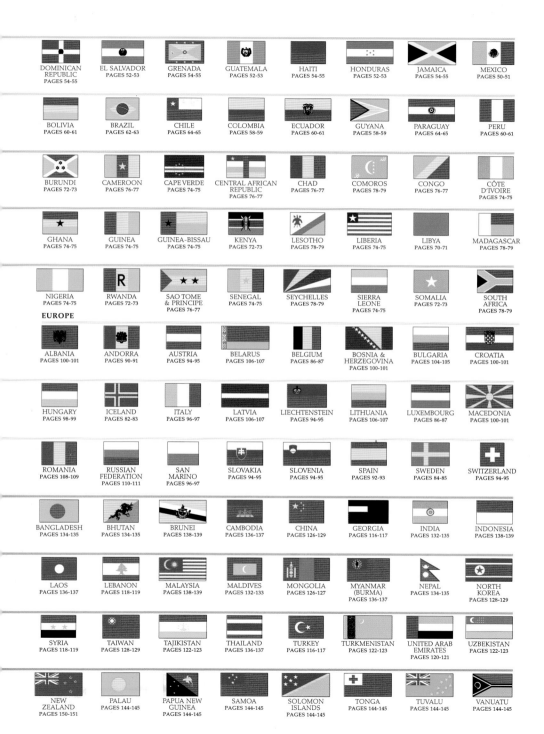

DOMINICAN REPUBLIC
PAGES 54-55

EL SALVADOR
PAGES 52-53

GRENADA
PAGES 54-55

GUATEMALA
PAGES 52-53

HAITI
PAGES 54-55

HONDURAS
PAGES 52-53

JAMAICA
PAGES 54-55

MEXICO
PAGES 50-51

BOLIVIA
PAGES 60-61

BRAZIL
PAGES 62-63

CHILE
PAGES 64-65

COLOMBIA
PAGES 58-59

ECUADOR
PAGES 60-61

GUYANA
PAGES 58-59

PARAGUAY
PAGES 64-65

PERU
PAGES 60-61

BURUNDI
PAGES 72-73

CAMEROON
PAGES 76-77

CAPE VERDE
PAGES 74-75

CENTRAL AFRICAN REPUBLIC
PAGES 76-77

CHAD
PAGES 76-77

COMOROS
PAGES 78-79

CONGO
PAGES 76-77

CÔTE D'IVOIRE
PAGES 74-75

GHANA
PAGES 74-75

GUINEA
PAGES 74-75

GUINEA-BISSAU
PAGES 74-75

KENYA
PAGES 72-73

LESOTHO
PAGES 78-79

LIBERIA
PAGES 74-75

LIBYA
PAGES 70-71

MADAGASCAR
PAGES 78-79

NIGERIA
PAGES 74-75

RWANDA
PAGES 72-73

SAO TOME & PRINCIPE
PAGES 76-77

SENEGAL
PAGES 74-75

SEYCHELLES
PAGES 78-79

SIERRA LEONE
PAGES 74-75

SOMALIA
PAGES 72-73

SOUTH AFRICA
PAGES 78-79

EUROPE

ALBANIA
PAGES 100-101

ANDORRA
PAGES 90-91

AUSTRIA
PAGES 94-95

BELARUS
PAGES 106-107

BELGIUM
PAGES 86-87

BOSNIA & HERZEGOVINA
PAGES 100-101

BULGARIA
PAGES 104-105

CROATIA
PAGES 100-101

HUNGARY
PAGES 98-99

ICELAND
PAGES 82-83

ITALY
PAGES 96-97

LATVIA
PAGES 106-107

LIECHTENSTEIN
PAGES 94-95

LITHUANIA
PAGES 106-107

LUXEMBOURG
PAGES 86-87

MACEDONIA
PAGES 100-101

ROMANIA
PAGES 108-109

RUSSIAN FEDERATION
PAGES 110-111

SAN MARINO
PAGES 96-97

SLOVAKIA
PAGES 94-95

SLOVENIA
PAGES 94-95

SPAIN
PAGES 92-93

SWEDEN
PAGES 84-85

SWITZERLAND
PAGES 94-95

BANGLADESH
PAGES 134-135

BHUTAN
PAGES 134-135

BRUNEI
PAGES 138-139

CAMBODIA
PAGES 136-137

CHINA
PAGES 126-129

GEORGIA
PAGES 116-117

INDIA
PAGES 132-135

INDONESIA
PAGES 138-139

LAOS
PAGES 136-137

LEBANON
PAGES 118-119

MALAYSIA
PAGES 138-139

MALDIVES
PAGES 132-133

MONGOLIA
PAGES 126-127

MYANMAR (BURMA)
PAGES 136-137

NEPAL
PAGES 134-135

NORTH KOREA
PAGES 128-129

SYRIA
PAGES 118-119

TAIWAN
PAGES 128-129

TAJIKISTAN
PAGES 122-123

THAILAND
PAGES 136-137

TURKEY
PAGES 116-117

TURKMENISTAN
PAGES 122-123

UNITED ARAB EMIRATES
PAGES 120-121

UZBEKISTAN
PAGES 122-123

NEW ZEALAND
PAGES 150-151

PALAU
PAGES 144-145

PAPUA NEW GUINEA
PAGES 144-145

SAMOA
PAGES 144-145

SOLOMON ISLANDS
PAGES 144-145

TONGA
PAGES 144-145

TUVALU
PAGES 144-145

VANUATU
PAGES 144-145

THE POLITICAL WORLD

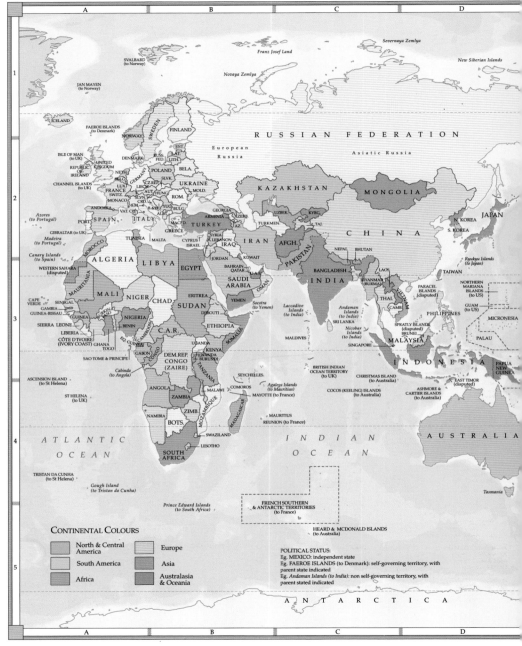

CONTINENTAL COLOURS

- North & Central America
- South America
- Africa
- Europe
- Asia
- Australasia & Oceania

POLITICAL STATUS:
Eg. MEXICO: independent state
Eg. FAEROE ISLANDS (to Denmark): self-governing territory, with parent state indicated
Eg. *Andaman Islands (to India)*: non self-governing territory, with parent stated indicated

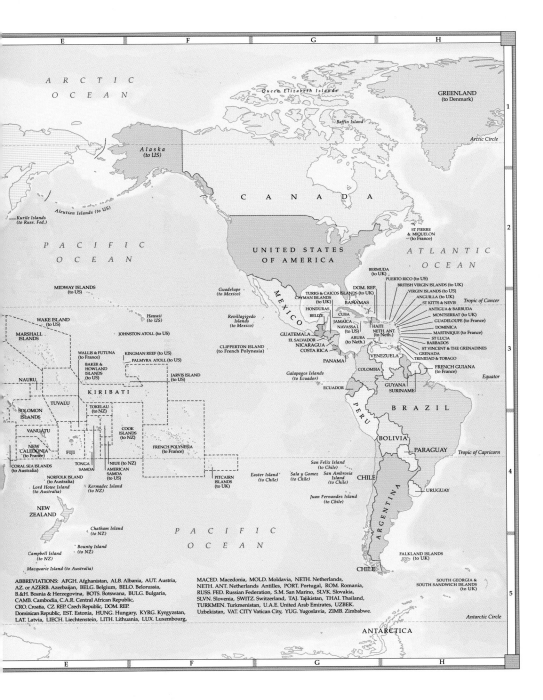

ARCTIC
OCEAN

Queen Elizabeth Islands

GREENLAND
(to Denmark)

Baffin Island

Arctic Circle

Alaska
(to US)

CANADA

Kurile Islands
(to Russ. Fed.)

Aleutian Islands (to US)

ST PIERRE
& MIQUELON
(to France)

PACIFIC
OCEAN

UNITED STATES
OF AMERICA

ATLANTIC
OCEAN

MIDWAY ISLANDS
(to US)

Hawaii
(to US)

Guadelupe
(to Mexico)

BERMUDA
(to UK)

PUERTO RICO (to US)
BRITISH VIRGIN ISLANDS (to UK)
VIRGIN ISLANDS (to US)
ANGUILLA (to UK)
ST KITTS & NEVIS

Tropic of Cancer

WAKE ISLAND
(to US)

MARSHALL
ISLANDS

JOHNSTON ATOLL (to US)

Revillagigedo
Islands
(to Mexico)

TURKS & CAICOS ISLANDS
(to UK)

DOM. REP.

BAHAMAS

HONDURAS

BELIZE

CUBA

JAMAICA

NAVASSA I.
(to US)

HAITI

NETH. ANT.
(to Neth.)

ANTIGUA & BARBUDA
MONTSERRAT (to UK)
GUADELOUPE (to France)
DOMINICA
MARTINIQUE (to France)
ST LUCIA
BARBADOS
ST VINCENT & THE GRENADINES

WALLIS & FUTUNA
(to France)

KINGMAN REEF (to US)

PALMYRA ATOLL (to US)

BAKER &
HOWLAND
ISLANDS
(to US)

JARVIS ISLAND
(to US)

NAURU

KIRIBATI

GUATEMALA
EL SALVADOR
NICARAGUA
COSTA RICA

PANAMA

ARUBA
(to Neth.)

GRENADA
TRINIDAD & TOBAGO

VENEZUELA

FRENCH GUIANA
(to France)

COLOMBIA

GUYANA
SURINAME

Equator

TUVALU

Galapagos Islands
(to Ecuador)

ECUADOR

SOLOMON
ISLANDS

TOKELAU
(to NZ)

COOK
ISLANDS
(to NZ)

PERU

BRAZIL

VANUATU

NEW
CALEDONIA
(to France)

FIJI

FRENCH POLYNESIA
(to France)

NIUE (to NZ)

BOLIVIA

PARAGUAY

Tropic of Capricorn

CORAL SEA ISLANDS
(to Australia)

NORFOLK ISLAND
(to Australia)

Lord Howe Island
(to Australia)

TONGA

SAMOA

AMERICAN
SAMOA
(to US)

Kermadec Island
(to NZ)

PITCAIRN
ISLANDS
(to UK)

Easter Island
(to Chile)

San Felix Island
(to Chile)

Sala y Gomez
(to Chile)

San Ambrosia
Island
(to Chile)

CHILE

ARGENTINA

URUGUAY

NEW
ZEALAND

Juan Fernandez Island
(to Chile)

Chatham Island
(to NZ)

Bounty Island
(to NZ)

Campbell Island
(to NZ)

PACIFIC

OCEAN

Macquarie Island (to Australia)

FALKLAND ISLANDS
(to UK)

CHILE

SOUTH GEORGIA &
SOUTH SANDWICH ISLANDS
(to UK)

ABBREVIATIONS: AFGH. Afghanistan, ALB. Albania, AUT. Austria,
AZ. or AZERB. Azerbaijan, BELG. Belgium, BELO. Belorussia,
B.&H. Bosnia & Herzegovina, BOTS. Botswana, BULG. Bulgaria,
CAMB. Cambodia, C.A.R. Central African Republic,
CRO. Croatia, CZ. REP Czech Republic, DOM. REP.
Dominican Republic, EST. Estonia, HUNG. Hungary, KYRG. Kyrgyzstan,
LAT. Latvia, LIECH. Liechtenstein, LITH. Lithuania, LUX. Luxembourg,

MACED. Macedonia, MOLD. Moldavia, NETH. Netherlands,
NETH. ANT. Netherlands Antilles, PORT. Portugal, ROM. Romania,
RUSS. FED. Russian Federation, S.M. San Marino, SLVK. Slovakia,
SLVN. Slovenia, SWITZ. Switzerland, TAJ. Tajikistan, THAI. Thailand,
TURKMEN. Turkmenistan, U.A.E. United Arab Emirates, UZBEK.
Uzbekistan, VAT. CITY Vatican City, YUG. Yugoslavia, ZIMB. Zimbabwe.

Antarctic Circle

ANTARCTICA

THE PHYSICAL WORLD

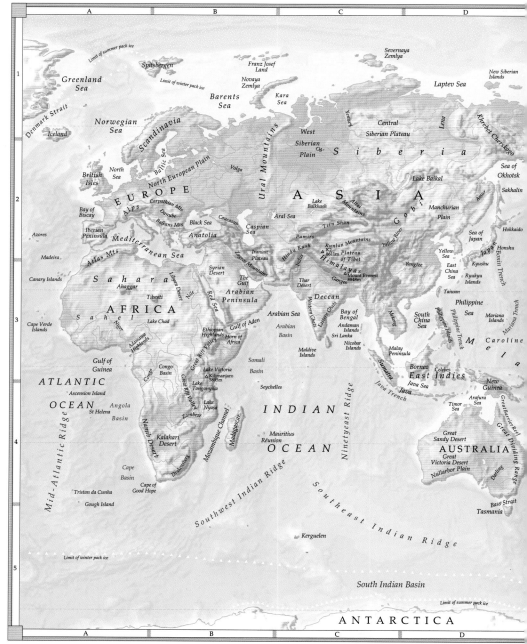

Greenland
Sea

Spitsbergen

Franz Josef
Land

Severnaya
Zemlya

New Siberian
Islands

Limit of summer pack ice

Novaya
Zemlya

Limit of winter pack ice

Barents
Sea

Kara
Sea

Laptev Sea

Denmark Strait

Iceland

Norwegian
Sea

Scandinavia

Baltic Sea

West
Siberian
Plain

Central
Siberian Plateau

Lena

Khrebet Cherskogo

British
Isles

North
Sea

North European Plain

Volga

Ural Mountains

Ob'

S i b e r i a

Sea of
Okhotsk

Bay of
Biscay

E U R O P E

Alps

Carpathian Mts

Danube

Balkans Mts

Black Sea

Caucasus

Lake
Balkhash

Altai
Mountains

A S I A

Amur

Sakhalin

Azores

Iberian
Peninsula

Mediterranean Sea

Anatolia

Aral Sea

Caspian
Sea

Tien Shan

Gobi

Manchurian
Plain

Hokkaido

Madeira

Atlas Mts

Zagros Mountains

Iranian
Plateau

Pamirs

Hindu Kush

Kunlun Mountains

K2
8611m

Plateau
of Tibet

Yellow
River

Yangtze

Sea of
Japan

Yellow
Sea

East
China
Sea

Japan

Honshu

Kyushu

Canary Islands

S a h a r a

Ahaggar

Syrian
Desert

The
Gulf

Indus

Himalayas

Mount Everest
8848m

Ganges

Ryukyu
Islands

Taiwan

Cape Verde
Islands

Tibesti

Niger

Lake Chad

Nile

Red Sea

Arabian
Peninsula

Thar
Desert

Deccan

Western Ghats

Eastern Ghats

Philippine
Sea

Mariana
Islands

Mariana Trench

S a h e l

AFRICA

Ethiopian
Highlands

Gulf of Aden

Arabian Sea

Bay of
Bengal

Andaman
Islands

Sri Lanka

Mekong

South
China
Sea

Philippine Islands

Philippine Trench

M

Caroline

Adamawa
Highlands

Horn of
Africa

Arabian
Basin

Nicobar
Islands

Malay
Peninsula

e

l

Gulf of
Guinea

Congo

Congo
Basin

Great Rift Valley

Lake Victoria

Kilimanjaro
5895m

Maldive
Islands

Somali
Basin

Sumatra

Borneo

Java Trench

Celebes

Java Sea

East Indies

Java

New
Guinea

Great Barrier Reef

a

ATLANTIC

Ascension Island

St Helena

Angola
Basin

Lake
Tanganyika

Lake
Nyasa

Seychelles

Timor
Sea

Arafura
Sea

OCEAN

Zambezi

I N D I A N

Mauritius
Réunion

Great
Sandy Desert

AUSTRALIA

Great Dividing Range

Mid-Atlantic Ridge

Namib Desert

Kalahari
Desert

Madagascar

Mozambique Channel

O C E A N

Ninetyeast Ridge

Great
Victoria Desert

Nullarbor Plain

Darling

Cape
Basin

Drakensberg

Cape of
Good Hope

Southwest Indian Ridge

Bass Strait

Tasmania

Tristan da Cunha

Gough Island

Kerguelen

Southeast Indian Ridge

Limit of winter pack ice

South Indian Basin

Limit of summer pack ice

ANTARCTICA

ARCTIC OCEAN

East Siberian Sea
Limit of summer pack ice
Beaufort Sea
Queen Elizabeth Islands
Ellesmere Island
Greenland
Baffin Bay
Baffin Island
Arctic Circle

Chukchi Sea
Brooks Range
Mackenzie
Great Bear Lake
Kamchatka
Bering Strait
Limit of winter pack ice
△ Mount McKinley (Denali) 6194m
Rocky Mountains
Great Slave Lake
Hudson Bay
Péninsula d'Ungava
Labrador Sea

Bering Sea
Aleutian Basin
Aleutian Islands
Aleutian Trench
Gulf of Alaska
Coast Ranges
Canadian Shield
Lake Winnipeg
Laurentian Mountains

Kurile Trench
Northwest Pacific Basin
Emperor Seamounts
Mendocino Fracture Zone
Vancouver Island
NORTH AMERICA
Great Lakes
Great Plains
Appalachian Mts
Mississippi
North American Basin
Grand Banks of Newfoundland
Mid-Atlantic Ridge

Murray Fracture Zone
Sierra Madre Occidental
Sierra Madre Oriental
Lower California
Gulf of Mexico
Tropic of Cancer

Mid-Pacific Mountains
Hawaiian Islands
Hawaii
Yucatan Peninsula
Greater Antilles
West Indies
ATLANTIC OCEAN

Central Pacific Basin
Marshall Islands
P o l y n e s i a
PACIFIC
Middle America Trench
Caribbean Sea
Lesser Antilles

Micronesia
slands
OCEAN
Line Islands

Solomon Islands
Phoenix Islands
Samoa
Marquesas Islands
Galapagos Islands
Guiana Highlands
Equator

Coral Sea
Vanuatu Fiji Tonga
Cook Islands
Tuamotu Islands
Amazon
Amazon Basin
SOUTH AMERICA
Brazil Basin

New Caledonia
Peru Basin
Peru
Andes
Planalto de Mato Grosso
Brazilian Highlands
Tropic of Capricorn

East Pacific Rise
Easter Island
Cerro Aconcagua 6959m △
Gran Chaco
Paraná
Juan Fernandez Islands
Chile Trench

Tasman Sea
Kermadec Trench
Southwest
North Island
New Zealand
Pacific
Basin
Pampas
Argentine Basin

South Island
Campbell Plateau
Patagonia
Falkland Islands
South Georgia

Tierra del Fuego
Cape Horn
Drake Passage
South Sandwich Islands

Limit of winter pack ice
Antarctic Peninsula
Antarctic Circle

ELEVATION
Below sea level
-4000m -3000m -2000m -1000m -500m   0   100m 250m 500m 1000m 2000m 4000m
-13 124ft -9843ft -6562ft -3281ft -1640ft -820ft/-250m 0
0   328ft 820ft 1640ft 3281ft 6562ft 13 124ft

TIME ZONES

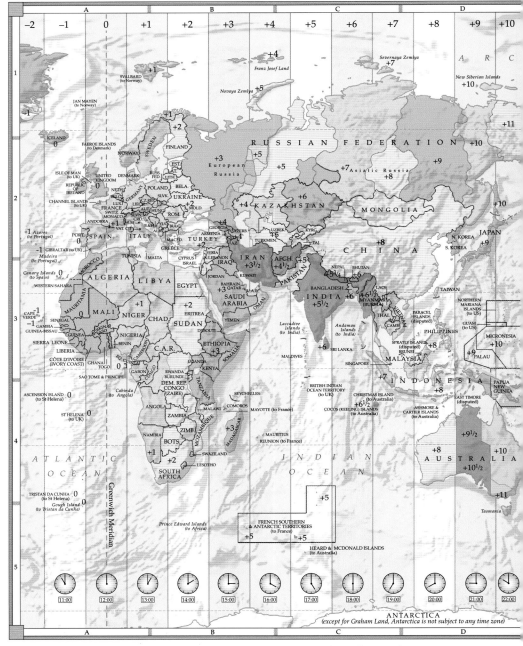

The numbers represented thus: +2/-2, indicate the number of hours each time zone is ahead or behind GMT (Greenwich Mean Time)

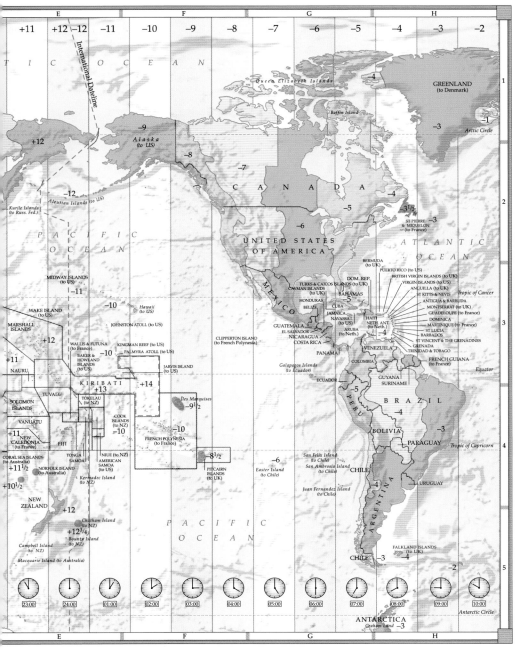

The clocks and 24-hour times given at the bottom of the map show the time in each time zone when it is 12.00 hours noon GMT

GEOLOGY & STRUCTURE

GEOLOGICAL REGIONS | Continental shield | Igneous rock types | MOUNTAIN RANGES | Hercynian (290 to 362 Ma) | Ma= millions of years ago

Sedimentary rocks | Coral formation | Alpine (5 to 23 Ma) | Caledonian (386 to 439 Ma)

14

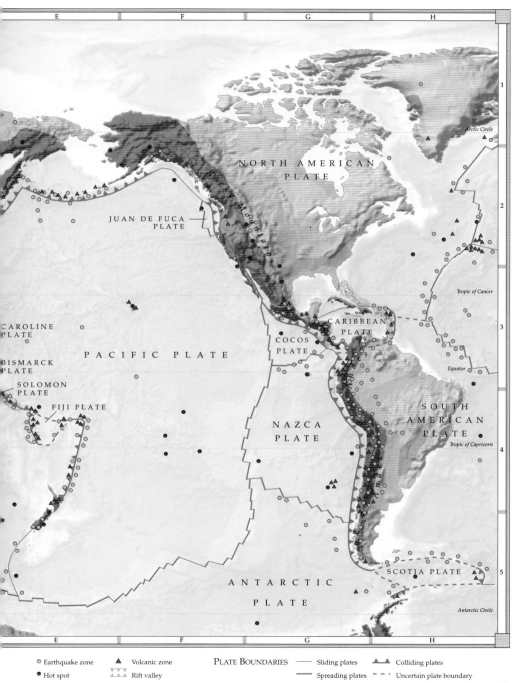

E   F   G   H

1

Arctic Circle

NORTH AMERICAN
PLATE

JUAN DE FUCA
PLATE

2

Rocky Mountains

Tropic of Cancer

CARIBBEAN
PLATE

3

CAROLINE
PLATE

COCOS
PLATE

Equator

PACIFIC PLATE

BISMARCK
PLATE

SOLOMON
PLATE

FIJI PLATE

SOUTH
AMERICAN
PLATE

Tropic of Capricorn

NAZCA
PLATE

4

SCOTIA PLATE

5

ANTARCTIC

PLATE

Antarctic Circle

E   F   G   H

○ Earthquake zone   ▲ Volcanic zone   PLATE BOUNDARIES   — Sliding plates   ▲▲ Colliding plates

● Hot spot   ▲▲▲ Rift valley   — Spreading plates   - - - Uncertain plate boundary

15

WORLD CLIMATE

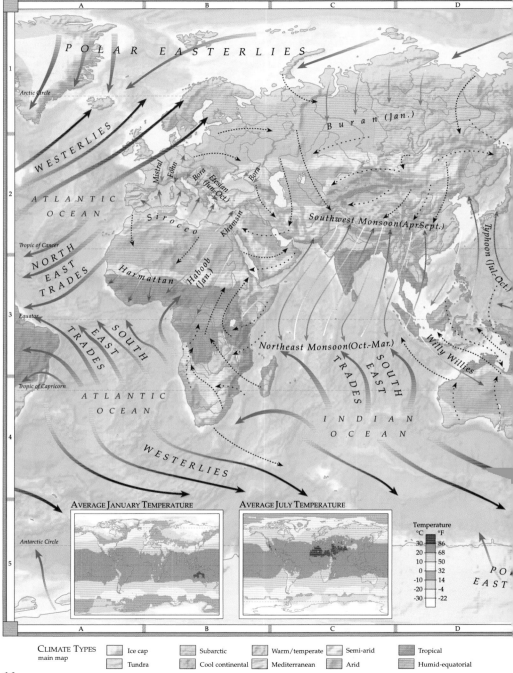

POLAR EASTERLIES

Arctic Circle

WESTERLIES

Buran (Jan.)

Mistral

Föhn

Bora

Etesian
(Jun.-Oct.)

Bora

ATLANTIC
OCEAN

Sirocco

Southwest Monsoon (Apr.-Sept.)

Tropic of Cancer

NORTH
EAST
TRADES

Harmattan

Haboob
(Jan.)

Khamsin

Typhoon (Jul.-Oct.)

Equator

SOUTH
EAST
TRADES

Northeast Monsoon (Oct.-Mar.)

SOUTH
EAST
TRADES

Willy Willies

Tropic of Capricorn

ATLANTIC
OCEAN

INDIAN
OCEAN

WESTERLIES

Antarctic Circle

PO
EAST

AVERAGE JANUARY TEMPERATURE

AVERAGE JULY TEMPERATURE

Temperature

°C	°F
30	86
20	68
10	50
0	32
-10	14
-20	-4
-30	-22

CLIMATE TYPES
main map

Ice cap	Subarctic	Warm/temperate
Tundra	Cool continental	Mediterranean

Semi-arid Tropical

Arid Humid-equatorial

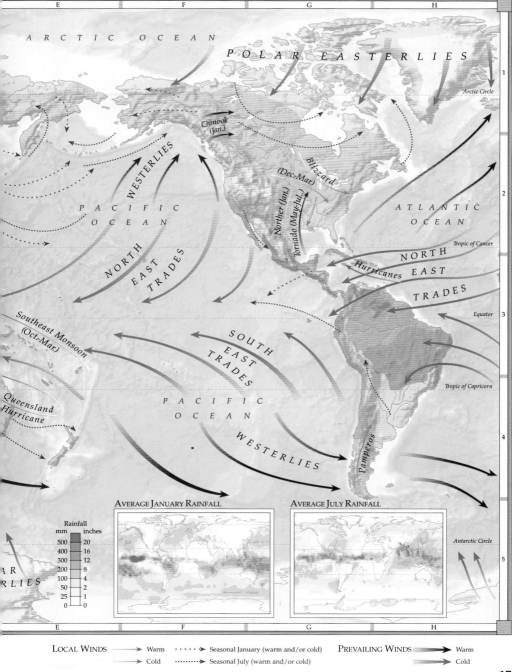

ARCTIC OCEAN

POLAR EASTERLIES

Arctic Circle

Chinook
(Jan.)

Blizzard
(Dec-Mar)

WESTERLIES

PACIFIC
OCEAN

ATLANTIC
OCEAN

Norther (Jan.)
Tornado (May-Jul.)

NORTH

EAST

Tropic of Cancer

NORTH

EAST

TRADES

Hurricanes

TRADES

Equator

Southeast Monsoon
(Oct-Mar)

SOUTH

EAST

TRADES

Queensland
Hurricane

PACIFIC
OCEAN

Tropic of Capricorn

WESTERLIES

Pamperos

AVERAGE JANUARY RAINFALL

AVERAGE JULY RAINFALL

WESTERLIES

Antarctic Circle

Rainfall
mm   inches
500   20
400   16
300   12
200   8
100   4
50   2
25   1
0   0

AR
RLIES

| LOCAL WINDS | → Warm | ..·····➤ Seasonal January (warm and/or cold) | PREVAILING WINDS | → Warm |
| | → Cold | ········➤ Seasonal July (warm and/or cold) | | → Cold |

OCEAN CURRENTS

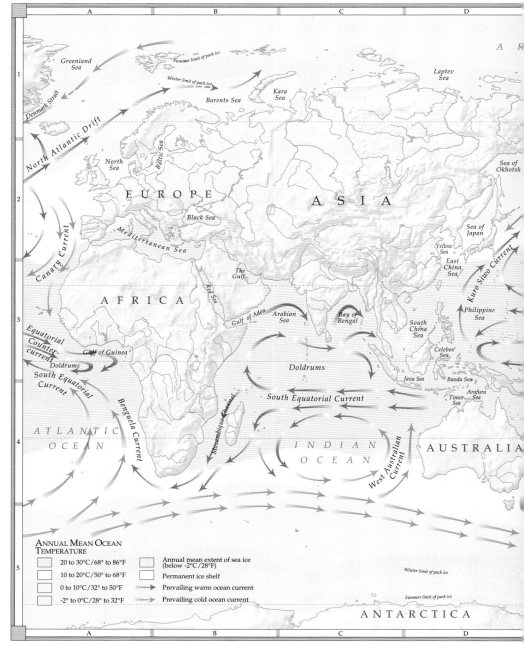

Greenland Sea

Summer limit of pack ice

Winter limit of pack ice

Laptev Sea

Denmark Strait

Barents Sea

Kara Sea

North Atlantic Drift

North Sea

Baltic Sea

Sea of Okhotsk

EUROPE

ASIA

Canary Current

Mediterranean Sea

Black Sea

Sea of Japan

Yellow Sea

East China Sea

Kuro Siwo Current

Red Sea

The Gulf

AFRICA

Gulf of Aden

Arabian Sea

Bay of Bengal

South China Sea

Philippine Sea

Equatorial Counter-current

Celebes Sea

Doldrums

Gulf of Guinea

Doldrums

Java Sea

Banda Sea

South Equatorial Current

South Equatorial Current

Arafura Sea

Timor Sea

Benguela Current

Mozambique Channel

ATLANTIC OCEAN

INDIAN OCEAN

AUSTRALIA

West Australian Current

ANNUAL MEAN OCEAN TEMPERATURE

20 to 30°C/68° to 86°F	Annual mean extent of sea ice (below -2°C/28°F)
10 to 20°C/50° to 68°F	Permanent ice shelf
0 to 10°C/32° to 50°F	Prevailing warm ocean current
-2° to 0°C/28° to 32°F	Prevailing cold ocean current

Winter limit of pack ice

Summer limit of pack ice

ANTARCTICA

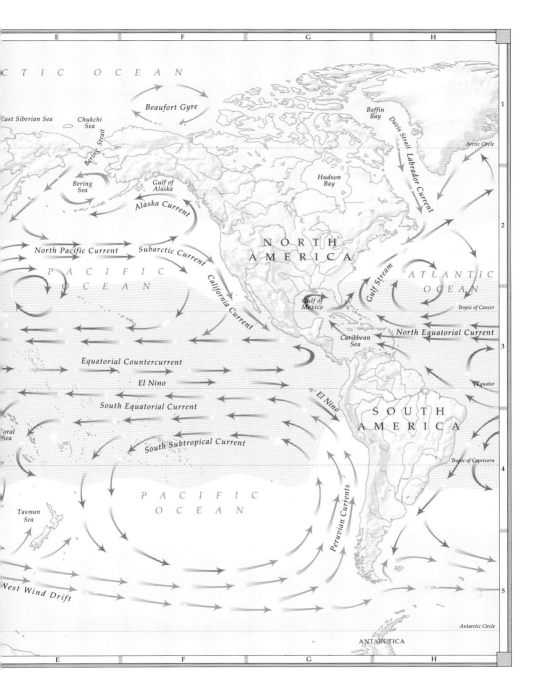

LIFE ZONES

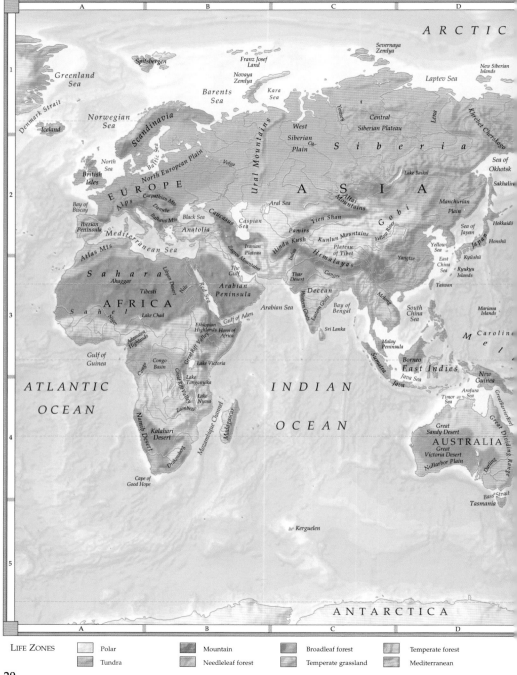

ARCTIC

Greenland Sea

Spitsbergen

Franz Josef Land

Novaya Zemlya

Severnaya Zemlya

New Siberian Islands

Laptev Sea

Denmark Strait

Iceland

Norwegian Sea

Barents Sea

Kara Sea

Khrebet Cherskogo

Scandinavia

Ural Mountains

West Siberian Plain

Central Siberian Plateau

Siberia

Yenisey

Lena

North Sea

British Isles

Baltic Sea

North European Plain

Volga

Ob

ASIA

Sea of Okhotsk

Sakhalin

EUROPE

Alps

Carpathian Mts

Danube

Black Sea

Caucasus

Caspian Sea

Aral Sea

Altai Mountains

Lake Baikal

Gobi

Manchurian Plain

Hokkaidō

Bay of Biscay

Iberian Peninsula

Mediterranean Sea

Balkans Mts

Anatolia

Iranian Plateau

Zagros Mountains

Pamirs

Tien Shan

Hindu Kush

Kunlun Mountains

Yellow River

Sea of Japan

Japan

Honshū

Atlas Mts

The Gulf

Plateau of Tibet

Yangtze

Yellow Sea

East China Sea

Kyūshū

Ryukyu Islands

Sahara

Ahaggar

Libyan Desert

Nile

Red Sea

Arabian Peninsula

Thar Desert

Himalayas

Indus

Ganges

Deccan

Western Ghats

Eastern Ghats

Bay of Bengal

Mekong

South China Sea

Mariana Islands

Caroline

M e l

Tibesti

AFRICA

Sahel

Niger

Lake Chad

Ethiopian Highlands

Gulf of Aden

Horn of Africa

Arabian Sea

Sri Lanka

Malay Peninsula

Adamawa Highlands

Great Rift Valley

Congo

Congo Basin

Lake Victoria

Lake Tanganyika

Lake Nyasa

Sumatra

Borneo

East Indies

Java Sea

Java

New Guinea

Gulf of Guinea

Arafura Sea

Timor Sea

Great Barrier Reef

Great Dividing Range

ATLANTIC

OCEAN

INDIAN

OCEAN

Zambezi

Mozambique Channel

Madagascar

Namib Desert

Kalahari Desert

Drakensberg

Great Sandy Desert

AUSTRALIA

Great Victoria Desert

Nullarbor Plain

Darling

Cape of Good Hope

Bass Strait

Tasmania

Kerguelen

ANTARCTICA

LIFE ZONES

Polar	Mountain	Broadleaf forest	Temperate forest
Tundra	Needleleaf forest	Temperate grassland	Mediterranean

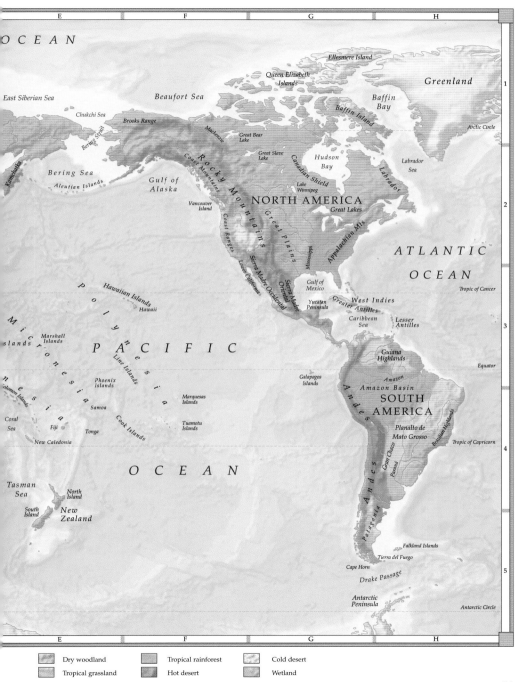

E   F   G   H

O C E A N

East Siberian Sea

Chukchi Sea

Ellesmere Island

Queen Elizabeth
Islands

Greenland

1

Beaufort Sea

*Baffin
Bay*

Baffin Island

Brooks Range

Mackenzie

Arctic Circle

Bering Strait

Kamchatka

Bering Sea

Aleutian Islands

Gulf of
Alaska

Rocky Mountains

Coast Mountains

Great Bear
Lake

Great Slave
Lake

*Hudson
Bay*

Canadian Shield

Labrador

Labrador
Sea

2

*Vancouver
Island*

Lake
Winnipeg

NORTH AMERICA

Great Lakes

Great Plains

Coast Ranges

*Sierra Madre
Occidental*

Lower California

Mississippi

Appalachian Mts

A T L A N T I C

O C E A N

Tropic of Cancer

P o l y n e s i a

Hawaiian Islands

Hawaii

Gulf of
Mexico

Yucatan
Peninsula

Greater Antilles

West Indies

*Sierra Madre
Oriental*

Caribbean
Sea

Lesser
Antilles

3

M i c r o n e s i a

Marshall
Islands

Islands

P A C I F I C

Line Islands

Phoenix
Islands

Guiana
Highlands

Amazon

*Galapagos
Islands*

Amazon Basin

SOUTH
AMERICA

Equator

n e s i a

Solomon Islands

Samoa

Marquesas
Islands

A n d e s

Brazilian Highlands

Coral
Sea

Fiji

Tonga

Cook Islands

Tuamotu
Islands

Planalto de
Mato Grosso

Tropic of Capricorn

4

New Caledonia

Gran Chaco

Paraná

O C E A N

Tasman
Sea

North
Island

South
Island

New
Zealand

A n d e s

Patagonia

Falkland Islands

Tierra del Fuego

Cape Horn

Drake Passage

5

Antarctic
Peninsula

Antarctic Circle

E   F   G   H

Dry woodland	Tropical rainforest	Cold desert	
Tropical grassland	Hot desert	Wetland	

POPULATION

POPULATION DENSITY PER SQUARE KILOMETRE
- More than 500
- 300 - 500
- 200 - 299
- 100 - 199
- 30 - 99
- Less than 30
- Data not available

AVERAGE LIFE EXPECTANCY
- More than 75
- 66 - 75
- 56 - 65
- 45 - 55
- Less than 45

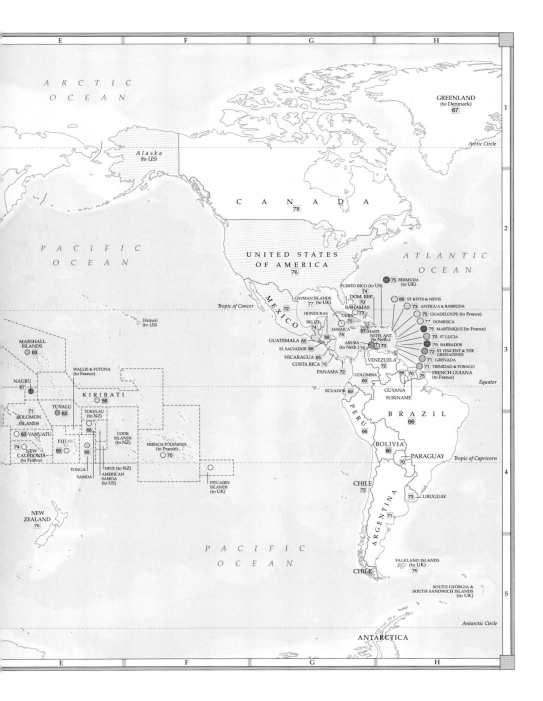

A R C T I C
O C E A N

GREENLAND
(to Denmark)
67

Arctic Circle

Alaska
(to US)

P A C I F I C
O C E A N

C A N A D A
78

A T L A N T I C

UNITED STATES
OF AMERICA
76

O C E A N

BERMUDA
75 (to UK)

Tropic of Cancer

Hawaii
(to US)

M E X I C O
72

CAYMAN ISLANDS
77 (to UK)

HONDURAS

BELIZE
74

CUBA
73

PUERTO RICO (to US)
74
DOM. REP.
70
BAHAMAS
73

ST KITTS & NEVIS
66

ANTIGUA & BARBUDA
73

GUADELOUPE (to France)
75

DOMINICA
77

MARSHALL
ISLANDS
63

GUATEMALA 65

EL SALVADOR 68

NICARAGUA 65

COSTA RICA 76

PANAMA 72

JAMAICA
74

68

HAITI
57
NETH. ANT.
(to Neth.)
73

ARUBA
(to Neth.) 76

MARTINIQUE (to France)
76

ST LUCIA
70

BARBADOS
76

ST VINCENT & THE
GRENADINES
72

GRENADA
71

VENEZUELA
72

COLOMBIA
69

65 70

TRINIDAD & TOBAGO
71

FRENCH GUIANA
75 (to France)

Equator

WALLIS & FUTUNA
(to France)

NAURU
67

K I R I B A T I
58

ECUADOR 69

GUYANA

SURINAME

TUVALU
63

TOKELAU
(to NZ)

PERÚ
66

B R A Z I L
66

SOLOMON
ISLANDS
71

63 VANUATU

COOK
ISLANDS
(to NZ)

68

FRENCH POLYNESIA
(to France)
70

BOLIVIA
80

PARAGUAY
70

Tropic of Capricorn

74
NEW
CALEDONIA
(to France)

FIJI
63

68

NIUE (to NZ)

PITCAIRN
ISLANDS
(to UK)

CHILE
72

73 URUGUAY

TONGA

SAMOA

AMERICAN
SAMOA
(to US)

A R G E N T I N A
71

NEW
ZEALAND
76

P A C I F I C

O C E A N

FALKLAND ISLANDS
(to UK)
76

CHILE

SOUTH GEORGIA &
SOUTH SANDWICH ISLANDS
(to UK)

Antarctic Circle

A N T A R C T I C A

LANGUAGES

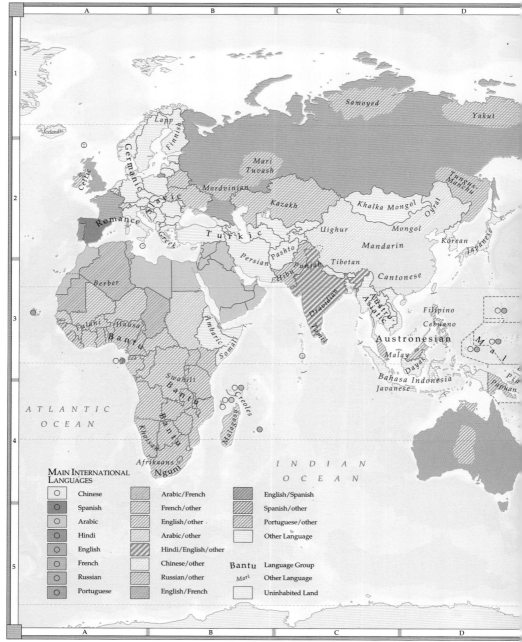

Samoyed

Yakut

Lapp

Icelandic

Finnish

Germanic

Celtic

Mari

Tuvash

Tungus-Manchu

Slavic

Mordvinian

Kazakh

Khalka Mongol

Oyat

Romance

Greek

Turkic

Uighur

Mongol

Korean

Japanese

Berber

Persian

Pashto

Punjab

Tibetan

Mandarin

Cantonese

Hibu

Fulani

Hausa

Amharic

Dravidian

Austro-Asiatic

Filipino

Bantu

Somali

Tamil

Cebuano

Austronesian

M a l

Swahili

Malay

Dayak

Bantu

Bahasa Indonesia

P i g

Bantu

Javanese

Papuan

Creoles

Khoisan

Malagasy

ATLANTIC
OCEAN

Afrikaans

Nguni

INDIAN
OCEAN

MAIN INTERNATIONAL LANGUAGES

○	Chinese		Arabic/French		English/Spanish
○	Spanish		French/other		Spanish/other
○	Arabic		English/other		Portuguese/other
○	Hindi		Arabic/other		Other Language
○	English		Hindi/English/other		
○	French		Chinese/other	Bantu	Language Group
○	Russian		Russian/other	Mari	Other Language
○	Portuguese		English/French		Uninhabited Land

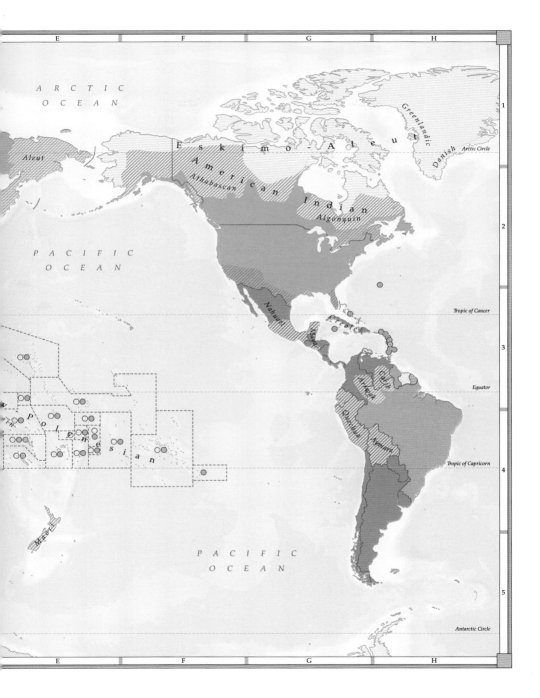

RELIGION

SVALBARD
(to Norway)

ICELAND

FAEROE ISLANDS
(to Denmark)

NORWAY SWEDEN FINLAND

RUSSIAN FEDERATION

European
Russia

Asiatic Russia

DENMARK RUSS.
FED.
EST.
LAT.
LITH.

UNITED KINGDOM
REPUBLIC
OF
IRELAND

NETH.
BELG.
LUX.

POLAND
BELA.

GERMANY CZECH REP.
LIECH.
AUT. HUNG.
SWITZ. SLVN.
MONACO

UKRAINE

MOLD.

KAZAKHSTAN

MONGOLIA

FRANCE

ANDORRA

PORT.

SPAIN

VAT. CITY

ITALY

SAN
MARINO

CRO.
B & H
SERB.
MON.

ROM.

BULG.

MACED.
ALB.

GREECE

GEORGIA
ARMENIA
AZERB.

TURKEY

CYPRUS
LEBANON
ISRAEL

SYRIA

IRAQ

UZBEK.

TURKMEN.

KYRG.

TAJ.

CHINA

N. KOREA JAPAN

S. KOREA

GIBRALTAR (to UK)

TUNISIA

MALTA

JORDAN

IRAN

AFGH.

PAKISTAN

NEPAL BHUTAN

BANGLADESH

TAIWAN

NORTHERN
MARIANA
ISLANDS
(to US)

MOROCCO

WESTERN SAHARA
(disputed)

ALGERIA

LIBYA

EGYPT

BAHRAIN
QATAR

KUWAIT

SAUDI
ARABIA

U.A.E.

OMAN

INDIA

LAOS

MYAN.
BURMA

THAI.

VIETNAM

CAMB.

PARACEL
ISLANDS
(disputed)

PHILIPPINES

MICRONESIA

MAURITANIA

MALI

NIGER

CHAD

SUDAN

ERITREA

DJIBOUTI

YEMEN

SRI LANKA

MALDIVES

SPRATLY ISLANDS
(disputed)
BRUNEI

MALAYSIA

SINGAPORE

PALAU

CAPE
VERDE

SENEGAL

GAMBIA

GUINEA-BISSAU

GUINEA

SIERRA LEONE

LIBERIA

CÔTE D'IVOIRE
(IVORY COAST)

BURKINA
FASO

GHANA

TOGO

BENIN

NIGERIA

CAMEROON

C.A.R.

ETHIOPIA

SOMALIA

UGANDA

KENYA

INDONESIA

EAST TIMOR
(disputed)

PAPUA
NEW
GUINEA

SAO TOME & PRINCIPE

EQ. GUINEA

GABON

CONGO

DEM. REP.
CONGO
(ZAIRE)

BURUNDI
RWANDA

TANZANIA

SEYCHELLES

ANGOLA

MALAWI

COMOROS

MAYOTTE (to France)

ZAMBIA

ZIMB.

MOZAMBIQUE

MADAGASCAR

MAURITIUS

REUNION (to France)

ATLANTIC
OCEAN

NAMIBIA

BOTS.

SWAZILAND

LESOTHO

SOUTH
AFRICA

INDIAN
OCEAN

AUSTRALIA

MAJORITY RELIGIONS

- Marxism / Maoism
- Protestant Christianity
- Catholic Christianity
- Orthodox Christianity
- Shi'a Islam
- Sunni Islam
- Hinduism
- Judaism
- Theravada Buddhism
- Mahayana Buddhism
- Tibetan Buddhism
- Other

STATE POLICY

▲ Secular ideologies governing
● Communist states during 20th century
■ Non-pluralist states

ANTARCTICA
(uninhabited)

26

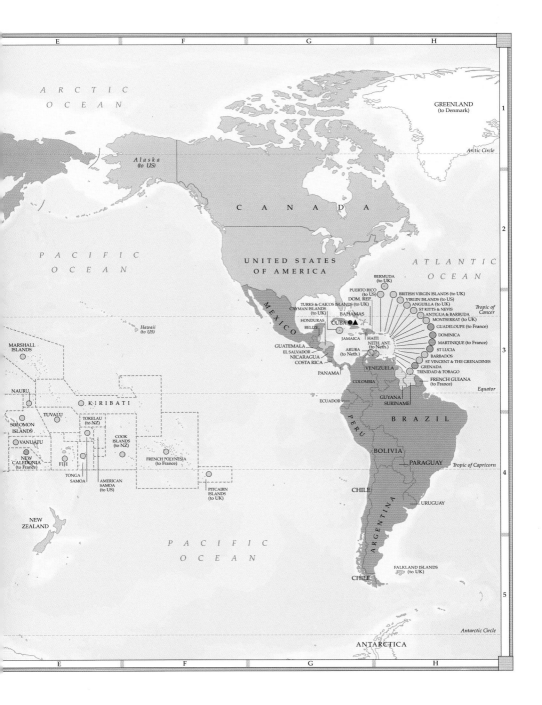

A R C T I C
O C E A N

GREENLAND
(to Denmark)

Arctic Circle

Alaska
(to US)

C A N A D A

P A C I F I C
O C E A N

UNITED STATES
OF AMERICA

A T L A N T I C
O C E A N

BERMUDA
(to UK)

PUERTO RICO
(to US)

Hawaii
(to US)

CAYMAN ISLANDS
(to UK)

TURKS & CAICOS ISLANDS (to UK)

DOM. REP.

BAHAMAS

BRITISH VIRGIN ISLANDS (to UK)
VIRGIN ISLANDS (to US)
ANGUILLA (to UK)
ST KITTS & NEVIS
ANTIGUA & BARBUDA
MONTSERRAT (to UK)

Tropic of
Cancer

GUADELOUPE (to France)

MARSHALL
ISLANDS

MEXICO

HONDURAS
BELIZE

CUBA

HAITI
JAMAICA

DOMINICA
MARTINIQUE (to France)
ST LUCIA
BARBADOS
ST VINCENT & THE GRENADINES
GRENADA

GUATEMALA
EL SALVADOR
NICARAGUA
COSTA RICA

NETH. ANT.
(to Neth.)

ARUBA
(to Neth.)

TRINIDAD & TOBAGO

FRENCH GUIANA
(to France)

NAURU

VENEZUELA

PANAMA

COLOMBIA

Equator

KIRIBATI

ECUADOR

GUYANA
SURINAME

TUVALU

TOKELAU
(to NZ)

P
E
R
U

B R A Z I L

SOLOMON
ISLANDS

VANUATU

COOK
ISLANDS
(to NZ)

NEW
CALEDONIA
(to France)

FIJI

FRENCH POLYNESIA
(to France)

BOLIVIA

PARAGUAY

Tropic of Capricorn

TONGA
SAMOA

AMERICAN
SAMOA
(to US)

PITCAIRN
ISLANDS
(to UK)

CHILE

A
R
G
E
N
T
I
N
A

URUGUAY

NEW
ZEALAND

P A C I F I C

O C E A N

CHILE

FALKLAND ISLANDS
(to UK)

Antarctic Circle

ANTARCTICA

THE GLOBAL ECONOMY

ECONOMIC PERFORMANCE

GNP per capita, 1995 ($US)

- more than 20 000
- 10 000 to 20 000
- 5000 to 10 000
- 1000 to 5000
- 500 to 1000
- 250 to 500
- less than 250
- data not available

Human Development Index (HDI)

- high human development

- poor human development

HDI is one of the best indicators of economic development. The single index is reached by measuring life expectancy at birth, per capita purchasing power, literacy rates and years of schooling

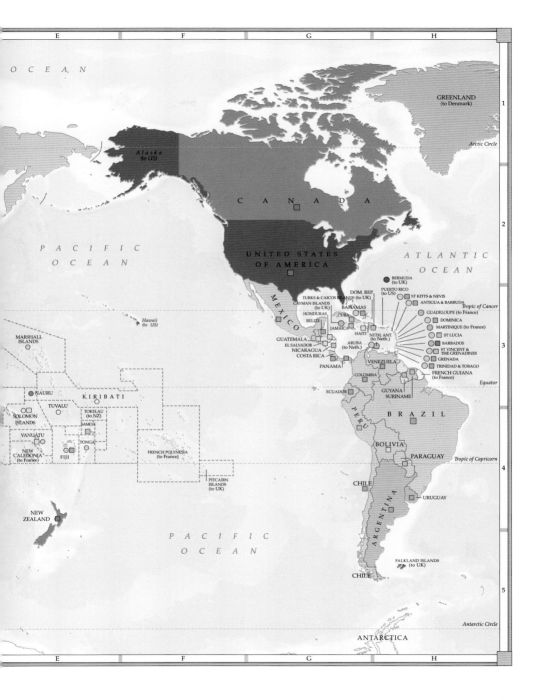

E F G H

OCEAN

GREENLAND
(to Denmark)

1

Arctic Circle

*Alaska
(to US)*

C A N A D A

2

*PACIFIC
OCEAN*

UNITED STATES
OF AMERICA

*ATLANTIC
OCEAN*

BERMUDA
(to UK)

*Hawaii
(to US)*

MEXICO

TURKS & CAICOS ISLANDS (to UK)
CAYMAN ISLANDS
(to UK)
HONDURAS
BELIZE
CUBA
JAMAICA

DOM. REP.

PUERTO RICO
(to US)

ST KITTS & NEVIS
ANTIGUA & BARBUDA

Tropic of Cancer

GUADELOUPE (to France)
DOMINICA
MARTINIQUE (to France)
ST LUCIA
BARBADOS

MARSHALL
ISLANDS

GUATEMALA
EL SALVADOR
NICARAGUA
COSTA RICA

HAITI
NETH. ANT.
(to Neth.)
ARUBA
(to Neth.)

ST VINCENT &
THE GRENADINES
GRENADA
TRINIDAD & TOBAGO

3

PANAMA

VENEZUELA
COLOMBIA

FRENCH GUIANA
(to France)

Equator

NAURU
K I R I B A T I

TUVALU
SOLOMON
ISLANDS

TOKELAU
(to NZ)
SAMOA

ECUADOR

GUYANA
SURINAME

B R A Z I L

VANUATU

NEW
CALEDONIA
(to France)

TONGA
FIJI

FRENCH POLYNESIA
(to France)

PERU

BOLIVIA

PARAGUAY

Tropic of Capricorn

PITCAIRN
ISLANDS
(to UK)

CHILE

4

NEW
ZEALAND

ARGENTINA

URUGUAY

*PACIFIC
OCEAN*

CHILE

FALKLAND ISLANDS
(to UK)

5

Antarctic Circle

ANTARCTICA

E F G H

29

GLOBAL CONFLICT

KEY

International conflict since 1975

Civil unrest since 1975

Disputed territories

.... Disputed border

----- Undefined border

O C E A N

GREENLAND
(to Denmark)

Arctic Circle

Alaska
(to US)

C A N A D A

Kurile Islands
(part of Russ.Fed.)

P A C I F I C

O C E A N

ST PIERRE
& MIQUELON
(to France)

UNITED STATES
OF AMERICA

A T L A N T I C

O C E A N

BERMUDA
(to UK)

PUERTO RICO (to US)
BRITISH VIRGIN ISLANDS (to UK)
VIRGIN ISLANDS (to US)
ANGUILLA (to UK)
ST KITTS & NEVIS
ANTIGUA & BARBUDA
MONTSERRAT (to UK)
GUADELOUPE (to France)
DOMINICA
MARTINIQUE (to France)
ST LUCIA
BARBADOS
ST VINCENT & THE GRENADINES
GRENADA
TRINIDAD & TOBAGO

DOM. REP.
TURKS & CAICOS ISLANDS (to UK)
CAYMAN ISLANDS
(to UK)
HONDURAS
BELIZE
CUBA
BAHAMAS
JAMAICA
NAVASSA
(to US)
HAITI
NETH. ANT.
(to Neth.)
ARUBA
(to Neth.)

M E X I C O

Hawaii
(to US)

MARSHALL
ISLANDS

WALLIS & FUTUNA
(to France)
KINGMAN REEF (to US)
PALMYRA ATOLL (to US)

BAKER &
HOWLAND
ISLANDS
(to US)

JARVIS ISLAND
(to US)

GUATEMALA
EL SALVADOR
NICARAGUA
COSTA RICA
PANAMA

VENEZUELA

COLOMBIA

GUYANA
SURINAME

FRENCH GUIANA
(to France)

Equator

NAURU

K I R I B A T I

ECUADOR

TUVALU

SOLOMON
ISLANDS

TOKELAU
(to NZ)

PERU

B R A Z I L

VANUATU

NEW
CALEDONIA
(to France)

FIJI

COOK
ISLANDS
(to NZ)

FRENCH POLYNESIA
(to France)

BOLIVIA

PARAGUAY

Tropic of Capricorn

TONGA
SAMOA

NIUE (to NZ)
AMERICAN
SAMOA
(to US)

PITCAIRN
ISLANDS
(to UK)

CHILE

URUGUAY

NEW
ZEALAND

P A C I F I C

O C E A N

A R G E N T I N A

CHILE

FALKLAND ISLANDS
(to UK)

Antarctic Circle

ANTARCTICA

31

THE
WORLD'S
REGIONS

NORTH & CENTRAL AMERICA

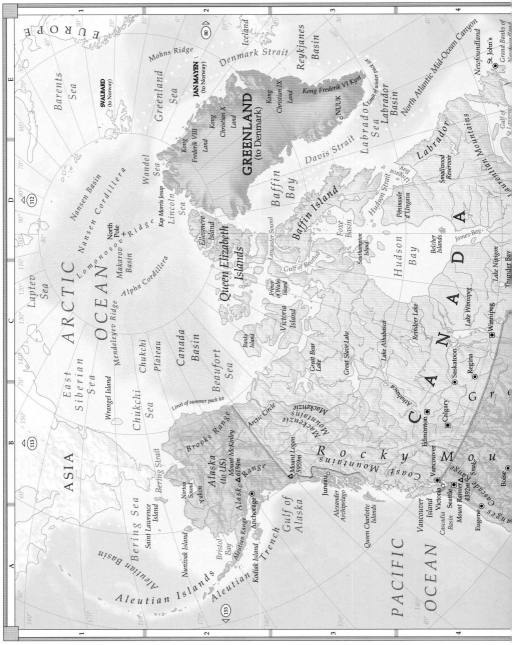

EUROPE

Barents Sea

Mohns Ridge

Iceland

Reykjanes Basin

Denmark Strait

SVALBARD (to Norway)

JAN MAYEN (to Norway)

Greenland Sea

Kong Christian IX Land

Kong Frederik VI Kyst

Kong Christian X Land

Kong Frederik VIII Land

NUUK

GREENLAND (to Denmark)

North Atlantic Mid-Ocean Canyon

Newfoundland

St. John's

Gulf of St Lawrence

Grand Banks of Newfoundland

Labrador Sea

Davis Strait

Labrador Basin

Labrador

Appalachian Mountains

Wandel Sea

Lincoln Sea

Kap Morris Jesup

Baffin Bay

Baffin Island

Hudson Strait

Peninsule d'Ungava

Ungava Bay

Smallwood Reservoir

Nansen Basin

Nansen Cordillera

North Pole

Makarov Basin

Lomonosov Ridge

Ellesmere Island

Queen Elizabeth Islands

Lancaster Sound

Gulf of Boothia

Foxe Basin

Southampton Island

James Bay

Belcher Islands

Hudson Bay

Lake Nipigon

Thunder Bay

ARCTIC OCEAN

Alpha Cordillera

Mendeleyev Ridge

Laptev Sea

East Siberian Sea

Wrangel Island

Chukchi Plateau

Chukchi Sea

Canada Plateau

Prince of Wales Island

Victoria Island

Great Bear Lake

Reindeer Lake

Lake Winnipeg

Winnipeg

Banks Island

Great Slave Lake

Lake Athabasca

Saskatoon

Regina

Gre

Beaufort Sea

Canada Basin

Limit of summer pack ice

Arctic Circle

Mackenzie Mountains

Mackenzie

Athabasca

Edmonton

Calgary

CANADA

Bering Strait

Brooks Range

Alaska (to US)

Mount McKinley 6194m

Alaska Range

Rocky Mountains

Coast Mountains

Mount Logan 5959m

ASIA

Bering Sea

Saint Lawrence Island

Norton Sound

Yukon

Nunivak Island

Bristol Bay

Anchorage

Juneau

Alexander Archipelago

Queen Charlotte Islands

Vancouver Island

Victoria

Seattle

Vancouver

Cascadia Basin

Mount Rainier 4392m

Cascade Range

Eugene

Snake

Boise

Mou

Aleutian Basin

Aleutian Islands

Aleutian Trench

Kodiak Island

Gulf of Alaska

PACIFIC OCEAN

---

0 km   1000

0 miles   1000

POPULATION   ● National capital

○ Less than 50,000   ○ 50,000 -100,000   ◉ 100,000 - 500,000   ◼ Over 500,000

ATLANTIC

OCEAN

Sargasso Sea

Nares Plain

Bermuda Rise

BERMUDA
(to UK)

Hatteras Plain

TURKS & CAICOS
ISLANDS
(to UK)

VIRGIN ISLANDS (to US)
BRITISH VIRGIN ISLANDS
(to UK) ANGUILLA (to UK)
ANTIGUA &
BARBUDA
GUADELOUPE
(to France)
DOMINICA

PUERTO
RICO
(to US)

ST KITTS & NEVIS
MONTSERRAT (to UK)
MARTINIQUE (to France)
ST LUCIA
ST VINCENT &
THE GRENADINES
GRENADA

LESSER
Antilles

BARBADOS
66
TRINIDAD
& TOBAGO

PORT-OF-SPAIN

DOMINICAN
REPUBLIC

SANTO
DOMINGO

NETHERLANDS
ANTILLES
(to Neth.)

MIQUELON
(to France)

Scotia
Halifax

Georges
Bank
Boston
Cape Cod
New York
Philadelphia
Baltimore
WASHINGTON DC
Richmond

Québec
Montreal
OTTAWA
Lake Ontario
Albany
Niagara
Falls
Lake Erie
Toronto
Detroit

St Lawrence

Appalachian Mountains

Great

Lakes
Lake Huron
Cleveland
Columbus
Lake Michigan
Milwaukee
Chicago

Lake Superior

Saint Paul
Madison
Des Moines
Lincoln

Raleigh

Columbia

Jacksonville

*Blake
Plateau*

Miami

Tampa

Straits of Florida

BAHAMAS
NASSAU

HAVANA
CUBA

HAITI
PORT-AU-PRINCE
JAMAICA
KINGSTON

CAYMAN
ISLANDS
(to UK)

Greater Antilles

Caribbean Sea

ARUBA
(to Neth.)

*Colombian
Basin*

SOUTH

AMERICA

Andes

56

PANAMA CITY

COSTA RICA
PANAMA
SAN JOSÉ

PANAMA
Basin

Cocos Ridge

Lake Nicaragua
NICARAGUA
MANAGUA

HONDURAS
TEGUCIGALPA

BELMOPAN
BELIZE

GUATEMALA
GUATEMALA CITY
SAN SALVADOR
EL SALVADOR
SAN SALVADOR

*Yucatan
Peninsula*

Gulf of Mexico

Middle America Trench

*Guatemala
Basin*

Colón Ridge

153

Galapagos Islands
(to Ecuador)

PACIFIC

OCEAN

East Pacific Rise

UNITED STATES

OF AMERICA

G r e a t
P l a i n s

Atlanta
Montgomery
Nashville
Memphis
Jackson
Baton Rouge
New Orleans

Indianapolis
Springfield
Columbia

Ohio

Little Rock
Arkansas
Red River

Oklahoma City

Topeka

Denver

Colorado

Santa Fe

P l

Houston

Austin
San Antonio

Dallas

Rio Grande

El Paso

Monterrey

Sierra Madre Oriental

MEXICO CITY
Volcán
Pico de Orizaba
5700m

MEXICO

Acapulco

Guadalajara

Sierra Madre Occidental

Revillagigedo
Islands
(to Mexico)

Phoenix

*Grand
Canyon*

△ Mount Whitney
4418m

Sierra Nevada
Great Basin

Sacramento
San Francisco
San Jose

Los Angeles
San Diego

Coast

Salt Lake City

Gulf of California
Lower California

CLIPPERTON ISLAND
(to French Polynesia)

Murray Fracture Zone

Clarion Fracture Zone

Tropic of Cancer

Equator

*Gallego
Rise*

N

153

Tropic of Cancer

Missouri

*Mississippi
Delta*

Mississippi

35

WESTERN CANADA & ALASKA

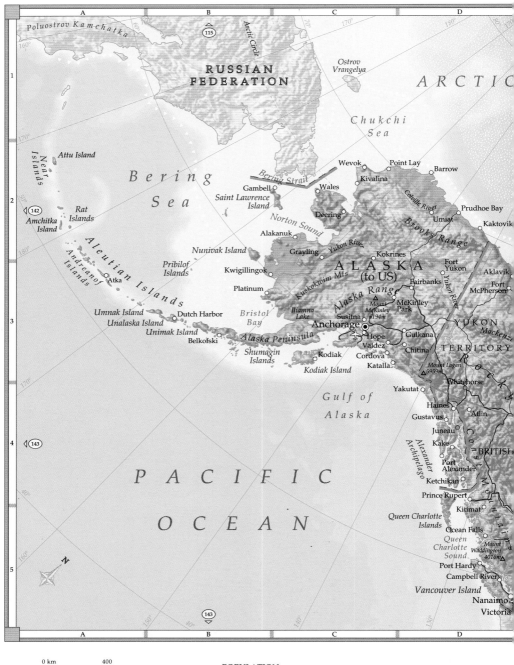

Poluostrov Kamchatka

115

Arctic Circle

RUSSIAN FEDERATION

Ostrov Vrangelya

A R C T I C

Chukchi Sea

Attu Island

Near Islands

*B e r i n g
S e a*

Bering Strait

Wevok
Point Lay
Barrow

Kivalina

Wales

Gambell

Saint Lawrence Island

Deering

Colville River

Umiat
Prudhoe Bay

Kaktovik

142

Rat Islands

Amchitka Island

Norton Sound

Alakanuk

Grayling
Yukon River
Kokrines

Brooks Range

Nunivak Island

Pribilof Islands

Kwigillingok

A L A S K A
(to US)

Fort Yukon

Aklavik

Aleutian Islands

Andreanof Islands
Atka

Platinum

Kuskokwim Mts

Fairbanks

Fort McPherson

Umnak Island
Unalaska Island

Dutch Harbor

Unimak Island

Belkofski

Iliamna Lake

Alaska Range

Mount McKinley 6194m

McKinley Park

Y U K O N

Bristol Bay

Susitna

Anchorage

Mackenz

Alaska Peninsula

Hope

Gulkana

T E R R I T O R Y

Shumagin Islands

Valdez
Cordova
Chitina

Katalla

Mount Logan 5959m

Kodiak

Kodiak Island

143

Yakutat

Whitehorse

*Gulf of
Alaska*

Haines

Gustavus
Atlin

Juneau

Kake

BRITISH

P A C I F I C

Alexander Archipelago

Port Alexander

Ketchikan

O C E A N

Prince Rupert

Queen Charlotte Islands

Kitimat

Ocean Falls

Queen Charlotte Sound

Mount Waddington 4016m

143

Port Hardy

Campbell River

Vancouver Island

Nanaimo

Victoria

A

B

C

D

0 km   400

0 miles   400

POPULATION

○ Less than 50,000   ○ 50,000 -100,000   ◉ 100,000 - 500,000   ■ Over 500,000

● Internal administrative capital

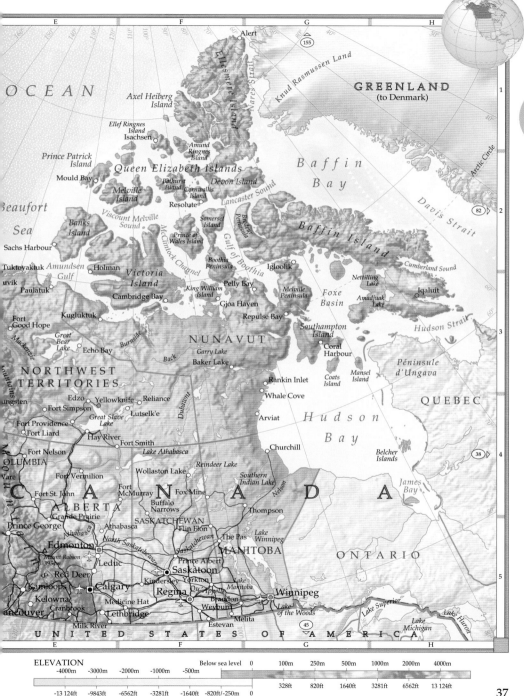

GREENLAND
(to Denmark)

OCEAN

*Axel Heiberg
Island*

Ellesmere Island

Alert

155

Knud Rasmussen Land

*Ellef Ringnes
Island*
Isachsen

*Prince Patrick
Island*

Mould Bay

Queen Elizabeth Islands

*Amund
Ringnes
Island*

*Bathurst
Island*
*Cornwallis
Island*
Resolute

Devon Island

Lancaster Sound

*Baffin
Bay*

Arctic Circle

82

Davis Strait

*Melville
Island*

*Beaufort
Sea*

*Banks
Island*

*Viscount Melville
Sound*

Sachs Harbour

McClintock Channel

*Somerset
Island*

*Prince of
Wales Island*

Gulf of Boothia

*Boothia
Peninsula*

Igloolik

Baffin Island

Cumberland Sound

Tuktoyaktuk *Amundsen
Gulf*

Holman

uvik
Paulatuk

*Victoria
Island*

Cambridge Bay

*King William
Island*

Pelly Bay

Gjoa Haven

*Melville
Peninsula*

*Nettilling
Lake*

*Foxe
Basin*

*Amadjuak
Lake*

Iqaluit

Fort
Good Hope

Kugluktuk

Repulse Bay

*Great
Bear
Lake*

Echo Bay

Mackenzie

Burnside

Back

NUNAVUT

Garry Lake

Baker Lake

*Southampton
Island*

Coral
Harbour

Hudson Strait

*Péninsule
d'Ungava*

NORTHWEST
TERRITORIES

ungsten

Edzo Yellowknife

Fort Simpson

Reliance

*Great Slave
Lake*

Lutselk'e

Dubawnt

Rankin Inlet

Whale Cove

Arviat

*Coats
Island*

*Mansel
Island*

*Hudson

Bay*

QUEBEC

Fort Providence
Fort Liard

Hay River
Fort Smith

Lake Athabasca

Fort Nelson

OLUMBIA

Vare

Fort Vermilion

Reindeer Lake

Wollaston Lake

*Southern
Indian Lake*

Nelson

Churchill

*Belcher
Islands*

*James
Bay*

38

CANADA

Fort St. John

Prince George

Fort
McMurray

Buffalo
Narrows

Fox Mine

Thompson

*Lake
Winnipeg*

ONTARIO

ALBERTA

Grande Prairie

Athabasca

Athabasca

SASKATCHEWAN

Flin Flon

The Pas

North Saskatchewan

Saskatchewan

MANITOBA

Edmonton

*Mount Robson
395?m*

Leduc

Prince Albert

Saskatoon

Red Deer

Kindersley

Yorkton

*Lake
Manitoba*

Kamloops

Calgary

Regina

Qu'Appelle

Brandon

Winnipeg

*Lake
of the Woods*

Lake Superior

Kelowna

Cranbrook

Medicine Hat

Weyburn

ancouver
Lethbridge

Milk River

Estevan

Melita

45

*Lake
Michigan*

*Lake
Huron*

UNITED STATES OF AMERICA

ELEVATION

					Below sea level	0	100m	250m	500m	1000m	2000m	4000m
-4000m	-3000m	-2000m	-1000m	-500m								

						328ft	820ft	1640ft	3281ft	6562ft	13 124ft
-13 124ft	-9843ft	-6562ft	-3281ft	-1640ft	-820ft/-250m	0					

EASTERN CANADA

NORTHWEST
TERRITORIES

NUNAVUT

SASKATCHEWAN

Churchill

Southern
Indian Lake

Nelson

Hayes

Coats
Island

Mansel
Island

Ottawa Islands

Hudson

Bay

Ivujivik

Charles
Island

Hudson

*Péninsule
d' Ungava*

Inukjuak

Koksoak

Lac
Minto

MANITOBA

Cedar
Lake

Lake
Winnipeg

Lake
Winnipegosis

Lake
Manitoba

Sandy Lake

Fort Severn

Severn

Winisk

Winisk

Belcher
Islands

*James
Bay*

Akimiski
Island

Attawapiskat

Attawapiskat

Lac
Bienvill

QUE

C

A

N

A

ONTARIO

Albany

Fort
Albany

Eastmain

Moosonee

Rivière de Rupert

Lac
Mistassini

Lac Seul

Armstrong

Moose

Harricana

Chibougamau

Kenora

Dryden

Lake of
the Woods

Lake
Nipigon

Longlac

Hearst

Kapuskasing

Cochrane

Réservoir
Gouin

Fort Frances

Atikokan

Nipigon

Marathon

Tip Top Mountain
△640m

Timmins

Amos

Rouyn-Noranda

NORTH
DAKOTA

Rainy
Lake

Thunder Bay

Wawa

Foleyet

Kirkland
Lake

Val-d'Or

Red River

Lake Superior

MINNESOTA

MICHIGAN

Sault Ste.Marie
Sudbury

North
Bay

Pembroke

Gatineau
Hull

Lava

SOUTH
DAKOTA

Manitoulin
Island

Georgian
Bay

OTTAWA

NEBRASKA

UNITED STATES

WISCONSIN

*Lake
Huron*

Midland

Peterborough

Kingston

Lake
Ontari

OF AMERICA

IOWA

Lake Michigan

Brampton

Oshawa

Toronto

Kitchener

Hamilton

St. Catharines

Sarnia

London

Niagara
Falls

NEW YORK

Windsor

Leamington

Lake Erie

OHIO

PENNSYLVANIA

ILLINOIS

Mississippi River

INDIANA

0 km   400

0 miles   400

POPULATION   ● National capital   ◎ Internal administrative capital

○ Less than 50,000   ○ 50,000 -100,000   ◉ 100,000 - 500,000   ◼ Over 500,000

E 65° 60° F 55° 60° 50° G 45° H

Baffin Island
Strait
Resolution Island
Button Islands
Akpatok Island
Ungava Bay
Kuujjuaq
Rivière à la Baleine
Caniapiscau
Nain
Hopedale
Makkovik
Cape Harrison
Schefferville
Labrador Sea
Labrador
NEWFOUNDLAND
Smallwood Reservoir
Lake Melville
Churchill
Cartwright
Réservoir de Caniapiscau
St.Anthony
B E C
D
Réservoir Manicouagan
Laurentian Mountains
A
Havre-St-Pierre
Strait of Belle Isle
Gander
Sept-Îles
Île d'Anticosti
Corner Brook
Grand Falls
St.John's
Baie-Comeau
St.Lawrence
Gaspé
Gulf of St. Lawrence
Newfoundland
Lac St-Jean
Péninsule de Gaspé
Île d'Anticosti
Channel-Port aux Basques
Cape Race
nquière
Chicoutimi
Matane
Îles de la Madeleine
Cabot Strait
ST PIERRE & MIQUELON
(to France)
Rimouski
Rivière-du-Loup
Bathurst
PRINCE EDWARD ISLAND
Glace Bay
Sydney
La Tuque
Edmundston
NEW BRUNSWICK
Charlottetown
Cape Breton Island
Charlesbourg
Québec
St-Georges
Moncton
Amherst
New Glasgow
Trois-Rivières
Drummondville
Fredericton
Oromocto
Truro
NOVA SCOTIA
Sable Island
Montréal
Saint John
Dartmouth
MAINE
Bay of Fundy
Halifax
Sherbrooke
Liverpool
VERMONT
Yarmouth
NEW HAMPSHIRE
ATLANTIC
MASSACHUSETTS
Cape Cod
CONNECTICUT
RHODE ISLAND
70°
OCEAN
65° 40° 60° 55°
N

E F G H

ELEVATION

| -4000m | -3000m | -2000m | -1000m | -500m | Below sea level | 0 | 100m | 250m | 500m | 1000m | 2000m | 4000m |

| | | | | | | 0 | 328ft | 820ft | 1640ft | 3281ft | 6562ft | 13 124ft |

| -13 124ft | -9843ft | -6562ft | -3281ft | -1640ft | -820ft/-250m | 0 | | | | | | |

39

USA: THE NORTHEAST

0 km 200

0 miles 200

POPULATION

● National capital   ● Internal administrative capital

○ Less than 50,000   ○ 50,000 -100,000   ◉ 100,000 - 500,000   ◼ Over 500,000

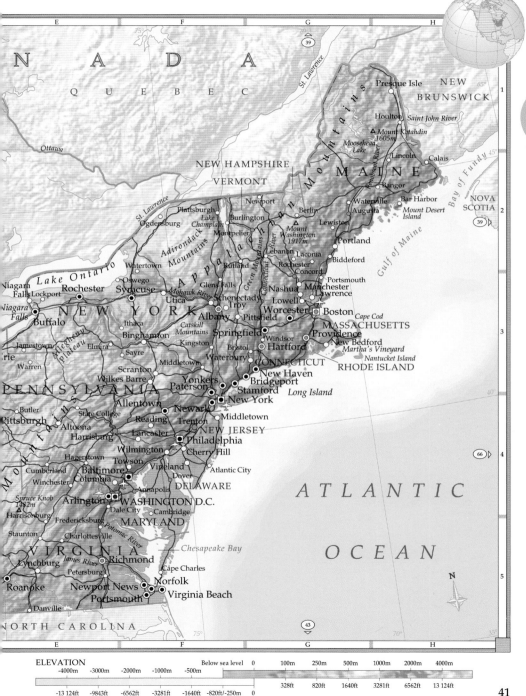

ELEVATION

-4000m	-3000m	-2000m	-1000m	-500m	Below sea level	0	100m	250m	500m	1000m	2000m	4000m

| -13 124ft | -9843ft | -6562ft | -3281ft | -1640ft | -820ft/-250m | 0 | 328ft | 820ft | 1640ft | 3281ft | 6562ft | 13 124ft |

USA: THE SOUTHEAST

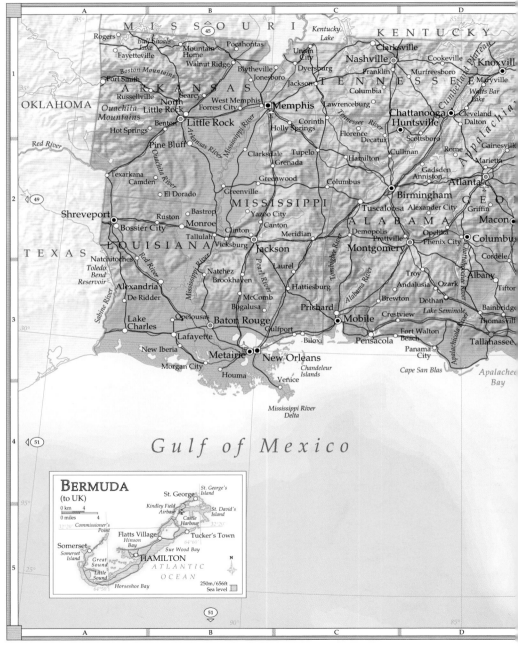

POPULATION

○ Less than 50,000 ○ 50,000 -100,000 ◉ 100,000 - 500,000 ■ Over 500,000

◎ Internal administrative capital

0 km 200

0 miles 200

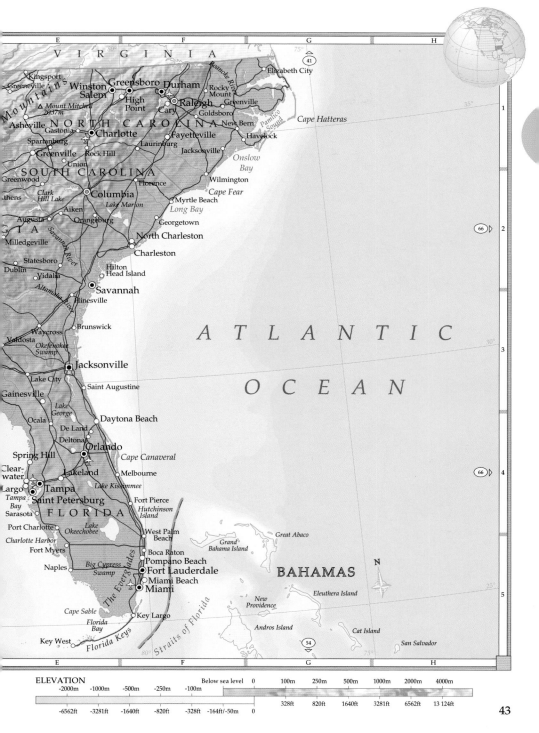

V I R G I N I A

41

Kingsport
Greeneville
Winston
Salem
High
Point
Greensboro
Durham
Raleigh
Cary
Rocky
Mount
Elizabeth City
75°

△ Mount Mitchell
2037m
Goldsboro
Greenville
New Bern
35°
Cape Hatteras

Asheville
Gastonia
Spartanburg
N O R T H   C A R O L I N A
Charlotte
Fayetteville
Havelock
Pamlico
Sound

Greenville
Union
Rock Hill
Laurinburg
Jacksonville
Onslow
Bay

S O U T H   C A R O L I N A
Greenwood
Clark
Hill Lake
Columbia
Florence
Wilmington
Cape Fear

thens
Aiken
Lake Marion
Myrtle Beach
Long Bay

Augusta
Orangeburg
Georgetown

Milledgeville
T A
Savannah River
North Charleston
66
2

Statesboro
Dublin
Vidalia
Altamaha River
Hilton
Head Island
Charleston

Savannah
Hinesville

Waycross
Brunswick
A T L A N T I C
Valdosta
Okefenokee
Swamp
30°
3

Jacksonville
Lake City
O C E A N
Saint Augustine

Gainesville
Lake
George

Ocala
Daytona Beach
De Land
Deltona

Spring Hill
Orlando
Cape Canaveral

Clear-
water
Lakeland
Melbourne
66
4

Largo
Tampa
Lake Kissimmee
Tampa
Bay
Saint Petersburg
Fort Pierce

Sarasota
F L O R I D A
Hutchinson
Island

Port Charlotte
Lake
Okeechobee
West Palm
Beach
Great Abaco

Charlotte Harbor
Fort Myers
Grand
Bahama Island

Naples
Big Cypress
Swamp
Boca Raton
Pompano Beach
Fort Lauderdale
Miami Beach
Miami
BAHAMAS
N

Cape Sable
The Everglades
Eleuthera Island

Key Largo
Straits of Florida
New
Providence
25°
5

Florida
Bay
Andros Island
Cat Island

Key West
Florida Keys
54
San Salvador
75°
80°

ELEVATION
-2000m -1000m -500m -250m -100m   Below sea level 0   100m   250m   500m   1000m   2000m   4000m

-6562ft -3281ft -1640ft -820ft -328ft -164ft/-50m 0   328ft   820ft   1640ft   3281ft   6562ft   13 124ft

USA: Central States

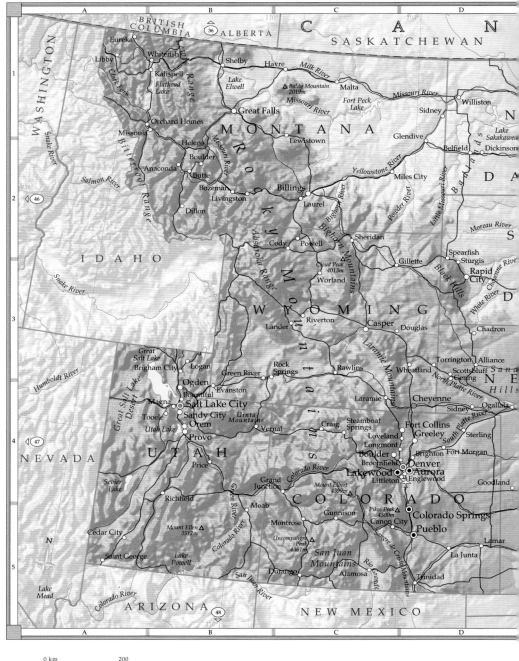

POPULATION

○ Less than 50,000 ○ 50,000 -100,000 ◉ 100,000 - 500,000 ■ Over 500,000

● Internal administrative capital

0 km 200

0 miles 200

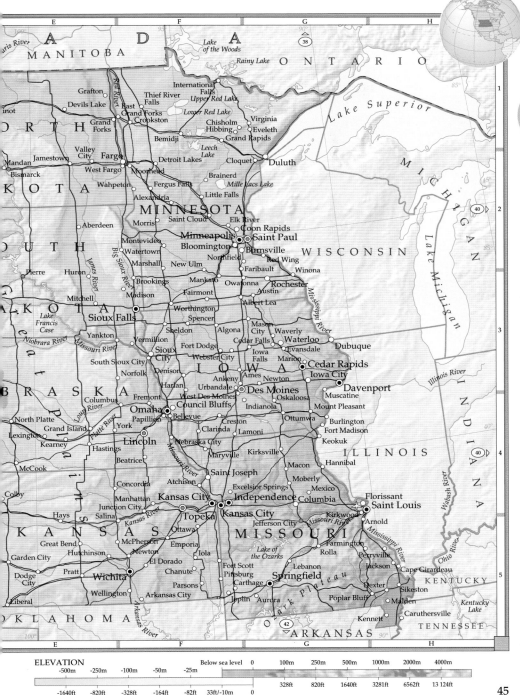

ELEVATION

					Below sea level	0		100m	250m	500m	1000m	2000m	4000m
-500m	-250m	-100m	-50m	-25m									
-1640ft	-820ft	-328ft	-164ft	-82ft	33ft/-10m	0		328ft	820ft	1640ft	3281ft	6562ft	13 124ft

USA: THE WEST

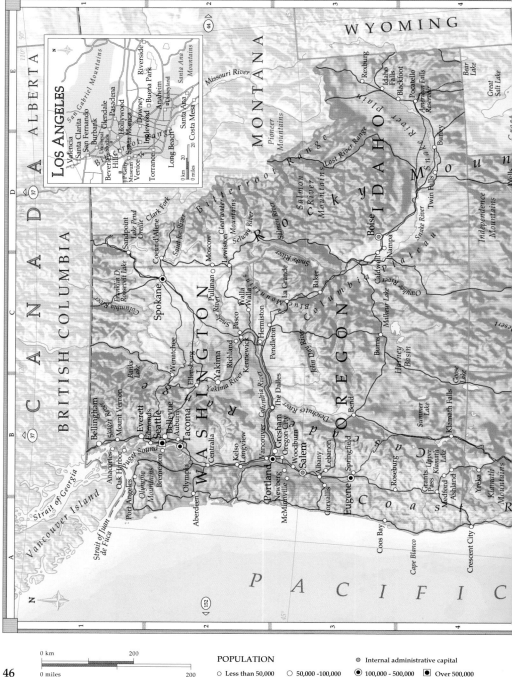

LOS ANGELES

San Gabriel Mountains
Valencia
Santa Clarita
San Fernando
Burbank
Universal Glendale
City Hollywood Pasadena
Beverly Studios Riverside
Hills J.P. Getty Santa Monica Downey Santa Ana Park
Museum Venice Inglewood Disneyland Mountains
Torrance Buena Park
Long Beach Anaheim
Costa Mesa

0 km 20
0 miles 20

WYOMING

MONTANA

IDAHO

OREGON

WASHINGTON

CANADA

BRITISH COLUMBIA

ALBERTA

Vancouver Island

Strait of Georgia

Strait of Juan de Fuca

PACIFIC

POPULATION

⦿ Internal administrative capital

○ Less than 50,000 ○ 50,000 -100,000 ◉ 100,000 - 500,000 ◾ Over 500,000

0 km 200

0 miles 200

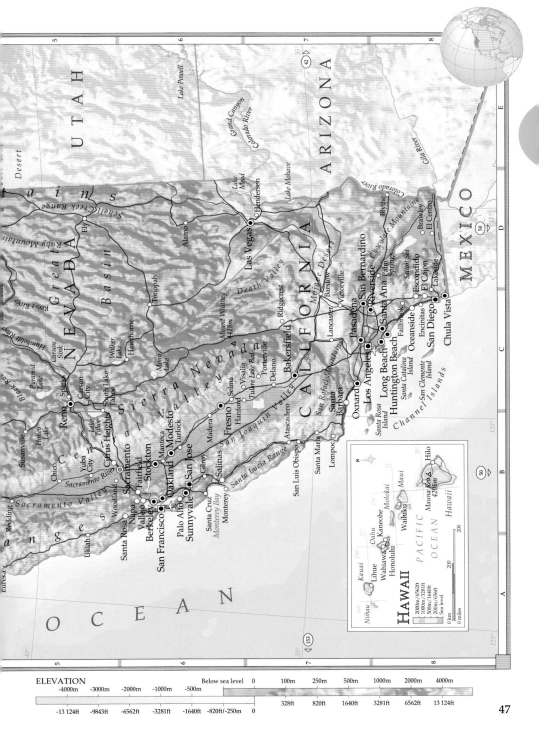

ELEVATION

-4000m	-3000m	-2000m	-1000m	-500m	Below sea level	0	100m	250m	500m	1000m	2000m	4000m

| -13 124ft | -9843ft | -6562ft | -3281ft | -1640ft | -820ft/-250m | 0 | | 328ft | 820ft | 1640ft | 3281ft | 6562ft | 13 124ft |

USA: THE SOUTHWEST

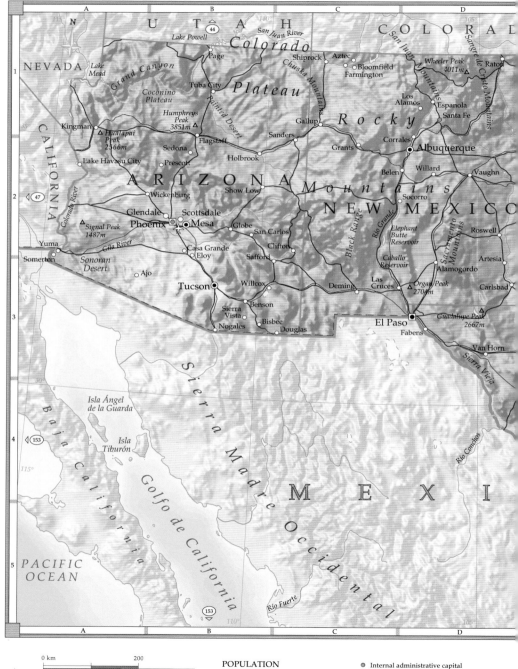

POPULATION

○ Less than 50,000   ○ 50,000 -100,000   ◉ 100,000 - 500,000   ◼ Over 500,000

◉ Internal administrative capital

0 km   200

0 miles   200

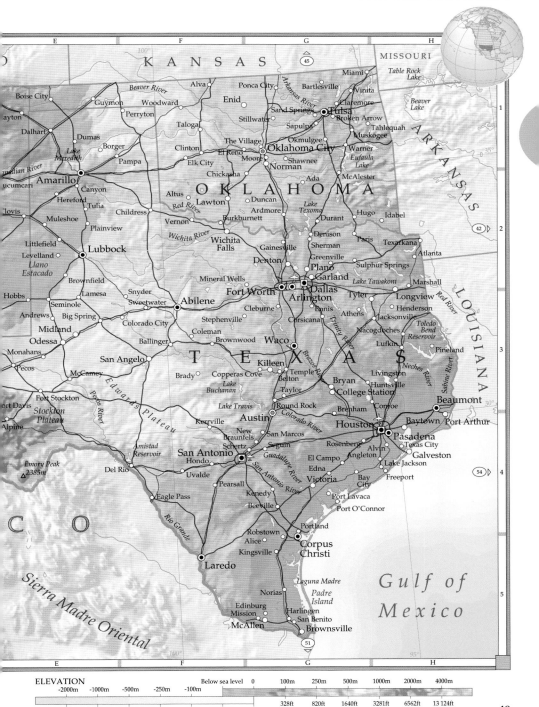

ELEVATION

				Below sea level	0	100m	250m	500m	1000m	2000m	4000m
-2000m	-1000m	-500m	-250m	-100m							
-6562ft	-3281ft	-1640ft	-820ft	-328ft	-164ft/-50m	0	328ft	820ft	1640ft	3281ft	6562ft	13 124ft

49

MEXICO

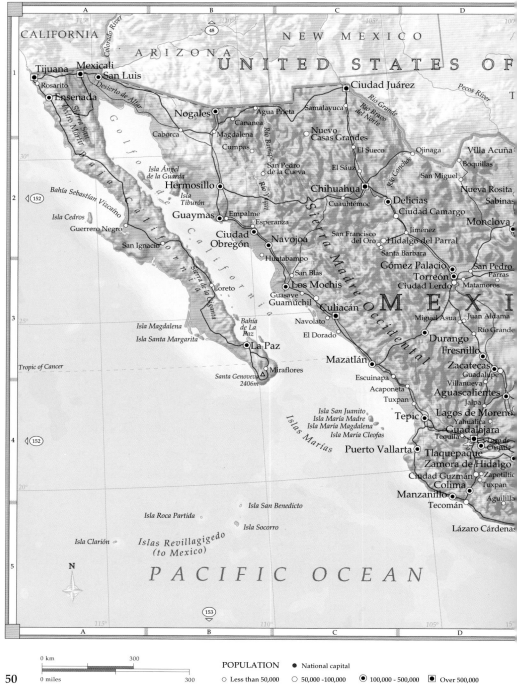

CALIFORNIA

ARIZONA

NEW MEXICO

UNITED STATES OF

Colorado River

48

Pecos River

Tijuana
Mexicali
San Luis
Rosarito
Ensenada

Desierto de Altar

Sierra San Pedro Mártir

Ciudad Juárez

Rio Grande
Rio Bravo del Norte

Nogales
Agua Prieta
Samalayuca
Cananea
Caborca
Magdalena
Cumpas
Nuevo Casas Grandes

El Sueco
Ojinaga
Villa Acuña
Boquillas

Golfo de California

Isla Ángel de la Guarda

San Pedro de la Cueva
El Sáuz
San Miguel
Nueva Rosita

Bahía Sebastián Vizcaíno

Isla Cedros

Hermosillo
Isla Tiburón
Río Yaqui

Chihuahua
Cuauhtémoc
Delicias
Ciudad Camargo

Sabinas
Monclova

Guerrero Negro

Guaymas
Empalme
Esperanza

San Francisco del Oro
Jiménez

San Ignacio

Ciudad Obregón
Navojoa
Hidalgo del Parral
Santa Barbara

Gómez Palacio
San Pedro
Parras

Huatabampo

Sierra Madre Occidental

Sierra de la Giganta

Loreto

San Blas
Los Mochis
Guasave
Guamúchil
Culiacán

Torreón
Ciudad Lerdo
Matamoros

MEXI

Miguel Asua
Juan Aldama
Río Grande

Isla Magdalena
Isla Santa Margarita

Bahía de La Paz

Navolato
El Dorado

Durango
Fresnillo

La Paz

Mazatlán

Zacatecas
Guadalupe
Villanueva
Aguascalientes
Jalpa

Tropic of Cancer

Santa Genoveva 2406m

Miraflores

Escuinapa
Acaponeta
Tuxpan

Isla San Juanito
Isla María Madre
Isla María Magdalena
Isla María Cleofas

Tepic

Lagos de Moreno
Yahualica
Guadalajara
Tequila
Lago de Chapala

Islas Marías

Puerto Vallarta
Tlaquepaque
Zamora de Hidalgo

Ciudad Guzmán
Zapotiltic
Colima
Tuxpan
Manzanillo
Tecomán
Aguililla

Isla San Benedicto

Isla Roca Partida

Isla Socorro

Lázaro Cárdenas

Isla Clarión

Islas Revillagigedo
(to Mexico)

N

PACIFIC OCEAN

153

POPULATION
● National capital
○ Less than 50,000   ○ 50,000 -100,000   ◉ 100,000 - 500,000   ◼ Over 500,000

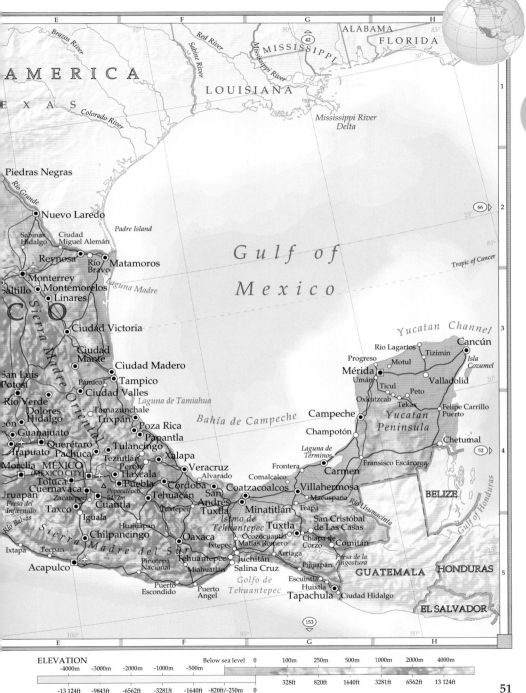

Gulf of Mexico

ELEVATION

Below sea level	0		100m	250m	500m	1000m	2000m	4000m
-4000m	-3000m	-2000m	-1000m	-500m				

					328ft	820ft	1640ft	3281ft	6562ft	13 124ft
-13 124ft	-9843ft	-6562ft	-3281ft	-1640ft	-820ft/-250m	0				

51

CENTRAL AMERICA

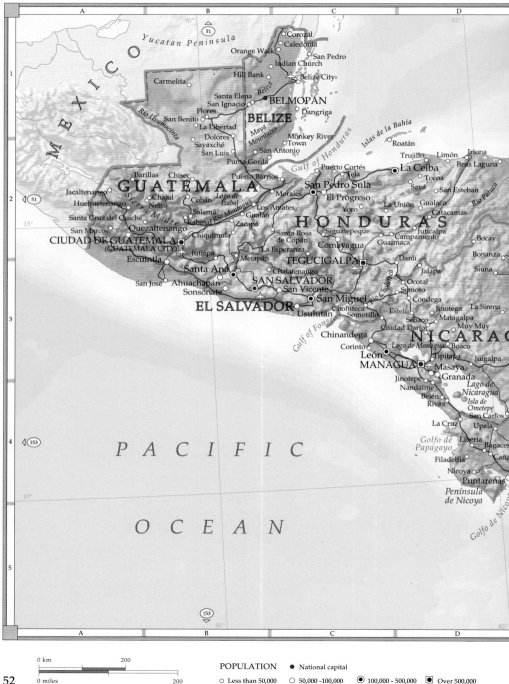

Yucatan Peninsula

MEXICO

Corozal
Caledonia
Orange Walk
San Pedro
Indian Church
Hill Bank
Belize City
Carmelita
Santa Elena
San Ignacio
Flores
BELMOPAN
San Benito
La Libertad
Dangriga
Dolores
BELIZE
Sayaxché
Maya
Mountains
Monkey River
Town
San Antonio
San Luis
Punta Gorda
Islas de la Bahía
Roatán
Trujillo
Limón
Iriona
Brus Laguna
Barillas
Chisec
Puerto Barrios
Puerto Cortés
Tela
La Ceiba
Tocoa
Jacaltenango
GUATEMALA
Morales
San Pedro Sula
Savá
San Esteban
Huehuetenango
Nebaj
Cobán
Lago de
Izabal
El Progreso
La Unión
Gualaco
Catacamas
Salamá
Rabinal
Gualán
Yoro
HONDURAS
Santa Cruz del Quiché
Santa Rosa
de Copán
Siguatepeque
Juticalpa
Bocay
San Marcos
Quezaltenango
Chiquimula
Zacapa
Campamento
Bonanza
CIUDAD DE GUATEMALA
(GUATEMALA CITY)
Jutiapa
Metapán
Comayagua
Guaimaca
Siuna
Escuintla
La Esperanza
TEGUCIGALPA
Danlí
Jalapa
San José
Ahuachapán
Santa Ana
Chalatenango
Ocotal
Somoto
Sonsonate
SAN SALVADOR
San Vicente
Condega
Jinotega
La Sirena
EL SALVADOR
San Miguel
Usulután
Choluteca
Somotillo
Estelí
Sébaco
Matagalpa
Gulf of Fonseca
Chinandega
Ciudad Darío
Muy Muy
NICARA
Corinto
Lago de Managua
Boaco
León
Tipitapa
Juigalpa
MANAGUA
Masaya
Jinotepe
Granada
Nandaime
Lago de
Nicaragua
Belén
Rivas
Isla de
Ometepe
San Carlos
La Cruz
Upala
Golfo de
Papagayo
Liberia
Bagaces
Filadelfia
Caña
Nicoya
Puntarenas
Península
de Nicoya
Golfo de Nicoya

PACIFIC

OCEAN

0 km   200

0 miles   200

POPULATION   ● National capital

○ Less than 50,000   ○ 50,000 -100,000   ◉ 100,000 - 500,000   ◼ Over 500,000

Islas Santanilla
(to Honduras)

Laguna de Caratasca
Puerto Lempira

Río Coco

Waspam

Cayos Miskitos

Tuapi

Yablis
Puerto Cabezas

Mosquito Coast

Prinzapolka

Barra de Río Grande

U A
Laguna de Perlas

El Rama
Islas del Maíz

Bluefields

Punta Gorda

San Juan del Norte

Río San Juan
uerto
Viejo
Quesada
juela
Heredia
SAN JOSÉ
Cartago

COSTA RICA
Siquirres
Limón

Guabito

Cerro Chirripó
Grande
3819m
uepos
Buenos Aires
Cortés

Palmar
Sur

Bahía
de Coronado
Península de Osa

La Concepción

Cordillera de
Talamanca

Almirante
Laguna
de Chiriquí

Volcán Barú 3475m
Boquete Cordillera Central

David

Golfo Dulce

Golfo de los
Mosquitos

Guarumal

Santiago

P A N A M A

Golfo
de Chiriquí

Isla de Coiba

Isla
Cébaco

Ocú

Las Tablas

Península de
Azuero

Bajo Nuevo
(to Colombia)

Cayo de Serranilla
(to Colombia)

Cayo de Serrana
(to Colombia)

Isla de Providencia
(to Colombia)

Isla de San Andrés
(to Colombia)

C a r i b b e a n

S e a

Istmo de Panamá

Portobelo
Colón
Cristóbal
Panama Canal
Lago Gatún
Balboa
Capira
PANAMÁ
(PANAMA CITY)
Penonomé
Aguadulce
Chitré

El Porvenir

Cordillera de San Blas

San Miguelito

Lago Bayano

Chimán

Archipiélago
de las Perlas

Isla
del Rey

La Palma

Yaviza

El Real

Garachiné

Jaqué

Golfo
de P a n a m á

Gulf of
Darien

Ailigandí

Serranía del Darién

Puerto Obaldía

COLOMBIA

N

54

55

58

58

80°

15°

75°

10°

80°

E   F   G   H

1

2

3

4

5

ELEVATION
-4000m   -3000m   -2000m   -1000m   -500m

Below sea level   0   100m   250m   500m   1000m   2000m   4000m

-13 124ft   -9843ft   -6562ft   -3281ft   -1640ft   -820ft/-250m   0

328ft   820ft   1640ft   3281ft   6562ft   13 124ft

53

THE CARIBBEAN

N

Gulf of Mexico

UNITED STATES OF AMERICA

The Everglades

Grand Bahama Island

Freeport

Marsh Harbour

Great Abaco

Bimini Islands

Berry Islands

Northeast Providence Channel

Florida Keys

Straits of Florida

Nicholls Town

NASSAU

New Providence

Eleuthera Island

Rock Sound

Cat Island

Tropic of Cancer

Cay Sal

Andros Town

Andros Island

Exuma Cays

Exuma Sound

San Salvador

LA HABANA (HAVANA)

Anguilla Cays

BAHAMAS

George Town

Rum Cay

Long Island

Guanabacoa

Great Exuma Island

Clarence Town

Crooked Island

Yucatan Channel

Artemisa

Cárdenas

Sagua la Grande

Archipiélago de Camagüey

Crooked Island Passage

Pinar del Río

Matanzas

Santa Clara

Acklins Island

Mayaguana Passage

Mayaguana

Consolación del Sur

Cienfuegos

Placetas

Caicos Passage

La Fé

Nueva Gerona

Morón

Ciego de Ávila

Ragged Island Range

Little Inagua

Isla de la Juventud

Cayo Largo

Sancti Spíritus

C U B A

Lake Rosa

Archipiélago de los Canarreos

Bahía de Cochinos

Camagüey

Nuevitas

Matthew Town

Great Inagua

Archipiélago de los Jardines de la Reina

Las Tunas

Holguín

Bayamo

Manzanillo

Palma Soriano

Guantánamo

Cap-Haïtien

Cayman Brac

Santiago de Cuba

Windward Passage

Gonaïves

GEORGE TOWN

Grand Cayman

NAVASSA ISLAND (to US)

Jérémie

HAÏTI

PORT-AU-PRINCE

CAYMAN ISLANDS (to UK)

G r e a t e r

Montego Bay

Jamaica Channel

Cayes

Jacm

Spanish Town

Portmore

KINGSTON

JAMAICA

Pedro Cays

C a r i b b e a n

A

HONDURAS

NICARAGUA

JAMAICA

Montego Bay

Lucea

Falmouth

Runaway Bay

St Ann's Bay

Ocho Rios

Caribbean Sea

The Cockpit Country

Cambridge

Christiana

Ewarton

Annotto Bay

Buff Bay

Port Antonio

Savanna-La-Mar

Mandeville

Spanish Town

Blue Mountain Peak 2258m

Black River

May Pen

Old Harbour

KINGSTON

Portmore

Morant Bay

N

Portland Bight

Caribbean Sea

2000m/6562ft
1000m/3281ft
500m/1640ft
200m/656ft
Sea level

0 km   20
0 miles   20

COSTA RICA

COLOMBIA

POPULATION

● National capital

○ Less than 50,000   ○ 50,000 -100,000   ◉ 100,000 - 500,000   ■ Over 500,000

0 km   200
0 miles   200

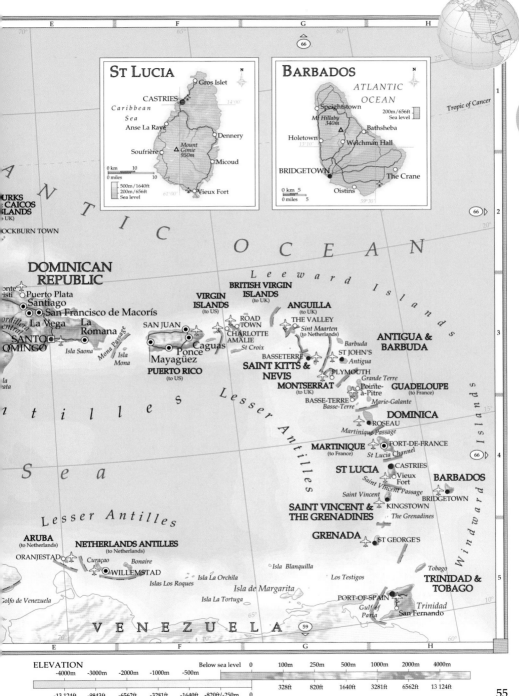

St Lucia

Gros Islet

CASTRIES

Caribbean Sea

Anse La Raye

Dennery

Soufrière

△ Mount Gimie 950m

Micoud

0 km 10
0 miles 10

500m/1640ft
200m/656ft
Sea level

Vieux Fort

Barbados

ATLANTIC OCEAN

Speightstown

Mt Hillaby 340m △

Bathsheba

200m/656ft
Sea level

Holetown

Welchman Hall

BRIDGETOWN

The Crane

Oistins

0 km 5
0 miles 5

Tropic of Cancer

TURKS & CAICOS ISLANDS
(to UK)

COCKBURN TOWN

DOMINICAN REPUBLIC

Puerto Plata
Santiago
San Francisco de Macorís
La Vega
La Romana

SANTO DOMINGO

Isla Saona

Mona Passage

Isla Mona

PUERTO RICO
(to US)

SAN JUAN

Caguas
Ponce
Mayagüez

Isla Mona

Greater Antilles

Sea

Lesser Antilles

A T L A N T I C   O C E A N

Leeward Islands

BRITISH VIRGIN ISLANDS
(to UK)

VIRGIN ISLANDS
(to US)

ROAD TOWN

CHARLOTTE AMALIE

St Croix

ANGUILLA
(to UK)

THE VALLEY

Sint Maarten
(to Netherlands)

BASSETERRE

SAINT KITTS & NEVIS

Antigua

Barbuda

ANTIGUA & BARBUDA

ST JOHN'S

MONTSERRAT
(to UK)

PLYMOUTH

Grande Terre

Pointe-a-Pitre

GUADELOUPE
(to France)

BASSE-TERRE
Basse-Terre

Marie-Galante

DOMINICA

ROSEAU

Martinique Passage

MARTINIQUE
(to France)

FORT-DE-FRANCE

St Lucia Channel

ST LUCIA

CASTRIES
Vieux Fort

BARBADOS

BRIDGETOWN

Saint Vincent Passage

Saint Vincent

SAINT VINCENT & THE GRENADINES

KINGSTOWN

The Grenadines

GRENADA

ST GEORGE'S

Lesser Antilles

ARUBA
(to Netherlands)

ORANJESTAD

NETHERLANDS ANTILLES
(to Netherlands)

Curaçao

Bonaire

WILLEMSTAD

Islas Los Roques

Isla La Orchila

Isla Blanquilla

Los Testigos

Tobago

TRINIDAD & TOBAGO

Windward Islands

Golfo de Venezuela

Isla de Margarita

Isla La Tortuga

PORT-OF-SPAIN

Gulf of Paria

Trinidad

San Fernando

V E N E Z U E L A

ELEVATION

					Below sea level	0	100m	250m	500m	1000m	2000m	4000m
-4000m	-3000m	-2000m	-1000m	-500m		0						
							328ft	820ft	1640ft	3281ft	6562ft	13 124ft
-13 124ft	-9843ft	-6562ft	-3281ft	-1640ft	-820ft/-250m	0						

55

SOUTH AMERICA

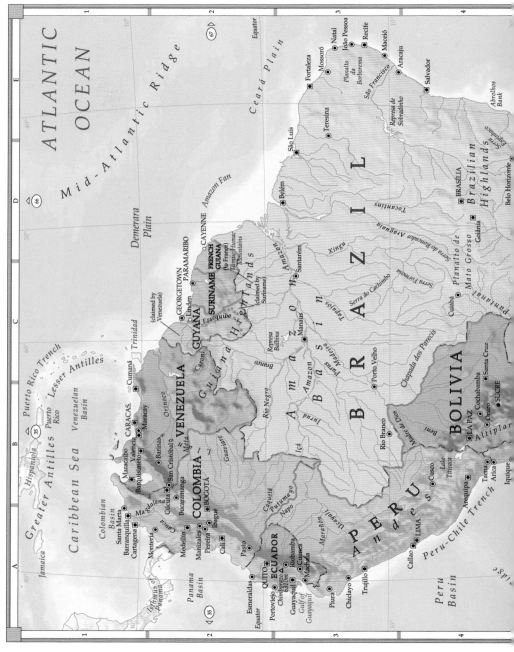

POPULATION   ● National capital

○ Less than 50,000   ◉ 50,000 -100,000   ◉ 100,000 - 500,000   ◼ Over 500,000

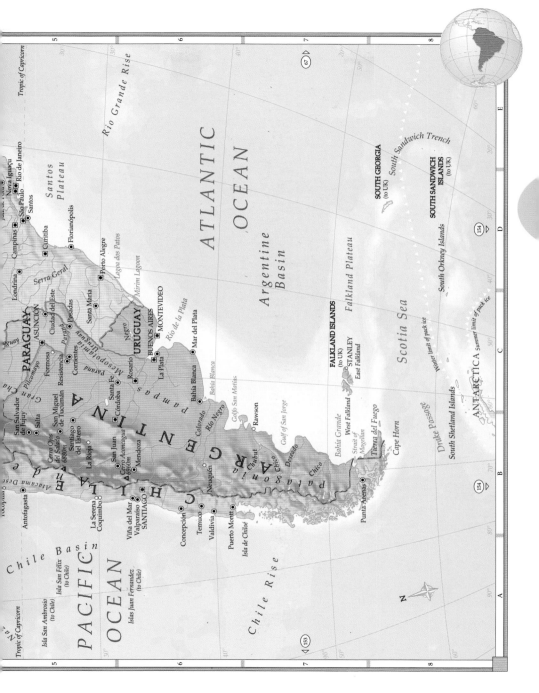

ATLANTIC

OCEAN

PACIFIC

OCEAN

Tropic of Capricorn

Rio Grande Rise

Santos Plateau

Nova Iguaçu
Rio de Janeiro
São Paulo
Santos
Campinas
Curitiba
Florianópolis
Londrina
Serra Geral
Porto Alegre
Lagoa dos Patos
Santa Maria
Mirim Lagoon

Argentine Basin

Falkland Plateau

PARAGUAY
ASUNCIÓN
Ciudad del Este
Desadas
Formosa
Resistencia
Corrientes
Paraná
Mesopotamia
Uruguay
URUGUAY
MONTEVIDEO
Río de la Plata
BUENOS AIRES
Mar del Plata
La Plata
Rosario
Santa Fe
Córdoba
Negro
Bahía Blanca
Pampas
Bahía Blanca
Colorado
Río Negro
Golfo San Matías
Rawson
Gulf of San Jorge
Chubut
Chico
Deseado
Chico

Gran Chaco
San Salvador de Jujuy
Salta
San Miguel de Tucumán
Santiago del Estero
La Rioja
San Juan
Mendoza
Cerro Ojos del Salado 6880m
Cerro Aconcagua 6960m
Neuquén
ARGENTINA
Patagonia

Atacama Desert
Antofagasta
CHILE
La Serena
Coquimbo
Viña del Mar
Valparaíso
SANTIAGO
Concepción
Temuco
Valdivia
Puerto Montt
Isla de Chiloé

Chile Basin
Isla San Félix *(to Chile)*
Isla San Ambrosio *(to Chile)*
Islas Juan Fernández *(to Chile)*

Chile Rise

Tropic of Capricorn

Bahía Grande
West Falkland
East Falkland
FALKLAND ISLANDS *(to UK)*
STANLEY
Strait of Magellan
Tierra del Fuego
Cape Horn
Punta Arenas
Drake Passage
South Shetland Islands

Scotia Sea

Winter limit of pack ice

Summer limit of pack ice
ANTARCTICA

South Orkney Islands

South Sandwich Trench

SOUTH GEORGIA *(to UK)*

SOUTH SANDWICH ISLANDS *(to UK)*

67

154

154

153

N

E

D

C

B

A

5

6

7

8

5

6

7

8

57

NORTHERN SOUTH AMERICA

Caribbean Sea

L e s s e r   A n t

ARUBA
(to Netherlands)

NETHERLANDS ANTILLES
(to Netherlands)

Curaçao

Bonaire

Islas Los Roques

Isla La Orch

Península de la Guajira

Ríohacha

Maicao

Puerto López

Punto Fijo

Golfo de Venezuela

Coro

Puerto Cumarebo

Santa Marta

Ciénaga

Dabajuro

Sabaneta

Puerto Cabello

CARACA

Barranquilla

Pico Cristóbal Colón
△ 5775m

Maracaibo

San Felipe

Maracay

Soledad

Sabanalarga

La Concepción

Cabimas

Cartagena

Valledupar

Machiques

Ciudad Ojeda

Carora

Barquisimeto

Valencia

San Juan de los Morr

El Carmen de Bolívar

Sincelejo

Magangué

San Carlos del Zulia

Lago de Maracaibo

Trujillo

Acarigua

Valle de la Pascua

Montería

Cereté

El Vigía

Mérida

Guanare

Calabozo

Planeta Rica

Aguachica

△ Pico Bolívar
5007m

Barinas

Caucasia

Ocaña

Río Guanare

San Fernand

PANAMA

Panama Canal

Golfo de Panamá

Dabeiba

Yarumal

Cúcuta

Pamplona

San Cristóbal

Río Apure

Río Arauca

L

a n

V E N I

Arauca

Río Meta

Puerto Carreño

Nuquí

Bello

Puerto Berrío

Bucaramanga

Medellín

Barrancabermeja

Itagüí

Quibdó

Sogamoso

Puerto Ayacuchc

Manizales

Tunja

Zipaquira

Yopal

Pereira

Armenia

BOGOTÁ

Río Meta

Río Orinoco

Tuluá

Ibagué

Girardot

Espinal

Villavicencio

Buenaventura

Buga

Palmira

C O L O M B I A

Río Guaviare

Puerto Inírida

Cali

Neiva

Popayán

Garzón

San José del Guaviare

Tumaco

Pitalito

PACIFIC OCEAN

Pasto

Mocoa

Florencia

Nevada de Cumbal △
4764m

Orito

Ipiales

Equator

Río Vaupés

Mitú

Río Apaporis

E C U A D O R

Río Putumayo

Río Napo

Río Caquetá

Río Japurá

A n

A n d e s

P E R U

Río Ipá

Amazon

Río Juru

0 km 200

0 miles 200

POPULATION   ● National capital

○ Less than 50,000   ○ 50,000 -100,000   ◉ 100,000 - 500,000   ■ Over 500,000

ATLANTIC

OCEAN

SAINT VINCENT &
THE GRENADINES

BARBADOS

Isla Blanquilla
GRENADA
Isla de
Margarita
Islas Los Testigos
La Asunción
Tobago
Tortuga
Porlamar
Carúpano
TRINIDAD &
umaná
Cariaco
Güiria
TOBAGO
Puerto La Cruz
Gulf of
Barcelona
San Mateo
Paria
Trinidad
Anaco
Maturín
araza
Cantaura
Tucupita
El Tigre

Río Orinoco
Ciudad Guayana
Embalse de Guri
Upata
Ciudad
Bolívar
Charity
Matthews
Ridge
El Callao
Spring Garden
GEORGETOWN
Parika
El Dorado
Aurora
New
Amsterdam
Peters Mine
Bartica
Salto
Rockstone
PARAMARIBO
Ángel
Linden
Totness
Nieuw Amsterdam
Kamarang
Nieuw
St-Laurent-
GUYANA
Nickerie
du-Maroni
Sinnamary
Mount Roraima
Orealla
Kaaimanston
Kourou
2810m
Apoera
CAYENNE
Kurupukari
W. J. van
Grand-
Ouanary
Blommesteinmeer
Santi
Pakaraima Mountains
SURINAME
Montagnes
St-Georges
FRENCH
de la Trinité
Juliana Top
GUIANA
(Venezuela claims all
1230m
Camopi
of Guyana west of
Lethem
(to France)
Essequibo River)
(claimed by
Suriname)
Río Orinoco
Highlands
Acarai Mountains
Tumuc Hunac Mountains
(claimed by
Suriname)
Río Negro
Equator

B   R   A   Z   I   L
Amazon
zon   Basin
Amazon
Amazon
Río Purus
Río Tapajós

Río Caura
Río Paragua
Río Caroní
El Tigre
ZUELA
Guiana

Cuyuni River
Essequibo River
Courantyne River
Maroni River

55
67
62
62

E   F   G   H

1

2

3

4

5

10°

5°

ELEVATION
-4000m   -3000m   -2000m   -1000m   -500m   Below sea level   0   100m   250m   500m   1000m   2000m   4000m
328ft   820ft   1640ft   3281ft   6562ft   13 124ft
-13 124ft   -9843ft   -6562ft   -3281ft   -1640ft   -820ft/-250m   0

59

WESTERN SOUTH AMERICA

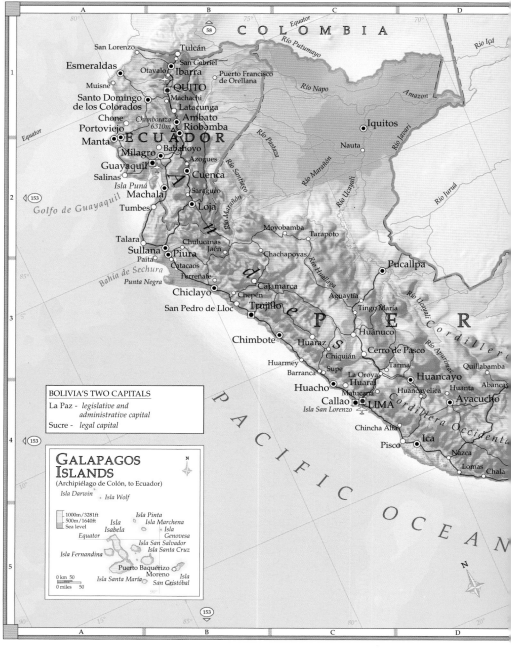

COLOMBIA

San Lorenzo
Tulcán
Esmeraldas
San Gabriel
Otavalo Ibarra
Muisne
Puerto Francisco
de Orellana
Santo Domingo
de los Colorados
QUITO
Machachi
Latacunga
Chone *Chimborazo* Ambato
6310m
Portoviejo Riobamba
Manta **ECUADOR**
Babahoyo
Milagro
Azogues
Guayaquil
Salinas Cuenca
Isla Puná
Machala Saraguro
Tumbes Loja

Iquitos
Nauta

Río Putumayo
Río Içá

Río Napo
Amazon
Río Javarí
Río Juruá

Equator

Golfo de Guayaquil

Talara
Chulucanas
Sullana Jaén
Paita Piura
Catacaos
Punta Negra Ferreñafe
Chiclayo Chepén
San Pedro de Lloc
Chimbote Huaraz
Huarmey
Barranca
Huacho
Callao
Isla San Lorenzo

Moyobamba
Tarapoto
Chachapoyas
Cajamarca
Aguaytía
Tingo María
Huánuco
Chiquián
Cerro de Pasco
Supe
La Oroya Tarma
Huaral
Matucana
Chincha Alta
LIMA

Pucallpa

Huancayo
Huancavelica Huanta Abancay
Quillabamba
Ayacucho

Cordillera Occidental

Bahía de Sechura

PERU

Cordillera

Río Pastaza
Río Santiago
Río Marañón
Río Ucayali
Río Huallaga
Río Ucayali
Río Apurímac

Ica
Pisco
Nazca
Lomas
Chala

BOLIVIA'S TWO CAPITALS

La Paz - *legislative and administrative capital*

Sucre - *legal capital*

GALAPAGOS ISLANDS
(Archipiélago de Colón, to Ecuador)

Isla Darwin
Isla Wolf

1000m/3281ft
500m/1640ft
Sea level

Isla Pinta
Isla Marchena
Isla Isabela
Isla Genovesa
Isla San Salvador
Isla Santa Cruz
Isla Fernandina
Puerto Baquerizo Moreno
Isla Santa María
Isla San Cristóbal

0 km 50
0 miles 50

PACIFIC OCEAN

POPULATION

● National capital

○ Less than 50,000
○ 50,000 -100,000
◉ 100,000 - 500,000
◼ Over 500,000

0 km 400
0 miles 400

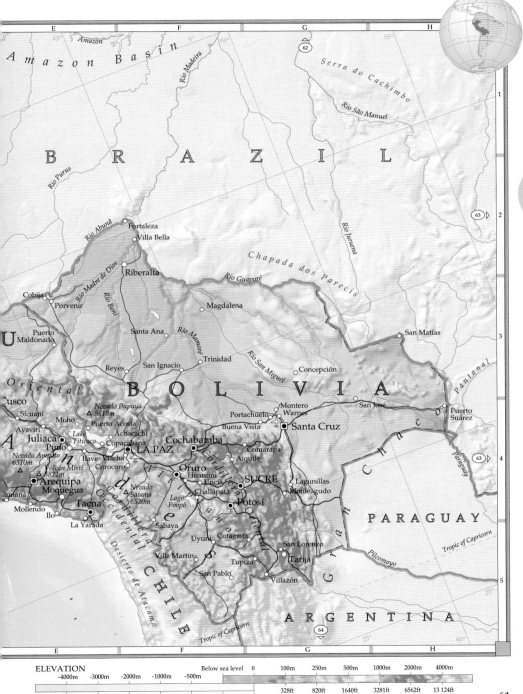

E   F   G   H

65°

Amazon

A m a z o n   B a s i n

5°

60°

55°

62

Serra do Cachimbo

10°

1

Rio Madeira

Rio São Manuel

B   R   A   Z   I   L

Rio Purus

Rio Iruena

63

2

15°

Fortaleza

Villa Bella

Rio Abunã

Chapada dos Parecis

Riberalta

Rio Madre de Dios

Rio Guaporé

Cobija

Porvenir

Rio Beni

Magdalena

Rio Mamoré

San Matías

55°

U

Puerto
Maldonado

Santa Ana

Rio San Miguel

3

Pantanal

O r i e n t a l

Reyes

San Ignacio

Trinidad

Concepción

usco

B   O   L   I   V   I   A

San José

20°

Puerto
Suárez

Sícuani

Nevado Pupuya
△ 5818m

Montero
Warnes

Portachuelo

C h a c o

Moho

Puerto Acosta

Buena Vista

Santa Cruz

63

4

Ayaviri

Achacachi

*Lake
Titicaca*

Copacabana

Cochabamba

Comarapa

Paraguay

*Nevado Ampato
6310m*
△

Juliaca

Puno

Ilave

Viacha

LA PAZ

Aiquile

Cordillera

Oruro

*Volcán Misti
5822m*

Corocoro

Huanuni

Lincia

SUCRE

Lagunillas

Arequipa

Moquegua

*Nevado
Sajama
6520m*

Challapata

Monteagudo

a m a ñ á

Tacna

*Lago
Poopó*

Potosí

P   A   R   A   G   U   A   Y

Mollendo

Ilo

La Yarada

Sabaya

O c c i d e n t a l

Uyuni

Cotagaita

O r i e n t a l

San Lorenzo

G r a n

Tropic of Capricorn

25°

Villa Martín

Tupiza

Tarija

Pilcomayo

C H I L E

San Pablo

Villazón

Desierto de Atacama

70°

Tropic of Capricorn

65°

A   R   G   E   N   T   I   N   A

60°

25°

64

5

E   F   G   H

ELEVATION

| -4000m | -3000m | -2000m | -1000m | -500m | Below sea level 0 | 100m | 250m | 500m | 1000m | 2000m | 4000m |

| -13 124ft | -9843ft | -6562ft | -3281ft | -1640ft | -820ft/-250m | 0 | 328ft | 820ft | 1640ft | 3281ft | 6562ft | 13 124ft |

61

BRAZIL

A   80°   B   70°   C   D   60°

58

VENEZUELA

GUYANA

COLOMBIA

Cordillera Occidental

Cordillera Oriental

Guiana Highland

Uraricoera
Boa Vista
Caracaraí

Roraima

Pico da Neblina
3014m

Río Putumayo

Río Negro

Represa Balbin

1

ECUADOR

Río Napo

Río Japurá

Río Içá

Amazon

Manaus

Tefé

Coari

Río Madeira

Equator

Galapagos Islands
(Archipiélago de Colón)
(to Ecuador)

Río Marañón

Río Javari

Río Juruá

A m a z o n   B a s

2

153

Japiim

Feijó

Río Purus

A c r e

Humaitá

Porto Velho

B R

Río Abunã

Río Ucayali

Rondônia

Río Jurueno

Vilhe

PERU

Chapada dos Parecis

Guaporé

Río Mamoré

P A C I F I C

A n d e s

Cordillera Oriental

Lake
Titicaca

Cordillera Occidental

3

Desierto de Atacama

BOLIVIA

Lago
Poopó

PARA

10°

O C E A N

Pilcomayo

Río Bermejo

4

153

20°

Tropic of Capricorn

C H I L E

A n d e s

G r a n

Río Salado

Paraguay

N

ARGENTINA

5

Paraná

153

90°   A   80°   B   70°   C   D   60°

30°

0 km   600

0 miles   600

POPULATION   ● National capital

○ Less than 50,000   ○ 50,000 -100,000   ◉ 100,000 - 500,000   ◼ Over 500,000

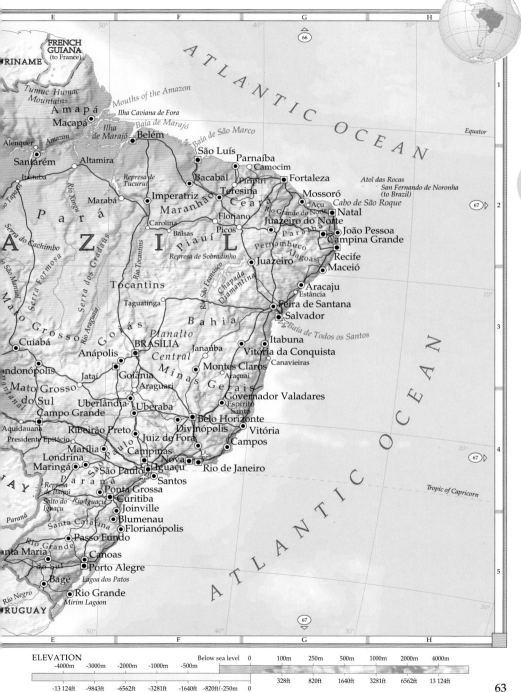

FRENCH GUIANA (to France)

SURINAME

Tumuc Humac Mountains

Mouths of the Amazon

A m a p á

Macapá

Ilha Caviana de Fora

Ilha de Marajó

Baía de Marajó

ATLANTIC

OCEAN

Alenquer

Amazon

Santarém

Altamira

Belém

Baía de São Marco

São Luís

Parnaíba

Camocim

Fortaleza

Equator

Ititbuba

Marabá

Imperatriz

Bacabal

Piripiri

Teresina

Mossoró

Atol das Rocas

San Fernando de Noronha (to Brazil)

Cabo de São Roque

P a r á

Maranhão

C e a r á

Açu

Natal

Rio Xingu

Carolina

Floriano

Rio Grande do Norte

Juazeiro do Norte

João Pessoa

Serra do Cachimbo

Rio Tapajós

A

Z

I

L

Balsas

Picos

P i a u í

P a r a í b a

Campina Grande

Pernambuco

Recife

Serra Formosa

Rio Tocantins

Represa de Sobradinho

Juazeiro

Alagoas

Maceió

n São Manuel

Serra dos Gradaús

T o c a n t i n s

Rio São Francisco

Chapada Diamantina

Aracaju

Estância

M a t o

Rio Araguaia

Taguatinga

B a h i a

Feira de Santana

Salvador

G r o s s o

Planalto

Itabuna

Baía de Todos os Santos

Cuiabá

Anápolis

BRASÍLIA

Central

Janaúba

Vitória da Conquista

Canavieiras

G o i á s

Montes Claros

ondonópolis

Jataí

M i n a s

Araçuaí

Mato Grosso do Sul

Goiânia

Araguari

Governador Valadares

Espírito Santo

antal

Uberlândia

Uberaba

G e r a i s

Campo Grande

Belo Horizonte

Aquidauana

Ribeirão Preto

Divinópolis

Vitória

Presidente Epitácio

Juiz de Fora

Campos

Marília

Campinas

Londrina

Nova

Maringá

Iguaçu

Rio de Janeiro

Tropic of Capricorn

P a r a n á

São Paulo

Santos

Represa de Itaipu

Ponta Grossa

Salto do Iguaçu

Rio Iguaçu

Curitiba

Paraná

Joinville

Santa Catarina

Blumenau

Florianópolis

Passo Fundo

Rio Grande

do Sul

anta Maria

Canoas

Porto Alegre

Bagé

Lagoa dos Patos

URUGUAY

Rio Negro

Rio Grande

Mirim Lagoon

ATLANTIC

OCEAN

50°

40°

30°

E

F

G

H

1

2

3

4

5

10°

20°

30°

Planalto de Mato Grosso

B R A Z I L

Pantanal

Tropic of Capricorn

Represa de Itaipú

63

PERU

B O L I V I A

Cordillera Oriental

Lago Poopó

Cordillera Occidental

61

Chuquicamata

Calama

Arica

Iquique

Lagunas

Tocopilla

Mejillones

Antofagasta

Taltal

Chañaral

Caldera

Copiapó

Vallenar

Domeyko

La Serena

Coquimbo

Ovalle

Illapel

Salamanca

La Ligua

Pichilemu

Viña del Mar

Valparaíso

San Antonio

Rancagua

Curicó

Talca

PARAGUAY

Capitán Pablo Lagerenza

General Eugenio A. Garay

Mariscal Estigarribia

Fuerte Olimpo

Pedro Juan Caballero

Concepción

Rosario

Las Lomitas

Pilcomayo

Las Lomitas

Río Bermejo

Formosa

Pilar

San Juan Bautista

Villarrica

Caazapá

Coronel Oviedo

Ciudad del Este

Eldorado

Encarnación

Posadas

Yuty

San Ramón de la Nueva Orán

San Salvador de Jujuy

Calafate

Cerro Galán 6100m

La Quiaca

Quiaca

Salta

Metán

San Miguel de Tucumán

Santiago del Estero

Añatuya

Frías

Deán Funes

Jesús María

Villa María

Río Cuarto

Villa Mercedes

San Luis

Pergamino

Junín

Rufino

Realicó

Trenque Lauquen

A N D E S

Cerro Ojos del Salado 6880m

Cerro Aconcagua 6959m

San Fernando del Valle de Catamarca

La Rioja

San Juan

Mendoza

Godoy Cruz

San Rafael

General Alvear

SANTIAGO

Monte Patria

La Calera

C H I L E

Desierto de Atacama

CORRIENTES

Resistencia

Santo Tomé

Mercedes

Goya

Vera

Reconquista

Rafaela

Santa Fe

Monte Caseros

Concordia

Paraná

Rosario

Guaycurú

Dolores

Zárate

BUENOS AIRES

La Plata

Lomas de Zamora

MONTEVIDEO

URUGUAY

Melo

Rivera

Artigas

Salto

Paysandú

Mercedes

Trinidad

Florida

Chuy

Mirim Lagoon

Lagoa dos Patos

Río de la Plata

Río Negro

Uruguay

Paraná

P A M P A S

Tropic of Capricorn

O C E A N

P A C I F I C

0 km   200

0 miles   200

POPULATION   ● National capital

○ Less than 50,000   ○ 50,000 -100,000   ◉ 100,000 - 500,000   ◼ Over 500,000

ATLANTIC

OCEAN

ARGENTINA

Mar del Plata
Balcarce
Tandil
Necochea
Coronel
Dorrego
Tres Arroyos
Bahía Blanca
Bahía Blanca
Punta Alta
Choele Choel
Río Negro
Cipolletti
Neuquén
Río Colorado
Zapala
San Antonio
Oeste
Golfo San Matías
Viedma
*Península
Valdés*
Golfo Nuevo
Rawson
Trelew
Río Chubut
San Carlos de Bariloche
*Lago
Nahuel Huapí*
Paso
de Indios
Esquel
Río Chico
Sarmiento
*Lago
Musters*
*Lago
Buenos Aires*
Comodoro Rivadavia
Golfo San Jorge
Caleta
Olivia
Puerto Deseado
Río Deseado
Perito
Moreno
Puerto
San Julián
El Calafate
Río Chico
Río Santa Cruz
Río Gallegos
*Bahía
Grande*
Strait of Magellan
Puerto Natales
Punta Arenas
Porvenir
Tierra del Fuego
Ushuaia
Beagle Channel
Cabo de Hornos
(Cape Horn)
Isla
de los Estados
Drake Passage

FALKLAND ISLANDS
(to UK)
*West
Falkland*
*East
Falkland*
STANLEY
Goose
Green

CHILE

Concepción
Los
Angeles
Lebu
Río Bío Bío
Temuco
Loncoche
Valdivia
Osorno
Puerto Varas
Puerto Montt
Ancud
Castro
Isla de Chiloé
Golfo Corcovado
*Archipiélago
de los Chonos*
Puerto Aisén
Coihaique
Chile Chico
Cochrane
*Cerro
San Valentín
4058m*
*Cerro
Militar Sur
3050m*
*Isla
Wellington*
Golfo de Penas
*Cerro Paine
2670m*
Cerro Fitz Roy
*Lago
Viedma*
*Lago
Argentino*

Tandil

N

⟨67⟩
⟨154⟩
⟨154⟩
⟨143⟩

THE ATLANTIC OCEAN

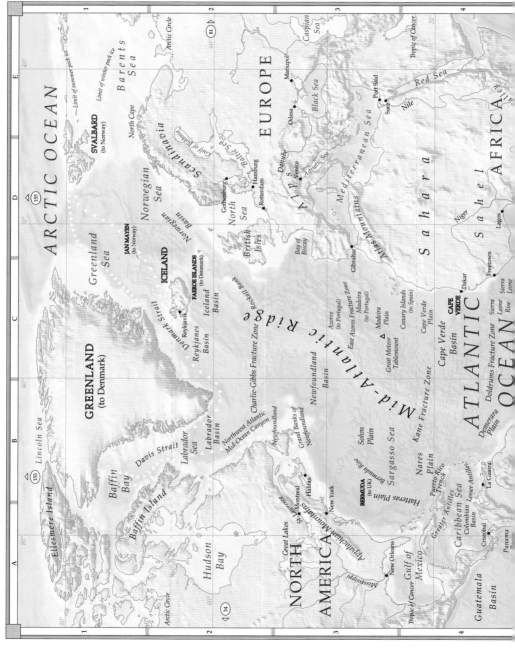

ARCTIC OCEAN

Lincoln Sea

Ellesmere Island

SVALBARD
(to Norway)

North Cape

Limit of summer pack ice

Limit of winter pack ice

Barents
Sea

Scandinavia

Gulf of Bothnia

Baltic Sea

EUROPE

Mariupol

Odessa

Black Sea

Caspian
Sea

Tropic of Cancer

Red Sea

Port Said

Suez

Nile

AFRICA

Valley

Danube

Venice

Hamburg

Rotterdam

North
Sea

Gothenburg

Alps

Adriatic Sea

Mediterranean Sea

Atlas Mountains

Gibraltar

Bay of
Biscay

British
Isles

Niger

Lagos

Sahara

Sahel

Freetown

Dakar

Sierra
Leone

CAPE
VERDE

JAN MAYEN
(to Norway)

ICELAND

FAROE ISLANDS
(to Denmark)

Reykjavik

Iceland
Basin

Reykjanes
Basin

Norwegian
Sea

Norwegian
Basin

Greenland
Sea

Greenland
(to Denmark)

Denmark Strait

Rockall Bank

Charlie-Gibbs Fracture Zone

Mid-Atlantic Ridge

Azores
(to Portugal)

East Azores Fracture Zone

Madeira
(to Portugal)

Madeira
Plain

Great Meteor
Tablemount

Canary Islands
(to Spain)

Cape Verde
Plain

Cape Verde
Basin

Doldrums Fracture Zone

ATLANTIC

OCEAN

Demerara
Plain

Baffin
Bay

Davis Strait

Labrador
Sea

Labrador
Basin

Baffin Island

Northwest Atlantic
Mid-Ocean Canyon

Newfoundland
Basin

Grand Banks of
Newfoundland

Newfoundland

Kane Fracture Zone

Sohm
Plain

Nares
Plain

Puerto Rico
Trench

La Guaira

Sierra
Leone
Basin

Greater Antilles

Lesser Antilles

Caribbean
Sea

Colombian
Basin

Cristobal

Panama

Hudson
Bay

Great Lakes

St. Lawrence

Montreal

Halifax

New York

BERMUDA
(to UK)

Bermuda Rise

Sargasso Sea

Hatteras Plain

NORTH

AMERICA

Appalachian Mountains

New Orleans

Mississippi

Gulf of
Mexico

Tropic of Cancer

Guatemala
Basin

Arctic Circle

Arctic Circle

0 km 1000

0 miles 1000

• Major port

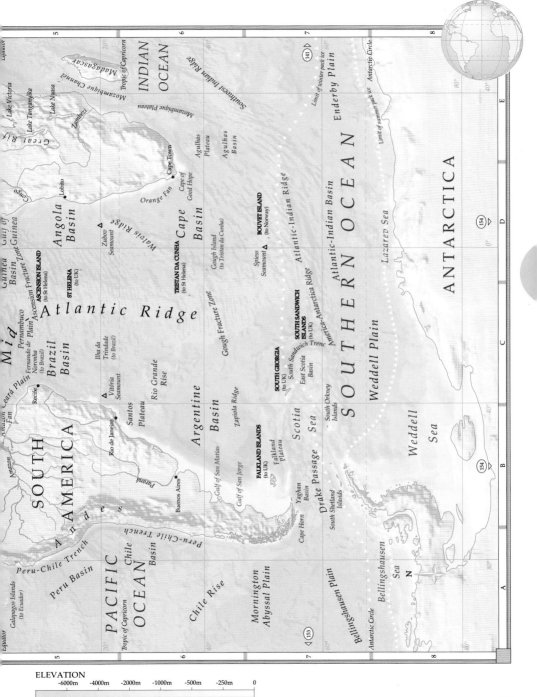

ELEVATION

| -6000m | -4000m | -2000m | -1000m | -500m | -250m | 0 |

| -19 686ft | -13 124ft | -6562ft | -3281ft | -1640ft | -820ft | 0 |

AFRICA

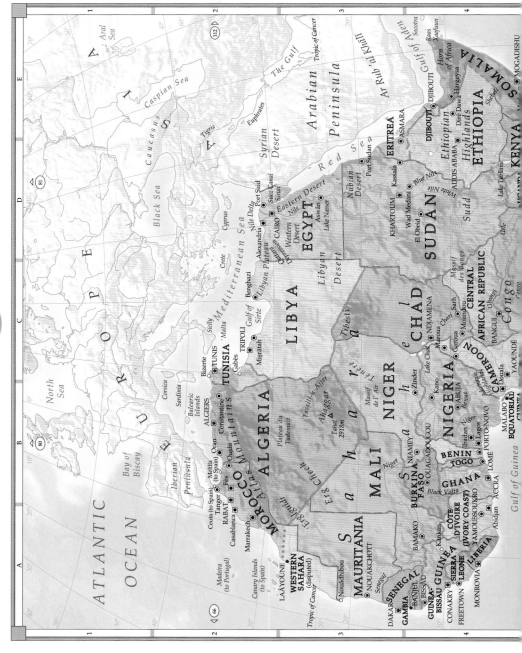

Aral Sea

Caspian Sea

Black Sea

Mediterranean Sea

The Gulf

Gulf of Aden

Socotra

Ras Xaafuun

Horn of Africa

SOMALIA

MOGADISHU

KENYA

Arabian Peninsula

Ar Rub' al Khālī

Syrian Desert

Red Sea

ERITREA

DJIBOUTI

DJIBOUTI

Ethiopian Highlands

ETHIOPIA

ASMARA

ADDIS ABABA

Dire Dawa

Hargeysa

Shebeli

Lake Turkana

Caucasus

Tigris

Euphrates

Cyprus

Crete

Suez Canal

Port Said

Nile Delta

Alexandria

CAIRO

Sinai

Qattara Depression

Eastern Desert

Nile

Aswan

Lake Nasser

EGYPT

Western Desert

Libyan Desert

Nubian Desert

Port Sudan

Kassala

Wad Medani

KHARTOUM

El Obeid

Blue Nile

White Nile

Sudd

SUDAN

Atbara

Nile

Tropic of Cancer

(112)

(81)

Benghazi

Libyan Plateau

Sirte

Gulf of Sirte

TRIPOLI

Miṣrātah

LIBYA

Tibesti

Tibesti

Massif des Bongo

CHAD

Central African Republic

Congo

Uele

Ubangi

BANGUI

YAOUNDÉ

Sicily

Malta

Gabes

Bizerte

TUNIS

TUNISIA

Corsica

Sardinia

Balearic Islands

ALGIERS

Constantine

Oujda

Fez

Meliila (to Spain)

Tindouf

Plateau du Tademaït

ALGERIA

Tassili-n-Ajjer

Massif de l'Aïr

Ahaggar

Tahat 2918m

Ténéré

Zinder

NIGER

NIAMEY

Lake Chad

NDJAMENA

Sarh

Moundou

Maroua

CAMEROON

Garoua

Kano

ABUJA

Benue

NIGERIA

Douala

MALABO

EQUATORIAL GUINEA

Ibadan

Lagos

PORTO-NOVO

BENIN

TOGO

LOMÉ

GHANA

ACCRA

Black Volta

Niger

North Sea

Bay of Biscay

Iberian Peninsula

Madeira (to Portugal)

Canary Islands (to Spain)

(80)

Ceuta (to Spain)

Tanger

RABAT

Casablanca

Marrakech

MOROCCO

Atlas Mountains

Oran

Sahara

MALI

BAMAKO

OUAGADOUGOU

BURKINA FASO

Kankan

CÔTE D'IVOIRE (IVORY COAST)

YAMOUSSOUKRO

Abidjan

Sahel

Niger

Senegal

Erg Chech

Erg Iguidi

WESTERN SAHARA (disputed)

LAÂYOUNE

Nouâdhibou

MAURITANIA

NOUAKCHOTT

DAKAR

SENEGAL

BANJUL

GAMBIA

BISSAU

GUINEA-BISSAU

CONAKRY

GUINEA

SIERRA LEONE

FREETOWN

MONROVIA

LIBERIA

Tropic of Cancer

(66)

ATLANTIC OCEAN

Gulf of Guinea

E U R O P E

A S I A

| 0 km | | 1000 |
| 0 miles | | 1000 |

POPULATION ● National capital

○ Less than 50,000 ○ 50,000 -100,000 ◉ 100,000 - 500,000 ◼ Over 500,000

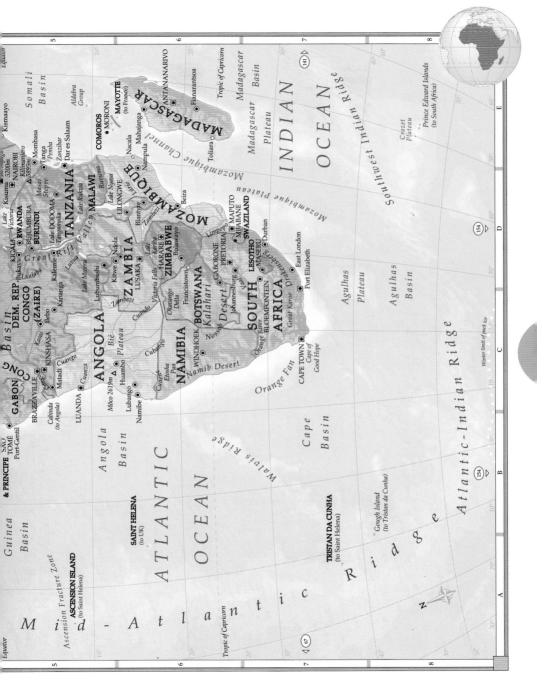

Equator

Somali
Basin

Aldabra
Group

Kismaayo

MAYOTTE
(to France)

COMOROS
MORONI

MADAGASCAR

ANTANANARIVO

Fianarantsoa

Toliara

Madagascar
Basin

Tropic of Capricorn

Mombasa
Tanga
Pemba
Zanzibar
Dar es Salaam

Nacala
Nampula

Mahajanga

Madagascar
Plateau

INDIAN

OCEAN

Mozambique Channel

Southwest Indian Ridge

Prince Edward Islands
(to South Africa)

Crozet
Plateau

NAIROBI
Kilimanjaro 5899m △
5200m △ Kisumu Lake
Victoria

KIGALI
RWANDA
BUJUMBURA
BURUNDI
Bukavu

Masai
Steppe

TANZANIA

DODOMA
Lake Tanganyika

LILONGWE

Lake Nyasa

MALAWI

Rovuma

Lake Rukwa

Beira

Zambezi

Mozambique Plateau

Mozambique Basin

DEM. REP.
CONGO
(ZAIRE)

Great

Rift Valley

Ruvuma

BLANTYRE

Limpopo

MOZAMBIQUE

CONGO

Basin

Lualaba

KINSHASA
Ilebo
Kananga
Kasai

Kalemie
Lake Mweru

Luangwa

Lake
Kariba
Kafue

MAPUTO

MBABANE

SWAZILAND

Lubumbashi

ZAMBIA

LUSAKA

HARARE

ZIMBABWE

Bulawayo

PRETORIA

Johannesburg

Durban

East London

Limpopo

GABORONE

BOTSWANA

MASERU

LESOTHO

Kitwe
Ndola

Victoria Falls

Cuando

Okavango
Delta

Kalahari
Desert

Francistown

WINDHOEK

Drakensberg

BLOEMFONTEIN

SOUTH

AFRICA

Port Elizabeth

Agulhas
Plateau

Agulhas
Basin

ANGOLA

Bié
Plateau

Huambo

Cuanza

Cuango

BRAZZAVILLE

GABON

SÃO TOMÉ
& PRINCIPE

Port-Gentil

Cabinda
(to Angola)

Matadi

LUANDA

Lubango

Namibe

Móco 2619m △

Namib Desert

Cunene

Etosha
Pan

NAMIBIA

Nossob

Orange River

Great Karoo

CAPE TOWN
Cape of
Good Hope

Orange Fan

Cape
Basin

SAINT HELENA
(to UK)

ASCENSION ISLAND
(to Saint Helena)

Ascension Fracture Zone

Guinea
Basin

Angola
Basin

ATLANTIC

OCEAN

Walvis Ridge

TRISTAN DA CUNHA
(to Saint Helena)

Gough Island
(to Tristan da Cunha)

Tropic of Capricorn

Equator

Mid-Atlantic

Ridge

Atlantic-Indian Ridge

Winter limit of pack ice

N

NORTHWEST AFRICA

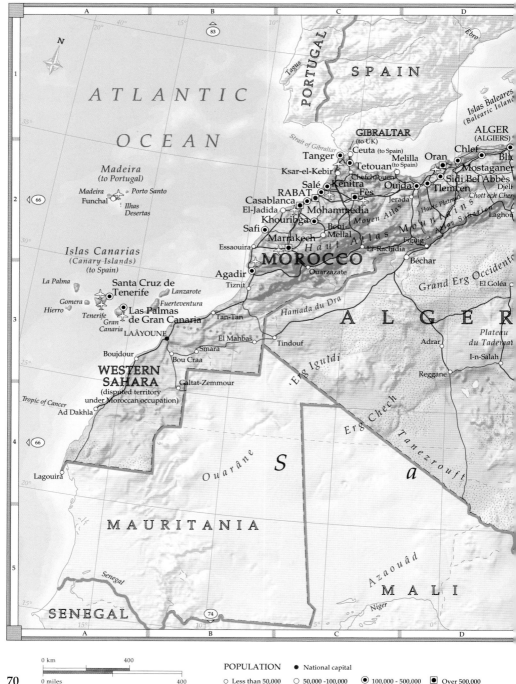

N

83

ATLANTIC

PORTUGAL

SPAIN

OCEAN

GIBRALTAR
(to UK)

ALGER
(ALGIERS)

Islas Baleares
(Balearic Islands)

Madeira
(to Portugal)

Ceuta (to Spain)

Melilla
(to Spain)

Tanger

Chlef

Blida

Madeira
Porto Santo

Ksar-el-Kebir

Tetouan

Oran

Mostaganem

Funchal

Illas
Desertas

Chefchaouen

Salé

Kenitra

Sidi Bel Abbès

Djelfa

RABAT

Fès

Oujda

Tlemcen

Islas Canarias
(Canary Islands)
(to Spain)

Casablanca

Mohammedia

Jerada

Chott ech Cher...

El-Jadida

Beni-

Moyen Atlas

Hauts Plateaux

Laghouat

Khouribga

Mellal

Safi

Marrakech

Atlas Mountains

Figuig

Atlas Saharien

Essaouira

Haut

Er-Rachidia

MOROCCO

Béchar

Grand Erg Occidental

La Palma

Agadir

Ouarzazate

El Goléa

Tiznit

Santa Cruz de
Tenerife

Lanzarote

Gomera

Fuerteventura

Hierro

Tenerife

Las Palmas
de Gran Canaria

Gran
Canaria

Tan-Tan

Hamada du Dra

A L G E R I A

LAÂYOUNE

El Mahbas

Tindouf

Plateau
du Tademait

Smara

Adrar

I-n-Salah

Boujdour

Bou Craa

Erg Iguidi

Reggane

WESTERN
SAHARA
(disputed territory
under Moroccan occupation)

Galtat-Zemmour

Tropic of Cancer

Ad Dakhla

Erg Chech

S

Ouarâne

a

Tanezrouft

Lagouira

M A U R I T A N I A

Azaouâd

M A L I

Senegal

Niger

SENEGAL

74

66

66

0 km   400
0 miles   400

POPULATION   ● National capital

70

○ Less than 50,000   ○ 50,000 -100,000   ◉ 100,000 - 500,000   ◼ Over 500,000

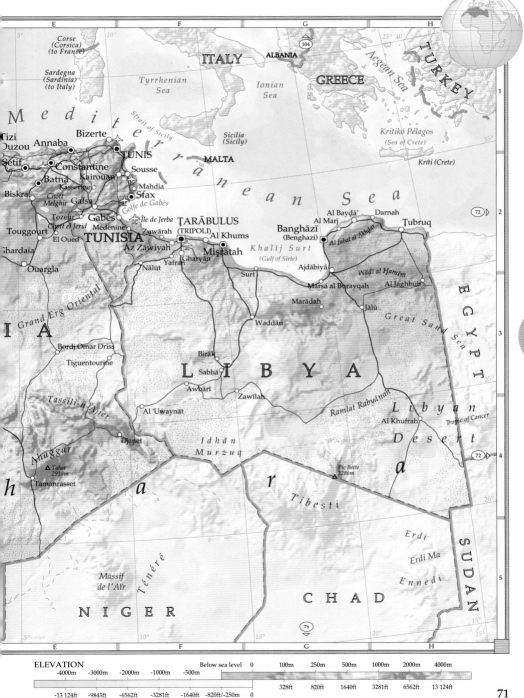

ELEVATION

	Below sea level	0	100m	250m	500m	1000m	2000m	4000m
-4000m	-3000m	-2000m	-1000m	-500m				
-13 124ft	-9843ft	-6562ft	-3281ft	-1640ft	-820ft/-250m	0	328ft	820ft	1640ft	3281ft	6562ft	13 124ft

71

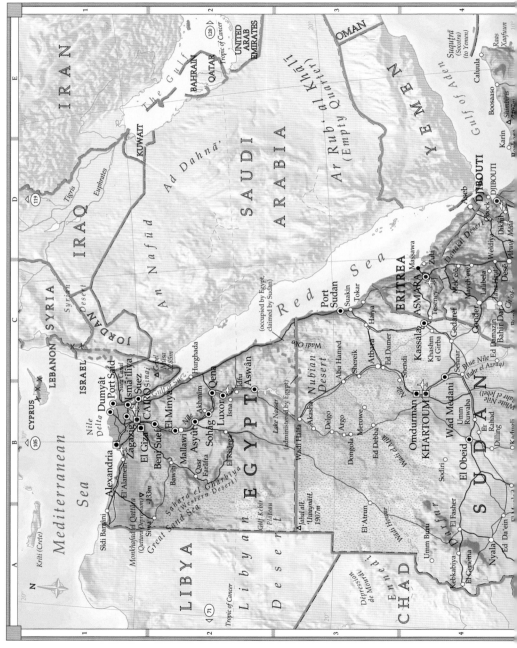

0 km   400

0 miles   400

POPULATION   ● National capital

○ Less than 50,000   ○ 50,000 -100,000   ◉ 100,000 - 500,000   ◼ Over 500,000

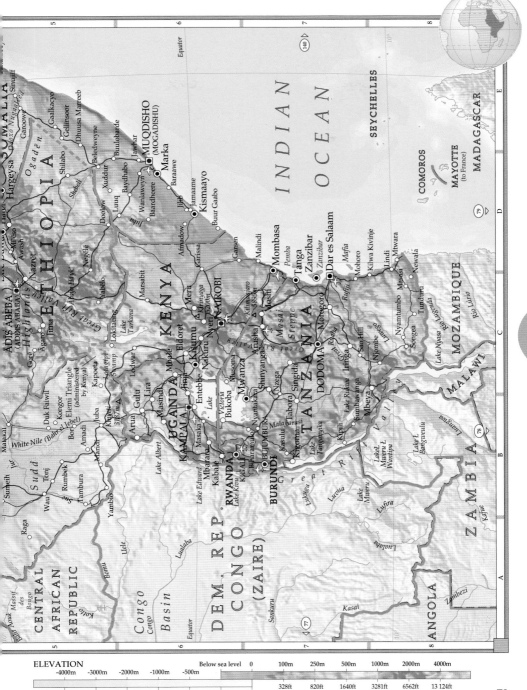

ELEVATION

					Below sea level	0	100m	250m	500m	1000m	2000m	4000m
-4000m	-3000m	-2000m	-1000m	-500m								

						328ft	820ft	1640ft	3281ft	6562ft	13 124ft
-13 124ft	-9843ft	-6562ft	-3281ft	-1640ft	-820ft/-250m	0					

N

Tropic of Cancer

WESTERN
SAHARA
(disputed territory
under Moroccan occupation)

Aïn Ben Tili

Bir Mogreïn

'Erg Iguîdi

Kâghet El Hank

Erg

Fdérik   Zouérat
Touâjil

Nouâdhibou   Choûm

Akchâr   Atâr   Chinguetti
Akjoujt   Oujeft

El Mreyyé

M A U R I T A N I A

S

CAPE
VERDE

Ilhas de Barlavento

Santo
Antão
Mindelo
São   Pedra Lume
Vicente São   Sal
Nicolau   Boa Vista

Santiago
Fogo   Maio
PRAIA

Ilhas de Sotavento

A T L A N T I C

NOUAKCHOTT   Idîni
Boutilimit   Magta   Tidjikja   Tîchît
Lahjar
Rkîz   Boûmdeïd   Aoukâr   Oualâta
Aleg   Tâmchekket
Rosso   Kaédi   Kiffa   'Ayoûn el 'Atroûs   Néma
Richard Toll Dagana   Amourj
Saint Louis   Louga   Matam   Timbedgha   Bassikounou
Mékhé   Sélibabi   Kobenni
DAKAR   Thiès   Mbaké   Nioro
Mbour   Diourbel
Sokone   Kaolack   Kayes   Ténenkou
BANJUL   Kaolack   Kolokani   Niger
GAMBIA   Tambacounda   Toukoto   Ségou   Bani
Bignona   Kolda   Gambia   Kita   Koulikoro   San
Ziguinchor Sédhiou   BAMAKO   Koutiala
Bafata   Gaoual   Sikass
BISSAU   Boké   Labé   Dinguiraye Niger
GUINEA-   Boké   Pita   Mamou   Siguiri   Bougouni
BISSAU   Kindia   Faranah   Kankan
G U I N E A   Tôkounou Odienné   Ferkessédougou
CONAKRY   Tengréla
SIERRA   Makeni   Kissidougou Boundiali Korhogo
FREETOWN   LEONE   Beyla   CÔTE
Bo   Kenema Nzérékoré   D'IVOIRE
Gbanga Danané Katiola (IVORY COAST)
Tubmanburg   Lako
MONROVIA   Harbel YAMOUSSOUKRO   Kossi
Buchanan Zwedru   Gagnoa
LIBERIA   Divo
Harper   Sassandra
San-Pédro

Senegal

Sénégal

Bafing

Gambia

Baoulé

Bagoé

Cavally

Sassandra

Bandama

O C E A N

67
67

0 km   400

0 miles   400

POPULATION   ● National capital

○ Less than 50,000   ○ 50,000 -100,000   ◉ 100,000 - 500,000   ▣ Over 500,000

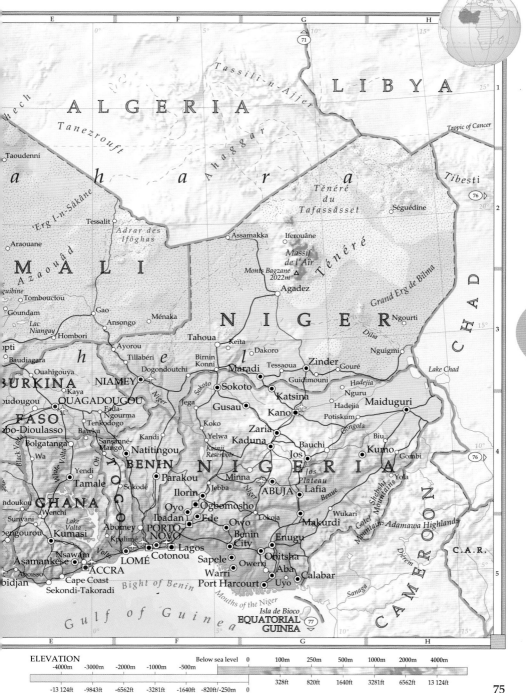

ALGERIA

LIBYA

Tassili-n-Ajjer

Tanezrouft

Ahaggar

S a h a r a

Taoudenni

Tropic of Cancer

Tibesti

'Erg I-n-Sâkâne

Ténéré
du
Tafassâsset

Séguédine

Araouane

Tessalit

Adrar des
Ifôghas

Assamakka

Iferouâne

MALI

Azaouâd

Massif
de l'Aïr

Ténéré

Grand Erg de Bilma

Monts Bagzane
2022m

guibine

Tombouctou

Agadez

Goundam

Gao

Ménaka

NIGER

Ngourti

CHAD

Lac
Niangay

Ansongo

Dilia

Nguigmi

pti

Hombori

Ayorou

Tahoua

Keita

Dakoro

Baudiagara

h

Tillabéri

e

Dogondoutchi

Birnin
Konni

l

Tessaoua

Zinder

Gouré

Lake Chad

Ouahigouya

NIAMEY

Maradi

Guidimouni

Hadejia

BURKINA

Kaya

Sokoto

Jega

Sokoto

Katsina

Kano

Nguru

Hadejia

Potiskum

Maiduguri

udougou

QUAGADOUGOU

Gusau

oo-Dioulasso

FASO

Fada-
Ngourma
Tenkodogo

Koko

Zaria

Bauchi

Gongola

Biu

Kumo

bo-Dioulasso

Bawku

Yelwa

Kaduna

Jos

Gombi

Bolgatanga

Sansanné-
Mango

Kandi

Kainji
Reservoir

Jos
Plateau

Yola

Wa

Natitingou

Yendi

BENIN

N I G E R I A

Minna

Lafia

Wukari

Tamale

Parakou

Ilorin

Jebba

ABUJA

Benue

Adamawa Highlands

GHANA

Sokodé

Oyo

Ogbomosho

Tokoja

Makurdi

C.A.R.

Wenchi

Ibadan

Ede

Owo

Sunyani

Lake
Volta

Abomey

PORTO-
NOVO

Benin
City

Enugu

engourou

Kumasi

Kpalimé

Lagos

Sapele

Onitsha

Kumasi

Nsawam

Cotonou

Owerri

Aba

Calabar

CAMEROON

Asamankese

LOMÉ

Warri

Port Harcourt

Uyo

koisso

ACCRA

Cape Coast

bidjan

Sekondi-Takoradi

Bight of Benin

Mouths of the Niger

Sanaga

Gulf of Guinea

Isla de Bioco

EQUATORIAL
GUINEA

ELEVATION

					Below sea level	0	100m	250m	500m	1000m	2000m	4000m
-4000m	-3000m	-2000m	-1000m	-500m								
-13 124ft	-9843ft	-6562ft	-3281ft	-1640ft	-820ft/-250m	0	328ft	820ft	1640ft	3281ft	6562ft	13 124ft

CENTRAL AFRICA

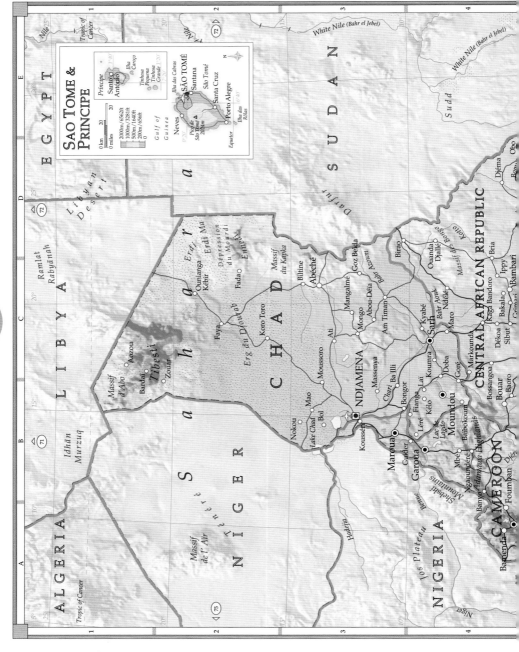

SAO TOME & PRINCIPE

Príncipe
Santo António
Santana
Santa Cruz
Tinhosa Pequena
Tinhosa Grande
SÃO TOMÉ
Ilha das Cabras
São Tomé
Neves
Porto Alegre
Ilha das Rólas
Gulf of Guinea
Equator

200m / 656ft
1000m / 3281ft
500m / 1640ft
200m / 656ft
0

Pico de São Tomé 2024m

0 km   20
0 miles   20

EGYPT

White Nile (Bahr el Jebel)

SUDAN

Sudd

White Nile (Bahr el Jebel)

Nile

Libyan Desert

Ramlat Rabyānah

LIBYA

Idhān Murzuq

ALGERIA

Tropic of Cancer

Massif de l' Aïr

NIGER

Ténéré

Massif d'Abo

Aozou

Bardaï

Zouar

Tibesti

Erdi

Erdi Ma

Dépression du Mourdi

Enneri

Ounianga Kébir

Fadao

Faya

Koro Toro

Erg du Djourab

Ati

Moussoro

Nokou

Mao

Bol

Lake Chad

S a h a r a

C H A D

Darfur

Massif du Kapka

Biltine

Abéché

Goz Beïda

Mangalmé

Mongo

Abou-Déïa

Am Timan

Bahr Azoum

Birao

Ouanda Djallé

Ndélé

Massif des Bongo

Koro

Bria

Ippy

Bambari

Bakala

Kaga Bandoro

Dékoa

Sibut

Grimari

Djéma

Obo

Bangassou

Oho

CENTRAL AFRICAN REPUBLIC

Kyabé

Sarh

Maro

Bahr Aouk

Koumra

Doba

Goré

Moundou

Baïbokoum

Markounda

Bossangoa

Bouar

Baoro

Bozoum

Kélo

Léré

Lac de Lagdo

Fianga

Laï

Bongor

Massenya

Ba Illi

Chari

NDJAMENA

Kousséri

Maroua

Guider

Garoua

Mbé

Ngaoundéré

Adamawa Highlands

Shebshi Mountains

Mandara Mountains

Bénoué

Banyo

Foumban

CAMEROON

Bamenda

Djérem

Plateau

Hadejia

NIGERIA

Niger

0 km   400
0 miles   400

POPULATION   ● National capital

○ Less than 50,000   ○ 50,000 -100,000   ◉ 100,000 - 500,000   ◼ Over 500,000

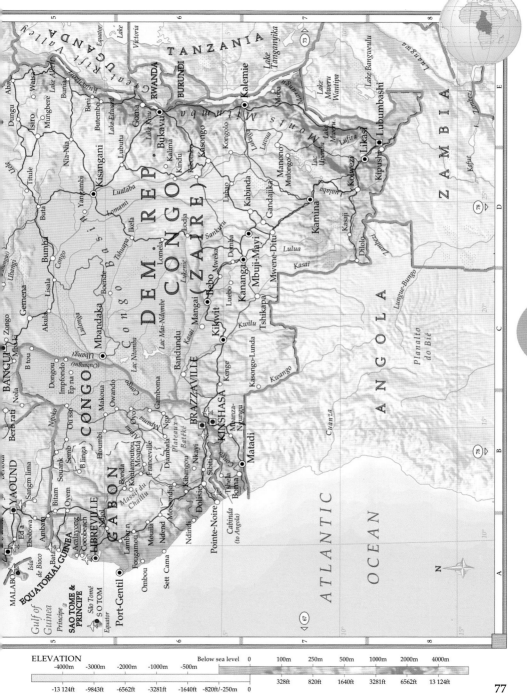

ELEVATION

					Below sea level	0	100m	250m	500m	1000m	2000m	4000m
-4000m	-3000m	-2000m	-1000m	-500m								
							328ft	820ft	1640ft	3281ft	6562ft	13 124ft
-13 124ft	-9843ft	-6562ft	-3281ft	-1640ft	-820ft/-250m	0						

77

SOUTHERN AFRICA

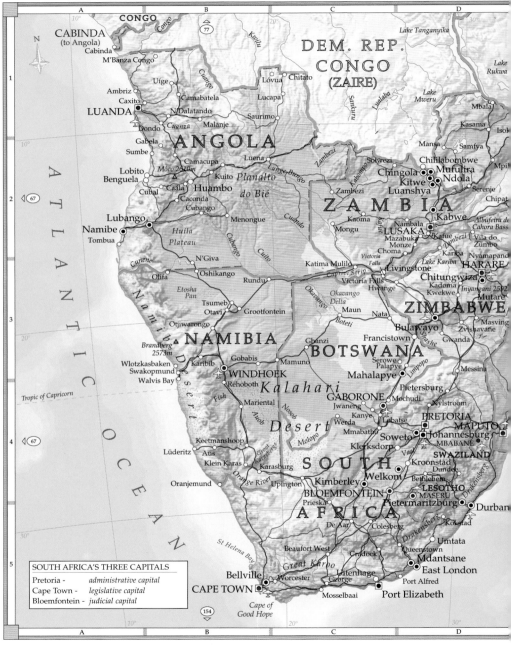

SOUTH AFRICA'S THREE CAPITALS

Pretoria - *administrative capital*
Cape Town - *legislative capital*
Bloemfontein - *judicial capital*

POPULATION

● National capital

○ Less than 50,000   ○ 50,000 -100,000   ◉ 100,000 - 500,000   ◼ Over 500,000

0 km   400
0 miles   400

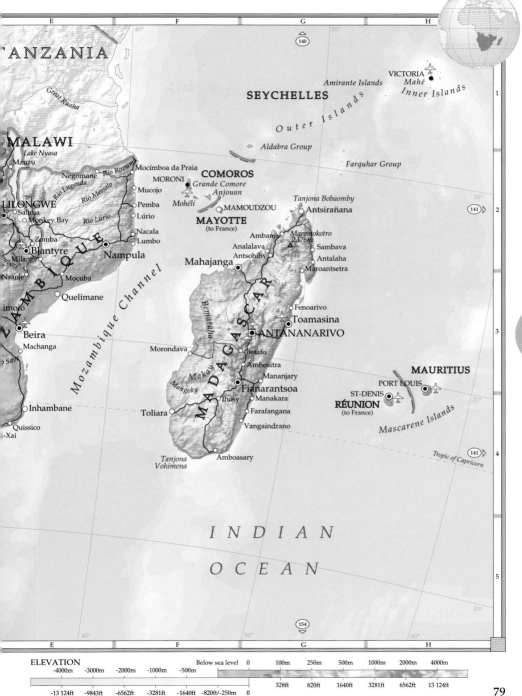

ELEVATION

Below sea level						0	100m	250m	500m	1000m	2000m	4000m
-4000m	-3000m	-2000m	-1000m	-500m								
-13 124ft	-9843ft	-6562ft	-3281ft	-1640ft	-820ft/-250m	0	328ft	820ft	1640ft	3281ft	6562ft	13 124ft

Reykjanes Basin
△ 155
REYKJAVÍK
ICELAND
Vatnajökull
Limit of winter pack ice
Arctic Circle

Charlie-Gibbs Fracture Zone

Reykjanes Ridge

Iceland Basin

Faeroe-Iceland Ridge

Norwegian Basin

Norwegian Sea

Lofo

◁ 66

Hatton Ridge

FAEROE ISLANDS
(to Denmark)

Faeroe-Shetland Trough

Shetland Islands

Trondheim ⊙

N O R W A Y

Rockall Bank

Outer Hebrides

Mid-Atlantic Ridge

Porcupine Plain

Rockall Trough

British Isles

Orkney Islands

Bergen ⊙

Stavanger ⊙

OSLO ⊙

Vä

ATLANTIC OCEAN

Ireland

Glasgow ⊙
⊙ Edinburgh
Belfast

REPUBLIC OF IRELAND

ISLE OF MAN
(to UK)
⊙ DUBLIN

UNITED KINGDOM

North Sea

Gothenburg ⊙
Ålborg ⊙
Jyllana
⊙ Jönköpin

Liverpool ⊙ ⊙ Manchester

DENMARK COPENHAG
Odense ⊙
⊙ Malmö

Celtic Sea

Britain

Celtic Shelf

Cardiff ⊙
LONDON ⊙
⊙ Birmingham

NETHERLANDS
THE ⊙⊙ AMSTERDAM
HAGUE ⊙ Rotterdam

⊙ Hamburg

Hannover ⊙

Elbe

N O

English Channel

BELGIUM ⊙ BRUSSELS

BERLIN ⊙

Pozn

CHANNEL IS.
(to UK)

le Havre ⊙

Liège ⊙
LUXEMBOURG

Bonn ⊙
GERMANY

Wrocław

Azores-Biscay Rise

Charcot Seamounts

Biscay Plain

Rennes ⊙

Seine

LUXEMBOURG ⊙
PARIS ⊙

⊙ Frankfurt
am Main

Rhine

PRAG

Nantes ⊙

Loire

⊙ Orléans

⊙ Strasbourg

⊙ Stuttgart

CZECH REPUBLIC

Iberian Plain

Bay of Biscay

A Coruña ⊙

FRANCE

Munich ⊙

Zürich ⊙
BERN ⊙
SWITZERLAND

BRATISL
VIENNA ⊙

Galicia Bank

Bordeaux ⊙

Lyon ⊙

LIECH.

⊙ Salzburg
Innsbruck AUSTRIA

Cordillera Cantábrica

Bilbao ⊙

Massif
Central

Mont Blanc △
4807m

A L P S

Milan ⊙
Po

SLOVENIA
⊙ LJUBLJAN

◁ 66

Porto ⊙

Duero

Pyrenees

Toulouse ⊙

Rhône

Turin ⊙

Venice ⊙
⊙ Trieste

ZA
CROA

PORTUGAL

Iberian

Zaragoza ⊙

Garonne

ANDORRA

Nice ⊙

⊙ Bologna

Horseshoe Seamounts

Tagus Plain

Duero

Ebro

⊙ Marseille

MONACO ◆

Pisa ⊙

SAN MARINO

BOS
& HE

Tagus

LISBON

⊙ MADRID

I T A L Y

SARAJE
Mostar

SPAIN

Iberian Peninsula

⊙ Barcelona

Corsica

Apennines

Adriatic Sea

Madeira
(to Portugal)

Guadalquivir

⊙ Valencia

Sardinia

VATICAN CITY ◉
ROME

Seville ⊙

Málaga ⊙

Palma ⊙

Balearic Islands

Algerian Basin

⊙ Naples
⊙ Bari

Tyrrhenian Sea

Canary Islands
(to Spain)

GIBRALTAR
(to UK)

Strait of Gibraltar

Ceuta
(to Spain)

Melilla
(to Spain)

Mediterranean

⊙ Palermo
Sicily

⊙ Cosenza

Mount Etna △
3340m
⊙ Catania

Ioni
Bas

N

Atlas Mountains

AFRICA
△ 68

MALTA ⊙ ☉
VALLETTA

e a

0 km   500

0 miles   500

POPULATION   ● National capital

○ Less than 50,000   ⊙ 50,000 -100,000   ◉ 100,000 - 500,000   ◼ Over 500,000

Barents Sea

North Cape

Ostrov Kolguyev

Arctic Circle

155

Ob'

80°

Irtysh

1

Murmansk
Kola
Peninsula

White
Sea

Archangel

Northern Dvina

Ural Mountains

R   U   S   S   I   A   N

FINLAND

Tampere

Åland Turku HELSINKI

STOCKHOLM TALLINN

Uppsala

ESTONIA

LATVIA

RĪGA
LITHUANIA

KALININGRAD
(to Russ Fed.)
liningrad
ansk

Kaunas
VILNIUS

dgoszcz

WARSAW

Brest

BELARUS

Babruysk

Homyel'

MINSK

OLAND

Vistula

Kraków

L'viv

Carpathian Mountains

VOVAKIA

Chernivtsi

UDAPEST

UNGARY Cluj-Napoca

Tisza

ROMANIA

Braşov

BELGRADE

BUCHAREST

YUGO-
SLAVIA

Danube

Constanţa

BULGARIA Varna

Balkan Mountains

SKOPJE

SOFIA

Burgas

MACED.

TIRANA

TURKEY

LBANIA

Pindus Mountains

Aegean
Sea

GREECE

ATHENS

Piraeus

Peloponnese

Sea

Irákleio

Crete

Lake Onega

Lake Ladoga

Saint Petersburg

Vologda

Yaroslavl'

MOSCOW

Vitsyebsk

Central
Russian
Upland

Pripet
Marshes

Dnieper Lowlands

KIEV

Dnieper

UKRAINE

Dniester

Bug

Dnipropetrovs'k

Donets'k

MOLDOVA

CHIŞINĂU

Odesa

Crimea

Simferopol'

Sea of
Azov

E u r o p e a n   P l a i n

Perm'

F   E   D   E   R   A   T   I   O   N

Ufa

Kazan'

Nizhniy
Novgorod

Ul'yanovsk

Samara

Orenburg

Volga Uplands

Volga

Ural

Voronezh

Don

Kharkiv

Volgograd

Astrakhan'

Ural

Syr Darya

Aral Sea

Amu Darya

112

70°

60°

50°

80°

2

3

A   S   I   A

Caspian Sea

Rostov-na-Donu

Stavropol'

C a u c a s u s

El'brus 5642m

Black Sea

A n a t o l i a

Cyprus

Tigris

Euphrates

118

Zagros Mountains

112

4

40°

60°

30°

5

81

THE NORTH ATLANTIC

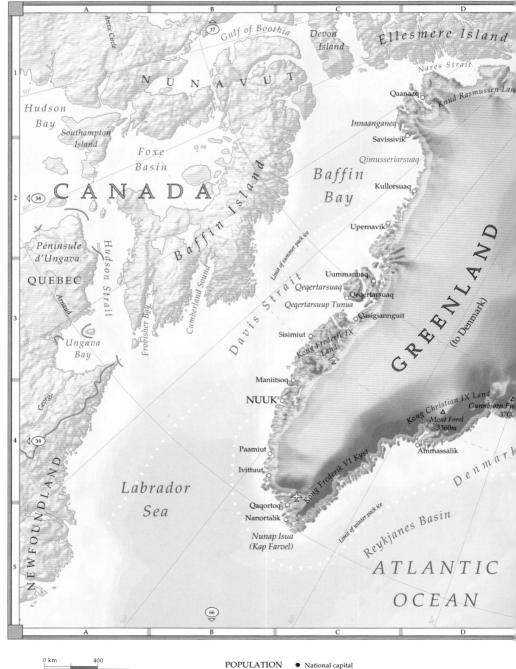

A
B
C
D

37

Gulf of Boothia

90°

Devon
Island

Ellesmere Island

Nares Strait

Arctic Circle

N U N A V U T

Qaanaaq

Knud Rasmussen Lan

Hudson
Bay

90°

Innaanganeq

Savissivik

1

Southampton
Island

Qimusseriarsuaq

Foxe
Basin

Baffin
Bay

Kullorsuaq

C A N A D A

80°

38

Upernavik

2

Limit of summer pack ice

Péninsule
d'Ungava

Baffin Island

Uummannaq

Qeqertarsuaq

Qeqertarsuaq

Davis Strait

QUEBEC

Hudson Strait

Qeqertarsuup Tunua

Qasigiannguit

GREENLAND

Cumberland Sound

Frobisher Bay

Sisimiut

Kong Frederik IX
Land

(to Denmark)

3

Arnaud

Ungava
Bay

Maniitsoq

NUUK

Kong Christian IX Land

Gunnbjørn Fje
370

Mont Forel
3360m

Paamiut

George

Ammassalik

4

39

Ivittuut

Kong Frederik VI Kyst

Denmark

Labrador
Sea

Qaqortoq

Nanortalik

NEWFOUNDLAND

Nunap Isua
(Kap Farvel)

Limit of winter pack ice

Reykjanes Basin

ATLANTIC

5

50°

66

40°

30°

OCEAN

A
B
C
D

0 km   400

0 miles   400

POPULATION   ● National capital

○ Less than 50,000   ○ 50,000 -100,000   ◉ 100,000 - 500,000   ◼ Over 500,000

Lincoln
Sea

ARCTIC

OCEAN

Kap Morris Jesup

Wandel
Sea

Independence Fjord

Nord

SVALBARD
(to Norway)

Kvitøya

Zemlya
Frantsa-Iosifa

Novaya
Zemlya

Nordaustlandet

Kong Karls Land

Spitsbergen

Barentsøya

Edgeøya

Barents

Sea

LONGYEARBYEN

Kong Frederik VIII Land

Barentsberg

Storfjorden

Greenland

Sea

Kong Christian X Land

Limit of winter pack ice

Daneborg

△ Petermann Bjerg
2940m

Limit of summer pack ice

Bjørnøya
(to Norway)

Nordkapp
(North Cape)

FINLAND

Kong Oscar Fjord

Mohns Ridge

Ittoqqortoormiit
Kangikajik

Kangertittivaq

JAN MAYEN
(to Norway)

Norwegian

Sea

Norwegian Basin

Vestfjorden

Arctic Circle

Strait

ICELAND

Bolungarvík

Siglufjördhur

Raufarhöfn

safjördhur

Húsavík

Akureyri

Seydhisfjördhur

Stykkishólmur

Neskaupstadhur

axaflói

REYKJAVÍK

Djúpivogur

Selfoss

Vatnajökull

Thorlákshöfn

Hvannadalshnúkur
2119m

Surtsey

Vestmannaeyjar

FAEROE ISLANDS
(to Denmark)

N

TÓRSHAVN

Shetland
Islands

S
W
E
D
E
N

Gulf
of
Bothnia

NORWAY

ELEVATION

-4000m	-3000m	-2000m	-1000m	-500m	Below sea level	0	100m	250m	500m	1000m	2000m	4000m

| -13 124ft | -9843ft | -6562ft | -3281ft | -1640ft | -820ft/-250m | 0 | 328ft | 820ft | 1640ft | 3281ft | 6562ft | 13 124ft |

SCANDINAVIA & FINLAND

RUSSIAN FEDERATION

FINLAND

Arctic Circle

Barents Sea

ARCTIC OCEAN

Nordkapp
(North Cape)

Lapland

Norwegian Sea

Arctic Circle

0 km   200

0 miles   200

POPULATION   ● National capital

○ Less than 50,000   ○ 50,000 -100,000   ◉ 100,000 - 500,000   ◼ Over 500,000

NORWAY

DENMARK

RUSS. FED.

ESTONIA

LATVIA

LITHUANIA

KALININGRAD
(to Russian
Federation)

POLAND

GERMANY

BELARUS

Baltic Sea

North Sea

Gulf of Finland

Gulf of Bothnia

Gulf of Riga

Skagerrak

Kattegat

HELSINKI
STOCKHOLM
OSLO
KØBENHAVN
Copenhagen
Tampere
Turku (Åbo)
Vantaa
Espoo
Bergen
Stavanger
Göteborg (Gothenburg)
Malmö
Århus
Aalborg
Odense

ELEVATION

Below sea level														
-2000m	-1000m	-500m	-250m	-100m		0	100m	250m	500m	1000m	2000m	4000m		
-6562ft	-3281ft	-1640ft	-820ft	-328ft	-164ft/-50m	0		328ft	820ft	1640ft	3281ft	6562ft	13 124ft	

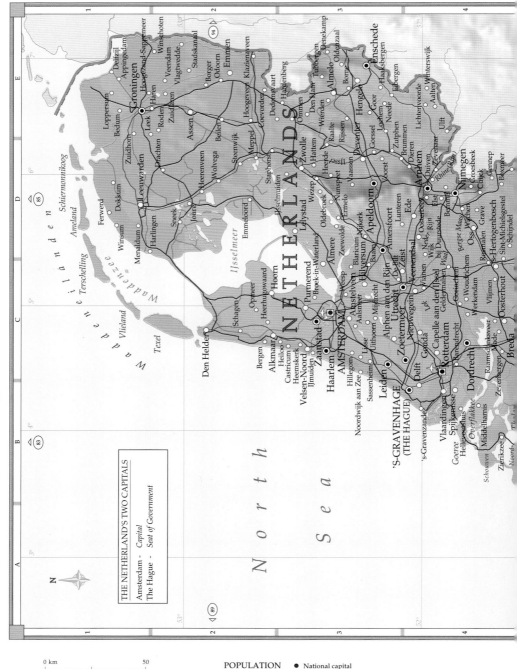

THE NETHERLAND'S TWO CAPITALS

Amsterdam -   *Capital*
The Hague -   *Seat of Government*

N

0 km   50

0 miles   50

POPULATION   ● National capital

○ Less than 50,000   ○ 50,000 -100,000   ◉ 100,000 - 500,000   ◼ Over 500,000

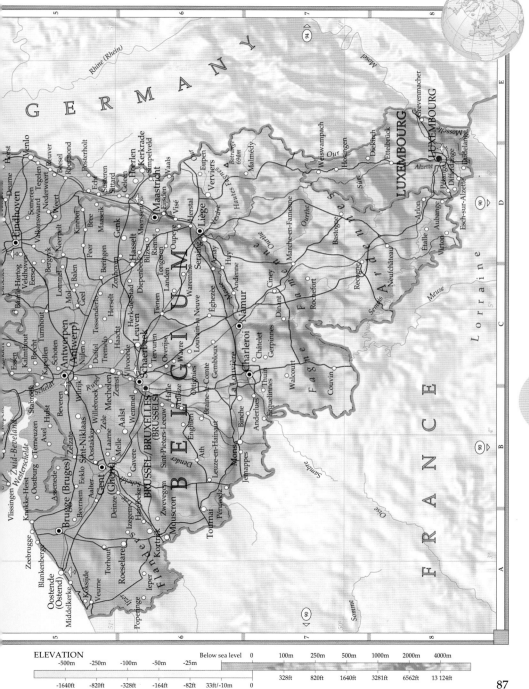

ELEVATION

-500m	-250m	-100m	-50m	-25m	Below sea level	0	100m	250m	500m	1000m	2000m	4000m
-1640ft	-820ft	-328ft	-164ft	-82ft	33ft/-10m	0	328ft	820ft	1640ft	3281ft	6562ft	13 124ft

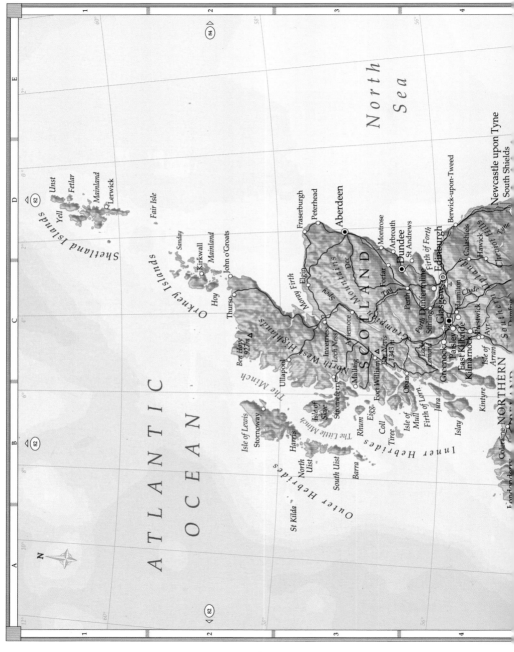

North Sea

ATLANTIC OCEAN

Shetland Islands

Unst
Yell
Fetlar
Mainland
Lerwick

Fair Isle

Orkney Islands

Sanday
Kirkwall
Mainland
Hoy
John o'Groats

Thurso

Ben Hope
927m

North West Highlands

The Minch

Ullapool

Stromeferry
Malaig
Isle of Skye

The Little Minch

Isle of Lewis
Stornoway

Harris

North Uist

South Uist

Barra

St Kilda

Outer Hebrides

Rhum
Eigg
Coll
Tiree
Isle of Mull
Firth of Lorn

Inner Hebrides

Jura
Islay

Kintyre
Isle of Arran

Moray Firth
Elgin
Spey
Inverness
Loch Ness
Aviemore
Ben Nevis
1343 m
Fort William
Loch Linnhe
Oban

SCOTLAND

Grampian Mountains
Dee
Tay

Fraserburgh
Peterhead
Aberdeen

Montrose
Arbroath
Dundee
St Andrews
Forfar
Perth

Firth of Forth
Dunfermline
Edinburgh
Stirling
Forth
Glasgow
Hamilton
Clyde
Paisley
Greenock
East Kilbride
Kilmarnock
Prestwick
Ayr

Berwick-upon-Tweed
Galashiels
Hawick
Cheviot Hills
Cheviot

Newcastle upon Tyne
South Shields
Tyne

Southern

Coleraine
NORTHERN

Londonderry

N

0 km 100
0 miles 100

POPULATION ● National capital ◎ Internal administrative capital
○ Less than 50,000 ○ 50,000 -100,000 ◉ 100,000 - 500,000 ◼ Over 500,000

ELEVATION

-2000m	-1000m	-500m	-250m	-100m	Below sea level	0	100m	250m	500m	1000m	2000m	4000m
-6562ft	-3281ft	-1640ft	-820ft	-328ft	-164ft/-50m	0	328ft	820ft	1640ft	3281ft	6562ft	13 124ft

FRANCE, ANDORRA & MONACO

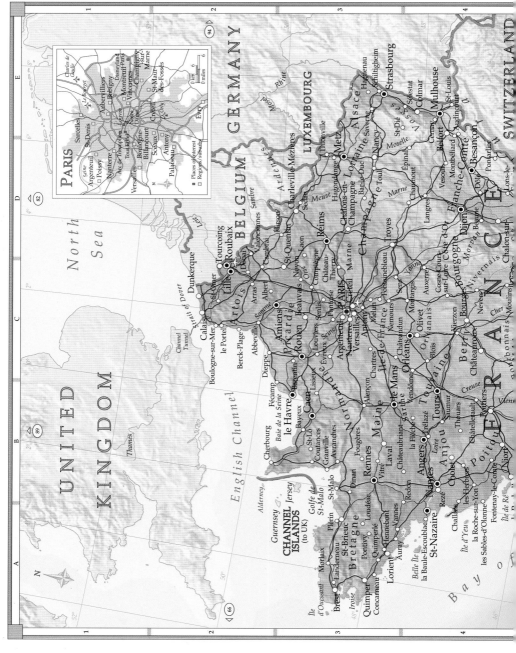

PARIS

Charles de Gaulle
Le Bourget
Sarcelles
Argenteuil
Nanterre
Arc de Triomphe
Versailles
Palaiseau
St-Denis
Aubervilliers
Bobigny
Louvre
Montreuil Paris
Vincennes
Créteil
Antony
Sceaux
Boulogne-Billancourt
Disneyland
Champigny-sur-Marne
St-Maur-des-Fossés
Evry
Seine

■ Places of interest
□ Regions / suburbs

North Sea

UNITED KINGDOM

Channel Tunnel

English Channel

North
Sea

Strait of Dover

Channel Islands
Guernsey
Jersey (to UK)
Alderney
CHANNEL ISLANDS (to UK)

GERMANY
BELGIUM
LUXEMBOURG
SWITZERLAND

Dunkerque
Tourcoing
Roubaix
St-Omer
Lille
Calais
Boulogne-sur-Mer
le Portel
Berck-Plage
Abbeville
Valenciennes
Cambrai
St-Quentin
Charleville-Mézières
Sedan
Reims
Châlons-en-Champagne
Bar-le-Duc
Metz
Thionville
Strasbourg
Haguenau
Schiltigheim
Sélestat
Colmar
Mulhouse
St-Louis
Belfort
Montbéliard
Besançon
Pontarlier
Lons-le-Saunier

Amiens
Beauvais
Senlis
Compiègne
Noyon
Laon
Soissons
Château-Thierry
Troyes
Chaumont
Langres
Dijon
Chalon-sur-Saône

Cherbourg
St-Lô
Coutances
Granville
Avranches
Bayeux
Caen
le Havre
Fécamp
Dieppe
Rouen
Évreux
Lisieux
Argentan
Alençon
Chartres
Dreux
Versailles
PARIS
Créteil
Melun
Fontainebleau
Nemours
Montargis
Auxerre
Nevers
Moulins

Brest
Morlaix
Landerneau
Quimper
Concarneau
Lorient
Hennebont
Quimperlé
Pontivy
St-Brieuc
Dinan
St-Malo
Rennes
Laval
le Mans
Angers
Nantes
St-Nazaire
la Baule-Escoublac
Challans
les Sables-d'Olonne
la Roche-sur-Yon
Fontenay-le-Comte
Poitiers
Châtellerault
les Herbiers
Cholet
Saumur
Thouars
Redon
Vannes
Auray
Loudéac
Vitré
Fougères
Mayenne
la Flèche
Blois
Orléans
Olivet
Vendôme
Tours
Amboise
Châteaudun
Pithiviers
Montereau
Sens
Joigny
Bourges
Vierzon
Romorantin-Lanthenay
Châteauroux
Issoudun
Nevers
Cosne-Cours-sur-Loire

FRANCE

Bay of

0 km 100
0 miles 100

POPULATION
● National capital
○ Less than 50,000
○ 50,000 –100,000
◉ 100,000 - 500,000
◼ Over 500,000

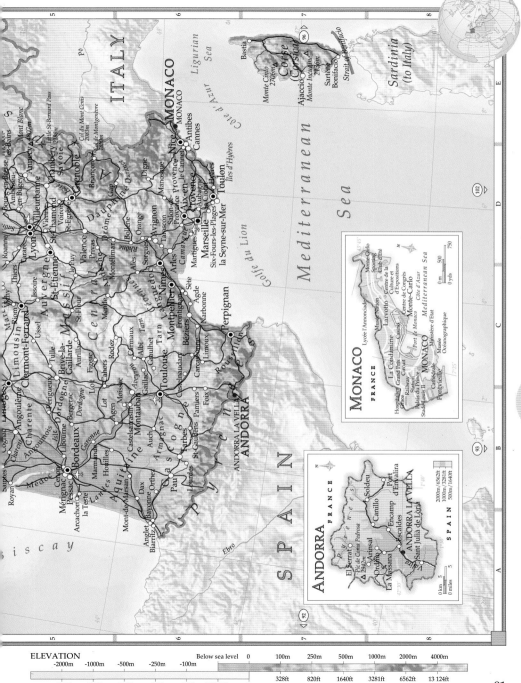

ELEVATION

Below sea level											
-2000m	-1000m	-500m	-250m	-100m	0	100m	250m	500m	1000m	2000m	4000m
-6562ft	-3281ft	-1640ft	-820ft	-328ft	-164ft/-50m	0	328ft	820ft	1640ft	3281ft	6562ft	13 124ft

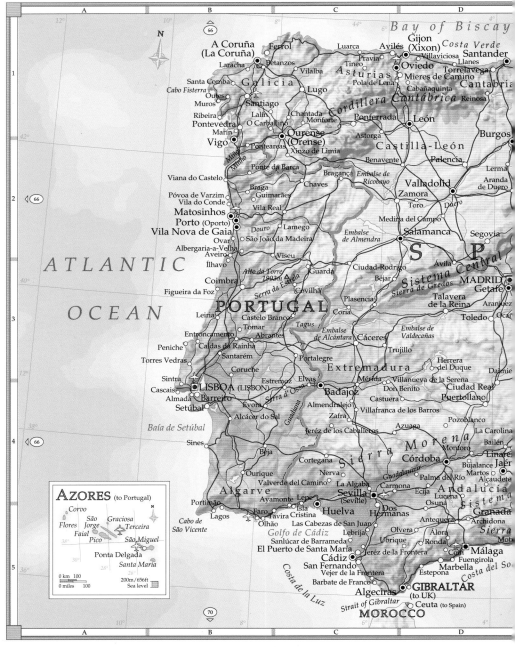

Bay of Biscay

Gijón (Xixon) · Costa Verde · Santander
A Coruña (La Coruña) · Ferrol · Luarca · Avilés · Villaviciosa · Llanes
Laracha · Betanzos · Tineo · Pravia · Oviedo · Torrelavega
Santa Comba · Vilalba · Mieres de Camino · Reinosa
Cabo Fisterra · Galicia · Pola de Lena · Cabañaquinta · Cantabria
Outes · Lugo · Cordillera Cantábrica
Muros · Santiago · Chantada · Ponferrada · León
Ribeira · Lalín · O Carballiño · Monforte · Astorga · Burgos
Pontevedra · Marín · Ourense (Orense) · Castilla-León
Vigo · Ponteareas · Xinzo de Limia · Benavente · Palencia · Lerma
Minho · Ponte da Barca · Braganza · Embalse de Ricobayo · Valladolid · Aranda de Duero
Viana do Castelo · Chaves · Zamora
Braga · Guimarães · Vila Real · Toro · Duero · Medina del Campo · Segovia
Póvoa de Varzim · Vila do Conde · Vila Real
Matosinhos · Porto (Oporto) · Embalse de Almendra · Salamanca
Vila Nova de Gaia · Douro · Lamego · S
Ovar · São João da Madeira · Ávila · MADRID
Albergaria-a-Velha · Viseu · Ciudad-Rodrigo · Sistema Central · Getafe
Aveiro · Ílhavo · Guarda · Béjar · Sierra de Gredos
ATLANTIC · Coimbra · Alto da Torre 1993m · Covilhã · Talavera de la Reina · Aranjuez
Figueira da Foz · Serra da Estrela · Plasencia · Toledo · Ocar
OCEAN · Leiria · Castelo Branco · Coria
Entroncamento · Tomar · Tagus · Embalse de Alcántara · Cáceres · Embalse de Valdecañas
Peniche · Caldas da Rainha · Abrantes · Trujillo · Herrera del Duque
Torres Vedras · Santarém · Portalegre · Extremadura · Daimie
Sintra · Coruche · Elvas · Mérida · Villanueva de la Serena · Ciudad Real
Cascais · Estremoz · Cristina · Don Benito · Puertollano
Almada · LISBOA (LISBON) · Badajoz · Castuera · Pozoblanco · La Carolina
Barreiro · Évora · Almendralejo · Villafranca de los Barros · Azuaga · Bailén
Setúbal · Alcácer do Sal · Zafra · Morena · Montoro · Linares
Baía de Setúbal · Jeréz de los Caballeros · Córdoba · Bujalance · Jaén
Sines · Beja · Martos · Alcaudete
Cortegana · Sierra · Guadalquivir · Palma del Río · Andalucía · Sistema
Ourique · Nerva · Carmona · Ecija · Lucena · Sierra
Valverde del Camino · La Algaba · Osuna · Granada
Portimão · Algarve · Ayamonte · Lepe · Sevilla (Seville) · Antequera · Archidona
Lagos · Faro · Tavira · Isla Cristina · Huelva · Dos Hermanas · Olvera · Mot
Cabo de São Vicente · Olhão · Las Cabezas de San Juan · Lebrija · Álora · Ronda · Sierra
Golfo de Cádiz · Sanlúcar de Barrameda · Ubrique · Estepona · Costa del So
El Puerto de Santa María · Jeréz de la Frontera · Málaga
Cádiz · Fuengirola
San Fernando · Vejer de la Frontera · Marbella
Barbate de Franco · Estepona
Costa de la Luz · Algeciras · GIBRALTAR (to UK)
Strait of Gibraltar · Ceuta (to Spain)
MOROCCO

AZORES (to Portugal)
Corvo
São Jorge · Graciosa
Flores · Faial · Terceira
Pico
São Miguel
Ponta Delgada
Santa Maria

0 km 100
0 miles 100
200m/656ft
Sea level

0 km 100
0 miles 100

POPULATION · ● National capital
○ Less than 50,000 · ○ 50,000 -100,000 · ◉ 100,000 - 500,000 · ◼ Over 500,000

FRANCE

redo
Bermeo
Zarautz
Eibar
Donostia-San Sebastián
Irún
Tolosa
Ilbao
País Vasco
Bergara
Pamplona
Vitoria-Gasteiz
(Iruña)
Miranda
de Ebro
Estella-Lizarra
Logroño
Navarra
Jaca
Monte Perdido
3348m
La Seu d'Urgel
ANDORRA

Golfe du Lion

Sistema
La Rioja
Arnedo
Calahorra
Huesca
Barbastro
Berga
Ripoll
 Banyoles
Figueres
Girona
(Gerona)
Palafrugell
Palamós

El Burgo
de Osma
Ejea de
los Caballeros
Monzón
Balaguer
Cervera
Manlleu
Vic
Blanes
Arenys de Mar

Soria
Tarazona
Tudela
Zaragoza
Lleida
(Lérida)
Tàrrega
Fraga
Sabadell
Terrassa
Barcelona
L'Hospitalet de Llobregat

Ibérico
Calatayud
Aragón
Daroca
Alcañiz
Vilafranca del Penedès
Valls
Reus
Sitges
El Vendrell
Tarragona

Guadalajara
Alcalá de Henares
rrejón de Ardoz
Medinaceli
Teruel
Tortosa
Amposta
Sant Carles de la Ràpita
Vinaròs

Tagus
Cuenca
Javalambre
2020m
Onda
Castelló de la Plana
Burriana

Tarancón
Castilla-La Mancha
Burjassot
Vall d' Uxó
Sagunto
Golfo de
Valencia

Mota del Cuervo
Campo de Criptana
Socuéllamos
La Roda
Xúcar
Torrente
Catarroja
Algemesí
Sueca
Cullera
Gandía
Oliva
Valencia

Tomelloso
Manzanares
La Solana
Idepeñas
Albacete
Almansa
Xàtiva
Ontinyent
Alcoy
Denia

Villanueva de los Infantes
Hellín
Jumilla
Elda
Benidorm
Villajoyosa

Beas de
Segura
Moratalla
Villena
Monóvar
San Juan de Alicante
Alicante

beda
Villacarrillo
Cazorla
Cieza
Mula
Elche
Callosa de Segura
Orihuela
Costa Blanca

Béticos
Huéscar
Murcia
Murcia
Totana
La Unión

Baza
Lorca
Aguilas
Cartagena

Guadix
Mulhacén
3481m
Mojácar

Nevada
Berja
Almería
Adra

Mediterranean Sea

Ciutadella de Menorca
Menorca
(Minorca)
Mahón

Pollença
Sa Pobla
Palma
Manacor
Llucmajor
Felanitx

Cabrera
Mallorca
(Majorca)

Islas Baleares
(Balearic Islands)

Eivissa
(Ibiza)
Eivissa
Formentera

ALGERIA

ELEVATION

-4000m	-3000m	-2000m	-1000m	-500m	Below sea level	0	100m	250m	500m	1000m	2000m	4000m
-13 124ft	-9843ft	-6562ft	-3281ft	-1640ft	-820ft/-250m	0	328ft	820ft	1640ft	3281ft	6562ft	13 124ft

GERMANY & THE ALPINE STATES

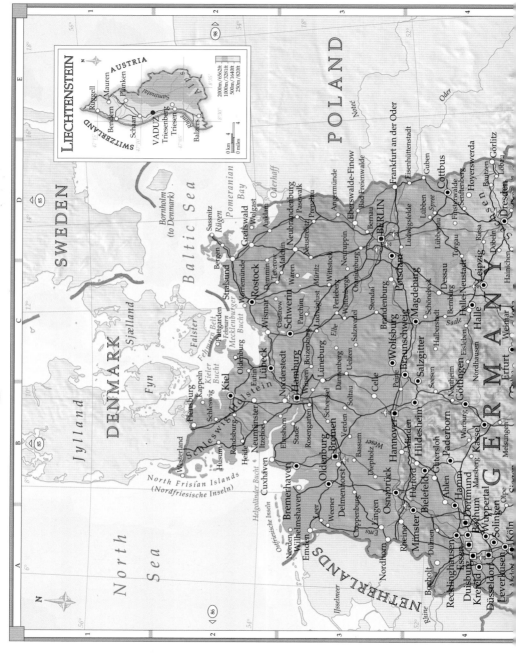

POLAND

SWEDEN

DENMARK

NETHERLANDS

LIECHTENSTEIN

AUSTRIA

SWITZERLAND

VADUZ
Triesenberg
Triesen
Balzers
Mauren
Planken
Schaan
Bendern
Ruggell

Samináhal

ALPS

Rhine

2000m/6562ft
1000m/3281ft
500m/1640ft
250m/820ft

0 km 4
0 miles 4

North Sea

Baltic Sea

Pomeranian Bay

Oderhaff

Jylland

Sjælland

Fyn

Falster

*Bornholm
(to Denmark)*

Oder

Notec

Görlitz
Löbau
Dresden
Bautzen
Hoyerswerda
Senftenberg
Finsterwalde
Döbeln
Riesa
Torgau
Lübben
Lübbenau
Spree
Guben
Cottbus
Eisenhüttenstadt
Eberswalde-Finow
Bad Freienwalde
Frankfurt an der Oder
Angermünde
Prenzlau
Pasewalk
Neubrandenburg
Anklam
Wolgast
Greifswald
Sassnitz
Rügen
Bergen
Stralsund
Warnemünde
Rostock
Wismar
Schwerin
Güstrow
Teterow
Demmin
Malchin
Waren
Müritz
Wittstock
Neustrelitz
Neuruppin
Oranienburg
Bernau
BERLIN
Potsdam
Ludwigsfelde
Brandenburg
Magdeburg
Schönebeck
Dessau
Bernburg
Halle-Neustadt
Halle
Leipzig
Weimar
Erfurt
Weißenfels
Eisleben
Nordhausen
Melsungen
Mühlhausen
Göttingen
Northeim
Warburg
Kassel
Marsberg
Seesen
Halberstadt
Salzgitter
Wolfsburg
Braunschweig
Peine
Celle
Soltau
Uelzen
Salzwedel
Stendal
Perleberg
Wittenberge
Ludwigslust
Parchim
Boizenburg
Dannenberg
Lüneburg
Lübeck
Eutin
Fehmarn
Plöngarden
Kieler Bucht
Kappeln
Flensburg
Schleswig
Kiel
Rendsburg
Husum
Heide
Neumünster
Itzehoe
Elmshorn
Stade
Norderstedt
Hamburg
Wedel
Rosengarten
Scheessel
Verden
Rotenburg
Bassum
Diepholz
Bremen
Delmenhorst
Oldenburg
Cuxhaven
Bremerhaven
Wilhelmshaven
Nordenham
Westerland
Schleswig-Holstein
Mecklenburg
Elbe
Saale
Weser
Ems
Aller
Leine

Rhein
Norden
Emden
Leer
Weener
Cloppenburg
Lingen
Rheine
Nordhorn
Meppen
Osnabrück
Ibbenbüren
Münster
Dülmen
Coesfeld
Bocholt
Recklinghausen
Gelsenkirchen
Bottrop
Oberhausen
Duisburg
Essen
Bochum
Dortmund
Hamm
Ahlen
Gütersloh
Bielefeld
Herford
Minden
Hannover
Hildesheim
Paderborn
Düsseldorf
Neuss
Krefeld
Leverkusen
Köln
Solingen
Wuppertal
Olpe

N Sea
Ostfriesische Inseln
Helgoländer Bucht
Ijsselmeer
Rhine

GERMANY

0 km 100
0 miles 100

POPULATION · National capital
○ Less than 50,000   ○ 50,000 -100,000   ◉ 100,000 - 500,000   ■ Over 500,000

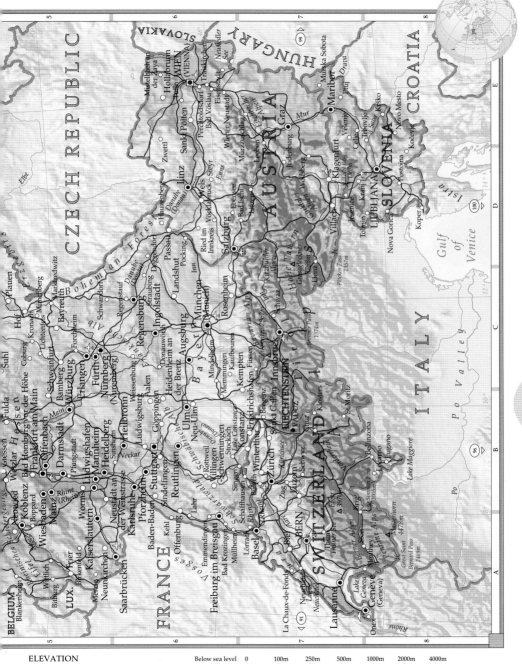

CROATIA

SLOVENIA

CZECH REPUBLIC

SLOVAKIA

HUNGARY

AUSTRIA

ITALY

Gulf
of
Venice

Po Valley

FRANCE

SWITZERLAND

BELGIUM

LUX.

ELEVATION

					Below sea level	0	100m	250m	500m	1000m	2000m	4000m
-500m	-250m	-100m	-50m	-25m								
-1640ft	-820ft	-328ft	-164ft	-82ft	33ft/-10m	0	328ft	820ft	1640ft	3281ft	6562ft	13 124ft

95

ITALY

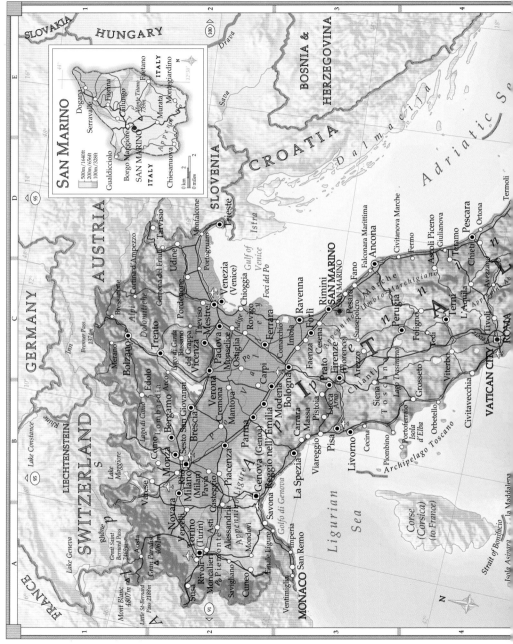

SAN MARINO

500m/1640ft
200m/656ft
100m/328ft

Dogana
Serravalle
Fiorina
Falciano
Montegiardino
Monte Titano
739m
Murata
SAN MARINO
ITALY
Gualdicciolo
Borgo Maggiore
Chiesanuova
ITALY
Montegiardino

0 km 2
0 miles 2

SLOVAKIA
HUNGARY
BOSNIA & HERZEGOVINA
CROATIA
Drava
Sava
Dalmacia
Adriatic Sea

Trieste
Monfalcone
Istra
Gulf of Venice

GERMANY
AUSTRIA
Inn
Brenner Pass 1371m
Bressanone
Alpi
Cortina d'Ampezzo
Merano
Dolomitiche
Gemona del Friuli
Udine
Tarvisio
Pordenone
Portogruaro
Venezia (Venice)
Chioggia
Foci del Po
Ravenna
Rimini
SAN MARINO
Fano
Pesaro
Falconara Marittima
Ancona
Civitanova Marche
Fermo
Ascoli Piceno
Giulianova
Teramo
Pescara
Ortona
Chieti
Termoli

Bolzano
Trento
Lago di Garda
del Grappa
Bassano
Treviso
Mestre
Vicenza
Padova
Mestre
Mira
Rovigo
Adige
Ostiglia
Ferrara
Comacchio
Imola
Faenza
Cesena
Forlì
Sansepolcro
Perugia
Foligno
Spoleto
Todi
Terni
Rieti
Avezzano
L'Aquila
Tivoli
ROMA

LIECHTENSTEIN
SWITZERLAND
Lake Constance
Rhine
Lake Maggiore
Lago di Como
Edolo
Lombardia
Bergamo
Brescia
Sesto San Giovanni
Monza
Como
Varese
Rho
Milano (Milan)
Pavia
Castegio
Cremona
Mantova
Parma
Reggio nell'Emilia
Modena
Carpi
Bologna
Emilia
Pistoia
Prato
Firenze (Florence)
Arezzo
Chianti
Toscana
Lago Trasimeno
Siena
Grosseto
Viterbo
Civitavecchia
VATICAN CITY

FRANCE
Mont Blanc 4807m
Great Saint Bernard Pass 2469m
Little St-Bernard Pass 2188m
Rhône
Gran Paradiso 4061m
Aosta
Susa
Rivoli
Torino (Turin)
Moncalieri
Piemonte
Savigliano
Cuneo
Mondovì
Asti
Alessandria
Vercelli
Novara
Appennino
Savona
Finale Ligure
Imperia
Ventimiglia
San Remo
MONACO
Golfo di Genova
Genova (Genoa)
Piacenza
Ligure
La Spezia
Carrara
Massa
Viareggio
Lucca
Pisa
Arno
Livorno
Cecina
Piombino
Portoferraio
Isola d'Elba
Orbetello
Archipelago Toscano
Corse (Corsica) (to France)
Strait of Bonifacio
Isola Asinara
la Maddalena
Ligurian Sea
Piombino

Appennino Marchigiano
Marche
Umbro-Marchigiano
Appennino Tosco-Emiliano

N

POPULATION

● National capital

○ Less than 50,000   ○ 50,000 –100,000   ◉ 100,000 – 500,000   ◼ Over 500,000

0 km 100
0 miles 100

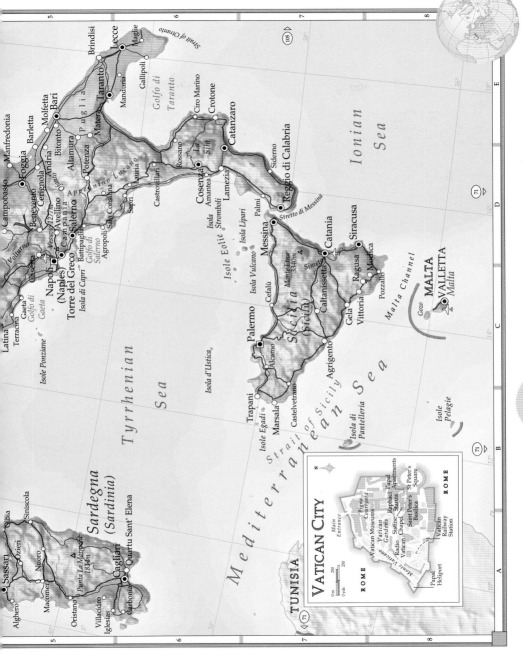

ITALY

Lecce
Brindisi
Maglie
Strait of Otranto
Taranto
Manduria
Gallipoli
Golfo di Taranto
Bari
Molfetta
Barletta
Bitonto
Andria
Matera
Cerignola
Altamura
Manfredonia
Foggia
Potenza
Campobasso
Benevento
Avellino
Salerno
Vesuvio 1277m
Napoli (Naples)
Caserta
Torre del Greco
Battipaglia
Golfo di Salerno
Agropoli
Isola di Capri
Gaeta
Golfo di Gaeta
Latina
Terracina
Isole Ponziane
Puglia
Ciro Marino
Crotone
Catanzaro
Rossano
La Sila
Cosenza
Amantea
Lamezia
Sapri
Castrovillari
Lauria
Sala Consilina Lucano
Apennino Lucano
Volturno
Campania
Reggio di Calabria
Sidero
Stretto di Messina
Palmi
Messina
Isola Lipari
Isole Eolie
Isola Vulcano
Isola Stromboli
Cefalù
Palermo
Alcamo
Trapani
Isole Egadi
Marsala
Castelvetrano
Strait of Sicily
Isola di Pantelleria
Sicilia (Sicily)
Caltanissetta
Agrigento
Gela
Vittoria
Ragusa
Modica
Pozzallo
Simeto
Monte Etna 3340m
Catania
Siracusa
Ionian Sea
Malta Channel
Gozo
MALTA
VALLETTA
Malta
Isole Pelagie
Tyrrhenian Sea
Mediterranean Sea
Isola d'Ustica
Sardegna (Sardinia)
Olbia
Siniscola
Sassari
Ozieri
Nuoro
Macomer
Oristano
Villacidro
Iglesias
Carbonia
Punta La Marmora 1834m
Cagliari
Quartu Sant' Elena
Sant' Elena
Alghero
TUNISIA

VATICAN CITY

N
Main Entrance
Pigna Courtyard
Vatican Museums
Vatican Gardens
Radio Vaticana
Raphael Stanza
Sistine Chapel
Papal Apartments
Saint Peter's Basilica
St Peter's Square
ROME
Monte Vaticano
Papal Heliport
Vatican Railway Station
ROME
ROME
0 m   200
0 yds   250

ELEVATION

					Below sea level	0	100m	250m	500m	1000m	2000m	4000m
-2000m	-1000m	-500m	-250m	-100m								
-6562ft	-3281ft	-1640ft	-820ft	-328ft	-164ft/-50m	0	328ft	820ft	1640ft	3281ft	6562ft	13 124ft

97

CENTRAL EUROPE

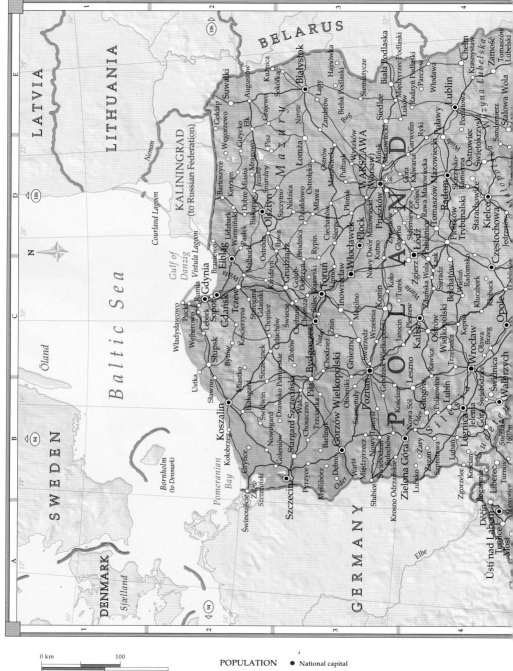

EUROPE

POLAND

0 km   100

0 miles   100

POPULATION

● National capital

○ Less than 50,000   ○ 50,000 - 100,000   ◉ 100,000 - 500,000   ◼ Over 500,000

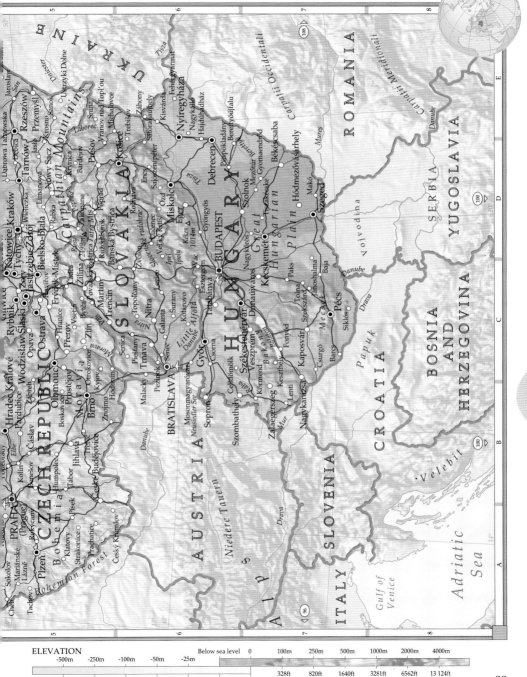

ELEVATION

					Below sea level	0	100m	250m	500m	1000m	2000m	4000m
-500m	-250m	-100m	-50m	-25m								
-1640ft	-820ft	-328ft	-164ft	-82ft	33ft/-10m	0	328ft	820ft	1640ft	3281ft	6562ft	13 124ft

SOUTHEAST EUROPE

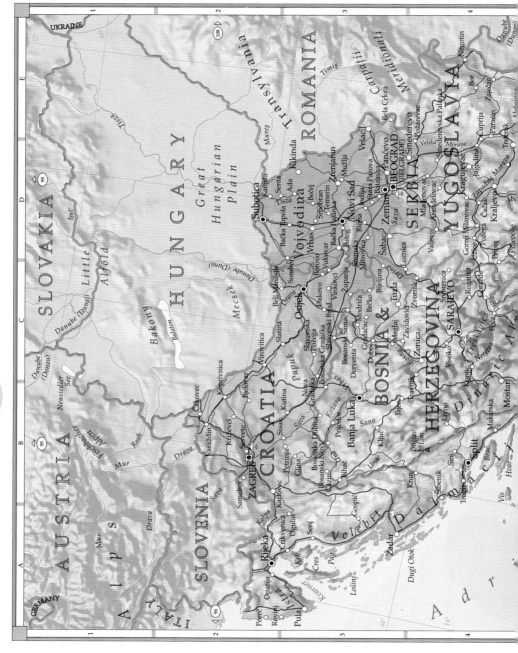

UKRAINE

SLOVAKIA

HUNGARY

Great
Hungarian
Plain

Little
Alföld

AUSTRIA

GERMANY

ITALY

SLOVENIA

CROATIA

ROMANIA

Transylvania

SERBIA

YUGOSLAVIA

BELGRADE
(BEOGRAD)

Vojvodina

Novi Sad

Subotica

Zemun

BOSNIA &
HERZEGOVINA

SARAJEVO

Banja Luka

Split

Zadar

Adriatic

Dinaric Alps

Velebit

Danube (Dunaj)

Danube (Donau)

Alps

Mur

Drava

Sava

Tisza

Danube (Duna)

Danube (Dunărea)

Mureş

Timiş

Carpaţii Meridionali

0 km   100

0 miles   100

POPULATION   ● National capital

○ Less than 50,000   ○ 50,000 -100,000   ◉ 100,000 - 500,000   ◼ Over 500,000

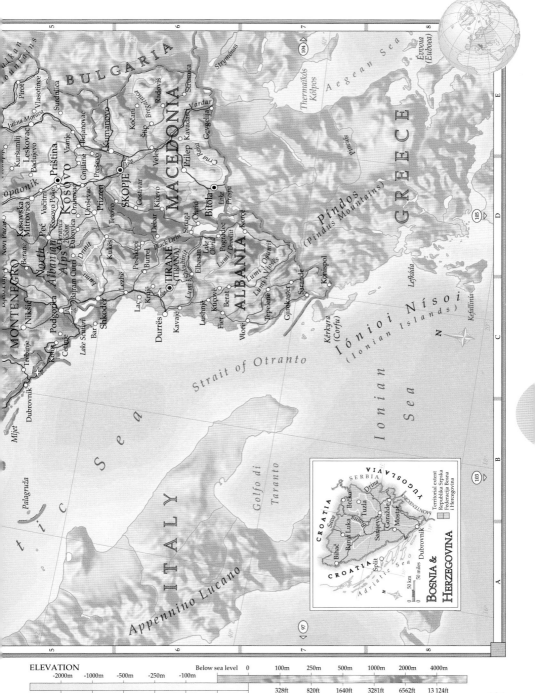

ELEVATION

| -2000m | -1000m | -500m | -250m | -100m | Below sea level | 0 | 100m | 250m | 500m | 1000m | 2000m | 4000m |

| -6562ft | -3281ft | -1640ft | -820ft | -328ft | -164ft/-50m | 0 | | 328ft | 820ft | 1640ft | 3281ft | 6562ft | 13 124ft |

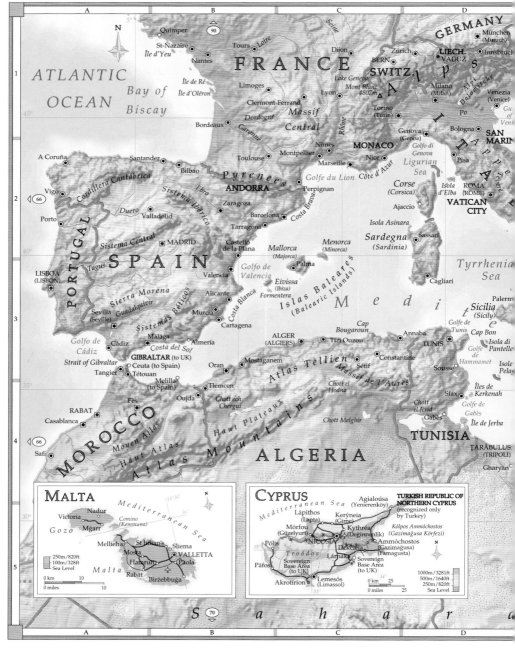

ELEVATION

| Below sea level | 0 | 100m | 250m | 500m | 1000m | 2000m | 4000m |

-4000m -3000m -2000m -1000m -500m

-13 124ft -9843ft -6562ft -3281ft -1640ft -820ft/-250m 0

328ft 820ft 1640ft 3281ft 6562ft 13 124ft

BULGARIA & GREECE

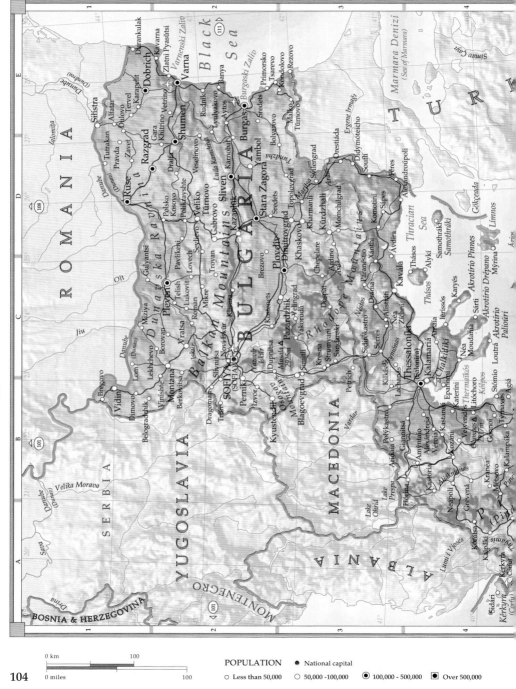

0 km   100

0 miles   100

POPULATION   ● National capital

○ Less than 50,000   ○ 50,000 -100,000   ◉ 100,000 - 500,000   ◼ Over 500,000

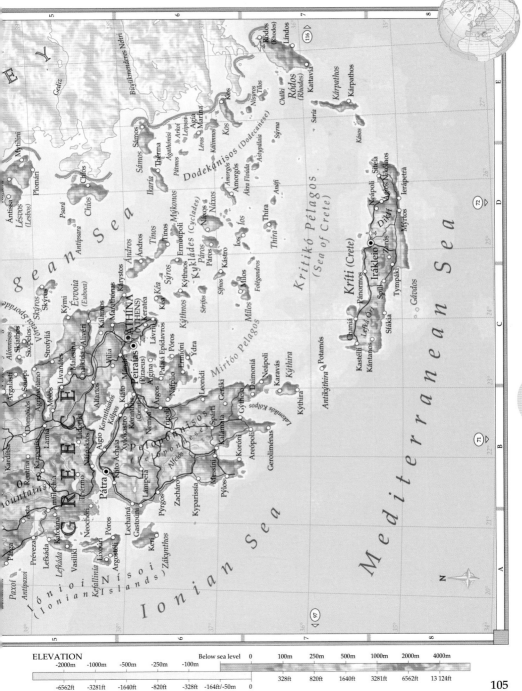

EY

Getiz

Büyükmenderes Nehri

Mytilíni

Antissa
Lésvos
(Lesbos)

Antipsara
Psará

Chíos
Chíos

Plomári

a e g e a n   S e a

Vóreis Sporádes

Alónnisos
Skiáthos
Skópelos
Strofyliá
Skýros
Skýros

Kými

Evvoia
(Euboea)

Sámos
Sámos

Ikaría

Therma

Patmos
Léros
Arkoí
Leipsoí
Agathónisi

Dodekánisos (Dodecanese)

Kálimnos

Kós
Kos

Nísiros
Tílos
Chálki

Agia
Marína

Ródos
(Rhodes)
Lindos

116

Ródos
(Rhodes)
Kattaviá

Kárpathos
Kárpathos

Sária
Kásos

Kárystos

Kálamos
Marathónas
Chalkída
Alivéri

Ándros
Ándros

Tínos
Tínos

Sýros
Sýros

Kýklades (Cyclades)

Mýkonos

Náxos
Náxos
Páros
Páros

Kéa
Kéa
Kýthnos
Kýthnos

Astypálaia
Amorgós
Amorgós

Akra Floúda

Nísiros

Sýrna

Anáfi

D

72

Mýrtos
Ierápetra

Lár

Ermoúpoli

Strofyliá
Livanátes
Malesína

Yília

ATHÍNA
(ATHENS)

Keratéa
Lávrio
Lávrio

Marína
Mégara

Peiraiás
(Piraeus)

Aígina
Póros

Opoúntioi
Palaiá Epídavros

Ermíoni
Ydra
Leonídi

Náfplio
Árgos

Kastro

Sífnos
Sérifos

Folégandros

Mílos
Mílos

Íos
Íos

Thíra
Thíra
Thíra

Kritikó Pélagos
(Sea of Crete)

Pánormos
Iráklio
Zarós
Spíli
Tympáki

Neápoli
Sitéa
Ágios Nikólaos
Díkti

Kríti (Crete)

Chaniá
Lefká Óri
Kantanos
Sfákia

Kastélli

Gávdos

KorinthiakósKólpos

Xylókastro
Korinthos
(Corinth)

Aígio
Kíáto

Nemea
Trípoli

Kto Achaía

Pátra

GREECE

Lamía
Karpenísi
Agrínio
Mólos

Kardítsa
Domokós

Trífilos
Náfpaktos
Aitolikó
Amfilochía

Préveza
Árta
Refína

Páxoi
Antípaxoi

Lefkáda
Vasilikí
Lixoúri
Argostóli

Kefallinía

Iónioi Nísoi
(Ionian Islands)

Zákynthos
Keri

Lechainá
Gastoúni

Pýrgos
Zacháro

Kyparissía

Pýlos
Messíni

Koróni

Areópoli
Gerolimếnas

Kalamáta
Koróni

Korinthos
Álfíos

Sparti
Geráki

Gýtheio

Peloponnísos

Mirtóo Pelagos

Lakonikós Kólpos

Daimoniá
Neápoli
Karavás

Kýthira
Kýthira

Antikýthira

Potamós

Mirtóo Pelagos

71

N

I o n i a n   S e a

M e d i t e r r a n e a n   S e a

97

ELEVATION

Below sea level										
-2000m	-1000m	-500m	-250m	-100m	0	100m	250m	500m	1000m	2000m	4000m
-6562ft	-3281ft	-1640ft	-820ft	-328ft	-164ft/-50m	0	328ft	820ft	1640ft	3281ft	6562ft	13 124ft

THE BALTIC STATES & BELARUS

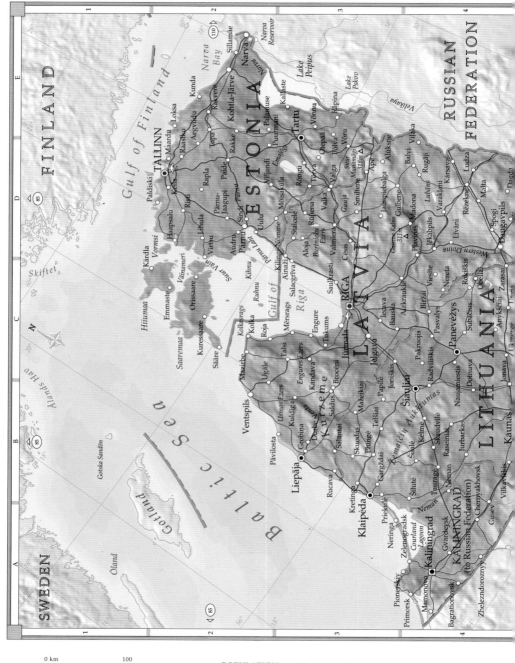

FINLAND

SWEDEN

RUSSIAN FEDERATION

ESTONIA

LATVIA

LITHUANIA

Gulf of Finland

Baltic Sea

Gulf of Riga

Gulf of Finland

Ålands Hav

Gotland

Öland

Skiftet

Gotska Sandön

Lake Peipus

Lake Pskov

Narva Bay

Narva Reservoir

TALLINN

RĪGA

KALININGRAD (to Russian Federation)

Narva
Sillamäe
Narva
Kohtla-Järve
Rakvere
Kunda
Loksa
Aegviidu
Kaasiku
Maardu
Paldiski
Keila
Tapa
Rakke
Paide
Põltsamaa
Puurmani
Paldise
Kallaste
Tartu
Võnnu
Otepää
Põlva
Võru
Tõrva
Valga
Ape
Balvi
Viļaka
Rūjiena
Alūksne
Smiltene
Jaunpiebalga
Gulbene
Munamägi 318m △
Sinti
Rūjiena
Valka
Gauja
Madona
Lubāns
Varakļāni
Rēzekne
Kārsava
Ludza
Malta
Spogi
Daugavpils
Dagda
Zilupe
Velikaya
Līvāni
Jēkabpils
Pļaviņas
Krustpils
Gaiziņa Kalns 311m △
Aknīste
Obeļiai
Rokiškis
Nereta
Viesīte
Neretta
Subačius
Biržai
Pasvalys
Radviliškis
Panevėžys
Anykščiai
Utena
Ukmergė
Jonava
Kaunas
Vilkaviškis
Gusev
Chernyakhovsk
Gvardeysk
Zelenogradsk
Kaliningrad
Mamonovo
Bagrationovsk
Zheleznodorozhny
Pionerskiy
Primorsk
Légoni
Neman
Neman
Šilutė
Kretinga
Priekulė
Neringa
Klaipėda
Gargždai
Plungė
Skuodas
Mažeikiai
Telšiai
Šiauliai
Kelmė
Raseiniai
Jurbarkas
Tauragė
Šilalė
Skaudvilė
Naujamiestis
Papilė
Joniškis
Pakruojis
Žemaičių Aukštumas
Žemaičių Aukštumas
Liepāja
Grobiņa
Pāvilosta
Ventspils
Kuldīga
Saldus
Sahtani
Rucava
Dobele
Broceni
Auce
Jelgava
Bauska
Iecava
Aizkraukle
Tukums
Jūrmala
Saulkrasti
Salacgrīva
Engure
Enguras Ezers
Mērsrags
Talsi
Roja
Kolka
Mazirbe
Ugāle
 Usmas Ezers
Kandava
Ventspils
Kolkasrags
Rēzekne
Aloja
Limbaži
Valmiera
Cēsis
Burtnieku Ezers
Ainaži
Kilingi-Nõmme
Pärnu
Sindi
Audru
Tõstamaa
Lihula
Pärnu Laht
Pärnu
Häädemeeste
Viljandi
Türi
Rapla
Haapsalu
Risti
Virtsu
Lihula
Väinameri
Suur Väin
Kärdla
Hiiumaa
Emmaste
Vormsi
Saaremaa
Kuressaare
Orissaare
Viinameri
Sõre
Kihnu
Ruhnu

0 km   100

0 miles   100

POPULATION   ● National capital

○ Less than 50,000   ○ 50,000 -100,000   ◉ 100,000 - 500,000   ◼ Over 500,000

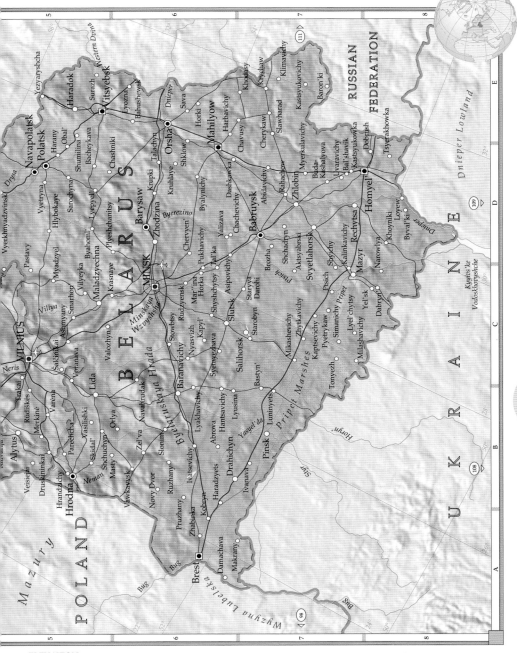

RUSSIAN FEDERATION

Dnieper Lowland

Yezvaryshcha
Haradok
Surazh
Vitsyebsk
Lyozna
Bahushevsk
Navapolatsk
Polatsk
Obal'
Harany
Shumilina
Bachey'kava
Chashniki
Dnieper
Sava
Horki
Klimavichy
Krychaw
Khodasy
Kastsyukovichy
Baron'ki
Shklow
Harbavichy
Cherykaw
Slawharad
Talachyn
Kruhlaye
Chavusy
Myerkulavichy
Mahilyow
Orsha
Krupki
Byalynichy
Dashkawka
Rahachow
Buda-Kashalyova
Uvaravichy
Bal'shavik
Tsyerakhowka
Dobrush
Myadzyel
Byahoml'
Lyepyel
Plyeshchanitsy
Byerezino
Zhodzina
Barysaw
Cheryven'
Pukhavichy
Abidavichy
Zhlobin
Bychykha
Homyel
Loyew
Byval'ki
Vyetryna
Hlybokaye
Vileyka
Krasnaye
Maladzyechna
Smarhon'
Ashmyany
Vilyeyka
Valozhyn
MINSK
Mar"ina Horka
Shyshchytsy
Asipovichy
Brozha
Shchadryn
Aktsyabrski
Rechytsa
Narowlya
Khoyniki
Mazyr
Svyetlahorsk
Ptsich
Kalinkavichy
Dabryn'
Yel'sk
Lyel'chytsy
Dnieper

Takai
Rudiskés
Merkiné
VILNIUS
Šalčininkai
Varéna
Voranava
Lida
Navahrudak
Baranavichy
Slutsk
Salihorsk
Starobyn
Bastyn'
Lyusina
Luninyets
Tonyezh
Simanichy
Pripet
Pyetrykaw
Kaptsevichy
Zhytkavichy
Pripet Marshes
Horyn'
Styr

POLAND
Hrodna
Neman
Masty
Shchuchyn
Skidal'
Pareéchcha
Zel'va
Ruzhany
Ivatsevichy
Zhabinka
Kobryn
Damachava
Makrany
Ivanava
Pinsk
Drahichyn
Yasyel'da
Haradzyets
Bug
Brest

Wyżyna Lubelska

UKRAINE, MOLDOVA & ROMANIA

POPULATION   ● National capital

○ Less than 50,000   ○ 50,000 -100,000   ◉ 100,000 - 500,000   ◼ Over 500,000

ELEVATION

					Below sea level	0	100m	250m	500m	1000m	2000m	4000m
-2000m	-1000m	-500m	-250m	-100m								
-6562ft	-3281ft	-1640ft	-820ft	-328ft	-164ft/-50m	0	328ft	820ft	1640ft	3281ft	6562ft	13 124ft

109

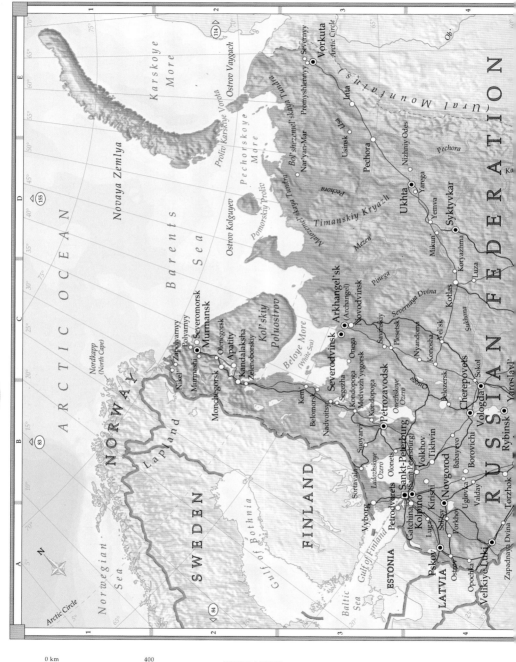

ARCTIC OCEAN

NORWAY

SWEDEN

FINLAND

ESTONIA

LATVIA

RUSSIAN FEDERATION

Barents Sea

Karskoye More

Novaya Zemlya

Kol'skiy Poluostrov

Beloye More
(White Sea)

Ural Mountains

Lapland

Norwegian Sea

Gulf of Bothnia

Baltic Sea

Gulf of Finland

Arctic Circle

Vorkuta
Severnyy
Promyshlennyy
Inta
Usinsk
Naryan-Mar
Pechora
Nizhniy Odes
Ukhta
Yarega
Yemva
Syktyvkar
Mikun'
Koryazhma
Luza
Kotlas
Vel'sk
Nyandoma
Konosha
Arkhangel'sk (Archangel)
Novodvinsk
Plesetsk
Severodvinsk
Onega
Medvezh'yegorsk
Belozersk
Sokol
Cherepovets
Vologda
Rybinsk
Yaroslavl'
Murmansk
Severomorsk
Polyarnyy
Zapolyarnyy
Nikel'
Monchegorsk
Olenegorsk
Apatity
Kandalaksha
Zelenoborskiy
Kem'
Belomorsk
Nadvoitsy
Segezha
Kondopoga
Petrozavodsk
Suoyarvi
Sortavala
Vyborg
Petrodvorets
Sankt-Peterburg (Saint Petersburg)
Gatchina
Kolpino
Volkhov
Tikhvin
Babayevo
Borovichi
Novgorod
Valday
Torzhok
Staraya Russa
Soltsy
Luga
Pskov
Ostrov
Opochka
Velikiye Luki

Timanskiy Kryazh

Severnaya Dvina

Pechora

Mezen'

Pinega

Ob'

Ka

Nordkapp (North Cape)

0 km 400
0 miles 400

POPULATION

● National capital
○ Less than 50,000
○ 50,000 –100,000
◉ 100,000 – 500,000
◼ Over 500,000

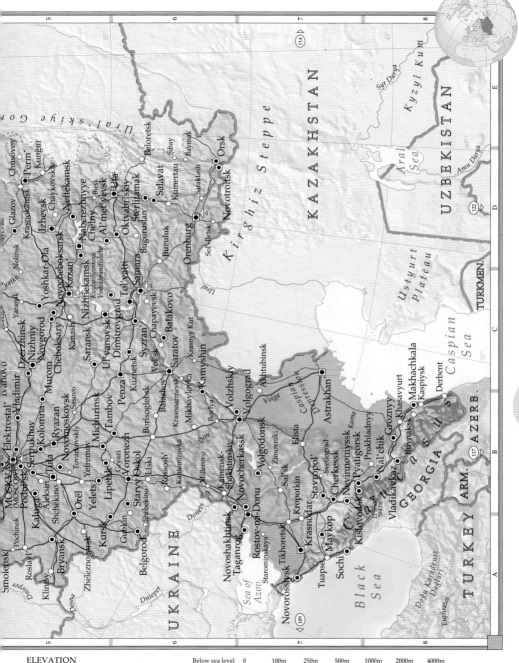

ELEVATION

-2000m	-1000m	-500m	-250m	-100m	Below sea level	0	100m	250m	500m	1000m	2000m	4000m
-6562ft	-3281ft	-1640ft	-820ft	-328ft	-164ft/-50m	0	328ft	820ft	1640ft	3281ft	6562ft	13 124ft

NORTH & WEST ASIA

Franz Josef Land

ARCTIC

Ostrov Komsomolets

Severnaya Zemlya

Ostrov Oktyabr'skoy Revolyutsii
Ostrov Bol'shevik

Novaya Zemlya

Kara Sea

Poluostrov Taymyr

Ozer
Tayn

North Siberia

Khela

Koni

Norwegian
Sea   North Cape

Barents
Sea

Ostrov
Kolguyev

Poluostrov
Yamal

Noril'sk

Central
Siberian
Plateau

Murmansk
Kola
Peninsula

Arctic Circle
81

White Sea

Archangel

R U S S I A N   F E

Kureyka

Lower Tunguska

S i

Gulf of Bothnia

Lake
Onega

Lake Ladoga

Northern
Dvina

Vologda

Perm'

Ural Mountains

Ob'

West Siberian
Plain

Ob'

Stony Tunguska

Angara

Saint Petersburg

Yaroslavl

Nizhniy
Novgorod

Yekaterinburg

Irtysh

Chulym

Tomsk

Krasnoyarsk

Baltic Sea

Kaliningrad

MOSCOW

Volga

Kazan'

Ufa

Chelyabinsk

Omsk

Novosibirsk

Novokuznetsk

KALININGRAD
(to Russ. Fed.)

Central
Russian
Upland

Ul'yanovsk

Samara

Ishim

A

S

Irk

Voronezh

Saratov

Orenburg

Ural'sk

ASTANA

Sayanskiy Khrebet

E U R O P E

Volgograd

Kirghiz
Steppe

Karaganda

Kazakh Uplands

Semipalatinsk

Altai Mountains

Rostov-na-Donu

Don

Ural

KAZAKHSTAN

Ozero
Zaysan

G

Astrakhan'

Aral'sk

Lake
Balkhash

Danube

Stavropol'

El'brus
5642m

Caucasus

Aktau

Ustyurt
Plateau

Aral
Sea

Sur Darya

Kyzyl
Kum

Kyzylorda

Ili

Taraz

Almaty

Black Sea

Istanbul

Küre Dağları

GEORGIA
T'BILISI

ARMENIA

AZERB.

BAKU

Dashkhovuz

UZBEKISTAN

Amu Darya

Kara Kum

TASHKENT

BISHKEK

Tien Shan

KYRGYZSTAN

ANKARA

YEREVAN

TURKMENISTAN

DUSHANBE

Anatolia

TURKEY

Lake
Van

Tabriz

ASHGABAT

TAJIKISTAN

Adana

Gaziantep

Mosul

TEHRAN

Hindu Kush

Kunlun Mountains

Mediterranean Sea

103

Tripoli

SYRIA

IRAQ

Qom

IRAN

KABUL

Jalalabad

Adana

DAMASCUS

BAGHDAD

Isfahan

Iranian
Plateau

Herat

Khyber Pass

BEIRUT

LEBANON

Syrian
Desert

Tigris

Euphrates

AFGHANISTAN

ISRAEL

Basra

Zagros Mountains

JERUSALEM

AMMAN

JORDAN

KUWAIT

KUWAIT

Shiraz

Zahedan

An Nafud

The Gulf

Bandar-e 'Abbas

Thar Desert

Himalayas

Ganges

Tropic of Cancer

MANAMA

BAHRAIN

Dubai

Gulf of Oman

Indus Fan

RIYADH

QATAR

DOHA

U.A.E.

MUSCAT

SAUDI ARABIA

ABU
DHABI

Sur

Murray Ridge

Ganges Fan

Mel

At Ta'if

Arabian
Peninsula

OMAN

Nile

Red Sea

Ar Rub' al Khali

AFRICA

SANA

YEMEN

Arabian
Sea

Bay of
Bengal

Ta'izz

Aden

Socotra
(to Yemen)

Gulf of Aden

69

Summer limit of pack ice

Winter limit of pack ice

East Novaya Zemlya Trench

0 km   800
0 miles   800

POPULATION   ● National capital

○ Less than 50,000   ○ 50,000 -100,000   ◉ 100,000 - 500,000   ◼ Over 500,000

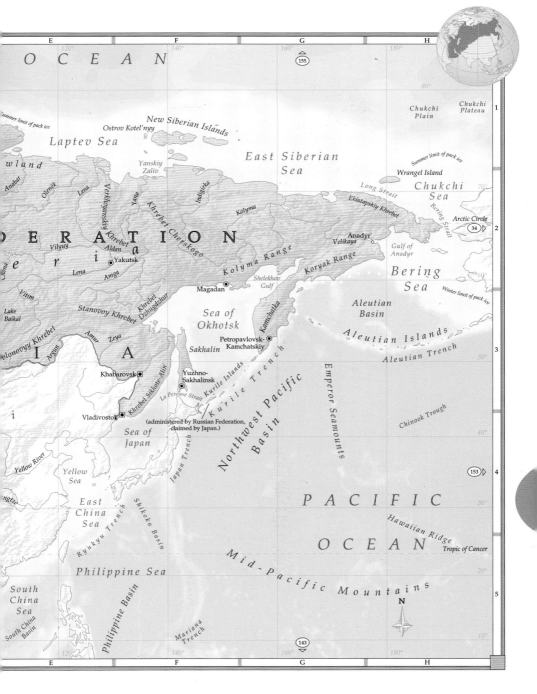

OCEAN

E 120° F 140° G 160° 155 H 180°

80°

1

Chukchi
Plain

Chukchi
Plateau

New Siberian Islands

Ostrov Kotel'nyy

summer limit of pack ice

Laptev Sea

East Siberian
Sea

Summer limit of pack ice

Wrangel Island

wland

Anabar

Yanskiy
Zaliv

Long Strait

70°

Chukchi
Sea

Olenek

Lena

Yana

Indigirka

Kolyma

Ekiatapskiy Khrebet

Bering Strait

Verkhoyanskiy Khrebet

Khrebet Cherskogo

Arctic Circle

34

2

ERATION

eria

Vilyuy

Aldan

a

Yakutsk

Anadyr'
Velikaya

Gulf of
Anadyr

Lena

Amga

Kolyma Range

Koryak Range

60°

onal

Vitim

Amur

Magadan

Shelekhov
Gulf

Bering
Sea

Lake
Baikal

Stanovoy Khrebet

Khrebet Dzhugdzhur

Sea of
Okhotsk

Kamchatka

Aleutian
Basin

Winter limit of pack ice

olonoryy Khrebet

IA

A

Zeya

Petropavlovsk-
Kamchatskiy

Aleutian Islands

50°

3

Khabarovsk

Sakhalin

Yuzhno-
Sakhalinsk

Aleutian Trench

Argun

Khrebet Sikhote-Alin'

Kurile Islands

Kurile Trench

Northwest Pacific

Emperor Seamounts

Chinook Trough

i

Vladivostok

La Perouse Strait

Basin

40°

153

4

(administered by Russian Federation,
claimed by Japan.)

Japan Trench

Sea of
Japan

Yellow River

Yellow
Sea

PACIFIC

30°

ngtze

East
China
Sea

Shikoku Basin

OCEAN

Hawaiian Ridge

Ryukyu Trench

Tropic of Cancer

Philippine Sea

Mid-Pacific Mountains

20°

5

South
China
Sea

Philippine Basin

South China
Basin

N

120°

Mariana
Trench

140°

160°

143

180°

10°

E F G H

RUSSIA & KAZAKHSTAN

POPULATION   ● National capital

0 km   800

0 miles   800

○ Less than 50,000   ○ 50,000 -100,000   ◉ 100,000 - 500,000   ■ Over 500,000

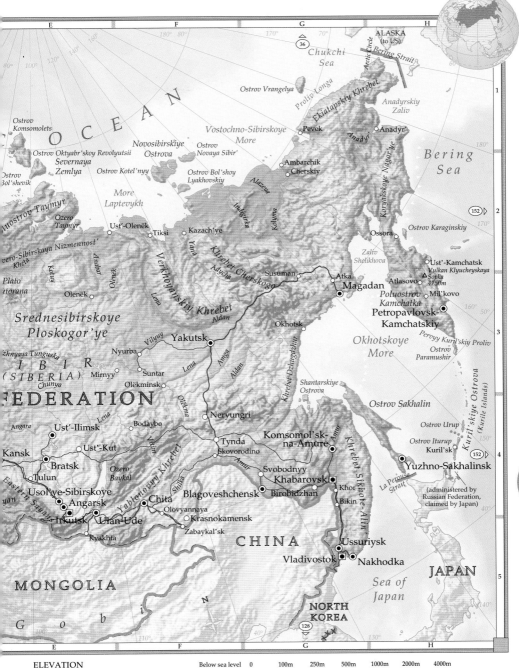

ALASKA
(to US)

Arctic Circle

Bering Strait

Chukchi
Sea

Ostrov Vrangelya

Prolit Longa

Ekiatapskiy Khrebet

Anadyrskiy
Zaliv

Vostochno-Sibirskoye
More

Pevek

Anadyr'

Bering
Sea

O C E A N

Ostrov
Komsomolets

Novosibirskiye
Ostrova

Ostrov
Novaya Sibir'

Ambarchik
Cherskiy

Anadyr'

Koryakskoye Nagor'ye

Ostrov Oktyabr'skoy Revolyutsii
Severnaya
Zemlya

Ostrov Kotel'nyy

Ostrov Bol'shoy
Lyakhovskiy

Ostrov
Bol'shevik

More
Laptevykh

Alazeya

Kolyma

Ossora

Ostrov Karaginskiy

Itostrov Taymyr

Ozero
Taymyr

Ust'-Olenёk

Tiksi

Kazach'ye

Indigirka

Zaliv
Shelikhova

Ust'-Kamchatsk
Vulkan Klyucheyskaya

vero-Sibirskaya Nizmennost'
Kheta

Anabar

Olenёk

Yana

Adycha

Khrebet Cherskogo

Susuman

Atka

Atlasovo

Sopka
2750m

Plato
torana

Kotuy

Olenёk

Lena

Magadan

Poluostrov
Kamchatka

Mil'kovo

Srednesibirskoye
Ploskogor'ye

Verkhoyanskiy Khrebet

Aldan

Okhotsk

Petropavlovsk-
Kamchatskiy

Petropavlovsk-
Kamchatskiy

Okhotskoye
More

Peroyy Kuril'skiy Proliv

zhnyaya Tunguska

Nyurba

Vilyuy

Yakutsk

Lena

Anga

Khrebet Dzhugdzhun

Ostrov
Paramushir

I B I R
(SIBERIA)

Chunya

Mirnyy

Suntar

Lena

Aldan

Shantarskiye
Ostrova

Ostrov Sakhalin

Kuril'skiye Ostrova
(Kurile Islands)

FEDERATION

Olёkminsk

Olёkma

Neryungri

Ostrov Urup

Angara

Ust'-Ilimsk

Bodaybo

Ostrov Iturup

Kuril'sk

Kansk

Ust'-Kut

Tynda
Skovorodino

Komsomol'sk-
na-Amure

Amur

Amur

Bratsk

Ozero
Baykal

Vitim

Yablonovyy Khrebet

Shilka

Svobodnyy

Khabarovsk

Birobidzhan

Khrebet Sikhote-Alin

Yuzhno-Sakhalinsk

Tulun

Usol'ye-Sibirskoye
Angarsk

Chita

Blagoveshchensk

Khor

La Perouse
Strait

Eastern Sayan
Irkutsk

Ulan-Ude

Olovyannaya

Krasnokamensk

Bikin

(administered by
Russian Federation,
claimed by Japan)

Kyakhta

Zabaykal'sk

CHINA

Ussuriysk

MONGOLIA

NORTH
KOREA

Vladivostok

Nakhodka

Sea of
Japan

JAPAN

G o b i

ELEVATION

-4000m -3000m -2000m -1000m -500m   Below sea level 0   100m 250m 500m 1000m 2000m 4000m

-13 124ft -9843ft -6562ft -3281ft -1640ft -820ft/-250m 0   328ft 820ft 1640ft 3281ft 6562ft 13 124ft

TURKEY & THE CAUCASUS

ROMANIA

UKRAINE

Lacul Razim
Lacul Sinoie

Kryms'kyy
Pivostriv

Danube

BULGARIA

Varnenski
Zaliv

B l a c k   S e a

Burgaski
Zaliv

Maritsa

Kırklareli

İnebolu
Sinop
Gerze

Cide

Edirne

Ergene Nehri

Zonguldak

Bartın
Küre Dağları
Kastamonu

Bafra

Çorlu

Karabük

Kargı

Samsun

Tekirdağ

Marmara Denizi
(Sea of Marmara)

İstanbul

Devrek

Çerkeş

Merzifon
Ünye

Ordu

İzmit

Adapazarı

Gerede

Kızıl Irmak

Çorum

Çanakkale

Bandırma

Yalova

İznik Gölü

Bolu

Çankırı

Alaca

Tokat

Za

Bursa

Bilecik

Kalecik

Sorgun

Yıldızeli

Çanakkale
Boğazı
(Dardanelles)

Balıkesir

Bozüyük

Eskişehir

ANKARA

Kırıkkale

Sivas

Edremit
Ayvalık

Kütahya

Polatlı

Hirfanlı
Barajı

Şarkışla
Boğazlıyan

Simav

Simav Çayı

T   U   R   K

Akhisar

Gediz

Kulu

Tuz Gölü

Bünyan

Hekim

Manisa

Uşak

Afyon

Nevşehir

İncesu

Gürün

İzmir

Gediz Nehri

Cihanbeyli

Kayseri

Alaşehir

Akşehir

Aksaray

Göksun

Gü

Ödemiş

Nazilli

Dinar

Beyşehir
Gölü

Niğde

Aydın

Büyükmenderes Nehri

Denizli

Konya

Kahramanmaraş

Söke

Milas

Burdur

Burdur
Gölü

Isparta

Suğla Gölü

Ereğli

Tavas

Karaman

Gaziant

Bodrum

Muğla

Toros Dağları

Ceyhan

Osmaniye

Marmaris

Dalaman

Antalya

Manavgat

Tarsus

Adana

Mersin

Kilis

Fethiye

Alanya

Mut

İskenderun

Kaş

Finike

Antalya
Körfezi

Silifke

Antakya

Kırıkhan

Ródos
(Rhodes)

Anamur

Orantes

GREECE

Lésvos

Chíos

Menemen

Sámos

Dodekánisos
(Dodecánese)

Kárpathos

M e d i t e r r a n e a n
S e a

CYPRUS

TURKISH REPUBLIC OF
NORTHERN CYPRUS
(recognised only by Turkey)

LEBANON

0 km		200
0 miles		200

POPULATION   ● National capital

○ Less than 50,000   ○ 50,000 -100,000   ◉ 100,000 - 500,000   ◼ Over 500,000

RUSSIAN

FEDERATION

Caspian

Sea

Caucasus

Gagra
Gudaut'a
Sokhumi
Och'amch'ire

Abkhazia

Enguri
Mestia

Kazbek
5047m

Greater Caucasus

Xaçmaz

Kut'aisi
Samtredia
P'ot'i
K'obulet'i
Bat'umi
Hopa
Ajaria

Gori
Tsalka

South
Ossetia

GEORGIA

T'BILISI
Rust'avi

Zaqatala

Quba

Siyäzän

122

Akhalts'ikhe

Lesser Caucasus

Şäki

Sumqayıt

BAKI
(BAKU)

Trabzon
Rize
Of
Pazar
Giresun
Gümüşhane

Dağ Karadeniz Dağları

Artvin

Gyumri

Kura

Vanadzor

Gäncä

Mingäçevir

Yevlax

Şamaxı

Kars
Artvin
Sarıkamış
İspir

ARMENIA

YEREVAN

Sevan
Sevana Lich

AZERBAIJAN

Nagornyy
Karabakh

İmişli

Qäzimämmäd
Äli-Bayramı
Kura

İahiye
Erzincan
Tercan
Kemah
Bingöl

Aşkale
Pasinler
Erzurum

Horasan
Ağrı
Doğubayazıt
Patnos

Büyükağrı Dağı
(Mount Ararat)
5137m

Artashat

Goris

Xankändi

Biläsuvar

Aras

Länkäran

Euphrates
(Fırat Nehri)

E
Y

Toroslar

Ergiş
Muradiye

Naxçıvan

AZERBAIJAN

Kemah
Malatya
Kebanı
Barajı
Bingöl
Elâzığ

Muş
Tatvan
Bitliş
Silvan

Van
Gölü

Van
Gevaş

*Daryācheh-ye
Orūmīyeh*

IRAN

Diyarbakır
Silverek
Atatürk
Barajı
Viranşehir
Şanlıurfa
Ceylanpınar
Adıyaman

Batman
Mardin
Şırnak
Nusaybin

Siirt

Kurdistan

Tigris

*Reshteh-ye Kühhä-ye Alborz
(Elburz Mountains)*

120

Al Jazīrah

Euphrates

IRAQ

Buhayrat
ath
Tharthār

*Kühhä-ye Zägros
(Zägros Mountains)*

Buhayrat
al Asad

Jabal Bishrī

RIA

120

THE NEAR EAST

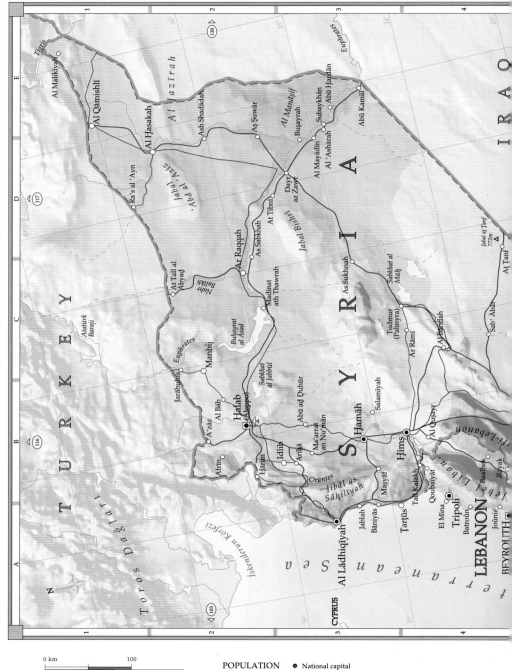

POPULATION ● National capital

○ Less than 50,000 ○ 50,000 -100,000 ◉ 100,000 - 500,000 ◼ Over 500,000

0 km 100

0 miles 100

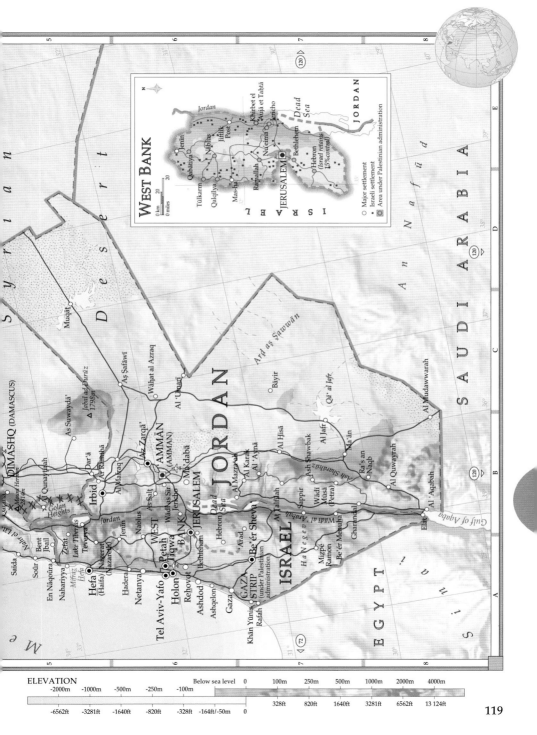

THE MIDDLE EAST

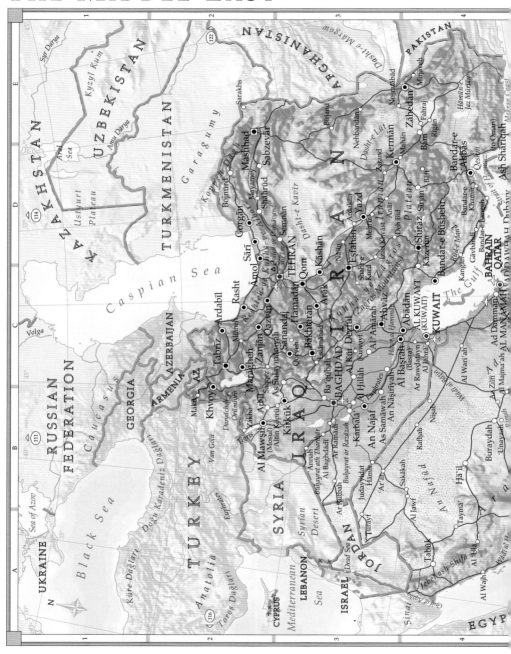

UKRAINE

RUSSIAN FEDERATION

KAZAKHSTAN

UZBEKISTAN

TURKMENISTAN

GEORGIA

AZERBAIJAN

ARMENIA

AZ

TURKEY

SYRIA

IRAQ

IRAN

AFGHANISTAN

PAKISTAN

JORDAN

ISRAEL

LEBANON

CYPRUS

EGYPT

BAHRAIN

QATAR

KUWAIT

AL KUWAYT
(KUWAIT)

Caspian Sea

Black Sea

Sea of Azov

Aral Sea

Mediterranean Sea

The Gulf

Dead Sea

Gulf of Aqaba

Syr Darya

Amu Darya

Volga

Kyzyl Kum

Ustyurt Plateau

Garagumy

Dasht-e Margow

Kara Karadeniz Dağları

Küre Dağları

Toros Dağları

Anatolia

Caucasus

Van Gölü

Euphrates

Tigris

Syrian Desert

An Nafūd

Jebel esh Shifa

Wādī al Bāţin

Koppeh Dāgh

Dasht-e Kavir

Dasht-e Lūt

Zagros Mountains (Kuhhā-ye Zāgros)

Kavīr-e Namak

Central Makran Range

Strait of Hormuz

Gulf of Oman

Hāmūn-e Jaz Mūriān

Kuhhā-ye Kūhī-ye Alborz

Mashhad

Sabzevār

Shāhrūd

Semnān

TEHRĀN

Qom

Kāshān

Eşfahān

Yazd

Kermān

Zābedān

Zāhedān

Mīrjāveh

Fahraj

Rīgān

Bam

Bāft

Sīrjān

Shīrāz

Kāzerūn

Bandar-e Bushehr

Bandar-e Abbās

Qeshm

Ardabīl

Tabrīz

Khvoy

Maku

Maragheh

Zanjān

Qazvīn

Rasht

Āmol

Sārī

Gorgān

Bojnūrd

Hamadān

Arāk

Sanandaj

Bākhtarān

Al Kūt

Dezfūl

Ahvāz

Ābādān

Al Başrah (Basra)

An Nāşirīyah

As Samāwah

An Najaf

Karbalā

Al Hillah

BAGHDĀD

Ba qūbah

Kirkūk

Arbīl

Al Mawşil (Mosul)

Zākho

Dahūk

As Sulaymānīyah

Al Başrah

Ad Dammām

Al Jubayl

AL MANĀMAH

AD DAWHAH

Buraydah

Hā'il

'Unayzah

Sakākah

Al Jawf

Tabūk

Taymā'

Rafhah

Nisāb

Al Ḥufūf

Riyadh

0 km 400

0 miles 400

POPULATION

- National capital

○ Less than 50,000

○ 50,000 -100,000

◉ 100,000 - 500,000

◼ Over 500,000

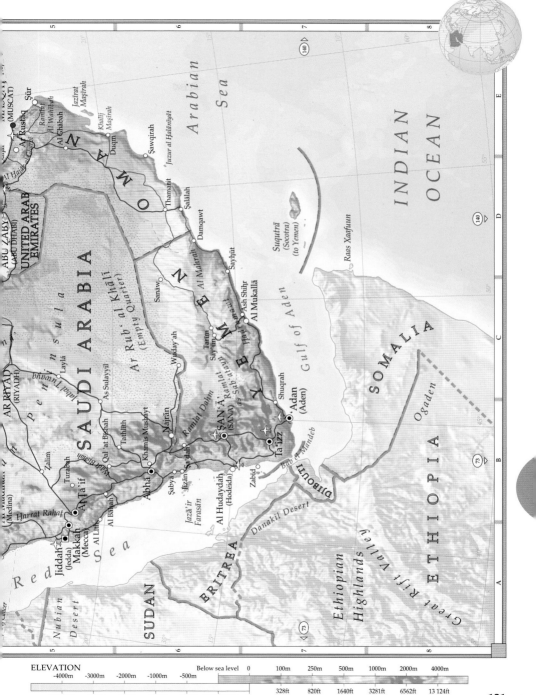

MUSCAT
Sūr
Al Rustāq
Jazīrat Maşīrah
Rāmiş
Al Wahībah
Al Ghābah
Khalūf
Maşīrah
Duqm

O M A N

Şawqirah

UNITED ARAB EMIRATES
ABU ZABY (ABU DHABI)
Al Hajar al Gharbi

Thamarīt
Şalālah
Damqawt

S A U D I   A R A B I A

Ar Rub' al Khālī
(Empty Quarter)

Sanaw
Al Mahrah
Sayḩūt

Ramlat Dahm

Wadī'ah

Ash Shiḩr
Al Mukallā
Haḑramawt

Layla
As Sulayyil

Najrān
Khamis Mushayt
Saḑah
Tathlīth
Qal'at Bishah

Ramlat Dahm

Tarīm
Sayūn

AR RIYAD (RIYADH)
Wadi al Dawasir
bnoan L

Peninsula

Arabian Sea

Jazīrat Maşīrah

Juzur al Ḩalānīyāt

Suquţrā (Socotra) (to Yemen)

Raas Xaafuun

INDIAN OCEAN

Gulf of Aden

SAN'Ā (SANA)
Ramlat as Sab'atayn
Y E M E N

Shuqrah
Adan (Aden)
Ta'izz

Turabah
Zalim
Aţ Ţā'if
Al Bāhah
Şabyā
Jīzān
Jazā'ir Farasān
Abhā

Al Hudaydah (Hodeida)
Zabīd

Bāb el Mandeb

SOMALIA

Ogaden

(Al Madīnah) (Medina)
Harrat Rahat
Jiddah (Jedda)
Makkah (Mecca)
Aş Şa'īd
Al Līth

Red Sea

SUDAN

Nubian Desert

ERITREA

DJIBOUTI

Danakil Desert

Ethiopian Highlands

Great Rift Valley

E T H I O P I A

ELEVATION

					Below sea level	0	100m	250m	500m	1000m	2000m	4000m
-4000m	-3000m	-2000m	-1000m	-500m									
-13 124ft	-9843ft	-6562ft	-3281ft	-1640ft	-820ft/-250m	0		328ft	820ft	1640ft	3281ft	6562ft	13 124ft

121

CENTRAL ASIA

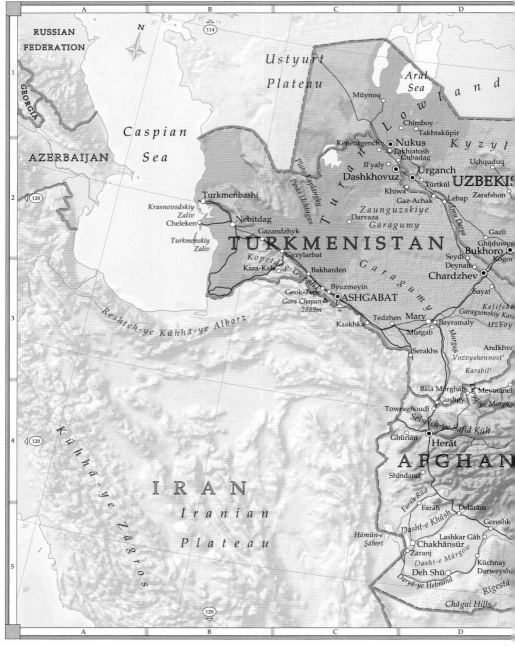

RUSSIAN
FEDERATION

GEORGIA

AZERBAIJAN

Caspian

Sea

Ustyurt

Plateau

Aral
Sea

Mŭynoq

Chimboy

Takhtakŭpir

Keneutgench
Takhiatosh
Il'yaly
Dashkhovuz
Nukus
Gubadag
Urganch
Türtkŭl
Khiwa

K y z y l

Uchquduq

UZBEKIS

Gaz-Achak
Lebap
Zarafshon

Plato Kaplangqy

Peski Uchtagan

Krasnovodskiy
Zaliv
Cheleken

Turkmenbashi

Nebitdag

Gazandzhyk

Zaunguzskiye
Darvaza
Garagumy

Gazli
Ghijduwo

Bukhoro
Kogon

Amu Darya

Turkmenskiy
Zaliv

Kopet
Gyzylarbat
Kara-Kala
Bakharden

Seydi
Deynau

Chardzhev

Geok-Tepe
Gora Chapan
2889m

Byuzmeyin
ASHGABAT

Garagumy

Sayat

Kelifs

Garagumskiy Kan

Kaakhka

Tedzhen
Murgab

Mary
Bayramaly

Uzboy

Serakhs

Murgab

Andkhv
Vozvyshennost'

Karabil'

Bālā Morghāb
Gushgy

Meymanel
-ye Morgha

Towraghoudī

Reshteh-ye Kūhhā-ye Alborz

Selseleh-ye Safid Kūh

TURKMENISTAN

Ghūrīān

Herāt

K ū h h ā - y e   Z ā g r o s

Shīndand

AFGHAN

IRAN

I r a n i a n

P l a t e a u

Farāh Rūd

Farāh
Delārām

Gereshk

Dasht-e Khāsh

Hāmūn-e
Şāberī

Lashkar Gāh
Chakhānsūr
Zaranj

Küchnay
Darweysha

Dasht-e Mārgow

Deh Shū

Darya-ye Helmand

Rīgestā

Chāgai Hills

0 km   200

0 miles   200

POPULATION   ● National capital

○ Less than 50,000   ○ 50,000 -100,000   ◉ 100,000 - 500,000   ◼ Over 500,000

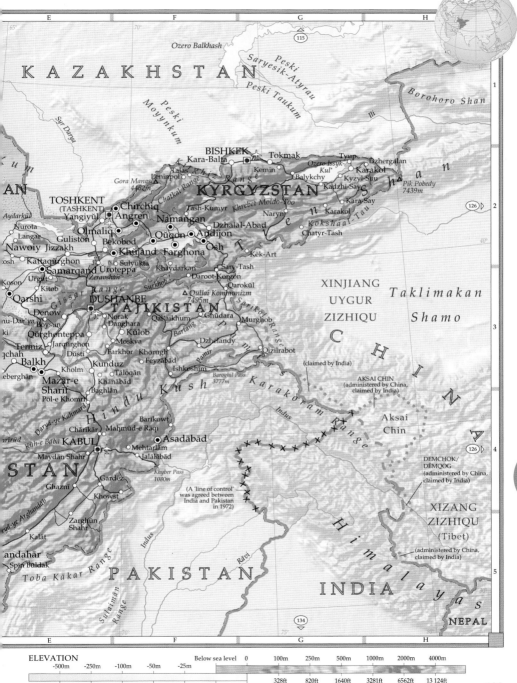

Ozero Balkhash

K A Z A K H S T A N

Peski Saryesik-Atyrau

Peski Taukum

Peski Moyynkum

Peski

Borohoro Shan

Ili

Syr Darya

BISHKEK
Kara-Balta
Tokmak
Tyup
Dzhergalan

AN
Kara
Lalas
Kemin
Ozero Issyk-Kul'
Karakol

Gora Manas
4482m
Keminpol
Balykchy
Kyzyl-Suu

TOSHKENT
(TASHKENT)
Chirchiq
KYRGYZSTAN
Kadzhi-Say
Pik Pobedy
7439m

Yangiyŭl
Angren
Tash-Kumyr
Khrebet Moldo-Too
Kara-Say

Nurota
Olmaliq
Namangan
Naryn
Karakol

Langar
Bekobod
Dzhalal-Abad
Kokshaal-Tau

Nawoiy
Jizzakh
Qŭqon
Andijon
Chatyr-Tash

osh
Kattaqŭrghon
Uroteppa
Khŭjand
Farghona
Osh
Kēk-Art

Koson
Samarqand
Sulyukta
Khaydarkan
Sary-Tash

Urgut
Kitob
Zeravshan
Daroot-Korgon

Qarshi
Range
Surkhob
Qarokŭl

Denow
DUSHANBE
Qullai Kommunizm
7495m

nu-Dar'ya
Boysun
TAJIKISTAN
Norak
Qalaikhum
Ghŭdara
Murghob

ki
Qŭrghonteppa
Danghara
Bartang
XINJIANG

Termiz
Jarqŭrghon
Kŭlob
Moskva
Dzhelandy
UYGUR

Dŭsti
Farkhor
Khorugh
Qizilrabot
ZIZHIQU

Balkh
Kunduz
Feyzābād
Ishkoshim
C

eberghān
Kholm
Tāloqān
Baroghil Pass
3777m
(claimed by India)

Mazār-e
Sharif
Khānābād
Karakoram
Range
Indus
AKSAI CHIN
(administered by China,
claimed by India)

Pol-e Khomri
Baghlān
Hindu
Kush
Aksai
Chin

Barīkowt
H

Chārīkār
Mahmūd-e Rāqi
Asadābād
DEMCHOK/
DÊMQOG
(administered by China,
claimed by India)

KĀBUL
Mehtarlām

Maydān Shahr
Jalālābād
XIZANG
ZIZHIQU

STAN
Khyber Pass
1080m
(Tibet)

Ghaznī
Gardēz
(A 'line of control'
was agreed between
India and Pakistan
in 1972)
(administered by China,
claimed by India)

Zarghūn
Shahr
Khowst

Kalāt
Indus

andahār
Spin Būldak
PAKISTAN
INDIA

Toba Kākar Range

Sulaimān Range

Ravi

NEPAL

Taklimakan

Shamo

CHINA

Himalayas

ELEVATION

					Below sea level	0	100m	250m	500m	1000m	2000m	4000m
-500m	-250m	-100m	-50m	-25m								
-1640ft	-820ft	-328ft	-164ft	-82ft	33ft/-10m	0	328ft	820ft	1640ft	3281ft	6562ft	13 124ft

123

SOUTH & EAST ASIA

Black Sea

40°

112

Irtysh

Yenisey

Lake Baikal

Aral Sea

Syr Darya

Lake Balkhash

Altai Mountains

Uvs Nuur

Hovsgol Nuur

Erdenet

Choybalsan

ULAN BATOR

Kerulen

MONGOLIA

Plateau of Mongolia

Caspian Sea

A S I A

Tien Shan

Tarim He

Tarim Basin

Urumqi

G o b i

Baotou

Daton

Ordos Desert

Taiyuar

Yellow River

Iranian Plateau

112

Hindu Kush

K2
8611m

Takla Makan Desert

Kunlun Mountains

Altun Shan

Qilian Shan

Qaidam Pendi

Xiqing Shan

Lanzhou

Xi'an

Peshawar

Indus

~ Aksai Chin
(administered by China,
claimed by India)

~ Demchok/Demqog
(administered by China,
claimed by India)

Plateau of Tibet

C H I N A

Sichuan Pendi

Yangtze

ISLAMABAD
Gujranwala
Lahore
Faisalabad
Multan

Jammu and Kashmir

Chengdu

Chongqing

Dong

Quetta

Sutlej

Ludhiana

Himalayas

Brahmaputra

Mekong

Salween

Guiyang

PAKISTAN

Delhi

NEW DELHI

Jaipur

Jumna

Ganges

NEPAL

KATHMANDU

Mount Everest 8848m

THIMPHU

BHUTAN

Guwahati

Imphal

Kunming

Xi Jia

The Gulf

Gulf of Oman

Hyderabad
Karachi

Thar Desert

Mouths of the Indus

Rann of Kachchh

Kanpur

Patna

Ganges

BANGLADESH

DHAKA

Chittagong

Nanning

Red River

Mandalay

VIETNAM

HANOI

Hai Phong

Arabian Peninsula

Arabian Sea

Ahmadabad

Vindhya Range

Indore

Narmada

Nagpur

Satpura Range

Khulna

Calcutta

Mouths of the Ganges

**MYANMAR
(BURMA)**

Chindwin

Irrawaddy

LAOS

Gulf of Tongking

Haine

Arabian Basin

Mumbai
(Bombay)

Pune

Solapur

Hyderabad

Deccan

Godavari

Eastern Ghats

Western Ghats

Vijayawada

Salween

Mekong

Louangphabang

Chiang Mai

Pegu

Vinh

VIENTIANE

Da Na

Owen Fracture Zone

*Laccadive Islands
(to India)*

Hubli

Bangalore

Mysore

Chennai
(Madras)

Bay of Bengal

Mouths of the Irrawaddy

RANGOON
Bassein

THAILAND

Pakxe

Carlsberg Ridge

Mid-Indian Ridge

Jaffna

SRI LANKA

COLOMBO

Gulf of Mannar

*Andaman Islands
(to India)*

Andaman Sea

BANGKOK

Tônlé Sap

CAMBODIA

PHNOM PENH

Hô Chi Mi

Equator

N

MALDIVES

MALE

Chagos-Laccadive Plateau

Ceylon Plain

INDIA

69

Nicobar Islands
(to India)

Gulf of Thailand

Mouths of the Mekong

Kota Bharu

Natuna Islands

Malay Peninsula

Medan

Danau Toba

M A L A

KUALA LUMPUR

**BRITISH INDIAN
OCEAN TERRITORY**
(to UK)

INDIAN OCEAN

Mid-Indian Basin

141

Ninetyeast Ridge

Cocos Basin

Strait of Malacca

Sumatra

Padang

Pekanbaru

SINGAPORE

G r e a t e

Pontianak

Palembang

Bangka

Mascarene Plateau

Java Trenc

JAKART
Semara

Bandung

Jav

0 km   1000

0 miles   1000

POPULATION   ● National capital

○ Less than 50,000   ○ 50,000 -100,000   ◉ 100,000 - 500,000   ■ Over 500,000

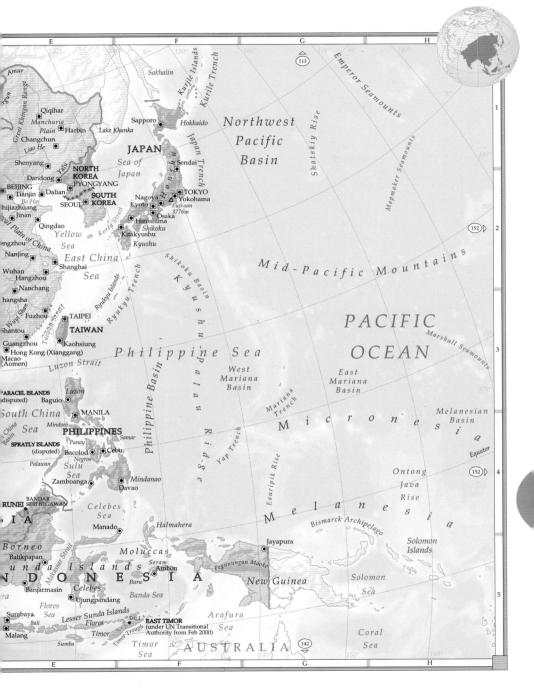

Amur
Qiqihar
Manchuria
Plain
Harbin
Lake Khanka
Changchun
Liao He
Great Khingan Range
Sakhalin
Kurile Islands
Kurile Trench
Emperor Seamounts
113
Sapporo
Hokkaido
Japan Trench
Northwest
Pacific
Basin
Shatskiy Rise
Shenyang
NORTH
KOREA
PYONGYANG
JAPAN
Sea of
Japan
Sendai
Manmaker Seamounts
BEIJING
Dandong
Tianjin
Dalian
SOUTH
KOREA
SEOUL
Nagoya
Honshu
TOKYO
Yokohama
hijiazhuang
Bo Hai
Jinan
Kyoto
Osaka
Fuji-san
3776m
152
ngzhou of China
Qingdao
Yellow
Sea
Korea Strait
Hiroshima
Shikoku
Kitakyushu
Kyushu
Nanjing
East China
Shanghai
Shikoku Basin
Mid-Pacific Mountains
Wuhan
Hangzhou
Sea
Ryukyu Islands
Ryukyu Trench
Kyushu
hangsha
Wugyi Shan
Fuzhou
TAIPEI
Taiwan Strait
PACIFIC
OCEAN
Marshall Seamounts
hantou
TAIWAN
Palau Ridge
Guangzhou
Kaohsiung
Hong Kong (Xianggang)
Macao
(Aomen)
Luzon Strait
Philippine Sea
West
Mariana
Basin
East
Mariana
Basin
ARACEL ISLANDS
(disputed)
Luzon
Baguio
Philippine Basin
Mariana Trench
Micronesia
Melanesian
Basin
South China
China
Sea
Basin
Mindoro
PHILIPPINES
SPRATLY ISLANDS
(disputed)
Panay
Samar
Bacolod
Cebu
Yap Trench
Eauripik Rise
Equator
152
Palawan
Negros
Sulu
Sea
Zamboanga
Mindanao
Davao
Ontong
Java
Rise
RUNEI
BANDAR
SERI BEGAWAN
Celebes
Sea
Melanesia
IA
Manado
Halmahera
Bismarck Archipelago
Solomon
Islands
Borneo
Balikpapan
Moluccas
Jayapura
Sunda Islands
Makassar Strait
Seram
Ambon
Pegunungan Maoke
Solomon
Sea
NDONESIA
Banjarmasin
Celebes
Buru
Banda Sea
New Guinea
Surabaya
Flores
Ujungpandang
Bali
Lesser Sunda Islands
Flores
Arafura
Sea
Coral
Sea
Malang
Sumba
Timor
DILI
Timor Trough
EAST TIMOR
(under UN Transitional
Authority from Feb 2000)
Timor
Sea
AUSTRALIA
142

WESTERN CHINA & MONGOLIA

RUSSIAN FED

KAZAKHSTAN

Kazakhskiy

Melkosopochnik

Kulunda Steppe

Ozero Balkhash

Ozero Zaysan

Hövsgöl Nuur

Uvs Nuur

Ulaangom

Olgiy

Moron

Altay

Chang Nuur

Hyargas Nuur

Hovd

Har Nuur

Tsetserleg

Karamay

Gurbantünggüt Shamo

Altay

Bayanhongor

M O N G O

Ulungur Hu

Ozero Issyk-Kul'

KYRGYZSTAN

Yining

Boro Shan

Kuytun

Shihezi

Fukang

Jimsar

Qitai

Aj Bogd Uul 3802m

Tien Shan

Ürümqi

Turpan

Hami

G

Pik Pobedy 7439m

Korla

Bosten Hu

Turpan Pendi

Atas Bogd 2702m

Go

TAJIKISTAN

Kashi

Yengisar

Shache

Tarim He

Tarim Basin

Kuruktag

Lop Nur

Xingxingxia

Ejin Qi

Q

AFGH.

XINJIANG UYGUR

ZIZHIQU

GANSU

Qilian Shan

Altun Shan

Danghe Nanshan

Yecheng (claimed by India)

Pishan

Moyu

Ruoqiang

Taklimakan Shamo

Hotan

Qira

Kunlun Shan

Qaidam Pendi

Golmud

Burhan Budai Shan

Dulan

Qinghai Hu

Anyêmaqên Sha

PAKISTAN

Karakoram Range

K2 8611m

AKSAI CHIN

AKSAI CHIN (administered by China, claimed by India)

Indus

Rutog

Qingzang Gaoyuan (Plateau of Tibet)

Tongtian He

C H I

QINGHAI

Bayan Har Shan

Yushu

Mekong

JAMMU AND KASHMIR

DEMCHOK/DÊMQOG (administered by China, claimed by India)

K a s h m i r

Yamuna

Gar

Zanda

X I Z A N G

ZIZHIQU (Tibet)

Nyima

Siling Co

Tanggula Shan

Amdo

Qamdo

Tangra Yumco

Ngangzê Co

Gyaring Co

Nam Co

Nagqu

Damxung

Salween

Nyainqêntanglha Shan

ARUNACHAL PRADESH (claimed by China)

Jinsha Jiang

Brahmaputra

Ganges

H i m a l a y a s

NEPAL

Lhazê

Xigazê

Maizhokunggar

Lhasa

Gonggar

Mount Everest 8848m

Gyangzê

INDIA

BHUTAN

INDIA

MYANMAR (BURMA)

0 km   400

0 miles   400

POPULATION   ● National capital   ◉ Internal administrative capital

○ Less than 50,000   ○ 50,000 -100,000   ◉ 100,000 - 500,000   ◼ Over 500,000

RUSS. FED.

Ozero Baykal

ERATION

Shilka

Ergun (Ergun He)

Amur (Heilong Jiang)

Ergun
Zuoqi
Jagdaqi

HEILONGJIANG

Selenga

Onon

Hailar

Manzhouli

Sühbaatar

Lake
Khanka

Darhan

Onon Gol

Choybalsan

Hulun
Nur

Da Hinggan Ling

ilgan

Erdenet

ULAANBAATAR
(ULAN BATOR)

Kerulen

Öndörhaan

Menengiyn
Tal

Hulingol

JILIN

Dzuunmod

Baruun-Urt

Tongliao

OLIA

Saynshand

Xilinhot

Chifeng

LIAONING

NORTH
KOREA

Sea
of
Japan

Dalandzadgad

Erenhot

Inner Mongolia

Liao He

128

aytn Nuruu

NEI MONGOL ZIZHIQU

Jining

BEIJING

Liaodong Wan

Korea
Bay

SOUTH
KOREA

b

Lang Shan

Hohhot

Baotou

TIANJIN

Bo Hai

ibrat Shan

Huang He

Wuhai

Mu Us
Shamo

Great Wall of China

HEBEI

JAPAN

Tengger
Shamo

SHANXI

SHANDONG

Yellow
Sea

NINGXIA
HUIZU
ZIZHIQU

iŋing

Huang He (Yellow River)

JIANGSU

N

GANSU

A

SHAANXI

HENAN

Han Shui

ANHUI

SHANGHAI

East
China
Sea

129

Chang Jiang (Yangtze)

HUBEI

ZHEJIANG

SICHUAN

CHONGQING

Nansei-shotō (to Japan)

JIANGXI

HUNAN

FUJIAN

YUNNAN

GUIZHOU

Tropic of Cancer

TAIWAN

129

ELEVATION

| -2000m | -1000m | -500m | -250m | -100m | Below sea level | 0 | 100m | 250m | 500m | 1000m | 2000m | 4000m |

| -6562ft | -3281ft | -1640ft | -820ft | -328ft | -164ft/-50m | 0 | 328ft | 820ft | 1640ft | 3281ft | 6562ft | 13 124ft |

EASTERN CHINA & KOREA

POPULATION   ● National capital   ◉ Internal administrative capital

○ Less than 50,000   ○ 50,000 -100,000   ◉ 100,000 - 500,000   ■ Over 500,000

JAPAN

East China Sea

Okinawa

Nansei-shotō
(Ryukyu Islands-Japan)

Tropic of Cancer

PACIFIC

OCEAN

PHILIPPINES

Chilung
TAIPEI
Taichung
T'aichung
Chiai
TAIWAN
T'ainan
Kaohsiung

Luzon Strait

Taiwan Strait

(China and Taiwan claim
all of each other's territory)

Yangzhou
Shanghai
Suzhou
Ningbo
Jiaxing
Wuxi
Wuhu
Hangzhou
Jinhua
Wenzhou
Nanjing
ZHEJIANG
Hefei
Anqing
Shangrao
Wuhu
ANHUI
Huangshi
Jingdezhen
Nanping
Fuzhou
Xinyang
HUBEI
Yichang
Jiujiang
Nanchang
Linchuan
FUJIAN
Yong'an
Quanzhou
JIANGXI
Xiangtan
Yueyang
Changsha
Hengyang
Xiamen
Nanyang
Wanxian
Lichuan
Dongting Hu
Loudi
HUNAN
Chenzhou
Longyan
Zhangzhou
Shantou
Shaoguan
Shaguan
Chongqing
Zunyi
Huaihua
Lengshuitan
Quanzhou
Gulin
Dongguan
Hong Kong
(Xianggang)
CHONGQING
GUIZHOU
Guiyang
Liuzhou
GUANGDONG
Guangzhou
Macao
(Aomen)
Jiangmen
Maoming
Anshun
Nanning
Yulin
GUANGXI
ZHUANGZU
Zhaoqing
Neijiang
Zigong
Gejiu
Qinzhou
Zhanjiang
Haikou
YUNNAN
Kunming
Beihai
Suxi
Xuwen
Dongfang
Danxian
HAINAN
Hainan Dao
Dali
Baoshan
Wuliang Shan
Mekong
Jinghong

South China Sea

PARACEL
ISLANDS
(disputed by China,
Taiwan and Vietnam)

Amphitrite Group
Crescent Group
Triton Island

Gulf of Tongking

SPRATLY ISLANDS
(disputed by China,
Malaysia, Philippines,
Taiwan and Vietnam)

Flat Island
Nanshan Island
Thitu Island
Loaita Island
Len Dao
Namyit Island
Spratly Island

VIETNAM

LAOS

THAILAND

CAMBODIA

Gulf of Thailand

MYANMAR
(BURMA)

INDIA

Tropic of Cancer

XIZANG
ZIZHIQU
(Tibet)

SICHUAN
Mianyang
Chengdu
Leshan
Xichang
Ya'an
Sichuan
Pendi
Hengduan Shan
Salween
Yalong Jiang
Jinsha Jiang
Min Jiang
Red River
Mekong

SHAANXI
Hanzhong
Guangyuan

Yangzhou

| | | |

ELEVATION

-2000m	-1000m	-500m	-250m	-100m	Below sea level	0	100m	250m	500m	1000m	2000m	4000m
-6562ft	-3281ft	-1640ft	-820ft	-328ft	-164ft/-50m	0	328ft	820ft	1640ft	3281ft	6562ft	13 124ft

JAPAN

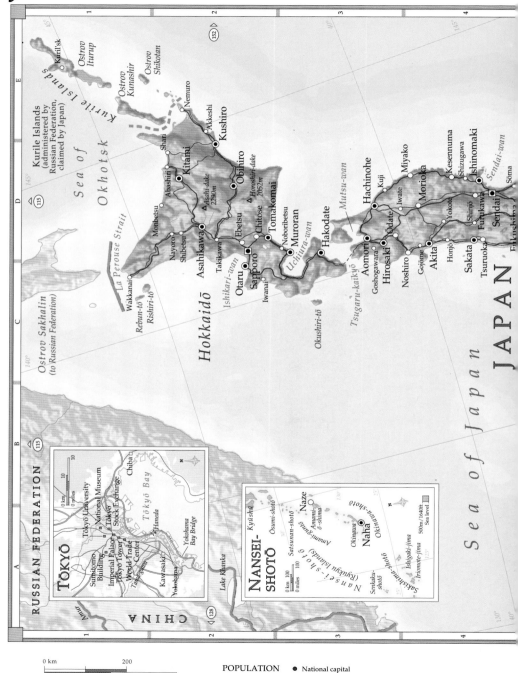

E

D

C

B

A

1

2

3

4

Kuril'sk
Ostrov Iturup
Ostrov Kunashir
Ostrov Shikotan
Kurile Islands
(administered by Russian Federation, claimed by Japan)

s p u r e l s l I   e l i r u K

Sea of Okhotsk

Nemuro
Akkeshi
Kushiro
Shari
Kitami
Abashiri
Obihiro
Asahi-dake 2290m
Hiroshiri-dake 2052m
Monbetsu
Nayoro
Shibetsu
Ebetsu
Chitose
Tomakomai
Noboribetsu
Muroran
Uchiura-wan
Hakodate
Takikawa
Asahikawa
Otaru
Sapporo
Iwanai
Hokkaidō
Ishikari-wan
Rebun-tō
Rishiri-tō
Wakkanai
Takikawa

La Perouse Strait

Ostrov Sakhalin
(to Russian Federation)

Okushiri-tō

Tsugaru-kaikyō

Mutsu-wan
Hachinohe
Kuji
Iwate
Miyako
Morioka
Yokote
Shinjo
Kesennuma
Shizugawa
Ishinomaki
Sendai-wan
Sōma
Aomori
Odate
Goshogawara
Hirosaki
Noshiro
Gojome
Akita
Honjo
Sakata
Tsuruoka
Sendai
Funikawa
Fukushima

Sea of Japan

J A P A N

115

115

128

CHINA

Amur

Lake Kunka

TŌKYŌ

0 km 10
0 miles 10

Chiba
Tōkyō University
National Museum
Tōkyō Stock Exchange
Sumitomo Building
Imperial Palace
Tōkyō Tower
World Trade Center
Tiananmen
Haneda
Kawasaki
Yokohama
Tōkyō Bay
Yokohama Bay Bridge

N

NANSEI-SHOTŌ

0 km 100
0 miles 100

Kyūshū
Ōsumi-shotō
Satsunan-shotō
Amami-guntō
Amami-ō-shima
Naze
Nansei-shotō
Okinawa
Naha
(Ryūkyū Islands)
Tokara-shotō
Sakishima-shotō
Ishigaki-jima
Iriomote-jima
Senkaku-shotō

N

145°

145°

140°

135°

130°

125°

45°

40°

40°

35°

30°

Sea level
500m/1640ft

N

0 km   200
0 miles   200

POPULATION   ● National capital

○ Less than 50,000   ○ 50,000 -100,000   ◉ 100,000 - 500,000   ■ Over 500,000

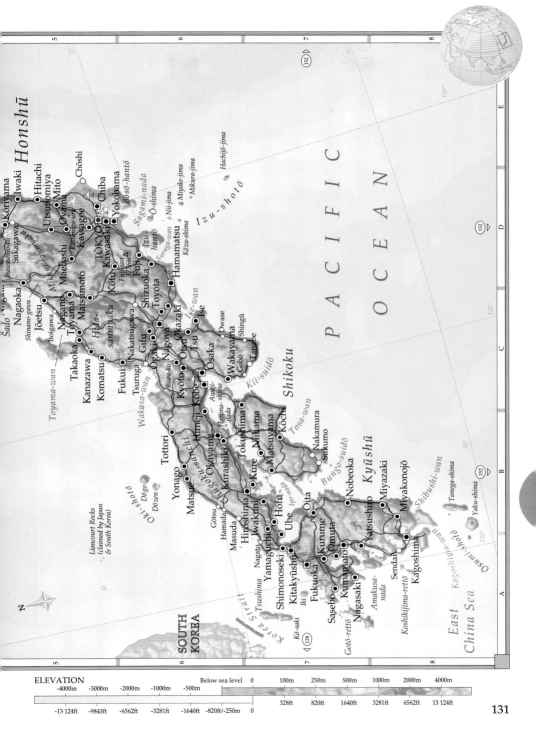

Honshū

Kōriyama
Iwaki
Hitachi
Utsunomiya
Mito
Oyama
Chōshi
Chiba
Kashima-ura
Yokohama
Bōsō-hantō
Sagami-nada
Sukagawa
Hitachi-nada
TOKYO
Kawagoe
Kawasaki
Sagami-wan
Ō-shima
Izu-shotō
Hachijō-jima
Miyake-jima
Nii-jima
Mikura-jima
Kōzu-shima

Nagaoka
Maebashi
Matsumoto
Hida-sanmyaku
Mikuni-sanmyaku
Jōetsu
Nagano
Toyama
Shinano-gawa
Shiga-gawa
Sado
Fuji
Kōfu
Fujisan 3776m △
Shizuoka
Izu-hantō
Suruga-wan
Hamamatsu

Kii-suidō
Takaoka
Nagoya
Toyota
Kanazawa
Komatsu
Hida
Gifu
Nakatsugawa
Okazaki
Tsu
Owase
Shingū
Toyama-wan
Fukui
Tsuruga
Ogaki
Ōtsu
Ise
Owase
Ise-wan
Wakayama
Gobō
Tanabe
Wakasa-wan
Kōbe
Kyōto
Biwa-ko
Ōsaka
Awaji-shima
Awaji-shima
Harima-nada
Chūgoku
Himeji
Okayama
Tottori
Chūgoku-sanchi
Yonago
Matsue
Kurashiki
Kure
Tokushima
Mihara
Shikoku
Tosa-wan
Kōchi
Matsuyama
Nakamura
Sukumo
Bungo-suidō
Oki-shotō
Dōgo
Dōzen
Gōtsu
Masuda
Hiroshima
Iwakuni
Hōfu
Ōita
Nobeoka
Kyūshū
Miyazaki
Liancourt Rocks (claimed by Japan & South Korea)
Nagato
Yamaguchi
Ube
Kurume
Ōmuta
Yatsushiro
Miyakonojō
Shibushi-wan
Tanega-shima
Shimonoseki
Kitakyūshū
Fukuoka
Kumamoto
Sendai
Kagoshima
Kagoshima-wan
Yaku-shima
Ōsumi-shotō
Tsushima
Iki
Saseboo
Nagasaki
Amakusa-nada
Koshikijima-rettō
Ko-saki
Gotō-rettō

SOUTH
KOREA

Korea Strait

Tsushima Strait

P A C I F I C

O C E A N

East

China Sea

N

SOUTHERN INDIA & SRI LANKA

Mumbai (Bombay)
Kalyān
Pune
Ahmadnagar
Nānded
Jagdalpur
Bārāmati
Nizāmābād
Karīmnagar
Vizianagaram
Solāpur
Secunderābād
Visākhapatna
Sāngli
Gulbarga
Hyderābād
Rājahmundr
Kolhāpur
Rāichūr
Kākināda
Belgaum
Gadag
Kurnool
Vijayawāda
Panaji
Hubli
Machilīpatnam
Chīrāla
Nandyāl
Ongole
Dāvangere
Tādpatri
Kāvali
Tungabhadra
Reservoir
Anantapur
Nellore
Shimoga
Bhadrāvati
Cuddapah
Udupi
Tumkūr
Mangalore
Bangalore
Vellore
Chennai (Madras)
Kāsargod
Mandya
Kānchīpuram
Krishnagiri
Tiruppattūr
Cannanore
Mysore
Salem
Pondicherry
Calicut
Erode
Neyveli
Coimbatore
Trichūr
Tiruchchirāppalli
Ernākulam
Dindigul
Madurai
Cochin
Jaffna
Alleppey
Rājapālaiyam
SRI LANKA
Quilon
Mannar
Vavuniya
Trincomalee
Trivandrum
Tuticorin
Anurādhapura
Nāgercoil
Puttalam
Batticaloa
Gulf of Mannar
Matale
Negombo
Kandy
COLOMBO
Sri Jayawardanapura
Kalutara
Ratnapura
Galle
Matara

Arabian Sea

Lakshadweep (Laccadive Islands) (to India)

Amīndīvi Islands

Kavaratti Island

Kalpeni Island

Nine Degree Channel

Minicoy Island

Eight Degree Channel

Ihavandippolhu Atoll

MALDIVES

Faadhippolhu Atoll

Horsburgh Atoll

Male' Atoll

Ari Atoll

MALE'

Felidhu Atoll

Mulaku Atoll

Kolhumadulu Atoll

Hadhdhunmathi Atoll

North Huvadhu Atoll

South Huvadhu Atoll

Equator

Gan

Addu Atoll

INDIAN

Malabar Coast

Coromandel Coast

Palk Strait

Tamil Nādu

Karnātaka

INDIA

Deccan

Andhra Pradesh

Western Ghats

Godāvari

Krishna

0 km 300
0 miles 300

POPULATION   ● National capital

○ Less than 50,000   ○ 50,000 -100,000   ◉ 100,000 - 500,000   ▣ Over 500,000

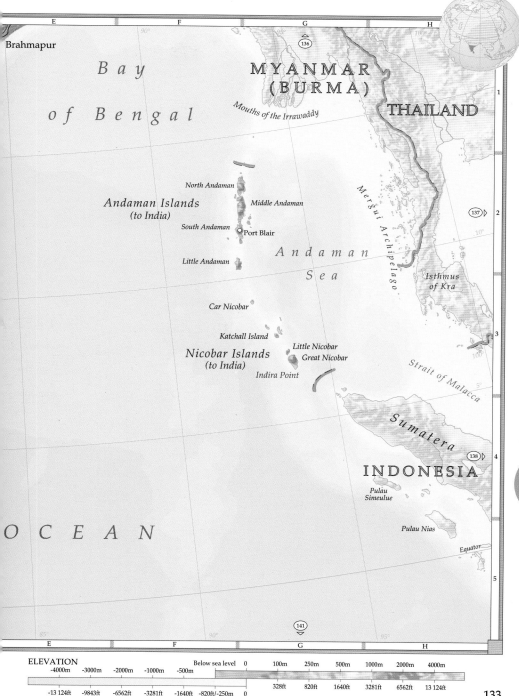

Brahmapur

B a y

o f   B e n g a l

MYANMAR
(BURMA)

THAILAND

Mouths of the Irrawaddy

North Andaman

Andaman Islands
(to India)

Middle Andaman

South Andaman

Port Blair

Little Andaman

A n d a m a n

S e a

Mergui Archipelago

Isthmus
of Kra

Car Nicobar

Katchall Island

Little Nicobar

Nicobar Islands
(to India)

Great Nicobar

Indira Point

Strait of Malacca

S u m a t e r a

INDONESIA

Pulau
Simeulue

Pulau Nias

Equator

O C E A N

ELEVATION

					Below sea level	0	100m	250m	500m	1000m	2000m	4000m
-4000m	-3000m	-2000m	-1000m	-500m								
-13 124ft	-9843ft	-6562ft	-3281ft	-1640ft	-820ft/-250m	0		328ft	820ft	1640ft	3281ft	6562ft	13 124ft

NORTHERN INDIA, PAKISTAN & BANGLADESH

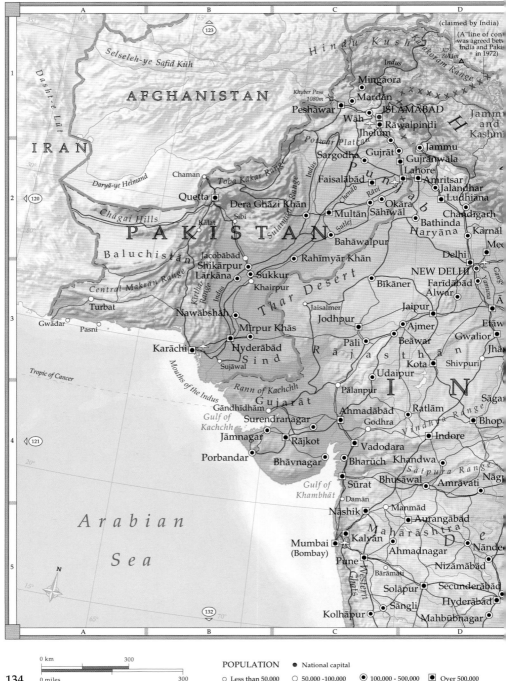

(claimed by India)

(A "line of con
was agreed betv
India and Pakis
in 1972)

K2
8611m

Hindu Kush

Karakoram Range

Selseleh-ye Safid Kūh

Dasht-e Lūt

AFGHANISTAN

Indus

Mingāora

Khyber Pass
1080m
Peshawar

Mardān

Wāh
ISLĀMĀBĀD
Rāwalpindi

Jhelum

IRAN

Potwar Plateau

Sargodha
Gujrāt

Jammu
and
Kashmi

Daryā-ye Helmand

Chaman

Toba Kākar Range

Jammu

Gujrānwāla

Lahore

Quetta

Dera Ghāzi Khān

Faisalābād

Chenāb
Rāvi

Amritsar
Jalandhar
Ludhiāna

Chāgai Hills

P A K I S T A N

Multān
Sāhīwāl

Okāra
Chandīgarh

Kālat
Sibi

Bahāwalpur

Haryāna
Karnāl

Mee

Baluchistān

Jacobābād
Shikārpur
Lārkāna

Sukkur
Rahīmyār Khān

Bīkāner

Delhi

NEW DELHI

Farīdābād
Alwar

Central Makrān Range

Kirthar Range
Indus

Khairpur

Thar Desert

Jaisalmer

Jaipur

A

Turbat

Nawābshāh

Jodhpur

Ajmer

Etaw

Gwādar
Pasni

Karāchi

Mīrpur Khās

Hyderābād

Sind

Pāli
Beāwar

Gwalior

Jha

Tropic of Cancer

Sujāwal

R ā j a s t h ā n

Kota
Shivpuri

Udaipur

Mouths of the Indus

Rann of Kachchh

Pālanpur

I N

Gāndhīdhām

G u j a r ā t

Gulf of
Kachchh

Surendranagar

Ahmadābād

Godhra

Ratlām

Sāga

Jāmnagar

Rājkot

Vadodara

Indore

Vindhya Range

Bhop

Porbandar

Bhāvnagar

Bharūch

Khandwa

Sātpura Range

Nāg

Sūrat

Bhusāwal

Amrāvati

Gulf of
Khambhāt

Daman

Nāshik

Manmād

A r a b i a n

S e a

N

Mumbai
(Bombay)

Kalyān

Aurangābād

Mahārāshtra

D   e

Nānde

Ahmadnagar

Pune

Bārāmati

Nizāmābād

Western Ghats

Solāpur

Secunderābād

Hyderābād

Kolhāpur

Sāngli

Mahbūbnagar

0 km   300

0 miles   300

POPULATION   ● National capital

○ Less than 50,000   ○ 50,000 -100,000   ◉ 100,000 - 500,000   ◼ Over 500,000

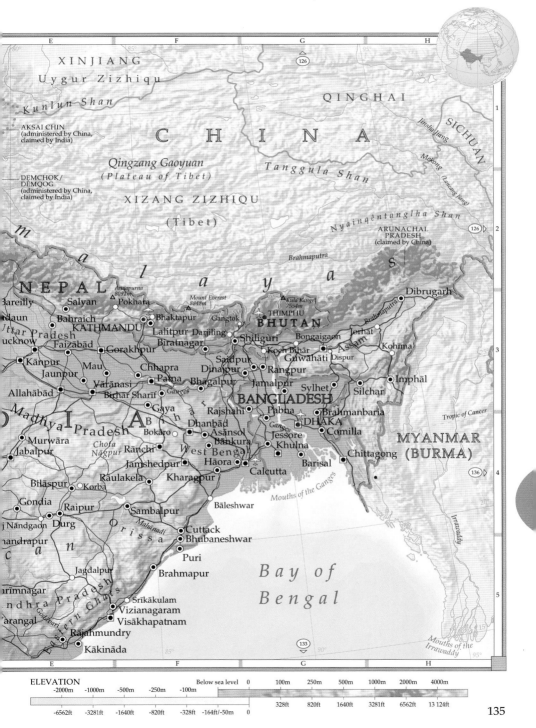

XINJIANG
Uygur Zizhiqu

Kunlun Shan

AKSAI CHIN
(administered by China,
claimed by India)

C H I N A

QINGHAI

SICHUAN

Jinshajiang

Mekong (Lancang Jiang)

Qingzang Gaoyuan
(Plateau of Tibet)

Tanggula Shan

DEMCHOK/
DEMQOG
(administered by China,
claimed by India)

XIZANG ZIZHIQU
(Tibet)

Nyainqêntanglha Shan

ARUNACHAL
PRADESH
(claimed by China)

126

Brahmaputra

m   a   l   a   y   a   s

Dibrugarh

Annapurna
8091m

NEPAL

Bareilly   Salyan   Pokhara
                            Bhaktapur   Gangtok
Idaun   Bahraich   Mount Everest
            KATHMANDU   8848m
Uttar Pradesh Lalitpur Darjiling
ucknow   Faizābād Gorakhpur   Biratnagar   Shiligūri
         Kānpur   Koch Bihār
              Mau   Chhapra   Dinajpur Rangpur
         Jaunpur   Patna
                 Varānasi Bhagalpur Jamalpur
Allahābād Bihār Sharīf   Ganges
                        Gaya   Rajshahi
Madhya   Pradesh B   i   h   a   r
Murwāra   Bokaro   Dhanbād   Asānsol
Jabalpur Chota   Ranchi   Bānkura
          Nāgpur   West Bengal   Khulna
Bilāspur Raulakela Jamshedpur Hāora
          Korba   Kharagpur   Calcutta
Gondia   Bāleshwar
j Nāndgaon Raipur   Sambalpur
      Durg O r i s s a
nandrapur   Mahānadi   Cuttack
c   a   Bhubaneshwar
              Jagdalpur   Puri
arimnagar   Brahmapur
ndhra   Pradesh
arangal   Godāvari   Srīkākulam
          Rajahmundry   Vizianagaram
              Kākināda   Visākhapatnam

THIMPHU   Kula Kangri
          7554m
BHUTAN
          Bongaigaon   Jorhat
Koch Bihār   Guwāhāti Assam   Kohīma
          Dispur
Rangpur   Imphāl
         Sylhet   Silchar
BANGLADESH
Pabna   Brāhmanbaria
        DHAKA
Ganges Comilla
Jessore
Khulna   Chittagong
         Barisal
              MYANMAR
              (BURMA)

Tropic of Cancer

126

136

Irrawaddy

Bay of
Bengal

Mouths of the Ganges

Mouths of the
Irrawaddy

133

Mainland Southeast Asia

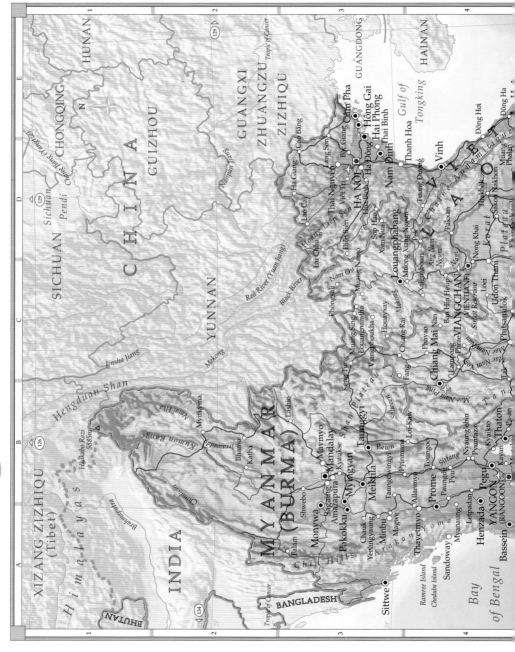

POPULATION

○ Less than 50,000　　● National capital

○ 50,000 -100,000　　◉ 100,000 - 500,000　　◼ Over 500,000

0 km　　200

0 miles　　200

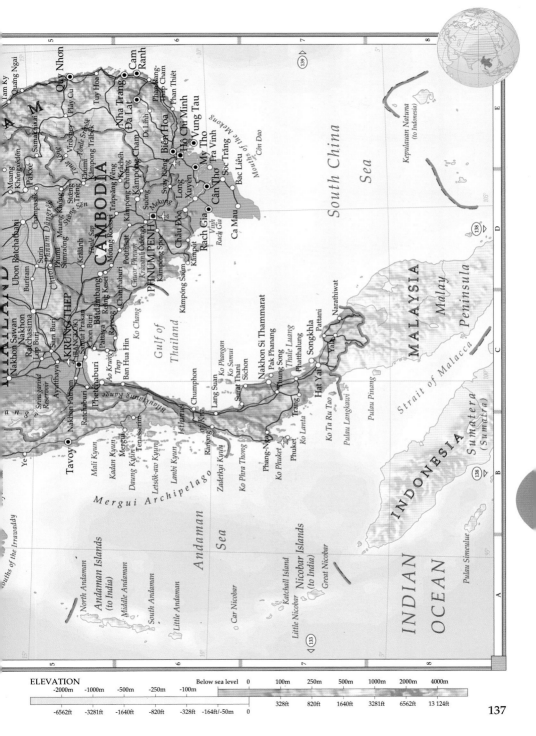

South China Sea

Kepulauan Natuna
(to Indonesia)

Gulf of Thailand

MALAYSIA

Malay Peninsula

Strait of Malacca

INDONESIA

Sumatera (Sumatra)

Andaman Sea

Mergui Archipelago

North Andaman
Andaman Islands (to India)
Middle Andaman
South Andaman
Little Andaman

Car Nicobar
Katchall Island
Nicobar Islands (to India)
Little Nicobar
Great Nicobar

INDIAN OCEAN

Pulau Simeulue

THAILAND
CAMBODIA

VIETNAM

PHNOM PENH
KRUNG THEP (BANGKOK)

Mouths of the Mekong

Mouths of the Irrawaddy

ELEVATION

					Below sea level	0	100m	250m	500m	1000m	2000m	4000m
-2000m	-1000m	-500m	-250m	-100m								
-6562ft	-3281ft	-1640ft	-820ft	-328ft	-164ft/-50m	0	328ft	820ft	1640ft	3281ft	6562ft	13 124ft

137

MARITIME SOUTHEAST ASIA

SINGAPORE

0 km 10
0 miles 10

MALAYSIA
Johore Strait

Causeway
Pulau Ubin
Pulau Tekong

Lim Chu Kang
Bukit Panjang New Town
Hougang
Choa Chu Kang
Bukit Timah 176m
Queenstown
Jurong Industrial Estate
Selat Pandan
Telok Blangah
Pulau Sudong
Sentosa
Pulau Pawai
Strait of Singapore

Changi
Bedok New Town
City

103°50'
104°
103°40'

Urban areas
Open areas
Nature reserves

MYANMAR (BURMA)
137
LAOS
VIETNAM
Gulf of Tongking
Hainan Dao (to China)
N
THAILAND
120
PARACEL ISLANDS
(disputed by China, Taiwan and Vietnam)
CAMBODIA
Mekong
South China Sea
SPRATLY ISLANDS
(disputed by China, Malaysia, Philippines, Taiwan and Vietnam)

133

Andaman Sea

Nicobar Islands
(to India)

Gulf of Thailand

Mouths of the Mekong

Balaba
Gunung Kinabalu
4101
Kota Kinabalu
BANDAR SERI BEGAWAN
BRUNEI
Miri
Taw
Sab

Bandaaceh
Sigli
Langsa
Meulaboh
Medan
Tebingtinggi
Pematangsiantar
Pulau Simeulue
Kepulauan Banyak
Sibolga
Pulau Nias

George Town
Pulau Pinang
Butterworth
Taiping
Ipoh
Kuala Lumpur
Klang
Seremban
Danau Toba
Melaka
Muar
Batu Pahat
Keluang
Johor Bahru
SINGAPORE

Kota Bharu
Kuala Terengganu
Dungun
Cukai
Kuantan

Kepulauan Natuna

Bintulu
Sibu
Sarawak
Batang Rajang
Sri Aman
Kuching
Singkawang
Sidas
Pontianak
Sungai Kapuas

Borneo
Peguntungan Muller
Sungai Mahakam
Samarinda
Balikpapan

Kalimantan
Sampit
Sungai Barito
Amuntai
Kandanga

Banjarmasin
Pulau Laut

Equator

Pekanbaru
Solok
Rengat
Kualatungkal
Jambi

Kepulauan Lingga
Bangka
Selat Karimata

Padang
Pulau Siberut
Batang Hari
Kepulauan Mentawai
Sungaipenuh
Pangkalpinang
Palembang
Lahat
Bengkulu
Kotabumi

Pulau Belitung

INDO

133

Sumatera
(Sumatra)
Bandarlampung
Serang
Bogor
Sukabumi
Bandung
Tasikmalaya
Cilacap
Magelang
Yogyakarta
Surakarta

JAKARTA
Selat Sunda

Cirebon
Tegal
Pekalongan
Semarang
Kudus

Java Sea
Pulau Madura
Surabaya
Probolinggo
Jomber
Malang
Kediri
Madiun

Maka

Matara
Bali
Denpasar
Pulau Lombok
N

INDIAN
OCEAN

Jawa
(Java)

10°
100°
110°

141

POPULATION

● National capital
○ Less than 50,000
○ 50,000 -100,000
◉ 100,000 - 500,000
■ Over 500,000

0 km 400
0 miles 400

ELEVATION

-4000ft	-3000ft	-2000ft	-1000ft	-500ft	Below sea level	0	100m	250m	500m	1000m	2000m	4000m
-13 124ft	-9843ft	-6562ft	-3281ft	-1640ft	-820ft/-250m	0	328ft	820ft	1640ft	3281ft	6562ft	13 124ft

THE INDIAN OCEAN

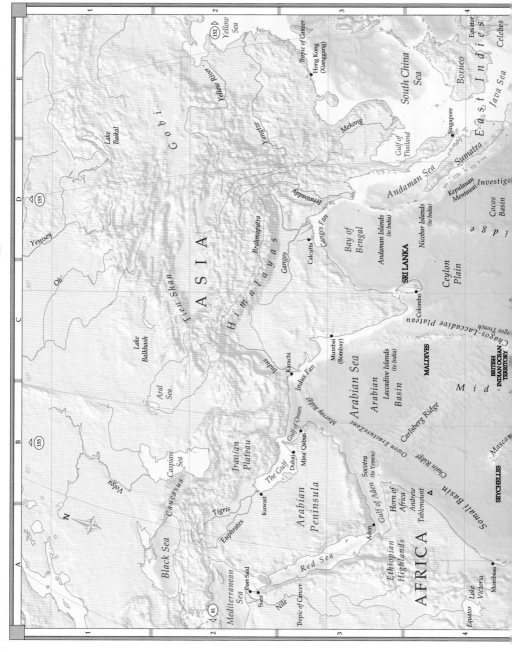

ASIA

AFRICA

Gobi

Yellow
Sea

Yellow River

Tropic of Cancer

Hong Kong
(Xianggang)

South China
Sea

Borneo

Celebes

East Indies

Equator

Java Sea

Lake
Baikal

Yangtze

Mekong

Gulf of
Thailand

Singapore

Sumatra

Andaman Sea

Kepulauan
Mentawai

Investiga

Irrawaddy

Brahmaputra

Ganges Fan

Bay of
Bengal

Andaman Islands
(to India)

Nicobar Islands
(to India)

Cocos
Basin

δ p i

Yenisey

Ob'

Tien Shan

Himalayas

Ganges

Calcutta

SRI LANKA

Ceylon
Plain

Lake
Balkhash

Indus

Karachi

Indus Fan

Mumbai
(Bombay)

Colombo

Chagos-Laccadive Plateau

gos Trench

Mi d

Aral
Sea

Murray Ridge

Arabian Sea

Arabian
Basin

Laccadive Islands
(to India)

MALDIVES

BRITISH
INDIAN OCEAN
TERRITORY

Caspian
Sea

Iranian
Plateau

Gulf of Oman

Queen Fracture Zone

Carlsberg Ridge

Masca

Volga

Dubai

Mina' Qabus

Socotra
(to Yemen)

Chain Ridge

Somali Basin

SEYCHELLES

The Gulf

Caucasus

Kuwait

Arabian
Peninsula

Gulf of Aden

Horn of
Africa

Andrew
Tablemount

Tigris

Euphrates

Aden

Black Sea

Ethiopian
Highlands

Mediterranean
Sea

Port Said

Red Sea

Equator

Lake
Victoria

Mombasa

Suez

Nile

Tropic of Cancer

N

0 km   1500

0 miles   1500

● Major port

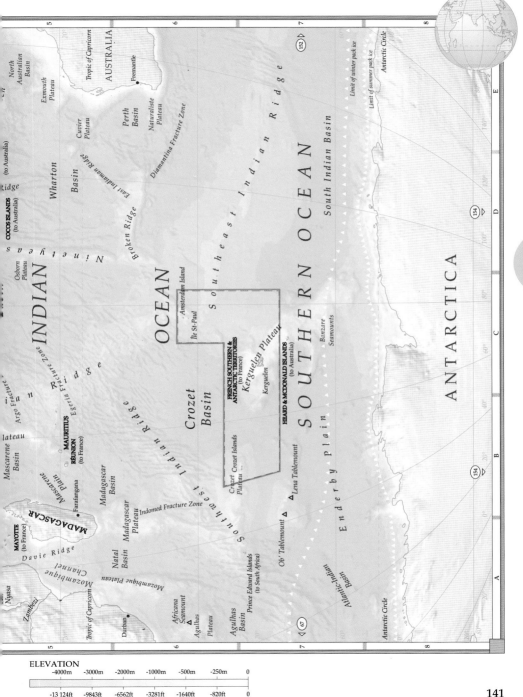

AUSTRALIA

Tropic of Capricorn

Fremantle

North Australian Basin

Exmouth Plateau

Cuvier Plateau

Perth Basin

Naturaliste Plateau

Perth Plateau

(to Australia)

COCOS ISLANDS (to Australia)

Wharton Basin

East Indiaman Ridge

Diamantina Fracture Zone

Broken Ridge

Ridge

Osborn Plateau

Ninetyeast

INDIAN

OCEAN

Amsterdam Island

Île St-Paul

South east Indian Ridge

SOUTHERN OCEAN

South Indian Basin

ANTARCTICA

Limit of winter pack ice

Limit of summer sea ice

Antarctic Circle

152

154

154

Mascarene Basin

Central Indian Ridge

Egeria Fracture Zone

Argo Fracture

Argo Fracture

MAURITIUS

RÉUNION (to France)

Madagascar Basin

Crozet Basin

Kerguelen Plateau

FRENCH SOUTHERN & ANTARCTIC TERRITORIES (to France)

Kerguelen

HEARD & McDONALD ISLANDS (to Australia)

Banzare Seamounts

plateau

Southwest Indian Ridge

Indomed Fracture Zone

Madagascar Plateau

MADAGASCAR

MAYOTTE (to France)

Mascarene Plateau

Farafangana

Mascarene Plain

Crozet Crozet Islands

Plateau

Ob' Tablemount

Lena Tablemount

Enderby Plain

Atlantic-Indian Basin

67

Nyasa

Zambezi

Davie Ridge

Mozambique Channel

Mozambique Plateau

Natal Basin

Tropic of Capricorn

Durban

Africana Seamount

Agulhas

Agulhas Plateau

Prince Edward Islands (to South Africa)

Agulhas Basin

Antarctic Circle

Antarctic Circle

ELEVATION

-4000m	-3000m	-2000m	-1000m	-500m	-250m	0
-13 124ft	-9843ft	-6562ft	-3281ft	-1640ft	-820ft	0

AUSTRALASIA & OCEANIA

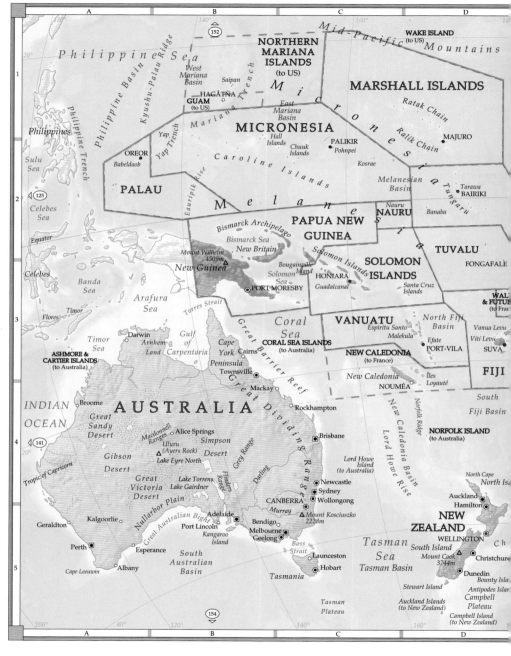

POPULATION   ● National capital

○ Less than 50,000   ○ 50,000 -100,000   ◉ 100,000 - 500,000   ◼ Over 500,000

0 km   1000

0 miles   1000

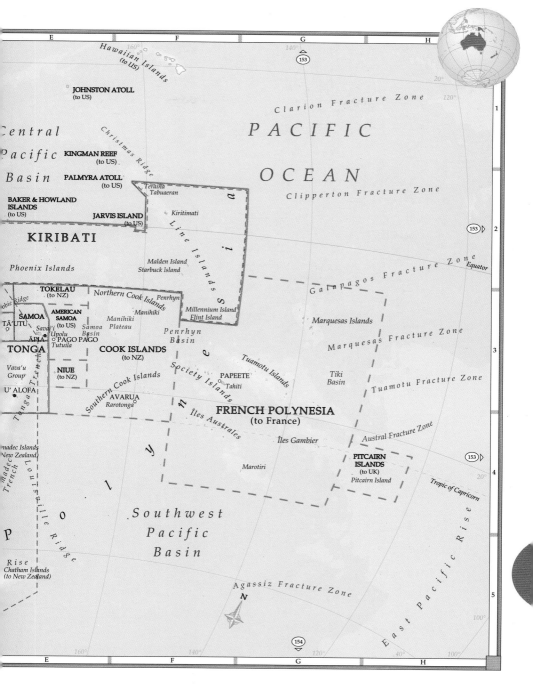

153

PACIFIC

Clarion Fracture Zone

20°

120°

OCEAN

Clipperton Fracture Zone

153

JOHNSTON ATOLL
(to US)

Central

Pacific

KINGMAN REEF
(to US)

Basin

PALMYRA ATOLL
(to US)

BAKER & HOWLAND
ISLANDS
(to US)

Christmas Ridge

Teraina
Tabuaeran

JARVIS ISLAND
(to US)

Kiritimati

KIRIBATI

Line Islands

Malden Island
Starbuck Island

Phoenix Islands

Galapagos Fracture Zone

Equator

TOKELAU
(to NZ)

Northern Cook Islands

Penrhyn

Marquesas Islands

Gobie Ridge

SAMOA

AMERICAN
SAMOA
(to US)

Manihiki

Manihiki

Marquesas Fracture Zone

TA'UTU

Savai'i

Samoa
Basin

Manihiki
Plateau

ÁPLA

Upolu

Tutuila

O PAGO PAGO

Penrhyn
Basin

Tuamotu Islands

TONGA

COOK ISLANDS
(to NZ)

Tiki
Basin

Tuamotu Fracture Zone

Vava'u
Group

NIUE
(to NZ)

PAPEETE
Tahiti

Society Islands

U' ALOFA

Southern Cook Islands

AVARUA
Rarotonga

FRENCH POLYNESIA
(to France)

Îles Australes

Austral Fracture Zone

Tonga Trench

Kermadec Islands
(to New Zealand)

Îles Gambier

153

20°

Louisville Ridge

Marotiri

PITCAIRN
ISLANDS
(to UK)

Pitcairn Island

Tropic of Capricorn

Kermadec Trench

P

Southwest

Pacific

Basin

Rise
Chatham Islands
(to New Zealand)

Rise

East Pacific Rise

100°

Agassiz Fracture Zone

N

40°

100°

154

5

160°

140°

120°

120°

THE SOUTHWEST PACIFIC

152

Tinian Saipan
Rota

NORTHERN MARIANA
ISLANDS
(to US)

GUAM
(to US)

HAGÁTÑA

MARSHALL
ISLANDS

MICRONESIA

Yap

Enewetak
Atoll

Bikini Atoll

Rongelap
Atoll

Ujelang Atoll

Kwajalein
Atoll
Namu Atoll
Ailinglaplap Atoll

Ailuk Atoll

Wotje Atoll

Maloelap

Majuro A

Jaluit Atoll

Mili Atoll

Babeldaob
OREOR

Chuuk
Islands

PALIKIR

Pohnpei

Caroline Islands

Kosrae

Ebon Atoll

Makir

PALAU

139

Equator

Tarau
BAIRIKI

Abema

Nonou

NAURU

Banaba

Admiralty
Islands

St.Matthias Group

Bismarck Archipelago

Bismarck Sea

New Ireland

New Guinea

Madang

PAPUA NEW GUINEA

Mount Wilhelm
4509m

Bougainville
Island

INDONESIA

Central Range

Lae

New
Britain

Choiseul

Santa Isabel

SOLOMON

Solomon Sea

Owen Stanley Range

New Georgia
Islands

Malaita

ISLANDS

Gulf of
Papua

HONIARA

PORT MORESBY

Arafura Sea

Torres Strait

D'Entrecasteaux
Islands

Guadalcanal

San Cristobal

Santa Cruz
Islands

Rennell

Louisiade
Archipelago

Arnhem
Land

Groote
Eylandt

Coral Sea

VANUATU

Banks Islands

Gulf of
Carpentaria

Cape
York
Peninsula

CORAL SEA ISLANDS
(to Australia)

Espiritu Santo

Maéwo

Pentecost

Barkly Tableland

Malekula

Ambrym
Epi

Efate

PORT-VILA

NEW
CALEDONIA
(to France)

Erromango

Tanna
Aneityum

NORTHERN

Tropic of Capricorn
Macdonnell

New
Caledonia

Îles Loyauté

Ouvéa

Lifou

Maré

TERRITORY

QUEENSLAND

NOUMÉA

Ranges

146

Great Barrier Reef

Great Dividing Range

AUSTRALIA

149

POPULATION

● National capital

○ Less than 50,000

○ 50,000 -100,000

◉ 100,000 - 500,000

◼ Over 500,000

0 km   750

0 miles   750

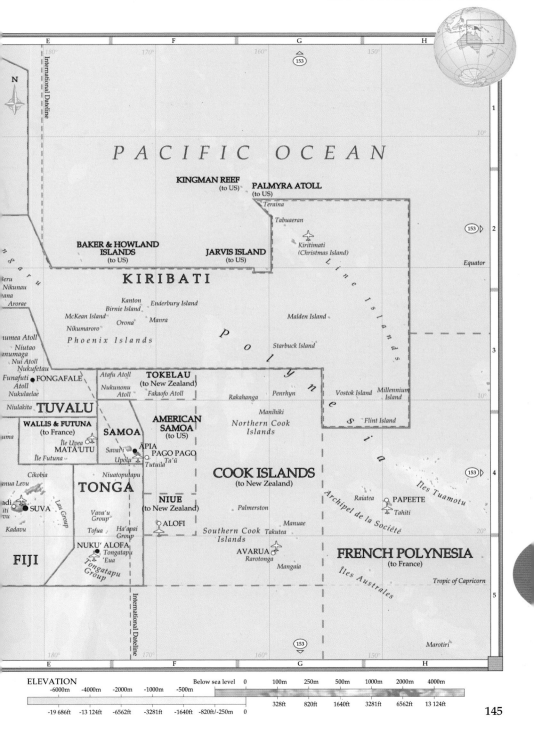

N

153

P A C I F I C   O C E A N

International Dateline

KINGMAN REEF
(to US)

PALMYRA ATOLL
(to US)

Teraina

Tabuaeran

BAKER & HOWLAND
ISLANDS
(to US)

JARVIS ISLAND
(to US)

Kiritimati
(Christmas Island)

153

Equator

K I R I B A T I

Beru
Nikunau
ana
Arorae

Kanton
Birnie Island
McKean Island
Nikumaroro
Orona
Enderbury Island
Manra

Malden Island

Line   Islands

P
o
l
y
n
e
s
i
a

Phoenix Islands

Starbuck Island

153

umea Atoll
Niutao
anumaga
Nui Atoll
Nukufetau
Funafuti
Atoll
Nukulaelae
Niulakita

FONGAFALE

Atafu Atoll

Nukunonu
Atoll

TOKELAU
(to New Zealand)

Fakaofo Atoll

Rakahanga

Penrhyn

Vostok Island

Millennium
Island

TUVALU

WALLIS & FUTUNA
(to France)
Île Uvea
MATA'UTU
Île Futuna

SAMOA

Savai'i
Upolu
AMERICAN
SAMOA
(to US)
ÁPIA
PAGO PAGO
Ta'ū
Tutuila

Manihiki

Northern Cook
Islands

Flint Island

uma

Cikobia
anua Levu
adi
iti
vu
Kadavu

TONGA

SUVA

Lau Group

Niuatoputapu

NIUE
(to New Zealand)

Vava'u
Group
Tofua
Ha'apai
Group
NUKU' ALOFA
Tongatapu
'Eua
Tongatapu
Group

ALOFI

Palmerston

COOK ISLANDS
(to New Zealand)

Raiatea
PAPEETE
Tahiti

Archipel de la Société

Îles Tuamotu

153

Manuae

Southern Cook
Islands

Takutea

FIJI

AVARUA
Rarotonga

Mangaia

FRENCH POLYNESIA
(to France)

Îles Australes

Tropic of Capricorn

International Dateline

153

Marotiri

ELEVATION

| -6000m | -4000m | -2000m | -1000m | -500m | Below sea level | 0 | 100m | 250m | 500m | 1000m | 2000m | 4000m |

| -19 686ft | -13 124ft | -6562ft | -3281ft | -1640ft | -820ft/-250m | 0 | | 328ft | 820ft | 1640ft | 3281ft | 6562ft | 13 124ft |

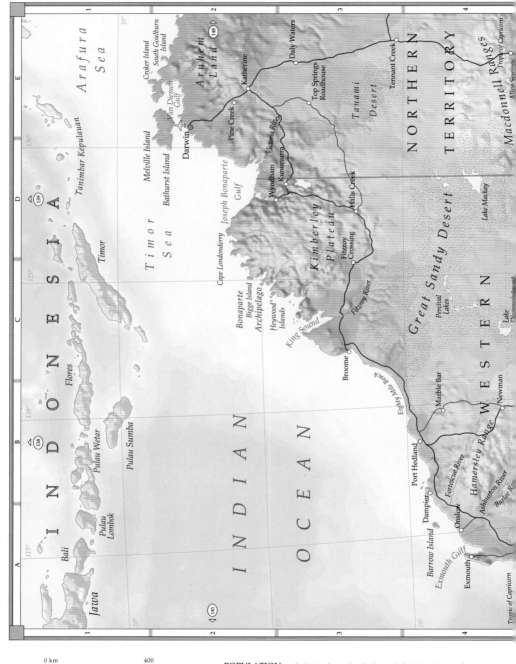

0 km   400

0 miles   400

POPULATION

● National capital   ● Internal administrative capital

○ Less than 50,000   ○ 50,000 -100,000   ◉ 100,000 - 500,000   ◼ Over 500,000

WESTERN AUSTRALIA

SOUTH AUSTRALIA

AUSTRALIA

Musgrave Ranges

Great Victoria Desert

Uluru (Ayers Rock) 863m

Coober Pedy

Tarcoola

Lake Everard

Penong

Lake Gairdner

Ceduna

Elliston

Port Lincoln

Lake Rebecca

Reid

Eucla

Nullarbor Plain

Great Australian Bight

INDIAN OCEAN

Lake Carnegie

Lake Wells

Lake Carey

Zanthus

Lake Cowan

Balladonia

Kalgoorlie

Coolgardie

Norseman

Esperance

Robinson Range

Lake Barlee

Meekatharra

Mount Magnet

Lake Moore

Southern Cross

Merredin

Brookton

Narrogin

Wagin

Katanning

Albany

Murchison River

Gascoyne River

Moora

Gingin

Perth

Northam

Collie

Manjimup

Fremantle

Rockingham

Mandurah

Bunbury

Busselton

Augusta

Carnavon

Bernier Island

Dorre Island

Shark Bay

Dirk Hartog Island

Denham

Kalbarri

Geraldton

N

ELEVATION

					Below sea level	0	100m	250m	500m	1000m	2000m	4000m
-4000m	-3000m	-2000m	-1000m	-500m								
-13 124ft	-9843ft	-6562ft	-3281ft	-1640ft	-820ft/-250m	0	328ft	820ft	1640ft	3281ft	6562ft	13 124ft

147

EASTERN AUSTRALIA

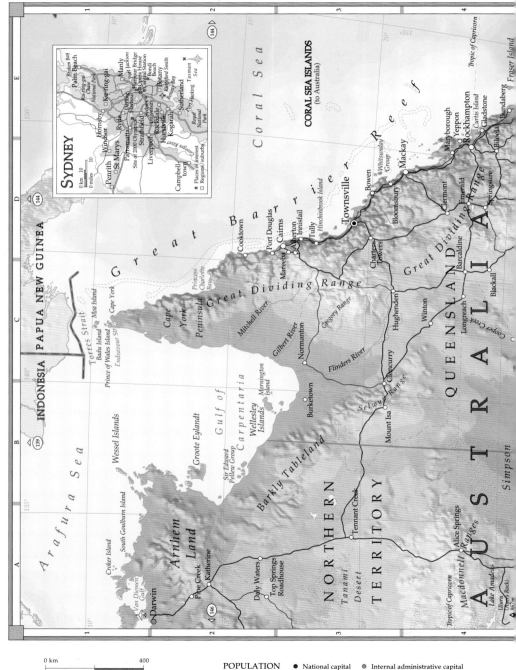

POPULATION

- ● National capital
- ◉ Internal administrative capital
- ○ Less than 50,000
- ○ 50,000 -100,000
- ◉ 100,000 - 500,000
- ■ Over 500,000

Tasman Sea

TASMANIA

SOUTH AUSTRALIA

NEW SOUTH WALES

VICTORIA

AUSTRALIAN CAPITAL TERRITORY

Great Victoria Desert

Great Dividing Range

Flinders Ranges

Grey Range

Barrier Range

Gympie
Caloundra
Brisbane
Gold Coast
Ipswich
Surfers Paradise
Murwillumbah
Lismore
Toowoomba
Warwick
Stanthorpe
Grafton
Coffs Harbour
Miles
Dalby
Moonie
Goondiwindi
Port Macquarie
Roma
St George
Warwick
Taree
Newcastle
Mitchell
Bollon
Moree
Narrabri
Tamworth
Muswellbrook
Gosford
Parramatta
Sydney
Wollongong
Cunnamulla
Bourke
Nyngan
Dubbo
Orange
Lithgow
Bathurst
Goulburn
CANBERRA
Cobar
Ivanhoe
Parkes
Cootamundra
Cooma
Bega
Broken Hill
Wilcannia
Hay
Wagga Wagga
Deniliquin
Albury
Wodonga
Wangaratta
Mount Kosciuszko
2228m
Bairnsdale
Tibooburra
Menindee
Mildura
Ouyen
Shepparton
Bendigo
Sale
Traralgon
Marree
Peterborough
Crystal Brook
Keith
Horsham
Sunbury
Melbourne
Ballarat
Geelong
Port Augusta
Whyalla
Port Pirie
Cawler
Adelaide
Tailem Bend
Naracoorte
Portland
Warrnambool
Elizabeth
Mount Gambier
Tarcoola
Coober Pedy
Lake Eyre North
Lake Eyre South
Lake Torrens
Lake Frome
Lake Blanche
Lake Callabonna
Penong
Ceduna
Elliston
Lake Everard
Lake Gairdner
Port Lincoln
Kangaroo Island
Spencer Gulf
Investigator Strait
Eyre Peninsula

Flinders Island
Cape Barren Island
Banks Strait
Launceston
Maria Island
Hobart
South Bruny Island
Burnie
Devonport
Marrawah
King Island
Hunter Island
Bass Strait
South East Point

Warrego River
Darling River
Murray River
Murrumbidgee River
Lachlan River
Darling River
Barwon River
Musgrave Ranges

N

ELEVATION

						Below sea level	0	100m	250m	500m	1000m	2000m	4000m
-4000m	-3000m	-2000m	-1000m	-500m									
-13 124ft	-9843ft	-6562ft	-3281ft	-1640ft	-820ft/-250m	0		328ft	820ft	1640ft	3281ft	6562ft	13 124ft

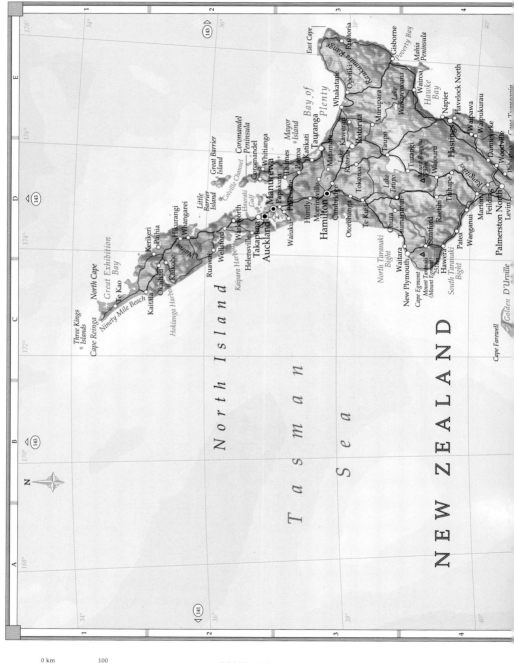

0 km   100

0 miles   100

POPULATION   ● National capital

○ Less than 50,000   ○ 50,000 -100,000   ◉ 100,000 - 500,000   ■ Over 500,000

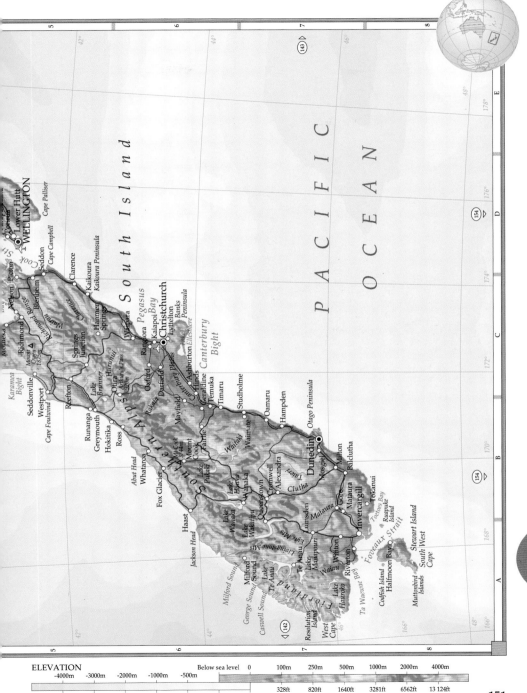

PACIFIC

OCEAN

South Island

Southern Alps

Fiordland

WELLINGTON
Lower Hutt
Porirua
Cape Palliser
Cape Campbell
Picton
Arapoa
Seddon
Blenheim
Clarence
Kaikoura
Kaikoura Peninsula
Richmond
Motueka
Mount Owen 1875m
Nelson
Richmond Range
Wairau
Waimea
Karamea Bight
Seddonville
Westport
Cape Foulwind
Reefton
Lake Brunner
Runanga
Greymouth
Hokitika
Ross
Otira
Arthur's Pass
Hurunui
Springs Junction
Hanmer Springs
Waipara
Rangiora
Rakaia
Christchurch
Lyttelton
Kaiapoi Bay
Banks Peninsula
Pegasus Bay
Canterbury Bight
Ellesmere
Ashburton
Darfield
Oxford
Methven
Mayfield
Rakaia
Canterbury Plains
Rolleston
Geraldine
Temuka
Timaru
Studholme
Oamaru
Hampden
Ashburton
Hinds
Tekapo
Waihao
Waimate
Fairlie
Abut Head
Whataroa
Fox Glacier
Haast
Jackson Head
Mount Cook/Aoraki
Lake Tekapo
Lake Pukaki
Lake Hawea
Lake Wanaka
Wanaka
Cromwell
Alexandra
Queenstown
Lake Wakatipu
Milford Sound
George Sound
Caswell Sound
Resolution Island
West Cape
Te Anau
Lake Te Anau
Lake Manapouri
Livingstone Mts
Eyre Mts
Mataura
Clutha
Lake Waihola
Lumsden
Gore
Mataura
Waiau
Lake Hauroko
Riverton
Winton
Invercargill
Tuatapere
Foveaux Strait
Ta Waewae Bay
Muttonbird Islands
Codfish Island
Halfmoon Bay
Stewart Island
Ruapuke Island
South West Cape
Toetoes Bay
Dunedin
Otago Peninsula
Mosgiel
Milton
Balclutha
Kaitangata
143
154
154
142

42°
44°
46°
48°
46°
48°
176°
178°
174°
172°
170°
168°
166°
160°

5 6 7 8
A B C D E

ELEVATION

					Below sea level	0	100m	250m	500m	1000m	2000m	4000m
-4000m	-3000m	-2000m	-1000m	-500m								
-13 124ft	-9843ft	-6562ft	-3281ft	-1640ft	-820ft/-250m	0	328ft	820ft	1640ft	3281ft	6562ft	13 124ft

151

THE PACIFIC OCEAN

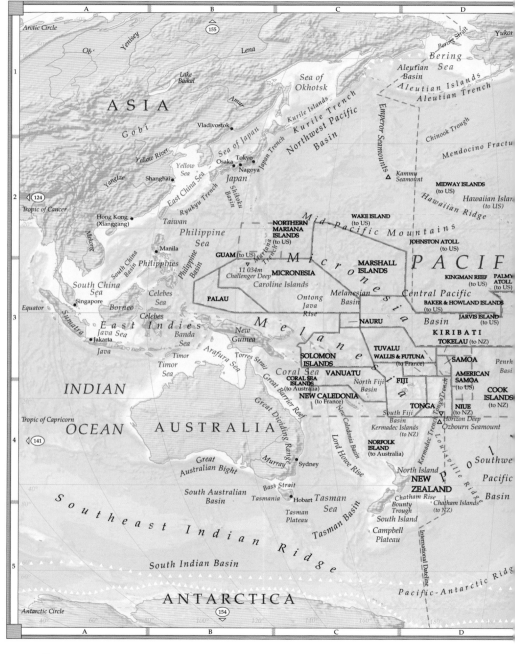

Arctic Circle
155
Lena
Yukor
Bering Strait
Bering Sea
Ob'
Yenisey
Aleutian Basin
Aleutian Islands
Aleutian Trench
ASIA
Lake Baikal
Sea of Okhotsk
Amur
Gobi
Kurile Islands
Kurile Trench
Chinook Trough
Vladivostok
Japan Trench
Northwest Pacific Basin
Emperor Seamounts
Mendocino Fractu
Sea of Japan
Yellow River
Yangtze
Osaka Tokyo
Nagoya
Kammu Seamount
MIDWAY ISLANDS (to US)
Yellow Sea
Japan
Shanghai
Shikoku Basin
Hawaiian Ridge
Hawaiian Islar (to US)
East China Sea
Tropic of Cancer
124
Hong Kong (Xianggang)
Taiwan
Ryukyu Trench
Mid-Pacific Mountains
WAKE ISLAND (to US)
Philippine Sea
NORTHERN MARIANA ISLANDS (to US)
Micronesia
PACIF
Manila
Mariana Trench
JOHNSTON ATOLL (to US)
Mekong
South China Basin
Philippines
GUAM (to US)
Philippine Basin
11 034m Challenger Deep
MICRONESIA
MARSHALL ISLANDS
Central Pacific
KINGMAN REEF (to US)
PALMY ATOLL (to US)
South China Sea
Celebes Sea
Caroline Islands
BAKER & HOWLAND ISLANDS (to US)
Singapore
Borneo
PALAU
Ontong Java Rise
Melanesian Basin
JARVIS ISLAND (to US)
Equator
East Indies
Celebes
Melanesia
Basin
KIRIBATI
Sumatra
Java Sea
New Guinea
NAURU
TOKELAU (to NZ)
Jakarta
Banda Sea
SOLOMON ISLANDS
TUVALU
WALLIS & FUTUNA (to France)
SAMOA
Penrh Basi
Java
Timor
Torres Strait
Great Barrier Reef
Coral Sea
VANUATU
CORAL SEA ISLANDS (to Australia)
North Fiji Basin
FIJI
AMERICAN SAMOA (to US)
COOK ISLANDS (to NZ)
Timor Sea
Arafura Sea
NEW CALEDONIA (to France)
TONGA
NIUE (to NZ)
INDIAN
Great Dividing Range
New Caledonia Basin
Tonga Trench
Tropic of Capricorn
141
OCEAN
AUSTRALIA
Lord Howe Rise
South Fiji Basin
Kermadec Islands (to NZ)
Horizon Deep
Ozbourn Seamount
Kermadec Trench
Louisville Ridge
Southwe
Pacific
NORFOLK ISLAND (to Australia)
North Island
NEW ZEALAND
Basin
Great Australian Bight
Murray
Sydney
Bass Strait
Tasman Sea
Chatham Rise
Chatham Islands (to NZ)
South Australian Basin
Tasmania
Hobart
Tasman Basin
Bounty Trough
South Island
Tasman Plateau
Campbell Plateau
Southeast Indian Ridge
South Indian Basin
Pacific-Antarctic Ridg
International Dateline
ANTARCTICA
154
Antarctic Circle

0 km   2000
● Major port
0 miles   2000

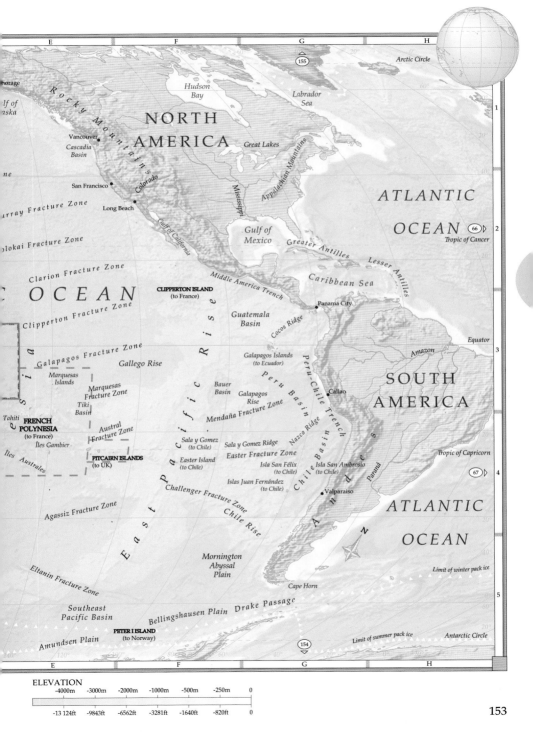

horage

Rocky Mountains

NORTH
AMERICA

Vancouver
Cascadia
Basin

San Francisco

Long Beach

Colorado

Gulf of California

Hudson
Bay

Great Lakes

Mississippi

Appalachian Mountains

155

Arctic Circle

Labrador
Sea

ATLANTIC

OCEAN 66

Tropic of Cancer

lf of
aska

ne

urray Fracture Zone

olokai Fracture Zone

Clarion Fracture Zone

OCEAN

Clipperton Fracture Zone

Galapagos Fracture Zone

Gallego Rise

Marquesas
Islands

Marquesas
Fracture Zone

Tiki
Basin

Tahiti FRENCH
POLYNESIA
(to France)

Îles Gambier

Austral
Fracture Zone

Îles Australes

PITCAIRN ISLANDS
(to UK)

CLIPPERTON ISLAND
(to France)

Middle America Trench

Guatemala
Basin

Cocos Ridge

Panama City

Greater Antilles

Caribbean Sea

Lesser Antilles

East Pacific Rise

Galapagos Islands
(to Ecuador)

Peru Basin

Bauer
Basin

Galapagos
Rise

Mendaña Fracture Zone

Sala y Gomez
(to Chile)

Sala y Gomez Ridge

Nazca Ridge

Easter Island
(to Chile)

Easter Fracture Zone

Isla San Félix
(to Chile)

Islas Juan Fernández
(to Chile)

Peru-Chile Trench

Callao

Amazon

Equator

SOUTH
AMERICA

Andes

Isla San Ambrosio
(to Chile)

Chile Basin

Tropic of Capricorn

67

Paraná

Valparaíso

Challenger Fracture Zone

Chile Rise

Agassiz Fracture Zone

Eltanin Fracture Zone

East Pacific Rise

Mornington
Abyssal
Plain

Cape Horn

ATLANTIC

OCEAN

Limit of winter pack ice

Southeast
Pacific Basin

Bellingshausen Plain

Drake Passage

Amundsen Plain

PETER I ISLAND
(to Norway)

154

Limit of summer pack ice

Antarctic Circle

1

2

3

4

5

ELEVATION

-4000m	-3000m	-2000m	-1000m	-500m	-250m	0
-13 124ft	-9843ft	-6562ft	-3281ft	-1640ft	-820ft	0

ANTARCTICA

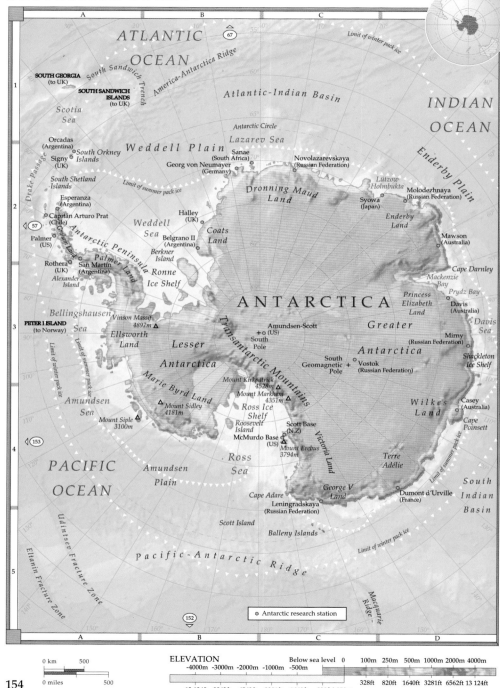

ATLANTIC
OCEAN

67

America-Antarctica Ridge

Limit of winter pack ice

INDIAN
OCEAN

SOUTH GEORGIA
(to UK)

SOUTH SANDWICH
ISLANDS
(to UK)

South Sandwich Trench

Atlantic-Indian Basin

Scotia
Sea

Antarctic Circle

Lazarev Sea

Enderby Plain

Orcadas
(Argentina)

South Orkney
Islands

Signy
(UK)

Weddell Plain

Sanae
(South Africa)

Georg von Neumayer
(Germany)

Novolazarevskaya
(Russian Federation)

Lützow
Holmbukta

Molodezhnaya
(Russian Federation)

South Shetland
Islands

Drake Passage

Limit of summer pack ice

Dronning Maud
Land

Syowa
(Japan)

Esperanza
(Argentina)

Capitán Arturo Prat
(Chile)

Halley
(UK)

Enderby
Land

57

Palmer
(US)

Weddell
Sea

Belgrano II
(Argentina)

Coats
Land

Mawson
(Australia)

Rothera
(UK)

San Martín
(Argentina)

Antarctic Peninsula

Berkner
Island

Cape Darnley

Graham Land

Palmer Land

Ronne
Ice Shelf

Mackenzie
Bay

Prydz Bay

Alexander
Island

Bellingshausen
Sea

Vinson Massif
4897m

ANTARCTICA

Princess
Elizabeth
Land

Davis
(Australia)

Davis
Sea

PETER I ISLAND
(to Norway)

Ellsworth
Land

Lesser
Antarctica

Amundsen-Scott
(US)

South
Pole

Greater

Antarctica

Mirny
(Russian Federation)

Shackleton
Ice Shelf

Limit of winter pack ice

Limit of summer pack ice

Transantarctic Mountains

South
Geomagnetic
Pole

Vostok
(Russian Federation)

Amundsen
Sea

Marie Byrd Land

Mount Kirkpatrick
4528m

Mount Markham
4351m

Wilkes
Land

Casey
(Australia)

Mount Sidley
4181m

Ross Ice
Shelf

Cape
Poinsett

Mount Siple
3100m

Roosevelt
Island

Scott Base
(N.Z)

McMurdo Base
(US)

Mount Erebus
3794m

Victoria Land

Terre
Adélie

South

Indian

Basin

PACIFIC

OCEAN

Amundsen
Plain

Ross
Sea

George V
Land

Dumont d'Urville
(France)

Cape Adare

Leningradskaya
(Russian Federation)

Eltanin Fracture Zone

Udintsev Fracture Zone

Scott Island

Balleny Islands

Macquarie
Ridge

Limit of winter pack ice

Pacific-Antarctic Ridge

152

○ Antarctic research station

153

ELEVATION

					Below sea level	0	100m	250m	500m	1000m	2000m	4000m
	-4000m	-3000m	-2000m	-1000m	-500m							

0 km   500

0 miles   500

-13 124ft -9843ft -6562ft -3281ft -1640ft -820ft/-250m   328ft   820ft   1640ft 3281ft 6562ft 13 124ft

ARCTIC OCEAN

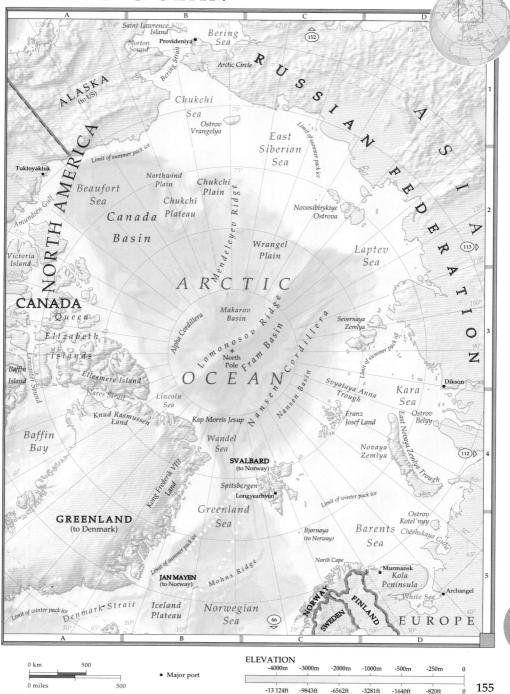

ALASKA (to US)

RUSSIAN FEDERATION

NORTH AMERICA

CANADA

Saint Lawrence Island

Norton Sound

Providéniya

Bering Strait

Bering Sea

152

Arctic Circle

Chukchi Sea

Ostrov Vrangelya

East Siberian Sea

Limit of summer pack ice

Tuktoyaktuk

Limit of summer pack ice

Northwind Plain

Chukchi Plain

Chukchi Plateau

Beaufort Sea

Canada Basin

Wrangel Plain

Novosibirskiye Ostrova

Laptev Sea

113

Amundsen Gulf

Victoria Island

ARCTIC

Makarov Basin

Mendeleyev Ridge

Alpha Cordillera

Lomonosov Ridge

North Pole

Fram Basin

Nansen Cordillera

Nansen Basin

Severnaya Zemlya

Queen Elizabeth Islands

OCEAN

Dikson

Kara Sea

Baffin Island

Ellesmere Island

Lancaster Sound

Nares Strait

Lincoln Sea

Kap Morris Jesup

Svyataya Anna Trough

East Novaya Zemlya Trough

Ostrov Belyy

Knud Rasmussen Land

Franz Josef Land

Baffin Bay

Wandel Sea

Svalbard (to Norway)

Novaya Zemlya

112

Kong Frederik VIII Land

Spitsbergen

Longyearbyen

Ostrov Kotel'nyy

GREENLAND (to Denmark)

Greenland Sea

Bjørnøya (to Norway)

Limit of winter pack ice

Barents Sea

Chëshskaya Guba

North Cape

Ostrov Belyy

JAN MAYEN (to Norway)

Mohns Ridge

Murmansk

Kola Peninsula

Archangel

White Sea

Limit of winter pack ice

Denmark Strait

Iceland Plateau

Norwegian Sea

66

NORWAY

SWEDEN

FINLAND

EUROPE

0 km 500

0 miles 500

● Major port

ELEVATION

-4000m -3000m -2000m -1000m -500m -250m 0

-13 124ft -9843ft -6562ft -3281ft -1640ft -820ft 0

OVERSEAS TERRITORIES & DEPENDENCIES

DESPITE THE RAPID process of global decolonization since the Second World War, around 10 million people in more than 50 territories around the world continue to live under the protection of France, Australia, the Netherlands, Denmark, Norway, New Zealand, the UK, or the USA. These remnants of former colonial empires may have persisted for economic, strategic or political reasons and are administered in a variety of ways.

AUSTRALIA

AUSTRALIA'S OVERSEAS TERRITORIES have not been an issue since Papua New Guinea became independent in 1975. Consequently there is no overriding policy toward them. Norfolk Island is inhabited by descendants of the H.M.S Bounty mutineers and more recent Australian migrants.

ASHMORE & CARTIER ISLANDS
Indian Ocean
STATUS: External territory
CLAIMED: 1978
CAPITAL: Not applicable
POPULATION: None
AREA: 5.2 sq km
(2 sq miles)

CHRISTMAS ISLAND
Indian Ocean
STATUS: External territory
CLAIMED: 1958
CAPITAL: Flying Fish Cove
POPULATION: 1,275
AREA: 134.6 sq km
(52 sq miles)

COCOS ISLANDS
Indian Ocean
STATUS: External territory
CLAIMED: 1955
CAPITAL: No official capital
POPULATION: 670
AREA: 14.24 sq km
(5.5 sq miles)

CORAL SEA ISLANDS
South Pacific
STATUS: External territory
CLAIMED: 1969
CAPITAL: None
POPULATION: 8 (meteorologists)
AREA: Less than 3 sq km
(1.16 sq miles)

HEARD & McDONALD IS.
Indian Ocean
STATUS: External territory
CLAIMED: 1947
CAPITAL: Not applicable
POPULATION: None
AREA: 417 sq km
(161 sq miles)

NORFOLK ISLAND
South Pacific
STATUS: External territory
CLAIMED: 1774
CAPITAL: Kingston
POPULATION: 2,181
AREA: 34.4 sq km
(13.3 sq miles)

DENMARK

THE FAEROE ISLANDS have been under Danish administration since Queen Margreth I of Denmark inherited Norway in 1380. The Home Rule Act of 1948 gave the Faeroese control over all their internal affairs. Greenland first came under Danish rule in 1380. Today, Denmark is responsible for the island's foreign affairs and defense.

FAEROE ISLANDS
North Atlantic
STATUS: External territory
CLAIMED: 1380
CAPITAL: Tórshavn
POPULATION: 43,382
AREA: 1,399 sq km
(540 sq miles)

GREENLAND
North Atlantic
STATUS: External territory
CLAIMED: 1380
CAPITAL: Nuuk
POPULATION: 56,076
AREA: 2,175,516 sq km
(840,000 sq miles)

FRANCE

FRANCE HAS DEVELOPED economic ties with its overseas territories, thereby stressing interdependence over independence. Overseas *départements*, officially part of France, have their own governments. Territorial *collectivités* and overseas *territoires* have varying degrees of autonomy.

CLIPPERTON ISLAND
East Pacific
STATUS: Dependency of French Polynesia
CLAIMED: 1930
CAPITAL: Not applicable
POPULATION: None
AREA: 7 sq km
(2.7 sq miles)

FRENCH GUIANA
South America
STATUS: Overseas department
CLAIMED: 1817
CAPITAL: Cayenne
POPULATION: 152,300
AREA: 90,996 sq km
(35,135 sq miles)

FRENCH POLYNESIA
South Pacific
STATUS: Overseas territory
CLAIMED: 1843
CAPITAL: Papeete
POPULATION: 219,521
AREA: 4,165 sq km
(1,608 sq miles)

GUADELOUPE
West Indies
STATUS: Overseas department
CLAIMED: 1635
CAPITAL: Basse-Terre
POPULATION: 419,500
AREA: 1,780 sq km
(687 sq miles)

MARTINIQUE
West Indies
STATUS: Overseas
department
CLAIMED: 1635
CAPITAL: Fort-de-France
POPULATION: 381,200
AREA: 1,100 sq km
(425 sq miles)

MAYOTTE
Indian Ocean
STATUS: Territorial
collectivity
CLAIMED: 1843
CAPITAL: Mamoudzou
POPULATION: 131,320
AREA: 374 sq km
(144 sq miles)

NEW CALEDONIA
South Pacific
STATUS: Overseas territory
CLAIMED: 1853
CAPITAL: Nouméa
POPULATION: 196,836
AREA: 19,103 sq km
(7,374 sq miles)

RÉUNION
Indian Ocean
STATUS: Overseas
department
CLAIMED: 1638
CAPITAL: Saint-Denis
POPULATION: 632,000
AREA: 2,512 sq km
(970 sq miles)

ST. PIERRE & MIQUELON
North America
STATUS: Territorial collectivity
CLAIMED: 1604
CAPITAL: Saint-Pierre
POPULATION: 6,600
AREA: 242 sq km
(93.4 sq miles)

WALLIS & FUTUNA
South Pacific
STATUS: Overseas territory
CLAIMED: 1842
CAPITAL: Matā'Utu
POPULATION: 15,000
AREA: 274 sq km
(106 sq miles)

NETHERLANDS

THE COUNTRY'S TWO REMAINING
overseas territories were formerly
part of the Dutch West Indies. Both
are now self-governing, but the
Netherlands remains responsible
for their defense.

ARUBA
West Indies
STATUS: Autonomous
part of the Netherlands
CLAIMED: 1643
CAPITAL: Oranjestad
POPULATION: 88,000
AREA: 194 sq km (75 sq miles)

NETHERLANDS ANTILLES
West Indies
STATUS: Autonomous
part of the Netherlands
CLAIMED: 1816
CAPITAL: Willemstad
POPULATION: 207,175
AREA: 800 sq km (308 sq miles)

NEW ZEALAND

NEW ZEALAND'S GOVERNMENT
has no desire to retain any overseas
territories. However, the economic
weakness of its dependent territory
Tokelau and its freely associated
states, Niue and the Cook Islands,
has forced New Zealand to
remain responsible for their
foreign policy and defense.

COOK ISLANDS
South Pacific
STATUS: Associated territory
CLAIMED: 1901
CAPITAL: Avarua
POPULATION: 20,200
AREA: 293 sq km
(113 sq miles)

NIUE
South Pacific
STATUS: Associated territory
CLAIMED: 1901
CAPITAL: Alofi
POPULATION: 2,080
AREA: 264 sq km
(102 sq miles)

TOKELAU
South Pacific
STATUS: Dependent territory
CLAIMED: 1926
CAPITAL: Not applicable
POPULATION: 1,577
AREA: 10.4 sq km (4 sq miles)

NORWAY

IN 1920, 41 nations signed the Spitsbergen Treaty recognizing Norwegian
sovereignty over Svalbard. There
is a NATO base on Jan Mayen.
Bouvet Island is a nature reserve.

BOUVET ISLAND
South Atlantic
STATUS: Dependency
CLAIMED: 1928
CAPITAL: Not applicable
POPULATION: None
AREA: 58 sq km (22 sq miles)

JAN MAYEN
North Atlantic
STATUS: Dependency
CLAIMED: 1929
CAPITAL: Not applicable
POPULATION: None
AREA: 381 sq km (147 sq miles)

PETER I. ISLAND
Southern Ocean
STATUS: Dependency
CLAIMED: 1931
CAPITAL: Not applicable
POPULATION: None
AREA: 180 sq km (69 sq miles)

SVALBARD
Arctic Ocean
STATUS: Dependency
CLAIMED: 1920
CAPITAL: Longyearbyen
POPULATION: 3,231
AREA: 62,906 sq km
(24,289 sq miles)

Continued on p.158

UNITED KINGDOM

THE UK STILL has the largest number of overseas territories. These are locally-governed by a mixture of elected representatives and appointed officials, and they all enjoy a large measure of internal self-government, but certain powers, such as foreign affairs and defense, are reserved for Governors of the British Crown.

ANGUILLA
West Indies
STATUS: Dependent territory
CLAIMED: 1650
CAPITAL: The Valley
POPULATION: 10,300
AREA: 96 sq km
(37 sq miles)

ASCENSION ISLAND
South Atlantic
STATUS: Dependency of St. Helena
CLAIMED: 1673
CAPITAL: Georgetown
POPULATION: 1,099
AREA: 88 sq km
(34 sq miles)

BERMUDA
North Atlantic
STATUS: Crown colony
CLAIMED: 1612
CAPITAL: Hamilton
POPULATION: 60,144
AREA: 53 sq km
(20.5 sq miles)

BRITISH INDIAN OCEAN TERRITORY
STATUS: Dependent territory
CLAIMED: 1814
CAPITAL: Diego Garcia
POPULATION: 930
AREA: 60 sq km
(23 sq miles)

BRITISH VIRGIN ISLANDS
West Indies
STATUS: Dependent territory
CLAIMED: 1672
CAPITAL: Road Town
POPULATION: 17,896
AREA: 153 sq km
(59 sq miles)

CAYMAN ISLANDS
West Indies
STATUS: Dependent territory
CLAIMED: 1670
CAPITAL: George Town
POPULATION: 35,000
AREA: 259 sq km (100 sq miles)

FALKLAND ISLANDS
South Atlantic
STATUS: Dependent territory
CLAIMED: 1832
CAPITAL: Stanley
POPULATION: 2,564
AREA: 12,173 sq km
(4,699 sq miles)

GIBRALTAR
Southwest Europe
STATUS: Crown colony
CLAIMED: 1713
CAPITAL: Gibraltar
POPULATION: 27,086
AREA: 6.5 sq km (2.5 sq miles)

GUERNSEY
Channel Islands
STATUS: Crown dependency
CLAIMED: 1066
CAPITAL: St. Peter Port
POPULATION: 56,681
AREA: 65 sq km (25 sq miles)

ISLE OF MAN
British Isles
STATUS: Crown dependency
CLAIMED: 1765
CAPITAL: Douglas
POPULATION: 71,714
AREA: 572 sq km (221 sq miles)

JERSEY
Channel Islands
STATUS: Crown dependency
CLAIMED: 1066
CAPITAL: St. Helier
POPULATION: 85,150
AREA: 116 sq km (45 sq miles)

MONTSERRAT
West Indies
STATUS: Dependent territory
CLAIMED: 1632
CAPITAL: Plymouth
(currently uninhabitable)
POPULATION: 2,850
AREA: 102 sq km (40 sq miles)

PITCAIRN ISLANDS
South Pacific
STATUS: Dependent territory
CLAIMED: 1887
CAPITAL: Adamstown
POPULATION: 55
AREA: 3.5 sq km (1.35 sq miles)

ST. HELENA
South Atlantic
STATUS: Dependent territory
CLAIMED: 1673
CAPITAL: Jamestown
POPULATION: 6,472
AREA: 122 sq km (47 sq miles)

SOUTH GEORGIA & THE SOUTH SANDWICH ISLANDS
South Atlantic
STATUS: Dependent territory
CLAIMED: 1775
CAPITAL: Not applicable
POPULATION: No permanent residents
AREA: 3,592 sq km (1,387 sq miles)

TRISTAN DA CUNHA
South Atlantic
STATUS: Dependency of St. Helena
CLAIMED: 1612
CAPITAL: Edinburgh
POPULATION: 297
AREA: 98 sq km (38 sq miles)

TURKS & CAICOS ISLANDS
West Indies
STATUS: Dependent territory
CLAIMED: 1766
CAPITAL: Cockburn Town
POPULATION: 13,800
AREA: 430 sq km (166 sq miles)

UNITED STATES OF AMERICA

AMERICA'S OVERSEAS TERRITORIES have been seen as strategically useful, if expensive, links with its "backyards." The US has, in most cases, given the local population a say in deciding their own status. A US Commonwealth territory, such as Puerto Rico, has a greater level of independence than that of a US unincorporated or external territory.

AMERICAN SAMOA
South Pacific
STATUS: Unincorporated territory
CLAIMED: 1900
CAPITAL: Pago Pago
POPULATION: 60,000
AREA: 195 sq km (75 sq miles)

BAKER & HOWLAND ISLANDS
South Pacific
STATUS: Unincorporated territory
CLAIMED: 1856
CAPITAL: Not applicable
POPULATION: None
AREA: 1.4 sq km (0.54 sq miles)

GUAM
West Pacific
STATUS: Unincorporated territory
CLAIMED: 1898
CAPITAL: Hagåtña
POPULATION: 149,249
AREA: 549 sq km (212 sq miles)

JARVIS ISLAND
South Pacific
STATUS: Unincorporated territory
CLAIMED: 1856
CAPITAL: Not applicable
POPULATION: None
AREA: 4.5 sq km (1.7 sq miles)

JOHNSTON ATOLL
Central Pacific
STATUS: Unincorporated territory
CLAIMED: 1858
CAPITAL: Not applicable
POPULATION: 327
AREA: 2.8 sq km (1 sq mile)

KINGMAN REEF
Central Pacific
STATUS: Administered territory
CLAIMED: 1856
CAPITAL: Not applicable
POPULATION: None
AREA: 1 sq km (0.4 sq miles)

MIDWAY ISLANDS
Central Pacific
STATUS: Administered territory
CLAIMED: 1867
CAPITAL: Not applicable
POPULATION: 453
AREA: 5.2 sq km (2 sq miles)

NAVASSA ISLAND
West Indies
STATUS: Unincorporated territory
CLAIMED: 1856
CAPITAL: Not applicable
POPULATION: None
AREA: 5.2 sq km (2 sq miles)

NORTHERN MARIANA ISLANDS
West Pacific
STATUS: Commonwealth territory
CLAIMED: 1947
CAPITAL: Saipan
POPULATION: 58,846
AREA: 457 sq km (177 sq miles)

PALMYRA ATOLL
Central Pacific
STATUS: Unincorporated territory
CLAIMED: 1898
CAPITAL: Not applicable
POPULATION: None
AREA: 12 sq km (5 sq miles)

PUERTO RICO
West Indies
STATUS: Commonwealth territory
CLAIMED: 1898
CAPITAL: San Juan
POPULATION: 3.8 million
AREA: 8,959 sq km (3,458 sq miles)

VIRGIN ISLANDS
West Indies
STATUS: Unincorporated territory
CLAIMED: 1917
CAPITAL: Charlotte Amalie
POPULATION: 101,809
AREA: 355 sq km (137 sq miles)

WAKE ISLAND
Central Pacific
STATUS: Unincorporated territory
CLAIMED: 1898
CAPITAL: Not applicable
POPULATION: 302
AREA: 6.5 sq km (2.5 sq miles)

GLOSSARY OF GEOGRAPHICAL TERMS

THE FOLLOWING GLOSSARY lists all geographical terms occuring on the maps and in the main-entry names in the Index–Gazetteer. These terms may precede, follow or be run together with the proper elements of the name; where they precede it the term is reversed for indexing purposes – thus Poluostov Yamal is indexed as Yamal, Poluostrov.

A

Å *Danish, Norwegian,* River
Alpen *German,* Alps
Altiplanicie *Spanish,* Plateau
Älv(en) *Swedish,* River
Anse *French,* Bay
Archipiélago *Spanish,* Archipelago
Arcipelago *Italian,* Archipelago
Arquipélago *Portuguese,* Archipelago
Aukštuma *Lithuanian,* Upland

B

Bahía *Spanish,* Bay
Baía *Portuguese,* Bay
Baḥr *Arabic,* River
Baie *French,* Bay
Bandao *Chinese,* Peninsula
Banjaran *Malay,* Mountain range
Batang *Malay,* Stream
-berg *Afrikaans, Norwegian,* Mountain
Birket *Arabic ,* Lake
Boğazı *Turkish,* Strait
Bucht *German,* Bay
Bugten *Danish,* Bay
Buḥayrat *Arabic,* Lake, reservoir
Buḥeiret *Arabic,* Lake
Bukit *Malay,* Mountain
-bukta *Norwegian,* Bay
bukten *Swedish,* Bay
Burnu *Turkish,* Cape, point
Buuraha *Somali,* Mountains

C

Cabo *Portuguese,* Cape
Cap *French,* Cape
Cascada *Portuguese,* Waterfall
Cerro *Spanish,* Mountain
Chaîne *French,* Mountain range
Chau *Cantonese,* Island
Chāy *Turkish,* Stream
Chhâk *Cambodian,* Bay
Chhu *Tibetan,* River
-chôsuji *Korean,* Reservoir

Chott *Arabic,* Salt lake, depression
Ch'ün-tao *Chinese,* Island group
Cordillera *Spanish,* Mountain range
Costa *Spanish,* Coast
Côte *French,* Coast
Cuchilla *Spanish,* Mountains

D

Dağı *Azerbaijani, Turkish,* Mountain
Dağları *Azerbaijani, Turkish,* Mountains
-dake *Japanese,* Peak
Danau *Indonesian,* Lake
Đao *Vietnamese,* Island
Daryā *Persian,* River
Daryācheh *Persian,* Lake
Dasht *Persian,* Plain, desert
Dawḥat *Arabic,* Bay
Dere *Turkish,* Stream
Dili *Azerbaijani,* Spit
-do *Korean,* Island
Dooxo *Somali,* Valley
Düzü *Azerbaijani,* Steppe
-dwīp *Bengali,* Island

E

Embalse *Spanish,* Reservoir
Erg *Arabic,* Dunes
Estany *Catalan,* Lake
Estrecho *Spanish,* Strait
-ey *Icelandic,* Island
Ezero *Bulgarian, Macedonian,* Lake

F

Fjord *Danish,* Fjord
-fjorden *Norwegian,* Fjord
-fjørdhur *Faeroese,* Fjord
Fleuve *French,* River
Fliegu *Maltese,* Channel
-fljór *Icelandic,* River

G

-gang *Korean,* River
Ganga *Nepali, Sinhala,* River
Gaoyuan *Chinese,* Plateau
-gawa *Japanese,* River
Gebel *Arabic,* Mountain

-gebirge *German,* Mountains
Ghubbat *Arabic,* Bay
Gjiri *Albanian,* Bay
Gol *Mongolian,* River
Golfe *French,* Gulf
Golfo *Italian, Spanish,* Gulf
Gora *Russian, Serbian,* Mountain
Gory *Russian,* Mountains
Guba *Russian,* Bay
Gunung *Malay,* Mountain

H

Ḥadd *Arabic,* Spit
-haehyŏp *Korean,* Strait
Haff *German,* Lagoon
Hai *Chinese,* Sea, bay
Ḥammādat *Arabic,* Plateau
Hāmūn *Persian,* Lake
Hawr *Arabic,* Lake
Hāyk' *Amharic,* Lake
He *Chinese,* River
Helodrano *Malagasy,* Bay
-hegység *Hungarian,* Mountain range
Hka *Burmese,* River
-ho *Korean,* Lake
Hô *Korean,* Reservoir
Holot *Hebrew,* Dunes
Hora *Belorussian,* Mountain
Hrada *Belorussian,* Mountains, ridge
Hsi *Chinese,* River
Hu *Chinese,* Lake

I

Île(s) *French,* Island(s)
Ilha(s) *Portuguese,* Island(s)
Ilhéu(s) *Portuguese,* Islet(s)
Irmak *Turkish,* River
Isla(s) *Spanish,* Island(s)
Isola (Isole) *Italian,* Island(s)

J

Jabal *Arabic,* Mountain
Jāl *Arabic,* Ridge
-järvi *Finnish,* Lake
Jazīrat *Arabic,* Island
Jazīreh *Persian,* Island
Jebel *Arabic,* Mountain

Jezero *Serbian/Croatian,* Lake
Jiang *Chinese,* River
-joki *Finnish,* River
-jökull *Icelandic,* Glacier
Juzur *Arabic,* Islands

K

Kaikyō *Japanese,* Strait
-kaise *Lappish,* Mountain
Kali *Nepali,* River
Kalnas *Lithuanian,* Mountain
Kalns *Latvian,* Mountain
Kang *Chinese,* Harbor
Kangri *Tibetan,* Mountain(s)
Kaôh *Cambodian,* Island
Kapp *Norwegian,* Cape
Kavīr *Persian,* Desert
K'edi *Georgian,* Mountain range
Kediet *Arabic,* Mountain
Kepulauan *Indonesian, Malay,* Island group
Khalîg, Khalīj *Arabic,* Gulf
Khawr *Arabic,* Inlet
Khola *Nepali,* River
Khrebet *Russian,* Mountain range
Ko *Thai,* Island
Kolpos *Greek,* Bay
-kopf *German,* Peak
Körfäzi *Azerbaijani,* Bay
Körfezi *Turkish,* Bay
Kõrgustik *Estonian,* Upland
Koshi *Nepali,* River
Kowtal *Persian,* Pass
Kūh(hā) *Persian,* Mountain(s)
-kundo *Korean,* Island group
-kysten *Norwegian,* Coast
Kyun *Burmese,* Island

L

Laaq *Somali,* Watercourse
Lac *French,* Lake
Lacul *Romanian,* Lake
Lago *Italian, Portuguese, Spanish,* Lake
Laguna *Spanish,* Lagoon, Lake

Laht *Estonian*, Bay
Laut *Indonesian*, Sea
Lembalemba *Malagasy*, Plateau
Lerr *Armenian*, Mountain
Lerrnashght'a *Armenian*, Mountain range
Les *Czech*, Forest
Lich *Armenian*, Lake
Liqeni *Albanian*, Lake
Lumi *Albanian*, River
Lyman *Ukrainian*, Estuary

M

Mae Nam *Thai*, River
-mägi *Estonian*, Hill
Maja *Albanian*, Mountain
-man *Korean*, Bay
Marios *Lithuanian*, Lake
-meer *Dutch*, Lake
Melkosopochnik *Russian*, Plain
-meri *Estonian*, Sea
Mifraz *Hebrew*, Bay
Monkhafad *Arabic*, Depression
Mont(s) *French*, Mountain(s)
Monte *Italian*, *Portuguese*, Mountain
More *Russian*, Sea
Mörön *Mongolian*, River

N

Nagor'ye *Russian*, Upland
Nahal *Hebrew*, River
Nahr *Arabic*, River
Nam *Laotian*, River
Nehri *Turkish*, River
Nevado *Spanish*, Mountain (snow-capped)
Nisoi *Greek*, Islands
Nizmennost' *Russian*, Lowland, plain
Nosy *Malagasy*, Island
Nur *Mongolian*, Lake
Nuruu *Mongolian*, Mountains
Nuur *Mongolian*, Lake
Nyzovyna *Ukrainian*, Lowland, plain

O

Ostrov(a) *Russian*, Island(s)
Oued *Arabic*, Watercourse
-oy *Faeroese*, Island
-øy(a) *Norwegian*, Island
Oya *Sinhala*, River
Ozero *Russian*, *Ukrainian*, Lake

P

Passo *Italian*, Pass
Pegunungan *Indonesian*, *Malay*, Mountain range
Pelagos *Greek*, Sea
Penisola *Italian*, Peninsula
Peski *Russian*, Sands
Phanom *Thai*, Mountain
Phou *Laotian*, Mountain
Pic *Catalan*, Peak
Pico *Portuguese*, *Spanish*, Peak
Pik *Russian*, Peak
Planalto *Portuguese*, Plateau
Planina, Planini *Bulgarian*, *Macedonian*, *Serbian*, *Croatian*, Mountain range
Ploskogor'ye *Russian*, Upland
Poluostrov *Russian*, Peninsula
Potamos *Greek*, River
Proliv *Russian*, Strait
Pulau *Indonesian*, *Malay*, Island
Pulu *Malay*, Island
Punta *Portuguese*, *Spanish*, Point

Q

Qā' *Arabic*, Depression
Qolleh *Persian*, Mountain

R

Raas *Somali*, Cape
-rags *Latvian*, Cape
Ramlat *Arabic*, Sands
Ra's *Arabic*, Cape, point, headland
Ravnina *Bulgarian*, *Russian*, Plain
Récif *French*, Reef
Represa (Rep.) *Spanish*, *Portuguese*, Reservoir
-rettō *Japanese*, Island chain
Riacho *Spanish*, Stream
Riban' *Malagasy*, Mountains
Rio *Portuguese*, River
Río *Spanish*, River
Riu *Catalan*, River
Rivier *Dutch*, River
Rivière *French*, River
Rowd *Pashtu*, River
Rūd *Persian*, River
Rudohorie *Slovak*, Mountains
Ruisseau *French*, Stream

S

Sabkhat *Arabic*, Salt marsh
Ṣaḥrā' *Arabic*, Desert
Samudra *Sinhala*, Reservoir
-san *Japanese*, *Korean*, Mountain
-sanchi *Japanese*, Mountains
-sanmaek *Korean*,
Sarīr *Arabic*, Desert
Sebkha, Sebkhet *Arabic*, Salt marsh, depression
See *German*, Lake
Selat *Indonesian*, Strait
-selkä *Finnish*, Ridge
Selseleh *Persian*, Mountain range
Serra *Portuguese*, Mountain
Serranía *Spanish*, Mountain
Sha'īb *Arabic*, Watercourse
Shamo *Chinese*, Desert
Shan *Chinese*, Mountain(s)
Shan-mo *Chinese*, Mountain range
Shaṭṭ *Arabic*, Distributary
-shima *Japanese*, Island
Shui-tao *Chinese*, Channel
Sierra *Spanish*, Mountains
Sôn *Vietnamese*, Mountain
Sông *Vietnamese*, River
-spitze *German*, Peak
Štít *Slovak*, Peak
Stoeng *Cambodian*, River
Stretto *Italian*, Strait
Su Anbarı *Azerbaijani*, Reservoir
Sungai *Indonesian*, *Malay*, River
Suu *Turkish*, River

T

Tal *Mongolian*, Plain
Tandavan' *Malagasy*, Mountain range
Tangorombohitr' *Malagasy*, Mountain massif
Tao *Chinese*, Island
Tassili *Berber*, Plateau, mountain
Tau *Russian*, Mountain(s)
Taungdan *Burmese*, Mountain range
Teluk *Indonesian*, *Malay*, Bay

Terara *Amharic*, Mountain
Tog *Somali*, Valley
Tônlé *Cambodian*, Lake
Top *Dutch*, Peak
-tunturi *Finnish*, Mountain
Tur'at *Arabic*, Channel

V

Väin *Estonian*, Strait
-vatn *Icelandic*, Lake
-vesi *Finnish*, Lake
Vinh *Vietnamese*, Bay
Vodokhranilishche (Vdkhr.) *Russian*, Reservoir
Vodoskhovyshche (Vdskh.) *Ukrainian*, Reservoir
Volcán *Spanish*, Volcano
Vozvyshennost' *Russian*, Upland, plateau
Vrh *Macedonian*, Peak
Vysochyna *Ukrainian*, Upland
Vysočina *Czech*, Upland

W

Waadi *Somali*, Watercourse
Wādī *Arabic*, Watercourse
Wāḥat, Wâhat *Arabic*, Oasis
Wald *German*, Forest
Wan *Chinese*, Bay
Wyżyna *Polish*, Upland

X

Xé *Laotian*, River

Y

Yarımadası *Azerbaijani*, Peninsula
Yazovir *Bulgarian*, Reservoir
Yoma *Burmese*, Mountains
Yü *Chinese*, Island

Z

Zaliv *Bulgarian*, *Russian*, Bay
Zatoka *Ukrainian*, Bay
Zemlya *Russian*, Land

CONTINENTAL FACTFILES

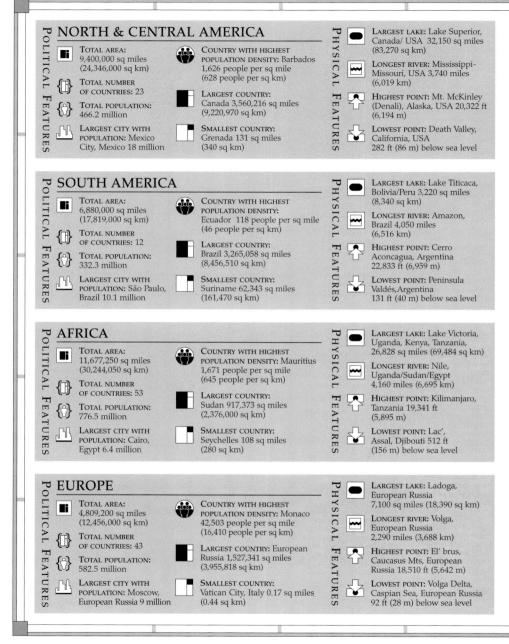

NORTH & CENTRAL AMERICA

POLITICAL FEATURES

TOTAL AREA:
9,400,000 sq miles
(24,346,000 sq km)

TOTAL NUMBER OF COUNTRIES: 23

TOTAL POPULATION:
466.2 million

LARGEST CITY WITH POPULATION: Mexico City, Mexico 18 million

COUNTRY WITH HIGHEST POPULATION DENSITY: Barbados 1,626 people per sq mile (628 people per sq km)

LARGEST COUNTRY:
Canada 3,560,216 sq miles
(9,220,970 sq km)

SMALLEST COUNTRY:
Grenada 131 sq miles
(340 sq km)

PHYSICAL FEATURES

LARGEST LAKE: Lake Superior, Canada/ USA 32,150 sq miles (83,270 sq km)

LONGEST RIVER: Mississippi-Missouri, USA 3,740 miles (6,019 km)

HIGHEST POINT: Mt. McKinley (Denali), Alaska, USA 20,322 ft (6,194 m)

LOWEST POINT: Death Valley, California, USA 282 ft (86 m) below sea level

SOUTH AMERICA

POLITICAL FEATURES

TOTAL AREA:
6,880,000 sq miles
(17,819,000 sq km)

TOTAL NUMBER OF COUNTRIES: 12

TOTAL POPULATION:
332.3 million

LARGEST CITY WITH POPULATION: São Paulo, Brazil 10.1 million

COUNTRY WITH HIGHEST POPULATION DENSITY:
Ecuador 118 people per sq mile
(46 people per sq km)

LARGEST COUNTRY:
Brazil 3,265,058 sq miles
(8,456,510 sq km)

SMALLEST COUNTRY:
Suriname 62,343 sq miles
(161,470 sq km)

PHYSICAL FEATURES

LARGEST LAKE: Lake Titicaca, Bolivia/Peru 3,220 sq miles (8,340 sq km)

LONGEST RIVER: Amazon, Brazil 4,050 miles (6,516 km)

HIGHEST POINT: Cerro Aconcagua, Argentina 22,833 ft (6,959 m)

LOWEST POINT: Peninsula Valdés, Argentina 131 ft (40 m) below sea level

AFRICA

POLITICAL FEATURES

TOTAL AREA:
11,677,250 sq miles
(30,244,050 sq km)

TOTAL NUMBER OF COUNTRIES: 53

TOTAL POPULATION:
776.5 million

LARGEST CITY WITH POPULATION: Cairo, Egypt 6.4 million

COUNTRY WITH HIGHEST POPULATION DENSITY: Mauritius 1,671 people per sq mile (645 people per sq km)

LARGEST COUNTRY:
Sudan 917,373 sq miles
(2,376,000 sq km)

SMALLEST COUNTRY:
Seychelles 108 sq miles
(280 sq km)

PHYSICAL FEATURES

LARGEST LAKE: Lake Victoria, Uganda, Kenya, Tanzania, 26,828 sq miles (69,484 sq km)

LONGEST RIVER: Nile, Uganda/Sudan/Egypt 4,160 miles (6,695 km)

HIGHEST POINT: Kilimanjaro, Tanzania 19,341 ft (5,895 m)

LOWEST POINT: Lac', Assal, Djibouti 512 ft (156 m) below sea level

EUROPE

POLITICAL FEATURES

TOTAL AREA:
4,809,200 sq miles
(12,456,000 sq km)

TOTAL NUMBER OF COUNTRIES: 43

TOTAL POPULATION:
582.5 million

LARGEST CITY WITH POPULATION: Moscow, European Russia 9 million

COUNTRY WITH HIGHEST POPULATION DENSITY: Monaco 42,503 people per sq mile (16,410 people per sq km)

LARGEST COUNTRY: European Russia 1,527,341 sq miles (3,955,818 sq km)

SMALLEST COUNTRY:
Vatican City, Italy 0.17 sq miles
(0.44 sq km)

PHYSICAL FEATURES

LARGEST LAKE: Ladoga, European Russia 7,100 sq miles (18,390 sq km)

LONGEST RIVER: Volga, European Russia 2,290 miles (3,688 km)

HIGHEST POINT: El' brus, Caucasus Mts, European Russia 18,510 ft (5,642 m)

LOWEST POINT: Volga Delta, Caspian Sea, European Russia 92 ft (28 m) below sea level

NORTH & WEST ASIA

POLITICAL FEATURES

TOTAL AREA:
9,585,550 sq miles
(24,826,600 sq km)

TOTAL NUMBER OF COUNTRIES: 24

TOTAL POPULATION:
478.6 million

LARGEST CITY WITH POPULATION: Istanbul, Turkey 6.5 million

COUNTRY WITH HIGHEST POPULATION DENSITY: Bahrain 2,350 people per sq mile (891 people per sq km)

LARGEST COUNTRY: Asiatic Russia 5,065,471 square miles (13,119,582 sq km)

SMALLEST COUNTRY: Bahrain 263 sq miles (680 sq km)

PHYSICAL FEATURES

LARGEST LAKE: Caspian Sea 142,243 sq miles (371,000 sq km)

LONGEST RIVER: Ob'-Irtysh, Asiatic Russia 3,461 miles (5,570 km)

HIGHEST POINT: Pik Pobedy, Kyrgyzstan/China 24,408 ft (7,439 m)

LOWEST POINT: Dead Sea, Israel/Jordan 1,286 ft (392 m) below sea level

SOUTH & EAST ASIA

POLITICAL FEATURES

TOTAL AREA:
7,936,200 sq miles
(20,554,700 sq km)

TOTAL NUMBER OF COUNTRIES: 23

TOTAL POPULATION:
3,300 million

LARGEST CITY WITH POPULATION: Tokyo, Japan 18.1 million

COUNTRY WITH HIGHEST POPULATION DENSITY: Singapore 15,285 people per sq mile (5,902 people per sq km)

LARGEST COUNTRY: China 3,600,926 sq miles (9,326,410 sq km)

SMALLEST COUNTRY: Maldives 116 sq miles (300 sq km)

PHYSICAL FEATURES

LARGEST LAKE: Tônlé Sap, Cambodia 100 sq miles (2,850 sq km)

LONGEST RIVER: Chang Jiang (Yangtze), China 3,965 miles (6,380 km)

HIGHEST POINT: Mount Everest, Nepal 29,030 ft (8,848 m)

LOWEST POINT: Turpan Hami (Turfan Basin), China 505 ft (154 m) below sea level

AUSTRALASIA & OCEANIA

POLITICAL FEATURES

TOTAL AREA:
3,376,700 sq miles
(8,745,750 sq km)

TOTAL NUMBER OF COUNTRIES: 14

TOTAL POPULATION:
28.6 million

LARGEST CITY WITH POPULATION: Sydney, Australia 3.7 million

COUNTRY WITH HIGHEST POPULATION DENSITY: Nauru 1,381 people per sq mile (548 people per sq km)

LARGEST COUNTRY: Australia 2,941,282 sq miles (7,617,930 sq km)

SMALLEST COUNTRY: Nauru 8 sq miles (21 sq km)

PHYSICAL FEATURES

LARGEST LAKE: Lake Eyre, Australia 3,430 sq miles (8,884 sq km)

LONGEST RIVER: Murray-Darling, Australia 2,330 miles (3,750 km)

HIGHEST POINT: Mt. Wilhelm Papua New Guinea 14,794 ft (4,509 m)

LOWEST POINT: Lake Eyre, Australia 52 ft (16 m) below sea level

ANTARCTICA

POLITICAL FEATURES

TOTAL AREA: 5,405,500 sq miles (14,000,000 sq km) of which approx. 324,300 sq miles (840,000 sq km) is ice-free

TOTAL NUMBER OF COUNTRIES: The Antarctic Treaty has 30 participating nations and 14 with observer status. Claims by Australia, France, New Zealand, Norway, Argentina, Chile and the UK are not recognized by other member states.

TOTAL POPULATION: No indigenous population. 74 research stations, (42 are staffed all year-round). Population varies between about 1,000 (winter) and 4,000 (summer).

PHYSICAL FEATURES

TOTAL VOLUME OF ICE: 7,200,000 cu miles (30,000,000 cu km): contains 90% of the Earth's fresh water

SEA ICE: 1,158,300 sq miles (3,000,000 sq km) in February. 7,722,000 sq miles (20,000,000 sq km) in October

LOWEST TEMPERATURE: Vostok Station -89.5°C (-129°F)

HIGHEST POINT: Vinson Massif 16,072 ft (4,897 m)

LOWEST POINT: Coastline 0ft/m

163

GEOGRAPHICAL COMPARISONS

LARGEST COUNTRIES

Russ. Fed.	.....6,592,812 sq miles	..(17,075,400 sq km)
China	........3,600,926 sq miles	...(9,326,410 sq km)
Canada	.......3,560,216 sq miles	...(9,220,970 sq km)
USA	.........3,539,224 sq miles	..(9,166,600 sq km)
Brazil	........3,265,058 sq miles	..(8,456,510 sq km)
Australia	.....2,941,282 sq miles	...(7,617,930 sq km)
India	..........1,147,948 sq miles	..(2,973,190 sq km)
Argentina	....1,056,636 sq miles	...(2,736,690 sq km)
Kazakhstan	....1,049,150 sq miles	..(2,717,300 sq km)
Sudan	..........917,373 sq miles	..(2,376,000 sq km)

SMALLEST COUNTRIES

Vatican City	.......0.17 sq miles	.......(0.44 sq km)
Monaco	............0.75 sq miles	......(1.95 sq km)
Nauru	...............8 sq miles	........(21 sq km)
Tuvalu	...............10 sq miles	.......(26 sq km)
San Marino	.........24 sq miles	......(61 sq km)
Liechtenstein	........62 sq miles	.....(160 sq km)
Marshall Islands	.....70 sq miles	......(181 sq km)
Seychelles	..........108 sq miles	......(280 sq km)
Maldives	..........116 sq miles	.....(300 sq km)
Malta	.............124 sq miles	......(320 sq km)

LARGEST ISLANDS

(TO THE NEAREST 1,000 - OR 100,000 FOR THE LARGEST)

Greenland	......849,400 sq miles	...(2,200,000 sq km)
New Guinea	.....312,000 sq miles	.....(808,000 sq km)
Borneo	..........292,222 sq miles	......(757,050 sq km)
Madagascar	.....229,300 sq miles	.....(594,000 sq km)
Sumatra	........202,300 sq miles	.....(524,000 sq km)
Baffin Island	.....183,800 sq miles	.....(476,000 sq km)
Honshu	..........88,800 sq miles	.....(230,000 sq km)
Britain	..........88,700 sq miles	.....(229,800 sq km)
Victoria Island	....81,900 sq miles	.....(212,000 sq km)
Ellesmere Island	.75,700 sq miles	.....(196,000 sq km)

RICHEST COUNTRIES

(GNP PER CAPITA, IN US$)

Liechtenstein	52,200
Luxembourg	45,360
Switzerland	39,980
Japan	38,160
Norway	36,100
Denmark	34,890
Singapore	32,810
USA	29,080
Germany	28,280
Austria	27,920

POOREST COUNTRIES

(GNP PER CAPITA, IN US$)

Somalia	100
Ethiopia	110
Congo, Dem. Rep. (Zaire)	110
Mozambique	140
Burundi	140
Sierra Leone	160
Niger	200
Tanzania	210
Malawi	210
Rwanda	210
Eritrea	230
Chad	230

MOST POPULOUS COUNTRIES

China	1,300,000,000
India	1,000,000,000
USA	278,400,000
Indonesia	212,000,000
Brazil	170,000,000
Pakistan	156,500,000
Russian Federation	147,000,000
Bangladesh	129,000,000
Japan	126,700,000
Nigeria	112,000,000

LEAST POPULOUS COUNTRIES

Vatican City	1,000
Tuvalu	11,100
Nauru	11,500
Palau	18,500
San Marino	26,000
Liechtenstein	32,000
Monaco	32,000
St. Kitts & Nevis	41,000
Marshall Islands	51,000
Andorra	66,000
Dominica	73,000
Seychelles	79,000

MOST DENSELY POPULATED COUNTRIES

Monaco	....42,503 people per sq mile	..(16,410 per sq km)
Singapore	..15,285 people per sq mile	...(5,902 per sq km)
Vatican City	.5,886 people per sq mile	...(2,273 per sq km)
Malta	.....3,148 people per sq mile	..(1,216 per sq km)
Bangladesh	.2,499 people per sq mile	....(965 per sq km)
Maldives	....2,469 people per sq mile	....(953 per sq km)
Bahrain	....2,350 people per sq mile	....(891 per sq km)
Taiwan	....1,756 people per sq mile	....(678 per sq km)
Mauritius	...1,671 people per sq mile	....(645 per sq km)
Barbados	...1,626 people per sq mile	....(628 per sq km)

MOST SPARSELY POPULATED COUNTRIES

Mongolia . . . . .4 people per sq mile . . . . . .(2 per sq km)
Namibia . . . . . .5 people per sq mile . . . . .(2 per sq km)
Australia . . . . . .6 people per sq mile . . . . . .(2 per sq km)
Mauritania . . . .6 people per sq mile . . . . .(2 per sq km)
Suriname . . . . .7 people per sq mile . . . . . .(3 per sq km)
Botswana . . . . .7 people per sq mile . . . . . .(3 per sq km)
Iceland . . . . . . .7 people per sq mile . . . . . .(3 per sq km)
Canada . . . . . . .8 people per sq mile . . . . . .(3 per sq km)
Libya . . . . .9 people per sq mile . . . . .(3 per sq km)
Guyana . . . . . .11 people per sq mile . . . . .(4 per sq km)

MOST WIDELY SPOKEN LANGUAGES

1. Chinese (Mandarin)   6. Arabic
2. English   7. Bengali
3. Hindi   8. Portuguese
4. Spanish   9. Malay-Indonesian
5. Russian   10. French

COUNTRIES WITH THE MOST LAND BORDERS

14: **China** *(Afghanistan, Bhutan, Myanmar, India, Kazakhstan, Kyrgyzstan, Laos, Mongolia, Nepal, North Korea, Pakistan, Russian Federation, Tajikistan, Vietnam)*

14: **Russian Federation** *(Azerbaijan, Belarus, China, Estonia, Finland, Georgia, Kazakhstan, Latvia, Lithuania, Mongolia, North Korea, Norway, Poland, Ukraine)*

10: **Brazil** *(Argentina, Bolivia, Colombia, French Guiana, Guyana, Paraguay, Peru, Suriname, Uruguay, Venezuela)*

9: **Congo, Dem. Rep. (Zaire)** *(Angola, Burundi, Central African Republic, Congo, Rwanda, Sudan, Tanzania, Uganda, Zambia)*

9: **Germany** *(Austria, Belgium, Czech Republic, Denmark, France, Luxembourg, Netherlands, Poland, Switzerland)*

9: **Sudan** *(Central African Republic, Chad, Congo, Dem. Rep. (Zaire), Egypt, Eritrea, Ethiopia, Kenya, Libya, Uganda)*

8: **Austria** *(Czech Republic, Germany, Hungary, Italy, Liechtenstein, Slovakia, Slovenia, Switzerland)*

8: **France** *(Andorra, Belgium, Germany, Italy, Luxembourg, Monaco, Spain, Switzerland)*

8: **Tanzania** *(Burundi, Congo, Dem. Rep. (Zaire), Kenya, Malawi, Mozambique, Rwanda, Uganda, Zambia)*

8: **Turkey** *(Armenia, Azerbaijan, Bulgaria, Georgia, Greece, Iran, Iraq, Syria)*

8: **Zambia** *(Angola, Botswana, Congo, Dem. Rep. (Zaire), Malawi, Mozambique, Namibia, Tanzania, Zimbabwe)*

LONGEST RIVERS

Nile (NE Africa) . . . . .4,160 miles . . . . . .(6,695 km)
Amazon (South America) . .4,049 miles . . . . . .(6,516 km)
Yangtze (China) . . . . .3,915 miles . . . . . .(6,299 km)
Mississippi/Missouri (US) .3,710 miles . . . . . .(5,969 km)
Ob'-Irtysh (Russ. Fed.) . . .3,461 miles . . . . . .(5,570 km)
Yellow River (China) . . . .3,395 miles . . . . . .(5,464 km)
Congo (Central Africa) . . . .2,900 miles . . . . . .(4,667 km)
Mekong (Southeast Asia) . .2,749 miles . . . . . .(4,425 km)
Lena (Russian Federation) . .2,734 miles . . . . . .(4,400 km)
Mackenzie (Canada) . . . . .2,640 miles . . . . . .(4,250 km)
Yenisey (Russ. Federation) .2,541 miles . . . . . .(4,090 km)

HIGHEST MOUNTAINS

(HEIGHT ABOVE SEA LEVEL)

Everest . . . . .29,030 ft . . . .(8,848 m)
K2 . . . . .28,253 ft . . . .(8,611 m)
Kanchenjunga I . . . . .28,210 ft . . . .(8,598 m)
Makalu I . . . . .27,767 ft . . . .(8,463 m)
Cho Oyu . . . . .26,907 ft . . . .(8,201 m)
Dhaulagiri I . . . . .26,796 ft . . . .(8,167 m)
Manaslu I . . . . .26,783 ft . . . .(8,163 m)
Nanga Parbat I . . . . .26,661 ft . . . .(8,126 m)
Annapurna I . . . . .26,547 ft . . . .(8,091 m)
Gasherbrum I . . . . .26,471 ft . . . .(8,068 m)

LARGEST BODIES OF INLAND WATER

(WITH AREA AND DEPTH)

Caspian Sea
143,243 sq miles (371,000 sq km) . . .3,215 ft (980 m)
Lake Superior
32,150 sq miles (83,270 sq km) . . . . .1,289 ft (393 m)
Lake Victoria
26,828 sq miles (69,484 sq km) . . . . . .328 ft (100 m)
Lake Huron
23,436 sq miles (60,700 sq km) . . . . . .751 ft (229 m)
Lake Michigan
22,402 sq miles (58,020 sq km) . . . . . .922 ft (281 m)
Lake Tanganyika
12,703 sq miles (32,900 sq km) . . .4,700 ft (1,435 m)
Great Bear Lake
12,274 sq miles (31,790 sq km) . . . . .1,047 ft (319 m)
Lake Baikal
11,776 sq miles (30,500 sq km) . . .5,712 ft (1,741 m)
Great Slave Lake
10,981 sq miles (28,440 sq km) . . . . . .459 ft (140 m)
Lake Erie
9,915 sq miles (25,680 sq km) . . . . .197 ft (60 m)

......continued on p.166

GEOGRAPHICAL COMPARISONS *continued*

DEEPEST OCEAN FEATURES

Challenger Deep, Marianas Trench (Pacific)
36,201 ft . . . . (11,034 m)
Vityaz III Depth, Tonga Trench (Pacific)
35,704 ft . . . . (10,882 m)
Vityaz Depth, Kurile-Kamchatka Trench (Pacific)
34,588 ft . . . . (10,542 m)
Cape Johnson Deep, Philippine Trench (Pacific)
34,441 ft . . . . (10,497 m)
Kermadec Trench (Pacific)
32,964 ft . . . . (10,047 m)
Ramapo Deep, Japan Trench (Pacific)
32,758 ft . . . .(9,984 m)
Milwaukee Deep, Puerto Rico Trench (Atlantic)
30,185 ft . . . .(9,200 m)
Argo Deep, Torres Trench (Pacific)
30,070 ft . . . .(9,165 m)
Meteor Depth, South Sandwich Trench (Atlantic)
30,000 ft . . . .(9,144 m)
Planet Deep, New Britain Trench (Pacific)
29,988 ft . . . .(9,140 m)

GREATEST WATERFALLS
(MEAN FLOW OF WATER)

Boyoma (Congo (Zaire) 600,400 cu. ft/sec (17,000 cu.m/sec)
Khône (Laos/Cambodia) 410,000 cu. ft/sec (11,600 cu.m/sec)
Niagara (USA/Canada) 195,000 cu. ft/sec (5,500 cu.m/sec)
Grande (Uruguay) . . . .160,000 cu. ft/sec (4,500 cu.m/sec)
Paulo Afonso (Brazil) 100,000 cu. ft/sec (2,800 cu.m/sec)
Urubupunga (Brazil) . .97,000 cu. ft/sec (2,750 cu.m/sec)
Iguaçu (Argentina/Brazil) 62,000 cu. ft/sec   (1,700 cu.m/sec)
Maribondo (Brazil) . . . .53,000 cu. ft/sec (1,500 cu.m/sec)
Victoria (Zimbabwe) . . .39,000 cu. ft/sec (1,100 cu.m/sec)
Kabalega (Uganda) . . . .42,000 cu. ft/sec (1,200 cu.m/sec)
Churchill (Canada) . . . .35,000 cu. ft/sec (1,000 cu.m/sec)
Cauvery (India) . . . . .33,000 cu. ft/sec   (900 cu.m/sec)

HIGHEST WATERFALLS

Angel (Venezuela) . . . . .3,212 ft . . . .(979 m)
Tugela (South Africa) . . . . . .3,110 ft . . . .(948 m)
Utigard (Norway) . . . . .2,625 ft . . . .(800 m)
Mongefossen (Norway) . . . .2,539 ft . . . .(774 m)
Mtarazi (Zimbabwe) . . . . . . .2,500 ft . . . .(762 m)
Yosemite (USA) . . . . .2,425 ft . . . .(739 m)
Ostre Mardola Foss (Norway) 2,156 ft . . . .(657 m)
Tyssestrengane (Norway) . .2,119 ft . . . .(646 m)
*Cuquenan (Venezuela) . . . .2,001 ft . . . .(610 m)
Sutherland (New Zealand) . .1,903 ft . . . .(580 m)
*Kjellfossen (Norway) . . . . .1,841 ft . . . .(561 m)

indicates that the total height is a single leap

LARGEST DESERTS

Sahara . . . . .3,450,000 sq miles . .(9,065,000 sq km)
Gobi . . . . .500,000 sq miles . .(1,295,000 sq km)
Ar Rub al Khali . .289,600 sq miles . . . .(750,000 sq km)
Great Victorian . .249,800 sq miles . . . .(647,000 sq km)
Sonoran . . . . .120,000 sq miles . . . .(311,000 sq km)
Kalahari . . . . .120,000 sq miles . . . .(310,800 sq km)
Kara Kum . . . . . . .115,800 sq miles . . . .(300,000 sq km)
Takla Makan . . . . .100,400 sq miles . . . .(260,000 sq km)
Namib . . . . .52,100 sq miles . . . .(135,000 sq km)
Thar . . . . .33,670 sq miles . . .(130,000 sq km)
*NB – Most of Antarctica is a polar desert, with only
50 mm of precipitation annually*

HOTTEST INHABITED PLACES

Djibouti (Djibouti) . . . . .86° F . . . .(30 °C)
Timbouctou (Mali) . . . . . . .84.7° F . . . .(29.3 °C)
Tirunelveli (India)
Tuticorin (India)
Nellore (India) . . . . .84.5° F . . . .(29.2 °C)
Santa Marta (Colombia) .
Aden (Yemen) . . . . .84° F . . . .(28.9 °C)
Madurai (India)
Niamey (Niger)
Hodeida (Yemen) . . . . .83.8° F . . . .(28.8 °C)
Ouagadougou (Burkina Faso)
Thanjavur (India)
Tiruchchirappalli (India)

DRIEST INHABITED PLACES

Aswân (Egypt) . . . . .0.02 in . . . . . .(0.5 mm)
Luxor (Egypt) . . . . .0.03 in . . . . . .(0.7 mm)
Arica (Chile) . . . . .0.04 in . . . . . .(1.1 mm)
Ica (Peru) . . . . .0.1 in . . . . . .(2.3 mm)
Antofagasta (Chile) . . . . .0.2 in . . . . . .(4.9 mm)
El Minya (Egypt) . . . . .0.2 in . . . . . .(5.1 mm)
Asyût (Egypt) . . . . .0.2 in . . . . . .(5.2 mm)
Callao (Peru) . . . . .0.5 in . . . . .(12.0 mm)
Trujillo (Peru) . . . . .0.55 in . . . . .(14.0 mm)
El Faiyûm (Egypt) . . . . .0.8 in . . . . .(19.0 mm)

WETTEST INHABITED PLACES

Buenaventura (Colombia) . . . . .265 in . . . . . .(6,743 mm)
Monrovia (Liberia) . . . . .202 in . . . . . .(5,131 mm)
Pago Pago (American Samoa) . . .196 in . . . . . .(4,990 mm)
Moulmein (Myanmar) . . . . .191 in . . . . . .(4,852 mm)
Lae (Papua New Guinea) . . . . . .183 in . . . . . .(4,645 mm)
Baguio (Luzon Island, Philippines)180 in . . . . . .(4,573 mm)
Sylhet (Bangladesh) . . . . .176 in . . . . . .(4,457 mm)
Padang (Sumatra, Indonesia) . .166 in . . . . . .(4,225 mm)
Bogor (Java, Indonesia) . . . . . . .166 in . . . . . .(4,225 mm)
Conakry (Guinea) . . . . .171 in . . . . . .(4,341 mm)

GLOSSARY OF ABBREVIATIONS

This Glossary provides a comprehensive guide to the abbreviations used in this Atlas, and in the Index.

A
abbrev. abbreviated
Afr. Afrikaans
Alb. Albanian
Amh. Amharic
anc. ancient
Ar. Arabic
Arm. Armenian
Az. Azerbaijani

B
Basq. Basque
Bel. Belorussian
Ben. Bengali
Bibl. Biblical
Bret. Breton
Bul. Bulgarian
Bur. Burmese

C
Cam. Cambodian
Cant. Cantonese
Cast. Castilian
Cat. Catalan
Chin. Chinese
Cro. Croat
Cz. Czech

D
Dan. Danish
Dut. Dutch

E
Eng. English
Est. Estonian
est. estimated

F
Faer. Faeroese
Fij. Fijian
Fin. Finnish
Flem. Flemish
Fr. French
Fris. Frisian

G
Geor. Georgian
Ger. German
Gk. Greek
Guj. Gujarati

H
Haw. Hawaiian
Heb. Hebrew
Hind. Hindi
hist. historical
Hung. Hungarian

I
Icel. Icelandic
Ind. Indonesian
In. Inuit
Ir. Irish
It. Italian

J
Jap. Japanese

K
Kaz. Kazakh
Kir. Kirghiz
Kor. Korean
Kurd. Kurdish

L
Lao. Laotian
Lapp. Lappish
Lat. Latin
Latv. Latvian
Lith. Lithanian
Lus. Lusatian

M
Mac. Macedonian
Mal. Malay
Malg. Malagasy
Malt. Maltese
Mong. Mongolian

N
Nepali. Nepali
Nor. Norwegian

O
off. officially

P
Pash. Pashtu
Per. Persian
Pol. Polish
Port. Portuguese
prev. previously

R
Rmsch. Romansch
Roman. Romanian
Rus. Russian

S
SCr. Serbo - Croatian
Serb. Serbian
Slvk. Slovak
Slvn. Slovene
Som. Somali
Sp. Spanish
Swa. Swahili
Swe. Swedish

T
Taj. Tajik
Th. Thai
Tib. Tibetan
Turk. Turkish
Turkm. Turkmenistan

U
Uigh. Uighur
Ukr. Ukrainian
Uzb. Uzbek

V
var. variant
Vtn. Vietnamese

W
Wel. Welsh

X
Xh. Xhosa

Y
Yugo. Yugoslavia

Key to country factboxes within the Index:

Formation
Date of independence

Population
Total population / population density - based on total *land* area .

Calorie consumption
Average number of calories consumed daily per person.

INDEX

A

Aachen *94 A4 Dut.* Aken, *Fr.* Aix-la-Chapelle; *anc.* Aquae Grani, Aquisgranum. Nordrhein-Westfalen, W Germany
Aaiún *see* Laâyoune
Aalborg *see* Ålborg
Aalen *95 B6* Baden-Württemberg, S Germany
Aalsmeer *86 C3* Noord-Holland, C Netherlands
Aalst *87 B6 Fr.* Alost. Oost-Vlaanderen, C Belgium
Aalten *86 E4* Gelderland, E Netherlands
Aalter *87 B5* Oost-Vlaanderen, NW Belgium
Äänekoski *85 D5* Länsi-Suomi, W Finland
Aar *see* Aare
Aare *95 A7 var.* Aar. *River* W Switzerland
Aarhus *see* Århus
Aat *see* Ath
Aba *75 G5* Abia, S Nigeria
Aba *77 E5* Orientale, NE Dem. Rep. Congo (Zaire)
Abā as Su'ūd *see* Najrān
Abaco Island *see* Great Abaco
Ābādān *120 C4* Khūzestān, SW Iran
Abai *see* Blue Nile
Abakan *114 D4* Respublika Khakasiya, S Russian Federation
Abancay *60 D4* Apurímac, SE Peru
Abariringa *see* Kanton
Abashiri *130 D2 var.* Abasiri. Hokkaidō, NE Japan
Abasiri *see* Abashiri
Ābaya Hāyk' *73 C5 Eng.* Lake Margherita, *It.* Abbaia. *Lake* SW Ethiopia
Ābay Wenz *see* Blue Nile
Abbeville *90 C2 anc.* Abbatis Villa. Somme, N France
'Abd al 'Azīz, Jabal *118 D2 mountain range* NE Syria
Abéché *76 C3 var.* Abécher, Abeshr. Ouaddaï, SE Chad
Abécher *see* Abéché
Abela *see* Ávila
Abemama *144 D2 var.* Apamama; *prev.* Roger Simpson Island. *Atoll* Tungaru, W Kiribati
Abengourou *75 E5* E Côte d'Ivoire
Aberdeen *88 D3 anc.* Devana. NE Scotland, UK
Aberdeen *45 E2* South Dakota, N USA
Aberdeen *46 B2* Washington, NW USA
Abergwaun *see* Fishguard
Abertawe *see* Swansea
Aberystwyth *89 C6* W Wales, UK
Abeshr *see* Abéché
Abhā *121 B6* 'Asīr, SW Saudi Arabia
Abidavichy *107 D7 Rus.* Obidovichi. Mahilyowskaya Voblasts', E Belarus
Abidjan *75 E5* S Côte d'Ivoire
Abilene *49 F3* Texas, SW USA
Abingdon *see* Pinta, Isla
Abkhazia *117 E1 autonomous republic* NW Georgia
Åbo *85 D6* Länsi-Suomi, W Finland
Aboisso *75 E5* SE Côte d'Ivoire
Abo, Massif d' *76 B1 mountain range* NW Chad
Abomey *75 F5* S Benin
Abou-Déïa *76 C3* Salamat, SE Chad
Abrantes *92 B3 var.* Abrántes. Santarém, C Portugal
Abrolhos Bank *56 E4 undersea feature* W Atlantic Ocean
Abrova *107 B6 Rus.* Obrovo. Brestskaya Voblasts', SW Belarus
Abrud *108 B4 Ger.* Gross-Schlatten, *Hung.* Abrudbánya. Alba, SW Romania

Abruzzese, Appennino *96 C4 mountain range* C Italy
Absaroka Range *44 B2 mountain range* Montana/Wyoming, NW USA
Abū aḏ Đuhūr *118 B3 Fr.* Aboudouhour. Idlib, NW Syria
Abu Dhabi *see* Abū Ẓaby
Abu Hamed *72 C3 River Nile, N Sudan
Abū Ḥardān *118 E3 var.* Hajîne. Dayr az Zawr, E Syria
Abuja *75 G4 country capital* (Nigeria) Federal Capital District, C Nigeria
Abū Kamāl *118 E3 Fr.* Abou Kémal. Dayr az Zawr, E Syria
Abula *see* Ávila
Abunã, Rio *62 C2 var.* Río Abuná. *River* Bolivia/Brazil
Abut Head *151 B6 headland* South Island, NZ
Ābuyē Mēda *72 D4 mountain* C Ethiopia
Abū Ẓabī *see* Abū Ẓaby
Abū Ẓaby *121 C5 var.* Abū Ẓabī, *Eng.* Abu Dhabi. *Country capital* (UAE) Abū Ẓaby, C UAE
Abyla *see* Ávila
Acalayong *77 A5* SW Equatorial Guinea
Acaponeta *50 D4* Nayarit, C Mexico
Acapulco *51 E5 var.* Acapulco de Juárez. Guerrero, S Mexico
Acapulco de Juárez *see* Acapulco
Acarai Mountains *59 F4 Sp.* Serra Acaraí. *Mountain range* Brazil/Guyana
Acarigua *58 D2* Portuguesa, N Venezuela
Accra *75 E5 country capital* (Ghana) SE Ghana
Achacachi *61 E4* La Paz, W Bolivia
Acklins Island *54 C2 island* SE Bahamas
Aconcagua, Cerro *64 B4 mountain* W Argentina
Açores *see* Azores
A Coruña *92 B1 Cast.* La Coruña, *Eng.* Corunna; *anc.* Caronium. Galicia, NW Spain
Acre *62 C2 off.* Estado do Acre. *State* W Brazil
Açu *63 G2 var.* Assu. Rio Grande do Norte, E Brazil
Ada *49 G2* Oklahoma, C USA
Ada *100 D3* Serbia, N Yugoslavia
Adalia, Gulf of *see* Antalya Körfezi
Adama *see* Nazrēt
Adamawa Highlands *76 B4 plateau* NW Cameroon
'Adan *121 B7 Eng.* Aden. SW Yemen
Adana *116 D4 var.* Seyhan. Adana, S Turkey
Adapazarı *116 B2 prev.* Ada Bazar. Sakarya, NW Turkey
Adare, Cape *154 B4 headland* Antarctica
Ad Dahnā' *120 C4 desert* E Saudi Arabia
Ad Dakhla *70 A4 var.* Dakhla. SW Western Sahara
Ad Dalanj *see* Dilling
Ad Damar *see* Ed Damer
Ad Damazin *see* Ed Damazin
Ad Dāmir *see* Ed Damer
Ad Dammām *120 C4 var.* Dammām. Ash Sharqīyah, NE Saudi Arabia
Ad Dāmūr *see* Damoûr
Ad Dawḥah *120 C4 Eng.* Doha. *Country capital* (Qatar) C Qatar
Aḏ Ḏiffah *see* Libyan Plateau
Addis Ababa *see* Ādīs Ābeba
Addu Atoll *132 A5 atoll* S Maldives
Adelaide *149 B6 state capital* South Australia
Aden *see* 'Adan
Aden, Gulf of *121 C7 gulf* SW Arabian Sea
Adige *96 C2 Ger.* Etsch. *River* N Italy

Adirondack Mountains 41 F2 *mountain range* New York, NE USA

Ādīs Ābeba 73 C5 *Eng.* Addis Ababa. *Country capital* (Ethiopia) C Ethiopia

Adıyaman 117 E4 Adıyaman, SE Turkey

Adjud 108 C4 Vrancea, E Romania

Admiralty Islands 144 B3 *island group* N PNG

Adra 93 E5 Andalucía, S Spain

Adrar 70 D3 C Algeria

Adrar des Iforas *see* Ifôghas, Adrar des

Adrian 40 C3 Michigan, N USA

Adriatic Sea 103 E2 *Alb.* Deti Adriatik, *It.* Mare Adriatico, *SCr.* Jadransko More, *Slvn.* Jadransko Morje. *Sea* N Mediterranean Sea

Adycha 115 F2 *river* NE Russian Federation

Aegean Sea 105 C5 *Gk.* Aigaíon Pélagos, Aigaío Pélagos, *Turk.* Ege Denizi. *Sea* NE Mediterranean Sea

Aegviidu 106 D2 *Ger.* Charlottenhof. Harjumaa, NW Estonia

Aelana *see* Al 'Aqabah

Aelok *see* Ailuk Atoll

Aelōnlaplap *see* Ailinglaplap Atoll

Aeolian Islands *see* Eolie, Isole

Afar Depression *see* Danakil Desert

Afghanistan 122 C4 *Per.* Dowlat-e Eslāmī-ye Afghānestān; *prev.* Republic of Afghanistan. *Country* C Asia

Afghanistan 122

Official name Islamic State of Afghanistan
Formation 1919
Capital Kabul
Population 22.7 million / 90 people per sq mile (35 people per sq km)
Total area 251,771 sq miles (652,090 sq km)
Languages Persian, Pashtu, Dari
Religions Sunni Muslim 84%, Shi'a Muslim 15%, other 1%
Ethnic mix Pashto 52%, Tajik 21%, Hazara 19%, Uzbek 5%, other 3%
Government Islamic regime
Currency Afghani = 100 puls
Literacy rate 31.5%
Calorie consumption 1,523 kilocalories

Afmadow 73 D6 Jubbada Hoose, S Somalia

Africa 68 *continent*

Africa, Horn of 68 E4 *physical region* Ethiopia/Somalia

Africana Seamount 141 A6 *undersea feature* SW Indian Ocean

'Afrīn 118 B2 Ḥalab, N Syria

Afyon 116 B3 *prev.* Afyonkarahisar. Afyon, W Turkey

Agadez 75 G3 *prev.* Agadès. Agadez, C Niger

Agadir 70 B3 SW Morocco

Agana/Agaña *see* Hagåtña

Āgaro 73 C5 C Ethiopia

Agassiz Fracture Zone 143 G5 *tectonic feature* S Pacific Ocean

Agathónisi 105 D6 *island* Dodekánisos, Greece, Aegean Sea

Agde 91 C6 *anc.* Agatha. Hérault, S France

Agedabia *see* Ajdābiyā

Agen 91 B5 *anc.* Aginnum. Lot-et-Garonne, SW France

Aghri Dagh *see* Büyükağrı Dağı

Agiá 104 B4 *var.* Ayiá. Thessalía, C Greece

Agialoúsa 102 D4 *var.* Yenierenköy. NE Cyprus

Agía Marína 105 E6 Léros, Dodekánisos, Greece, Aegean Sea

Ágios Nikólaos 105 D8 *var.* Áyios Nikólaos. Kríti, Greece, E Mediterranean Sea

Āgra 134 D3 Uttar Pradesh, N India

Agram *see* Zagreb

Ağrı 117 F3 *var.* Karaköse; *prev.* Karakılısse. Ağrı, NE Turkey

Agri Dagi *see* Büyükağrı Dağı

Agrigento 97 C7 *Gk.* Akragas; *prev.* Girgenti. Sicilia, Italy, C Mediterranean Sea

Agriovótano 105 C5 Évvoia, C Greece

Agropoli 97 D5 Campania, S Italy

Aguachica 58 B2 Cesar, N Colombia

Aguadulce 53 F5 Coclé, S Panama

Agua Prieta 50 B1 Sonora, NW Mexico

Aguascalientes 50 D4 Aguascalientes, C Mexico

Aguaytía 60 C3 Ucayali, C Peru

Aguilas 93 E4 Murcia, SE Spain

Aguililla 50 D4 Michoacán de Ocampo, SW Mexico

Agulhas Basin 69 D8 *undersea feature* SW Indian Ocean

Agulhas Plateau 67 D6 *undersea feature* SW Indian Ocean

Ahaggar 75 F2 *high plateau region* SE Algeria

Ahlen 94 B4 Nordrhein-Westfalen, W Germany

Ahmadābād 134 C4 *var.* Ahmedabad. Gujarāt, W India

Ahmadnagar 134 C5 *var.* Ahmednagar. Mahārāshtra, W India

Ahmedabad *see* Ahmadābād

Ahmednagar *see* Ahmadnagar

Ahuachapán 52 B3 Ahuachapán, W El Salvador

Ahvāz 120 C3 *var.* Ahwāz; *prev.* Nāsiri. Khūzestān, SW Iran

Ahvenanmaa *see* Åland

Ahwāz *see* Ahvāz

Aïdin *see* Aydın

Aígina 105 C6 *var.* Aíyina, Egina. Aígina, C Greece

Aígio 105 B5 *var.* Egio; *prev.* Aíyion. Dytikí Ellás, S Greece

Aiken 43 E2 South Carolina, SE USA

Ailigandí 53 G4 San Blas, NE Panama

Ailinglaplap Atoll 144 D2 *var.* Aelōnlaplap. *Atoll* Ralik Chain, S Marshall Islands

Ailuk Atoll 144 D1 *var.* Aelok. *Atoll* Ratak Chain, NE Marshall Islands

Ainaži 106 D3 *Est.* Heinaste, *Ger.* Hainasch. Limbaži, N Latvia

'Aïn Ben Tili 74 D1 Tiris Zemmour, N Mauritania

Aintab *see* Gaziantep

Aïoun el Atrous *see* 'Ayoûn el 'Atroûs

Aïoun el Atroûss *see* 'Ayoûn el 'Atroûs

Aiquile 61 F4 Cochabamba, C Bolivia

Aïr *see* Aïr, Massif de l'

Air du Azbine *see* Aïr, Massif de l'

Aïr, Massif de l' 75 G2 *var.* Aïr, Air du Azbine, Asben. *Mountain range* NC Niger

Aiud 108 B4 *Ger.* Strassburg, *Hung.* Nagyenyed; *prev.* Engeten. Alba, SW Romania

Aix *see* Aix-en-Provence

Aix-en-Provence 91 D6 *var.* Aix; *anc.* Aquae Sextiae. Bouches-du-Rhône, SE France

Aíyina *see* Aígina

Aíyion *see* Aígio

Aizkraukle 106 C4 Aizkraukle, S Latvia

Ajaccio 91 E7 Corse, France, C Mediterranean Sea

Ajaria 117 F2 *autonomous republic* SW Georgia

Aj Bogd Uul 126 D2 *mountain* SW Mongolia

Ajdābiyā 71 G2 *var.* Agedabia, Ajdābiyah. NE Libya

Ajdābiyah *see* Ajdābiyā

Ajjinena *see* El Geneina

Ajmer 134 D3 *var.* Ajmere. Rājasthān, N India

Ajmere *see* Ajmer

Ajo 48 A3 Arizona, SW USA

Akaba *see* Al 'Aqabah

Akamagaseki *see* Shimonoseki

Akasha 72 B3 Northern, N Sudan

Akchâr 74 C2 *desert* W Mauritania

Akhalts'ikhe 117 F2 SW Georgia

Akhisar 116 A3 Manisa, W Turkey

Akhmîm 72 B2 *anc.* Panopolis. C Egypt

Akhtubinsk 111 C7 Astrakhanskaya Oblast', SW Russian Federation

Akimiski Island 38 C3 *island* Northwest Territories, C Canada

Akinovka 109 F4 Zaporiz'ka Oblast', S Ukraine

Akita 130 D4 Akita, Honshū, C Japan

Akjoujt 74 C2 *prev.* Fort-Repoux. Inchiri, W Mauritania

Akkeshi 130 E2 Hokkaidō, NE Japan

Aklavik 36 D3 Northwest Territories, NW Canada

Akmola *see* Astana

Akpatok Island 39 E1 *island* Northwest Territories, E Canada

Akra Dhrepanon *see* Drépano, Akrotírio

Akra Kanestron *see* Palioúri, Akrotírio

Akron 40 D4 Ohio, N USA

Akrotiri *see* Akrotírion

Akrotírion 102 C5 *var.* Akrotiri. *UK air base* S Cyprus

Aksai Chin 124 B2 *Chin.* Aksayqin. *Disputed region* China/India

Aksaray 116 C4 Aksaray, C Turkey

Akşehir 116 B4 Konya, W Turkey

Aktau 114 A4 *Kaz.* Aqtaū; *prev.* Shevchenko. Mangistau, W Kazakhstan

Aktsyabrski 107 C7 *Rus.* Oktyabr'skiy; *prev.* Karpilovka. Homyel'skaya Voblasts', SE Belarus

Aktyubinsk 114 B4 *Kaz.* Aqtöbe. Aktyubinsk, NW Kazakhstan

Akula 77 C5 Equateur, NW Dem. Rep. Congo (Zaire)

Akureyri 83 E4 Nordhurland Eystra, N Iceland

Akyab *see* Sittwe

Alabama 51 G1 *off.* State of Alabama; also known as Camellia State, Heart of Dixie, The Cotton State, Yellowhammer State. *State* S USA

Alabama River 42 C3 *river* Alabama, S USA

Alaca 116 C3 Çorum, N Turkey

Alagoas 63 G2 *off.* Estado de Alagoas. *State* E Brazil

Alajuela 53 E4 Alajuela, C Costa Rica

Alakanuk 36 C2 Alaska, USA

Al 'Alamayn *see* El 'Alamein

Al 'Amārah 120 C3 *var.* Amara. E Iraq

Alamo 47 D6 Nevada, W USA

Alamogordo 48 D3 New Mexico, SW USA

Alamosa 44 C5 Colorado, C USA

Åland 85 D6 *var.* Aland Islands, *Fin.* Ahvenanmaa. *Island group* SW Finland

Aland Islands *see* Åland

Aland Sea *see* Ålands Hav

Ålands Hav 85 C6 *var.* Aland Sea. *Strait* Baltic Sea/Gulf of Bothnia

Alanya 116 C4 Antalya, S Turkey

Alappuzha *see* Alleppey

Al 'Aqabah 119 B8 *var.* Akaba, Aqaba, 'Aqaba; *anc.* Aelana, Elath. Ma'ān, SW Jordan

Alasca, Golfo de *see* Alaska, Gulf of

Alaşehir 116 A4 Manisa, W Turkey

Al 'Ashārah 118 E3 *var.* Ashara. Dayr az Zawr, E Syria

Alaska 36 C3 *off.* State of Alaska; also known as Land of the Midnight Sun, The Last Frontier, Seward's Folly; *prev.* Russian America. *State* NW USA

Alaska, Gulf of 36 C4 *var.* Golfo de Alasca. *Gulf* Canada/USA

Alaska Peninsula 36 C3 *peninsula* Alaska, USA

Alaska Range 34 B2 *mountain range* Alaska, USA

Al-Asnam *see* Chlef

Al Awaynāt *see* Al 'Uwaynāt

Al 'Aynā 119 B7 Al Karak, W Jordan

Alazeya 115 G2 *river* NE Russian Federation

Al Bāb 118 B2 Ḥalab, N Syria

Albacete 93 E3 Castilla-La Mancha, C Spain

Al Baghdādī 120 B3 *var.* Khān al Baghdādī. SW Iraq

Al Bāha *see* Al Bāḩah

Al Bāḩah 121 B5 *var.* Al Bāha. Al Bāḩah, SW Saudi Arabia

Al Baḩr al Mayyit *see* Dead Sea

Alba Iulia 108 B4 *Ger.* Weissenburg, *Hung.* Gyulafehérvár; *prev.* Bălgrad, Karlsburg, Károly-Fehérvár. Alba, W Romania

Albania 101 C7 *Alb.* Republika e Shqipërisë, Shqipëria; *prev.* People's Socialist Republic of Albania. *Country* SE Europe

Albania 101

Official name Republic of Albania
Formation 1912
Capital Tiranë
Population 3 million/293 people per sq mile (113 people per sq km)
Total area 10,579 sq miles (27,400 sq km) sq miles
Languages Albanian, Greek
Religions Sunni Muslim 70%, Greek Orthodox 20%, Roman Catholic 10%
Ethnic mix Albanian 96%, Greek 2%, other (including Macedonian) 2%
Government Multiparty republic
Currency Lek = 100 qindars
Literacy rate 85%
Calorie consumption 2,605 kilocalories

Albany 38 C3 *river* Ontario, S Canada

Albany 41 F3 *state capital* New York, NE USA

Albany 42 D3 Georgia, SE USA

Albany 46 B3 Oregon, NW USA

Albany 147 B7 Western Australia

Al Bāridah 118 C4 *var.* Bāridah. Ḩimş, C Syria

Al Başrah 120 C3 *Eng.* Basra; *hist.* Busra, Bussora. SE Iraq

Al Batrūn *see* Batroûn

Al Baydā' 71 G2 *var.* Beida. NE Libya

Albemarle Island *see* Isabela, Isla

Albemarle Sound 43 G1 *inlet* W Atlantic Ocean

Albergaria-a-Velha 92 B2 Aveiro, N Portugal

Albert 90 C3 Somme, N France

Alberta 37 C4 *province* SW Canada

Albert Edward Nyanza *see* Edward, Lake

Albert, Lake 73 B6 *var.* Albert Nyanza, Lac Mobutu Sese Seko. *Lake* Uganda/Dem. Rep. Congo (Zaire)

Albert Lea 45 F3 Minnesota, N USA

Albert Nyanza *see* Albert, Lake

Albi 91 C6 *anc.* Albiga. Tarn, S France

Ålborg 80 D3 *var.* Aalborg, Ålborg-Nørresundby; *anc.* Alburgum. Nordjylland, N Denmark

Ålborg-Nørresundby *see* Ålborg

Alborz, Reshteh-ye Kūhhā-ye 120 C2 *Eng.* Elburz Mountains. *Mountain range* N Iran

Albuquerque 48 D2 New Mexico, SW USA

Al Burayqah *see* Marsá al Burayqah

Alburgum *see* Ålborg

Albury 149 C7 New South Wales, SE Australia

Alcácer do Sal 92 B4 Setúbal, W Portugal

Alcalá de Henares 93 E3 *Ar.* Alkal'a; *anc.* Complutum. Madrid, C Spain

Alcamo 97 C7 Sicilia, Italy,
C Mediterranean Sea
Alcañiz 93 F2 Aragón, NE Spain
Alcántara, Embalse de 92 C3
reservoir W Spain
Alcaudete 92 D4 Andalucía,
S Spain
Alcázar *see* Ksar-el-Kebir
Alcoi *see* Alcoy
Alcoy 93 F4 *var.* Alcoi. País
Valenciano, E Spain
Aldabra Group 79 G2 *island group*
SW Seychelles
Aldan 115 F3 *river* NE Russian
Federation
al Dar al Baida *see* Rabat
Alderney 90 A2 *island* Channel
Islands
Aleg 74 C3 Brakna, SW Mauritania
Aleksandropol' *see* Gyumri
Aleksin 111 B5 Tul'skaya Oblast',
W Russian Federation
Aleksinac 100 E4 Serbia,
SE Yugoslavia
Alençon 90 B3 Orne, N France
Alenquer 63 E2 Pará, NE Brazil
Aleppo *see* Ḥalab
Alert 37 F1 Ellesmere Island,
Nunavut, N Canada
Alès 91 C6 *prev.* Alais. Gard,
S France
Aleşd 108 B3 Hung. Élesd. Bihor,
SW Romania
Alessandria 96 B2 Fr. Alexandrie.
Piemonte, N Italy
Ålesund 85 A5 Møre og Romsdal,
S Norway
Aleutian Basin 113 G3 *undersea*
feature Bering Sea
Aleutian Islands 36 A3 *island group*
Alaska, USA
Aleutian Range 34 A2 *mountain*
range Alaska, USA
Aleutian Trench 113 H3 *undersea*
feature S Bering Sea
Alexander Archipelago 36 D4 *island*
group Alaska, USA
Alexander City 42 D2 Alabama,
S USA
Alexander Island 154 A3 *island*
Antarctica
Alexandra 151 B7 Otago, South
Island, NZ
Alexándreia 104 B4 *var.* Alexándria.
Kentrikí Makedonía, N Greece
Alexandria 72 B1 Ar.
Al Iskandarīyah. N Egypt
Alexándria *see* Alexándreia
Alexandria 42 B3 Louisiana, S USA
Alexandria 45 F2 Minnesota,
N USA
Alexandria 108 C5 Teleorman,
S Romania
Alexandroúpoli 104 D3 *var.*
Alexandroúpolis, *Turk.* Dedeağaç,
Dedeagach. Anatolikí Makedonía
kai Thráki, NE Greece
Alexandroúpolis *see*
Alexandroúpoli
Al Fāshir *see* El Fasher
Alfatar 104 E1 Silistra, NE Bulgaria
Alfeiós 105 B6 *prev.* Alfiós, *anc.*
Alpheius, Alpheus. *River* S Greece
Alföld *see* Great Hungarian Plain
Alga 114 B4 Kaz. Alghа.
Aktyubinsk, NW Kazakhstan
Algarve 92 B4 *cultural region*
S Portugal
Algeciras 92 C5 Andalucía,
SW Spain
Algemesí 93 F3 País Valenciano,
E Spain
Al-Genain *see* El Geneina
Alger 71 E1 *var.* Algiers, El Djazaïr,
Al Jazair. *Country capital* (Algeria)
N Algeria
Algeria 70 C3 *Country* N Africa

Algeria 70

Official name Democratic and
Popular Republic of Algeria
Formation 1962
Capital Algiers
Population 31.5 million / 34 people
per sq mile (13 people per sq km)

Algeria (continued)

Total area 919,590 sq miles
(2,381,740 sq km)
Languages Arabic, Berber,
French
Religions Sunni Muslim 99%,
other 1%
Ethnic mix Arab 75%, Berber 24%,
European 1%
Government Multiparty republic
Currency Algerian dinar
= 100 centimes
Literacy rate 60.3%
Calorie consumption 2,897
kilocalories

Algerian Basin 80 C5 *var.* Balearic
Plain *undersea feature*
W Mediterranean Sea
Al Ghābah 121 E5 *var.* Ghaba.
C Oman
Alghero 97 A5 Sardegna, Italy,
C Mediterranean Sea
Al Ghurdaqah *see* Hurghada
Algiers *see* Alger
Al Golea *see* El Goléa
Algona 45 F3 Iowa, C USA
Al Hajār al Gharbī 121 D5 *mountain*
range N Oman
Al Ḥasakah 118 D2 *var.* Al Hasijah,
El Haseke, Fr. Hassetché.
Al Ḥasakah, NE Syria
Al Hasijah *see* Al Ḥasakah
Al Ḥillah 120 B3 *var.* Hilla. C Iraq
Al Ḥīsā 119 B7 Aṭ Ṭafīlah,
W Jordan
Al Ḥudaydah 121 B6 *Eng.* Hodeida.
W Yemen
Al Hufūf 120 C4 *var.* Hofuf. Ash
Sharqīyah, NE Saudi Arabia
Aliákmonas 104 B4 *prev.* Aliákmon,
anc. Haliacmon. *River* N Greece
Alíartos 105 C5 Stereá Ellás,
C Greece
Alicante 93 F4 *Cat.* Alacant;. País
Valenciano, SE Spain
Alice 49 G5 Texas, SW USA
Alice Springs 148 A4 Northern
Territory, C Australia
Aliki *see* Alykí
Alima 77 B6 *river* C Congo
Alindao 76 C4 Basse-Kotto,
S Central African Republic
Aliquippa 40 D4 Pennsylvania,
NE USA
Alistráti 104 C3 Kentrikí
Makedonía, NE Greece
Alivéri 105 C5 *var.* Alivérion.
Évvoia, C Greece
Alivérion *see* Alivéri
Al Jabal al Akhḍar 71 G2 *mountain*
range NE Libya
Al Jabal ash Sharqī *see* Anti-
Lebanon
Al Jafr 119 B7 Maʿān,
S Jordan
Al Jaghbūb 71 H3 NE Libya
Al Jahrāʾ 120 C4 *var.* Al Jahrah,
Jahra. C Kuwait
Al Jahrah *see* Al Jahrāʾ
Al Jawf 120 B4 *var.* Jauf. Al Jawf,
NW Saudi Arabia
Al Jazair *see* Alger
Al Jazīrah 118 E2 *physical region*
Iraq/Syria
Al Jīzah *see* El Gīza
Al Junaynah *see* El Geneina
Al Karak 119 B7 *var.* El Kerak,
Karak, *anc.* Kir Moab, Kir
of Moab. Al Karak, W Jordan
Al-Kasr al-Kebir *see* Ksar-el-Kebir
Al Khalīl *see* Hebron
Al Khārijah *see* El Khârga
Al Khufrah 71 H4 SE Libya
Al Khums 71 F2 *var.* Homs, Khoms,
Khums. NW Libya
Alkmaar 86 C2 Noord-Holland,
NW Netherlands
Al Kūt 120 C4 *var.* Kūt al ʿAmārah,
Kut al Imara. E Iraq
Al-Kuwait *see* Al Kuwayt
Al Kuwayt 120 C4 *var.* Al-Kuwait,
Eng. Kuwait, Kuwait City; *prev.*
Qurein. *Country capital* (Kuwait)
E Kuwait

Al Lādhiqīyah 118 A3 *Eng.* Latakia,
Fr. Lattaquié; *anc.* Laodicea,
Laodicea ad Mare. Al Lādhiqīyah,
W Syria
Allahābād 135 E3 Uttar Pradesh,
N India
Allanmyo 136 B4 Magwe,
C Myanmar
Allegheny Plateau 41 E3 *mountain*
range New York/Pennsylvania,
NE USA
Allentown 41 F4 Pennsylvania,
NE USA
Alleppey 132 C3 *var.* Alappuzha;
prev. Alleppi. Kerala, SW India
Alleppi *see* Alleppey
Alliance 44 D3 Nebraska, C USA
Al Līth 121 B5 Makkah, SW Saudi
Arabia
Alma-Ata *see* Almaty
Almada 92 B4 Setúbal, W Portugal
Al Madīnah 121 A5 *Eng.* Medina.
Al Madīnah, W Saudi Arabia
Al Mafraq 119 B6 *var.* Mafraq.
Al Mafraq, N Jordan
Al Mahdīyah *see* Mahdia
Al Mahrah 121 C6 *mountain range*
E Yemen
Al Majmaʿah 120 B4 Ar Riyāḍ,
C Saudi Arabia
Al Mālikīyah 118 E1 Al Ḥasakah,
NE Syria
Al Manāmah 120 C4 *Eng.* Manama.
Country capital (Bahrain)
N Bahrain
Al Manāşif 118 E3 *mountain range*
E Syria
Almansa 93 F4 Castilla-La Mancha,
C Spain
Al Marj 71 G2 *var.* Barka, *It.* Barce.
NE Libya
Almaty 114 C5 *var.* Alma-Ata.
Almaty, SE Kazakhstan
Al Mawşil 120 B2 *Eng.* Mosul.
N Iraq
Al Mayādīn 118 D3 *var.* Mayadin,
Fr. Meyadine. Dayr az Zawr,
E Syria
Al Mazraʿ *see* Al Mazraʿah
Al Mazraʿah 119 B6 *var.* Al Mazraʿ,
Mazraʿa. Al Karak, W Jordan
Almelo 86 E3 Overijssel,
E Netherlands
Almere-stad *see* Almere
Almería 93 E5 Ar. Al-Mariyya; *anc.*
Unci, *Lat.* Portus Magnus.
Andalucía, S Spain
Alʾmetʾyevsk 111 D5 Respublika
Tatarstan, W Russian Federation
Al Mīnāʾ *see* El Mina
Al Minyā *see* El Minya
Almirante 53 E4 Bocas del Toro,
NW Panama
Al Mudawwarah 119 B8 Maʿān,
SW Jordan
Al Mukallā 121 C6 *var.* Mukalla.
SE Yemen
Al Obayyid *see* El Obeid
Alofi 145 F4 *dependent territory*
capital (Niue) W Niue
Aloja 106 D3 Limbaži, N Latvia
Alónnisos 105 C5 *island* Vóreioi
Sporádes, Greece, Aegean Sea
Álora 92 D5 Andalucía, S Spain
Alor, Kepulauan 139 E5 *island group*
E Indonesia
Al Oued *see* El Oued
Alpen *see* Alps
Alpena 40 D2 Michigan, N USA
Alpes *see* Alps
Alpha Cordillera 155 B3 *var.* Alpha
Ridge. *Undersea feature* Arctic
Ocean
Alpha Ridge *see* Alpha Cordillera
Alphen *see* Alphen aan den Rijn
Alphen aan den Rijn 86 C3 *var.*
Alphen. Zuid-Holland,
C Netherlands
Alpi *see* Alps
Alpine 49 E4 Texas, SW USA
Alpi Transilvaniei *see* Carpaţii
Meridionali
Alps 102 C1 Fr. Alpes, Ger.
Alpen, It. Alpi. *Mountain range*
C Europe

Al Qaḍārif *see* Gedaref
Al Qāmishlī 118 E1 *var.* Kamishli,
Qamishly. Al Ḥasakah, NE Syria
Al Qaşrayn *see* Kasserine
Al Qayrawān *see* Kairouan
Al-Qsar *see* Ksar-el-Kebir
Al Qubayyāt *see* Qoubaïyât
Al Qunayţirah 119 B5 *var.*
El Kuneitra, El Quneitra,
Kuneitra, Qunaytra.
Al Qunayţirah, SW Syria
Al Quşayr 118 B4 *var.* El Quseir,
Quşayr, *Fr.* Kousseir. Ḥimş,
W Syria
Al Quwayrah 119 B8 *var.*
El Quweira. Maʿān, SW Jordan
Alsace 90 E3 *cultural region*
NE France
Alsdorf 94 A4 Nordrhein-Westfalen,
W Germany
Alt *see* Olt
Alta 84 D2 Fin. Alattio. Finnmark,
N Norway
Altai *see* Altai Mountains
Altai Mountains 126 C2 *var.* Altai,
Chin. Altay Shan, *Rus.* Altay.
Mountain range Asia/Europe
Altamaha River 43 E3 *river* Georgia,
SE USA
Altamira 63 E2 Pará, NE Brazil
Altamura 97 E5 *anc.* Lupatia.
Puglia, SE Italy
Altar, Desierto de 50 A1 *var.*
Sonoran Desert. *Desert*
Mexico/USA *see also* Sonoran
Desert
Altay 126 C2 Chin. A-le-t'ai, *Mong.*
Sharasume; *prev.* Ch'eng-hua,
Chenghwa. Xinjiang Uygur
Zizhiqu, NW China
Altay *see* Altai Mountains
Altay 126 D2 Govĭ-Altay,
W Mongolia
Altay Shan *see* Altai Mountains
Altin Köprü 120 B3 *var.* Altun
Kupri. N Iraq
Altiplano 61 F4 *physical region*
W South America
Alton 40 B5 Illinois, N USA
Alton 40 B4 Missouri, C USA
Altoona 41 E4 Pennsylvania,
NE USA
Alto Paraná *see* Paraná
Altun Kupri *see* Altin Köprü
Altun Shan 126 C3 *var.* Altyn Tagh.
Mountain range NW China
Altus 49 F2 Oklahoma, C USA
Altyn Tagh *see* Altun Shan
Al Ubayyiḍ *see* El Obeid
Alūksne 106 D3 Ger. Marienburg.
Alūksne, NE Latvia
Al ʿUlā 120 A4 Al Madīnah,
NW Saudi Arabia
Al ʿUmarī 119 C6 ʿAmmān,
E Jordan
Alupka 109 F5 Respublika Krym,
S Ukraine
Alushta 109 F5 Respublika Krym,
S Ukraine
Al ʿUwaynāt 71 F4 *var.* Al Awaynāt.
SW Libya
Alva 49 F1 Oklahoma, C USA
Alvarado 51 F4 Veracruz-Llave,
E Mexico
Alvin 49 H4 Texas, SW USA
Al Wajh 120 A4 Tabūk, NW Saudi
Arabia
Alwar 134 D3 Rājasthān, N India
Al Wariʿah 120 C4 Ash Sharqīyah,
N Saudi Arabia
Alykí 104 C4 *var.* Aliki. Thásos,
N Greece
Alytus 107 B5 Pol. Olita. Alytus,
S Lithuania
Alzette 87 D8 *river* S Luxembourg
Amadeus, Lake 147 D5 *seasonal lake*
Northern Territory, C Australia
Amadi 73 B5 Western Equatoria,
SW Sudan
Amadjuak Lake 37 G3 *lake* Baffin
Island, Nunavut, N Canada
Amakusa-nada 131 A7 *gulf* Kyūshū,
SW Japan
Åmål 85 B6 Västra Götaland,
S Sweden
Amami-guntō 130 A3 *island group*
SW Japan

Amami-Ō-shima 130 A3 *island*
S Japan
Amantea 97 D6 Calabria, SW Italy
Amapá 63 E1 Amapá, NE Brazil
Amara *see* Al 'Amārah
Amarapura 136 B3 Mandalay,
C Myanmar
Amarillo 49 E2 Texas, SW USA
Amay 87 C6 Liège, E Belgium
Amazon 63 E1 *Sp.* Amazonas. *River*
Brazil/Peru
Amazon Basin 62 D2 *basin* N South
America
Amazon, Mouths of the 63 F1 *delta*
NE Brazil
Ambam 77 B5 Sud, S Cameroon
Ambanja 79 G2 Antsiraňana,
N Madagascar
Ambarchik 115 G2 Respublika
Sakha (Yakutiya), NE Russian
Federation
Ambato 60 B1 Tungurahua,
C Ecuador
Ambérieu-en-Bugey 91 D5 Ain,
E France
Amboasary 79 F4 Toliara,
S Madagascar
Ambon 139 F4 *prev.* Amboina,
Amboyna. Pulau Ambon,
E Indonesia
Ambositra 79 G3 Fianarantsoa,
SE Madagascar
Ambrim *see* Ambrym
Ambriz 78 A1 Bengo, NW Angola
Ambrym 144 D4 *var.* Ambrim.
Island C Vanuatu
Amchitka Island 36 A2 *island*
Aleutian Islands, Alaska, USA
Amdo 126 C5 Xizang Zizhiqu,
W China
Ameland 86 D1 *Fris.* It Amelân.
Island Waddeneilanden,
N Netherlands
America-Antarctica Ridge 67 C7
undersea feature S Atlantic Ocean
American Falls Reservoir 46 E4
reservoir Idaho, NW USA
American Samoa 145 E4 *US
unincorporated territory*
W Polynesia
Amersfoort 86 D3 Utrecht,
C Netherlands
Ames 45 F3 Iowa, C USA
Amfilochía 105 A5 *var.* Amfilokhía.
Dytikí Ellás, C Greece
Amfilokhía *see* Amfilochía
Amga 115 F3 *river* NE Russian
Federation
Amherst 39 F4 Nova Scotia,
SE Canada
Amida *see* Diyarbakır
Amiens 90 C3 *anc.* Ambianum,
Samarobriva. Somme, N France
Amíndaion *see* Amýntaio
Amindeo *see* Amýntaio
Amīndīvi Islands 132 A2 *island
group* Lakshadweep, India,
N Indian Ocean
Amirante Islands 79 G1 *var.*
Amirantes Group. *Island group*
C Seychelles
Amirantes Group *see* Amirante
Islands
Amistad Reservoir 49 F4 *var.* Presa
de la Amistad. *Reservoir*
Mexico/USA
'Ammān 119 B6 *var.* Amman; *anc.*
Philadelphia, *Bibl.* Rabbah
Ammon, Rabbath Ammon.
Country capital (Jordan) 'Ammān,
NW Jordan
Amman *see* 'Ammān
Ammassalik 82 D4 *var.*
Angmagssalik. S Greenland
Ammóchostos 102 D5 *var.*
Famagusta, Gazimağusa.
E Cyprus
Āmol 120 D2 *var.* Amul.
Māzandarān, N Iran
Amorgós 105 D6 *island* Kykládes,
Greece, Aegean Sea
Amorgós 105 D6 Amorgós,
Kykládes, Greece, Aegean Sea
Amos 38 D4 Québec, SE Canada
Amourj 74 D3 Hodh ech Chargui,
SE Mauritania
Amoy *see* Xiamen

Ampato, Nevado 61 E4 *mountain*
S Peru
Amposta 93 F2 Cataluña,
NE Spain
Amrāvati 134 D4 *prev.* Amraoti.
Mahārāshtra, C India
Amritsar 134 D2 Punjab, N India
Amstelveen 86 C3 Noord-Holland,
C Netherlands
Amsterdam 86 C3 *country capital*
(Netherlands) Noord-Holland,
C Netherlands
Amsterdam Island 141 C6 *island*
NE French Southern and
Antarctic Territories
Am Timan 76 C3 Salamat,
SE Chad
Amu Darya 122 D2 *Rus.*
Amudar'ya, *Taj.* Dar"yoi Amu,
Turkm. Amyderya, *Uzb.*
Amudaryo; *anc.* Oxus. *River*
C Asia
Amu-Dar'ya 123 E3 Lebapskiy
Velayat, NE Turkmenistan
Amul *see* Āmol
Amund Ringnes Island 37 F2 *island*
Nunavut, N Canada
Amundsen Basin *see* Fram Basin
Amundsen Gulf 37 E2 *gulf*
Northwest Territories, N Canada
Amundsen Plain 154 A4 *undersea
feature* S Pacific Ocean
Amundsen-Scott 154 B3 *US research
station* Antarctica
Amundsen Sea 154 A4 *sea* S Pacific
Ocean
Amuntai 138 D4 *prev.* Amoentai.
Borneo, C Indonesia
Amur 115 G4 *Chin.* Heilong Jiang.
River China/Russian Federation
Amvrosiyivka 109 H3 *Rus.*
Amvrosiyevka. Donets'ka Oblast',
SE Ukraine
Amýntaio 104 B4 *var.* Amindeo;
prev. Amíndaion. Dytikí
Makedonía, N Greece
Anabar 115 E2 *river* NE Russian
Federation
An Abhainn Mhór *see* Blackwater
Anaco 59 E2 Anzoátegui,
NE Venezuela
Anaconda 44 B2 Montana, NW USA
Anacortes 46 B1 Washington,
NW USA
Anadolu Dağları *see* Doğu
Karadeniz Dağları
Anadyr' 115 G1 *river* NE Russian
Federation
Anadyr' 115 H1 Chukotskiy
Avtonomnyy Okrug, NE Russian
Federation
Anadyr, Gulf of *see* Anadyrskiy
Zaliv
Anadyrskiy Zaliv 115 H1 *Eng.* Gulf
of Anadyr. *Gulf* NE Russian
Federation
Anáfi 105 D7 *anc.* Anaphe. *Island*
Kykládes, Greece, Aegean Sea
'Anah *see* 'Annah
Anaheim 46 E2 California, W USA
Anaiza *see* 'Unayzah
Analalava 79 G2 Mahajanga,
NW Madagascar
Anamur 116 C5 İçel, S Turkey
Anantapur 132 C2 Andhra Pradesh,
S India
Anápolis 63 F3 Goiás, C Brazil
Anār 120 D3 Kermān, C Iran
Anatolia 116 C4 *plateau* C Turkey
Anatom *see* Aneityum
Añatuya 64 C3 Santiago del Estero,
N Argentina
An Bhearú *see* Barrow
Anchorage 36 C3 Alaska, USA
Ancona 96 C3 Marche, C Italy
Ancud 65 B6 *prev.* San Carlos de
Ancud. Los Lagos, S Chile
Åndalsnes 85 A5 Møre og Romsdal,
S Norway
Andalucía 92 D4 *cultural region*
S Spain
Andalusia 42 C3 Alabama, S USA
Andaman Islands 124 B4 *island
group* India, NE Indian Ocean
Andaman Sea 124 C4 *sea* NE Indian
Ocean
Andenne 87 C6 Namur, SE Belgium

Anderlues 87 B7 Hainaut,
S Belgium
Anderson 40 C4 Indiana, N USA
Andes 64 B3 *mountain range*
W South America
Andhra Pradesh 135 E5 *state*
E India
Andijon 123 F2 *Rus.* Andizhan.
Andijon Wiloyati, E Uzbekistan
Andikíthira *see* Antikýthira
Andipaxi *see* Antípaxoi
Andípsara *see* Antípsara
Ándissa *see* Ántissa
Andkhvoy 122 D3 Fāryāb,
N Afghanistan
Andorra 91 A7 *Cat.* Valls
d'Andorra, *Fr.* Vallée d'Andorre.
Country SW Europe

Andorra 91

Official name Principality of
Andorra
Formation 1278
Capital Andorra la Vella
Population 66,000 / 367 people
per sq mile (142 people per sq km)
Total area 180 sq miles
(465 sq km)
Languages Catalan, Spanish,
French Portuguese
Religions Roman Catholic 94%,
other 6%
Ethnic mix Catalan 61%, Spanish
Castilian 30%, other 9%
Government Parliamentary
democracy
Currency French franc and Spanish
peseta
Literacy rate 99%
Calorie consumption 3,708
kilocalories

Andorra *see* Andorra la Vella
Andorra la Vella 91 A8 *var.*
Andorra, *Fr.* Andorre la Vielle, *Sp.*
Andorra la Vieja. *Country capital*
(Andorra) C Andorra
Andorra la Vieja *see* Andorra la
Vella
Andorre la Vielle *see* Andorra la
Vella
Andover 89 D7 S England, UK
Andøya 84 C2 *island* C Norway
Andreanof Islands 36 A3 *island
group* Aleutian Islands, Alaska,
USA
Andrews 49 E3 Texas, SW USA
Andrew Tablemount 140 A4 *var.*
Gora Andryu. *Undersea feature*
W Indian Ocean
Andria 97 D5 Puglia, SE Italy
An Droichead Nua *see* Newbridge
Ándros 105 C6 *island* Kykládes,
Greece, Aegean Sea
Ándros 105 D6 Ándros, Kykládes,
Greece, Aegean Sea
Andros Island 54 B2 *island*
NW Bahamas
Andros Town 54 C1 Andros Island,
NW Bahamas
Aneityum 144 D5 *var.* Anatom; *prev.*
Kéamu. Island S Vanuatu
Ānewetak *see* Enewetak Atoll
Angara 115 E4 *river* C Russian
Federation
Angarsk 115 E4 Irkutskaya Oblast',
S Russian Federation
Ånge 85 C5 Västernorrland,
C Sweden
Ángel de la Guarda, Isla 50 B2
island NW Mexico
Angeles 139 E1 *off.* Angeles City.
Luzon, N Philippines
Angel Falls *see* Ángel, Salto
Ángel, Salto 59 E3 *Eng.* Angel Falls.
Waterfall E Venezuela
Ångermanälven 84 C4 *river*
N Sweden
Angermünde 94 D3 Brandenburg,
NE Germany
Angers 90 B4 *anc.* Juliomagus.
Maine-et-Loire, NW France
Anglesey 89 C5 *island*
NW Wales, UK
Anglet 91 A6 Pyrénées-Atlantiques,
SW France

Angleton 49 H4 Texas, SW USA
Angmagssalik *see* Ammassalik
Ang Nam Ngum 136 C4 *lake* C Laos
Angola 78 B2 *prev.* People's
Republic of Angola, Portuguese
West Africa. *Country* SW Africa

Angola 78

Official name Republic of Angola
Formation 1975
Capital Luanda
Population 13 million /27 people
per sq mile (10 people per sq km)
Total area 481,351 sq miles
(1,246,700 sq km)
Languages Portuguese, Umbundu,
Kimbundu, Kikongo
Religions Roman
Catholic/Protestant 64%,
Traditional beliefs 34%, other 2%
Ethnic mix Ovimbundu 37%,
Mbundu 25%, Bakongo 13%,
other 25%
Government Multiparty republic
Currency Readjusted kwanza
= 100 lwei
Literacy rate 45%
Calorie consumption 1,839
kilocalories

Angola Basin 69 B5 *undersea feature*
E Atlantic Ocean
Angostura, Presa de la 51 G5
reservoir SE Mexico
Angoulême 91 B5 *anc.* Iculisma.
Charente, W France
Angoumois 91 B5 *cultural region*
W France
Angren 123 F2 Toshkent Wiloyati,
E Uzbekistan
Anguilla 55 G3 *UK dependent
territory* E West Indies
Anguilla Cays 54 B2 *islets*
SW Bahamas
Anhui 128 C5 *var.* Anhui Sheng,
Anhwei, Wan. Admin. region
province E China
Anhui Sheng *see* Anhui
Anhwei *see* Anhui
Anina 108 A4 *Ger.* Steierdorf, *Hung.*
Stájerlakanina; *prev.* Ştaierdorf-
Anina, Steierdorf-Anina,
Steyerlak-Anina. Caraş-Severin,
SW Romania
Anjou 90 B4 *cultural region*
NW France
Anjouan 79 F2 *var.* Nzwani,
Johanna Island. *Island*
SE Comoros
Ankara 116 C3 *prev.* Angora, *anc.*
Ancyra. *Country capital* (Turkey)
Ankara, C Turkey
Ankeny 45 F3 Iowa, C USA
Anklam 94 D2 Mecklenburg-
Vorpommern, NE Germany
Anykščiai 106 C4 Anykščiai,
E Lithuania
An Longfort *see* Longford
An Mhuir Cheilteach *see* Celtic Sea
Annaba 71 E1 *prev.* Bône.
NE Algeria
An Nafūd 120 B4 *desert* NW Saudi
Arabia
'Annah 120 B3 *var.* 'Ānah. NW Iraq
An Najaf 120 B3 *var.* Najaf. S Iraq
Annamitique, Chaîne 136 D4
mountain range C Laos
Annapolis 41 F4 *state capital*
Maryland, NE USA
Annapurna 135 E3 *mountain*
C Nepal
An Nāqūrah *see* En Nâqoûra
Ann Arbor 40 C3 Michigan, N USA
An Nāşirīyah 120 C3 *var.* Nasiriya.
SE Iraq
Annecy 91 D5 *anc.* Anneciacum.
Haute-Savoie, E France
An Nîl al Azraq *see* Blue Nile
Anniston 42 D2 Alabama, S USA
Annotto Bay 54 B4 C Jamaica
An Ómaigh *see* Omagh
Anqing 128 D5 Anhui, E China
Anse La Raye 55 F1 NW Saint
Lucia
Anshun 128 B6 Guizhou, S China
Ansongo 75 E3 Gao, E Mali

An Srath Bán *see* Strabane
Antakya 116 D4 *anc.* Antioch, Antiochia. Hatay, S Turkey
Antalaha 79 G2 Antsiraňana, NE Madagascar
Antalya 116 B4 *prev.* Adalia, *anc.* Attaleia, *Bibl.* Attalia. Antalya, SW Turkey
Antalya, Gulf of *see* Antalya Körfezi
Antalya Körfezi 116 B4 *var.* Gulf of Adalia, *Eng.* Gulf of Antalya. *Gulf* SW Turkey
Antananarivo 79 G3 *prev.* Tananarive. *Country capital* (Madagascar) Antananarivo, C Madagascar
Antarctica 154 B3 *continent*
Antarctic Peninsula 154 A2 *peninsula* Antarctica
Antep *see* Gaziantep
Antequera 92 D5 *anc.* Anticaria, Antiquaria. Andalucía, S Spain
Antequera *see* Oaxaca
Antibes 91 D6 *anc.* Antipolis. Alpes-Maritimes, SE France
Anticosti, Île d' 39 F3 *Eng.* Anticosti Island. *Island* Québec, E Canada
Antigua 55 G3 *island* S Antigua and Barbuda, Leeward Islands
Antigua and Barbuda 55 G3 *country* E West Indies

Antigua and Barbuda 55

Official name Antigua and Barbuda
Formation 1981
Capital St. John's
Population 69,000 / 404 people per sq mile (156 people per sq km)
Total area 170 sq miles (440 sq km)
Languages English, English patois
Religions Anglican 44%, other Protestant 86%, Roman Catholic 10%, Rastafarian 1%, other 3%
Ethnic mix Black 98%, other 2%
Government Parliamentary democracy
Currency Eastern Caribbean dollar = 100 cents
Literacy rate 95%
Calorie consumption 2,458 kilocalories

Antikýthira 105 B7 *var.* Andikíthira. *Island* S Greece
Anti-Lebanon 118 B4 *var.* Jebel esh Sharqi, *Ar.* Al Jabal ash Sharqī, *Fr.* Anti-Liban. *Mountain range* Lebanon/Syria
Anti-Liban *see* Anti-Lebanon
Antípaxoi 105 A5 *var.* Andipaxi. *Island* Iónioi Nísoi, Greece, C Mediterranean Sea
Antipodes Islands 142 D5 *island group* S NZ
Antípsara 105 D5 *var.* Andípsara. *Island* E Greece
Ántissa 105 D5 *var.* Ándissa. Lésvos, E Greece
An Tlúr *see* Newry
Antofagasta 64 B2 Antofagasta, N Chile
Antony 90 E2 Hauts-de-Seine, N France
Antserana *see* Antsiraňana
An tSionainn *see* Shannon
Antsiraňana 79 G2 *var.* Antserana; *prev.* Antsirane, Diégo-Suarez. Antsiraňana, N Madagascar
Antsirane *see* Antsiraňana
Antsohíhy 79 G2 Mahajanga, NW Madagascar
An-tung *see* Dandong
Antwerp *see* Antwerpen
Antwerpen 87 C5 *Eng.* Antwerp, *Fr.* Anvers. Antwerpen, N Belgium
Anuradhapura 132 D3 North Central Province, C Sri Lanka
Anyang 128 C4 Henan, C China
A'nyêmaqên Shan 126 D4 *mountain range* C China
Anzio 97 C5 Lazio, C Italy
Aomen *see* Macao

Aomori 130 D3 Aomori, Honshū, C Japan
Aóos *see* Vjosës, Lumi i
Aosta 96 A1 *anc.* Augusta Praetoria. Valle d'Aosta, NW Italy
Ao Thai *see* Thailand, Gulf of
Aoukâr 74 D3 *var.* Aouker. *Plateau* C Mauritania
Aouk, Bahr 76 C4 *river* Central African Republic/Chad
Aouker *see* Aoukâr
Aozou 76 C1 Borkou-Ennedi-Tibesti, N Chad
Apalachee Bay 42 D3 *bay* Florida, SE USA
Apalachicola River 42 D3 *river* Florida, SE USA
Apamama *see* Abemama
Apaporis, Río 58 C4 *river* Brazil/Colombia
Apatity 110 C2 Murmanskaya Oblast', NW Russian Federation
Ape 106 D3 Alūksne, NE Latvia
Apeldoorn 86 D3 Gelderland, E Netherlands
Apennines *see* Appennino
Āpia 145 F4 *country capital* (Samoa) Upolu, SE Samoa
Apoera 59 G3 Sipaliwini, NW Suriname
Apostle Islands 40 B1 *island group* Wisconsin, N USA
Appalachian Mountains 35 D5 *mountain range* E USA
Appennino 96 E2 *Eng.* Apennines. *Mountain range* Italy/San Marino
Appingedam 86 E1 Groningen, NE Netherlands
Appleton 40 B2 Wisconsin, N USA
Apure, Río 58 C2 *river* W Venezuela
Apurímac, Río 60 D3 *river* S Peru
Apuseni, Munţii 108 A4 *mountain range* W Romania
'Aqaba *see* Al 'Aqabah
Aqaba, Gulf of 120 A4 *var.* Gulf of Elat, *Ar.* Khalīj al 'Aqabah; *anc.* Sinus Aelaniticus. *Gulf* NE Red Sea
Āqchah 123 E3 *var.* Āqcheh. Jowzjān, N Afghanistan
Āqcheh *see* Āqchah
Aquae Augustae *see* Dax
Aquae Sextiae *see* Aix-en-Provence
Aquae Tarbelicae *see* Dax
Aquidauana 63 E4 Mato Grosso do Sul, S Brazil
Aquila *see* L'Aquila
Aquila degli Abruzzo *see* L'Aquila
Aquitaine 91 B6 *cultural region* SW France
'Arabah, Wādī al 135 B7 *Heb.* Ha'Arava. *Dry watercourse* Israel/Jordan
Arabian Basin 124 A4 *undersea feature* N Arabian Sea
Arabian Desert *see* Eastern Desert
Arabian Peninsula 121 B5 *peninsula* SW Asia
Arabian Sea 124 A3 *sea* NW Indian Ocean
Aracaju 63 G3 *state capital* Sergipe, E Brazil
Araçuaí 63 F3 Minas Gerais, SE Brazil
Arad 108 A4 Arad, W Romania
'Arad 119 B7 Southern, S Israel
Arafura Sea 142 A3 *Ind.* Laut Arafuru. *Sea* W Pacific Ocean
Aragón 93 E2 *cultural region* E Spain
Araguaia, Río 63 E3 *var.* Araguaya. *River* C Brazil
Araguari 63 F3 Minas Gerais, SE Brazil
Araguaya *see* Araguaia, Río
Arāk 120 C3 *prev.* Sultānābād. Markazī, W Iran
Arakan Yoma 136 A3 *mountain range* W Myanmar
Aral Sea 122 C1 *Kaz.* Aral Tengizi, *Rus.* Aral'skoye More, *Uzb.* Orol Dengizi. *Inland sea* Kazakhstan/Uzbekistan
Aral'sk 114 B4 *Kaz.* Aral. Kyzylorda, SW Kazakhstan
Aranda de Duero 92 D2 Castilla-León, N Spain

Aranđelovac 100 D4 *prev.* Arandjelovac. Serbia, C Yugoslavia
Aranjuez 92 D3 *anc.* Ara Jovis. Madrid, C Spain
Araouane 75 E2 Tombouctou, N Mali
'Ar'ar 120 B3 Al Ḥudūd ash Shamālīyah, NW Saudi Arabia
Aras 117 G3 *Arm.* Arak's, *Az.* Araz Nehri, *Per.* Rūd-e Aras, *Rus.* Araks; *prev.* Araxes. *River* SW Asia
Arauca 58 C2 Arauca, NE Colombia
Arauca, Río 58 C2 *river* Colombia/Venezuela
Arbela *see* Arbīl
Arbīl 120 B2 *var.* Erbil, Irbīl, *Kurd.* Hawlēr; *anc.* Arbela. N Iraq
Arbroath 88 D3 *anc.* Aberbrothock. E Scotland, UK
Arbyzynka 109 E3 *Rus.* Arbuzinka. Mykolayivs'ka Oblast', S Ukraine
Arcachon 91 B5 Gironde, SW France
Arcata 46 A4 California, W USA
Archangel *see* Arkhangel'sk
Archangel Bay *see* Chëshskaya Guba
Archidona 92 D5 Andalucía, S Spain
Archipel des Australes *see* Australes, Îles
Archipel des Tuamotu *see* Tuamotu, Îles
Archipel de Tahiti *see* Société, Archipel de la
Arco 96 C2 Trentino-Alto Adige, N Italy
Arctic-Mid Oceanic Ridge *see* Nansen Cordillera
Arctic Ocean 172 B3 *ocean*
Arda 104 C3 *var.* Ardhas, *Gk.* Ardas. *River* Bulgaria/Greece *see also* Ardas
Arda *see* Ardas
Ardabīl 120 C2 *var.* Ardebil. Ardabīl, NW Iran
Ardakān 120 D3 Yazd, C Iran
Ardas 104 D3 *var.* Ardhas, *Bul.* Arda. *River* Bulgaria/Greece *see also* Arda
Ardas *see* Arda
Arḍ aş Şawwān 119 C7 *var.* Ardh es Suwwān. *Plain* S Jordan
Ardebil *see* Ardabīl
Ardèche 91 C5 *cultural region* E France
Ardennes 87 C8 *plateau* W Europe
Ardhas *see* Ardas
Ardh es Suwwān *see* Arḍ aş Şawwān
Ardino 104 D3 Kŭrdzhali, S Bulgaria
Ard Mhacha *see* Armagh
Ardmore 49 G2 Oklahoma, C USA
Arelas *see* Arles
Arelate *see* Arles
Arendal 85 A6 Aust-Agder, S Norway
Arenys de Mar 93 G2 Cataluña, NE Spain
Areópoli 105 B7 *prev.* Areópolis. Pelopónnisos, S Greece
Arequipa 61 E4 Arequipa, SE Peru
Arezzo 96 C3 *anc.* Arretium. Toscana, C Italy
Argalastí 105 C5 Thessalía, C Greece
Argenteuil 90 D1 Val-d'Oise, N France
Argentina 65 B5 *Country* S South America

Argentina 65

Official name Argentine Republic
Formation 1816
Capital Buenos Aires
Population 30 million / 35 people per sq mile (14 people per sq km)
Total area 1,056,636 sq miles (2,736,690 sq km)
Languages Spanish, Italian, Amerindian languages
Religions Roman Catholic 90%, Jewish 2%, Protestant 2%,

Argentina (continued)

other 6%
Ethnic mix European 85%, other 15%
Government Multiparty republic
Currency Argentine peso = 100 centavos
Literacy rate 95%
Calorie consumption 2,880 kilocalories

Argentina Basin *see* Argentine Basin
Argentine Basin 57 C7 *var.* Argentina Basin. *Undersea feature* SW Atlantic Ocean
Argentine Rise *see* Falkland Plateau
Arghandāb, Daryā-ye 123 E5 *river* SE Afghanistan
Argirocastro *see* Gjirokastër
Argo 72 B3 Northern, N Sudan
Argo Fracture Zone 141 C5 *tectonic feature* C Indian Ocean
Árgos 105 B6 Pelopónnisos, S Greece
Argostóli 105 A5 *var.* Argostólion. Kefallinía, Iónioi Nísoi, Greece, C Mediterranean Sea
Argostólion *see* Argostóli
Argun 125 E1 *Chin.* Ergun He, *Rus.* Argun'. *River* China/Russian Federation
Argyrokastron *see* Gjirokastër
Århus 85 B7 *var.* Aarhus. Århus, C Denmark
Aria *see* Herāt
Ari Atoll 132 A4 *atoll* C Maldives
Arica 64 B1 *hist.* San Marcos de Arica. Tarapacá, N Chile
Aridaía 104 B3 *var.* Aridea, Aridhaía. Dytikí Makedonía, N Greece
Aridea *see* Aridaía
Aridhaía *see* Aridaía
Arīḥā 118 B3 *var.* Arīhā. Idlib, W Syria
Arīḥā *see* Jericho
Arinsal 91 A7 NW Andorra
Arizona 48 A2 *off.* State of Arizona; also known as Copper State, Grand Canyon State. Admin. region *state* SW USA
Arkansas 42 A1 *off.* State of Arkansas; also known as The Land of Opportunity. *State* S USA
Arkansas City 45 F5 Kansas, C USA
Arkansas River 49 G1 *river* C USA
Arkhangel'sk 114 B2 *Eng.* Archangel. Arkhangel'skaya Oblast', NW Russian Federation
Arkoí 105 E6 *island* Dodekánisos, Greece, Aegean Sea
Arles 91 D6 *var.* Arles-sur-Rhône; *anc.* Arelas, Arelate. Bouches-du-Rhône, SE France
Arles-sur-Rhône *see* Arles
Arlington 49 G2 Texas, SW USA
Arlington 41 E4 Virginia, NE USA
Arlon 87 D8 *Dut.* Aarlen, *Ger.* Arel; *Lat.* Orolaunum. Luxembourg, SE Belgium
Armagh 89 B5 *Ir.* Ard Mhacha. S Northern Ireland, UK
Armagnac 91 B6 *cultural region* S France
Armenia 117 F3 *var.* Ajastan, *Arm.* Hayastani Hanrapetut'yun; *prev.* Armenian Soviet Socialist Republic. *Country* SW Asia

Armenia 117

Official name Republic of Armenia
Formation 1991
Capital Yerevan
Population 3.5 million / 304 people per sq mile (117 people per sq km)
Total area 11,506 sq miles (29,800 sq km)
Languages Armenian, Russian
Religions The Armenian Apostolic Church 94%, other 6%

Armenia (continued)

Ethnic mix Armenian 93%,Azeri
3%, Russian 2%, other 2%
Government Multiparty republic
Currency Dram = 100 louma
Literacy rate 99%
Calorie consumption
not available

Armenia 58 B3 Quindío,
W Colombia
Armidale 149 D6 New South Wales,
SE Australia
Armstrong 38 B3 Ontario, S Canada
Armyans'k 109 F4 Rus. Armyansk.
Respublika Krym, S Ukraine
Arnaía 104 C4 var. Arnea. Kentrikí
Makedonía, N Greece
Arnaud 82 A3 river Québec,
E Canada
Arnea see Arnaía
Arnedo 93 E2 La Rioja, N Spain
Arnhem 86 D4 Gelderland,
SE Netherlands
Arnhem Land 148 A2 physical region
Northern Territory, N Australia
Arno 96 B3 river C Italy
Arnold 45 G4 Missouri, C USA
Arorae 145 E3 atoll Tungaru,
W Kiribati
Arquipélago da Madeira see
Madeira
Arquipélago dos Açores see Azores
Ar Rahad see Er Rahad
Ar Ramādī 120 B3 var. Ramadi,
Rumadiya. SW Iraq
Ar Rāmī 118 C4 Ḥimṣ, C Syria
Ar Ramthā 119 B5 var. Ramtha.
Irbid, N Jordan
Arran, Isle of 88 C3 island
SW Scotland, UK
Ar Raqqah 118 C2 var. Rakka; anc.
Nicephorium. Ar Raqqah, N Syria
Arras 90 C2 anc. Nemetocenna. Pas-
de-Calais, N France
Ar Rawdatayn 120 C4 var.
Raudhatain. N Kuwait
Arriaga 51 F5 Chiapas, SE Mexico
Ar Riyāḍ 121 C5 Eng. Riyadh.
Country capital (Saudi Arabia) Ar
Riyāḍ, C Saudi Arabia
Ar Rub 'al Khālī 121 C6 Eng.
Empty Quarter, Great Sandy
Desert. Desert SW Asia
Ar Rustāq 121 E5 var. Rostak,
Rustaq. N Oman
Ar Ruṭbah 120 B3 var. Rutba.
SW Iraq
Árta 105 A5 anc. Ambracia. Ípeiros,
W Greece
Artashat 117 F3 S Armenia
Artemisa 54 B2 La Habana, W Cuba
Artesia 48 D3 New Mexico, SW USA
Arthur's Pass 151 C6 pass South
Island, NZ
Artigas 64 D3 prev. San Eugenio,
San Eugenio del Cuareim.
Artigas, N Uruguay
Art'ik 117 F2 W Armenia
Artois 90 C2 cultural region
N France
Artsyz 108 D4 Rus. Artsiz. Odes'ka
Oblast', SW Ukraine
Artvin 117 F2 Artvin, NE Turkey
Arua 73 B6 NW Uganda
Aruângua see Luangwa
Aruba 58 C1 var. Oruba. Dutch
autonomous region S West Indies
Aru, Kepulauan 139 G4 Eng. Aru
Islands; prev. Aroe Islands. Island
group E Indonesia
Arunāchal Pradesh 135 G3 cultural
region NE India
Arusha 73 C7 Arusha, N Tanzania
Arviat 37 G4 prev. Eskimo Point.
Nunavut, C Canada
Arvidsjaur 84 C4 Norrbotten,
N Sweden
Arys' 114 B5 Kaz. Arys. Yuzhnyy
Kazakhstan, S Kazakhstan
Asadābād 123 F4 var. Asadābād;
prev. Chaghasarāy. Kunar,
E Afghanistan
Asad, Buḥayrat al 134 C2 Eng. Lake
Assad. Lake N Syria

Asahi-dake 130 D2 mountain
Hokkaidō, N Japan
Asahikawa 130 D2 Hokkaidō,
N Japan
Asamankese 75 E5 SE Ghana
Āsānsol 135 F4 West Bengal,
NE India
Asben see Aïr, Massif de l'
Ascension Fracture Zone 69 A5
tectonic feature C Atlantic Ocean
Ascension Island 85 A5 dependency
of St. Helena C Atlantic Ocean
Ascoli Piceno 96 C4 anc. Asculum
Picenum. Marche, C Italy
Aseb 72 D4 var. Assab, Amh. Āseb.
SE Eritrea
Ashara see Al 'Ashārah
Ashburton 151 C6 Canterbury,
South Island, NZ
Ashburton River 146 A4 river
Western Australia
Ashdod 119 A6 anc. Azotos, Lat.
Azotus. Central, W Israel
Asheville 43 E1 North Carolina,
SE USA
Ashgabat 122 C3 prev. Ashkhabad,
Poltoratsk. Country capital
(Turkmenistan) Akhalskiy
Velayat, C Turkmenistan
Ashkelon see Ashqelon
Ashland 46 B4 Oregon, NW USA
Ashland 40 B1 Wisconsin, N USA
Ashmore and Cartier Islands 142
A3 Australian external territory
E Indian Ocean
Ashmyany 107 C5 Rus. Oshmyany.
Hrodzyenskaya Voblasts',
W Belarus
Ashqelon 119 A6 var. Ashkelon.
Southern, C Israel
Ash Shaddādah 118 D2 var. Ash
Shaddādah, Jisr ash Shadadi,
Shaddādī, Shedadi, Tell Shedadi.
Al Ḥasakah, NE Syria
Ash Shaddādah see Ash Shaddādah
Ash Shām see Dimashq
Ash Sharāh 119 B7 var. Esh Sharā.
Mountain range W Jordan
Ash Shāriqah 120 D4 Eng. Sharjah.
Ash Shāriqah, NE UAE
Ash Shawbak 119 B7 Ma'ān,
W Jordan
Ash Shiḥr 121 C6 SE Yemen
Asia 25 C2 continent
Asinara, Isola 96 A4 island W Italy
Asipovichy 107 D6 Rus. Osipovichi.
Mahilyowskaya Voblasts',
C Belarus
Aşkale 117 E3 Erzurum, NE Turkey
Askersund 85 C6 Örebro, C Sweden
Asmara 72 C4 Amh. Āsmera.
Country capital (Eritrea) C Eritrea
Assab see Aseb
As Sabkhah 118 D2 var. Sabkha. Ar
Raqqah, NE Syria
Aş Şafāwī 119 C6 Al Mafraq,
N Jordan
Aş Şaḥrā' al Gharbīyah see Sahara
el Gharbīya
Aş Şaḥrā' al Lībīyah see Libyan
Desert
Aş Şaḥrā' ash Sharqīyah see
Eastern Desert
As Salamīyah see Salamīyah
As Salṭ 119 B6 var. Salt. Al Balqā',
NW Jordan
Assamaka see Assamakka
Assamakka 75 F2 var. Assamaka.
Agadez, NW Niger
As Samāwah 120 B3 var. Samawa.
S Iraq
Assen 86 E2 Drenthe,
NE Netherlands
Assenede 87 B5 Oost-Vlaanderen,
NW Belgium
Assiout see Asyūt
Assiut see Asyūt
Assouan see Aswān
Assu see Açu
Assuan see Aswān
As Sukhnah 118 C3 var. Sukhne, Fr.
Soukhné. Ḥimṣ, C Syria
As Sulaymānīyah 120 C3 var.
Sulaimaniya, Kurd. Slēmānī.
NE Iraq
As Sulayyil 121 B5 Ar Riyāḍ,
S Saudi Arabia

Aş Şuwār 118 D2 var. Şuwār. Dayr
az Zawr, E Syria
As Suwaydā' 119 B5 var.
El Suweida, Es Suweida,
Suweida, Fr. Soueida. As
Suwaydā', SW Syria
Astacus see İzmit
Astana 114 C4 prev. Akmola,
Akmolinsk, Tselinograd, Kaz.
Aqmola. country capital
(Kazakhstan) Akmola, N
Kazakhstan
Astarabad see Gorgān
Asterābād see Gorgān
Asti 96 A2 anc. Asta Colonia, Asta
Pompeia, Hasta Colonia, Hasta
Pompeia. Piemonte, NW Italy
Astipálaia see Astypálaia
Astorga 92 C1 anc. Asturica
Augusta. Castilla-León, N Spain
Astrabad see Gorgān
Astrakhan' 111 C7 Astrakhanskaya
Oblast', SW Russian Federation
Asturias 92 C1 cultural region
NW Spain
Astypálaia 105 D7 var. Astipálaia,
It. Stampalia. Island Kykládes,
Greece, Aegean Sea
Asunción 64 D2 country capital
(Paraguay) Central, S Paraguay
Aswān 72 B2 var. Assouan, Assuan;
anc. Syene. SE Egypt
Asyūt 72 B2 var. Assiout, Assiut,
Siut; anc. Lycopolis. C Egypt
Atacama Desert see Atacama,
Desierto de
Atacama, Desierto de 64 B2 Eng.
Atacama Desert. Desert N Chile
Atafu Atoll 145 E3 island
NW Tokelau
Aţār 74 C2 Adrar, W Mauritania
Atas Bogd 126 D3 mountain
SW Mongolia
Atascadero 47 B7 California,
W USA
Atatürk Barajı 117 E4 reservoir
S Turkey
Atbara 72 C3 var. 'Aţbārah. River
Nile, NE Sudan
'Aţbārah see Atbara
Atbasar 114 C4 Akmola,
N Kazakhstan
Atchison 45 F4 Kansas, C USA
Ath 87 B6 var. Aat. Hainaut,
SW Belgium
Athabasca 37 E5 var. Athabaska.
River Alberta, SW Canada
Athabasca 37 E5 Alberta,
SW Canada
Athabasca, Lake 37 F4 lake
Alberta/Saskatchewan,
SW Canada
Athabaska see Athabasca
Athens see Athína
Athens 43 E2 Georgia, SE USA
Athens 40 D4 Ohio, N USA
Athens 49 G3 Texas, SW USA
Atherton 148 D3 Queensland,
NE Australia
Athína 105 C6 Eng. Athens; prev.
Athínai, anc. Athenae. Country
capital (Greece) Attikí, C Greece
Athlone 89 B5 Ir. Baile Átha Luain.
C Ireland
Ath Thawrah see Madīnat ath
Thawrah
Ati 76 C3 Batha, C Chad
Atikokan 38 B4 Ontario, S Canada
Atka 36 A3 Atka Island, Alaska,
USA
Atka 115 G3 Magadanskaya Oblast',
E Russian Federation
Atlanta 42 D2 state capital Georgia,
SE USA
Atlanta 49 H2 Texas, SW USA
Atlantic City 41 F4 New Jersey,
NE USA
Atlantic-Indian Basin 67 D7
undersea feature SW Indian Ocean
Atlantic-Indian Ridge 69 B8
undersea feature
SW Indian Ocean
Atlantic Ocean 66 B4 ocean
Atlas Mountains 70 C2 mountain
range NW Africa
Atlasovo 115 H3 Kamchatskaya
Oblast', E Russian Federation

Atlas Saharien 70 D2 var. Saharan
Atlas. Mountain range
Algeria/Morocco
Atlas Tellien 102 C3 Eng. Tell Atlas.
Mountain range N Algeria
Atlin 36 D4 British Columbia,
W Canada
Aţ Ţafilah 119 B7 var. Et Tafila,
Tafila. Aţ Ţafilah, W Jordan
Aţ Ţā'if 121 B5 Makkah, W Saudi
Arabia
At Tall al Abyaḍ 118 C2 var. Tall
al Abyaḍ, Tell Abyaḍ, Fr. Tell
Abiad. Ar Raqqah, N Syria
Aţ Ţanf 118 D4 Ḥimṣ, S Syria
Attapu see Samakhixai
Attawapiskat 38 C3 river Ontario,
S Canada
Attawapiskat 38 C3 Ontario,
C Canada
At Tibnī 118 D2 var. Tibnī. Dayr az
Zawr, NE Syria
Attopeu see Samakhixai
Attu Island 36 A2 island Aleutian
Islands, Alaska, USA
Atyrau 114 B4 prev. Gur'yev.
Atyrau, W Kazakhstan
Aubagne 91 D6 anc. Albania.
Bouches-du-Rhône, SE France
Aubange 87 D8 Luxembourg,
SE Belgium
Aubervilliers 90 E1 Seine-St-Denis,
N France
Auburn 46 B2 Washington, NW USA
Auch 91 B6 Lat. Augusta
Auscorum, Elimberrum. Gers,
S France
Auckland 150 D2 Auckland, North
Island, NZ
Auckland Islands 142 C5 island
group S NZ
Audincourt 90 E4 Doubs, E France
Audru 106 D2 Ger. Audern.
Pärnumaa, SW Estonia
Augathella 149 D5 Queensland,
E Australia
Augsburg 95 C6 Fr. Augsbourg; anc.
Augusta Vindelicorum. Bayern,
S Germany
Augusta 41 G2 state capital Maine,
NE USA
Augusta 43 E2 Georgia, SE USA
Augusta 147 A7 Western Australia
Augustów 98 E2 Rus. Avgustov.
Podlaskie, NE Poland
'Aujā et Tahtā see. Khirbet el 'Aujā
et Tahtā
Aulie Ata/Auliye-Ata see Taraz
Auob 78 B4 var. Oup. River
Namibia/South Africa
Aurangābād 134 D5 Mahārāshtra,
C India
Auray 90 A3 Morbihan, NW France
Aurès, Massif de l' 102 C4 mountain
range NE Algeria
Aurillac 91 C5 Cantal, C France
Aurora 44 D4 Colorado, C USA
Aurora 40 B3 Illinois, N USA
Aurora 45 G5 Missouri, C USA
Aurora 59 F2 NW Guyana
Aus 78 B4 Karas, SW Namibia
Ausa see Vic
Austin 49 G3 state capital Texas,
S USA
Austin 45 G3 Minnesota, N USA
Australes, Îles 143 F4 var. Archipel
des Australes, Îles Tubuai, Tubuai
Islands, Eng. Austral Islands.
Island group SW French Polynesia
Austral Fracture Zone 143 H4
tectonic feature S Pacific Ocean
Australia 142 A4 Country

Australia 142

Official name Commonwealth of
Australia
Formation 1901
Capital Canberra
Population 19 million / 6 people
per sq mile (2 people per sq km)
Total area 2,941,282 sq miles
(7,617,930 sq km)
Languages English, Greek, Italian,
Vietnamese, Aboriginal languages
Religions Christian 64%, other 34%

Australia (continued)

Ethnic mix European 95%, Asian 4%, Aboriginal and other 1%
Government Parliamentary democracy
Currency Australian dollar = 100 cents
Literacy rate 99%
Calorie consumption 3,179 kilocalories

Australian Alps *149 C7 mountain range* SE Australia
Australian Capital Territory *149 D7 prev.* Federal Capital Territory. *Territory* SE Australia
Austral Islands *see* Australes, Îles
Austria *95 D7 Ger.* Österreich. *Country* C Europe

Austria 95

Official name Republic of Austria
Formation 1920
Capital Vienna
Population 8.2 million / 257 people per sq mile (99 people per sq km)
Total area 31,942 sq miles (82,730 sq km)
Languages German, Croatian, Slovene
Religions Roman Catholic 78%, non-religious 9%, Protestant 5%, Muslim 2%, other (including Jewish) 6%
Ethnic mix German 93%, Croatian, Slovene, Hungarian 6%, other 1%
Government Multiparty republic
Currency Schilling = 100 groschen
Literacy rate 99%
Calorie consumption 3,497 kilocalories

Auvergne *91 C5 cultural region* C France
Auxerre *90 C4 anc.* Autesiodorum, Autissiodorum. Yonne, C France
Avarua *145 G5 dependent territory capital* (Cook Islands) Rarotonga, S Cook Islands
Ávdira *104 C3* Anatolikí Makedonía kai Thráki, NE Greece
Aveiro *92 B2 anc.* Talabriga. Aveiro, W Portugal
Avela *see* Ávila
Avellino *97 D5 anc.* Abellinum. Campania, S Italy
Avesta *85 C6* Kopparberg, C Sweden
Aveyron *91 C6 river* S France
Avezzano *96 C4* Abruzzo, C Italy
Aviemore *88 C3* N Scotland, UK
Avignon *91 D6 anc.* Avenio. Vaucluse, SE France
Avila *see* Ávila
Ávila *92 D3 var.* Avila; *anc.* Abela, Abula, Abyla, Avela. Castilla-León, C Spain
Avilés *92 C1* Asturias, NW Spain
Avranches *90 B3* Manche, N France
Awaji-shima *131 C6 island* SW Japan
Āwash *73 D5 var.* Hawash. *River* C Ethiopia
Awbārī *71 F3* SW Libya
Ax *see* Dax
Axel *87 B5* Zeeland, SW Netherlands
Axel Heiberg Island *37 E1 var.* Axel Heiburg. *Island* Nunavut, N Canada
Axel Heiburg *see* Axel Heiberg Island
Ayacucho *60 D4* Ayacucho, S Peru
Ayagoz *130 C5 var.* Ayaguz, *Kaz.* Ayaköz; *prev.* Sergiopol. Vostochnyy Kazakhstan, E Kazakhstan
Ayaguz *see* Ayagoz
Ayaköz *see* Ayagoz
Ayamonte *92 C4* Andalucía, S Spain

Ayaviri *61 E4* Puno, S Peru
Aydarkŭl *123 E2 Rus.* Ozero Aydarkul'. *Lake* C Uzbekistan
Aydın *116 A4 var.* Aïdin; *anc.* Tralles. Aydın, SW Turkey
Ayers Rock *see* Uluru
Ayeyarwady *see* Irrawaddy
Ayiá *see* Agiá
Ayios Evstrátios *see* Efstrátios, Ágios
Áyios Nikólaos *see* Ágios Nikólaos
Ayorou *75 E3* Tillabéri, W Niger
'Ayoûn el 'Atroûs *74 D3 var.* Aïoun el Atrous, Aïoun el Atroûss. Hodh el Gharbi, SE Mauritania
Ayr *88 C4* W Scotland, UK
Ayteke Bi *130 B4 . Kaz.* Zhangaqazaly, *prev.* Novokazalinsk Kyzylorda, SW Kazakhstan
Aytos *104 E2* Burgas, E Bulgaria
Ayutthaya *137 C5 var.* Phra Nakhon Si Ayutthaya. Phra Nakhon Si Ayutthaya, C Thailand
Ayvalık *116 A3* Balıkesir, W Turkey
Azahar, Costa del *93 F3 coastal region* E Spain
Azaouâd *75 E3 desert* C Mali
A'zāz *118 B2* Ḩalab, NW Syria
Azerbaijan *117 G2 Az.* Azărbaycan, Azărbaycan Respublikası; *prev.* Azerbaijan SSR. *Country* SW Asia

Azerbaijan 117

Official name Republic of Azerbaijan
Formation 1991
Capital Baku
Population 7.7 million / 230 people per sq mile (89 people per sq km)
Total area 33,436 sq miles (86,600 sq km)
Languages Azerbaijani, Russian
Religions Muslim 83%, Armenian Apostolic and Russian Orthodox 17 %
Ethnic mix Azeri 83%, Armenian 6%, Russian 5%, Daghestani 3%, other 3%
Government Multiparty republic
Currency Manat = 100 gopik
Literacy rate 96.3%
Calorie consumption not available

Azimabad *see* Patna
Azogues *60 B2* Cañar, S Ecuador
Azores *92 A4 var.* Açores, Ilhas dos Açores, *Port.* Arquipélago dos Açores. *Island group* Portugal, NE Atlantic Ocean
Azores-Biscay Rise *80 A3 undersea feature* E Atlantic Ocean
Azoum, Bahr *76 C3 seasonal river* SE Chad
Azov, Sea of *103 H1 Rus.* Azovskoye More, *Ukr.* Azovs'ke More. *Sea* NE Black Sea
Azraq, Wāḥat al *135 C6 oasis* N Jordan
Aztec *48 C1* New Mexico, SW USA
Azuaga *92 C4* Extremadura, W Spain
Azuero, Península de *53 F5 peninsula* S Panama
Azul *65 D5* Buenos Aires, E Argentina
Azur, Côte d' *107 E6 Coastal region* SE France
Az Zaqāzīq *see* Zagazig
Az Zarqā' *119 B6 var.* Zarqa. Az Zarqā', NW Jordan
Az Zāwiyah *71 F2 var.* Zawia. NW Libya
Az Zilfī *120 B4* Ar Riyāḍ, N Saudi Arabia
Æsernia *see* Isernia

B

Ba *100 D3 prev.* Mba. Viti Levu, W Fiji
Baalbek *118 B4 var.* Ba'labakk; *anc.* Heliopolis. E Lebanon
Bá an Daingin *see* Dingle Bay

Baardheere *73 D6 var.* Bardere, *It.* Bardera. Gedo, SW Somalia
Baarle-Hertog *87 C5* Antwerpen, N Belgium
Baarn *86 C3* Utrecht, C Netherlands
Babadag *108 D5* Tulcea, SE Romania
Babahoyo *60 B2 prev.* Bodegas. Los Ríos, C Ecuador
Bāb, Kūh-e *123 E4 mountain range* C Afghanistan
Babayevo *110 B4* Vologodskaya Oblast', NW Russian Federation
Babeldaob *144 A1 var.* Babeldaop, Babelthuap. *Island* N Palau
Babeldaop *see* Babeldaob
Bab el Mandeb *121 B7 strait* Gulf of Aden/Red Sea
Babelthuap *see* Babeldaob
Bá Bheanntraí *see* Bantry Bay
Babruysk *107 D7 Rus.* Bobruysk. Mahilyowskaya Voblasts', E Belarus
Babuyan Channel *139 E1 channel* N Philippines
Babuyan Island *139 E1 island* N Philippines
Bacabal *63 F2* Maranhão, E Brazil
Bacău *108 C4 Hung.* Bákó. Bacău, NE Romania
Băc Giang *136 D3* Ha Băc, N Vietnam
Bacheykava *107 D5 Rus.* Bocheykovo. Vitsyebskaya Voblasts', N Belarus
Back *37 F3 river* Nunavut, N Canada
Bačka Palanka *100 D3 prev.* Palanka. Serbia, NW Yugoslavia
Bačka Topola *100 D3 Hung.* Topolya; *prev. Hung.* Bácstopolya. Serbia, N Yugoslavia
Bac Liêu *137 D6 var.* Vinh Loi. Minh Hai, S Vietnam
Bacolod *125 E4 off.* Bacolod City. Negros, C Philippines
Bacolod City *see* Bacolod
Bácsszenttamás *see* Srbobran
Badajoz *92 C4 anc.* Pax Augusta. Extremadura, W Spain
Baden-Baden *95 B6 anc.* Aurelia Aquensis. Baden-Württemberg, SW Germany
Bad Freienwalde *94 D3* Brandenburg, NE Germany
Bad Hersfeld *94 B4* Hessen, C Germany
Bad Homburg *see* Bad Homburg vor der Höhe
Bad Homburg vor der Höhe *95 B5 var.* Bad Homburg. Hessen, W Germany
Bá Dhún na nGall *see* Donegal Bay
Bad Ischl *95 D7* Oberösterreich, N Austria
Bad Krozingen *95 A6* Baden-Württemberg, SW Germany
Badlands *44 D2 physical region* North Dakota, N USA
Badu Island *148 C1 island* Queensland, NE Australia
Bad Vöslau *95 E6* Niederösterreich, NE Austria
Baetic Cordillera *see* Béticos, Sistemas
Baetic Mountains *see* Béticos, Sistemas
Bafatá *74 C4* C Guinea-Bissau
Baffin Bay *37 G2 bay* Canada/Greenland
Baffin Island *37 G2 island* Nunavut, NE Canada
Bafing *74 C3 river* W Africa
Bafoussam *76 A4* Ouest, W Cameroon
Bafra *116 D2* Samsun, N Turkey
Bāft *120 D4* Kermān, S Iran
Bagaces *52 D4* Guanacaste, NW Costa Rica
Bagdad *see* Baghdād
Bagé *63 E5* Rio Grande do Sul, S Brazil
Baghdād *120 B3 var.* Bagdad, *Eng.* Baghdad. *Country capital* (Iraq) C Iraq
Baghlān *123 E3* Baghlān, NE Afghanistan

Bago *see* Pegu
Bagoé *74 D4 river* Côte d'Ivoire/Mali
Bagrationovsk *106 A4 Ger.* Preussisch Eylau. Kaliningradskaya Oblast', W Russian Federation
Bagrax Hu *see* Bosten Hu
Baguio *139 E1 off.* Baguio City. Luzon, N Philippines
Bagzane, Monts *75 F3 mountain* N Niger
Bahama Islands *see* Bahamas
Bahamas *54 C2 Country* N West Indies

Bahamas 54

Official name Commonwealth of the Bahamas
Formation 1973
Capital Nassau
Population 307,000 / 79 people per sq mile (31 people per sq km)
Total area 3,864 sq miles (10,010 sq km)
Languages English, English Creole, French Creole
Religions Baptist 32%, Anglican 20%, Roman Catholic 19%, Church of God 6%, Methodist 6%, other 17%
Ethnic mix Black 85%, White 15%
Government Parliamentary democracy
Currency Bahamian dollar = 100 cents
Literacy rate 95.8%
Calorie consumption 2,624 kilocalories

Bahamas *35 D6 var.* Bahama Islands. *Island group* N West Indies
Bahāwalpur *134 C2* Punjab, E Pakistan
Bahía *63 F3 off.* Estado da Bahia. *State* E Brazil
Bahía Blanca *65 C5* Buenos Aires, E Argentina
Bahía, Islas de la *52 C1 Eng.* Bay Islands. *Island group* N Honduras
Bahir Dar *72 C4 var.* Bahr Dar, Bahrdar Giyorgis. NW Ethiopia
Bahraich *135 E3* Uttar Pradesh, N India
Bahrain *120 C4 Ar.* Al Baḥrayn; *prev.* Bahrein, *anc.* Tylos or Tyros. *Country* SW Asia

Bahrain 120

Official name State of Bahrain
Formation 1971
Capital Manama
Population 617,000 / 2,350 people per sq mile (891 people per sq km)
Total area 263 sq miles (680 sq km)
Languages Arabic, English
Religions Muslim (mainly Shi'a) 85%, Christian 7%, other 8%
Ethnic mix Bahraini 70%, Iranian, Indian, Pakistani 24%, other Arab 6%
Government Monarchy with Consultative Council
Currency Bahrain dinar = 1,000 fils
Literacy rate 86.3%
Calorie consumption not available

Baḥr al Milḥ *see* Razāzah, Buḥayrat ar
Baḥrat Lūt *see* Dead Sea
Bahrat Tabariya *see* Tiberias, Lake
Bahr Dar *see* Bahir Dar
Bahrdar Giyorgis *see* Bahir Dar
Bahr el Azraq *see* Blue Nile
Bahr el Jebel *see* White Nile
Bahret Lut *see* Dead Sea

Bahr Tabariya, Sea of *see* Tiberias, Lake
Bahushewsk 107 E6 *Rus.* Bogushëvsk. Vitsyebskaya Voblasts', NE Belarus
Baia Mare 108 B3 *Ger.* Frauenbach, *Hung.* Nagybánya; *prev.* Neustadt. Maramureş, NW Romania
Baia Sprie 108 B3 *Ger.* Mittelstadt, *Hung.* Felsőbánya. Maramureş, NW Romania
Baïbokoum 76 B4 Logone-Oriental, SW Chad
Baidoa *see* Baydhabo
Baie-Comeau 39 E3 Québec, SE Canada
Baikal, Lake *see* Baykal, Ozero
Baile Átha Luain *see* Athlone
Bailén 92 D4 Andalucía, S Spain
Baile na Mainistreach *see* Newtownabbey
Băileşti 108 B5 Dolj, SW Romania
Ba Illi 76 B3 Chari-Baguirmi, SW Chad
Bainbridge 42 D3 Georgia, SE USA
Bā'ir *see* Bāyir
Baireuth *see* Bayreuth
Bairiki 144 D2 *country capital* (Kiribati) Tarawa, NW Kiribati
Bairnsdale 149 C7 Victoria, SE Australia
Baishan 129 E3 *prev.* Hunjiang. Jilin, NE China
Baiyin 128 B4 Gansu, C China
Baja 99 C7 Bács-Kiskun, S Hungary
Baja California 48 A4 *Eng.* Lower California. *Peninsula* NW Mexico
Baja California 50 B2 *state* NW Mexico
Bajo Boquete *see* Boquete
Bajram Curri 101 D3 Kukës, N Albania
Bakala 76 C4 Ouaka, C Central African Republic
Bakan *see* Shimonoseki
Baker 46 C3 Oregon, NW USA
Baker and Howland Islands 145 E2 *US unincorporated territory* W Polynesia
Baker Lake 37 F3 Nunavut, N Canada
Bakersfield 47 C7 California, W USA
Bakharden 122 C3 *Turkm.* Bäherden; *prev.* Bakherden. Akhalskiy Velayat, C Turkmenistan
Bakhchysaray 109 F5 *Rus.* Bakhchisaray. Respublika Krym, S Ukraine
Bakhmach 109 F1 Chernihivs'ka Oblast', N Ukraine
Bākhtarān 120 C3 *prev.* Kermānshāh, Qahremānshahr. Kermānshāhb. W Iran
Bakı 117 H2 *Eng.* Baku. *Country capital* (Azerbaijan) E Azerbaijan
Bakony 99 C7 *Eng.* Bakony Mountains, *Ger.* Bakonywald. *Mountain range* W Hungary
Baku *see* Bakı
Balabac Island 129 C8 *island* W Philippines
Balabac Strait 138 D2 *var.* Selat Balabac. *Strait* Malaysia/Philippines
Ba'labakk *see* Baalbek
Balaguer 93 F2 Cataluña, NE Spain
Balakovo 111 C6 Saratovskaya Oblast', W Russian Federation
Bālā Morghāb 122 D4 Laghmān, NW Afghanistan
Balashov 111 B6 Saratovskaya Oblast', W Russian Federation
Balaton *C7 var.* Lake Balaton, *Ger.* Plattensee. *Lake* W Hungary
Balaton, Lake *see* Balaton
Balbina, Represa 62 D1 *reservoir* NW Brazil
Balboa 53 G4 Panamá, C Panama
Balcarce 65 D5 Buenos Aires, E Argentina
Balclutha 151 B7 Otago, South Island, NZ
Baldy Mountain 44 C1 *mountain* Montana, NW USA

Bâle *see* Basel
Baleares, Islas 93 G3 *Eng.* Balearic Islands. *Island group* Spain, W Mediterranean Sea
Balearic Islands *see* Baleares, Islas
Balearic Plain *see* Algerian Basin
Baleine, Rivière à la 39 E2 *river* Québec, E Canada
Balen 87 C5 Antwerpen, N Belgium
Bāleshwar 135 F4 *prev.* Balasore. Orissa, E India
Bali 138 D5 *island* C Indonesia
Balıkesir 116 A3 Balıkesir, W Turkey
Balīkh 118 C2 *river* N Syria
Balikpapan 138 D4 Borneo, C Indonesia
Balkan Mountains 104 C2 *Bul./SCr.* Stara Planina. *Mountain range* Bulgaria/Yugoslavia
Balkh 123 E3 *anc.* Bactra. Balkh, N Afghanistan
Balkhash 114 C5 *Kaz.* Balqash. Karaganda, SE Kazakhstan
Balkhash, Lake *see* Balkhash, Ozero
Balkhash, Ozero 114 C5 *Eng.* Lake Balkhash, *Kaz.* Balqash. *Lake* SE Kazakhstan
Balladonia 147 C6 Western Australia
Ballarat 149 C7 Victoria, SE Australia
Balleny Islands 154 B5 *island group* Antarctica
Ballinger 49 F3 Texas, SW USA
Balochistān *see* Baluchistān
Balş 108 B5 Olt, S Romania
Balsas 63 F2 Maranhão, E Brazil
Balsas, Río 51 E5 *var.* Río Mexcala. *River* S Mexico
Bal'shavik 107 D7 *Rus.* Bol'shevik. Homyel'skaya Voblasts', SE Belarus
Balta 108 D3 Odes'ka Oblast', SW Ukraine
Bălţi 108 D3 *Rus.* Bel'tsy. N Moldova
Baltic Sea 85 C7 *Ger.* Ostee, *Rus.* Baltiskoye More. *Sea* N Europe
Baltimore 41 F4 Maryland, NE USA
Baltkrievija *see* Belarus
Baluchistān 134 B3 *var.* Balochistān, Beluchistan. Admin. region *province* SW Pakistan
Balvi 106 D4 Balvi, NE Latvia
Balykchy 123 G2 *Kir.* Ysyk-Köl; *prev.* Issyk-Kul', Rybach'ye. Issyk-Kul'skaya Oblast', NE Kyrgyzstan
Balzers 94 E2 S Liechtenstein
Bam 120 E4 Kermān, SE Iran
Bamako 74 D4 *country capital* (Mali) Capital District, SW Mali
Bambari 76 C4 Ouaka, C Central African Republic
Bamberg 95 C5 Bayern, SE Germany
Bamenda 76 A4 Nord-Ouest, W Cameroon
Banaba 144 D2 *var.* Ocean Island. *Island* Tungaru, W Kiribati
Bandaaceh 138 A3 *var.* Banda Atjeh; *prev.* Koetaradja, Kutaradja, Kutaraja. Sumatera, W Indonesia
Banda Atjeh *see* Bandaaceh
Bandama 74 D5 *var.* Bandama Fleuve. *River* S Côte d'Ivoire
Bandama Fleuve *see* Bandama
Bandar 'Abbās *see* Bandar-e 'Abbās
Bandarbeyla 73 E5 *var.* Bender Beila, Bender Beyla. Bari, NE Somalia
Bandar-e 'Abbās 120 D4 *var.* Bandar 'Abbās; *prev.* Gombroon. Hormozgan, S Iran
Bandar-e Büshehr 120 C4 *var.* Büshehr, *Eng.* Bushire. Büshehr, S Iran
Bandar-e Khamīr 120 D4 Hormozgan, S Iran
Bandar-e Langeh 120 D4 *var.* Bandar-e Lengeh, Lingeh. Hormozgan, S Iran
Bandar-e Lengeh *see* Bandar-e Langeh

Bandar Kassim *see* Boosaaso
Bandarlampung 138 C4 *prev.* Tanjungkarang, Teloekbetoeng, Telukbetung. Sumatera, W Indonesia
Bandar Maharani *see* Muar
Bandar Masulipatnam *see* Machilīpatnam
Bandar Seri Begawan 138 D3 *prev.* Brunei Town. *Country capital* (Brunei) N Brunei
Bandar Sri Aman *see* Sri Aman
Banda Sea 139 F5 *var.* Laut Banda. *Sea* E Indonesia
Bandiagara 75 E3 Mopti, C Mali
Bandırma 116 A3 *var.* Penderma. Balıkesir, NW Turkey
Bandundu 77 C6 *prev.* Banningville. Bandundu, W Dem. Rep. Congo (Zaire)
Bandung 138 C5 *prev.* Bandoeng. Jawa, C Indonesia
Bangalore 132 C2 Karnātaka, S India
Bangassou 76 D4 Mbomou, SE Central African Republic
Banggai, Kepulauan 139 E4 *island group* C Indonesia
Banghāzī 71 G2 *Eng.* Bengazi, Benghazi, *It.* Bengasi. NE Libya
Bangka, Pulau 138 C4 *island* W Indonesia
Bangkok *see* Krung Thep
Bangkok, Bight of *see* Krung Thep, Ao
Bangladesh 135 G3 *prev.* East Pakistan. *Country* S Asia

Bangladesh 135

Official name	People's Republic of Bangladesh
Formation	1971
Capital	Dhaka
Population	129 million / 2,499 people per sq mile (965 people per sq km)
Total area	51,702 sq miles (133,910 sq km)
Languages	Bengali, Urdu, Chakma, Marma (Magh), Garo, Khasi, Santhali
Religions	Muslim (mainly Sunni) 87%, Hindu 12%, other 1%
Ethnic mix	Bengali 98%, other 2%
Government	Multiparty republic
Currency	Taka = 100 paisa
Literacy rate	40%
Calorie consumption	2,019 kilocalories

Bangor 89 B5 *Ir.* Beannchar. E Northern Ireland, UK
Bangor 41 G2 Maine, NE USA
Bangor 89 C6 NW Wales, UK
Bangui 75 B5 *country capital* (Central African Republic) Ombella-Mpoko, SW Central African Republic
Bangweulu, Lake 73 B8 *var.* Lake Bengweulu. *Lake* N Zambia
Ban Hat Yai *see* Hat Yai
Ban Hin Heup 136 C4 Viangchan, C Laos
Ban Houayxay *see* Houayxay
Ban Houei Sai *see* Houayxay
Ban Hua Hin 137 C6 *var.* Hua Hin. Prachuap Khiri Khan, SW Thailand
Bani 74 D3 *river* S Mali
Banias *see* Bāniyās
Banī Suwayf *see* Beni Suef
Bāniyās 118 B3 *var.* Banias, Baniyas, Paneas. Tarṭūs, W Syria
Baniyas *see* Bāniyās
Banja Luka 100 B3 Republika Srpska, NW Bosnia and Herzegovina
Banjarmasin 138 D4 *prev.* Bandjarmasin. Borneo, C Indonesia
Banjul 74 B3 *prev.* Bathurst. *Country capital* (Gambia) W Gambia
Banks Island 37 E2 *island* Banks Island, Northwest Territories, NW Canada
Banks Islands 144 D4 *Fr.* Îles Banks. *Island group* N Vanuatu

Banks Lake 46 B1 *reservoir* Washington, NW USA
Banks Peninsula 151 C6 *peninsula* South Island, NZ
Banks Strait 149 C8 *strait* SW Tasman Sea
Bānkura 135 F4 West Bengal, NE India
Ban Mak Khaeng *see* Udon Thani
Banmo *see* Bhamo
Bañolas *see* Banyoles
Ban Pak Phanang *see* Pak Phanang
Ban Sichon *see* Sichon
Banská Bystrica 99 C6 *Ger.* Neusohl, *Hung.* Besztercebánya. Banskobystrický Kraj, C Slovakia
Bantry Bay 89 A7 *Ir.* Bá Bheanntraí. *Bay* SW Ireland
Banya 104 E2 Burgas, E Bulgaria
Banyak, Kepulauan 138 A3 *prev.* Kepulauan Banjak. *Island group* NW Indonesia
Banyo 76 B4 Adamaoua, NW Cameroon
Banyoles 93 G2 *var.* Bañolas. Cataluña, NE Spain
Banzare Seamounts 141 C7 *undersea feature* S Indian Ocean
Baoji 128 B4 *var.* Pao-chi, Paoki. Shaanxi, C China
Baoro 76 B4 Nana-Mambéré, W Central African Republic
Baoshan 128 A6 *var.* Pao-shan. Yunnan, SW China
Baotou 127 F3 *var.* Pao-t'ou, Paotow. Nei Mongol Zizhiqu, N China
Ba'qūbah 120 B3 *var.* Qubba. C Iraq
Baquerizo Moreno *see* Puerto Baquerizo Moreno
Bar 101 C5 *It.* Antivari. Montenegro, SW Yugoslavia
Baraawe 73 D6 *It.* Brava. Shabeellaha Hoose, S Somalia
Baraji, Hirfanli 116 C3 *lake* C Turkey
Bārāmati 134 C5 Mahārāshtra, W India
Baranavichy 107 B6 *Pol.* Baranowicze, *Rus.* Baranovichi. Brestskaya Voblasts', SW Belarus
Barbados 55 G1 *country* SE West Indies

Barbados 55

Official name	Barbados
Formation	1966
Capital	Bridgetown
Population	270,000 / 1,626 people per sq mile (628 people per sq km)
Total area	166 sq miles (430 sq km)
Languages	English, Bajan (Barbadian English)
Religions	Anglican 40%, non-religious 17%, Pentecostal 8%, Methodist 7%, Catholic 4%, other 24%
Ethnic mix	Black 80%, mixed 15%, White 4%, other 1%
Government	Parliamentary democracy
Currency	Barbados dollar = 100 cents
Literacy rate	97.6%
Calorie consumption	3,207 kilocalories

Barbastro 93 F2 Aragón, NE Spain
Barbate de Franco 92 C5 Andalucía, S Spain
Barbuda 55 G3 *island* N Antigua and Barbuda
Barcaldine 148 C4 Queensland, E Australia
Barce *see* Al Marj
Barcelona 93 G2 *anc.* Barcino, Barcinona. Cataluña, E Spain
Barcelona 59 E2 Anzoátegui, NE Venezuela
Barcoo *see* Cooper Creek
Barcs 99 C7 Somogy, SW Hungary
Bardaï 76 C1 Borkou-Ennedi-Tibesti, N Chad
Bardejov 99 D5 *Ger.* Bartfeld, *Hung.* Bártfa. Prešovský Kraj, E Slovakia

Bardera *see* Baardheere
Bardere *see* Baardheere
Bareilly 135 E3 *var.* Bareli. Uttar Pradesh, N India
Bareli *see* Bareilly
Barendrecht 86 C4 Zuid-Holland, SW Netherlands
Barentin 90 C3 Seine-Maritime, N France
Barentsberg 83 G2 Spitsbergen, W Svalbard
Barentsøya 83 G2 *island* E Svalbard
Barents Sea 110 C2 *Nor.* Barents Havet, *Rus.* Barentsevo More. *Sea* Arctic Ocean
Barents Trough 81 E1 *undersea feature* SW Barents Sea
Bar Harbor 41 H2 Mount Desert Island, Maine, NE USA
Bari 97 E5 *var.* Bari delle Puglie; *anc.* Barium. Puglia, SE Italy
Bāridah *see* Al Bāridah
Bari delle Puglie *see* Bari
Barikot *see* Barīkowṭ
Barīkowṭ 123 F4 *var.* Barikot. Kunar, NE Afghanistan
Barillas 52 A2 *var.* Santa Cruz Barillas. Huehuetenango, NW Guatemala
Barinas 58 C2 Barinas, W Venezuela
Barisal 135 G4 Khulna, S Bangladesh
Barisan, Pegunungan 138 B4 *mountain range* Sumatera, W Indonesia
Barito, Sungai 138 D4 *river* Borneo, C Indonesia
Barium *see* Bari
Barka *see* Al Marj
Barkly Tableland 148 B3 *plateau* Northern Territory/Queensland, N Australia
Bârlad 108 D4 *prev.* Bîrlad. Vaslui, E Romania
Barlavento, Ilhas de 74 A2 *var.* Windward Islands. *Island group* N Cape Verde
Bar-le-Duc 90 D3 *var.* Bar-sur-Ornain. Meuse, NE France
Barlee, Lake 147 B6 *lake* Western Australia
Barlee Range 146 A4 *mountain range* Western Australia
Barletta 97 D5 *anc.* Barduli. Puglia, SE Italy
Barlinek 98 B3 *Ger.* Berlinchen. Zachodniopomorskie, NW Poland
Barmouth 89 C6 NW Wales, UK
Barnaul 114 C4 Altayskiy Kray, C Russian Federation
Barnet 89 A7 SE England, UK
Barnstaple 89 C7 SW England, UK
Baroghil Pass 123 F3 *var.* Kowtal-e Barowghīl. *Pass* Afghanistan/Pakistan
Baron'ki 107 E7 *Rus.* Boron'ki. Mahilyowskaya Voblasts', E Belarus
Barquisimeto 58 C2 Lara, NW Venezuela
Barra 88 B3 *island* NW Scotland, UK
Barra de Río Grande 53 E3 Región Autónoma Atlántico Sur, E Nicaragua
Barragem de Sobradinho *see* Sobradinho, Represa de
Barranca 60 C3 Lima, W Peru
Barrancabermeja 58 B2 Santander, N Colombia
Barranquilla 58 B1 Atlántico, N Colombia
Barreiro 92 B4 Setúbal, W Portugal
Barrier Range 149 C6 *hill range* New South Wales, SE Australia
Barrow 89 B6 *Ir.* An Bhearú. *River* SE Ireland
Barrow 36 D2 Alaska, USA
Barrow-in-Furness 89 C5 NW England, UK
Barrow Island 146 A4 *island* Western Australia
Barstow 47 C7 California, W USA
Bar-sur-Ornain *see* Bar-le-Duc
Bartang 123 F3 *river* SE Tajikistan
Bartica 59 F3 N Guyana
Bartın 116 C2 Bartın NW Turkey

Bartlesville 49 G1 Oklahoma, C USA
Bartoszyce 98 D2 *Ger.* Bartenstein. Warmińsko-Mazurskie, NE Poland
Baruun-Urt 127 F2 Sühbaatar, E Mongolia
Barú, Volcán 53 E5 *var.* Volcán de Chiriquí. *Volcano* W Panama
Barwon River 149 D5 *river* New South Wales, SE Australia
Barysaw 107 D6 *Rus.* Borisov. Mínskaya Voblasts', NE Belarus
Basarabeasca 108 D4 *Rus.* Bessarabka. SE Moldova
Basel 95 A7 *Eng.* Basle, *Fr.* Bâle. Basel-Stadt, NW Switzerland
Basilan 139 E3 *island* SW Philippines
Basle *see* Basel
Basra *see* Al Başrah
Bassano del Grappa 96 C2 Veneto, NE Italy
Bassein 136 A4 *var.* Pathein. Irrawaddy, SW Myanmar
Basse-Terre 55 G4 *dependent territory capital* (Guadeloupe) Basse Terre, SW Guadeloupe
Basse Terre 55 G4 *island* W Guadeloupe
Basseterre 55 G3 *country capital* (Saint Kitts and Nevis) Saint Kitts, Saint Kitts and Nevis
Bassikounou 74 D3 Hodh ech Chargui, SE Mauritania
Bass Strait 149 C7 *strait* SE Australia
Bassum 94 B3 Niedersachsen, NW Germany
Bastia 91 E7 Corse, France, C Mediterranean Sea
Bastogne 87 D7 Luxembourg, SE Belgium
Bastrop 42 B2 Louisiana, S USA
Bastyn' 107 B7 *Rus.* Bostyn'. Brestskaya Voblasts', SW Belarus
Basuo *see* Dongfang
Bata 77 A5 NW Equatorial Guinea
Batabanó, Golfo de 54 A2 *gulf* W Cuba
Batajnica 100 D3 Serbia, N Yugoslavia
Batangas 139 E2 *off.* Batangas City. Luzon, N Philippines
Bătdâmbâng 137 C5 *prev.* Battambang. Bătdâmbâng, NW Cambodia
Batéké, Plateaux 77 B6 *plateau* S Congo
Bath 89 D7 *hist.* Akermanceaster, *anc.* Aquae Calidae, Aquae Solis. SW England, UK
Bathinda 134 D2 Punjab, NW India
Bathsheba 55 G1 E Barbados
Bathurst 39 F4 New Brunswick, SE Canada
Bathurst 149 D6 New South Wales, SE Australia
Bathurst Island 146 D2 *island* Northern Territory, N Australia
Bathurst Island 37 F2 *island* Parry Islands, Nunavut, N Canada
Bāţin, Wādī al 136 C4 *dry watercourse* SW Asia
Batman 117 E4 *var.* İluh. Batman, SE Turkey
Batna 71 E2 NE Algeria
Baton Rouge 42 B3 *state capital* Louisiana, S USA
Batroûn 118 A4 *var.* Al Batrūn. N Lebanon
Batticaloa 132 D3 Eastern Province, E Sri Lanka
Battipaglia 97 D5 Campania, S Italy
Bat'umi 117 F2 W Georgia
Batu Pahat 138 B3 *prev.* Bandar Penggaram. Johor, Peninsular Malaysia
Bauchi 75 G4 Bauchi, NE Nigeria
Bauer Basin 153 F3 *undersea feature* E Pacific Ocean
Bauld, Cape *see* Al Bayḑā'
Bauska 106 C3 *Ger.* Bauske. Bauska, S Latvia
Bautzen 94 D4 *Lus.* Budyšin. Sachsen, E Germany
Bavarian Alps 95 C7 *Ger.* Bayrische Alpen. *Mountain range* Austria/Germany

Bavispe, Río 50 C2 *river* NW Mexico
Bawîti 72 B2 N Egypt
Bawku 75 E4 N Ghana
Bayamo 54 C3 Granma, E Cuba
Bayan Har Shan 126 D4 *var.* Bayan Khar. *Mountain range* C China
Bayanhongor 126 D2 Bayanhongor, C Mongolia
Bayan Khar *see* Bayan Har Shan
Bayano, Lago 53 G4 *lake* E Panama
Bay City 40 C3 Michigan, N USA
Bay City 49 G4 Texas, SW USA
Baydhabo 73 D6 *var.* Baydhowa, Isha Baydhabo, *It.* Baidoa. Bay, SW Somalia
Baydhowa *see* Baydhabo
Bayern 95 C6 *cultural region* SE Germany
Bayeux 90 B3 *anc.* Augustodurum. Calvados, N France
Bāyir 117 C7 *var.* Bā'ir. Ma'ān, S Jordan
Baykal, Ozero 115 E4 *Eng.* Lake Baikal. *Lake* S Russian Federation
Baymak 111 D6 Respublika Bashkortostan, W Russian Federation
Bayonne 91 A6 *anc.* Lapurdum. Pyrénées-Atlantiques, SW France
Bayramaly 122 D3 *prev.* Bayram-Ali. Maryyskiy Velayat, S Turkmenistan
Bayreuth 95 C5 *var.* Baireuth. Bayern, SE Germany
Bayrūt *see* Beyrouth
Baytown 49 H4 Texas, SW USA
Baza 93 E4 Andalucía, S Spain
Beagle Channel 65 C8 *channel* Argentina/Chile
Béal Feirste *see* Belfast
Beannchar *see* Bangor
Bear Lake 46 E4 *lake* Idaho/Utah, NW USA
Beas de Segura 93 E4 Andalucía, S Spain
Beata, Isla 55 E3 *island* SW Dominican Republic
Beatrice 45 F4 Nebraska, C USA
Beaufort Sea 34 D2 *sea* Arctic Ocean
Beaufort West 78 C5 *Afr.* Beaufort-Wes. Western Cape, SW South Africa
Beaumont 49 H3 Texas, SW USA
Beaune 90 D4 Côte d'Or, C France
Beauvais 90 C3 *anc.* Bellovacum, Caesaromagus. Oise, N France
Beaver Island 40 C2 *island* Michigan, N USA
Beaver Lake 49 H1 *reservoir* Arkansas, C USA
Beaver River 49 F1 *river* Oklahoma, C USA
Beāwar 134 C3 Rājasthān, N India
Bečej 100 D3 *Ger.* Altbetsche, *Hung.* Óbecse, Rácz-Becse; *prev.* Magyar-Becse, Stari Bečej. Serbia, N Yugoslavia
Béchar 70 D2 *prev.* Colomb-Béchar. W Algeria
Beckley 40 D5 West Virginia, NE USA
Bedford 89 D6 E England, UK
Bedum 86 E1 Groningen, NE Netherlands
Be'ér Menuẖa 119 B7 *var* Be'er Menukha. Southern, S Israel
Be'er Menukha *see* Be'ér Menuẖa
Beernem 87 A5 West-Vlaanderen, NW Belgium
Beersheba *see* Be'er Sheva'
Be'ér Sheva' 119 A7 *var.* Beersheba, *Ar.* Bir es Saba. Southern, S Israel
Beesel 87 D5 Limburg, SE Netherlands
Beeville 49 G4 Texas, SW USA
Bega 149 D7 New South Wales, SE Australia
Beida *see* Al Bayḑā'
Beihai 128 B6 Guangxi Zhuangzu Zizhiqu, S China
Beijing 128 C3 *var.* Pei-ching, *Eng.* Peking; *prev.* Pei-p'ing. *Country/municipality capital* (China) Beijing Shi, E China
Beilen 86 E2 Drenthe, NE Netherlands

Beira 79 E3 Sofala, C Mozambique
Beirut *see* Beyrouth
Beit Leẖm *see* Bethlehem
Beiuş 108 B3 *Hung.* Belényes. Bihor, NW Romania
Beja 92 B4 *anc.* Pax Julia. Beja, SE Portugal
Béjar 92 C3 Castilla-León, N Spain
Bejraburi *see* Phetchaburi
Békéscsaba 99 D7 *Rom.* Bichiş-Ciaba. Békés, SE Hungary
Bekobod 123 E2 *Rus.* Bekabad; *prev.* Begovat. Toshkent Wiloyati, E Uzbekistan
Bela Crkva 100 E3 *Ger.* Weisskirchen, *Hung.* Fehértemplom. Serbia, W Yugoslavia
Belarus 107 B6 *var.* Belorussia, *Latv.* Baltkrievija; *prev.* Belorussian SSR, *Rus.* Belorusskaya SSR. *Country* E Europe

---

Belarus 107

Official name	Republic of Belarus
Formation	1991
Capital	Minsk
Population	10.2 million / 127 people per sq mile (49 people per sq km)
Total area	80,154 sq miles (207,600 sq km)
Languages	Belorussian, Russian
Religions	Russian Orthodox 60%, Roman Catholic 8%, other 32%
Ethnic mix	Belorussian 78%, Russian 13%, Polish 4%, other 5%
Government	Multiparty republic
Currency	Belorussian rouble = 100 kopeks
Literacy rate	99%
Calorie consumption	not available

Belau *see* Palau
Belchatow *see* Belchatów
Belchatów 98 C4 *var.* Belchatow. Łódzkie, C Poland
Belcher Islands 38 C2 *Fr.* Îles Belcher. *Island group* Northwest Territories, SE Canada
Beledweyne 73 D5 *var.* Belet Huen, *It.* Belet Uen. Hiiraan, C Somalia
Belém 63 F1 *var.* Pará. *State capital* Pará, N Brazil
Belen 48 D2 New Mexico, SW USA
Belén 52 D4 Rivas, SW Nicaragua
Belet Huen *see* Beledweyne
Belet Uen *see* Beledweyne
Belfast 89 E1 *Ir.* Béal Feirste. *Admin capital* E Northern Ireland, UK
Belfield 44 D2 North Dakota, N USA
Belfort 90 E4 Territoire-de-Belfort, E France
Belgaum 132 B1 Karnātaka, W India
Belgium 87 *Bel* Dut. België, Fr. Belgique. *Country* NW Europe

---

Belgium 87

Official name	Kingdom of Belgium
Formation	1830
Capital	Brussels
Population	10.2 million / 805 people per sq mile (311 people per sq km)
Total area	12,671 sq miles 32,820 sq km)
Languages	Flemish, French, German
Religions	Roman Catholic 88%, Muslim 2%, other 10%
Ethnic mix	Fleming 58%, Walloon 33%, Italian 2%, Moroccan 1%, other 6%
Government	Constitutional monarchy
Currency	Franc = 100 centimes
Literacy rate	99%
Calorie consumption	3,681 kilocalories

Belgorod 111 A6 Belgorodskaya Oblast', W Russian Federation

Belgrade see Beograd
Belgrano II 154 A2 *Argentinian research station* Antarctica
Belice see Belize City
Beligrad see Berat
Beli Manastir 100 C3 *Hung.* Pélmonostor; *prev.* Monostor. Osijek-Baranja, NE Croatia
Bélinga 77 B5 Ogooué-Ivindo, NE Gabon
Belitung, Pulau 138 C4 *island* W Indonesia
Belize 52 B1 *Sp.* Belice; *prev.* British Honduras, Colony of Belize. *Country* Central America

Belize 52

Official name Belize
Formation 1981
Capital Belmopan
Population 200,000 /23 people per sq mile (9 people per sq km)
Total area 8,803 sq miles (22,800 sq km)
Languages English, English Creole, Spanish, Maya, Garifuna (Carib)
Religions Christian 87%, other 13%
Ethnic mix Mestizo 44%, Creole 30%, Maya 11%, Garifuna 7%, Asian 4%, other 4%
Government Parliamentary democracy
Currency Belizean dollar = 100 cents
Literacy rate 75%
Calorie consumption 2,662 kilocalories

Belize 52 B1 *river* Belize/Guatemala
Belize see Belize City
Belize City 52 C1 *var.* Belize, *Sp.* Belice. Belize, NE Belize
Belkofski 36 B3 Alaska, USA
Belle Île 90 A4 *island* NW France
Belle Isle, Strait of 39 G3 *strait* Newfoundland and Labrador, E Canada
Belleville 40 B4 Illinois, N USA
Bellevue 45 F4 Iowa, C USA
Bellevue 46 B2 Washington, NW USA
Bellingham 46 B1 Washington, NW USA
Belling Hausen Mulde see Southeast Pacific Basin
Bellingshausen Abyssal Plain see Bellingshausen Plain
Bellingshausen Plain 153 F5 *var.* Bellingshausen Abyssal Plain. *Undersea feature* SE Pacific Ocean
Bellingshausen Sea 154 A3 *sea* Antarctica
Bellinzona 95 B8 *Ger.* Bellenz. Ticino, S Switzerland
Bello 58 B2 Antioquia, W Colombia
Bellville 78 B5 Western Cape, SW South Africa
Belmopan 52 C1 *country capital* (Belize) Cayo, C Belize
Belogradchik 104 B1 Vidin, NW Bulgaria
Belo Horizonte 63 F4 *prev.* Bello Horizonte. *State capital* Minas Gerais, SE Brazil
Belomorsk 110 B3 Respublika Kareliya, NW Russian Federation
Beloretsk 111 D6 Respublika Bashkortostan, W Russian Federation
Belorussia/Belorussian SSR see Belarus
Belorusskaya SSR see Belarus
Beloye More 110 C3 *Eng.* White Sea. *Sea* NW Russian Federation
Belozersk 110 B4 Vologodskaya Oblast', NW Russian Federation
Belton 49 G3 Texas, SW USA
Beluchistan see Baluchistän
Belukha, Gora 114 D5 *mountain* Kazakhstan/Russian Federation
Belyy, Ostrov 114 D2 *island* N Russian Federation
Bemaraha 79 F3 *var.* Plateau du Bemaraha. *Mountain range* W Madagascar

Bemidji 45 F1 Minnesota, N USA
Bemmel 86 D4 Gelderland, SE Netherlands
Benaco see Garda, Lago di
Benavente 92 D2 Castilla-León, N Spain
Bend 46 B3 Oregon, NW USA
Bender Beila see Bandarbeyla
Bender Beyla see Bandarbeyla
Bender Cassim see Boosaaso
Bendern 94 E1 NW Liechtenstein
Bender Qaasim see Boosaaso
Bendigo 149 C7 Victoria, SE Australia
Beneŝov 99 B5 *Ger.* Beneschau. Středočesky Kraj, W Czech Republic
Benevento 97 D5 *anc.* Beneventum, Malventum. Campania, S Italy
Bengal, Bay of 124 C4 *bay* N Indian Ocean
Bengbu 128 D5 *var.* Peng-pu. Anhui, E China
Benghazi see Banghāzī
Bengkulu 138 B4 *prev.* Bengkoeloe, Benkoelen, Benkulen. Sumatera, W Indonesia
Benguela 78 A2 *var.* Benguella. Benguela, W Angola
Benguella see Benguela
Bengweulu, Lake see Bangweulu, Lake
Ben Hope 88 B2 *mountain* N Scotland, UK
Beni 56 B4 *var.* El Beni. Admin. region *department* N Bolivia
Beni 77 E5 Nord Kivu, NE Dem. Rep. Congo (Zaire)
Benidorm 93 F4 País Valenciano, SE Spain
Beni-Mellal 70 C2 C Morocco
Benin 75 F4 *prev.* Dahomey. *Country* W Africa

Benin 75

Official name Republic of Benin
Formation 1960
Capital Porto-Novo
Population 6 million / 143 people per sq mile (55 people per sq km)
Total area 42,710 sq miles (110,620 sq km)
Languages French, Fon, Bariba, Yoruba, Adja, Houeda, Somba
Religions Traditional beliefs 70%, Muslim 15%, Christian 15%
Ethnic mix Fon 39%, Yoruba 12%, Adja 10%, other tribal groups 39%
Government Multiparty republic
Currency CFA franc = 100 centimes
Literacy rate 34%
Calorie consumption 2,532 kilocalories

Benin, Bight of 75 F5 *gulf* W Africa
Benin City 75 F5 Edo, SW Nigeria
Beni, Río 61 E3 *river* N Bolivia
Beni Suef 72 B2 *var.* Banī Suwayf. N Egypt
Ben Nevis 88 C3 *mountain* N Scotland, UK
Benson 48 B3 Arizona, SW USA
Bent Jbaïl 119 A5 *var.* Bint Jubayl. S Lebanon
Benton 42 B1 Arkansas, C USA
Benue 76 B4 *Fr.* Bénoué. *River* Cameroon/Nigeria
Benue 75 G4 *state* SE Nigeria
Beograd 100 D3 *Eng.* Belgrade, *Ger.* Belgrad; *anc.* Singidunum. *Country capital* (Yugoslavia) Serbia, N Yugoslavia
Berane 101 D5 *prev.* Ivangrad. Montenegro, SW Yugoslavia
Berat 101 C6 *var.* Berati, *SCr.* Beligrad. Berat, C Albania
Berati see Berat
Berau 138 D4 *var.* MacCluer Gulf. *Bay* Irian Jaya, E Indonesia
Berbera 72 D4 Woqooyi Galbeed, NW Somalia
Berbérati 77 B5 Mambéré-Kadéï, SW Central African Republic
Berck-Plage 90 C2 Pas-de-Calais, N France

Berdyans'k 109 G4 *Rus.* Berdyansk; *prev.* Osipenko. Zaporiz'ka Oblast', SE Ukraine
Berdychiv 108 D2 *Rus.* Berdichev. Zhytomyrs'ka Oblast', N Ukraine
Berehove 108 B3 *Cz.* Berehovo, *Hung.* Beregszász, *Rus.* Beregovo. Zakarpats'ka Oblast', W Ukraine
Berettyó 99 D7 *Rom.* Barcău; *prev.* Berătău, Beretău. *River* Hungary/Romania
Berettyóújfalu 99 D6 Hajdú-Bihar, E Hungary
Berezhany 108 C2 *Pol.* Brzeżany. Ternopil's'ka Oblast', W Ukraine
Berezniki 111 D5 Permskaya Oblast', NW Russian Federation
Berga 93 G2 Cataluña, NE Spain
Bergamo 96 B2 *anc.* Bergomum. Lombardia, N Italy
Bergara 93 E1 País Vasco, N Spain
Bergen 85 A5 Hordaland, S Norway
Bergen 94 D2 Mecklenburg-Vorpommern, NE Germany
Bergen 86 C2 Noord-Holland, NW Netherlands
Bergerac 91 B5 Dordogne, SW France
Bergeyk 87 C5 Noord-Brabant, S Netherlands
Bergse Maas 86 D4 *river* S Netherlands
Beringen 87 C5 Limburg, NE Belgium
Bering Sea 36 A2 *sea* N Pacific Ocean
Bering Strait 36 C2 *Rus.* Beringov Proliv. *Strait* Bering Sea/Chukchi Sea
Berja 93 E5 Andalucía, S Spain
Berkeley 47 B6 California, W USA
Berkner Island 154 A2 *island* Antarctica
Berkovitsa 104 C2 Montana, NW Bulgaria
Berlin 94 D3 *country capital* (Germany) Berlin, NE Germany
Berlin 41 G2 New Hampshire, NE USA
Bermejo, Río 64 C2 *river* N Argentina
Bermeo 93 E1 País Vasco, N Spain
Bermuda 35 D6 *var.* Bermuda Islands, Bermudas; *prev.* Somers Islands. *UK crown colony* NW Atlantic Ocean
Bermuda Islands see Bermuda
Bermuda Rise 35 E6 *undersea feature* C Sargasso Sea
Bermudas see Bermuda
Bern 95 A7 *Fr.* Berne. *Country capital* (Switzerland) Bern, W Switzerland
Bernau 94 D3 Brandenburg, NE Germany
Bernburg 94 C4 Sachsen-Anhalt, C Germany
Berne see Bern
Berner Alpen 95 A7 *var.* Berner Oberland, *Eng.* Bernese Oberland. *Mountain range* SW Switzerland
Berner Oberland see Berner Alpen
Bernese Oberland see Berner Alpen
Bernier Island 147 A5 *island* Western Australia
Berry 90 C4 *cultural region* C France
Berry Islands 54 C1 *island group* N Bahamas
Bertoua 77 B5 Est, E Cameroon
Beru 145 E2 *var.* Peru. *Atoll* Tungaru, W Kiribati
Berwick-upon-Tweed 88 D4 N England, UK
Berytus see Beyrouth
Besançon 90 D4 *anc.* Besontium, Vesontio. Doubs, E France
Beskra see Biskra
Betafo 79 G3 Antananarivo, C Madagascar
Betanzos 92 B1 Galicia, NW Spain
Bethlehem 119 B6 *Ar.* Beit Lahm, *Heb.* Bet Lehem. C West Bank
Bethlehem 78 D4 Free State, C South Africa

Béticos, Sistemas 92 D4 *var.* Sistema Penibético, *Eng.* Baetic Cordillera, Baetic Mountains. *Mountain range* S Spain
Bet Lehem see Bethlehem
Bétou 77 C5 La Likouala, N Congo
Bette, Pic 71 G4 *var.* Bikkū Bïttï, *It.* Picco Bette. *Mountain* S Libya
Bette, Picco see Bette, Pic
Beulah 40 C2 Michigan, N USA
Beuthen see Bytom
Beveren 87 B5 Oost-Vlaanderen, N Belgium
Beverley 89 D5 E England, UK
Bexley 89 B8 SE England, UK
Beyla 74 D4 Guinée-Forestière, SE Guinea
Beyrouth 118 A4 *var.* Bayrūt, *Eng.* Beirut; *anc.* Berytus. *Country capital* (Lebanon) W Lebanon
Beyşehir 116 B4 Konya, SW Turkey
Beyşehir Gölü 116 B4 *lake* C Turkey
Béziers 91 C6 *anc.* Baeterrae, Baeterrae Septimanorum, Julia Beterrae. Hérault, S France
Bhadrāvati 132 C2 Karnātaka, SW India
Bhāgalpur 135 F3 Bihār, NE India
Bhaktapur 135 F3 Central, C Nepal
Bhamo 136 B2 *var.* Banmo. Kachin State, N Myanmar
Bharūch 134 C4 Gujarāt, W India
Bhāvnagar 134 C4 *prev.* Bhaunagar. Gujarāt, W India
Bhopāl 134 D4 Madhya Pradesh, C India
Bhubaneswar 135 F5 *prev.* Bhubaneswar, Bhuvaneshwar. Orissa, E India
Bhuket see Phuket
Bhusāwal 134 D4 *prev.* Bhusaval. Mahārāshtra, C India
Bhutan 135 G3 *var.* Druk-yul. *Country* S Asia

Bhutan 135

Official name Kingdom of Bhutan
Formation 1656
Capital Thimpu
Population 2.1 million/ 116 people per sq mile (45 people per sq km)
Total area 18,147 sq miles (47,000 sq km)
Languages Dzongkha, Nepali, Assamese
Religions Mahayana Buddhist 70%, Hindu 24%, other 6%
Ethnic mix Bhote 60%, Nepalese 25%, Indigenous tribes 15%
Government Absolute monarchy
Currency Ngultrum = 100 chetrum
Literacy rate 44.2%
Calorie consumption 2,553 kilocalories

Biak, Pulau 139 G4 *island* E Indonesia
Biała Podlaska 98 E3 Lubelskie, E Poland
Białogard 98 B2 *Ger.* Belgard. Zachodniopomorskie, NW Poland
Białystok 98 E3 *Rus.* Belostok, Bielostok. Podlaskie, NE Poland
Biarritz 91 A6 Pyrénées-Atlantiques, SW France
Bicaz 108 C3 *Hung.* Békás. Neamţ, NE Romania
Biddeford 41 G2 Maine, NE USA
Bideford 89 C7 SW England, UK
Biel 95 A7 *Fr.* Bienne. Bern, W Switzerland
Bielefeld 94 B4 Nordrhein-Westfalen, NW Germany
Bielsko-Biała 99 C5 *Ger.* Bielitz, Bielitz-Biala. Śląskie, S Poland
Bielsk Podlaski 98 E3 Podlaskie, NE Poland
Bien Bien see Điên Biên
Biên Hoa 137 E6 Đông Nai, S Vietnam
Bienville, Lac 38 D2 *lake* Québec, C Canada
Bié, Planalto do 78 B2 *var.* Bié Plateau. *Plateau* C Angola

Bié Plateau *see* Bié, Planalto do
Big Cypress Swamp *43 E5 wetland* Florida, SE USA
Bigge Island *146 C2 island* Western Australia
Bighorn Mountains *44 C2 mountain range* Wyoming, C USA
Bighorn River *44 C2 river* Montana/Wyoming, NW USA
Bignona *74 B3* SW Senegal
Big Sioux River *45 E2 river* Iowa/South Dakota, N USA
Big Spring *49 E3* Texas, SW USA
Bihać *100 B3* Federacija Bosna I Hercegovina, NW Bosnia and Herzegovina
Bihār *135 F4 prev.* Behar. Admin. region *state* N India
Biharamulo *73 B7* Kagera, NW Tanzania
Bihosava *107 D5 Rus.* Bigosovo. Vitsyebskaya Voblasts', NW Belarus
Bijeljina *100 C3* Republika Srpska, NE Bosnia and Herzegovina
Bijelo Polje *101 D5* Montenegro, SW Yugoslavia
Bīkāner *134 C3* Rājasthān, NW India
Bikin *115 G4* Khabarovskiy Kray, SE Russian Federation
Bikini Atoll *144 C1 var.* Pikinni. *Atoll* Ralik Chain, NW Marshall Islands
Bikkū Bīttī *see* Bette, Pic
Bilāspur *135 E4* Madhya Pradesh, C India
Biläsuvar *117 H3 Rus.* Bilyasuvar; *prev.* Pushkino. SE Azerbaijan
Bila Tserkva *109 E2 Rus.* Belaya Tserkov'. Kyyivs'ka Oblast', N Ukraine
Bilauktaung Range *137 C6 var.* Thanintari Taungdan. *Mountain range* Myanmar/Thailand
Bilbao *93 E1 Basq.* Bilbo. País Vasco, N Spain
Bilecik *116 B3* Bilecik, NW Turkey
Billings *44 C2* Montana, NW USA
Bilma, Grand Erg de *75 H3 desert* NE Niger
Biloela *148 D4* Queensland, E Australia
Biloxi *42 C3* Mississippi, S USA
Biltine *76 C3* Biltine, E Chad
Bilwi *see* Puerto Cabezas
Bilzen *87 D6* Limburg, NE Belgium
Bimini Islands *54 C1 island group* W Bahamas
Binche *87 B7* Hainaut, S Belgium
Bindloe Island *see* Marchena, Isla
Binghamton *41 F3* New York, NE USA
Bingöl *117 E3* Bingöl, E Turkey
Bint Jubayl *see* Bent Jbaïl
Bintulu *138 D3* Sarawak, East Malaysia
Binzhou *128 D4* Shandong, E China
Bío Bío, Río *65 B5 river* C Chile
Bioco, Isla de *77 A5 var.* Bioko, *Eng.* Fernando Po, *Sp.* Macías Nguema Biyogo. *Island* NW Equatorial Guinea
Bioko *see* Bioco, Isla de
Birāk *71 F3 var.* Brak. C Libya
Birao *76 D3* Vakaga, NE Central African Republic
Biratnagar *135 F3* Eastern, SE Nepal
Bir es Saba *see* Be'ér Sheva'
Birhār Sharīf *135 F3* Bihar, N India
Bīrjand *120 E3* Khorāsān, E Iran
Birkenfeld *95 A5* Rheinland-Pfalz, SW Germany
Birkenhead *89 C5* NW England, UK
Birmingham *42 C2* Alabama, S USA
Birmingham *89 C6* C England, UK
Bir Moghrein *see* Bîr Moghreïn
Bîr Moghreïn *74 C1 var.* Bir Moghrein; *prev.* Fort-Trinquet. Tiris Zemmour, N Mauritania
Birnie Island *145 E3 atoll* Phoenix Islands, C Kiribati
Birni-Nkonni *see* Birnin Konni
Birnin Konni *75 F3 var.* Birni-Nkonni. Tahoua, SW Niger

Birobidzhan *115 G4* Yevreyskaya Avtonomnaya Oblast', SE Russian Federation
Birsk *111 D5* Respublika Bashkortostan, W Russian Federation
Biržai *106 C4 Ger.* Birsen. Biržai, NE Lithuania
Birżebbuġa *102 B5* SE Malta
Bisbee *48 B3* Arizona, SW USA
Biscay, Bay of *80 B4 Sp.* Golfo de Vizcaya, *Port.* Baía de Biscaia. *Bay* France/Spain
Biscay Plain *80 B3 undersea feature* SE Bay of Biscay
Bīshah, Wādī *121 B5 dry watercourse* C Saudi Arabia
Bishkek *123 G2 var.* Pishpek; *prev.* Frunze. *Country capital* (Kyrgyzstan) Chuyskaya Oblast', N Kyrgyzstan
Bishop's Lynn *see* King's Lynn
Bishrī, Jabal *118 D3 mountain range* E Syria
Biskara *see* Biskra
Biskra *71 E2 var.* Beskra, Biskara. NE Algeria
Biskupiec *98 D2 Ger.* Bischofsburg. Warmińsko-Mazurskie, NE Poland
Bislig *139 F2* Mindanao, S Philippines
Bismarck *45 E2 state capital* North Dakota, N USA
Bismarck Archipelago *144 B3 island group* NE PNG
Bismarck Sea *144 B3 sea* W Pacific Ocean
Bisnulok *see* Phitsanulok
Bissau *74 B4 country capital* (Guinea-Bissau) W Guinea-Bissau
Bistriţa *108 B3 Ger.* Bistritz, *Hung.* Beszterce; *prev.* Nösen. Bistriţa-Năsăud, N Romania
Bitam *77 B5* Woleu-Ntem, N Gabon
Bitburg *95 A5* Rheinland-Pfalz, SW Germany
Bitlis *117 F3* Bitlis, SE Turkey
Bitola *101 D6 Turk.* Monastir; *prev.* Bitolj. S FYR Macedonia
Bitonto *97 D5 anc.* Butuntum. Puglia, SE Italy
Bitterroot Range *46 D2 mountain range* Idaho/Montana, NW USA
Bitung *139 F3 prev.* Bitoeng. Sulawesi, C Indonesia
Biu *75 H4* Borno, E Nigeria
Biwa-ko *131 C6 lake* Honshū, SW Japan
Bizerte *71 E1 Ar.* Banzart, *Eng.* Bizerta. N Tunisia
Bjelovar *100 B2 Hung.* Belovár. Bjelovar-Bilogora, N Croatia
Bjørnøya *83 F3 Eng.* Bear Island. *Island* N Norway
Blackall *148 C4* Queensland, E Australia
Black Drin *101 D6 Alb.* Lumi i Drinit të Zi, *SCr.* Crni Drim. *River* Albania/FYR Macedonia
Blackfoot *46 E4* Idaho, NW USA
Black Forest *see* Schwarzwald
Black Hills *44 D3 mountain range* South Dakota/Wyoming, N USA
Blackpool *89 C5* NW England, UK
Black Range *48 C2 mountain range* New Mexico, SW USA
Black River *136 C3 Chin.* Babian Jiang, Lixian Jiang, *Fr.* Rivière Noire, *Vtn.* Sông Đa. *River* China/Vietnam
Black River *54 A5* W Jamaica
Black Rock Desert *47 C5 desert* Nevada, W USA
Black Sand Desert *see* Garagumy
Black Sea *116 B1 var.* Euxine Sea, *Bul.* Cherno More, *Rom.* Marea Neagră, *Rus.* Chernoye More, *Turk.* Karadeniz, *Ukr.* Chorne More. *Sea* Asia/Europe
Black Sea Lowland *109 E4 Ukr.* Prychornomors'ka Nyzovyna. *Depression* SE Ukraine
Black Volta *75 E4 var.* Borongo, Mouhoun, Moun Hou, *Fr.* Volta Noire. *River* W Africa
Blackwater *89 A6 Ir.* An Abhainn Mhór. *River* S Ireland

Blagoevgrad *104 C3 prev.* Gorna Dzhumaya. Blagoevgrad, SW Bulgaria
Blagoveshchensk *115 G4* Amurskaya Oblast', SE Russian Federation
Blake Plateau *35 D6 var.* Blake Terrace. *Undersea feature* W Atlantic Ocean
Blake Terrace *see* Blake Plateau
Blanca, Bahía *65 C5 bay* E Argentina
Blanca, Costa *93 F4 physical region* SE Spain
Blanche, Lake *149 B5 lake* South Australia
Blanc, Mont *91 D5 It.* Monte Bianco. *Mountain* France/Italy
Blanco, Cape *46 A4 headland* Oregon, NW USA
Blanes *93 G2* Cataluña, NE Spain
Blankenberge *87 A5* West-Vlaanderen, NW Belgium
Blankenheim *95 A5* Nordrhein-Westfalen, W Germany
Blanquilla, Isla *59 E1 var.* La Blanquilla. *Island* N Venezuela
Blantyre *79 E2 var.* Blantyre-Limbe. Southern, S Malawi
Blantyre-Limbe *see* Blantyre
Blaricum *86 C3* Noord-Holland, C Netherlands
Blenheim *151 C5* Marlborough, South Island, NZ
Blida *70 D2 var.* El Boulaida, El Boulaïda. N Algeria
Bloemfontein *78 C4 var.* Mangaung. *Country capital* (South Africa-judicial capital) Free State, C South Africa
Blois *90 C4 anc.* Blesae. Loir-et-Cher, C France
Bloomfield *48 C1* New Mexico, SW USA
Bloomington *40 B4* Illinois, N USA
Bloomington *40 C4* Indiana, N USA
Bloomington *45 F2* Minnesota, N USA
Bloomsbury *148 D3* Queensland, NE Australia
Bluefield *40 D5* West Virginia, NE USA
Bluefields *53 E3* Región Autónoma Atlántico Sur, SE Nicaragua
Blue Mountain Peak *54 B5 mountain* E Jamaica
Blue Mountains *46 C3 mountain range* Oregon/Washington, NW USA
Blue Nile *68 D4 var.* Abai, Bahr el Azraq, *Amh.* Ābay Wenz, *Ar.* An Nīl al Azraq. *River* Ethiopia/Sudan
Blue Nile *72 C4 state* E Sudan
Blumenau *63 E5* Santa Catarina, S Brazil
Blythe *47 D8* California, W USA
Blytheville *42 C1* Arkansas, C USA
Bo *74 C4* S Sierra Leone
Boaco *52 D3* Boaco, S Nicaragua
Boa Vista *74 A3 island* Ilhas de Barlavento, E Cape Verde
Boa Vista *62 D1 state capital* Roraima, NW Brazil
Bobaomby, Tanjona *79 G2 Fr.* Cap d'Ambre. *Headland* N Madagascar
Bobigny *90 E1* Seine-St-Denis, N France
Bobo-Dioulasso *74 D4* SW Burkina faso
Bobrynets' *109 E3 Rus.* Bobrinets. Kirovohrads'ka Oblast', C Ukraine
Boca Raton *43 F5* Florida, SE USA
Bocay *52 D2* Jinotega, N Nicaragua
Bocche del Po *see* Po, Foci del
Bocholt *94 A4* Nordrhein-Westfalen, W Germany
Bochum *94 A4* Nordrhein-Westfalen, W Germany
Boçsa *108 A4 Ger.* Bokschen, *Hung.* Boksánbánya. Caraş-Severin, SW Romania
Bodaybo *115 F4* Irkutskaya Oblast', E Russian Federation
Boden *84 D4* Norrbotten, N Sweden

Bodmin *89 C7* SW England, UK
Bodø *84 C3* Nordland, C Norway
Bodrum *116 A4* Muğla, SW Turkey
Boende *77 C5* Equateur, C Dem. Rep. Congo (Zaire)
Boetoeng *see* Buton, Pulau
Bogale *136 B4* Irrawaddy, SW Myanmar
Bogatynia *98 B4 Ger.* Reichenau. Dolnośląskie, SW Poland
Boğazlıyan *116 D3* Yozgat, C Turkey
Bogor *138 C5 Dut.* Buitenzorg. Jawa, C Indonesia
Bogotá *58 B3 prev.* Santa Fe, Santa Fe de Bogotá. *Country capital* (Colombia) Cundinamarca, C Colombia
Bo Hai *128 D4 var.* Gulf of Chihli. *Gulf* NE China
Bohemia *99 A5 Cz.* Čechy, *Ger.* Böhmen. *Cultural and historical region* W Czech Republic
Bohemian Forest *95 C5 Cz.* Český Les, Šumava, *Ger.* Böhmerwald. *Mountain range* C Europe
Böhmisch-Krumau *see* Český Krumlov
Bohol Sea *139 E2 var.* Mindanao Sea. *Sea* S Philippines
Bohoro Shan *126 B2 mountain range* NW China
Bohuslav *109 E2 Rus.* Boguslav. Kyyivs'ka Oblast', N Ukraine
Boise *46 D3 var.* Boise City. *State capital* Idaho, NW USA
Boise City *see* Boise
Boise City *49 E1* Oklahoma, C USA
Boizenburg *94 C3* Mecklenburg-Vorpommern, N Germany
Bojador *see* Boujdour
Bojnūrd *120 D2 var.* Bujnurd. Khorāsān, N Iran
Bokāro *135 F4* Bihār, N India
Boké *74 C4* Guinée-Maritime, W Guinea
Bokhara *see* Bukhoro
Boknafjorden *85 A6 fjord* S Norway
Bol *76 B3* Lac, W Chad
Bolgatanga *75 E4* N Ghana
Bolhrad *108 D4 Rus.* Bolgrad. Odes'ka Oblast', SW Ukraine
Bolívar, Pico *58 C2 mountain* W Venezuela
Bolivia *61 F3 Country* W South America

Bolivia 61

Official name Republic of Bolivia
Formation 1825
Capital Sucre (official)/La Paz (administrative)
Population 8.3 million / 20 people per sq mile (8 people per sq km)
Total area 418,682 sq miles (1,084,390 sq km)
Languages Spanish, Aymara, Quechua
Religions Roman Catholic 93%, other 7%
Ethnic mix Quechua 37%, Aymara 32%, mixed 13%, European 10%, other 8%
Government Multiparty republic
Currency Boliviano = 100 centavos
Literacy rate 83.6%
Calorie consumption 2,094 kilocalories

Bollène *91 D6* Vaucluse, SE France
Bollnäs *85 C5* Gävleborg, C Sweden
Bollon *149 D5* Queensland, C Australia
Bologna *96 C3* Emilia-Romagna, N Italy
Bol'shevik, Ostrov *115 E2 island* Severnaya Zemlya, N Russian Federation
Bol'shezemel'skaya Tundra *110 E3 physical region* NW Russian Federation

Bol'shoy Lyakhovskiy, Ostrov 115 *F2 island* NE Russian Federation
Bolton 89 *D5 prev.* Bolton-le-Moors. NW England, UK
Bolu 116 *B3* Bolu, NW Turkey
Bolungarvík 83 *E4* Vestfirdhir, NW Iceland
Bolyarovo 104 *D3 prev.* Pashkeni. Yambol, E Bulgaria
Bolzano 96 *C1 Ger.* Bozen; *anc.* Bauzanum. Trentino-Alto Adige, N Italy
Boma 77 *B6* Bas-Zaïre, W Dem. Rep. Dem. Rep. Congo (Zaire)
Bombay *see* Mumbai
Bomu 76 *D4 var.* Mbomou, Mbomu, M'Bomu. *River* Central African Republic/Dem. Rep. Congo (Zaire)
Bonaire 55 *F5 island* E Netherlands Antilles
Bonanza 52 *D2* Región Autónoma Atlántico Norte, NE Nicaragua
Bonaparte Archipelago 146 *C2 island group* Western Australia
Bon, Cap 102 *D3 headland* N Tunisia
Bonda 77 *B6* Ogooué-Lolo, C Gabon
Bondoukou 75 *E4* E Côte d'Ivoire
Bone *see* Watampone
Bone, Teluk 139 *E4 bay* Sulawesi, C Indonesia
Bongaigaon 135 *G3* Assam, NE India
Bongo, Massif des 76 *D4 var.* Chaîne des Mongos. *Mountain range* NE Central African Republic
Bongor 76 *B3* Mayo-Kébbi, SW Chad
Bonifacio 91 *E7* Corse, France, C Mediterranean Sea
Bonifacio, Strait of 96 *A4 Fr.* Bouches de Bonifacio, *It.* Bocche de Bonifacio. *Strait* C Mediterranean Sea
Bonn 95 *A5* Nordrhein-Westfalen, W Germany
Bononia *see* Boulogne-sur-Mer
Boosaaso 72 *E4 var.* Bandar Kassim, Bender Qaasim, Bosaso, *It.* Bender Cassim. Bari, N Somalia
Boothia, Gulf of 37 *F2 gulf* Nunavut, NE Canada
Boothia Peninsula 37 *F2 prev.* Boothia Felix. *Peninsula* Nunavut, NE Canada
Boppard 95 *A5* Rheinland-Pfalz, W Germany
Boquete 53 *E5 var.* Bajo Boquete. Chiriquí, W Panama
Boquillas 50 *D2 var.* Boquillas del Carmen. Coahuila de Zaragoza, NE Mexico
Boquillas del Carmen *see* Boquillas
Bor 73 *B5* Jonglei, S Sudan
Bor 100 *E4* Serbia, E Yugoslavia
Borås 85 *B7* Västra Götaland, S Sweden
Borborema, Planalto da 56 *E3 plateau* NE Brazil
Bordeaux 91 *B5 anc.* Burdigala. Gironde, SW France
Bordj Omar Driss 71 *E3* E Algeria
Børgefjellet 84 *C4 mountain range* C Norway
Borger 86 *E2* Drenthe, NE Netherlands
Borger 49 *E1* Texas, SW USA
Borgholm 85 *C7* Kalmar, S Sweden
Borgo Maggiore 96 *E1* NW San Marino
Borisoglebsk 111 *B6* Voronezhskaya Oblast', W Russian Federation
Borlänge 85 *C6* Kopparberg, C Sweden
Borne 86 *E3* Overijssel, E Netherlands
Borneo 138 *C4 island* Brunei/Indonesia/Malaysia
Bornholm 85 *B8 island* E Denmark
Borohoro Shan 123 *H1 mountain range* NW China
Borongo *see* Black Volta
Borovan 104 *C2* Vratsa, NW Bulgaria

Borovichi 110 *B4* Novgorodskaya Oblast', W Russian Federation
Borovo 100 *C3* Vukovar-Srijem, NE Croatia
Borşa 108 *C3 Hung.* Borsa. Maramureş, N Romania
Boryslav 108 *B2 Pol.* Borysław, *Rus.* Borislav. L'viv's'ka Oblast', NW Ukraine
Bosanska Dubica 100 *B3 var.* Kozarska Dubica. Republika Srpska, NW Bosnia and Herzegovina
Bosanska Gradiška 100 *B3 var.* Gradiška. Republika Srpska, N Bosnia and Herzegovina
Bosanski Novi 100 *B3 var.* Novi Grad. Republika Srpska, NW Bosnia and Herzegovina
Bosanski Šamac 100 *C3 var.* Šamac, Republika Srpska, N Bosnia and Herzegovina
Bosaso *see* Boosaaso
Boskovice 99 *B5 Ger.* Boskowitz. Brněnský Kraj, SE Czech Republic
Bosna 100 *C4 river* N Bosnia and Herzegovina
Bosna I Hercegovina, Federacija *Admin. region republic* Bosnia and Herzegovina
Bosnia and Herzegovina 100 *B3 Country* SE Europe

Bosnia and Herzegovina 100

Official name Republic of Bosnia and Herzegovina
Formation 1992
Capital Sarajevo
Population 4 million /203 people per sq mile (78 people per sq km)
Total area 19,741 sq miles (51,130 sq km)
Languages Serbian, Croatian
Religions Muslim 40%, Serbian Orthodox 31%, other 29%
Ethnic mix Bosnian 44%, Serb 33%, Croat 17%, other 6%
Government Multiparty republic
Currency Marka = 100 pfenniga
Literacy rate 92.7%
Calorie consumption not available

Bōsō-hantō 131 *D6 peninsula* Honshū, S Japan
Bosphorus *see* İstanbul Boğazı
Bosporus *see* İstanbul Boğazı
Bosporus Cimmerius *see* Kerch Strait
Bosporus Thracius *see* İstanbul Boğazı
Bossangoa 76 *C4* Ouham, C Central African Republic
Bossembélé 76 *C4* Ombella-Mpoko, C Central African Republic
Bossier City 42 *A2* Louisiana, S USA
Bosten Hu 126 *C3 var.* Bagrax Hu. *Lake* NW China
Boston 89 *E6 prev.* St.Botolph's Town. E England, UK
Boston 41 *G3 state capital* Massachusetts, NE USA
Boston Mountains 42 *B1 mountain range* Arkansas, C USA
Botany 148 *E2* New South Wales, SE Australia
Botany Bay 148 *E2 inlet* New South Wales, SE Australia
Boteti 78 *C3 var.* Botletle. *River* N Botswana
Bothnia, Gulf of 85 *D5 Fin.* Pohjanlahti, *Swe.* Bottniska Viken. *Gulf* N Baltic Sea
Botletle *see* Boteti
Botoşani 108 *C3 Hung.* Botosány. Botoşani, NE Romania
Botou 128 *C4 prev.* Bozhen. Hebei, E China
Botrange 87 *D6 mountain* E Belgium

Botswana 78 *C3 Country* S Africa

Botswana 78

Official name Republic of Botswana
Formation 1966
Capital Gaborone
Population 1.6 million /7 people per sq mile (3 people per sq km)
Total area 218,814 sq miles (566,730 sq km)
Languages English, Tswana, Shona, San, Khoikhoi, Ndebele
Religions Traditional beliefs 50%, Christian 50%
Ethnic mix Tswana 98%, other 2%
Government Multiparty republic
Currency Pula = 100 thebe
Literacy rate 74.4%
Calorie consumption 2,266 kilocalories

Bouar 76 *B4* Nana-Mambéré, W Central African Republic
Bou Craa 70 *B3 var.* Bu Craa. NW Western Sahara
Bougainville Island 142 *B3 island* NE PNG
Bougaroun, Cap 102 *C3 headland* NE Algeria
Bougouni 74 *D4* Sikasso, SW Mali
Boujdour 70 *A3 var.* Bojador. W Western Sahara
Boulder 44 *C4* Colorado, C USA
Boulder 44 *B2* Montana, NW USA
Boulogne *see* Boulogne-sur-Mer
Boulogne-Billancourt 90 *D1 prev.* Boulogne-sur-Seine. Hauts-de-Seine, N France
Boulogne-sur-Mer 90 *C2 var.* Boulogne; *anc.* Bononia, Gesoriacum, Gessoriacum. Pas-de-Calais, N France
Boûmdeïd 74 *C3 var.* Boumdeït. Assaba, S Mauritania
Boumdeït *see* Boûmdeïd
Boundiali 74 *D4* N Côte d'Ivoire
Bountiful 44 *B4* Utah, W USA
Bounty Basin *see* Bounty Trough
Bounty Islands 142 *D5 island group* S NZ
Bounty Trough 152 *C5 var.* Bounty Basin. *Undersea feature* S Pacific Ocean
Bourbonnais 90 *C4* Illinois, N USA
Bourg *see* Bourg-en-Bresse
Bourgas *see* Burgas
Bourge-en-Bresse *see* Bourg-en-Bresse
Bourg-en-Bresse 91 *D5 var.* Bourg, Bourge-en-Bresse. Ain, E France
Bourges 90 *C4 anc.* Avaricum. Cher, C France
Bourgogne 90 *C4 Eng.* Burgundy. *Cultural region* E France
Bourke 149 *C5* New South Wales, SE Australia
Bournemouth 89 *D7* S England, UK
Boutilimit 74 *C3* Trarza, SW Mauritania
Bouvet Island 67 *D7 Norwegian dependency* S Atlantic Ocean
Bowen 148 *D3* Queensland, NE Australia
Bowling Green 40 *B5* Kentucky, S USA
Bowling Green 40 *C3* Ohio, N USA
Boxmeer 86 *D4* Noord-Brabant, SE Netherlands
Boyarka 109 *E2* Kyyivs'ka Oblast', N Ukraine
Boysun 123 *E3 Rus.* Baysun. Surkhondaryo Wiloyati, S Uzbekistan
Bozeman 44 *B2* Montana, NW USA
Bozüyük 116 *B3* Bilecik, NW Turkey
Brač 100 *B4 var.* Brach, *It.* Brazza; *anc.* Brattia. *Island* S Croatia
Brach *see* Brač
Bradford 89 *D5* N England, UK
Brady 49 *F3* Texas, SW USA
Braga 92 *B2 anc.* Bracara Augusta. Braga, NW Portugal

Bragança 92 *C2 Eng.* Braganza; *anc.* Julio Briga. Bragança, NE Portugal
Brahmanbaria 135 *G4* Chittagong, E Bangladesh
Brahmapur 135 *F5* Orissa, E India
Brahmaputra 135 *H3 var.* Padma, Tsangpo, *Ben.* Jamuna, *Chin.* Yarlung Zangbo Jiang, *Ind.* Bramaputra, Dihang, Siang. *River* S Asia
Brăila 108 *D4* Brăila, E Romania
Braine-le-Comte 87 *B6* Hainaut, SW Belgium
Brainerd 45 *F2* Minnesota, N USA
Brak *see* Birāk
Bramaputra *see* Brahmaputra
Brampton 38 *D5* Ontario, S Canada
Branco, Rio 56 *C3 river* N Brazil
Brandberg 78 *A3 mountain* NW Namibia
Brandenburg 94 *C3 var.* Brandenburg an der Havel. Brandenburg, NE Germany
Brandenburg an der Havel *see* Brandenburg
Brandon 37 *F5* Manitoba, S Canada
Braniewo 98 *D2 Ger.* Braunsberg. Warmińsko-Mazurskie, NE Poland
Brasília 63 *F3 country capital* (Brazil) Distrito Federal, C Brazil
Braşov 108 *C4 Ger.* Kronstadt, *Hung.* Brassó; *prev.* Oraşul Stalin. Braşov, C Romania
Bratislava 99 *C6 Ger.* Pressburg, *Hung.* Pozsony. *Country capital* (Slovakia) Bratislavský Kraj, SW Slovakia
Bratsk 115 *E4* Irkutskaya Oblast', C Russian Federation
Brattia *see* Brač
Braunschweig 94 *C4 Eng./Fr.* Brunswick. Niedersachsen, N Germany
Brava, Costa 93 *H2 coastal region* NE Spain
Bravo del Norte *see* Grande, Rio
Bravo del Norte, Río *see* Bravo, Río
Bravo del Norte, Río *see* Bravo, Río
Bravo del Norte, Río *see* Grande, Rio
Bravo, Río 50 *C1 var.* Río Bravo del Norte, Rio Grande. *River* Mexico/USA
Bravo, Río *see* Grande, Rio
Brawley 47 *D8* California, W USA
Brazil 62 *C2 Port.* Repùblica Federativa do Brasil, *Sp.* Brasil; *prev.* United States of Brazil. *Country* South America

Brazil 62

Official name Federative Republic of Brazil
Formation 1822
Capital Brasilia
Population 170 million / 52 people per sq mile (20 people per sq km)
Total area 3,265,058 sq miles (8,456,510 sq km)
Languages Portuguese, German, Italian, Spanish, Polish, Japanese
Religions Roman Catholic 89%, Protestant 6%, other 5%
Ethnic mix White 66%, other 34%
Government Multiparty republic
Currency Real = 100 centavos
Literacy rate 84%
Calorie consumption 2,824 kilocalories

Brazil Basin 67 *C5 var.* Brazilian Basin, Brazil'skaya Kotlovina. *Undersea feature* W Atlantic Ocean
Brazilian Basin *see* Brazil Basin
Brazilian Highlands *see* Central, Planalto
Brazil'skaya Kotlovina *see* Brazil Basin
Brazos River 49 *G3 river* Texas, SW USA
Brazza *see* Brač
Brazzaville 77 *B6 country capital* (Congo) Capital District, S Congo
Brecht 87 *C5* Antwerpen, N Belgium

Brecon Beacons *89 C6 mountain range* S Wales, UK
Breda *86 C4* Noord-Brabant, S Netherlands
Bree *87 D5* Limburg, NE Belgium
Bregalnica *101 E6 river* E FYR Macedonia
Bregenze *57 B7 anc.* Brigantium. Vorarlberg, W Austria
Bregovo *104 B1* Vidin, NW Bulgaria
Brčko *100 C3* Republika Srpska, NE Bosnia and Herzegovina
Bremen *94 B3 Fr.* Brême. Bremen, NW Germany
Bremerhaven *94 B3* Bremen, NW Germany
Bremerton *46 B2* Washington, NW USA
Brenham *49 G3* Texas, SW USA
Brenner Pass *96 C1 var.* BrennerSattel, *Fr.* Col du Brenner, *Ger.* Brennerpass, *It.* Passo del Brennero. *Pass* Austria/Italy
Brennerpass *see* Brenner Pass
Brenner Sattel *see* Brenner Pass
Brescia *96 C1 Ger.* Brixia. Lombardia, N Italy
Bressanone *96 C1 Ger.* Brixen. Trentino-Alto Adige, N Italy
Brest *107 A6 Pol.* Brześć nad Bugiem, *Rus.* Brest-Litovsk; *prev.* Brześć Litewski. Brestskaya Voblasts', SW Belarus
Brest *90 A3* Finistère, NW France
Bretagne *90 A3 Eng.* Brittany; *Lat.* Britannia Minor. *Cultural region* NW France
Brewton *42 C3* Alabama, S USA
Brezovo *104 D2 prev.* Abrashlare. Plovdiv, C Bulgaria
Bria *76 D4* Haute-Kotto, C Central African Republic
Briançon *91 D5 anc.* Brigantio. Hautes-Alpes, SE France
Bridgeport *41 F3* Connecticut, NE USA
Bridgetown *55 G2 country capital* (Barbados) SW Barbados
Bridlington *89 D5* E England, UK
Bridport *89 D7* S England, UK
Brig *95 A7 Fr.* Brigue, *It.* Briga. Valais, SW Switzerland
Brigham City *44 B3* Utah, W USA
Brighton *44 D4* Colorado, C USA
Brighton *89 E7* SE England, UK
Brindisi *97 E5 anc.* Brundisium, Brundusium. Puglia, SE Italy
Brisbane *149 E5 state capital* Queensland, E Australia
Bristol *89 D7 anc.* Bricgstow. SW England, UK
Bristol *41 F3* Connecticut, NE USA
Bristol *40 D5* Virginia, NE USA
Bristol Bay *36 B3 bay* Alaska, USA
Bristol Channel *89 C7 inlet* England/Wales, UK
Britain *80 C3 var.* Great Britain. *Island* UK
British Columbia *36 D4 Fr.* Colombie-Britannique. *Province* SW Canada
British Indian Ocean Territory *141 B5 UK dependent territory* C Indian Ocean
British Isles *89 island group* NW Europe
British Virgin Islands *55 F3 var.* Virgin Islands. *UK dependent territory* E West Indies
Brive-la-Gaillarde *91 C5 prev.* Brive, *anc.* Briva Curretia. Corrèze, C France
Brno *99 B5 Ger.* Brünn. Brněnský Kraj, SE Czech Republic
Brocéni *106 B3* Saldus, SW Latvia
Brodeur Peninsula *37 F2 peninsula* Baffin Island, Nunavut, NE Canada
Brodnica *98 C3 Ger.* Buddenbrock. Kujawski-pomorskie, C Poland
Broek-in-Waterland *86 C3* Noord-Holland, C Netherlands
Broken Arrow *49 G1* Oklahoma, C USA
Broken Bay *148 E1 bay* New South Wales, SE Australia
Broken Hill *149 B6* New South Wales, SE Australia

Broken Ridge *141 D6 undersea feature* S Indian Ocean
Bromley *89 B8* SE England, UK
Brookhaven *42 B3* Mississippi, S USA
Brookings *45 F3* South Dakota, N USA
Brooks Range *36 D2 mountain range* Alaska, USA
Brookton *147 B6* Western Australia
Broome *146 B3* Western Australia
Broomfield *44 D4* Colorado, C USA
Broucsella *see* Brussel
Brovary *109 E2* Kyyivs'ka Oblast', N Ukraine
Brownfield *49 E2* Texas, SW USA
Brownville *49 G5* Texas, SW USA
Brownwood *49 F3* Texas, SW USA
Brozha *107 D7* Mahilyowskaya Voblasts', E Belarus
Brugge *87 A5 Fr.* Bruges. West-Vlaanderen, NW Belgium
Brummen *86 D3* Gelderland, E Netherlands
Brunei *138 D3Mal.* Negara Brunei Darussalam. *Country* SE Asia

---

Brunei 138

Official name Sultanate of Brunei
Formation 1984
Capital Bandar Seri Begawan
Population 328,000 / 161 people per sq mile (62 people per sq km)
Total area 2,034 sq miles (5,270 sq km)
Languages Malay, English, Chinese
Religions Muslim 63%, Buddhist 14%, Christian 10%, other 13%
Ethnic mix Malay 67%, Chinese 16%, Indigenous 6%, other 11%
Government Absolute monarchy
Currency Brunei dollar = 100 cents
Literacy rate 90%
Calorie consumption 2,745 kilocalories

Brunner, Lake *151 C5 lake* South Island, NZ
Brunswick *43 E3* Georgia, SE USA
Brusa *see* Bursa
Brus Laguna *52 D2* Gracias a Dios, E Honduras
Brussa *see* Bursa
Brussel *var.* Brussels, *Fr.* Bruxelles, *Ger.* Brüssel; *anc.* Broucsella. *Country capital* (Belgium) Brussels, C Belgium *see also* Bruxelles
Brüssel *see* Brussel
Brussels *see* Brussel
Bruxelles *see* Brussel
Bryan *49 G3* Texas, SW USA
Bryansk *111 A5* Bryanskaya Oblast', W Russian Federation
Brzeg *98 C4 Ger.* Brieg; *anc.* Civitas Altae Ripae. Opolskie, S Poland
Bucaramanga *58 B2* Santander, N Colombia
Buchanan *74 C5 prev.* Grand Bassa. SW Liberia
Buchanan, Lake *49 F3 reservoir* Texas, SW USA
Bucharest *see* Bucureşti
Bu Craa *see* Bou Craa
Bucureşti *108 C5 Eng.* Bucharest, *Ger.* Bukarest; *prev.* Altenburg, *anc.* Cetatea Dâmboviţei. *Country capital* (Romania) Bucureşti, S Romania
Buda-Kashalyova *107 D7 Rus.* Buda-Koshelëvo. Homyel'skaya Voblasts', SE Belarus
Budapest *99 C6 off.* Budapest Fōváros, *SCr.* Budimpešta. *Country capital* (Hungary) Pest, N Hungary
Budaun *134 D3* Uttar Pradesh, N India
Buena Park *46 E2* California, W USA
Buenaventura *58 A3* Valle del Cauca, W Colombia
Buena Vista *93 H5* S Gibraltar
Buena Vista *61 G4* Santa Cruz, C Bolivia

Buenos Aires *64 D4 hist.* Santa Maria del Buen Aire. *Country capital* (Argentina) Buenos Aires, E Argentina
Buenos Aires *53 E5* Puntarenas, SE Costa Rica
Buenos Aires, Lago *65 B6 var.* Lago General Carrera. *Lake* Argentina/Chile
Buffalo *41 E3* New York, NE USA
Buffalo Narrows *37 F4* Saskatchewan, C Canada
Buff Bay *54 B5* E Jamaica
Buftea *108 C5* Bucureşti, S Romania
Bug *81 E3 Bel.* Zakhodni Buh, *Eng.* Western Bug, *Rus.* Zapadnyy Bug, *Ukr.* Zakhidnyy Buh. *River* E Europe
Buga *58 B3* Valle del Cauca, W Colombia
Bughotu *see* Santa Isabel
Buguruslan *111 D6* Orenburgskaya Oblast', W Russian Federation
Buḩayrat Naṣir *see* Nasser, Lake
Buheirat Nâsir *see* Nasser, Lake
Bujalance *92 D4* Andalucía, S Spain
Bujanovac *101 E5* Serbia, SE Yugoslavia
Bujnurd *see* Bojnûrd
Bujumbura *73 B7 prev.* Usumbura. *Country capital* (Burundi) W Burundi
Bukavu *77 E6 prev.* Costermansville. Sud Kivu, E Dem. Rep. Congo (Zaire)
Bukhara *see* Bukhoro
Bukhoro *122 D2 var.* Bokhara, *Rus.* Bukhara. Bukhoro Wiloyati, C Uzbekistan
Bukoba *73 B6* Kagera, NW Tanzania
Bülach *95 B7* Zürich, NW Switzerland
Bulawayo *78 D3 var.* Buluwayo. Matabeleland North, SW Zimbabwe
Buldur *see* Burdur
Bulgan *127 E2* Bulgan, N Mongolia
Bulgaria *104 C2 Bul.* Bŭlgariya; *prev.* People's Republic of Bulgaria. *Country* SE Europe

---

Bulgaria 104

Official name Republic of Bulgaria
Formation 1908
Capital Sofia
Population 8.2 million / 194 people per sq mile (74 people per sq km)
Total area 42,683 sq miles (110,550 sq km)
Languages Bulgarian, Turkish, Macedonian, Romany, Armenian, Russian
Religions Bulgarian Orthodox 84%, Muslim 13%, other 3%
Ethnic mix Bulgarian 85%, Turkish 9%, Macedonian 3%, Romany 3%
Government Multiparty republic
Currency Lev = 100 stotinki
Literacy rate 98.2%
Calorie consumption 2,831 kilocalories

Bull Shoals Lake *42 B1 reservoir* Arkansas/Missouri, C USA
Bulukumba *139 E4 prev.* Boeloekoemba. Sulawesi, C Indonesia
Buluwayo *see* Bulawayo
Bumba *77 D5* Equateur, N Dem. Rep. Congo (Zaire)
Bunbury *147 A7* Western Australia
Bundaberg *148 E4* Queensland, E Australia
Bungo-suidō *131 B7 strait* SW Japan
Bunia *77 E5* Orientale, NE Dem. Rep. Congo (Zaire)
Bünyan *116 D3* Kayseri, C Turkey
Buraida *see* Buraydah
Buraydah *120 B4 var.* Buraida. Al Qaşim, N Saudi Arabia

Burdur *116 B4 var.* Buldur. Burdur, SW Turkey
Burdur Gölü *116 B4 salt lake* SW Turkey
Burē *72 C4* C Ethiopia
Burgas *104 E2 var.* Bourgas. Burgas, E Bulgaria
Burgaski Zaliv *104 E2 gulf* E Bulgaria
Burgos *92 D2* Castilla-León, N Spain
Burhan Budai Shan *126 D4 mountain range* C China
Buri Ram *see* Buriram
Buriram *137 D5 var.* Buri Ram, Puriramya. Buri Ram, E Thailand
Burjassot *93 F3* País Valenciano, E Spain
Burkburnett *49 F2* Texas, SW USA
Burketown *148 B3* Queensland, NE Australia
Burkina *see* Burkina Faso
Burkina Faso *75 E4 var.* Burkina; *prev.* Upper Volta. *Country* W Africa

---

Burkina Faso 75

Official name Burkina Faso
Formation 1960
Capital Ouagadougou
Population 11.6 million / 113 people per sq mile (43 people per sq km)
Total area 105,714 sq miles (273,800 sq km)
Languages French, Mossi,Fulani, Tuareg, Dyula, Songhai
Religions Traditional beliefs 55%, Muslim 35%, Roman Catholic 9%, other Christian 1%
Ethnic mix Mossi 50%, other 50%
Government Multiparty republic
Currency CFA franc = 100 centimes
Literacy rate 20.7%
Calorie consumption 2,387 kilocalories

Burley *46 D4* Idaho, NW USA
Burlington *45 G4* Iowa, C USA
Burlington *41 F2* Vermont, NE USA
Burma *see* Myanmar
Burnie *149 C8* Tasmania, SE Australia
Burns *46 C3* Oregon, NW USA
Burnside *37 F3 river* Nunavut, NW Canada
Burnsville *45 F2* Minnesota, N USA
Burrel *101 D6 var.* Burreli. Dibër, C Albania
Burreli *see* Burrel
Burriana *93 F3* País Valenciano, E Spain
Bursa *116 B3 var.* Brussa; *prev.* Brusa, *anc.* Prusa. Bursa, NW Turkey
Burtnieks *see* Burtnieku Ezers
Burtnieku Ezers *106 C3 var.* Burtnieks. *Lake* N Latvia
Burundi *73 B7 prev.* Kingdom of Burundi, Urundi. *Country* C Africa

---

Burundi 73

Official name Republic of Burundi
Formation 1962
Capital Bujumbura
Population 6.7 million / 677 people per sq mile (261 people per sq km)
Total area 9,903 sq miles (25,650 sq km)
Languages Kirundi, French, Swahili
Religions Christian 68%, Traditional beliefs 32%
Ethnic mix Hutu 85%, Tutsi 14%, Twa 1%
Government Multiparty republic
Currency Burundi franc = 100 centimes
Literacy rate 44.6%
Calorie consumption 1,941 kilocalories

Buru, Pulau *139 F4 prev.* Boeroe. *Island* E Indonesia
Buşayrah *118 D3* Dayr az Zawr, E Syria
Büshehr *see* Bandar-e Büshehr
Bushire *see* Bandar-e Büshehr
Busselton *147 A7* Western Australia
Buta *77 D5* Orientale, N Dem. Rep. Congo (Zaire)
Butembo *77 E5* Nord Kivu, NE Dem. Rep. Congo (Zaire)
Butler *41 E4* Pennsylvania, NE USA
Buton, Pulau *139 E4 var.* Pulau Butung; *prev.* Boetoeng. *Island* C Indonesia
Butte *44 B2* Montana, NW USA
Butterworth *138 B3* Pinang, Peninsular Malaysia
Button Islands *37 L2 island group* Northwest Territories, NE Canada
Butuan *139 F2 off.* Butuan City. Mindanao, S Philippines
Buulobarde *73 D5 var.* Buulo Berde. Hiiraan, C Somalia Africa
Buulo Berde *see* Buulobarde
Buur Gaabo *73 D6* Jubbada Hoose, S Somalia
Buynaksk *111 B8* Republika Dagestan, SW Russian Federation
Büyükağrı Dağı *117 F3 var.* Aghri Dagh, Agri Dagi, Koh I Noh, Masis, *Eng.* Great Ararat, Mount Ararat. *Mountain* E Turkey
Büyükmenderes Nehri *116 A4 river* SW Turkey
Buzău *108 C4* Buzău, SE Romania
Buzuluk *111 D6* Akmola, C Kazakhstan
Byahoml' *107 D5 Rus.* Begoml'. Vitsyebskaya Voblasts', N Belarus
Byalynichy *107 D6 Rus.* Belynichi. Mahilyowskaya Voblasts', E Belarus
Bydgoszcz *98 C3 Ger.* Bromberg. Kujawskie-pomorskie, C Poland
Byelaruskaya Hrada *107 B6 Rus.* Belorusskaya Gryada. *Ridge* N Belarus
Byerezino *107 D6 Rus.* Berezina. *River* C Belarus
Byron Island *see* Nikunau
Bytom *99 C5 Ger.* Beuthen. Śląskie, S Poland
Bytča *99 C5* Žilinský Kraj, N Slovakia
Bytów *98 C2 Ger.* Bütow. Pomorskie, N Poland
Byuzmeyin *122 C3 Turkm.* Büzmeyin; *prev.* Bezmein. Akhalskiy Velayat, C Turkmenistan
Byval'ki *107 D8* Homyel'skaya Voblasts', SE Belarus
Byzantium *see* İstanbul

C

Caála *78 B2 var.* Kaala, Robert Williams, *Port.* Vila Robert Williams. Huambo, C Angola
Caazapá *64 D3* Caazapá, S Paraguay
Caballo Reservoir *48 C3 reservoir* New Mexico, SW USA
Cabañaquinta *92 D1* Asturias, N Spain
Cabanatuan *139 E1 off.* Cabanatuan City. Luzon, N Philippines
Cabimas *58 C1* Zulia, NW Venezuela
Cabinda *78 A1 var.* Kabinda. Cabinda, NW Angola
Cabinda *78 A1 var.* Kabinda. Admin. region *province* NW Angola
Cabora Bassa, Lake *see* Cahora Bassa, Albufeira de
Caborca *50 B1* Sonora, NW Mexico
Cabot Strait *39 G4 strait* E Canada
Cabras, Ilha das *76 E2 island* S Sao Tome and Principe
Cabrera *93 G3 anc.* Capraria. *Island* Islas Baleares, Spain, W Mediterranean Sea
Cáceres *92 C3 Ar.* Qazris. Extremadura, W Spain
Cachimbo, Serra do *63 E2 mountain range* C Brazil

Caconda *78 B2* Huíla, C Angola
Čadca *99 C5 Hung.* Csaca. Žilinský Kraj, N Slovakia
Cadillac *40 C2* Michigan, N USA
Cadiz *139 E2 off.* Cadiz City. Negros, C Philippines
Cádiz *92 C5 anc.* Gades, Gadier, Gadir, Gadire. Andalucía, SW Spain
Cádiz, Golfo de *92 B5 Eng.* Gulf of Cadiz. *Gulf* Portugal/Spain
Cadiz, Gulf of *see* Cádiz, Golfo de
Caen *90 B3* Basse-Normandie, N France
Caene *see* Qena
Caenepolis *see* Qena
Caerdydd *see* Cardiff
Caer Gybi *see* Holyhead
Caesarea Mazaca *see* Kayseri
Cafayate *64 C2* Salta, N Argentina
Cagayan de Oro *139 E2 off.* Cagayan de Oro City. Mindanao, S Philippines
Cagliari *97 A6 anc.* Caralis. Sardegna, Italy, C Mediterranean Sea
Caguas *55 F3* E Puerto Rico
Cahora Bassa, Albufeira de *78 D2 var.* Lake Cabora Bassa. *Reservoir* NW Mozambique
Cahors *91 C5 anc.* Cadurcum. Lot, S France
Cahul *108 D4 Rus.* Kagul. S Moldova
Caicos Passage *54 D2 strait* Bahamas/Turks and Caicos Islands
Caiffa *see* Hefa
Cailungo *96 E1* N San Marino
Caiphas *see* Hefa
Cairns *148 D3* Queensland, NE Australia
Cairo *72 B2 Ar.* Al Qāhirah, *var.* El Qâhira. *Country capital* (Egypt) N Egypt
Caisleán an Bharraigh *see* Castlebar
Cajamarca *60 B3 prev.* Caxamarca. Cajamarca, NW Peru
Čakovec *100 B2 Ger.* Csakathurn, *Hung.* Csáktornya; *prev. Ger.* Tschakathurn. Medimurje, N Croatia
Calabar *75 G5* Cross River, S Nigeria
Calabozo *58 D2* Guárico, C Venezuela
Calafat *108 B5* Dolj, SW Romania
Calafate *see* El Calafate
Calahorra *93 E2* La Rioja, N Spain
Calais *41 H2* Maine, NE USA
Calais *90 C2* Pas-de-Calais, N France
Calama *64 B2* Antofagasta, N Chile
Calamianes *see* Calamian Group
Calamian Group *129 C7 var.* Calamianes. *Island group* W Philippines
Cãlãras *see* Cãlãraşi
Cãlãraşi *108 D3 var.* Cãlãras, *Rus.* Kalarash. C Moldova
Cãlãraşi *150 C5* Cãlãraşi, SE Romania
Calatayud *93 E2* Aragón, NE Spain
Calbayog *139 E2 off.* Calbayog City. Samar, C Philippines
Calcutta *135 G4* West Bengal, NE India
Caldas da Rainha *92 B3* Leiria, W Portugal
Caldera *64 B3* Atacama, N Chile
Caldwell *46 C3* Idaho, NW USA
Caledonia *52 C1* Corozal, N Belize
Caleta *see* Catalan Bay
Caleta Olivia *65 B6* Santa Cruz, SE Argentina
Calgary *37 E5* Alberta, SW Canada
Cali *58 B3* Valle del Cauca, W Colombia
Calicut *132 C2 var.* Kozhikode. Kerala, SW India
California *47 B7 off.* State of California; also known as El Dorado, The Golden State. *State* W USA
California, Golfo de *50 B2 Eng.* Gulf of California; *prev.* Sea of Cortez. *Gulf* W Mexico

California, Gulf of *see* California, Golfo de
Cãlimãneşti *108 B4* Vâlcea, SW Romania
Callabonna, Lake *149 B5 lake* South Australia
Callao *60 C4* Callao, W Peru
Callosa de Segura *93 F4* País Valenciano, E Spain
Calmar *see* Kalmar
Caloundra *149 E5* Queensland, E Australia
Caltanissetta *97 C7* Sicilia, Italy, C Mediterranean Sea
Caluula *72 E4* Bari, NE Somalia
Camabatela *78 B1* Cuanza Norte, NW Angola
Camacupa *78 B2 var.* General Machado, *Port.* General Machado. Bié, C Angola
Camagüey *54 C2 prev.* Puerto Príncipe. Camagüey, C Cuba
Camagüey, Archipiélago de *54 C2 island group* C Cuba
Camaná *61 E4* Arequipa, SW Peru
Camargue *91 D6 physical region* SE France
Ca Mau *137 D6 prev.* Quan Long. Minh Hai, S Vietnam
Cambodia *137 D5 var.* Democratic Kampuchea, Roat Kampuchea, *Cam.* Kampuchea; *prev.* People's Democratic Republic of Kampuchea. *Country* SE Asia

Cambodia 137

Official name Kingdom of Cambodia
Formation 1953
Capital Phnom Penh
Population 11.2 million / 164 people per sq mile (63 people per sq km)
Total area 68,154 sq miles (176,520 sq km)
Languages Khmer, French, Chinese, Vietnamese, Cham
Religions Buddhist 95%, other 5%
Ethnic mix Khmer 94%, Chinese 4%, Vietnamese 1%, other 1%
Government Constitutional monarchy
Currency Riel = 100 sen
Literacy rate 66%
Calorie consumption 2,021 kilocalories

Cambrai *90 C2 Flem.* Kambryk; *prev.* Cambray, *anc.* Cameracum. Nord, N France
Cambrian Mountains *89 C6 mountain range* C Wales, UK
Cambridge *89 E6 Lat.* Cantabrigia. E England, UK
Cambridge *41 F4* Maryland, NE USA
Cambridge *40 D4* Ohio, NE USA
Cambridge *54 A4* W Jamaica
Cambridge *150 D3* Waikato, North Island, NZ
Cambridge Bay *37 F3 district capital* Victoria Island, Nunavut, NW Canada
Camden *42 B2* Arkansas, C USA
Cameroon *76 A4 Fr.* Cameroun. *Country* W Africa

Cameroon 76

Official name Republic of Cameroon
Formation 1960
Capital Yaoundé
Population 15 million / 84 people per sq mile (32 people per sq km)
Total area 179,690 sq miles (465,400 sq km)
Languages English, French, Bamileke, Fang, Fulani
Religions Traditional beliefs 25%, Christian 53%, Muslim 22%
Ethnic mix Cameroon highlanders 31%, Bantu 19%, Kirdi 11%, other 39%

Cameroon (continued)

Government Multiparty republic
Currency CFA franc = 100 centimes
Literacy rate 72%
Calorie consumption 1,981 kilocalories

Camocim *63 F2* Ceará, E Brazil
Camopi *59 H3* E French Guiana
Campamento *52 C2* Olancho, C Honduras
Campania *97 D5 cultural region* SE Italy
Campbell, Cape *151 D5 headland* South Island, NZ
Campbell Island *142 D5 island* S NZ
Campbell Plateau *142 D5 undersea feature* SW Pacific Ocean
Campbell River *36 D5* Vancouver Island, British Columbia, SW Canada
Campeche *51 G4* Campeche, SE Mexico
Campeche, Bahía de *51 F4 Eng.* Bay of Campeche. *Bay* E Mexico
Câm Pha *136 E3* Quang Ninh, N Vietnam
Câmpina *108 C4 prev.* Cîmpina. Prahova, SE Romania
Campina Grande *63 G2* Paraíba, E Brazil
Campinas *63 F4* São Paulo, S Brazil
Campobasso *97 D5* Molise, C Italy
Campo Criptana *see* Campo de Criptana
Campo de Criptana *93 E3 var.* Campo Criptana. Castilla-La Mancha, C Spain
Campo dos Goitacazes *see* Campos
Campo Grande *63 E4 state capital* Mato Grosso do Sul, SW Brazil
Campos *63 F4 var.* Campo dos Goitacazes. Rio de Janeiro, SE Brazil
Câmpulung *108 B4 prev.* Câmpulung-Muşcel, Cîmpulung. Argeş, S Romania
Campus Stellae *see* Santiago
Cam Ranh *137 E6* Khanh Hoa, S Vietnam
Canada *34 B4 country* N North America

Canada 34

Official name Canada
Formation 1867
Capital Ottawa
Population 31 million / 9 people per sq mile (3 people per sq km)
Total area 3,560,216 sq miles (9,220,970 sq km)
Languages English, French, Chinese
Religions Roman Catholic 47%, Protestant 41%, non-religious 12%
Ethnic mix British origin 44%, French origin 25%, other European 20%, other (including indigenous Indian) 11%
Government Parliamentary democracy
Currency Canadian dollar = 100 cents
Literacy rate 99%
Calorie consumption 3,094 kilocalories

Canada Basin *34 C2 undersea feature* Arctic Ocean
Canadian River *49 E2 river* SW USA
Çanakkale *116 A3 var.* Dardanelli; *prev.* Chanak, Kale Sultanie. Çanakkale, W Turkey
Çanakkale Boğazı *116 A2 Eng.* Dardanelles. *Strait* NW Turkey
Cananea *50 B1* Sonora, NW Mexico
Canarias, Islas *70 A2 Eng.* Canary Islands. *Island group* Spain, NE Atlantic Ocean
Canarreos, Archipiélago de los *54 B2 island group* W Cuba

Canary Islands *see* Canarias, Islas
Cañas 52 D4 Guanacaste, NW Costa Rica
Canaveral, Cape 43 E4 *headland* Florida, SE USA
Canavieiras 63 G3 Bahia, E Brazil
Canberra 142 C4 *country capital* (Australia) Australian Capital Territory, SE Australia
Cancún 51 H3 Quintana Roo, SE Mexico
Candia *see* Irákleio
Canea *see* Chaniá
Cangzhou 128 D4 Hebei, E China
Caniapiscau 39 E2 *river* Québec, E Canada
Caniapiscau, Réservoir de 38 D3 *reservoir* Québec, C Canada
Canik Dağları 116 D2 *mountain range* N Turkey
Canillo 91 A7 C Andorra
Çankırı 116 C3 *var.* Chankiri; *anc.* Gangra, Germanicopolis. Çankırı, N Turkey
Cannanore 132 B2 *var.* Kananur, Kannur. Kerala, SW India
Cannes 91 D6 Alpes-Maritimes, SE France
Canoas 63 E5 Rio Grande do Sul, S Brazil
Canon City 44 C5 Colorado, C USA
Cantabria 92 D1 *cultural region* N Spain
Cantábrica, Cordillera 92 C1 *mountain range* N Spain
Cantaura 59 E2 Anzoátegui, NE Venezuela
Canterbury 89 E7 *hist.* Cantwaraburh, *anc.* Durovernum, *Lat.* Cantuaria. SE England, UK
Canterbury Bight 151 C6 *bight* South Island, NZ
Canterbury Plains 151 C6 *plain* South Island, NZ
Cần Thơ 137 E6 Cần Thơ, S Vietnam
Canton *see* Guangzhou
Canton 42 B2 Mississippi, S USA
Canton 40 D4 Ohio, N USA
Canton Island *see* Kanton
Canyon 49 E2 Texas, SW USA
Cao Băng 136 D3 *var.* Caobang. Cao Băng, N Vietnam
Caobang *see* Cao Băng
Cape Barren Island 149 C8 *island* Furneaux Group, Tasmania, SE Australia
Cape Basin 69 B7 *undersea feature* S Atlantic Ocean
Cape Breton Island 39 G4 *Fr.* Île du Cap-Breton. Nova Scotia, SE Canada
Cape Charles 41 F5 Virginia, NE USA
Cape Coast 75 E5 *prev.* Cape Coast Castle. S Ghana
Cape Farewell *see* Uummannarsuaq
Cape Girardeau 45 H5 Missouri, C USA
Cape Horn *see* Hornos, Cabo de
Capelle aan den IJssel 86 C4 Zuid-Holland, SW Netherlands
Cape Palmas *see* Harper
Cape Town 78 B5 *var.* Ekapa, *Afr.* Kaapstad, Kapstad. *Country capital* (South Africa-legislative capital) Western Cape, SW South Africa
Cape Verde 74 A2 *Port.* Cabo Verde, Ilhas do Cabo Verde. *Country* E Atlantic Ocean

---

Cape Verde 74

Official name Republic of Cape Verde
Formation 1975
Capital Praia
Population 428,000/ 275 people per sq mile (106 people per sq km)
Total area 1,556 sq miles (4,030 sq km)
Languages Portuguese, Portuguese Creole

Cape Verde (continued)

Religions Roman Catholic 97%,Protestant 1%, other 2%
Ethnic mix Creole 60%, African 30%, other 10%
Government Multiparty republic
Currency Cape Verde escudo = 100 centavos
Literacy rate 71%
Calorie consumption 2,805 kilocalories

Cape Verde Basin 66 C4 *undersea feature* E Atlantic Ocean
Cape Verde Plain 66 C4 *undersea feature* E Atlantic Ocean
Cape York Peninsula 148 C2 *peninsula* Queensland, N Australia
Cap-Haïtien 54 D3 *var.* Le Cap. N Haiti
Capira 53 G5 Panamá, C Panama
Capitán Arturo Prat 154 A2 *Chilean research station* South Shetland Islands, Antarctica
Capitán Pablo Lagerenza 64 D1 *var.* Mayor Pablo Lagerenza. Chaco, N Paraguay
Capri, Isola di 97 C5 *island* S Italy
Caprivi Strip 78 C3 *Ger.* Caprivizipfel; *prev.* Caprivi Concession. *Cultural region* NE Namibia
Caquetá 56 B3 *off.* Departamanto del Caquetá. *Province* S Colombia
Caquetá, Río 58 C5 *var.* Rio Japurá, Yapurá. *River* Brazil/Colombia *see also* Japurá, Rio
CAR *see* Central African Republic
Caracal 108 B5 Olt, S Romania
Caracaraí 62 D1 Rondônia, W Brazil
Caracas 58 D1 *country capital* (Venezuela) Distrito Federal, N Venezuela
Caratasca, Laguna de 53 E2 *lagoon* NE Honduras
Carballiño *see* O Carballiño
Carbondale 40 B5 Illinois, N USA
Carbonia 97 A6 *var.* Carbonia Centro. Sardegna, Italy, C Mediterranean Sea
Carbonia Centro *see* Carbonia
Carcassonne 91 C6 *anc.* Carcaso. Aude, S France
Cárdenas 54 B2 Matanzas, W Cuba
Cardiff 89 C7 *Wel.* Caerdydd. *Admin capital* S Wales, UK
Cardigan Bay 89 C6 *bay* W Wales, UK
Carei 108 B3 *Ger.* Gross-Karol, Karol, *Hung.* Nagykároly; *prev.* Careii-Mari. Satu Mare, NW Romania
Carey, Lake 147 B6 *lake* Western Australia
Cariaco 59 E1 Sucre, NE Venezuela
Caribbean Sea 54 C4 *sea* W Atlantic Ocean
Carlisle 89 C4 *anc.* Caer Luel, Luguvallium, Luguvallum. NW England, UK
Carlow 89 B6 *Ir.* Ceatharlach. SE Ireland
Carlsbad 48 D3 New Mexico, SW USA
Carlsberg Ridge 140 B4 *undersea feature* S Arabian Sea
Carlsruhe *see* Karlsruhe
Carmana *see* Kvarner
Carmarthen 89 C6 SW Wales, UK
Carmaux 91 C6 Tarn, S France
Carmel 40 C4 Indiana, N USA
Carmelita 52 B1 Petén, N Guatemala
Carmen 51 G4 *var.* Ciudad del Carmen. Campeche, SE Mexico
Carmona 92 C4 Andalucía, S Spain
Carnaro *see* Kvarner
Carnarvon 147 A5 Western Australia
Carnegie, Lake 147 B5 *salt lake* Western Australia
Car Nicobar 133 F3 *island* Nicobar Islands, India, NE Indian Ocean
Caroço, Ilha 76 E1 *island* N Sao Tome and Principe
Carolina 56 F2 Maranhão, E Brazil
Caroline Island *see* Millennium Island

Caroline Islands 106 C2 *island group* C Micronesia
Caroní, Río 59 E3 *river* E Venezuela
Caronium *see* A Coruña
Carora 58 C1 Lara, N Venezuela
Carpathian Mountains 81 E4 *var.* Carpathians, *Cz./Pol.* Karpaty, *Ger.* Karpaten. *Mountain range* E Europe
Carpathians *see* Carpathian Mountains
Carpaţii Meridionali 108 B4 *var.* Alpi Transilvaniei, Carpaţii Sudici, *Eng.* South Carpathians, Transylvanian Alps, *Ger.* Südkarpaten, Transsylvanische Alpen, *Hung.* Déli-Kárpátok, Erdélyi-Havasok. *Mountain range* C Romania
Carpaţii Occidentali 99 E7 *Eng.* Western Carpathians. *Mountain range* W Romania
Carpaţii Sudici *see* Carpaţii Meridionali
Carpentaria, Gulf of 148 B2 *gulf* N Australia
Carpi 96 C2 Emilia-Romagna, N Italy
Carrara 96 B3 Toscana, C Italy
Carson City 47 C5 *state capital* Nevada, W USA
Carson Sink 47 C5 *salt flat* Nevada, W USA
Cartagena 93 F4 *anc.* Carthago Nova. Murcia, SE Spain
Cartagena 58 B1 *var.* Cartagena de los Indes. Bolívar, NW Colombia
Cartagena de los Indes *see* Cartagena
Cartago 53 E4 Cartago, C Costa Rica
Carthage 45 F5 Missouri, C USA
Cartwright 39 F2 Newfoundland and Labrador, E Canada
Carúpano 59 E1 Sucre, NE Venezuela
Caruthersville 45 H5 Missouri, C USA
Cary 43 F1 North Carolina, SE USA
Casablanca 70 C2 *Ar.* Dar-el-Beida. NW Morocco
Casa Grande 48 B2 Arizona, SW USA
Cascade Range 46 B3 *mountain range* Oregon/Washington, NW USA
Cascadia Basin 34 A4 *undersea feature* NE Pacific Ocean
Cascais 92 B4 Lisboa, C Portugal
Caserta 97 D5 Campania, S Italy
Casey 154 D4 *Australian research station* Antarctica
Casino 91 C8 New South Wales, SE Australia
Casper 44 C3 Wyoming, C USA
Caspian Depression 111 B7 *Kaz.* Kaspiy Mangy Oypaty, *Rus.* Prikaspiyskaya Nizmennost'. *Depression* Kazakhstan/Russian Federation
Caspian Sea 114 A4 *Az.* Xäzär Dänizi, *Kaz.* Kaspiy Tengizi, *Per.* Baḩr-e Khazar, Daryā-ye Khazar, *Rus.* Kaspiyskoye More. *Inland sea* Asia/Europe
Cassai *see* Kasai
Castamoni *see* Kastamonu
Casteggio 96 B2 Lombardia, N Italy
Castelló de la Plana 93 F3 *var.* Castellón. País Valenciano, E Spain
Castellón *see* Castelló de la Plana
Castelnaudary 91 C6 Aude, S France
Castelo Branco 92 C3 Castelo Branco, C Portugal
Castelsarrasin 91 B6 Tarn-et-Garonne, S France
Castelvetrano 97 C7 Sicilia, Italy, C Mediterranean Sea
Castilla-La Mancha 93 E3 *cultural region* NE Spain
Castilla-León 92 C2 *cultural region* NW Spain

Castlebar 89 A5 *Ir.* Caisleán an Bharraigh. W Ireland
Castleford 89 D5 N England, UK
Castle Harbour 42 B5 *inlet* Bermuda, NW Atlantic Ocean
Castricum 86 C3 Noord-Holland, W Netherlands
Castries 55 F1 *country capital* (Saint Lucia) N Saint Lucia
Castro 65 B6 Los Lagos, W Chile
Castrovillari 97 D6 Calabria, SW Italy
Castuera 92 D4 Extremadura, W Spain
Caswell Sound 151 A7 *sound* South Island, NZ
Catacamas 52 D2 Olancho, C Honduras
Catacaos 60 B3 Piura, NW Peru
Catalan Bay 93 H4 *var.* Caleta. *Bay* E Gibraltar
Cataluña 93 G2 *cultural region* N Spain
Catamarca *see* San Fernando del Valle de Catamarca
Catania 97 D7 Sicilia, Italy, C Mediterranean Sea
Catanzaro 97 D6 Calabria, SW Italy
Catarroja 93 F3 País Valenciano, E Spain
Cat Island 54 C1 *island* C Bahamas
Catskill Mountains 41 F3 *mountain range* New York, NE USA
Cauca, Río 58 B2 *river* N Colombia
Caucasia 58 B2 Antioquia, NW Colombia
Caucasus 81 G4 *Rus.* Kavkaz. *Mountain range* Georgia/Russian Federation
Caura, Río 59 E3 *river* C Venezuela
Cavalla 74 D5 *var.* Cavally, Cavally Fleuve. *River* Côte d'Ivoire/Liberia
Cavally *see* Cavalla
Cavally Fleuve *see* Cavalla
Caviana de Fora, Ilha 63 E1 *var.* Ilha Caviana. Island N Brazil
Caxito 78 B1 Bengo, NW Angola
Cayenne 59 H3 *dependent territory capital* (French Guiana) NE French Guiana
Cayes 54 D3 *var.* Les Cayes. SW Haiti
Cayman Brac 54 B3 *island* E Cayman Islands
Cayman Islands 54 B3 *UK dependent territory* W West Indies
Cay Sal 54 B2 *islet* SW Bahamas
Cazin 100 B3 Federacija Bosna I Hercegovina, NW Bosnia and Herzegovina
Cazorla 93 E4 Andalucía, S Spain
Ceadâr-Lunga *see* Ciadir-Lunga
Ceará 63 F2 *off.* Estado do Ceará. *State* C Brazil
Ceara Abyssal Plain *see* Ceará Plain
Ceará Plain 56 E3 *var.* Ceara Abyssal Plain. *Undersea feature* W Atlantic Ocean
Ceatharlach *see* Carlow
Cébaco, Isla 53 F5 *island* SW Panama
Cebu 139 E2 *off.* Cebu City. Cebu, C Philippines
Cecina 96 B3 Toscana, C Italy
Cedar City 44 A5 Utah, W USA
Cedar Falls 45 G3 Iowa, C USA
Cedar Lake 38 A2 *lake* Manitoba, C Canada
Cedar Rapids 45 G3 Iowa, C USA
Cedros, Isla 50 A2 *island* W Mexico
Ceduna 149 A6 South Australia
Cefalù 97 C7 *anc.* Cephaloedium. Sicilia, Italy, C Mediterranean Sea
Celebes *see* Sulawesi
Celebes Sea 139 E3 *Ind.* Laut Sulawesi. *Sea* Indonesia/Philippines
Celje 95 E7 *Ger.* Cilli. C Slovenia
Celldömölk 99 C6 Vas, W Hungary
Celle 94 B3 *var.* Zelle. Niedersachsen, N Germany
Celtic Sea 89 B7 *Ir.* An Mhuir Cheilteach. *Sea* SW British Isles

Celtic Shelf 80 B3 *undersea feature*
E Atlantic Ocean
Cenderawasih, Teluk 139 G4 *var.*
Teluk Irian, Teluk Sarera. *Bay* W
Pacific Ocean
Cenon 91 B5 Gironde, SW France
Central African Republic 76 C4 *var.*
République Centrafricaine, *abbrev.*
CAR; *prev.* Ubangi-Shari,
Oubangui-Chari, Territoire de
l'Oubangui-Chari. *Country*
C Africa

Central African Republic 76

Official name Central African
Republic
Formation 1960
Capital Bangui
Population 3.6 million /
15 people per sq mile
(6 people per sq km)
Total area 240,532 sq miles
(622,980 sq km)
Languages French, Sango, Banda,
Gbaya
Religions Christian 50%,
Traditional beliefs 24%,
Muslim 15%, other 11%
Ethnic mix Baya 34%, Banda 27%,
Mandjia 21%, Sara 10%, other 8%
Government Multiparty republic
Currency CFA franc
= 100 centimes
Literacy rate 42.4%
Calorie consumption 1,690
kilocalories

Central, Cordillera 55 E3 *mountain range* C Dominican Republic
Central, Cordillera 53 F5 *mountain range* C Panama
Central, Cordillera 139 E1 *mountain range* Luzon, N Philippines
Central, Cordillera 58 B3 *mountain range* W Colombia
Central Group *see* Inner Islands
Centralia 46 B2 Washington,
NW USA
Central Indian Ridge *see* Mid-
Indian Ridge
Central Makrān Range 134 A3 *mountain range* W Pakistan
Central Pacific Basin 142 D1 *undersea feature* C Pacific
Ocean
Central, Planalto 63 F3 *var.*
Brazilian Highlands. *Mountain range* E Brazil
Central Range 144 B3 *mountain range* NW PNG
Central Russian Upland *see*
Srednerusskaya Vozvyshennost'
Central Siberian Plateau *see*
Srednesibirskoye Ploskogor'ye
Central Siberian Uplands *see*
Srednesibirskoye Ploskogor'ye
Central, Sistema 92 D3 *mountain range* C Spain
Central Valley 47 B6 *valley*
California, W USA
Cephaloedium *see* Cefalu
Ceram *see* Seram, Pulau
Ceram Sea 139 F4 *Ind.* Laut Seram.
Sea E Indonesia
Cerasus *see* Giresun
Cereté 58 B2 Córdoba,
NW Colombia
Cerignola 97 D5 Puglia, SE Italy
Cerigo *see* Kýthira
Çerkeş 116 C2 Çankırı, N Turkey
Cernay 90 E4 Haut-Rhin,
NE France
Cerro Chirripó *see* Chirripó
Grande, Cerro
Cerro de Mulhacén *see*
Mulhacén
Cerro de Pasco 60 C3 Pasco,
C Peru
Cervera 93 F2 Cataluña, NE Spain
Cesena 96 C3 *anc.* Caesena. Emilia-
Romagna, N Italy
Cēsis 106 D3 *Ger.* Wenden. Cēsis,
C Latvia
České Budějovice 99 B5 *Ger.*
Budweis. Budějovický Kraj,
S Czech Republic

Český Krumlov 99 A5 *var.*
Böhmisch-Krumau, *Ger.*
Krummau. Budějovický Kraj,
S Czech Republic
Cetinje 101 C5 *It.* Cettigne.
Montenegro, SW Yugoslavia
Ceuta 70 C2 *enclave* Spain, N Africa
Cévennes 91 C6 *mountain range*
S France
Ceyhan 116 D4 Adana, S Turkey
Ceylanpınar 117 E4 Şanlıurfa,
SE Turkey
Ceylon Plain 124 B4 *undersea feature*
N Indian Ocean
Ceyre to the Caribs *see* Marie-
Galante
Chachapoyas 60 B2 Amazonas,
NW Peru
Chachevichy 107 D6 *Rus.*
Chechevichi. Mahilyowskaya
Voblasts', E Belarus
Chaco *see* Gran Chaco
Chad 76 C3 *Fr.* Tchad. *Country*
C Africa

Chad 76

Official name Republic of Chad
Formation 1960
Capital N'Djamena
Population 7.7 million /
16 people per sq mile
(6 people per sq km)
Total area 486,177 sq miles
(1,259,200 sq km)
Languages French, Arabic, Sara,
Maba
Religions Muslim 50%,
Traditional beliefs 43%,
Christian 7%
Ethnic mix Over 200 ethnic
groups divided between the Arabic
nomads (north) and black Africans
(south)
Government Multiparty republic
Currency CFA franc
= 100 centimes
Literacy rate 50.3%
Calorie consumption 1,989
kilocalories

Chad, Lake 76 B3 *Fr.* Lac Tchad.
Lake C Africa
Chadron 44 D3 Nebraska, C USA
Chadyr-Lunga *see* Ciadîr-Lunga
Chāgai Hills 134 A2 *var.* Chāh Gay.
Mountain range
Afghanistan/Pakistan
Chaghasarāy *see* Asadābād
Chagos-Laccadive Plateau 124 B4 *undersea feature* N Indian Ocean
Chagos Trench 141 C5 *undersea feature* N Indian Ocean
Chāh Gay *see* Chāgai Hills
Chaillu, Massif du 77 B6 *mountain range* C Gabon
Chaîne des Dangrek *see* Dângrêk,
Chuŏr Phnum
Chaîne des Mitumba *see* Mitumba,
Monts
Chaîne des Mongos *see* Bongo,
Massif des
Chain Ridge 140 B4 *undersea feature*
W Indian Ocean
Chajul 52 B2 Quiché, W Guatemala
Chakhānsūr 122 D5 Nīmrūz,
SW Afghanistan
Chala 60 D4 Arequipa, SW Peru
Chalatenango 52 C3 Chalatenango,
N El Salvador
Chalcidice *see* Chalkidikí
Chalcis *see* Chalkída
Chálki 105 E7 *island* Dodekánisos,
Greece, Aegean Sea
Chalkída 105 C5 *var.* Halkida; *prev.*
Khalkís, *anc.* Chalcis. Evvoia,
E Greece
Chalkidikí 104 C4 *var.* Khalkidhikí;
anc. Chalcidice. *Peninsula*
NE Greece
Challans 90 B4 Vendée,
NW France
Challapata 61 F4 Oruro, SW Bolivia
Challenger Deep 152 B3 *undersea feature* W Pacific Ocean
Challenger Fracture Zone 153 F4 *tectonic feature* SE Pacific Ocean

Châlons-en-Champagne 90 D3 *prev.*
Châlons-sur-Marne, *hist.* Arcae
Remorum, *anc.* Carolopois.
Marne, NE France
Chalon-sur-Saône 90 D4 *anc.*
Cabillonum. Saône-et-Loire,
C France
Cha Mai *see* Thung Song
Chaman 134 B2 Baluchistān,
SW Pakistan
Chambéry 91 D5 *anc.* Cambaria.
Savoie, E France
Champagne 90 D3 Yukon Territory,
W Canada
Champaign 40 B4 Illinois, N USA
Champasak 137 D5 Champasak,
S Laos
Champlain, Lake 41 F2 *lake*
Canada/USA
Champotón 51 G4 Campeche,
SE Mexico
Chanak *see* Çanakkale
Chañaral 64 B3 Atacama, N Chile
Chanchiang *see* Zhanjiang
Chandeleur Islands 42 C3 *island group* Louisiana, S USA
Chandīgarh 134 D2 Punjab,
N India
Chandrapur 135 E5 Mahārāshtra,
C India
Changan *see* Xi'an
Changane 79 E3 *river*
S Mozambique
Changchun 128 D3 *var.*
Ch'angch'un, Chang-ch'un; *prev.*
Hsinking. Jilin, NE China
Changkiakow *see* Zhangjiakou
Chang, Ko 137 C6 *island* S Thailand
Changsha 128 C5 *var.* Ch'angsha,
Ch'ang-sha. Hunan, S China
Ch'angsha *see* Changsha
Changzhi 128 C4 Shanxi, C China
Chaniá 105 C7 *var.* Hania, Khaniá,
Eng. Canea; *anc.* Cydonia. Kríti,
Greece, E Mediterranean Sea
Chañi, Nevado de 64 B2 *mountain*
NW Argentina
Chankiri *see* Çankırı
Channel Islands 89 C8 *Fr.* Îles
Normandes. *Island group*
S English Channel
Channel Islands 47 B8 *island group*
California, W USA
Channel-Port aux Basques 39 G4
Newfoundland, Newfoundland
and Labrador, SE Canada
Channel, The *see* English Channel
Channel Tunnel 90 C2 *tunnel*
France/UK
Chantabun *see* Chanthaburi
Chantaburi *see* Chanthaburi
Chantada 92 C1 Galicia, NW Spain
Chanthaburi 137 C6 *var.*
Chantabun, Chantaburi.
Chantaburi, S Thailand
Chanute 45 F5 Kansas, C USA
Chaouèn *see* Chefchaouen
Chaoyang 128 D3 Liaoning,
NE China
Chapala, Lago de 50 D4 *lake*
C Mexico
Chapan, Gora 122 B3 *mountain*
C Turkmenistan
Chapayevsk 111 C6 Samarskaya
Oblast', W Russian Federation
Chaplynka 109 F4 Khersons'ka
Oblast', S Ukraine
Charcot Seamounts 80 B3 *undersea feature* E Atlantic Ocean
Chardzhev 122 D3 *prev.* Chardzhou,
Chardzhui, Leninsk-Turkmenski,
Turkm. Chärjew. Lebapskiy
Velayat, E Turkmenistan
Charente 91 B5 *cultural region*
W France
Charente 91 B5 *river* W France
Chari 76 B3 *var.* Shari. *River* Central
African Republic/Chad
Chārīkār 123 E4 Parwān,
NE Afghanistan
Charity 59 F2 NW Guyana
Charkhlik *see* Ruoqiang
Charkhliq *see* Ruoqiang

Charleroi 87 C7 Hainaut,
S Belgium
Charlesbourg 39 E4 Québec,
SE Canada
Charles de Gaulle 90 E1 *international airport* (Paris) Seine-
et-Marne, N France
Cha Mai *see* Thung Song —
Charles Island 38 D1 *island*
Northwest Territories, NE Canada
Charles Island *see* Santa María, Isla
Charleston 40 D5 *state capital* West
Virginia, NE USA
Charleston 43 F2 South Carolina,
SE USA
Charleville 149 D5 Queensland,
E Australia
Charleville-Mézières 90 D3
Ardennes, N France
Charlie-Gibbs Fracture Zone 66 B2 *tectonic feature* N Atlantic Ocean
Charlotte 43 E1 North Carolina,
SE USA
Charlotte Amalie 55 F3 *prev.* Saint
Thomas. *Dependent territory capital*
(Virgin Islands (US)) Saint
Thomas, N Virgin Islands (US)
Charlotte Harbor 43 E5 *inlet*
Florida, SE USA
Charlottesville 41 E5 Virginia,
NE USA
Charlottetown 39 F4 Prince Edward
Island, Prince Edward Island,
SE Canada
Charsk *see* Shar
Charters Towers 148 D3
Queensland, NE Australia
Chartres 90 C3 *anc.* Autricum,
Civitas Carnutum. Eure-et-Loir,
C France
Charus Nuur 126 C2 *lake*
NW Mongolia
Chashniki 107 D5 *Rus.* Chashniki.
Vitsyebskaya Voblasts', N Belarus
Châteaubriant 90 B4 Loire-
Atlantique, NW France
Châteaudun 90 C3 Eure-et-Loir,
C France
Châteauroux 90 C4 *prev.* Indreville.
Indre, C France
Château-Thierry 90 C3 Aisne,
N France
Châtelet 87 C7 Hainaut, S Belgium
Châtelherault *see* Châtellerault
Châtellerault 90 B4 *var.*
Châtelherault. Vienne, W France
Chatham Island *see* San Cristóbal,
Isla
Chatham Island Rise *see* Chatham
Rise
Chatham Islands 143 E5 *island group* NZ, SW Pacific Ocean
Chatham Rise 142 D5 *var.* Chatham
Island Rise. *Undersea feature*
S Pacific Ocean
Chatkal Range 123 F2 *Rus.*
Chatkal'skiy Khrebet. *Mountain range* Kyrgyzstan/Uzbekistan
Chattahoochee River 42 D3 *river*
SE USA
Chattanooga 42 D1 Tennessee,
S USA
Chatyr-Tash 123 G2 Narynskaya
Oblast', C Kyrgyzstan
Châu Độc 137 D6 *var.* Chauphu,
Chau Phu. An Giang, S Vietnam
Chauk 136 A3 Magwe, W Myanmar
Chaumont 90 D4 *prev.* Chaumont-
en-Bassigny. Haute-Marne,
N France
Chau Phu *see* Châu Độc
Chaves 92 C2 *anc.* Aquae Flaviae.
Vila Real, N Portugal
Chávez, Isla *see* Santa Cruz, Isla
Chavusy 107 E6 *Rus.* Chausy.
Mahilyowskaya Voblasts',
E Belarus
Chaykovskiy 111 D5 Permskaya
Oblast', NW Russian Federation
Cheb 99 A5 *Ger.* Eger. Karlovarský
Kraj, W Czech Republic
Cheboksary 111 C5 Chuvashskaya
Respublika, W Russian Federation
Cheboygan 40 C2 Michigan, N USA
Chechaouèn *see* Chefchaouen
Chech, Erg 74 D1 *desert*
Algeria/Mali
Che-chiang *see* Zhejiang

Cheduba Island 136 A4 island
W Myanmar
Chefchaouen 70 C2 var. Chaouèn,
Chechaouèn, Sp. Xauen.
N Morocco
Chefoo see Yantai
Cheju-do 129 E4 Jap. Saishū;
prev. Quelpart. Island S South
Korea
Cheju Strait 129 E4 strait S South
Korea
Chekiang see Zhejiang
Cheleken 122 B2 Balkanskiy
Velayat, W Turkmenistan
Chelkar 114 B4 Aktyubinsk,
W Kazakhstan
Chełm 98 E4 Rus. Kholm.
Lubelskie, E Poland
Chełmno 98 C3 Ger. Culm, Kulm.
Kujawski-pomorskie, C Poland
Chełmża 98 C3 Ger. Culmsee,
Kulmsee. Kujawski-pomorskie, C
Poland
Cheltenham 89 D6 C England, UK
Chelyabinsk 114 C3
Chelyabinskaya Oblast',
C Russian Federation
Chemnitz 94 D4 prev. Karl-Marx-
Stadt. Sachsen, E Germany
Chenāb 134 C2 river India/Pakistan
Chengchiatun see Liaoyuan
Ch'eng-chou see Zhengzhou
Chengchow see Zhengzhou
Chengde 128 D3 var. Jehol. Hebei,
E China
Chengdu 128 B5 var. Chengtu,
Ch'eng-tu. Sichuan, C China
Chenghsien see Zhengzhou
Ch'eng-tu see Chengdu
Chennai 132 D2 prev Madras. Tamil
Nādu, S India
Chenxian see Chenzhou
Chen Xian see Chenzhou
Chen Xiang see Chenzhou
Chenzhou 128 C6 var. Chenxian,
Chen Xian, Chen Xiang. Hunan,
S China
Chepelare 104 C3 Smolyan,
S Bulgaria
Chepén 60 B3 La Libertad, C Peru
Cher 90 C4 river C France
Cherbourg 90 B3 anc. Carusbur.
Manche, N France
Cherepovets 110 B4 Vologodskaya
Oblast', NW Russian Federation
Chergui, Chott ech 70 D2 salt lake
NW Algeria
Cherkasy 109 E2 Rus. Cherkassy.
Cherkas'ka Oblast', C Ukraine
Cherkessk 111 B7 Karachayevo-
Cherkesskaya Respublika,
SW Russian Federation
Chernihiv 109 E1 Rus. Chernigov.
Chernihivs'ka Oblast',
NE Ukraine
Chernivtsi 108 C3 Ger. Czernowitz,
Rom. Cernǎuţi, Rus. Chernovtsy.
Chernivets'ka Oblast', W Ukraine
Cherno More see Black Sea
Chernoye More see Black Sea
Chernyakhovsk 106 A4 Ger.
Insterburg. Kaliningradskaya
Oblast', W Russian Federation
Cherry Hill 41 F4 New Jersey,
NE USA
Cherski Range see Cherskogo,
Khrebet
Cherskiy 115 G2 Respublika Sakha
(Yakutiya), NE Russian
Federation
Cherskogo, Khrebet 115 F2 var.
Cherski Range. Mountain range
NE Russian Federation
Chervonohrad 108 C2 Rus.
Chervonograd. L'vivs'ka Oblast',
NW Ukraine
Chervyen' 107 D6 Rus. Cherven'.
Minskaya Voblasts', C Belarus
Cherykaw 107 E7 Rus. Cherikov.
Mahilyowskaya Voblasts',
E Belarus
Chesapeake Bay 41 F5 inlet
NE USA
Chesha Bay see Chëshskaya Guba
Chëshskaya Guba 172 D5 var.
Archangel Bay, Chesha Bay, Dvina
Bay. Bay NW Russian Federation

Chester 89 C6 Wel. Caerleon; hist.
Legaceaster, Lat. Deva, Devana
Castra. C England, UK
Chetumal 51 H4 var. Payo Obispo.
Quintana Roo, SE Mexico
Cheviot Hills 88 D4 hill range
England/Scotland, UK
Cheyenne 44 D4 state capital
Wyoming, C USA
Cheyenne River 44 D3 river South
Dakota/Wyoming, N USA
Chhapra 135 F3 prev. Chapra. Bihār,
N India
Chiai 128 D6 var. Chia-i, Chiayi,
Kiayi, Jiayi, Jap. Kagi. C Taiwan
Chia-i see Chiai
Chiang-hsi see Jiangxi
Chiang Mai 136 B4 var. Chiangmai,
Chiengmai, Kiangmai. Chiang
Mai, NW Thailand
Chiangmai see Chiang Mai
Chiang Rai 136 C3 var. Chianpai,
Chienrai, Muang Chiang Rai.
Chiang Rai, NW Thailand
Chiang-su see Jiangsu
Chian-ning see Nanjing
Chianpai see Chiang Rai
Chianti 96 C3 cultural region
C Italy
Chiapa see Chiapa de Corzo
Chiapa de Corzo 51 G5 var. Chiapa.
Chiapas, SE Mexico
Chiayi see Chiai
Chiba 130 B1 var. Tiba. Chiba,
Honshū, S Japan
Chibougamau 38 D3 Québec,
SE Canada
Chicago 40 B3 Illinois, N USA
Ch'i-ch'i-ha-erh see Qiqihar
Chickasha 49 G2 Oklahoma, C USA
Chiclayo 60 B3 Lambayeque,
NW Peru
Chico 47 B5 California, W USA
Chico, Río 65 B6 river S Argentina
Chico, Río 65 B7 river SE Argentina
Chicoutimi 39 E4 Québec,
SE Canada
Chiengmai see Chiang Mai
Chienrai see Chiang Rai
Chiesanuova 96 D2 SW San
Marino
Chieti 96 D4 var. Teate. Abruzzo,
C Italy
Chifeng 127 G2 var. Ulanhad. Nei
Mongol Zizhiqu, N China
Chih-fu see Yantai
Chihli see Hebei
Chihli, Gulf of see Bo Hai
Chihuahua 50 C2 Chihuahua,
NW Mexico
Childress 49 F2 Texas, SW USA
Chile 64 B3 Country SW South
America

Chile 64

Official name Republic of Chile
Formation 1818
Capital Santiago
Population 15.2 million /
53 people per sq mile
(20 people per sq km)
Total area 289,111 sq miles
(748,800 sq km)
Languages Spanish, Amerindian
languages
Religions Roman Catholic 80%,
other and non-religious 20%
Ethnic mix Mixed and European
90%, Indian 10%
Government Multiparty republic
Currency Chilean peso
= 100 centavos
Literacy rate 95.2%
Calorie consumption 2,582
kilocalories

Chile Basin 57 A5 undersea feature
E Pacific Ocean
Chile Chico 65 B6 Aisén, W Chile
Chile Rise 57 A7 undersea feature
SE Pacific Ocean
Chililabombwe 78 D2 Copperbelt,
C Zambia
Chi-lin see Jilin
Chillán 65 B5 Bío Bío, C Chile
Chillicothe 40 D4 Ohio, N USA

Chiloé, Isla de 65 A6 var. Isla
Grande de Chiloé. Island W Chile
Chilpancingo 51 E5 var.
Chilpancingo de los Bravos.
Guerrero, S Mexico
Chilpancingo de los Bravos see
Chilpancingo
Chilung 128 D6 var. Keelung, Jap.
Kirun, Kirun'; prev. Sp. Santissima
Trinidad. N Taiwan
Chimán 53 G5 Panamá, E Panama
Chimborazo 60 A1 volcano
C Ecuador
Chimbote 60 C3 Ancash, W Peru
Chimboy 122 D1 Rus. Chimbay.
Qoraqalpoghiston Respublikasi,
NW Uzbekistan
Chimoio 79 E3 Manica,
C Mozambique
China 124 C2 Chin. Chung-hua Jen-
min Kung-ho-kuo, Zhonghua
Renmin Gongheguo; prev. Chinese
Empire. Country E Asia

China 124

Official name People's
Republic of China
Formation 1949
Capital Beijing
Population 1.3 billion /
355 people per sq mile
(137 people per sq km)
Total area 3,600,926 sq miles
(9,326,410 sq km)
Languages Mandarin, Wu,
Cantonese, Hsiang, Min, Hakka,
Kan
Religions Non-religious 59%,
Traditional beliefs 20%, other 21%
Ethnic mix Han 93%, other 7%
Government Single-party
republic
Currency Yuan = 10 jiao
Literacy rate 84%
Calorie consumption 2,727
kilocalories

Chi-nan see Jinan
Chinandega 52 C3 Chinandega,
NW Nicaragua
Chincha Alta 60 D4 Ica, SW Peru
Chin-chiang see Quanzhou
Chin-chou see Jinzhou
Chinchow see Jinzhou
Chindwin 136 B2 river
N Myanmar
Ch'ing Hai see Qinghai Hu
Chingola 78 D2 Copperbelt,
C Zambia
Ching-Tao see Qingdao
Chinguetti 74 C2 var. Chinguetti.
Adrar, C Mauritania
Chin Hills 136 A3 mountain range
W Myanmar
Chinhsien see Jinzhou
Chinnereth see Tiberias, Lake
Chinook Trough 113 H4 undersea
feature N Pacific Ocean
Chioggia 96 C2 anc. Fossa Claudia.
Veneto, NE Italy
Chíos 105 D5 var. Hios, Khíos, It.
Scio, Turk. Sakiz-Adasi. Chíos,
E Greece
Chíos 105 D5 var. Khíos. Island
E Greece
Chipata 78 D2 prev. Fort Jameson.
Eastern, E Zambia
Chiquián 60 C3 Ancash, W Peru
Chiquimula 52 B2 Chiquimula,
SE Guatemala
Chīrāla 132 D1 Andhra Pradesh,
E India
Chirchiq 123 E2 Rus. Chirchik.
Toshkent Wiloyati, E Uzbekistan
Chiriquí, Golfo de 53 E5 Eng.
Chiriqui Gulf. Gulf SW Panama
Chiriquí, Laguna de 53 E5 lagoon
NW Panama
Chirripó Grande, Cerro 52 D4 var.
Cerro Chirripó. Mountain
SE Costa Rica
Chisec 52 B2 Alta Verapaz,
C Guatemala
Chisholm 45 F1 Minnesota, N USA
Chisimaio see Kismaayo
Chisimayu see Kismaayo

Chişinău 108 D4 Rus. Kishinev.
Country capital (Moldova)
C Moldova
Chita 115 F4 Chitinskaya Oblast',
S Russian Federation
Chitato 78 C1 Lunda Norte,
NE Angola
Chitina 36 D3 Alaska, USA
Chitose 130 D2 var. Titose.
Hokkaidō, NE Japan
Chitré 53 F5 Herrera, S Panama
Chittagong 135 G4 Ben. Chāttagām.
Chittagong, SE Bangladesh
Chitungwiza 78 D3 prev.
Chitangwiza. Mashonaland East,
NE Zimbabwe
Chlef 70 D2 var. Ech Cheliff, Ech
Chleff; prev. Al-Asnam, El Asnam,
Orléansville. NW Algeria
Chocolate Mountains 47 D8
mountain range California, W USA
Chodzież 98 C3 Wielkopolskie, C
Poland
Choele Choel 65 C5 Río Negro,
C Argentina
Choiseul 144 C3 var. Lauru. Island
NW Solomon Islands
Chojnice 98 C2 Ger. Knoitz.
Pomorskie, N Poland
Ch'ok'ē 72 C4 var. Choke
Mountains. Mountain range
NW Ethiopia
Choke Mountains see Ch'ok'ē
Cholet 90 B4 Maine-et-Loire,
NW France
Choluteca 52 C3 Choluteca,
S Honduras
Choluteca, Río 52 C3 river
SW Honduras
Choma 78 D2 Southern, S Zambia
Chomutov 98 A4 Ger. Komotau.
Ústecký Kraj, NW Czech Republic
Chona 113 E2 river C Russian
Federation
Chon Buri 137 C5 prev. Bang Pla
Soi. Chon Buri, S Thailand
Chone 60 A1 Manabí, W Ecuador
Ch'ŏngjin 129 E3 NE North Korea
Chongqing 128 B5 var. Ch'ung-
ching, Ch'ung-ch'ing, Chungking,
Pahsien, Tchongking, Yuzhou.
Chongqing, C China
Chongqing 128 B5 Admin. region
province C China
Chonos, Archipiélago de los 65 A6
island group S Chile
Chorne More see Black Sea
Chornomors'ke 109 E4 Rus.
Chernomorskoye. Respublika
Krym, S Ukraine
Chortkiv 108 C2 Rus. Chortkov.
Ternopil's'ka Oblast', W Ukraine
Chorum see Çorum
Chorzów 99 C5 Ger. Königshütte;
prev. Królewska Huta. Śląskie,
S Poland
Chōshi 131 D5 var. Tyôsi. Chiba,
Honshū, S Japan
Choszczno 98 B3 Ger. Arnswalde.
Zachodniopomorskie, NW Poland
Chota Nāgpur 135 E4 plateau
N India
Chott el-Hodna see Hodna, Chott
El
Chott Melrhir see Melghir, Chott
Choûm 74 C2 Adrar, C Mauritania
Choybalsan 127 F2 Dornod,
E Mongolia
Christchurch 151 C6 Canterbury,
South Island, NZ
Christiana 54 B5 C Jamaica
Christiansand see Kristiansand
Christianshåb see Qasigiannguit
Christiansund see Kristiansund
Christmas Island 141 D5 Australian
external territory E Indian Ocean
Christmas Ridge 143 E1 undersea
feature C Pacific Ocean
Chuan see Sichuan
Ch'uan-chou see Quanzhou
Chubut 57 B7 off. Provincia de
Chubut. Admin. region province
S Argentina
Chubut, Río 65 B6 river
SE Argentina
Ch'u-chiang see Shaoguan
Chūgoku-sanchi 131 B6 mountain
range Honshū, SW Japan

Chuí *see* Chuy
Chukai *see* Cukai
Chukchi Plain 155 B2 *undersea feature* Arctic Ocean
Chukchi Plateau 34 C2 *undersea feature* Arctic Ocean
Chukchi Sea 34 B2 *Rus.* Chukotskoye More. *Sea* Arctic Ocean
Chula Vista 47 C8 California, W USA
Chulucanas 60 B2 Piura, NW Peru
Chulym 114 D4 *river* C Russian Federation
Chumphon 137 C6 *var.* Jumporn. Chumphon, SW Thailand
Ch'unch'ŏn 129 E4 *Jap.* Shunsen. N South Korea
Ch'ung-ching *see* Chongqing
Chungking *see* Chongqing
Chunya 115 E3 *river* C Russian Federation
Chuquicamata 64 B2 Antofagasta, N Chile
Chur 95 B7 *Fr.* Coire, *It.* Coira, *Rmsch.* Cuera, Quera; *anc.* Curia Rhaetorum. Graubünden, E Switzerland
Churchill 38 B2 *river* Manitoba/Saskatchewan, C Canada
Churchill 39 F2 *river* Newfoundland and Labrador, E Canada
Churchill 37 G4 Manitoba, C Canada
Chuska Mountains 48 C1 *mountain range* Arizona/New Mexico, SW USA
Chusovoy 111 D5 Permskaya Oblast', NW Russian Federation
Chuuk Islands 144 B2 *var.* Hogoley Islands; *prev.* Truk Islands. *Island group* Caroline Islands, C Micronesia
Chuy 64 E4 *var.* Chuí. Rocha, E Uruguay
Chyhyryn 109 E2 *Rus.* Chigirin. Cherkas'ka Oblast', N Ukraine
Ciadîr-Lunga 108 D4 *var.* Ceadâr-Lunga, *Rus.* Chadyr-Lunga. S Moldova
Cide 116 C2 Kastamonu, N Turkey
Ciechanów 98 D3 *prev.* Zichenau. Mazowieckie, C Poland
Ciego de Ávila 54 C2 Ciego de Ávila, C Cuba
Ciénaga 58 B1 Magdalena, N Colombia
Cienfuegos 54 B2 Cienfuegos, C Cuba
Cieza 93 E4 Murcia, SE Spain
Cihanbeyli 116 C3 Konya, C Turkey
Cikobia 145 E4 *prev.* Thikombia. *Island* N Fiji
Cilacap 138 C5 *prev.* Tjilatjap. Jawa, C Indonesia
Cill Airne *see* Killarney
Cill Chainnigh *see* Kilkenny
Cill Mhantáin *see* Wicklow
Cincinnati 40 C4 Ohio, N USA
Ciney 87 C7 Namur, SE Belgium
Cinto, Monte 91 E7 *mountain* Corse, France, C Mediterranean Sea
Cipolletti 65 B5 Río Negro, C Argentina
Cirebon 138 C4 *prev.* Tjirebon. Jawa, S Indonesia
Ciro Marino 97 E6 Calabria, S Italy
Cisnădie 108 B4 *Ger.* Heltau, *Hung.* Nagydisznód. Sibiu, SW Romania
Citlaltépetl *see* Orizaba, Volcán Pico de
Citrus Heights 47 B5 California, W USA
Ciudad Bolívar 59 E2 *prev.* Angostura. Bolívar, E Venezuela
Ciudad Acuña *see* Villa Acuña
Ciudad Camargo 50 D2 Chihuahua, N Mexico
Ciudad Cortés *see* Cortés
Ciudad Darío 52 D3 *var.* Dario. Matagalpa, W Nicaragua
Ciudad de Dolores Hidalgo *see* Dolores Hidalgo

Ciudad de Guatemala 52 B2 *var.* Gautemala City *Eng.* Guatemala City; *prev.* Santiago de los Caballeros. *Country capital* (Guatemala) Guatemala, C Guatemala
Ciudad del Carmen *see* Carmen
Ciudad del Este 64 E2 *prev.* Cuidad Presidente Stroessner, Presidente Stroessner, Puerto Presidente Stroessner. Alto Paraná, SE Paraguay
Ciudad Delicias *see* Delicias
Ciudad de México *see* México
Ciudad de Panamá *see* Panamá
Ciudad Guayana 59 E2 *prev.* San Tomé de Guayana, Santo Tomé de Guayana. Bolívar, NE Venezuela
Ciudad Guzmán 50 D4 Jalisco, SW Mexico
Ciudad Hidalgo 51 G5 Chiapas, SE Mexico
Ciudad Juárez 50 C1 Chihuahua, N Mexico
Ciudad Lerdo 50 D3 Durango, C Mexico
Ciudad Madero 51 E3 *var.* Villa Cecilia. Tamaulipas, C Mexico
Ciudad Mante 51 E3 Tamaulipas, C Mexico
Ciudad Miguel Alemán 51 E2 Tamaulipas, C Mexico
Ciudad Obregón 50 B2 Sonora, NW Mexico
Ciudad Ojeda 58 C1 Zulia, NW Venezuela
Ciudad Porfirio Díaz *see* Piedras Negras
Ciudad Quesada *see* Quesada
Ciudad Real 92 D3 Castilla-La Mancha, C Spain
Ciudad-Rodrigo 92 C3 Castilla-León, N Spain
Ciudad Valles 51 E3 San Luis Potosí, C Mexico
Ciudad Victoria 51 E3 Tamaulipas, C Mexico
Ciutadella *see* Ciutadella de Menorca
Ciutadella de Menorca 93 H3 *var.* Ciutadella. Menorca, Spain, W Mediterranean Sea
Civitanova Marche 96 D3 Marche, C Italy
Civitavecchia 96 C4 *anc.* Centum Cellae, Trajani Portus. Lazio, C Italy
Claremore 49 G1 Oklahoma, C USA
Clarence 151 C5 *river* South Island, NZ
Clarence 151 C5 Canterbury, South Island, NZ
Clarence Town 54 D2 Long Island, C Bahamas
Clarinda 45 F4 Iowa, C USA
Clarion Fracture Zone 153 E2 *tectonic feature* NE Pacific Ocean
Clarión, Isla 50 A5 *island* W Mexico
Clark Fork 44 A1 *river* Idaho/Montana, NW USA
Clark Hill Lake 43 E2 *var.* J.Storm Thurmond Reservoir. *Reservoir* Georgia/South Carolina, SE USA
Clarksburg 40 D4 West Virginia, NE USA
Clarksdale 42 B2 Mississippi, S USA
Clarksville 42 C1 Tennessee, S USA
Clayton 49 E1 New Mexico, SW USA
Clearwater 43 E4 Florida, SE USA
Clearwater Mountains 46 D2 *mountain range* Idaho, NW USA
Cleburne 49 G3 Texas, SW USA
Clermont 148 D4 Queensland, E Australia
Clermont-Ferrand 91 C5 Puy-de-Dôme, C France
Cleveland 40 D3 Ohio, N USA
Cleveland 42 D1 Tennessee, S USA
Clifton 48 C2 Arizona, SW USA
Clinton 42 B2 Mississippi, S USA
Clinton 49 F1 Oklahoma, C USA
Clipperton Fracture Zone 153 E3 *tectonic feature* E Pacific Ocean

Clipperton Island 35 A7 French dependency of French Polynesia E Pacific Ocean
Cloncurry 148 B3 Queensland, C Australia
Clonmel 89 B6 *Ir.* Cluain Meala. S Ireland
Cloppenburg 94 B3 Niedersachsen, NW Germany
Cloquet 45 G2 Minnesota, N USA
Cloud Peak 44 C3 *mountain* Wyoming, C USA
Clovis 49 E2 New Mexico, SW USA
Cluain Meala *see* Clonmel
Cluj-Napoca 108 B3 *Ger.* Klausenburg, *Hung.* Kolozsvár; *prev.* Cluj. Cluj, NW Romania
Clutha 151 B7 *river* South Island, NZ
Clyde 88 C4 *river* W Scotland, UK
Coari 62 D2 Amazonas, N Brazil
Coast Mountains 36 D4 *Fr.* Chaîne Côtière. *Mountain range* Canada/USA
Coast Ranges 46 A4 *mountain range* W USA
Coats Island 37 G3 *island* Nunavut, NE Canada
Coats Land 154 B2 *physical region* Antarctica
Coatzacoalcos 51 G4 *var.* Quetzalcoalco; *prev.* Puerto México. Veracruz-Llave, E Mexico
Cobán 52 B2 Alta Verapaz, C Guatemala
Cobar 149 C6 New South Wales, SE Australia
Cobija 61 E3 Pando, NW Bolivia
Coburg 95 C5 Bayern, SE Germany
Coca *see* Puerto Francisco de Orellana
Cochabamba 61 F4 *hist.* Oropeza. Cochabamba, C Bolivia
Cochin 132 C3 *var.* Kochi. Kerala, SW India
Cochinos, Bahía de 54 B2 *Eng.* Bay of Pigs. *Bay* SE Cuba
Cochrane 65 B7 Aisén, S Chile
Cochrane 38 C4 Ontario, S Canada
Cocibolca *see* Nicaragua, Lago de
Cockburn Town 55 E2 *var.* Grand Turk. *dependent territory capital* (Turks and Caicos Islands) Grand Turk Island, SE Turks and Caicos Islands
Cockpit Country, The 54 A4 *physical region* W Jamaica
Cocobeach 77 A5 Estuaire, NW Gabon
Coconino Plateau 48 B1 *plain* Arizona, SW USA
Coco, Río 53 E2 *var.* Río Wanki, Segovino Wangkí. *River* Honduras/Nicaragua
Cocos Basin 134 C5 *undersea feature* E Indian Ocean
Cocos Island Ridge *see* Cocos Ridge
Cocos Islands 141 D5 *island group* E Indian Ocean
Cocos Ridge 35 C8 *var.* Cocos Island Ridge. *Undersea feature* E Pacific Ocean
Cod, Cape 41 G3 *headland* Massachusetts, NE USA
Codfish Island 151 A8 *island* SW NZ
Codlea 108 C4 *Ger.* Zeiden, *Hung.* Feketehalom. Braşov, C Romania
Cody 44 C2 Wyoming, C USA
Coeur d'Alene 46 C2 Idaho, NW USA
Coevorden 86 E2 Drenthe, NE Netherlands
Coffs Harbour 149 E6 New South Wales, SE Australia
Cognac 91 B5 *anc.* Compniacum. Charente, W France
Coiba, Isla de 53 E5 *island* SW Panama
Coihaique 65 B6 *var.* Coyhaique. Aisén, S Chile
Coimbatore 132 C3 Tamil Nādu, S India
Coimbra 92 B3 *anc.* Conimbria, Conimbriga. Coimbra, W Portugal

Coín 92 D5 Andalucía, S Spain
Coirib, Loch *see* Corrib, Lough
Colby 45 E4 Kansas, C USA
Colchester 89 E6 *hist.* Colneceaste, *anc.* Camulodunum. E England, UK
Col du Brenner *see* Brenner Pass
Coleman 49 F3 Texas, SW USA
Coleraine 88 B4 *Ir.* Cúil Raithin. N Northern Ireland, UK
Colesberg 78 C5 Northern Cape, C South Africa
Colima 50 D4 Colima, S Mexico
Coll 88 B3 *island* W Scotland, UK
College Station 49 G3 Texas, SW USA
Collie 147 A7 Western Australia
Colmar 90 E4 *Ger.* Kolmar. Haut-Rhin, NE France
Cöln *see* Köln
Cologne *see* Köln
Colombia 58 B3 *Country* N South America

Colombia 58

Official name	Republic of Columbia
Formation	1819
Capital	Bogotá
Population	42.3 million / 105 people per sq mile (41 people per sq km)
Total area	401,042 sq miles (1,038,700 sq km)
Languages	Spanish, Amerindian languages, English Creole
Religions	Roman Catholic 95%, other 5%
Ethnic mix	Mestizo 58%, other 42%
Government	Multiparty republic
Currency	Colombian peso = 100 centavos
Literacy rate	91%
Calorie consumption	2,677 kilocalories

Colombian Basin 56 A1 *undersea feature* SW Caribbean Sea
Colombo 132 C4 *country capital* (Sri Lanka) Western Province, W Sri Lanka
Colón 53 G4 *prev.* Aspinwall. Colón, C Panama
Colonia Agrippina *see* Köln
Colón Ridge 35 B8 *undersea feature* E Pacific Ocean
Colorado 44 C4 *off.* State of Colorado; also known as Centennial State, Silver State. *State* C USA
Colorado City 49 F3 Texas, SW USA
Colorado Plateau 48 B1 *plateau* W USA
Colorado, Río 65 C5 *river* E Argentina
Colorado, Río *see* Colorado River
Colorado River 35 B5 *var.* Río Colorado. *River* Mexico/USA
Colorado River 49 G4 *river* Texas, SW USA
Colorado Springs 44 D5 Colorado, C USA
Columbia 46 B3 *river* Canada/USA
Columbia 43 E2 *state capital* South Carolina, SE USA
Columbia 41 E4 Maryland, NE USA
Columbia 45 G4 Missouri, C USA
Columbia 42 C1 Tennessee, S USA
Columbia Plateau 46 C3 *plateau* Idaho/Oregon, NW USA
Columbus 40 D4 *state capital* Ohio, N USA
Columbus 42 D2 Georgia, SE USA
Columbus 40 C4 Indiana, N USA
Columbus 42 C2 Mississippi, S USA
Columbus 45 F4 Nebraska, C USA
Colville Channel 150 D2 *channel* North Island, NZ
Colville River 36 D2 *river* Alaska, USA

Comacchio *96 C3 var.* Commachio; *anc.* Comactium. Emilia-Romagna, N Italy
Comactium *see* Comacchio
Comalcalco *51 G4* Tabasco, SE Mexico
Coma Pedrosa, Pic de *91 A7 mountain* NW Andorra
Comarapa *61 F4* Santa Cruz, C Bolivia
Comayagua *52 C2* Comayagua, W Honduras
Comer See *see* Como, Lago di
Comilla *135 G4 Ben.* Kumillā. Chittagong, E Bangladesh
Comino *102 A5 Malt.* Kemmuna. *Island* C Malta
Comitán *51 G5 var.* Comitán de Domínguez. Chiapas, SE Mexico
Comitán de Domínguez *see* Comitán
Commachio *see* Comacchio
Commissioner's Point *42 A5 headland* W Bermuda
Communism Peak *see* Kommunizm, Qullai
Como *96 B2 anc.* Comum. Lombardia, N Italy
Como, Lago di *B2 var.* Lario, *Eng.* Lake Como, *Ger.* Comer See. *Lake* N Italy
Como, Lake *see* Como, Lago di
Comoros *79 F2 Fr.* République Fédérale Islamique des Comores. *Country* W Indian Ocean

Comoros 79

Official name Federal Islamic Republic of the Comoros
Formation 1975
Capital Moroni
Population 694,000 / 806 people per sq mile (311 people per sq km)
Total area 861 sq miles (2,230 sq km)
Languages Arabic, French, Comoran
Religions Muslim (mainly Sunni) 98%, Roman Catholic 1%, other 1%
Ethnic mix Comorian 96%, other 4%
Government Islamic republic
Currency Comoros franc = 100 centimes
Literacy rate 55.4%
Calorie consumption 1,897 kilocalories

Compiègne *90 C3* Oise, N France
Compostella *see* Santiago
Comrat *108 D4 Rus.* Komrat. S Moldova
Conakry *74 C4 country capital* (Guinea) Conakry, SW Guinea
Concarneau *90 A3* Finistère, NW France
Concepción *64 D2 var.* Villa Concepción. Concepción, C Paraguay
Concepción *see* La Concepción
Concepción *65 B5* Bío Bío, C Chile
Concepción *61 G3* Santa Cruz, E Bolivia
Concepción de la Vega *see* La Vega
Conchos, Río *50 D2 river* C Mexico
Conchos, Río *48 D4 river* NW Mexico
Concord *41 G3 state capital* New Hampshire, NE USA
Concordia *64 D4* Entre Ríos, E Argentina
Concordia *45 E4* Kansas, C USA
Côn Ðao *137 E7 var.* Con Son. *Island* S Vietnam
Condate *see* Cosne-Cours-sur-Loire
Condega *52 D3* Estelí, NW Nicaragua
Congo *77 D5 Fr.* Moyen-Congo; *prev.* Middle Congo. *Country* C Africa

Congo 77

Official name Republic of the Congo
Formation 1960
Capital Brazzaville
Population 3 million / 22 people per sq mile (8 people per sq km)
Total area 131,853 sq miles (341,500 sq km)
Languages French, Kongo, Teke, Lingala
Religions Christian 50%, Traditional beliefs 48%, other 2%
Ethnic mix Bakongo 48%, Sangha 20%, Teke 17%, Mbochi 12%, other 3%
Government Multiparty republic
Currency CFA franc = 100 centimes
Literacy rate 77%
Calorie consumption 2,296 kilocalories

Congo *77 C6 prev.* Zaire, Belgian Congo, Congo (Kinshasa). *Country* C Africa

Congo (Zaire) 77

Official name Democratic Republic of the Congo
Formation 1960
Capital Kinshasa
Population 51.3 million / 59 people per sq mile (22 people per sq km)
Total area 875,520 sq miles (2,267,600 sq km)
Languages French, Kiswahili, Tshiluba
Religions Traditional beliefs 50%, Roman Catholic 37%, Protestant 13%
Ethnic mix Bantu and Hamitic 45%, other 55%
Government Single-party republic
Currency Franc = 100 centimes
Literacy rate 77%
Calorie consumption 2,060 kilocalories

Congo *77 C6 var.* Kongo, *Fr.* Zaire. *River* C Africa
Congo Basin *77 C6 drainage basin* W Dem. Rep. Congo (Zaire)
Connacht *see* Connaught
Connaught *89 A5 var.* Connacht, *Ir.* Chonnacht, Cúige. *Cultural region* W Ireland
Connecticut *41 F3 off.* State of Connecticut; also known as Blue Law State, Constitution State, Land of Steady Habits, Nutmeg State. *State* NE USA
Connecticut *41 G3 river* Canada/USA
Conroe *49 G3* Texas, SW USA
Consolación del Sur *54 A2* Pinar del Río, W Cuba
Con Son *see* Côn Ðao
Constance *see* Konstanz
Constance, Lake *B7 Ger.* Bodensee. *Lake* C Europe
Constanţa *108 D5 var.* Küstendje, *Eng.* Constanza, *Ger.* Konstanza, *Turk.* Küstence. Constanţa, SE Romania
Constantia *see* Konstanz
Constantine *71 E2 var.* Qacentina, *Ar.* Qoussantína. NE Algeria
Constantinople *see* İstanbul
Constanz *see* Konstanz
Constanza *see* Constanţa
Coober Pedy *149 A5* South Australia
Cookeville *42 D1* Tennessee, S USA
Cook Islands *145 F4 territory in free association with* NZ S Pacific Ocean
Cook, Mount *151 B6 prev.* Aoraki, Aorangi. *Mountain* South Island, NZ
Cook Strait *151 D5 var.* Raukawa. *Strait* NZ

Cooktown *148 D2* Queensland, NE Australia
Coolgardie *147 B6* Western Australia
Cooma *149 D7* New South Wales, SE Australia
Coon Rapids *45 F2* Minnesota, N USA
Cooper Creek *148 C4 var.* Barcoo, Cooper's Creek. *Seasonal river* Queensland/South Australia
Cooper's Creek *see* Cooper Creek
Coos Bay *46 A3* Oregon, NW USA
Cootamundra *149 D6* New South Wales, SE Australia
Copacabana *61 E4* La Paz, W Bolivia
Copenhagen *see* København
Copiapó *64 B3* Atacama, N Chile
Copperas Cove *49 G3* Texas, SW USA
Coppermine *see* Kugluktuk
Coquimbo *64 B3* Coquimbo, N Chile
Corabia *108 B5* Olt, S Romania
Coral Harbour *37 G3* Southampton Island, Nunavut, NE Canada
Coral Sea *142 B3 sea* SW Pacific Ocean
Coral Sea Islands *144 B4 Australian external territory* SW Pacific Ocean
Corantijn Rivier *see* Courantyne River
Corcaigh *see* Cork
Corcovado, Golfo *65 B6 gulf* S Chile
Cordele *42 D3* Georgia, SE USA
Cordillera Ibérica *see* Ibérico, Sistema
Cordoba *see* Córdoba
Córdoba *92 D4 var.* Cordoba, *Eng.* Cordova; *anc.* Corduba. Andalucía, SW Spain
Córdoba *64 C3* Córdoba, C Argentina
Córdoba *51 F4* Veracruz-Llave, E Mexico
Cordova *see* Córdoba
Cordova *36 C3* Alaska, USA
Corduba *see* Córdoba
Corentyne River *see* Courantyne River
Corfu *see* Kérkyra
Coria *92 C3* Extremadura, W Spain
Corinth *see* Kórinthos
Corinth *42 C1* Mississippi, S USA
Corinth, Gulf of *see* Korinthiakós Kólpos
Corinthiacus Sinus *see* Korinthiakós Kólpos
Corinto *52 C3* Chinandega, NW Nicaragua
Cork *89 A6 Ir.* Corcaigh. S Ireland
Çorlu *116 A2* Tekirdağ, NW Turkey
Corner Brook *39 G3* Newfoundland, Newfoundland and Labrador, E Canada
Corn Islands *see* Maíz, Islas del
Cornwallis Island *37 F2 island* Nunavut, N Canada
Coro *58 C1 prev.* Santa Ana de Coro. Falcón, NW Venezuela
Corocoro *61 F4* La Paz, W Bolivia
Coromandel *150 D2* Waikato, North Island, NZ
Coromandel Coast *132 D2 coast* E India
Coromandel Peninsula *150 D2 peninsula* North Island, NZ
Coronado, Bahía de *52 D5 bay* S Costa Rica
Coronel Dorrego *65 C5* Buenos Aires, E Argentina
Coronel Oviedo *64 D2* Caaguazú, SE Paraguay
Corozal *52 C1* Corozal, N Belize
Corpus Christi *49 G4* Texas, SW USA
Corrales *48 D2* New Mexico, SW USA
Corrib, Lough *89 A5 Ir.* Loch Coirib. *Lake* W Ireland
Corrientes *64 D3* Corrientes, NE Argentina
Corriza *see* Korçë
Corse *91 E7 Eng.* Corsica. *Island* France, C Mediterranean Sea
Corsica *see* Corse

Corsicana *49 G3* Texas, SW USA
Cortegana *92 C4* Andalucía, S Spain
Cortés *53 E5 var.* Ciudad Cortés. Puntarenas, SE Costa Rica
Cortina d'Ampezzo *96 C1* Veneto, NE Italy
Coruche *92 B3* Santarém, C Portugal
Çoruh Nehri *117 E3 Geor.* Chorokhi, *Rus.* Chorokh. *River* Georgia/Turkey
Çorum *116 D3 var.* Chorum. Çorum, N Turkey
Corunna *see* A Coruña
Corvallis *46 A3* Oregon, NW USA
Corvo *92 A5 var.* Ilha do Corvo. *Island* Azores, Portugal, NE Atlantic Ocean
Cosenza *97 D6 anc.* Consentia. Calabria, SW Italy
Cosne-Cours-sur-Loire *90 C4 var.* Cosne-sur-Loire; *anc.* Condate. Nièvre, C France
Cosne-sur-Loire *see* Cosne-Cours-sur-Loire
Costa Mesa *46 D2* California, W USA
Costa Rica *53 E4 Country* Central America

Costa Rica 53

Official name Republic of Costa Rica
Formation 1838
Capital San José
Population 4 million / 203 people per sq mile (78 people per sq km)
Total area 19,714 sq miles (51,060 sq km)
Languages Spanish, English Creole, Bribri, Cabecar
Religions Roman Catholic 76%, other (including Protestant) 24%
Ethnic mix White 96%, Black 2%, other 2%
Government Multiparty republic
Currency Costa Rican colón = 100 centimes
Literacy rate 95%
Calorie consumption 2,883 kilocalories

Cotagaita *61 F5* Potosí, S Bolivia
Côte d'Ivoire *74 D4 Eng.* Ivory Coast, Republic of the Ivory Coast. *Country* W Africa

Côte d'Ivoire 74

Official name Republic of Côte d'Ivoire
Formation 1960
Capital Yamoussoukro
Population 14.8 million / 121 people per sq mile (47 people per sq km)
Total area 122,779 sq miles (318,000 sq km)
Languages French, Akan, Kru, Voltaic
Religions Traditional beliefs 63%, Muslim 25%, Christian 12%
Ethnic mix Baoule 23%, Bete 18%, Kru 17%, Malinke 15%, other 27%
Government Multiparty republic
Currency CFA franc = 100 centimes
Literacy rate 42.6%
Calorie consumption 2,491 kilocalories

Côte d'Or *90 D4 cultural region* C France
Cotonou *75 F5 var.* Kotonu. S Benin
Cotrone *see* Crotone
Cotswold Hills *89 D6 var.* Cotswolds. *Hill range* S England, UK
Cotswolds *see* Cotswold Hills
Cottbus *94 D4 prev.* Kottbus. Brandenburg, E Germany
Council Bluffs *45 F4* Iowa, C USA
Courantyne River *59 G4 var.* Corantijn Rivier, Corentyne River. *River* Guyana/Suriname

Courland Lagoon 106 A4 *Ger.*
Kurisches Haff, *Rus.* Kurskiy
Zaliv. *Lagoon* Lithuania/Russian
Federation
Coutances 90 B3 *anc.* Constantia.
Manche, N France
Couvin 87 C7 Namur, S Belgium
Coventry 89 D6 *anc.* Couentrey.
C England, UK
Covilhã 92 C3 Castelo Branco,
E Portugal
Cowan, Lake 147 B6 *lake* Western
Australia
Coxen Hole *see* Roatán
Coxin Hole *see* Roatán
Coyhaique *see* Coihaique
Cozumel, Isla 51 H3 *island*
SE Mexico
Cradock 78 C5 Eastern Cape,
S South Africa
Craig 44 C4 Colorado, C USA
Craiova 108 B5 Dolj, SW Romania
Cranbrook 37 E5 British Columbia,
SW Canada
Crane *see* The Crane
Crawley 89 E7 SE England, UK
Cremona 96 B2 Lombardia, N Italy
Cres 100 A3 *It.* Cherso; *anc.* Crexa.
Island W Croatia
Crescent City 46 A4 California,
W USA
Crescent Group 128 C7 *island group*
C Paracel Islands
Creston 45 F4 Iowa, C USA
Crestview 42 D3 Florida, SE USA
Crete *see* Kríti
Créteil 90 E2 Val-de-Marne,
N France
Crete, Sea of *see* Kritikó Pélagos
Creuse 90 B4 *river* C France
Crewe 89 D6 C England, UK
Crikvenica 100 A3 *It.* Cirquenizza;
prev. Cirkvenica, Crjkvenica.
Primorje-Gorski Kotar,
NW Croatia
Crimea 81 F4 *var.* Krym, *Eng.*
Crimea, Crimean Oblast; *prev.*
Rus. Krymskaya ASSR,
Krymskaya Oblast'. Admin.
region *province* SE Ukraine
Crimean Oblast *see* Crimea
Cristóbal 53 G4 Colón, C Panama
Cristóbal Colón, Pico 58 B1
mountain N Colombia
Cristuru Secuiesc 108 C4 *prev.*
Cristur, Cristuru Săcuiesc, Sitaş
Cristuru, *Ger.* Kreutz, *Hung.*
Székelykeresztúr, Szitás-
Keresztúr. Harghita, C Romania
Crna Reka 101 D6 *river* S FYR
Macedonia
Croatia 100 B3 *Ger.* Kroatien, *SCr.*
Hrvatska. *Country* SE Europe

Croatia 100

Official name Republic of Croatia
Formation 1991
Capital Zagreb
Population 4.5 million /
206 people per sq mile
(80 people per sq km)
Total area 21,830 sq miles
(56,540 sq km)
Languages Croatian, Serbian
Religions Roman Catholic 76%,
Orthodox 11%, Muslim 1%,
other 12%
Ethnic mix Croat 78%, Serb 12%,
Yugoslav 2%, other 8%
Government Multiparty republic
Currency Kuna = 100 lipa
Literacy rate 97.7%
Calorie consumption
not available

Crocodile *see* Limpopo
Croia *see* Krujë
Croker Island 146 E2 *island*
Northern Territory, N Australia
Cromwell 151 B7 Otago, South
Island, NZ
Crooked Island 54 D2 *island*
SE Bahamas
Crooked Island Passage 54 D2
channel SE Bahamas
Crookston 45 F1 Minnesota, N USA

Croton *see* Crotone
Crotona *see* Crotone
Crotone 97 E6 *var.* Cotrone; *anc.*
Croton, Crotona. Calabria,
SW Italy
Croydon 89 A8 SE England, UK
Crozet Basin 141 B6 *undersea feature*
S Indian Ocean
Crozet Islands 141 B7 *island group*
French Southern and Antarctic
Territories
Crozet Plateau 141 B7 *var.* Crozet
Plateaus. *Undersea feature*
SW Indian Ocean
Crozet Plateaus *see* Crozet Plateau
Crystal Brook 149 B6 South
Australia
Csorna 99 C6 Győr-Moson-Sopron,
NW Hungary
Csurgó 99 C7 Somogy,
SW Hungary
Cuando 78 C2 *var.* Kwando. *River*
S Africa
Cuango 78 B1 *var.* Kwango. *River*
Angola/Dem. Rep. Congo (Zaire)
see also Kwango
Cuan na Gaillimhe *see* Galway Bay
Cuanza 78 B1 *var.* Kwanza. *River*
C Angola
Cuauhtémoc 50 C2 Chihuahua,
N Mexico
Cuautla 51 E4 Morelos, S Mexico
Cuba 54 B2 *Country* W West Indies

Cuba 54

Official name Republic of Cuba
Formation 1902
Capital Havana
Population 11.2 million /
262 people per sq mile
(101 people per sq km)
Total area 42,803 sq miles
(110,860 sq km)
Languages Spanish
Religions Non-religious 49%,
Roman Catholic 40%, Protestant 1%,
other 10%
Ethnic mix White 66%, European-
African 22%, Black 12%
Government Socialist republic
Currency Cuban peso
= 100 centavos
Literacy rate 96%
Calorie consumption 2,833
kilocalories

Cubal 78 B2 Benguela, W Angola
Cubango 78 B2 *var.* Kavango,
Kavengo, Kubango, Okavango,
Okavanggo. *River* S Africa *see also*
Okavango
Cubango 78 B2 *var.* Kuvango, *Port.*
Vila Artur de Paiva, Vila da Ponte.
Huíla, SW Angola
Cúcuta 58 C2 *var.* San José de
Cúcuta. Norte de Santander,
N Colombia
Cuddapah 132 C2 Andhra Pradesh,
S India
Cuenca 93 E3 *anc.* Conca. Castilla-
La Mancha, C Spain
Cuenca 60 B2 Azuay, S Ecuador
Cuernavaca 51 E4 Morelos,
S Mexico
Cuiabá 63 E3 *prev.* Cuyabá. *State
capital* Mato Grosso, SW Brazil
Cúige *see* Connaught
Cúige Laighean *see* Leinster
Cúige Mumhan *see* Munster
Cuijck 86 D4 Noord-Brabant,
SE Netherlands
Cúil Raithin *see* Coleraine
Cuito 78 B2 *var.* Kwito. *River*
SE Angola
Cukai 138 B3 *var.* Chukai,
Kemaman. Terengganu,
Peninsular Malaysia
Culiacán 50 C3 *var.* Culiacán
Rosales, Culiacán-Rosales.
Sinaloa, C Mexico
Culiacán-Rosales *see* Culiacán
Cullera 93 F3 País Valenciano,
E Spain
Cullman 42 C2 Alabama, S USA
Culmsee *see* Chełmża
Culpepper Island *see* Darwin, Isla

Cumaná 59 E1 Sucre, NE Venezuela
Cumbal, Nevada de 58 A4 *mountain*
SW Colombia
Cumberland 41 E4 Maryland,
NE USA
Cumberland Plateau 42 D1 *plateau*
E USA
Cumberland Sound 37 H3 *inlet*
Baffin Island, Nunavut,
NE Canada
Cumpas 50 B2 Sonora, NW Mexico
Cunene 69 C6 *var.* Kunene. *River*
Angola/Namibia *see also* Kunene
Cunene 78 A3 *province* S Angola
Cuneo 96 A2 *Fr.* Coni. Piemonte,
NW Italy
Cunnamulla 149 C5 Queensland,
E Australia
Ćuprija 100 E4 Serbia, E Yugoslavia
Curaçao 55 E5 *island* Netherlands
Antilles
Curicó 64 B4 Maule, C Chile
Curitiba 63 E4 *prev.* Curytiba. *State
capital* Paraná, S Brazil
Curtea de Argeş 108 C4 *var.* Curtea-
de-Arges. Argeş, S Romania
Curtea-de-Arges *see* Curtea de
Argeş
Curtici 108 A4 *Ger.* Kurtitsch, *Hung.*
Kürtös. Arad, W Romania
Curtis Island 148 E4 *island*
Queensland, SE Australia
Cusco 61 E4 *var.* Cuzco. Cusco,
C Peru
Cusset 91 C5 Allier, C France
Cutch, Gulf of *see* Kachchh, Gulf of
Cuttack 135 F4 Orissa, E India
Cuvier Plateau 141 E6 *undersea
feature* E Indian Ocean
Cuxhaven 94 B2 Niedersachsen,
NW Germany
Cuyuni, Río *see* Cuyuni River
Cuyuni River 59 F3 *var.* Río
Cuyuni. *River* Guyana/Venezuela
Cuzco *see* Cusco
Cyclades *see* Kykládes
Cydonia *see* Chaniá
Cymru *see* Wales
Cyprus 102 C4 *Gk.* Kypros, *Turk.*
Kıbrıs, Kıbrıs Cumhuriyeti.
Country E Mediterranean Sea

Cyprus 102

Official name Republic of Cyprus
Formation 1960
Capital Nicosia
Population 786,000 / 220 people
per sq mile (85 people per sq km)
Total area 3,567 sq miles
(9,240 sq km)
Languages Greek, Turkish, English
Religions Greek Orthodox 77%,
Muslim 18%, other 5%
Ethnic mix Greek 77%,
Turkish 18%,
other (mainly British) 5%
Government Multiparty republic
Currency Cyprus pound/
Turkish lira
Literacy rate 96%
Calorie consumption 3,779
kilocalories

Cythera *see* Kýthira
Cythnos *see* Kýthnos
Czech Republic 99 A5 *Cz.* Česká
Republika. *Country* C Europe

Czech Republic 99

Official name Czech Republic
Formation 1993
Capital Prague
Population 10.2 million /
335 people per sq mile
(129 people per sq km)
Total area 30,449 sq miles
(78,864 sq km)
Languages Czech, Slovak,
Hungarian
Religions Non-religious 40%,
Roman Catholic 39%, Protestant 2%,
other 19%
Ethnic mix Czech 85%, Moravian
13%, other 2%

Czech Republic (continued)

Government Multiparty republic
Currency Czech koruna
= 100 halura
Literacy rate 99%
Calorie consumption 3,156
kilocalories

Częstochowa 98 C4 *Ger.*
Czenstochau, Tschenstochau, *Rus.*
Chenstokhov. Śląskie, S Poland
Człuchów 98 C3 *Ger.* Schlochau.
Pomorskie, N Poland

D

Dabajuro 58 C1 Falcón,
NW Venezuela
Dabeiba 58 B2 Antioquia,
NW Colombia
Dąbrowa Tarnowska 99 D5
Małopolskie, S Poland
Dabryn' 107 C8 *Rus.* Dobryn'.
Homyel'skaya Voblasts',
SE Belarus
Dagana 74 B3 N Senegal
Dagda 106 D4 Krāslava, SE Latvia
Dagenham 89 B8 SE England, UK
Dağlıq Qarabağ *see* Nagornyy
Karabakh
Dagupan 139 E1 *off.* Dagupan City.
Luzon, N Philippines
Da Hinggan Ling 127 G1 *Eng.*
Great Khingan Range. *Mountain
range* NE China
Dahm, Ramlat 121 B6 *desert*
NW Yemen
Daimiel 92 D3 Castilla-La Mancha,
C Spain
Daimoniá 105 B7 Pelopónnisos,
S Greece
Dairen *see* Dalian
Dakar 74 B3 *country capital*
(Senegal) W Senegal
Dakhla *see* Ad Dakhla
Dakoro 75 G3 Maradi, S Niger
Đakovica 101 D5 *var.* Djakovica,
Alb. Gjakovë. Serbia, S Yugoslavia
Đakovo 100 C3 *var.* Djakovo, *Hung.*
Diakovár. Osijek-Baranja,
E Croatia
Dalai *see* Hulun Nur
Dalain Hob *see* Ejin Qi
Dalaman 116 A4 Muğla,
SW Turkey
Dalandzadgad 127 E3 Ömnögovĭ,
S Mongolia
Đa Lat 137 E6 Lâm Đông,
S Vietnam
Dalby 149 D5 Queensland,
E Australia
Dale City 41 E4 Virginia, NE USA
Dalhart 49 E1 Texas, SW USA
Dali 128 A6 *var.* Xiaguan. Yunnan,
SW China
Dalian 128 D4 *var.* Dairen, Dalien,
Lüda, Ta-lien, *Rus.* Dalny.
Liaoning, NE China
Dalien *see* Dalian
Dallas 49 G2 Texas, SW USA
Dalmacija 100 B4 *Eng.* Dalmatia,
Ger. Dalmatien, *It.* Dalmazia.
Cultural region S Croatia
Dalny *see* Dalian
Dalton 42 D1 Georgia, SE USA
Daly Waters 148 A2 Northern
Territory, N Australia
Damachava 107 A6 *var.*
Damachova, *Pol.* Domaczewo,
Rus. Domachëvo. Brestskaya
Voblasts', SW Belarus
Damachova *see* Damachava
Damān 134 C4 Damān and Diu,
W India
Damara 76 C4 Ombella-Mpoko,
S Central African Republic
Damas *see* Dimashq
Damasco *see* Dimashq
Damascus *see* Dimashq
Damāvand, Qolleh-ye 120 D3
mountain N Iran
Dammām *see* Ad Dammām
Damoûr 119 A5 *var.* Ad Dāmūr.
W Lebanon
Dampier 146 A4 Western Australia

Dampier, Selat 139 F4 *strait* Irian Jaya, E Indonesia
Damqawt 121 D6 *var.* Damqut. E Yemen
Damqut *see* Damqawt
Damxung 126 C5 Xizang Zizhiqu, W China
Danakil Desert 72 D4 *var.* Afar Depression, Danakil Plain. *Desert* E Africa
Danakil Plain *see* Danakil Desert
Danané 74 D5 W Côte d'Ivoire
Đa Nang 137 E5 *prev.* Tourane. Quang Nam-Đa Nang, C Vietnam
Danborg *see* Danneborg
Dandong 128 D3 *var.* Tan-tung; *prev.* An-tung. Liaoning, NE China
Daneborg 83 E3 *var.* Danborg. N Greenland
Dänew *see* Deynau
Dangerous Archipelago *see* Tuamotu, Îles
Danghara 123 E3 *Rus.* Dangara. SW Tajikistan
Danghe Nanshan 126 D3 *mountain range* W China
Dangla *see* Tanggula Shan
Dângrêk, Chuŏr Phnum 137 D5 *var.* Phanom Dang Raek, Phanom Dong Rak, *Fr.* Chaîne des Dangrek. *Mountain range* Cambodia/Thailand
Dangriga 52 C1 *prev.* Stann Creek. Stann Creek, E Belize
Danish West Indies *see* Virgin Islands (US)
Danlí 52 D2 El Paraíso, S Honduras
Danmarksstraedet *see* Denmark Strait
Dannenberg 94 C3 Niedersachsen, N Germany
Dannevirke 150 D4 Manawatu-Wanganui, North Island, NZ
Danube 81 E4 *Bul.* Dunav, Cz. Dunaj, *Ger.* Donau, *Hung.* Duna, *Rom.* Dunărea. *River* C Europe
Danville 41 E5 Virginia, NE USA
Dan Xian *see* Danzhou
Danxian/Dan Xian *see* Danzhou
Danzhou 128 C7 *prev.* Dan Xian, Danxian, Nada. Hainan, S China
Danziger Bucht *see* Danzig, Gulf of
Danzig, Gulf of 98 C2 *var.* Gulf of Pomorskie, *Ger.* Danziger Bucht, *Pol.* Zakota Pomorskiea, *Rus.* Gdan'skaya Bukhta. *Gulf* N Poland
Daqm *see* Duqm
Dar'ā 119 B5 *var.* Der'a, *Fr.* Déraa. Dar'ā, SW Syria
Darabani 108 C3 Botoșani, NW Romania
Daraut-Kurgan *see* Daroot-Korgon
Dardanelli *see* Çanakkale
Dar es Salaam 73 C7 Dar es Salaam, E Tanzania
Darfield 151 C6 Canterbury, South Island, NZ
Darfur 72 A4 *var.* Darfur Massif. *Cultural region* W Sudan
Darfur Massif *see* Darfur
Darhan 127 E2 Selenge, N Mongolia
Darién, Gulf of 58 A2 *var.* Golfo del Darién. *Gulf* S Caribbean Sea
Darién, Serranía del 53 H5 *mountain range* Colombia/Panama
Dario *see* Ciudad Darío
Darjeeling *see* Darjiling
Darjiling 135 F3 *prev.* Darjeeling. West Bengal, NE India
Darling River 149 C6 *river* New South Wales, SE Australia
Darlington 89 D5 N England, UK
Darmstadt 95 B5 Hessen, SW Germany
Darnah 71 G2 *var.* Dérna. NE Libya
Darnley, Cape 154 D2 *headland* Antarctica
Daroca 93 E2 Aragón, NE Spain
Daroot-Korgon 123 F3 *var.* Daraut-Kurgan. Oshskaya Oblast', SW Kyrgyzstan
Dartford 89 B8 SE England, UK
Dartmoor 89 C7 *moorland* SW England, UK
Dartmouth 39 F4 Nova Scotia, SE Canada

Darvaza 122 C2 *Turkm.* Derweze. Akhalskiy Velayat, C Turkmenistan
Darwin 146 D2 *prev.* Palmerston, Port Darwin. *Territory capital* Northern Territory, N Australia
Darwin, Isla 60 A4 *var.* Culpepper Island. *Island* W Ecuador
Daryācheh-ye Hāmūn *see* Şāberī, Hāmūn-e
Daryācheh-ye Sīstān *see* Şāberī, Hāmūn-e
Daryā-ye Morghāb *see* Murgab
Daryā-ye Pāmīr *see* Pamir
Daryoi Pomir *see* Pamir
Dashkawka 107 D6 Rus.
Dashkhovuz 122 C2 *Turkm.* Dashhowuz; *prev.* Tashauz. Dashkhovuzskiy Velayat, N Turkmenistan
Datong 128 C3 *var.* Tatung, Ta-t'ung. Shanxi, C China
Daugavpils 106 D4 *Ger.* Dünaburg; *prev.* Rus. Dvinsk. *Municipality* Daugvapils, SE Latvia
Daung Kyun 137 B6 *island* S Myanmar
Dauphiné 91 D5 *cultural region* E France
Dāvangere 132 C2 Karnātaka, W India
Davao 139 F3 *off.* Davao City. Mindanao, S Philippines
Davao Gulf 139 F3 *gulf* Mindanao, S Philippines
Davenport 45 G3 Iowa, C USA
David 53 E5 Chiriquí, W Panama
Davie Ridge 141 A5 *undersea feature* W Indian Ocean
Davis 154 D3 *Australian research station* Antarctica
Davis Sea 154 D3 *sea* Antarctica
Davis Strait 82 B3 *strait* Baffin Bay/Labrador Sea
Dawei *see* Tavoy
Dax 91 B6 *var.* Ax; *anc.* Aquae Augustae, Aquae Tarbelicae. Landes, SW France
Dayr az Zawr 118 D3 *var.* Deir ez Zor. Dayr az Zawr, E Syria
Dayton 40 C4 Ohio, N USA
Daytona Beach 43 F4 Florida, SE USA
De Aar 78 C5 Northern Cape, C South Africa
Dead Sea 119 B6 *var.* Bahret Lut, Lacus Asphaltites, *Ar.* Al Bahr al Mayyit, Bahrat Lūt, *Heb.* Yam HaMelah. *Salt lake* Israel/Jordan
Dealnu *see* Tana
Deán Funes 64 C3 Córdoba, C Argentina
Death Valley 47 C7 *valley* California, W USA
Debar 101 D6 *Ger.* Dibra, *Turk.* Debre. W FYR Macedonia
Debica 99 D5 Podkarpackie, SE Poland
De Bildt *see* De Bilt
De Bilt 86 C3 *var.* De Bildt. Utrecht, C Netherlands
Dębno 98 B3 Zachodniopomorskie, NW Poland
Debrecen 99 D6 *Ger.* Debreczin, *Rom.* Debrețin; *prev.* Debreczen. Hajdú-Bihar, E Hungary
Decatur 42 C1 Alabama, S USA
Decatur 40 B4 Illinois, N USA
Deccan 134 D5 *Hind.* Dakshin. *Plateau* C India
Děčín 98 B4 Ger. Tetschen. Ústecký Kraj, NW Czech Republic
Dedeagac *see* Alexandroúpoli
Dedeagach *see* Alexandroúpoli
Dedemsvaart 86 E3 Overijssel, E Netherlands
Dee 88 C3 *river* NE Scotland, UK
Deering 36 C2 Alaska, USA
Deggendorf 95 D6 Bayern, SE Germany
Değirmenlik 102 C5 N Cyprus
Deh Bīd 120 D3 Fārs, C Iran
Dehli *see* Delhi
Deh Shū 122 D5 *var.* Deshu. Helmand, S Afghanistan
Deinze 87 B5 Oost-Vlaanderen, NW Belgium

Deir ez Zor *see* Dayr az Zawr
Deirgeirt, Loch *see* Derg, Lough
Dej 108 B3 *Hung.* Dés; *prev.* Deés. Cluj, NW Romania
Dékoa 76 C4 Kémo, 188C Central African Republic
De Land 43 E4 Florida, SE USA
Delano 47 C7 California, W USA
Delārām 122 D5 Farāh, SW Afghanistan
Delaware 41 F4 *off.* State of Delaware; also known as Blue Hen State, Diamond State, First State. *State* NE USA
Delaware 40 D4 Ohio, N USA
Delft 86 B4 Zuid-Holland, W Netherlands
Delfzijl 86 E1 Groningen, NE Netherlands
Delgo 72 B3 Northern, N Sudan
Delhi 134 D3 *var.* Dehli, *Hind.* Dilli; *hist.* Shahjahanabad. Delhi, N India
Delicias 50 D2 *var.* Ciudad Delicias. Chihuahua, N Mexico
Déli-Kárpátok *see* Carpații Meridionali
Delmenhorst 94 B3 Niedersachsen, NW Germany
Del Rio 49 F4 Texas, SW USA
Deltona 43 E4 Florida, SE USA
Demba 77 D6 Kasai Occidental, C Dem. Rep. Congo (Zaire)
Dembia 76 D4 Mbomou, SE Central African Republic
Demchok *var.* Dêmqog. *Disputed region* China/India *see also* Dêmqog
Demchok 126 A4 *var.* Dêmqog. China/India *see also* Dêmqog
Demerara Plain 66 B3 *undersea feature* W Atlantic Ocean
Deming 48 C3 New Mexico, SW USA
Demmin 94 C2 Mecklenburg-Vorpommern, NE Germany
Demopolis 42 C2 Alabama, S USA
Dêmqog *var.* Demchok. *Disputed region* China/India *see also* Demchok
Denali *see* McKinley, Mount
Dender 87 B6 *Fr.* Dendre. *River* W Belgium
Denekamp 86 E3 Overijssel, E Netherlands
Den Haag *see* 's-Gravenhage
Den Ham 86 E3 Overijssel, E Netherlands
Denham 147 A5 Western Australia
Den Helder 86 C2 Noord-Holland, NW Netherlands
Denia 93 F4 País Valenciano, E Spain
Deniliquin 149 C7 New South Wales, SE Australia
Denison 45 F3 Iowa, C USA
Denison 49 G2 Texas, SW USA
Denizli 116 B4 Denizli, SW Turkey
Denmark 85 A7 Dan. Danmark; *anc.* Hafnia. *Country* N Europe

Denmark Strait 82 D4 *var.* Danmarksstraedet. *Strait* Greenland/Iceland
Dennery 55 F1 E Saint Lucia
Denow 123 E3 Rus. Denau. Surkhondaryo Wiloyati, S Uzbekistan
Denpasar 138 D5 *prev.* Paloe. Bali, C Indonesia
Denton 49 G2 Texas, SW USA
D'Entrecasteaux Islands 144 B3 *island group* SE PNG
Denver 44 D4 *state capital* Colorado, C USA
Der'a *see* Dar'ā
Déraa *see* Dar'ā
Dera Ghāzi Khān 134 C2 *var.* Dera Ghāzīkhān. Punjab, C Pakistan
Dera Ghāzīkhān *see* Dera Ghāzi Khān
Đeravica 101 D5 *mountain* S Yugoslavia
Derbent 111 B8 Respublika Dagestan, SW Russian Federation
Derby 89 D6 C England, UK
Dereli *see* Gónnoi
Derg, Lough 89 A6 *Ir.* Loch Deirgeirt. *Lake* W Ireland
Derhachi 109 G2 Rus. Dergachi. Kharkivs'ka Oblast', E Ukraine
De Ridder 42 A3 Louisiana, S USA
Dérna *see* Darnah
Derry *see* Londonderry
Derventa 100 B3 Republika Srpska, N Bosnia and Herzegovina
Deschutes River 46 B3 *river* Oregon, NW USA
Desē 72 C4 *var.* Desse, *It.* Dessie. N Ethiopia
Deseado, Río 65 B7 *river* S Argentina
Desertas, Ilhas 70 A2 *island group* Madeira, Portugal, NE Atlantic Ocean
Deshu *see* Deh Shū
Desierto de Altar *see* Sonoran Desert
Des Moines 45 F3 *state capital* Iowa, C USA
Desna 109 E2 *river* Russian Federation/Ukraine
Dessau 94 C4 Sachsen-Anhalt, E Germany
Desse *see* Desē
Dessie *see* Desē
Detroit 40 D3 Michigan, N USA
Detroit Lakes 45 F2 Minnesota, N USA
Deurne 87 D5 Noord-Brabant, SE Netherlands
Deva 108 B4 Ger. Diemrich, *Hung.* Déva. Hunedoara, W Romania
Devdelija *see* Gevgelija
Deventer 86 D3 Overijssel, E Netherlands
Devils Lake 45 E1 North Dakota, N USA
Devoll *see* Devollit, Lumi i
Devollit, Lumi i 101 D6 *var.* Devoll. *River* SE Albania
Devon Island 37 F2 *prev.* North Devon Island. *Island* Parry Islands, Nunavut, NE Canada
Devonport 149 C8 Tasmania, SE Australia
Devrek 116 C2 Zonguldak, N Turkey
Dexter 45 H5 Missouri, C USA
Deynau 122 D3 *var.* Dyanev, *Turkm.* Dänew. Lebapskiy Velayat, NE Turkmenistan
Dezfūl 120 C3 *var.* Dizful. Khūzestān, SW Iran
Dezhou 128 D4 Shandong, E China
Dhaka 135 G4 *prev.* Dacca. *Country capital* (Bangladesh) Dhaka, C Bangladesh
Dhanbād 135 F4 Bihār, NE India
Dhekélia 102 C5 *Eng.* Dhekelia. *Gk.* Dekéleia. *UK air base* SE Cyprus
Dhidhimótikhon *see* Didymóteicho
Dhíkti Ori *see* Díkti
Dhodhekánisos *see* Dodekánisos
Dhomokós *see* Domokós
Dhráma *see* Dráma
Dhrepanon, Akrotírio *see* Drépano Akrotírio

Denmark 85

Official name	Kingdom of Denmark
Formation	AD 950
Capital	Copenhagen (Koebenhavn)
Population	5.3 million / 324 people per sq mile (125 people per sq km)
Total area	16,359 sq miles (42,370 sq km)
Languages	Danish
Religions	Evangelical Lutheran 89%, Roman Catholic 1%, other 10%
Ethnic mix	Danish 96%, Faeroe and Inuit 1%, other (including Scandinavian) 3%
Government	Constitutional monarchy
Currency	Danish krone = 100 ore
Literacy rate	99%
Calorie consumption	3,664 kilocalories

Dhuusa Marreeb 73 E5 *var.* Dusa Marreb, *It.* Dusa Mareb. Galguduud, C Somalia
Diakovár *see* Đakovo
Diamantina, Chapada 63 F3 *mountain range* E Brazil
Diamantina Fracture Zone 141 E6 *tectonic feature* E Indian Ocean
Diarbekr *see* Diyarbakır
Dibrugarh 135 H3 Assam, NE India
Dickinson 44 D2 North Dakota, N USA
Didimotiho *see* Didymóteicho
Didymóteicho 104 D3 *var.* Dhidhimótikhon, Didimotiho. Anatolikí Makedonía kai Thráki, NE Greece
Diégo-Suarez *see* Antsirañana
Diekirch 87 D7 Diekirch, C Luxembourg
Điên Biên 136 D3 *var.* Bien Bien, Dien Bien Phu. Lai Châu, N Vietnam
Dien Bien Phu *see* Điên Biên
Diepenbeek 87 D6 Limburg, NE Belgium
Diepholz 94 B3 Niedersachsen, NW Germany
Dieppe 90 C2 Seine-Maritime, N France
Dieren 86 D4 Gelderland, E Netherlands
Differdange 87 D8 Luxembourg, SW Luxembourg
Digne 91 D6 *var.* Digne-les-Bains. Alpes-de-Haute-Provence, SE France
Digne-les-Bains *see* Digne
Digoin 90 C4 Saône-et-Loire, C France
Digul, Sungai 139 H5 *prev.* Digoel. *River* Irian Jaya, E Indonesia
Dihang *see* Brahmaputra
Dijon 90 D4 *anc.* Dibio. Côte d'Or, C France
Dikhil 72 D4 SW Djibouti
Dikson 114 D2 Taymyrskiy (Dolgano-Nenetskiy) Avtonomnyy Okrug, N Russian Federation
Díkti 105 D8 *var.* Dhíkti Ori. *Mountain range* Kriti, Greece, E Mediterranean Sea
Dili 139 F5 *var.* Dilli, Dilly. *Dependent territory capital* (East Timor), N East Timor
Dilia 75 G3 *var.* Dillia. *River* SE Niger
Di Linh 137 E6 Lâm Đông, S Vietnam
Dilli *see* Delhi
Dilli *see* Dili
Dillia *see* Dilia
Dilling 72 B4 *var.* Ad Dalanj. Southern Kordofan, C Sudan
Dillon 44 B2 Montana, NW USA
Dilly *see* Dili
Dilolo 77 D7 Ngounié, S Gabon
Dimashq 119 B5 *var.* Ash Shām, Esh Sham, *Eng.* Damascus, *Fr.* Damas, *It.* Damasco. *Country capital* (Syria) Dimashq, SW Syria
Dimitrovgrad 104 D3 Khaskovo, S Bulgaria
Dimitrovgrad 111 C6 Ul'yanovskaya Oblast', W Russian Federation
Dimovo 104 B1 Vidin, NW Bulgaria
Dinajpur 135 F3 Rajshahi, NW Bangladesh
Dinan 90 B3 Côtes d'Armor, NW France
Dinant 87 C7 Namur, S Belgium
Dinar 116 B4 Afyon, SW Turkey
Dinara *see* Dinaric Alps
Dinaric Alps 100 C4 *var.* Dinara. *Mountain range* Bosnia and Herzegovina/Croatia
Dindigul 132 C3 Tamil Nādu, SE India
Dingle Bay 89 A6 *Ir.* Bá an Daingin. *Bay* SW Ireland
Dinguiraye 74 C4 Haute-Guinée, N Guinea
Diourbel 74 B3 W Senegal
Dirē Dawa 73 D5 E Ethiopia

Dirk Hartog Island 147 A5 *island* Western Australia
Disappointment, Lake 146 C4 *salt lake* Western Australia
Dispur 135 G3 Assam, NE India
Divinópolis 63 F4 Minas Gerais, SE Brazil
Divo 74 D5 S Côte d'Ivoire
Diyarbakır 117 E4 *var.* Diarbekr; *anc.* Amida. Diyarbakır, SE Turkey
Dizful *see* Dezfūl
Djajapura *see* Jayapura
Djakovica *see* Đakovica
Djakovo *see* Đakovo
Djambala 77 B6 Plateaux, C Congo
Djambi *see* Jambi
Djanet 71 E4 *prev.* Fort Charlet. SE Algeria
Djéblé *see* Jablah
Djelfa 70 D2 *var.* El Djelfa. N Algeria
Djéma 76 D4 Haut-Mbomou, E Central African Republic
Djérablous *see* Jarābulus
Djerba *see* Jerba, Île de
Djérem 76 B4 *river* C Cameroon
Djevdjelija *see* Gevgelija
Djibouti 72 D4 *var.* Jibuti; *prev.* French Somaliland, French Territory of the Afars and Issas, *Fr.* Côte Française des Somalis, Territoire Français des Afars et des Issas. *Country* E Africa

Djibouti 72

Official name Republic of Djibouti
Formation 1977
Capital Djibouti
Population 638,000 / 71 people per sq mile (28 people per sq km)
Total area 8,949 sq miles (23,180 sq km)
Languages French, Arabic, Somali, Afar
Religions Christian 87%, other 13%
Ethnic mix Issa 60%, Afar 35%, other 5%
Government Multiparty republic
Currency Djibouti franc = 100 centimes
Literacy rate 48.6%
Calorie consumption 2,338 kilocalories

Djibouti 72 D4 *var.* Jibuti. *Country capital* (Djibouti) E Djibouti
Djourab, Erg du 76 C2 *dunes* N Chad
Djúpivogur 83 E5 Austurland, SE Iceland
Dnieper 81 F4 *Bel.* Dnyapro, *Rus.* Dnepr, *Ukr.* Dnipro. *River* E Europe
Dnieper Lowland 109 E2 *Bel.* Prydnyaprowskaya Nizina, *Ukr.* Prydniprovs'ka Nyzovyna. *Lowlands* Belarus/Ukraine
Dniester 81 E4 *Rom.* Nistru, *Rus.* Dnestr, *Ukr.* Dnister; *anc.* Tyras. *River* Moldova/Ukraine
Dnipro *see* Dnieper
Dniprodzerzhyns'k 109 F3 *Rus.* Dneprodzerzhinsk; *prev.* Kamenskoye. Dnipropetrovs'ka Oblast', E Ukraine
Dniprodzerzhyns'ke Vodoskhovyshche 109 F3 *Rus.* Dneprodzerzhinskoye Vodokhranilishche. *Reservoir* C Ukraine
Dnipropetrovs'k 109 F3 *Rus.* Dnepropetrovsk; *prev.* Yekaterinoslav. Dnipropetrovs'ka Oblast', E Ukraine
Dniprorudne 109 F3 *Rus.* Dneprorudnoye. Zaporiz'ka Oblast', SE Ukraine
Doba 76 C4 Logone-Oriental, S Chad
Döbeln 94 D4 Sachsen, E Germany
Doberai, Jazirah 139 G4 *Dut.* Vogelkop. *Peninsula* Irian Jaya, E Indonesia

Doboj 100 C3 Republika Srpska, N Bosnia and Herzegovina
Dobre Miasto 98 D2 *Ger.* Guttstadt. Warmińsko-Mazurskie, NE Poland
Dobrich 104 E1 *Rom.* Bazargic; *prev.* Tolbukhin. Dobrich, NE Bulgaria
Dobrush 107 D7 Homyel'skaya Voblasts', SE Belarus
Dodécanèse *see* Dodekánisos
Dodekánisos 105 D6 *var.* Nóties Sporádes, *Eng.* Dodecanese; *prev.* Dhodhekánisos. *Island group* SE Greece
Dodge City 45 E5 Kansas, C USA
Dodoma 69 D5 *country capital* (Tanzania) Dodoma, C Tanzania
Dodoma 73 C7 *region* C Tanzania
Dogana 96 E1 NE San Marino
Dōgo 131 B6 *island* Oki-shotō, SW Japan
Dogondoutchi 75 F3 Dosso, SW Niger
Doğubayazıt 117 F3 Ağrı, E Turkey
Doğu Karadeniz Dağları 117 E3 *var.* Anadolu Dağları. *Mountain range* NE Turkey
Doha *see* Ad Dawḥah
Doire *see* Londonderry
Dokkum 86 D1 Friesland, N Netherlands
Dokuchayevs'k 109 G3 *var.* Dokuchayevsk. Donets'ka Oblast', SE Ukraine
Dokuchayevsk *see* Dokuchayevs'k
Doldrums Fracture Zone 66 C4 *tectonic feature* W Atlantic Ocean
Dôle 90 D4 Jura, E France
Dolisie 77 B6 *prev.* Loubomo. Le Niari, S Congo
Dolomites *see* Dolomitiche, Alpi
Dolomiti *see* Dolomitiche, Alpi
Dolomitiche, Alpi 96 C1 *var.* Dolomiti, *Eng.* Dolomites. *Mountain range* NE Italy
Dolores 64 D4 Buenos Aires, E Argentina
Dolores 52 B1 Petén, N Guatemala
Dolores 64 D4 Soriano, SW Uruguay
Dolores Hidalgo 51 E4 *var.* Ciudad de Dolores Hidalgo. Guanajuato, C Mexico
Dolyna 108 B2 *Rus.* Dolina. Ivano-Frankivs'ka Oblast', W Ukraine
Dolyns'ka 109 F3 *Rus.* Dolinskaya. Kirovohrads'ka Oblast', S Ukraine
Domachëvo *see* Damachava
Domaczewo *see* Damachava
Dombås 85 B5 Oppland, S Norway
Domel Island *see* Letsôk-aw Kyun
Domeyko 64 B3 Atacama, N Chile
Dominica 55 H4 *Country* E West Indies

Dominica 55

Official name Commonwealth of Dominica
Formation 1978
Capital Roseau
Population 73,000 / 252 people per sq mile (97 people per sq km)
Total area 290 sq miles (750 sq km)
Languages English, French Creole
Religions Roman Catholic 77%, Protestant 15%, other 8%
Ethnic mix Black 98%, Amerindian 2%
Government Multiparty republic
Currency East Caribbean dollar = 100 cents
Literacy rate 94%
Calorie consumption 2,778 kilocalories

Dominica Channel *see* Martinique Passage
Dominican Republic 55 E2 *country* C West Indies

Dominican Republic 55

Official name Dominican Republic

Dominican Republic (continued)

Formation 1865
Capital Santo Domingo
Population 8.45 million / 455 people per sq mile (176 people per sq km)
Total area 18,679 sq miles (48,380 sq km)
Languages Spanish, French Creole
Religions Roman Catholic 92%, other and non-religious 8%
Ethnic mix European-African 73%, White 16%, Black 11%
Government Multiparty republic
Currency Dominican Republic peso = 100 centavos
Literacy rate 82.6%
Calorie consumption 2,286 kilocalories

Domokós 105 B5 *var.* Dhomokós. Stereá Ellás, C Greece
Don 111 B6 *var.* Duna, Tanais. *River* SW Russian Federation
Donau *see* Danube
Donauwörth 95 C6 Bayern, S Germany
Don Benito 92 C3 Extremadura, W Spain
Doncaster 89 D5 *anc.* Danum. N England, UK
Dondo 78 B1 Cuanza Norte, NW Angola
Donegal 89 B5 *Ir.* Dún na nGall. NW Ireland
Donegal Bay 89 A5 *Ir.* Bá Dhún na nGall. *Bay* NW Ireland
Donets 109 G2 *var.* Sivers'kyy Donets', *Rus.* Severskiy Donets. Serra Acaraí. *river* Russian Federation/Ukraine
Donets'k 109 G3 *Rus.* Donetsk; *prev.* Stalino. Donets'ka Oblast', E Ukraine
Dongfang 128 B7 *var.* Basuo. Hainan, S China
Dongguan 128 C6 Guangdong, S China
Đông Ha 136 E4 Quang Tri, C Vietnam
Đông Hoi 136 D4 Quang Binh, C Vietnam
Dongliao *see* Liaoyuan
Dongola 72 B3 *var.* Donqola, Dunqulah. Northern, N Sudan
Dongou 77 C5 La Likouala, NE Congo
Dongting Hu 128 C5 *var.* Tung-t'ing Hu.. Lake S China
Donji Vakuf *var.* Srbobran, Federacija Bosna I Hercegovina, N Yugoslavia
Donostia-San Sebastián 93 E1 País Vasco, N Spain
Donqola *see* Dongola
Doolow 73 D5 E Ethiopia
Doornik *see* Tournai
Door Peninsula 40 C2 *peninsula* Wisconsin, N USA
Dooxo Nugaaleed 73 E5 *var.* Nogal Valley. *Valley* E Somalia
Dordogne 91 B5 *cultural region* SW France
Dordogne 91 B5 *river* W France
Dordrecht 86 C4 *var.* Dordt, Dort. Zuid-Holland, SW Netherlands
Dordt *see* Dordrecht
Dorohoi 108 C3 Botoşani, NE Romania
Dorotea 84 C4 Västerbotten, N Sweden
Dorre Island 147 A5 *island* Western Australia
Dort *see* Dordrecht
Dortmund 94 A4 Nordrhein-Westfalen, W Germany
Dos Hermanas 92 C4 Andalucía, S Spain
Dospad Dagh *see* Rhodope Mountains
Dospat 104 C3 Smolyan, S Bulgaria
Dothan 42 D3 Alabama, S USA

Dotnuva 106 B4 Kėdainiai,
C Lithuania
Douai 90 C2 prev. Douay, anc.
Duacum. Nord, N France
Douala 77 A5 var. Duala. Littoral,
W Cameroon
Douglas 89 C5 dependent territory
capital (Isle of Man) E Isle of Man
Douglas 48 C3 Arizona, SW USA
Douglas 44 D3 Wyoming, C USA
Douro 92 B2 Sp. Duero. River
Portugal/Spain see also Duero
Dover 89 E7 Fr. Douvres; Lat.
Dubris Portus. SE England, UK
Dover 41 F4 state capital Delaware,
NE USA
Dover, Strait of 90 C2 var. Straits of
Dover, Fr. Pas de Calais. Strait
England, UK/France
Dover, Straits of see Dover, Strait
of
Dovrefjell 85 B5 plateau S Norway
Downpatrick 89 B5 Ir. Dún Pádraig.
SE Northern Ireland, UK
Dōzen 131 B6 island Oki-shotō,
SW Japan
Drač see Durrës
Drachten 86 D2 Friesland,
N Netherlands
Drăgăşani 108 B5 Vâlcea,
SW Romania
Dragoman 104 B2 Sofiya,
W Bulgaria
Dra, Hamada du 70 C3 var.
Hammada du Drâa, Haut Plateau
du Dra. Plateau W Algeria
Drahichyn 107 B6 Pol. Drohiczyn
Poleski, Rus. Drogichin.
Brestskaya Voblasts', SW Belarus
Drakensberg 78 D5 mountain range
Lesotho/South Africa
Drake Passage 57 B8 passage
Atlantic Ocean/Pacific Ocean
Dralfa 104 D2 Tŭrgovishte,
N Bulgaria
Dráma 104 C4 var. Dhráma.
Anatolikí Makedonía kai Thráki,
NE Greece
Drammen 85 B6 Buskerud,
S Norway
Drau see Drava
Drava 100 C3 var. Drau, Eng. Drave,
Hung. Dráva. River C Europe see
also Drau
Dráva see Drava
Drave see Drava
Drawsko Pomorskie 98 B3 Ger.
Dramburg. Zachodniopomorskie,
NW Poland
Drépano, Akrotírio 104 C4 var.
Akra Dhrepanon. Headland
N Greece
Dresden 94 D4 Sachsen,
E Germany
Drin see Drinit, Lumi i
Drina 100 C3 river Bosnia and
Herzegovina/Yugoslavia
Drinit, Lumi i 101 D5 var. Drin.
River NW Albania
Drobeta-Turnu Severin 108 B5 prev.
Turnu Severin. Mehedinţi,
SW Romania
Drogheda 89 B5 Ir. Droichead Átha.
NE Ireland
Drohobych 108 B2 Pol. Drohobycz,
Rus. Drogobych. L'vivs'ka Oblast',
NW Ukraine
Droichead Átha see Drogheda
Drôme 91 D5 cultural region
SE France
Dronning Maud Land 154 B2
physical region Antarctica
Drummondville 39 E4 Québec,
SE Canada
Druskininkai 107 B5 Pol.
Druskienniki. Druskininkai,
S Lithuania
Dryden 38 B3 Ontario, C Canada
Drysa 107 D5 Rus. Drissa. River
N Belarus
Duala see Douala
Dubai see Dubayy
Dubăsari 108 D3 Rus. Dubossary.
NE Moldova
Dubawnt 37 F4 river Northwest
Territories/Nunavut,
NW Canada

Dubayy 120 D4 Eng. Dubai.
Dubayy, NE UAE
Dubbo 127 D6 New South Wales,
SE Australia
Dublin 89 B5 Ir. Baile Átha Cliath;
anc. Eblana. Country capital
(Ireland), E Ireland
Dublin 43 E2 Georgia, SE USA
Dubno 108 C2 Rivnens'ka Oblast',
NW Ukraine
Dubrovnik 101 B5 It. Ragusa.
Dubrovnik-Neretva, SE Croatia
Dubuque 45 G3 Iowa, C USA
Dudelange 87 D8 var. Forge du
Sud, Ger. Dudelingen.
Luxembourg, S Luxembourg
Dudelingen see Dudelange
Duero 92 D2 Port. Douro. River
Portugal/Spain see also Douro
Duesseldorf see Düsseldorf
Duffel 87 C5 Antwerpen,
C Belgium
Dugi Otok 100 A4 var. Isola Grossa,
It. Isola Lunga. Island W Croatia
Duisburg 94 A4 prev. Duisburg-
Hamborn. Nordrhein-Westfalen,
W Germany
Duiven 86 D4 Gelderland,
E Netherlands
Duk Faiwil 73 B5 Jonglei, SE Sudan
Dulan 126 D4 var. Qagan Us.
Qinghai, C China
Dulce, Golfo 53 E5 gulf S Costa
Rica
Dülmen 94 A4 Nordrhein-
Westfalen, W Germany
Dulovo 104 E1 Silistra, NE Bulgaria
Duluth 45 G2 Minnesota, N USA
Dūmā 119 B5 Fr. Douma. Dimashq,
SW Syria
Dumas 49 E1 Texas, SW USA
Dumfries 88 C4 S Scotland, UK
Dumont d'Urville 154 C4 French
research station Antarctica
Dumyât 72 B1 Eng. Damietta.
N Egypt
Duna see Danube
Duna see Don
Dunaj see Danube
Dunaújváros 99 C7 prev.
Dunapentele, Sztálinváros. Fejér,
C Hungary
Dunav see Danube
Dunavska Ravnina 104 C2 Eng.
Danubian Plain. Plain N Bulgaria
Duncan 49 G2 Oklahoma, C USA
Dundalk 89 B5 Ir. Dún Dealgan.
NE Ireland
Dún Dealgan see Dundalk
Dundee 88 C4 E Scotland, UK
Dundee 78 D4 KwaZulu/Natal,
E South Africa
Dunedin 151 B7 Otago, South
Island, NZ
Dunfermline 88 C4 C Scotland,
UK
Dungu 77 E5 Orientale, NE Dem.
Rep. Congo (Zaire)
Dungun 138 B3 var. Kuala Dungun.
Terengganu, Peninsular Malaysia
Dunkerque 90 C2 Eng. Dunkirk,
Flem. Duinekerke; prev.
Dunquerque. Nord, N France
Dún Laoghaire 89 B6 Eng.
Dunleary; prev. Kingstown.
E Ireland
Dún na nGall see Donegal
Dún Pádraig see Downpatrick
Dunqulah see Dongola
Dunărea see Danube
Dupnitsa 104 C2 prev. Marek,
Stanke Dimitrov. Kyustendil,
W Bulgaria
Duqm 121 E5 var. Daqm. E Oman
Durance 91 D6 river SE France
Durango 50 D3 var. Victoria de
Durango. Durango, W Mexico
Durango 44 C5 Colorado, C USA
Durankulak 104 E1 Rom. Răcari;
prev. Blatnitsa, Duranulac.
Dobrich, NE Bulgaria
Durant 49 G2 Oklahoma, C USA
Durazzo see Durrës
Durban 78 D4 var. Port Natal.
KwaZulu/Natal, E South Africa
Durbe 106 B3 Ger. Durben. Liepāja,
W Latvia

Durg 135 E4 prev. Drug. Madhya
Pradesh, C India
Durham 89 D5 hist. Dunholme.
N England, UK
Durham 43 F1 North Carolina,
SE USA
Durostorum see Silistra
Durrës 101 C6 var. Durrësi, Dursi,
It. Durazzo, SCr. Drač, Turk. Draç.
Durrës, W Albania
Durrësi see Durrës
Dursi see Durrës
Durūz, Jabal ad 119 C5 mountain
SW Syria
D'Urville Island 150 C4 island
C NZ
Dusa Mareb see Dhuusa Marreeb
Dusa Marreb see Dhuusa Marreeb
Dushanbe 123 E3 var. Dyushambe;
prev. Stalinabad, Taj. Stalinobod.
Country capital (Tajikistan)
W Tajikistan
Düsseldorf 94 A4 var. Duesseldorf.
Nordrhein-Westfalen, W Germany
Düsti 123 E3 Rus. Dusti.
SW Tajikistan
Dutch Harbor 36 B3 Unalaska
Island, Alaska, USA
Dutch New Guinea see Irian Jaya
Duzdab see Zāhedān
Dvina see Severnaya Dvina
Dvina Bay see Chëshskaya Guba
Dyanev see Deynau
Dyersburg 42 C1 Tennessee, S USA
Dyushambe see Dushanbe
Dza Chu see Mekong
Dzerzhinsk 111 C5
Nizhegorodskaya Oblast',
W Russian Federation
Dzhalal-Abad 123 F2 Kir. Jalal-
Abad. Dzhalal-Abadskaya
Oblast', W Kyrgyzstan
Dzhambul see Taraz
Dzhankoy 109 F4 Respublika
Krym, S Ukraine
Dzhelandy 123 F3 SE Tajikistan
Dzhergalan 123 G2 Kir. Jyrgalan.
Issyk-Kul'skaya Oblast',
NE Kyrgyzstan
Dzhugdzhur, Khrebet 115 G3
mountain range E Russian
Federation
Dzhusaly 114 B4 Kaz. Zholsaly.
Kyzylorda, SW Kazakhstan
Działdowo 98 D3 Warmińsko-
Mazurskie, NE Poland
Dzuunmod 127 E2 Töv, C Mongolia

E

Eagle Pass 49 F4 Texas, SW USA
East Açores Fracture Zone see East
Azores Fracture Zone
East Antarctica see Greater
Antarctica
East Australian Basin see Tasman
Basin
East Azores Fracture Zone 66 C3
var. East Açores Fracture Zone.
Tectonic feature E Atlantic Ocean
Eastbourne 89 E7 SE England, UK
East Cape 150 E3 headland North
Island, NZ
East China Sea 125 E2 Chin. Dong
Hai. Sea W Pacific Ocean
Easter Fracture Zone 153 G4 tectonic
feature E Pacific Ocean
Easter Island 153 F4 var. Rapa Nui,
island E Pacific Ocean
Eastern Desert 68 D3 var. Aş Şaḥrā'
ash Sharqīyah, Eng. Arabian
Desert, Eastern Desert. Desert
E Egypt
Eastern Ghats 124 B3 mountain
range SE India
Eastern Sayans 115 E4 Mong.
Dzüün Soyonï Nuruu, Rus.
Vostochnyy Sayan. Mountain range
Mongolia/Russian Federation
East Falkland 65 D8 var. Isla
Soledad. Island E Falkland Islands
East Grand Forks 45 F1 Minnesota,
N USA
East Indiaman Ridge 141 D6
undersea feature E Indian Ocean
East Indies 152 A3 island group
SE Asia

East Kilbride 88 C4 S Scotland, UK
East Korea Bay 129 E3 bay E North
Korea
Eastleigh 89 D7 S England, UK
East London 78 D5 Afr. Oos-
Londen; prev. Emonti, Port Rex.
Eastern Cape, S South Africa
Eastmain 38 D3 river Québec,
C Canada
East Mariana Basin 142 B1 undersea
feature W Pacific Ocean
East Novaya Zemlya Trench 112 C1
var. Novaya Zemlya Trench.
Undersea feature W Kara Sea
East Pacific Rise 153 F4 undersea
feature E Pacific Ocean
East Saint Louis 40 B4 Illinois,
N USA
East Scotia Basin 67 C7 undersea
feature SE Scotia Sea
East Sea see Japan, Sea of
East Siberian Sea see Vostochno-
Sibirskoye More
East Timor 139 F5 var. Loro Sae
prev. Portuguese Timor, Timor
Timur. Dependent territory,
disputed territory, SE Asia
Eau Claire 40 A2 Wisconsin, N USA
Eauripik Rise 142 B2 undersea
feature W Pacific Ocean
Ebensee 95 D6 Oberösterreich,
N Austria
Eberswalde-Finow 94 D3
Brandenburg, E Germany
Ebetsu 130 D2 var. Ebetu.
Hokkaidō, NE Japan
Ebetu see Ebetsu
Ebolowa 77 A5 Sud, S Cameroon
Ebon Atoll 144 D2 var. Epoon. Atoll
Ralik Chain, S Marshall Islands
Ebro 93 E2 river NE Spain
Ebusus see Eivissa
Ech Cheliff see Chlef
Ech Chleff see Chlef
Echo Bay 37 E3 Northwest
Territories, NW Canada
Echt 87 D5 Limburg,
SE Netherlands
Ecija 92 D4 anc. Astigi. Andalucía,
SW Spain
Ecuador 60 B1 Country NW South
America

Ecuador 60

Official name Republic of
Ecuador
Formation 1830
Capital Quito
Population 12.4 million /
118 people per sq mile
(46 people per sq km)
Total area 106,887 sq miles
(276,840 sq km)
Languages Spanish, Quechua,
other Amerindian languages
Religions Roman Catholic 93%,
Protestant, Jewish and other 7%
Ethnic mix Mestizo 55%, Indian
25%, Black 10%, White 10%
Government Multiparty republic
Currency Sucre = 100 centavos
Literacy rate 90.7%
Calorie consumption 2,583
kilocalories

Ed Da'ein 72 A4 Southern Darfur,
W Sudan
Ed Damazin 72 C4 var. Ad
Damazin. Blue Nile, E Sudan
Ed Damer 72 C3 var. Ad Damar, Ad
Dāmir. River Nile, NE Sudan
Ed Debba 72 B3 Northern, N Sudan
Ede 86 D4 Gelderland,
C Netherlands
Ede 75 F5 Osun, SW Nigeria
Edéa 77 A5 Littoral, SW Cameroon
Edeyin Murzuq see Murzuq, Idhān
Edfu see Idfu
Edgeøya 83 G2 island S Svalbard
Edgware 89 A7 SE England, UK
Edinburg 49 G5 Texas, SW USA
Edinburgh 88 C4 admin capital
S Scotland, UK
Edirne 116 A2 Eng. Adrianople; anc.
Adrianopolis, Hadrianopolis.
Edirne, NW Turkey

Edmonds 46 B2 Washington, NW USA
Edmonton 37 E5 Alberta, SW Canada
Edmundston 39 E4 New Brunswick, SE Canada
Edna 49 G4 Texas, SW USA
Edolo 96 B1 Lombardia, N Italy
Edremit 116 A3 Balıkesir, NW Turkey
Edward, Lake 77 E5 var. Albert Edward Nyanza, Edward Nyanza, Lac Idi Amin, Lake Rutanzige. *Lake* Uganda/Zaire
Edward Nyanza *see* Edward, Lake
Edwards Plateau 49 F3 *plain* Texas, SW USA
Eeklo 87 B5 var. Eekloo. Oost-Vlaanderen, NW Belgium
Edzo 53 E4 *prev.* Rae-Edzo. Northwest Territories, NW Canada
Eekloo *see* Eeklo
Eersel 87 C5 Noord-Brabant, S Netherlands
Efate 144 D4 var. Éfaté *Fr.* Vaté; *prev.* Sandwich Island. *Island* C Vanuatu
Effingham 40 B4 Illinois, N USA
Eforie Sud 108 D5 Constanța, E Romania
Efstrátios, Ágios 104 D4 *var.* Ayios Evstratios. *Island* E Greece
Egadi, Isole 97 B7 *island group* S Italy
Eger 99 D6 *Ger.* Erlau. Heves, NE Hungary
Egeria Fracture Zone 141 C5 *tectonic feature* W Indian Ocean
Éghezèe 87 C6 Namur, C Belgium
Egina *see* Aígina
Egio *see* Aígio
Egmont, Mount *see* Taranaki, Mount
Egmont, Cape 150 C4 *headland* North Island, NZ
Egoli *see* Johannesburg
Egypt 72 B2 Ar. Jumhūrīyah Miṣr al 'Arabīyah; *prev.* United Arab Republic, *anc.* Aegyptus. *Country* NE Africa

Egypt 72

Official name Arab Republic of Egypt
Formation 1936
Capital Cairo
Population 68.5 million / 178 people per sq mile (69 people per sq km)
Total area 384,343 sq miles (995,450 sq km)
Languages Arabic, French, English
Religions Muslim (mainly Sunni) 94%, Coptic Christian and other 6%
Ethnic mix Eastern Hamitic 90%, other (Nubian, Armenian, Greek) 10%
Government Multiparty republic
Currency Egyptian pound = 100 piastres
Literacy rate 52.7%
Calorie consumption 3,335 kilocalories

Eibar 93 E1 País Vasco, N Spain
Eibergen 86 E3 Gelderland, E Netherlands
Eidfjord 85 A5 Hordaland, S Norway
Eier-Berg *see* Suur Munamägi
Eifel 95 A5 *plateau* W Germany
Eiger 95 B7 *mountain* C Switzerland
Eigg 88 B3 *island* W Scotland, UK
Eight Degree Channel 132 B3 *channel* India/Maldives
Eighty Mile Beach 146 B4 *beach* Western Australia
Eijsden 87 D6 Limburg, SE Netherlands
Eilat *see* Elat
Eindhoven 87 D5 Noord-Brabant, S Netherlands

Eipel *see* Ipel'
Eipel *see* Ipoly
Eisenhüttenstadt 94 D4 Brandenburg, E Germany
Eisenstadt 95 E6 Burgenland, E Austria
Eisleben 94 C4 Sachsen-Anhalt, C Germany
Eivissa 93 G3 var. Iviza, *Cast.* Ibiza; *anc.* Ebusus. *Island* Islas Baleares, Spain, W Mediterranean Sea
Eivissa 93 G3 var. Iviza, *Cast.* Ibiza; *anc.* Ebusus. Eivissa, Spain, W Mediterranean Sea
Ejea de los Caballeros 93 E2 Aragón, NE Spain
Ejin Qi 126 D3 *var.* Dalain Hob. Nei Mongol Zizhiqu, N China
Ekapa *see* Cape Town
Ekiatapskiy Khrebet 115 G1 *mountain range* NE Russian Federation
El 'Alamein 72 B1 *var.* Al 'Alamayn. N Egypt
El Asnam *see* Chlef
Elat 119 B8 *var.* Eilat, Elath. Southern, S Israel
Elat, Gulf of *see* Aqaba, Gulf of
Elath *see* Al 'Aqabah
Elath *see* Elat
El'Atrun 72 B3 Northern Darfur, NW Sudan
Elâzığ 117 E3 *var.* Elâziz. Elâzığ, E Turkey
Elâziz *see* Elâzığ
Elba, Isola d' 96 B4 *island* Archipelago Toscano, C Italy
Elbasan 101 D6 *var.* Elbasani. Elbasan, C Albania
Elbasani *see* Elbasan
Elbe 80 D3 Cz. Labe. *River* Czech Republic/Germany
El Beni *see* Beni
Elbert, Mount 44 C4 *mountain* Colorado, C USA
Elbing *see* Elbląg
Elbląg 98 C2 *var.* Elblag, *Ger.* Elbing. Warmińsko-Mazurskie, NE Poland
El Boulaida *see* Blida
El'brus 111 A8 *var.* Gora El'brus. *Mountain* SW Russian Federation
El Burgo de Osma 93 E2 Castila-León, C Spain
El Cajon 47 C8 California, W USA
El Calafate 65 B7 *var.* Calafate. Santa Cruz, S Argentina
El Callao 59 E2 Bolívar, E Venezuela
El Campo 49 G4 Texas, SW USA
El Carmen de Bolívar 58 B2 Bolívar, NW Colombia
El Centro 47 D8 California, W USA
Elche 93 F4 *var.* Elx-Elche; *anc.* Ilici, *Lat.* Illicis. País Valenciano, E Spain
Elda 93 F4 País Valenciano, E Spain
El Djazaïr *see* Alger
El Djelfa *see* Djelfa
El Dorado 42 B2 Arkansas, C USA
El Dorado 59 F2 Bolívar, E Venezuela
El Dorado 45 F5 Kansas, C USA
El Dorado 50 C3 Sinaloa, C Mexico
Eldorado 64 E3 Misiones, NE Argentina
Eldoret 73 C6 Rift Valley, W Kenya
Elektrostal' 111 B5 Moskovskaya Oblast', W Russian Federation
Elemi Triangle 73 B5 *disputed region* Kenya/Sudan
Elephant Butte Reservoir 48 C2 *reservoir* New Mexico, SW USA
Eleuthera Island 54 C1 *island* N Bahamas
El Fasher 72 A4 *var.* Al Fāshir. Northern Darfur, W Sudan
El Ferrol *see* Ferrol
El Ferrol del Caudillo *see* Ferrol
El Gedaref *see* Gedaref
El Geneina 72 A4 *var.* Ajjinena, Al-Genain, Al Junaynah. Western Darfur, W Sudan
Elgin 40 B3 Illinois, N USA
Elgin 88 C3 NE Scotland, UK
El Gîza 72 B1 *var.* Al Jizah, Gîza, Gizeh. N Egypt

El Goléa 70 D3 *var.* Al Golea. C Algeria
El Hank 74 D1 *cliff* N Mauritania
El Haseke *see* Al Ḥasakah
Elista 111 B7 Respublika Kalmykiya, SW Russian Federation
Elizabeth 149 B6 South Australia
Elizabeth City 43 G1 North Carolina, SE USA
Elizabethtown 40 C5 Kentucky, S USA
El-Jadida 70 C2 *prev.* Mazagan. W Morocco
Elk 98 E2 *Ger.* Lyck. Warmińsko-Mazurskie, NE Poland
Elk City 49 F1 Oklahoma, C USA
El Kerak *see* Al Karak
El Khalīl *see* Hebron
El Khârga 72 B2 *var.* Al Khārijah. C Egypt
Elkhart 40 C3 Indiana, N USA
Elk River 45 F2 Minnesota, N USA
El Kuneitra *see* Al Qunayṭirah
Ellef Ringnes Island 37 E1 *island* Nunavut, N Canada
Ellen, Mount 44 B5 *mountain* Utah, W USA
Ellensburg 46 B2 Washington, NW USA
Ellesmere Island 37 F1 *island* Queen Elizabeth Islands, Nunavut, N Canada
Ellesmere, Lake 151 C6 *lake* South Island, NZ
Elliston 149 A6 South Australia
Ellsworth Land 154 A3 *physical region* Antarctica
El Mahbas 70 B3 *var.* Mahbés. SW Western Sahara
El Mina 118 B4 *var.* Al Mīnā'. N Lebanon
El Minya 72 B2 *var.* Al Minyā, Minya. C Egypt
Elmira 41 E3 New York, NE USA
El Mreyyé 74 D2 *desert* E Mauritania
Elmshorn 94 B3 Schleswig-Holstein, N Germany
El Muglad 72 B4 Western Kordofan, C Sudan
El Obeid 72 B4 *var.* Al Obayyid, Al Ubayyiḍ. Northern Kordofan, C Sudan
El Ouâdi *see* El Oued
El Oued 71 E2 *var.* Al Oued, El Ouâdi, El Wad. NE Algeria
Eloy 48 B2 Arizona, SW USA
El Paso 48 D3 Texas, SW USA
El Porvenir 53 G4 San Blas, N Panama
El Progreso 52 C2 Yoro, NW Honduras
El Puerto de Santa María 92 C5 Andalucía, S Spain
El Quds *see* Jerusalem
El Quneitra *see* Al Qunayṭirah
El Quseir *see* Al Quṣayr
El Quweira *see* Al Quwayrah
El Rama 53 E3 Región Autónoma Atlántico Sur, SE Nicaragua
El Real 53 H5 *var.* El Real de Santa María. Darién, SE Panama
El Real de Santa María *see* El Real
El Reno 49 F1 Oklahoma, C USA
El Salvador 52 B3 *Country* Central America

El Salvador 52

Official name Republic of El Salvador
Formation 1856
Capital San Salvador
Population 6.3 million / 788 people per sq mile (304 people per sq km)
Total area 7,999 sq miles (20,720 sq km)
Languages Spanish
Religions Roman Catholic 80%, Evangelical 18%, other 2%

El Salvador (continued)

Ethnic mix Mestizo 89%, Indian 10%, White 1%
Government Multiparty republic
Currency Salvadorean colón = 100 centavos
Literacy rate 77%
Calorie consumption 2,663 kilocalories

El Sáuz 50 C2 Chihuahua, N Mexico
El Serrat 91 A7 N Andorra
Elst 86 D4 Gelderland, E Netherlands
El Sueco 50 C2 Chihuahua, N Mexico
El Suweida *see* As Suwaydā'
Eltanin Fracture Zone 153 E5 *tectonic feature* SE Pacific Ocean
El Tigre 59 E2 Anzoátegui, NE Venezuela
Elvas 92 C4 Portalegre, C Portugal
El Vendrell 93 G2 Cataluña, NE Spain
El Vigía 58 C2 Mérida, NW Venezuela
El Wad *see* El Oued
Elwell, Lake 44 B1 *reservoir* Montana, NW USA
Elx-Elche *see* Elche
Ely 47 D5 Nevada, W USA
El Yopal *see* Yopal
Emajõgi 106 D3 *Ger.* Embach. *River* SE Estonia
Emba 114 B4 *Kaz.* Embi. Aktyubinsk, W Kazakhstan
Emden 94 A3 Niedersachsen, NW Germany
Emerald 148 D4 Queensland, E Australia
Emerald Isle *see* Montserrat
Emesa *see* Ḥimṣ
Emmaste 106 C2 Hiiumaa, W Estonia
Emmeloord 86 D2 Flevoland, N Netherlands
Emmen 86 E2 Drenthe, NE Netherlands
Emmendingen 95 A6 Baden-Württemberg, SW Germany
Emory Peak 49 E4 *mountain* Texas, SW USA
Empalme 50 B2 Sonora, NW Mexico
Emperor Seamounts 113 G3 *undersea feature* NW Pacific Ocean
Emporia 45 F5 Kansas, C USA
Empty Quarter *see* Ar Rub 'al Khālī
Ems 94 A3 *Dut.* Eems. *River* NW Germany
Encamp 91 A8 C Andorra
Encarnación 64 D3 Itapúa, S Paraguay
Encinitas 47 C8 California, W USA
Encs 99 D6 Borsod-Abaúj-Zemplén, NE Hungary
Endeavour Strait 148 C1 *strait* Queensland, NE Australia
Enderbury Island 145 F3 *atoll* Phoenix Islands, C Kiribati
Enderby Land 154 C2 *physical region* Antarctica
Enderby Plain 154 D2 *undersea feature* S Indian Ocean
Enewetak Atoll 144 C1 *var.* Ånewetak, Eniwetok. *Atoll* Ralik Chain, W Marshall Islands
Enfield 89 A7 SE England, UK
Engannim *see* Jenīn
Enghien 87 B6 *Dut.* Edingen. Hainaut, SW Belgium
England 89 D5 *Lat.* Anglia. *National region* UK
Englewood 44 D4 Colorado, C USA
English Channel 89 D8 *var.* The Channel, *Fr.* la Manche. *Channel* NW Europe
Engure 106 C3 Tukums, W Latvia
Engures Ezers 106 B3 *lake* NW Latvia
Enguri 117 F1 *Rus.* Inguri. *River* NW Georgia
Enid 49 F1 Oklahoma, C USA
Enikale Strait *see* Kerch Strait

Eniwetok see Enewetak Atoll
En Nâqoûra 119 A5 var. An
  Nâqûrah. SW Lebanon
Ennedi 76 D2 plateau E Chad
Ennis 89 A6 Ir. Inis. W Ireland
Ennis 49 G3 Texas, SW USA
Enniskillen 89 B5 var. Inniskilling,
  Ir. Inis Ceithleann. SW Northern
  Ireland, UK
Enns 95 D6 river C Austria
Enschede 86 E3 Overijssel,
  E Netherlands
Ensenada 50 A1 Baja California,
  NW Mexico
Entebbe 73 B6 S Uganda
Entroncamento 92 B3 Santarém,
  C Portugal
Enugu 75 G5 Enugu, S Nigeria
Eolie, Isole 97 C6 var. Isole Lipari,
  Eng. Aeolian Islands, Lipari
  Islands. Island group S Italy
Epanomí 104 B4 Kentrikí
  Makedonía, N Greece
Epéna 77 B5 La Likouala,
  NE Congo
Eperies see Prešov
Eperjes see Prešov
Epi 144 D4 var. Épi. Island
  C Vanuatu
Épi see Epi
Épinal 90 D4 Vosges, NE France
Epiphania see Ḥamāh
Epitoli see Pretoria
Epoon see Ebon Atoll
Epsom 89 A8 SE England, UK
Equatorial Guinea 77 A5 Country
  C Africa

Equatorial Guinea 77

Official name Republic of
  Equatorial Guinea
Formation 1968
Capital Malabo
Population 453,000 / 42 people
  per sq mile (16 people per sq km)
Total area 10,830 sq miles
  (28,050 sq km)
Languages Spanish, Fang, Bubi
Religions Roman Catholic 90%,
  other 10%
Ethnic mix Fang 72%, Bubi 14%,
  Duala 3%, other 11%
Government Multiparty republic
Currency CFA franc
  = 100 centimes
Literacy rate 80%
Calorie consumption
  not available

Erautini see Johannesburg
Erbil see Arbīl
Erciş 117 F3 Van, E Turkey
Erdélyi-Havasok see Carpaţii
  Meridionali
Erdenet 127 E2 Bulgan,
  N Mongolia
Erdi 76 C2 plateau NE Chad
Erdi Ma 76 D2 desert NE Chad
Erebus, Mount 154 B4 mountain
  Ross Island, Antarctica
Ereğli 116 C4 Konya, S Turkey
Erenhot 127 F2 var. Erlian. Nei
  Mongol Zizhiqu, NE China
Erevan see Yerevan
Erfurt 94 C4 Thüringen,
  C Germany
Ergene Irmaği 116 A2 var. Ergene
  Irmaği. River NW Turkey
Erg Iguid see Iguîdi, 'Erg
Ergun He see Argun
Ergun Zuoqi 127 F1 Nei Mongol
  Zizhiqu, N China
Erie 40 D3 Pennsylvania, NE USA
Erie, Lake 40 D3 Fr. Lac Érié. Lake
  Canada/USA
Eritrea 72 C4 Tig. Ērtra. Country
  E Africa

Eritrea 72

Official name State of Eritrea
Formation 1993
Capital Asmara
Population 4 million / 86 people
  per sq mile (33 people per sq km)

Eritrea (continued)

Total area 45,405 sq miles
  (117,600 sq km)
Languages Tigrinya, Tigre,
  Afar, Arabic, Bilen, Kunama,
  Nara, Saho
Religions Christian 45%,
  Muslim 45%, other 10%
Ethnic mix Tigray (majority),
  Afars
Government Transitional
Currency Nafka = 100 cents
Literacy rate 25%
Calorie consumption 1,610
  kilocalories

Erivan see Yerevan
Erlangen 95 C5 Bayern, S Germany
Erlian see Erenhot
Ermelo 86 D3 Gelderland,
  C Netherlands
Ermióni 105 C6 Pelopónnisos,
  S Greece
Ermoúpoli 105 D6 var.
  Hermoupolis; prev. Ermoúpolis.
  Sýros, Kykládes, Greece,
  Aegean Sea
Ermoúpolis see Ermoúpoli
Ernākulam 132 C3 Kerala, SW India
Erode 132 C2 Tamil Nādu, SE India
Erquelinnes 87 B7 Hainaut,
  S Belgium
Er-Rachidia 70 C2 var. Ksar
  al Soule. E Morocco
Er Rahad 72 B4 var. Ar Rahad.
  Northern Kordofan, C Sudan
Erromango 144 D4 island S Vanuatu
Ertis see Irtysh
Erzgebirge 95 C5 Cz. Krušné Hory,
  Eng. Ore Mountains. Mountain
  range Czech Republic/Germany
  see also Krušné Hory
Erzincan 117 E3 var. Érzinjan.
  Erzincan, E Turkey
Erzinjan see Erzincan
Erzurum 117 E3 prev. Erzerum.
  Erzurum, NE Turkey
Esbjerg 85 A7 Ribe, W Denmark
Escaldes 91 A8 C Andorra
Escanaba 40 C2 Michigan, N USA
Esch-sur-Alzette 87 D8
  Luxembourg, S Luxembourg
Escondido 47 C8 California,
  W USA
Escuinapa 50 D3 var. Escuinapa de
  Hidalgo. Sinaloa, C Mexico
Escuinapa de Hidalgo see
  Escuinapa
Escuintla 51 G5 Chiapas,
  SE Mexico
Escuintla 52 B2 Escuintla,
  S Guatemala
Eşfahān 120 C3 Eng. Isfahan; anc.
  Aspadana. Eşfahān, C Iran
Esh Sham see Dimashq
Esh Sharā see Ash Sharāh
Eskişehir 116 B3 var. Eskishehr.
  Eskişehir, W Turkey
Eskishehr see Eskişehir
Eslāmābād 120 C3 var. Eslāmābād-e
  Gharb; prev. Harunabad,
  Shāhābād. Kermānshāhān, W Iran
Eslāmābād-e Gharb
  see Eslāmābād
Esmeraldas 60 A1 Esmeraldas,
  N Ecuador
Esna see Isna
Espanola 48 D1 New Mexico,
  SW USA
Esperance 147 B7 Western Australia
Esperanza 154 A2 Argentinian
  research station Antarctica
Esperanza 50 B2 Sonora,
  NW Mexico
Espinal 58 B3 Tolima, C Colombia
Espinhaço, Serra do 56 D4 mountain
  range SE Brazil
Espírito Santo 63 F4 off. Estado do
  Espírito Santo. State E Brazil
Espíritu Santo 144 C4 var. Santo.
  Island W Vanuatu
Espoo 85 D6 Swe. Esbo. Etelä-
  Suomi, S Finland
Esquel 65 B6 Chubut,
  SW Argentina

Essaouira 70 B2 prev. Mogador.
  W Morocco
Es Semara see Smara
Essen 94 A4 var. Essen an der Ruhr.
  Nordrhein-Westfalen,
  W Germany
Essen 87 C5 Antwerpen,
  N Belgium
Essen an der Ruhr see Essen
Essequibo River 59 F3 river
  C Guyana
Es Suweida see As Suwaydā'
Estacado, Llano 49 E2 plain New
  Mexico/Texas, SW USA
Estados, Isla de los 65 C8
  prev. Eng. Staten Island. Island
  S Argentina
Estância 63 G3 Sergipe, E Brazil
Estelí 52 D3 Estelí, NW Nicaragua
Estella see Estella-Lizarra
Estella-Lizarra 93 E1 Bas. Lizarra
  var. Estella. Navarra, N Spain
Estepona 92 D5 Andalucía,
  S Spain
Estevan 37 F5 Saskatchewan,
  S Canada
Estonia 106 D2 Est. Eesti Vabariik,
  Ger. Estland, Latv. Igaunija; prev.
  Estonian SSR, Rus. Éstonskaya
  SSR. Country NE Europe

Estonia 106

Official name Republic of
  Estonia
Formation 1991
Capital Tallinn
Population 1.4 million / 80 people
  per sq mile (31 people per sq km)
Total area 17,422 sq miles
  (45,125 sq km)
Languages Estonian, Russian
Religions Evangelical Lutheran
  98%, Eastern Orthodox or
  Baptist 2%
Ethnic mix Russian 62%,
  Estonian 30%, other 8%
Government Multiparty republic
Currency Kroon = 100 cents
Literacy rate 99%
Calorie consumption
  not available

Estrela, Serra da 92 C3 mountain
  range C Portugal
Estremoz 92 C4 Évora, S Portugal
Esztergom 99 C6 Ger. Gran; anc.
  Strigonium. Komárom-Esztergom,
  N Hungary
Étalle 87 D8 Luxembourg,
  SE Belgium
Etāwah 134 D3 Uttar Pradesh,
  N India
Ethiopia 73 C5 prev. Abyssinia,
  People's Democratic Republic of
  Ethiopia. Country E Africa

Ethiopia 73

Official name Federal Democratic
  Republic of Ethiopia
Formation 1896
Capital Addis Ababa
Population 62.6 million /
  179 people per sq mile
  (69 people per sq km)
Total area 349,490 sq miles
  (905,450 sq km)
Languages Amharic, Tigrinya,
  Galla
Religions Muslim 40%, Ethiopian
  Orthodox 40%, other 20%
Ethnic mix Oromo 40%, Amhara
  25%, Sidamo 9%, Shankella 6%,
  other 20%
Government Multiparty republic
Currency Ethiopian birr
  = 100 cents
Literacy rate 35.4%
Calorie consumption 1,610
  kilocalories

Ethiopian Highlands 73 C5 var.
  Ethiopian Plateau. Plateau
  N Ethiopia
Ethiopian Plateau see Ethiopian
  Highlands

Etna, Monte 97 C7 Eng. Mount
  Etna. Volcano Sicilia, Italy,
  C Mediterranean Sea
Etna, Mount see Etna, Monte
Etosha Pan 78 B3 salt lake
  N Namibia
Etoumbi 77 B5 Cuvette, NW Congo
Et Tafila see Aţ Ţafīlah
Ettelbrück 87 D8 Diekirch,
  C Luxembourg
'Eua 145 E5 prev. Middleburg
  Island. Island Tongatapu Group,
  SE Tonga
Euboea see Évvoia
Eucla 147 D6 Western Australia
Euclid 40 D3 Ohio, N USA
Eufaula Lake 49 G1 var. Eufaula
  Reservoir. Reservoir Oklahoma,
  C USA
Eufaula Reservoir see Eufaula Lake
Eugene 46 B3 Oregon, NW USA
Eupen 87 D6 Liège, E Belgium
Euphrates 112 B4 Ar. Al Furāt, Turk.
  Firat Nehri. River SW Asia
Eureka 47 A5 California, W USA
Eureka 44 A1 Montana, NW USA
Europa Point 93 H5 headland
  S Gibraltar
Europe 34 E1 continent
Eutin 94 C2 Schleswig-Holstein,
  N Germany
Euxine Sea see Black Sea
Evansdale 45 G3 Iowa, C USA
Evanston 40 B3 Illinois, N USA
Evanston 44 B4 Wyoming, C USA
Evansville 40 B5 Indiana, N USA
Eveleth 45 G1 Minnesota, N USA
Everard, Lake 149 A6 salt lake South
  Australia
Everest, Mount 126 B5 Chin.
  Qomolangma Feng, Nep.
  Sagarmatha. Mountain
  China/Nepal
Everett 46 B2 Washington,
  NW USA
Everglades, The 43 F5 wetland
  Florida, SE USA
Evje 85 A6 Aust-Agder, S Norway
Évora 92 B4 anc. Ebora, Lat.
  Liberalitas Julia.Évora, C Portugal
Évreux 90 C3 anc. Civitas
  Eburovicum. Eure, N France
Évros see Maritsa
Évry 90 E2 Essonne, N France
Évvoia 101 E8 Lat. Euboea. Island
  C Greece
Ewarton 54 B5 C Jamaica
Excelsior Springs 45 F4 Missouri,
  C USA
Exe 89 C7 river SW England, UK
Exeter 89 C7 anc. Isca
  Damnoniorum. SW England, UK
Exmoor 89 C7 moorland
  SW England, UK
Exmouth 89 C7 SW England, UK
Exmouth 146 A4 Western Australia
Exmouth Gulf 146 A4 gulf Western
  Australia
Exmouth Plateau 141 E5 undersea
  feature E Indian Ocean
Extremadura 92 C3 cultural region
  W Spain
Exuma Cays 54 C1 islets C Bahamas
Exuma Sound 54 C1 sound
  C Bahamas
Eyre Mountains 151 A7 mountain
  range South Island, NZ
Eyre North, Lake 149 A5 salt lake
  South Australia
Eyre Peninsula 149 A6 peninsula
  South Australia
Eyre South, Lake 149 A5 salt lake
  South Australia

F

Faadhippolhu Atoll 132 B4 var.
  Fadiffolu, Lhaviyani Atoll. Atoll
  N Maldives
Fabens 48 D3 Texas, SW USA
Fada 76 C2 Borkou-Ennedi-Tibesti,
  E Chad
Fada-Ngourma 75 E4 E Burkina
  faso
Fadiffolu see Faadhippolhu Atoll
Faenza 96 C3 anc. Faventia. Emilia-
  Romagna, N Italy

Faeroe-Iceland Ridge *80 C1*
undersea feature NW Norwegian
Sea
Faeroe-Shetland Trough *80 C2*
undersea feature NE Atlantic Ocean
Faeroes Islands *83 E5 Dan.*
Færøerne, *Faer.* Føroyar. *Danish
external territory* N Atlantic
Ocean
Faetano *96 E2* E San Marino
Făgăraş *108 C4 Ger.* Fogarasch,
Hung. Fogaras. Braşov,
C Romania
Fagibina, Lake *see* Faguibine, Lac
Fagne *87 C7 hill range* S Belgium
Faguibine, Lac *75 E3 var.* Lake
Fagibina. *Lake* NW Mali
Fahlun *see* Falun
Fahraj *120 E4* Kermān, SE Iran
Faial *92 A5 var.* Ilha do Faial. *Island*
Azores, Portugal, NE Atlantic
Ocean
Fairbanks *36 D3* Alaska, USA
Fairfield *47 B6* California, W USA
Fair Isle *88 D2 island* NE Scotland,
UK
Fairlie *151 B6* Canterbury, South
Island, NZ
Fairmont *45 F3* Minnesota, N USA
Faisalābād *134 C2 prev.* Lyallpur.
Punjab, NE Pakistan
Faizābād *see* Feyẕābād
Faizābād *135 E3* Uttar Pradesh,
N India
Fakaofo Atoll *145 F3 island*
SE Tokelau
Falam *136 A3* Chin State,
W Myanmar
Falconara Marittima *96 C3* Marche,
C Italy
Falkland Islands *65 D7 var.*
Falklands, Islas Malvinas. *UK
dependent territory* SW Atlantic
Ocean
Falkland Plateau *57 D7 var.*
Argentine Rise. *Undersea feature*
SW Atlantic Ocean
Falklands *see* Falkland Islands
Fallbrook *47 C8* California, W USA
Falmouth *89 C7* SW England, UK
Falmouth *54 A4* W Jamaica
Falster *85 B8 island* SE Denmark
Fălticeni *108 C3 Hung.* Falticsén.
Suceava, NE Romania
Falun *85 C6 var.* Fahlun.
Kopparberg, C Sweden
Famagusta *see* Ammóchostos
Famagusta Bay *see* Kólpos
Ammóchostos
Famenne *87 C7 physical region*
SE Belgium
Fang *136 C3* Chiang Mai,
NW Thailand
Fano *96 C3 anc.* Colonia Julia
Fanestris, Fanum Fortunae.
Marche, C Italy
Farafangana *79 G4* Fianarantsoa,
SE Madagascar
Farāh *122 D4 var.* Farah, Fararud.
Farāh, W Afghanistan
Farāh Rūd *122 D4 river*
W Afghanistan
Faranah *74 C4* Haute-Guinée,
S Guinea
Fararud *see* Farāh
Farasān, Jazāʾir *121 A6 island group*
SW Saudi Arabia
Farewell, Cape *150 C4 headland*
South Island, NZ
Farewell, Cape *see* Nunap Isua
Farghona *123 F2 Rus.* Fergana; *prev.*
Novyy Margilan. Farghona
Wiloyati, E Uzbekistan
Fargo *45 F2* North Dakota, N USA
Faribault *45 F2* Minnesota, N USA
Farīdābād *134 D3* Haryāna, N India
Farkhor *123 E3 Rus.* Parkhar.
SW Tajikistan
Farmington *45 G5* Missouri, C USA
Farmington *48 C1* New Mexico,
SW USA
Faro *92 B5* Faro, S Portugal
Farquhar Group *79 G2 island group*
S Seychelles
Farvel, Kap *see* Nunap Isua
Fastiv *109 E2 Rus.* Fastov. Kyyivsʹka
Oblastʹ, NW Ukraine

Fauske *84 C3* Nordland,
C Norway
Faxaflói *82 D5 Eng.* Faxa Bay. *Bay*
W Iceland
Faya *76 C2 prev.* Faya-Largeau,
Largeau. Borkou-Ennedi-Tibesti,
N Chad
Fayetteville *42 A1* Arkansas, C USA
Fayetteville *43 F1* North Carolina,
SE USA
Fdérick *see* Fdérik
Fdérik *74 C2 var.* Fdérick, *Fr.* Fort
Gouraud. Tiris Zemmour,
NW Mauritania
Fear, Cape *43 F2 headland* Bald
Head Island, North Carolina,
SE USA
Fécamp *90 B3* Seine-Maritime,
N France
**Federation of the separate
territories of** *see* Malaysia
Fehérgyarmat *99 E6* Szabolcs-
Szatmár-Bereg, E Hungary
Fehmarn *94 C2 island* N Germany
Fehmarn Belt *94 C2 Ger.*
Fehmarnbelt. *Strait*
Denmark/Germany
Feijó *62 C2* Acre, W Brazil
Feilding *150 D4* Manawatu-
Wanganui, North Island, NZ
Feira *see* Feira de Santana
Feira de Santana *63 G3 var.* Feira.
Bahia, E Brazil
Felanitx *93 G3 anc.* Canati,
Felaniche. Mallorca, Spain,
W Mediterranean Sea
Felidhu Atoll *132 B4 atoll*
C Maldives
Felipe Carrillo Puerto *51 H4*
Quintana Roo, SE Mexico
Felixstowe *89 E6* E England, UK
Femunden *85 B5 lake* S Norway
Fengcheng *128 D3 var.* Feng-cheng,
Fenghwangcheng. Liaoning,
NE China
Feng-cheng *see* Fengcheng
Fenghwangcheng *see* Fengcheng
Fengtien *see* Liaoning
Fenoarivo *79 G3* Toamasina,
E Madagascar
Fens, The *89 E6 wetland* E England,
UK
Feodosiya *109 F5 var.* Kefe, *It.* Kaffa;
anc. Theodosia. Respublika Krym,
S Ukraine
Féres *104 D3* Anatolikí Makedonía
kai Thráki, NE Greece
Fergus Falls *45 F2* Minnesota,
N USA
Ferkessédougou *74 D4* N Côte
d'Ivoire
Fermo *96 C4 anc.* Firmum Picenum.
Marche, C Italy
Fernandina, Isla *60 A5 var.*
Narborough Island. *Island*
Galapagos Islands, Ecuador,
E Pacific Ocean
Fernando de Noronha *63 H2 island*
E Brazil
Fernando Po *see* Bioco, Isla de
Fernando Póo *see* Bioco, Isla de
Ferrara *96 C2 anc.* Forum Alieni.
Emilia-Romagna, N Italy
Ferreñafe *60 B3* Lambayeque,
W Peru
Ferro *see* Hierro
Ferrol *92 B1 var.* El Ferrol; *prev.*
El Ferrol del Caudillo. Galicia,
NW Spain
Ferwerd *86 D1 Fris.* Ferwert.
Friesland, N Netherlands
Fès *70 C2 Eng.* Fez. N Morocco
Feteşti *108 D5* Ialomiţa,
SE Romania
Fethiye *116 B4* Muğla, SW Turkey
Fetlar *88 D1 island* NE Scotland,
UK
Feyẕābād *123 F3 var.* Faizabad,
Faizābād, Feyzābād, Fyzabad.
Badakhshān, NE Afghanistan
Fianarantsoa *79 F3* Fianarantsoa,
C Madagascar
Fianga *76 B4* Mayo-Kébbi,
SW Chad
Fier *101 C6 var.* Fieri. Fier,
SW Albania
Fieri *see* Fier

Figeac *91 C5* Lot, S France
Figig *see* Figuig
Figueira da Foz *92 B3* Coimbra,
W Portugal
Figueres *93 G2* Cataluña, E Spain
Figuig *70 D2 var.* Figig. E Morocco
Fiji *145 E5 Fij.* Viti. *Country*
SW Pacific Ocean

Fiji 145

Official name Republic of Fiji
Formation 1970
Capital Suva
Population 817,000 / 116 people
per sq mile (45 people per sq km)
Total area 7,054 sq miles
(18,270 sq km)
Languages Fijian, English, Hindi,
Urdu, Tamil, Telegu
Religions Hindu 38%, Methodist
37%, Roman Catholic 9%,
other 16%
Ethnic mix Indian 49%,
Indigenous Fijian 46%, other 5%
Government Multiparty republic
Currency Fiji dollar = 100 cents
Literacy rate 91.8%
Calorie consumption 3,089
kilocalories

Filadelfia *52 D4* Guanacaste,
W Costa Rica
Filiaşi *108 B5* Dolj, SW Romania
Filipstad *85 B6* Värmland,
C Sweden
Finale Ligure *96 A3* Liguria,
NW Italy
Finchley *89 A7* SE England, UK
Findlay *40 C4* Ohio, N USA
Finike *116 B4* Antalya, SW Turkey
Finland *84 D4 Fin.* Suomen
Tasavalta, Suomi. *Country*
N Europe

Finland 84

Official name Republic of Finland
Formation 1917
Capital Helsinki
Population 5.2 million / 44 people
per sq mile (17 people per sq km)
Total area 117,609 sq miles
(304,610 sq km)
Languages Finnish, Swedish,
Lappish
Religions Evangelical Lutheran
89%, Finnish Orthodox 1%, Roman
Catholic 1%, other 9%
Ethnic mix Finnish 93%,
Swedish 6%, other
(including Sami) 1%
Government Multiparty republic
Currency Markka = 100 pennia
Literacy rate 99%
Calorie consumption 3,018
kilocalories

Finland, Gulf of *85 D6 Est.* Soome
Laht, *Fin.* Suomenlahti, *Ger.*
Finnischer Meerbusen, *Rus.*
Finskiy Zaliv, *Swe.* Finska Viken.
Gulf E Baltic Sea
Finnmarksvidda *84 D2 physical
region* N Norway
Finsterwalde *94 D4* Brandenburg,
E Germany
Fiordland *151 A7 physical region*
South Island, NZ
Fiorina *96 E1* NE San Marino
Firenze *96 C3 Eng.* Florence; *anc.*
Florentia. Toscana, C Italy
Fischbacher Alpen *95 E7 mountain
range* E Austria
Fish *78 B4 var.* Vis. *River* S Namibia
Fishguard *89 C6 Wel.* Abergwaun.
SW Wales, UK
Fisterra, Cabo *92 B1 headland*
NW Spain
Fitzroy Crossing *146 C3* Western
Australia
Fitzroy River *146 C3 river* Western
Australia
Flagstaff *48 B2* Arizona, SW USA
Flanders *87 A6 Dut.* Vlaanderen, *Fr.*
Flandre. *Cultural region*
Belgium/France

Flathead Lake *44 B1 lake* Montana,
NW USA
Flat Island *128 C8 island* NE Spratly
Islands
Flatts Village *42 B5 var.* The Flatts
Village. C Bermuda
Flensburg *94 B2* Schleswig-
Holstein, N Germany
Flinders Island *149 C8 island*
Furneaux Group, Tasmania,
SE Australia
Flinders Ranges *149 B6 mountain
range* South Australia
Flinders River *148 C3 river*
Queensland, NE Australia
Flin Flon *37 F5* Manitoba,
C Canada
Flint *40 C3* Michigan, N USA
Flint Island *145 G4 island* Line
Islands, E Kiribati
Floreana, Isla *see* Santa María, Isla
Florence *see* Firenze
Florence *42 C1* Alabama, S USA
Florence *43 F2* South Carolina,
SE USA
Florencia *58 B4* Caquetá,
S Colombia
Florentia *see* Firenze
Flores *92 A5 island* Azores,
Portugal, NE Atlantic Ocean
Flores *139 E5 island* Nusa Tenggara,
C Indonesia
Flores *52 B1* Petén, N Guatemala
Flores Sea *138 D5 Ind.* Laut Flores.
Sea C Indonesia
Floriano *63 F2* Piauí, E Brazil
Florianópolis *63 F5 prev.* Destêrro.
State capital Santa Catarina,
S Brazil
Florida *43 E4 off.* State of Florida;
also known as Peninsular State,
Sunshine State. *State* SE USA
Florida *64 D4* Florida, S Uruguay
Florida Bay *43 E5 bay* Florida,
SE USA
Florida Keys *43 E5 island group*
Florida, SE USA
Florida, Straits of *54 B1 strait*
Atlantic Ocean/Gulf of Mexico
Flórina *104 B4 var.* Phlórina. Dytikí
Makedonía, N Greece
Florissant *45 G4* Missouri, C USA
Florida, Akrotírio *105 D7 headland*
Astypálaia, Kykládes, Greece,
Aegean Sea
Foča *100 C4 var.* Srbinje, Republika
Srpska, SE Bosnia and
Herzegovina
Focşani *108 C4* Vrancea, E Romania
Foggia *97 D5* Puglia, SE Italy
Fogo *74 A3 island* Ilhas de
Sotavento, SW Cape Verde
Foix *91 B6* Ariège, S France
Folégandros *105 C7 island*
Kykládes, Greece, Aegean Sea
Foleyet *38 C4* Ontario, S Canada
Foligno *96 C4* Umbria, C Italy
Folkestone *89 E7* SE England, UK
Fond du Lac *40 B2* Wisconsin,
N USA
Fongafale *145 E3 var.* Funafuti.
Country capital (Tuvalu) Funafuti
Atoll, SE Tuvalu
Fonseca, Gulf of *52 C3 Sp.* Golfo de
Fonseca. *Gulf* Central America
Fontainebleau *90 C3* Seine-et-
Marne, N France
Fontenay-le-Comte *90 B4* Vendée,
NW France
Fontvieille *91 B8* SW Monaco
Fonyód *99 C7* Somogy,
W Hungary
Foochow *see* Fuzhou
Forchheim *95 C5* Bayern,
SE Germany
Forel, Mont *82 D4 mountain*
SE Greenland
Forfar *88 C3* E Scotland, UK
Forge du Sud *see* Dudelange
Forlì *96 C3 anc.* Forum Livii. Emilia-
Romagna, N Italy
Formentera *93 G4 anc.* Ophiusa,
Lat. Frumentum. *Island* Islas
Baleares, Spain, W Mediterranean
Sea
Formosa *64 D2* Formosa,
NE Argentina

Formosa, Serra *63 E3 mountain range* C Brazil
Formosa Strait *see* Taiwan Strait
Forrest City *42 B1* Arkansas, C USA
Fort Albany *38 C3* Ontario, C Canada
Fortaleza *63 G2 prev.* Ceará. *State capital* Ceará, NE Brazil
Fortaleza *61 F2* Pando, N Bolivia
Fort-Bayard *see* Zhanjiang
Fort-Cappolani *see* Tidjikja
Fort Collins *44 D4* Colorado, C USA
Fort Davis *49 E3* Texas, SW USA
Fort-de-France *55 H4 prev.* Fort-Royal. *Dependent territory capital* (Martinique) W Martinique
Fort Dodge *45 F3* Iowa, C USA
Fortescue River *146 A4 river* Western Australia
Fort Frances *38 B4* Ontario, S Canada
Fort Good Hope *37 E3 var.* Good Hope. Northwest Territories, NW Canada
Fort Gouraud *see* Fdérik
Forth *88 C4 river* C Scotland, UK
Forth, Firth of *88 C4 estuary* E Scotland, UK
Fort-Lamy *see* Ndjamena
Fort Lauderdale *43 F5* Florida, SE USA
Fort Liard *37 E4 var.* Liard. Northwest Territories, W Canada
Fort Madison *45 G4* Iowa, C USA
Fort McMurray *37 E4* Alberta, C Canada
Fort McPherson *36 D3 var.* McPherson. Northwest Territories, NW Canada
Fort Morgan *44 D4* Colorado, C USA
Fort Myers *43 E5* Florida, SE USA
Fort Nelson *37 E4* British Columbia, W Canada
Fort Peck Lake *44 C1 reservoir* Montana, NW USA
Fort Pierce *43 F4* Florida, SE USA
Fort Providence *37 E4 var.* Providence. Northwest Territories, W Canada
Fort St.John *37 E4* British Columbia, W Canada
Fort Scott *45 F5* Kansas, C USA
Fort Severn *38 C2* Ontario, C Canada
Fort-Shevchenko *114 A4* Mangistau, W Kazakhstan
Fort Simpson *37 E4 var.* Simpson. Northwest Territories, W Canada
Fort Smith *37 E4 district capital* Northwest Territories, W Canada
Fort Smith *42 B1* Arkansas, C USA
Fort Stockton *49 E3* Texas, SW USA
Fort-Trinquet *see* Bîr Mogreïn
Fort Vermilion *37 E4* Alberta, W Canada
Fort Walton Beach *42 C3* Florida, SE USA
Fort Wayne *40 C4* Indiana, N USA
Fort William *88 C3* N Scotland, UK
Fort Worth *49 G2* Texas, SW USA
Fort Yukon *36 D3* Alaska, USA
Fougamou *77 A6* Ngounié, C Gabon
Fougères *90 B3* Ille-et-Vilaine, NW France
Fou-hsin *see* Fuxin
Foulwind, Cape *151 B5 headland* South Island, NZ
Foumban *76 A4* Ouest, NW Cameroon
Fou-shan *see* Fushun
Foveaux Strait *151 A8 strait* S NZ
Foxe Basin *37 G3 sea* Nunavut, N Canada
Fox Glacier *151 B6* West Coast, South Island, NZ
Fox Mine *37 F4* Manitoba, C Canada
Fraga *93 F2* Aragón, NE Spain
Fram Basin *155 C3 var.* Amundsen Basin. *Undersea feature* Arctic Ocean

France *90 B4 It./Sp.* Francia; *prev.* Gaul, Gaule, *Lat.* Gallia. *Country* W Europe

France 90

Official name French Republic
Formation AD 486
Capital Paris
Population 59 million /
278 people per sq mile
(107 people per sq km)
Total area 212,393 sq miles
(550,100 sq km)
Languages French, Provenial, German, Breton, Catalan, Basque
Religions Roman Catholic 88%, Muslim 8%, Protestant 2%, other 2%
Ethnic mix French 90%, North African 6%, German 2%, other 2%
Government Multiparty republic
Currency French franc = 100 centimes
Literacy rate 99%
Calorie consumption 3,633 kilocalories

Franceville *77 B6 var.* Massoukou, Masuku. Haut-Ogooué, E Gabon
Francfort prev *see* Frankfurt am Main
Franche-Comté *90 D4 cultural region* E France
Francis Case, Lake *45 E3 reservoir* South Dakota, N USA
Francisco Escárcega *51 G4* Campeche, SE Mexico
Francistown *78 D3* North East, NE Botswana
Franconian Jura *see* Fränkische Alb
Frankenalb *see* Fränkische Alb
Frankenstein *see* Ząbkowice Śląskie
Frankenstein in Schlesien *see* Ząbkowice Śląskie
Frankfort *40 C5 state capital* Kentucky, S USA
Frankfort on the Main *see* Frankfurt am Main
Frankfurt *see* Frankfurt am Main
Frankfurt am Main *95 B5 var.* Frankfurt, *Fr.* Francfort; *prev. Eng.* Frankfort on the Main. Hessen, SW Germany
Frankfurt an der Oder *94 D3* Brandenburg, E Germany
Fränkische Alb *95 C6 var.* Frankenalb, *Eng.* Franconian Jura. *Mountain range* S Germany
Franklin *42 C1* Tennessee, S USA
Franklin D.Roosevelt Lake *46 C1 reservoir* Washington, NW USA
Frantsa-Iosifa, Zemlya *114 D1 Eng.* Franz Josef Land. *Island group* N Russian Federation
Franz Josef Land *see* Frantsa-Iosifa, Zemlya
Fraserburgh *88 D3* NE Scotland, UK
Fraser Island *148 E4 var.* Great Sandy Island. *Island* Queensland, E Australia
Fredericksburg *41 E5* Virginia, NE USA
Fredericton *39 F4* New Brunswick, SE Canada
Frederikshåb *see* Paamiut
Fredrikstad *85 B6* Østfold, S Norway
Freeport *54 C1* Grand Bahama Island, N Bahamas
Freeport *49 H4* Texas, SW USA
Freetown *74 C4 country capital* (Sierra Leone) W Sierra Leone
Freiburg *see* Freiburg im Breisgau
Freiburg im Breisgau *95 A6 var.* Freiburg, *Fr.* Fribourg-en-Brisgau. Baden-Württemberg, SW Germany
Fremantle *147 A6* Western Australia
Fremont *45 F4* Nebraska, C USA
French Guiana *59 H3 var.* Guiana, Guyane. *French overseas department* N South America
French Polynesia *143 F4 French overseas territory* C Polynesia

French Southern and Antarctic Territories *141 B7 Fr.* Terres Australes et Antarctiques Françaises. *French overseas territory* S Indian Ocean
Fresnillo *50 D3 var.* Fresnillo de González Echeverría. Zacatecas, C Mexico
Fresnillo de González Echeverría *see* Fresnillo
Fresno *47 C6* California, W USA
Frías *64 C3* Catamarca, N Argentina
Fribourg-en-Brisgau *see* Freiburg im Breisgau
Friedrichshafen *95 B7* Baden-Württemberg, S Germany
Frobisher Bay *82 B3 inlet* Baffin Island, Northwest Territories, NE Canada
Frohavet *84 B4 sound* C Norway
Frome, Lake *149 B6 salt lake* South Australia
Frontera *51 G4* Tabasco, SE Mexico
Froñtignan *91 C6* Hérault, S France
Frostviken *see* Kvarnbergsvattnet
Frøya *84 A4 island* W Norway
Frunze *see* Bishkek
Frýdek-Místek *99 C5 Ger.* Friedek-Mistek. Ostravský Kraj, E Czech Republic
Fu-chien *see* Fujian
Fu-chou *see* Fuzhou
Fuengirola *92 D5* Andalucía, S Spain
Fuerte Olimpo *64 D2 var.* Olimpo. Alto Paraguay, NE Paraguay
Fuerte, Río *48 C5 river* C Mexico
Fuerteventura *70 B3 island* Islas Canarias, Spain, NE Atlantic Ocean
Fuhkien *see* Fujian
Fu-hsin *see* Fuxin
Fuji *131 D6 var.* Huzi. Shizuoka, Honshū, S Japan
Fujian *128 D6 var.* Fu-chien, Fuhkien, Fujian Sheng, Fukien, Min. Admin. region *province* SE China
Fujian Sheng *see* Fujian
Fuji-san *131 C6 var.* Fujiyama, *Eng.* Mount Fuji. *Mountain* Honshū, SE Japan
Fujiyama *see* Fuji-san
Fukang *126 C2* Xinjiang Uygur Zizhiqu, W China
Fukien *see* Fujian
Fukui *131 C6 var.* Hukui. Fukui, Honshū, SW Japan
Fukuoka *131 A7 var.* Hukuoka; *hist.* Najima. Fukuoka, Kyūshū, SW Japan
Fukushima *130 D4 var.* Hukusima. Fukushima, Honshū, C Japan
Fulda *95 B5* Hessen, C Germany
Funafuti *see* Fongafale
Funafuti Atoll *145 E3 atoll* C Tuvalu
Funchal *70 A2* Madeira, Portugal, NE Atlantic Ocean
Fundy, Bay of *39 F5 bay* Canada/USA
Furnes *see* Veurne
Fürth *95 D5* Bayern, S Germany
Furukawa *130 D4 var.* Hurukawa. Miyagi, Honshū, C Japan
Fushun *128 D3 var.* Fou-shan, Fu-shun. Liaoning, NE China
Fu-shun *see* Fushun
Fusin *see* Fuxin
Füssen *95 C7* Bayern, S Germany
Futog *100 D3* Serbia, NW Yugoslavia
Futuna, Île *145 E4 island* S Wallis and Futuna
Fuxin *128 D3 var.* Fou-hsin, Fu-hsin, Fusin. Liaoning, NE China
Fuzhou *128 D6 var.* Foochow, Fu-chou. Fujian, SE China
Fuzhou *see* Linchuan
Fyn *85 B8 Ger.* Fünen. *Island* C Denmark
Fyzabad *see* Feyzābād

G

Gaafu Alifu Atoll *see* North Huvadhu Atoll

Gaafu Dhaalu Atoll *see* South Huvadhu Atoll
Gaalkacyo *73 E5 var.* Galka'yo, *It.* Galcaio. Mudug, C Somalia
Gabela *78 B2* Cuanza Sul, W Angola
Gabès *71 E2 var.* Qâbis. E Tunisia
Gabès, Golfe de *71 F2 Ar.* Khalīj Qâbis. *Gulf* E Tunisia
Gabon *77 B6 Country* C Africa

Gabon 77

Official name Gabonese Republic
Formation 1960
Capital Libreville
Population 1.2 million /
12 people per sq mile
(5 people per sq km)
Total area 99,486 sq miles
(257,670 sq km)
Languages French, Fang, Punu, Sira, Nzebi, Mpongwe
Religions Christian 96%, Muslim 2%, other 2%
Ethnic mix Fang 35%, other Bantu 29%, Eshira 25%, other 11%
Government Multiparty republic
Currency CFA franc = 100 centimes
Literacy rate 66%
Calorie consumption 2,500 kilocalories

Gaborone *78 C4 prev.* Gaberones. *Country capital* (Botswana) South East, SE Botswana
Gabrovo *104 D2* Gabrovo, N Bulgaria
Gadag *132 C1* Karnātaka, W India
Gadsden *42 D2* Alabama, S USA
Gaeta *97 C5* Lazio, C Italy
Gaeta, Golfo di *97 C5 var.* Gulf of Gaeta. *Gulf* C Italy
Gaeta, Gulf of *see* Gaeta, Golfo di
Gäfle *see* Gävle
Gafsa *71 E2 var.* Qafşah. W Tunisia
Gagnoa *74 D5* C Côte d'Ivoire
Gagra *117 E1* NW Georgia
Gaillac *91 C6 var.* Gaillac-sur-Tarn. Tarn, S France
Gaillac-sur-Tarn *see* Gaillac
Gaillimh *see* Galway
Gainesville *43 E3* Florida, SE USA
Gainesville *42 D2* Georgia, SE USA
Gainesville *49 G2* Texas, SW USA
Gairdner, Lake *149 A6 salt lake* South Australia
Gaizin *see* Gaizina Kalns
Gaizina Kalns *106 C3 var.* Gaizin. *Mountain* E Latvia
Galán, Cerro *64 B3 mountain* NW Argentina
Galanta *99 C6 Hung.* Galánta. Trnavský Kraj, W Slovakia
Galapagos Fracture Zone *153 E3 tectonic feature* E Pacific Ocean
Galapagos Islands *153 F3 var.* Islas de los Galápagos, *Tortoise Islands. Island group* Ecuador, E Pacific Ocean
Galapagos Rise *153 F3 undersea feature* E Pacific Ocean
Galashiels *88 C4* SE Scotland, UK
Galaţi *108 D4 Ger.* Galatz. Galaţi, E Romania
Galcaio *see* Gaalkacyo
Galesburg *40 B3* Illinois, N USA
Galicia *92 B1 cultural region* NW Spain
Galicia Bank *80 B4 undersea feature* E Atlantic Ocean
Galilee, Sea of *see* Tiberias, Lake
Galka'yo *see* Gaalkacyo
Galle *132 D4 prev.* Point de Galle. Southern Province, SW Sri Lanka
Gallego Rise *153 F3 undersea feature* E Pacific Ocean
Gallegos *see* Río Gallegos
Gallipoli *97 E6* Puglia, SE Italy
Gällivare *84 C3* Norrbotten, N Sweden
Gallup *48 C1* New Mexico, SW USA
Galtat-Zemmour *70 B3* C Western Sahara
Galveston *49 H4* Texas, SW USA

Galway 89 A5 Ir. Gaillimh.
W Ireland
Galway Bay 89 A6 Ir. Cuan na
Gaillimhe. Bay W Ireland
Gambell 36 C2 Saint Lawrence
Island, Alaska, USA
Gambia 74 C3 Fr. Gambie. River
W Africa
Gambia 74 B3 Country W Africa

Gambia 74

Official name Republic of The
Gambia
Formation 1965
Capital Banjul
Population 1.3 million /
338 people per sq mile
(131 people per sq km)
Total area 3,861 sq miles
(10,000 sq km)
Languages English, Mandinka,
Fulani, Wolof, Diola, Soninke
Religions Muslim 90%, Christian
9%, Traditional beliefs 1%
Ethnic mix Mandingo 42%, Fulani
18%, Wolof 16%, Jola 10%, Serahuli
9%, other 5%
Government Multiparty republic
Currency Dalasi = 100 butut
Literacy rate 33%
Calorie consumption 2,360
kilocalories

Gambier, Îles 143 G4 island group
E French Polynesia
Gamboma 77 B6 Plateaux, E Congo
Gan see Gansu
Gan see Jiangxi
Gan 132 B5 Addu Atoll, C Maldives
Gäncä 117 G2 Rus. Gyandzha; prev.
Kirovabad, Yelisavetpol.
W Azerbaijan
Gandajika 77 D7 Kasai Oriental,
S Dem. Rep. Congo (Zaire)
Gander 39 G3 Newfoundland,
Newfoundland and Labrador,
SE Canada
Gāndhīdhām 134 C4 Gujarāt,
W India
Gandía 93 F3 País Valenciano,
E Spain
Ganges 135 F3 Ben. Padma. River
Bangladesh/India see also Padma
Ganges Cone see Ganges Fan
Ganges Fan 140 D3 var. Ganges
Cone. Undersea feature N Bay of
Bengal
Ganges, Mouths of the 135 G4 delta
Bangladesh/India
Gangra see Çankırı
Gangtok 135 F3 Sikkim, N India
Gansu 128 B4 var. Gan, Gansu
Sheng, Kansu. Admin. region
province N China
Gansu Sheng see Gansu
Ganzhou 128 D6 Jiangxi, S China
Gao 75 E3 Gao, E Mali
Gaoual 74 C4 Moyenne-Guinée,
N Guinea
Gaoxiong see Kaohsiung
Gap 91 D5 anc. Vapincum. Hautes-
Alpes, SE France
Gar 126 A4 var. Gar Xincun. Xizang
Zizhiqu, W China
Garachiné 53 G5 Darién,
SE Panama
Garagum see Garagumy
Garagum Kanaly see Garagumskiy
Kanal
Garagumskiy Kanal 122 D3 var.
Kara Kum Canal, Karakumskiy
Kanal, Turkm. Garagum Kanaly.
Canal C Turkmenistan
Garagumy 122 C3 var. Qara Qum,
Eng. Black Sand Desert, Kara
Kum, Turkm. Garagum; prev. Peski
Karakumy. Desert C Turkmenistan
Gara Khitríno 104 D2 Shumen,
NE Bulgaria
Garda, Lago di C2 var. Benaco,
Eng. Lake Garda, Ger. Gardasee.
Lake NE Italy
Garda, Lake see Garda, Lago di
Gardasee see Garda, Lago di
Garden City 45 E5 Kansas, C USA
Gardeyz see Gardēz

Gardēz 123 E4 var. Gardeyz,
Gordiaz. Paktīā, E Afghanistan
Gargždai 106 B3 Gargždai,
W Lithuania
Garissa 73 D6 Coast, E Kenya
Garland 49 G2 Texas, SW USA
Garman, Loch see Wexford
Garoe see Garoowe
Garonne 91 B5 anc. Garumna. River
S France
Garoowe 73 E5 var. Garoe. Nugaal,
N Somalia
Garoua 76 B4 var. Garua. Nord,
N Cameroon
Garrygala see Kara-Kala
Garry Lake 37 F3 lake Nunavut,
N Canada
Garsen 73 D6 Coast, S Kenya
Garua see Garoua
Garwolin 98 D4 Mazowieckie,
C Poland
Gar Xincun see Gar
Gary 40 B3 Indiana, N USA
Garzón 58 B4 Huila, S Colombia
Gascogne 91 B6 Eng. Gascony.
Cultural region S France
Gascoyne River 147 A5 river
Western Australia
Gaspé 39 F3 Québec, SE Canada
Gaspé, Péninsule de 39 E4 var.
Péninsule de la Gaspésie.
Peninsula Québec, SE Canada
Gastonia 43 E1 North Carolina,
SE USA
Gastoúni 105 B6 Dytikí Ellás,
S Greece
Gatchina 110 B4 Leningradskaya
Oblast', NW Russian Federation
Gatineau 38 D4 Québec, SE Canada
Gatún, Lago 53 F4 reservoir
C Panama
Gauja 106 D3 Ger. Aa. River
Estonia/Latvia
Gauteng see Johannesburg
Gāvbandī 120 D4 Hormozgān,
S Iran
Gávdos, Isla 105 C8 island SE Greece
Gavere 87 B6 Oost-Vlaanderen,
NW Belgium
Gävle 85 C6 var. Gäfle; prev. Gefle.
Gävleborg, C Sweden
Gawler 149 B6 South Australia
Gaya 135 F3 Bihār, N India
Gayndah 149 E5 Queensland,
E Australia
Gaza 119 A6 Ar. Ghazzah, Heb.
'Azza. NE Gaza Strip
Gaz-Achak 122 D2 Turkm. Gazojak.
Lebapskiy Velayat,
NE Turkmenistan
Gazandzhyk 122 B2 Turkm.
Gazanjyk; prev. Kazandzhik.
Balkanskiy Velayat,
W Turkmenistan
Gaza Strip 119 A7 Ar. Qiṭā'
Ghazzah. Disputed region SW Asia
Gazi Antep see Gaziantep
Gaziantep 116 D4 var. Gazi Antep;
prev. Aintab, Antep. Gaziantep,
S Turkey
Gazimağusa see Ammóchostos
Gazimağusa Körfezi see Kólpos
Ammóchostos
Gazli 122 D2 Bukhoro Wiloyati,
C Uzbekistan
Gbanga 74 D5 var. Gbarnga.
N Liberia
Gbarnga see Gbanga
Gdańsk 98 C2 Fr. Dantzig, Ger.
Danzig. Pomorskie, N Poland
Gdan'skaya Bukhta see Danzig,
Gulf of
Pomorskie, Gulf of see Danzig,
Gulf of
Gdynia 98 C2 Ger. Gdingen.
Pomorskie, N Poland
Gedaref 72 C4 var. Al Qaḍārif,
El Gedaref. Gedaref, E Sudan
Gediz 116 B3 Kütahya, W Turkey
Gediz Nehri 116 A3 river W Turkey
Geel 87 C5 var. Gheel. Antwerpen,
N Belgium
Geelong 149 C7 Victoria,
SE Australia
Ge'e'mu see Golmud
Gefle see Gävle
Geilo 85 A5 Buskerud, S Norway

Gejiu 128 B6 var. Kochiu. Yunnan,
S China
Gëkdepe see Geok-Tepe
Gela 97 C7 prev. Terranova di
Sicilia. Sicilia, Italy,
C Mediterranean Sea
Geldermalsen 86 C4 Gelderland,
C Netherlands
Geleen 87 D6 Limburg,
SE Netherlands
Gelinsoor see Gellinsoor
Gellinsoor 73 E5 var. Gelinsoor.
Mudug, NE Somalia
Gembloux 87 C6 Namur, Belgium
Gemena 77 C5 Equateur, NW Dem.
Rep. Congo (Zaire)
Gemona del Friuli 96 D2 Friuli-
Venezia Giulia, NE Italy
Genck see Genk
General Alvear 64 B4 Mendoza,
W Argentina
General Eugenio A.Garay 64 C1
Guairá, S Paraguay
General Machado see Camacupa
General Santos 139 F3 off. General
Santos City. Mindanao,
S Philippines
Geneva see Genève
Geneva, Lake A7 Fr. Lac de
Genève, Lac Léman, le Léman,
Ger. Genfer See. Lake
France/Switzerland
Genève 95 A7 Eng. Geneva, Ger.
Genf, It. Ginevra. Genève,
SW Switzerland
Genf see Genève
Genk 87 D6 var. Genck. Limburg,
NE Belgium
Gennep 86 D4 Limburg,
SE Netherlands
Genoa see Genova
Genova 102 D1 Eng. Genoa, Fr.
Gênes; anc. Genua. Liguria,
NW Italy
Genova, Golfo di 96 A3 Eng. Gulf
of Genoa. Gulf NW Italy
Genovesa, Isla 60 B5 var. Tower
Island. Island Galapagos Islands,
Ecuador, E Pacific Ocean
Gent 87 B5 Eng. Ghent, Fr. Gand.
Oost-Vlaanderen, NW Belgium
Geok-Tepe 122 C3 var. Gëkdepe,
Turkm. Gökdepe. Akhalskiy
Velayat, C Turkmenistan
George 82 A4 river Newfoundland
and Labrador/Québec, E Canada
George 78 C5 Western Cape,
S South Africa
George, Lake 43 E3 lake Florida,
SE USA
Georges Bank 35 D5 undersea
feature W Atlantic Ocean
George Sound 151 A7 sound South
Island, NZ
Georges River 148 D2 river New
South Wales, SE Australia
George Town 54 B3 var.
Georgetown. Dependent territory
capital (Cayman Islands) Grand
Cayman, SW Cayman Islands
George Town 138 B3 var. Penang,
Pinang. Pinang, Peninsular
Malaysia
George Town 54 C2 Great Exuma
Island, C Bahamas
Georgetown 59 F2 country capital
(Guyana) N Guyana
Georgetown 43 F2 South Carolina,
SE USA
George V Land 154 C4 physical
region Antarctica
Georgia 117 F2 Geor. Sak'art'velo,
Rus. Gruzinskaya SSR, Gruziya;
prev. Georgian SSR. Country
SW Asia

Georgia 117

Official name Republic of
Georgia
Formation 1991
Capital Tbilisi
Population 5 million / 186 people
per sq mile (72 people per sq km)
Total area 26,911 sq miles
(69,700 sq km)

Georgia (continued)

Languages Georgian, Russian
Religions Georgian
Orthodox 70%, Russian Orthodox
10%, other 20%
Ethnic mix Georgian 70%,
Armenian 8%, Russian 6%,
Azeri 6%, Ossetian 3%, other 7%
Government Multiparty republic
Currency Lari = 100 tetri
Literacy rate 99%
Calorie consumption
not available

Georgia 42 D2 off. State of Georgia;
also known as Empire State of the
South, Peach State. State SE USA
Georgian Bay 40 D2 lake bay
Ontario, S Canada
Georgia, Strait of 46 A1 strait
British Columbia, W Canada
Georg von Neumayer 154 A2
German research station Antarctica
Gera 94 C4 Thüringen, E Germany
Geráki 105 B6 Pelopónnisos,
S Greece
Geraldine 151 B6 Canterbury, South
Island, NZ
Geraldton 147 A6 Western Australia
Geral, Serra 57 D5 mountain range
S Brazil
Gerede 116 C2 Bolu, N Turkey
Gereshk 122 D5 Helmand,
SW Afghanistan
Gering 44 D3 Nebraska, C USA
Germanicopolis see Çankırı
Germany 94 B4 Ger.
Bundesrepublik Deutschland,
Deutschland. Country N Europe

Germany 94

Official name Federal Republic of
Germany
Formation 1871
Capital Berlin
Population 82.2 million /
609 people per sq mile
(235 people per sq km)
Total area 134,949 sq miles
(349,520 sq km)
Languages German
Religions Protestant 36%,
Roman Catholic 35%, Muslim 2%,
other 27%
Ethnic mix German 92%,
other 8%
Government Multiparty republic
Currency Deutsche Mark
= 100 pfennigs
Literacy rate 99%
Calorie consumption 3,344
kilocalories

Gerolimémas 105 B7 Pelopónnisos,
S Greece
Gerona see Girona
Gerpinnes 87 C7 Hainaut,
S Belgium
Gerunda see Girona
Gerze 116 D2 Sinop, N Turkey
Gesoriacum see Boulogne-sur-Mer
Gessoriacum see Boulogne-sur-Mer
Getafe 92 D3 Madrid, C Spain
Gevaş 117 F3 Van, SE Turkey
Gevgeli see Gevgelija
Gevgelija 101 E6 var. Đevđelija,
Djevdjelija, Turk. Gevgeli. SE FYR
Macedonia
Ghaba see Al Ghābah
Ghana 75 E5 Country W Africa

Ghana 75

Official name Republic of Ghana
Formation 1957
Capital Accra
Population 20.2 million /
227 people per sq mile
(88 people per sq km)
Total area 88,810 sq miles
(230,020 sq km)
Languages English, Twi, Fanti,
Ewe, Ga, Adangbe, Gurma,
Dagomba

Ghana (continued)

Religions Christian 43%, Traditional beliefs 38%, Muslim 11%, other 8%
Ethnic mix Akan 44%, Moshi-Dagomba 16%, Ewe 13%, Ga 8%, other 19%
Government Multiparty republic
Currency Cedi = 100 pesewas
Literacy rate 66.4% ,
Calorie consumption 2,199 kilocalories

Ghanzi 78 C3 *var.* Khanzi. Ghanzi, W Botswana
Gharandal 119 B7 Maʿān, SW Jordan
Ghardaïa 70 D2 N Algeria
Gharvān *see* Gharyān
Gharyān 71 F2 *var.* Gharvān. NW Libya
Ghaznī 123 E4 *var.* Ghazni. Ghaznī, E Afghanistan
Ghazni *see* Ghaznī
Gheel *see* Geel
Gheorgheni 108 C4 *prev.* Gheorghieni, Sînt-Miclăuş, *Ger.* Niklasmarkt, *Hung.* Gyergyószentmiklós. Harghita, C Romania
Ghijduwon 122 D2 *Rus.* Gizhduvan. Bukhoro Wiloyati, C Uzbekistan
Ghūdara 123 F3 *var.* Gudara, *Rus.* Kudara. SE Tajikistan
Ghurdaqah *see* Hurghada
Ghūriān 122 D4 Herāt, W Afghanistan
Giannitsá 104 B4 *var.* Yiannitsá. Kentrikí Makedonía, N Greece
Gibraltar 93 G4 UK *dependent territory* SW Europe
Gibraltar, Bay of 93 G5 *bay* Gibraltar/Spain
Gibraltar, Strait of 92 C5 *Fr.* Détroit de Gibraltar, *Sp.* Estrecho de Gibraltar. *Strait* Atlantic Ocean/Mediterranean Sea
Gibson Desert 147 B5 *desert* Western Australia
Giedraičiai 107 C5 Molėtai, E Lithuania
Giessen 95 B5 Hessen, W Germany
Gifu 131 C6 *var.* Gihu. Gifu, Honshū, SW Japan
Giganta, Sierra de la 50 B3 *mountain range* W Mexico
Gihu *see* Gifu
Gijón 92 D1 *var.* Xixón. Asturias, NW Spain
Gilani *see* Gnjilane
Gila River 48 A2 *river* Arizona, SW USA
Gilbert River 148 C3 *river* Queensland, NE Australia
Gilf Kebir Plateau 72 A2 Ar. Haḍabat al Jilf al Kabīr. *Plateau* SW Egypt
Gillette 44 D3 Wyoming, C USA
Gilroy 47 B6 California, W USA
Gimie, Mount 55 F1 *mountain* C Saint Lucia
Gimma *see* Jīma
Ginevra *see* Genève
Gingin 147 A6 Western Australia
Giohar *see* Jawhar
Girardot 58 B3 Cundinamarca, C Colombia
Giresun 117 E2 *var.* Kerasunt; *anc.* Cerasus, Pharnacia. Giresun, NE Turkey
Girin *see* Jilin
Girne *see* Kerýneia
Girona 93 G2 *var.* Gerona; *anc.* Gerunda. Cataluña, NE Spain
Gisborne 150 E3 Gisborne, North Island, NZ
Gissar Range 123 E3 *Rus.* Gissarskiy Khrebet. *Mountain range* Tajikistan/Uzbekistan
Githio *see* Gýtheio
Giulianova 96 D4 Abruzzo, C Italy
Giumri *see* Gyumri
Giurgiu 108 C5 Giurgiu, S Romania

Gîza *see* El Gîza
Gizeh *see* El Gîza
Giżyeko 98 D2 Warmiúsko-Mazurskie, NE Poland
Gjakovë *see* Đakovica
Gjilan *see* Gnjilane
Gjinokastër *see* Gjirokastër
Gjirokastër 101 C7 *var.* Gjirokastra; *prev.* Gjinokastër, *Gk.* Argyrokastron, *It.* Argirocastro. Gjirokastër, S Albania
Gjirokastra *see* Gjirokastër
Gjoa Haven 37 F3 King William Island, Nunavut, NW Canada
Gjøvik 85 B5 Oppland, S Norway
Glace Bay 39 G4 Cape Breton Island, Nova Scotia, SE Canada
Gladstone 148 E4 Queensland, E Australia
Glåma 85 B5 *river* SE Norway
Glasgow 88 C4 S Scotland, UK
Glavn'a Morava *see* Velika Morava
Glazov 111 D5 Udmurtskaya Respublika, NW Russian Federation
Glendale 48 B2 Arizona, SW USA
Glendive 44 D2 Montana, NW USA
Glens Falls 41 F3 New York, NE USA
Glina 100 B3 Sisak-Moslavina, NE Croatia
Glittertind 85 A5 *mountain* S Norway
Gliwice 99 C5 Ger. Gleiwitz. Śląskie, S Poland
Globe 48 B2 Arizona, SW USA
Głogów 98 B4 *Ger.* Glogau, Glogow. Dolnośląskie
Gloucester 89 D6 *hist.* Caer Glou, *Lat.* Glevum. C England, UK
Głowno 98 D4 Łódź, C Poland
Gniezno 98 C4 *Ger.* Gnesen. Wielkopolskie, C Poland
Gnjilane 101 D5 *var.* Gilani, *Alb.* Gjilan. Serbia, S Yugoslavia
Goa *see* Panaji
Gobabis 78 B3 Omaheke, E Namibia
Gobi 126 D3 *desert* China/Mongolia
Gobō 131 C6 Wakayama, Honshū, SW Japan
Godāvari 124 B3 *var.* Godavari. *River* C India
Godhavn *see* Qeqertarsuaq
Godhra 134 C4 Gujarāt, W India
Godoy Cruz 64 B4 Mendoza, W Argentina
Godthaab *see* Nuuk
Godthåb *see* Nuuk
Goeree 86 B4 *island* SW Netherlands
Goes 87 B5 Zeeland, SW Netherlands
Goettingen *see* Göttingen
Gogebic Range 40 B1 *hill range* Michigan/Wisconsin, N USA
Goiânia 63 E3 *prev.* Goyania. State capital Goiás, C Brazil
Goiás 63 E3 Goiás, C Brazil
Gojōme 130 D4 Akita, Honshū, NW Japan
Gökçeada 104 D4 *var.* Imroz Adası, *Gk.* Imbros. *Island* NW Turkey
Gökdepe *see* Geok-Tepe
Göksun 116 D4 Kahramanmaraş, C Turkey
Gol 85 A5 Buskerud, S Norway
Golan Heights 119 B5 *Ar.* Al Jawlān, *Heb.* HaGolan. *Mountain range* SW Syria
Goldap 98 E2 *Ger.* Goldap. Warmińsko-Mazurskie, NE Poland
Gold Coast 149 E5 *cultural region* Queensland, E Australia
Golden Bay 150 C4 *bay* South Island, NZ
Goldsboro 43 F1 North Carolina, SE USA
Goleniów 98 B3 *Ger.* Gollnow. Zachodniopomorskie, NW Poland
Golmo *see* Golmud
Golub-Dobrzyń 98 C3 Kujawski-pomorskie, C Poland
Golmud 126 D4 *var.* Ge'e'mu, Golmo, *Chin.* Ko-erh-mu. Qinghai, C China

Goma 77 E6 Nord Kivu, NE Dem. Rep. Congo (Zaire)
Gombi 75 H4 Adamawa, E Nigeria
Gombroon *see* Bandar-e 'Abbās
Gomera 70 A3 *island* Islas Canarias, Spain, NE Atlantic Ocean
Gómez Palacio 50 D3 Durango, C Mexico
Gonaïves 54 D3 *var.* Les Gonaïves. N Haiti
Gonâve, Île de la 54 D3 *island* C Haiti
Gondar *see* Gonder
Gonder 72 C4 *var.* Gondar. N Ethiopia
Gondia 135 E4 Mahārāshtra, C India
Gonggar 126 C5 Xizang Zizhiqu, W China
Gongola 75 G4 *river* E Nigeria
Gonni *see* Gónnoi
Gónnoi 104 B4 *var.* Gonni, Gónnos; *prev.* Derelí. Thessalía, C Greece
Gónnos *see* Gónnoi
Good Hope *see* Fort Good Hope
Good Hope, Cape of 78 B5 *Afr.* Kaap de Goede Hoop, Kaap die Goeie Hoop. *Headland* SW South Africa
Goodland 44 D4 Kansas, C USA
Goondiwindi 149 D5 Queensland, E Australia
Goor 86 E3 Overijssel, E Netherlands
Goose Green 65 D7 *var.* Prado del Ganso. East Falkland, Falkland Islands
Goose Lake 46 B4 *var.* Lago dos Gansos. *Lake* California/Oregon, W USA
Göppingen 95 B6 Baden-Württemberg, SW Germany
Gora Andryu *see* Andrew Tablemount
Gora El'brus *see* El'brus
Góra Kalwaria 114 D4 Mazowieckie, C Poland
Gorakhpur 135 E3 Uttar Pradesh, N India
Goražde 100 C4 Federacija Bosna I Hercegovina, SE Bosnia and Herzegovina
Gordiaz *see* Gardēz
Gore 151 B7 Southland, South Island, NZ
Gorē 73 C5 C Ethiopia
Goré 76 C4 Logone-Oriental, S Chad
Gorgān 120 D2 *var.* Astarabad, Astrabad, Gurgan; *prev.* Asterābād, *anc.* Hyrcania. Golestān, N Iran
Gori 117 F2 C Georgia
Gorinchem 86 C4 *var.* Gorkum. Zuid-Holland, C Netherlands
Goris 117 G3 SE Armenia
Gorkum *see* Gorinchem
Görlitz 94 D4 Sachsen, E Germany
Gornji Milanovac 100 C4 Serbia, C Yugoslavia
Gorontalo 139 E4 Sulawesi, C Indonesia
Gorontalo, Teluk *see* Tomini, Gulf of
Gorssel 86 D3 Gelderland, E Netherlands
Gory Putorana *see* Putorana, Plato
Gorzów Wielkopolski 98 B3 *Ger.* Landsberg, Landsberg an der Warthe. Lubuskie, W Poland
Gosford 149 D6 New South Wales, SE Australia
Goshogawara 130 D3 *var.* Gosyogawara. Aomori, Honshū, C Japan
Gospić 100 A3 Lika-Senj, C Croatia
Gostivar 101 D6 W FYR Macedonia
Gosyogawara *see* Goshogawara
Göteborg 85 B7 *Eng.* Gothenburg. Västra Götaland, S Sweden
Gotel Mountains 75 G5 *mountain range* E Nigeria
Gotha 94 C4 Thüringen, C Germany
Gothenburg *see* Göteborg
Gothenburg 80 D3 Nebraska, C USA

Gotland 85 C7 *island* SE Sweden
Gotō-rettō 131 A7 *island group* SW Japan
Gotska Sandön 106 B1 *island* SE Sweden
Gōtsu 131 B6 *var.* Gôtu. Shimane, Honshū, SW Japan
Göttingen 94 B4 *var.* Goettingen. Niedersachsen, C Germany
Gôtu *see* Gōtsu
Gouda 86 C4 Zuid-Holland, C Netherlands
Gough Fracture Zone 67 C6 *tectonic feature* S Atlantic Ocean
Gough Island 69 B8 *island* Tristan da Cunha, S Atlantic Ocean
Gouin, Réservoir 38 D4 *reservoir* Québec, SE Canada
Goulburn 149 D6 New South Wales, SE Australia
Goundam 75 E3 Tombouctou, NW Mali
Gouré 75 G3 Zinder, SE Niger
Governador Valadares 63 F4 Minas Gerais, SE Brazil
Govī Altayn Nuruu 127 E3 *mountain range* S Mongolia
Goya 64 D3 Corrientes, NE Argentina
Goz Beïda 76 C3 Ouaddaï, SE Chad
Gozo 97 C8 *Malt.* Ghawdex. *Island* N Malta
Graciosa 92 A5 *var.* Ilha Graciosa. *Island* Azores, Portugal, NE Atlantic Ocean
Gradačac 100 C3 Federacija Bosna I Hercegovina, N Bosnia and Herzegovina
Gradaús, Serra dos 63 E3 *mountain range* C Brazil
Gradiška *see* Bosanska Gradiška
Grafton 149 E5 New South Wales, SE Australia
Grafton 45 E1 North Dakota, N USA
Graham Land 154 A2 *physical region* Antarctica
Grajewo 98 E3 Podlaskie, NE Poland
Grampian Mountains 88 C3 *mountain range* C Scotland, UK
Granada 92 D5 Andalucía, S Spain
Granada 52 D3 Granada, SW Nicaragua
Gran Canaria 70 A3 *var.* Grand Canary. *Island* Islas Canarias, Spain, NE Atlantic Ocean
Gran Chaco 62 D2 *var.* Chaco. *Lowland plain* South America
Grand *see* Cockburn Town
Grand Bahama Island 54 B1 *island* N Bahamas
Grand Banks of Newfoundland 34 E4 *undersea feature* NW Atlantic Ocean
Grand Canary *see* Gran Canaria
Grand Canyon 48 A1 *canyon* Arizona, SW USA
Grand Cayman 54 B3 *island* SW Cayman Islands
Grande, Bahía 65 B7 *bay* S Argentina
Grande Comore 79 F2 *var.* Njazidja, Great Comoro. *Island* NW Comoros
Grande de Chiloé, Isla *see* Chiloé, Isla de
Grand Prairie 37 E4 Alberta, W Canada
Grand Erg Occidental 70 D3 *desert* W Algeria
Grand Erg Oriental 71 E3 *desert* Algeria/Tunisia
Grande, Rio 35 B6 *var.* Río Bravo, *Sp.* Río Bravo del Norte, Bravo del Norte. *River* Mexico/USA
Grande, Rio 49 F4 *river* Texas, SW USA
Grande, Rio *see* Bravo, Río
Grande, Rio 51 E2 *river* S Mexico
Grande Terre 55 G3 *island* E West Indies
Grand Falls 39 G3 Newfoundland, Newfoundland and Labrador, SE Canada
Grand Forks 45 E1 North Dakota, N USA

Grand Island 45 E4 Nebraska, C USA
Grand Junction 44 C4 Colorado, C USA
Grand Rapids 40 C3 Michigan, N USA
Grand Rapids 45 F1 Minnesota, N USA
Grand-Santi 59 G3 W French Guiana
Gran Lago see Nicaragua, Lago de
Gran Malvina, Isla see West Falkland
Gran Paradiso 96 A2 Fr. Grand Paradis. Mountain NW Italy
Gran Santiago see Santiago
Grants 48 C2 New Mexico, SW USA
Grants Pass 46 B4 Oregon, NW USA
Granville 90 B3 Manche, N France
Graulhet 91 C6 Tarn, S France
Grave 86 D4 Noord-Brabant, SE Netherlands
Grayling 36 C2 Alaska, USA
Graz 95 E7 prev. Gratz. Steiermark, SE Austria
Great Abaco 54 C1 var. Abaco Island. Island N Bahamas
Great Alfold see Great Hungarian Plain
Great Ararat see Büyükağrı Dağı
Great Australian Bight 147 D7 bight S Australia
Great Barrier Island 150 D2 island N NZ
Great Barrier Reef 148 D2 reef Queensland, NE Australia
Great Basin 47 C5 basin W USA
Great Bear Lake 37 E3 Fr. Grand Lac de l'Ours. Lake Northwest Territories, NW Canada
Great Belt see Storebælt
Great Bend 45 E5 Kansas, C USA
Great Bermuda see Bermuda
Great Britain see Britain
Great Comoro see Grande Comore
Great Dividing Range 148 D4 mountain range NE Australia
Greater Antarctica 154 C3 var. East Antarctica. Physical region Antarctica
Greater Antilles 54 D3 island group West Indies
Greater Caucasus 117 G2 Az. Bas Qafqaz Silsiläsi, Geor. Kavkasioni, Rus. Bol'shoy Kavkaz. Mountain range Asia/Europe
Greater Sunda Islands 124 D5 var. Sunda Islands. Island group Indonesia
Great Exhibition Bay 150 C1 inlet North Island, NZ
Great Exuma Island 54 C2 island C Bahamas
Great Falls 44 B1 Montana, NW USA
Great Hungarian Plain 99 C7 var. Great Alfold, Plain of Hungary, Hung. Alföld. Plain SE Europe
Great Inagua 54 D2 var. Inagua Islands. Island S Bahamas
Great Indian Desert see Thar Desert
Great Karroo see Great Karoo
Great Lakes 35 C5 lakes Ontario, Canada/USA
Great Meteor Seamount see Great Meteor Tablemount
Great Meteor Tablemount 66 B3 var. Great Meteor Seamount. Undersea feature E Atlantic Ocean
Great Nicobar 133 G3 island Nicobar Islands, India, NE Indian Ocean
Great Plain of China 125 E2 plain E China
Great Plains 45 E3 var. High Plains. Plains Canada/USA
Great Rift Valley 73 C5 var. Rift Valley. Depression Asia/Africa
Great Ruaha 73 C7 river S Tanzania
Great Saint Bernard Pass 96 A1 Fr. Col du Grand-Saint-Bernard, It. Passo di Gran San Bernardo. Pass Italy/Switzerland
Great Salt Desert see Kavīr, Dasht-e

Great Salt Lake 44 A3 salt lake Utah, W USA
Great Salt Lake Desert 44 A4 plain Utah, W USA
Great Sand Sea 71 H3 desert Egypt/Libya
Great Sandy Desert 146 C4 desert Western Australia
Great Sandy Island see Fraser Island
Great Slave Lake 37 E4 Fr. Grand Lac des Esclaves. Lake Northwest Territories, NW Canada
Great Sound 42 A5 bay Bermuda, NW Atlantic Ocean
Great Victoria Desert 147 C5 desert South Australia/Western Australia
Great Wall of China 128 C4 ancient monument N China
Great Yarmouth 89 E6 var. Yarmouth. E England, UK
Gredos, Sierra de 92 D3 mountain range W Spain
Greece 111 C6 Gk. Ellás; anc. Hellas. Country SE Europe

Greece 105

Official name Hellenic Republic
Formation 1829
Capital Athens
Population 10.6 million / 210 people per sq mile (81 people per sq km)
Total area 50,520 sq miles (130,850 sq km)
Languages Greek, Turkish, Macedonian, Albanian
Religions Greek Orthodox 98%, Muslim 1%, other 1%
Ethnic mix Greek 98%, other 2%
Government Multiparty republic
Currency Drachma = 100 lepta
Literacy rate 96.6%
Calorie consumption 3,815 kilocalories

Greece 81 E5 New York, NE USA
Greeley 44 D4 Colorado, C USA
Green Bay 40 B2 lake bay Michigan/Wisconsin, N USA
Green Bay 40 B2 Wisconsin, N USA
Greeneville 43 E1 Tennessee, S USA
Greenland 82 D3 Dan. Grønland, Inuit Kalaallit Nunaat. Danish external territory NE North America
Greenland Sea 83 F2 sea Arctic Ocean
Green Mountains 41 G2 mountain range Vermont, NE USA
Greenock 88 C4 W Scotland, UK
Green River 40 C5 river Kentucky, C USA
Green River 44 B4 river Utah, W USA
Green River 44 B3 Wyoming, C USA
Greensboro 43 F1 North Carolina, SE USA
Greenville 42 B2 Mississippi, S USA
Greenville 43 F1 North Carolina, SE USA
Greenville 43 E1 South Carolina, SE USA
Greenville 49 G2 Texas, SW USA
Greenwich 89 B8 SE England, UK
Greenwood 42 B2 Mississippi, S USA
Greenwood 43 E2 South Carolina, SE USA
Gregory Range 148 C3 mountain range Queensland, E Australia
Greifswald 94 D2 Mecklenburg-Vorpommern, NE Germany
Grenada 55 G5 country SE West Indies

Grenada 55

Official name Grenada
Formation 1974
Capital St. George's

Grenada (continued)

Population 96,000 / 731 people per sq mile (282 people per sq km)
Total area 131 sq miles (340 sq km)
Languages English, English Creole
Religions Roman Catholic 68%, Anglican 17%, other 15%
Ethnic mix Black 84%, European-African 13%, South Asian 3%
Government Parliamentary democracy
Currency East Caribbean dollar = 100 cents
Literacy rate 96%
Calorie consumption 2,402 kilocalories

Grenada 42 C2 Mississippi, S USA
Grenadines, The 55 H4 island group Grenada/St Vincent and the Grenadines
Grenoble 91 D5 anc. Cularo, Gratianopolis. Isère, E France
Gresham 46 B3 Oregon, NW USA
Grevená 104 B4 Dytikí Makedonía, N Greece
Grevenmacher 87 E8 Grevenmacher, E Luxembourg
Greymouth 151 B5 West Coast, South Island, NZ
Grey Range 149 C5 mountain range New South Wales/Queensland, E Australia
Greytown see San Juan del Norte
Griffin 42 D2 Georgia, SE USA
Grimari 76 C4 Ouaka, C Central African Republic
Grimsby 89 E5 prev. Great Grimsby. E England, UK
Grobiņa 106 B3 Ger. Grobin. Liepāja, W Latvia
Grodzisk Wielkopolski 98 B3 Wielkopolskie, C Poland
Groesbeek 86 D4 Gelderland, SE Netherlands
Grójec 98 D4 Mazowieckie, C Poland
Groningen 86 E1 Groningen, NE Netherlands
Groote Eylandt 148 B2 island Northern Territory, N Australia
Grootfontein 78 B3 Otjozondjupa, N Namibia
Groot Karasberge 78 B4 mountain range S Namibia
Groot Karoo see Great Karoo
Gros Islet 55 F1 N Saint Lucia
Grosse Morava see Velika Morava
Grosseto 96 B4 Toscana, C Italy
Grossglockner 95 C7 mountain W Austria
Groznyy 111 B8 Chechenskaya Respublika, SW Russian Federation
Grudziądz 98 C3 Ger. Graudenz. Kujawski-pomorskie, C Poland
Grums 85 B6 Värmland, C Sweden
Gryazi 111 B6 Lipetskaya Oblast', W Russian Federation
Gryfice 98 B2 Ger. Greifenberg, Greifenberg in Pommern. Zachodniopomorskie, NW Poland
Guabito 53 E4 Bocas del Toro, NW Panama
Guadalajara 93 E3 Ar. Wad Al-Hajarah; anc. Arriaca. Castilla-La Mancha, C Spain
Guadalajara 50 D4 Jalisco, C Mexico
Guadalcanal 144 C3 island C Solomon Islands
Guadalquivir 92 D4 river W Spain
Guadalupe 50 D3 Zacatecas, C Mexico
Guadalupe Peak 48 D3 mountain Texas, SW USA
Guadalupe River 49 G4 river SW USA
Guadarrama, Sierra de 93 E2 mountain range C Spain
Guadeloupe 55 H3 French overseas department E West Indies

Guadiana 92 C4 river Portugal/Spain
Guadix 93 E4 Andalucía, S Spain
Guaimaca 52 C2 Francisco Morazán, C Honduras
Guajira, Península de la 58 B1 peninsula N Colombia
Gualaco 52 D2 Olancho, C Honduras
Gualán 52 B2 Zacapa, C Guatemala
Gualdicciolo 96 D1 NW San Marino
Gualeguaychú 64 D4 Entre Ríos, E Argentina
Guam 144 B1 US unincorporated territory W Pacific Ocean
Guamúchil 50 C3 Sinaloa, C Mexico
Guanabacoa 54 B2 La Habana, W Cuba
Guanajuato 51 E4 Guanajuato, C Mexico
Guanare 58 C2 Portuguesa, N Venezuela
Guanare, Río 58 D2 river W Venezuela
Guangdong 128 C6 var. Guangdong Sheng, Kuang-tung, Kwangtung, Yue. Admin. region province S China
Guangdong Sheng see Guangdong
Guangxi see Guangxi Zhuangzu Zizhiqu
Guangxi Zhuangzu Zizhiqu 128 C6 var. Guangxi, Gui, Kuang-hsi, Kwangsi, Eng. Kwangsi Chuang Autonomous Region. Admin. region autonomous region S China
Guangyuan 128 B5 var. Kuang-yuan, Kwangyuan. Sichuan, C China
Guangzhou 128 C6 var. Kuang-chou, Kwangchow, Eng. Canton. Guangdong, S China
Guantánamo 54 D3 Guantánamo, SE Cuba
Guaporé, Río 62 D3 var. Río Iténez. River Bolivia/Brazil see also Iténez, Río
Guarda 92 C3 Guarda, N Portugal
Guarumal 53 F5 Veraguas, S Panama
Guasave 50 C3 Sinaloa, C Mexico
Guatemala 52 A2 Country Central America

Guatemala 52

Official name Republic of Guatemala
Formation 1838
Capital Guatemala City
Population 11.4 million / 272 people per sq mile (105 people per sq km)
Total area 41,864 sq miles (108,430 sq km)
Languages Spanish, Quiché, Mam, Cakchiquel, Kekchí
Religions Christian 99%, other 1%
Ethnic mix Amerindian 60%, Mestizo 30%, other 10%
Government Multiparty republic
Currency Quetzal = 100 centavos
Literacy rate 66.6%
Calorie consumption 2,255 kilocalories

Guatemala Basin 35 B7 undersea feature E Pacific Ocean
Guatemala City see Ciudad de Guatemala
Guaviare 56 B2 off. Comisaría Guaviare. Province N Colombia
Guaviare, Río 58 D3 river E Colombia
Guayaquil 60 A2 var. Santiago de Guayaquil. Guayas, SW Ecuador
Guayaquil, Golfo de 60 A2 var. Gulf of Guayaquil. Gulf SW Ecuador
Guayaquil, Gulf of see Guayaquil, Golfo de
Guaymas 50 B2 Sonora, NW Mexico
Gubadag 122 C2 Turkm. Tel'man; prev. Tel'mansk. Dashkhovuzskiy Velayat, N Turkmenistan

Guben *94 D4 var.* Wilhelm-Pieck-Stadt. Brandenburg, E Germany
Gubkin *111 B6* Belgorodskaya Oblast', W Russian Federation
Gudara *see* Ghŭdara
Gudaut'a *117 E1* NW Georgia
Guéret *90 C4* Creuse, C France
Guernsey *89 D8 UK dependent territory* NW Europe
Guerrero Negro *50 A2* Baja California Sur, NW Mexico
Gui *see* Guangxi Zhuangzu Zizhiqu
Guiana *see* French Guiana
Guiana Highlands *62 D1 var.* Macizo de las Guayanas. *Mountain range* N South America
Guidder *see* Guider
Guider *76 B4 var.* Guidder. Nord, N Cameroon
Guidimouni *75 G3* Zinder, S Niger
Guildford *89 D7* SE England, UK
Guilin *128 C6 var.* Kuei-lin, Kweilin. Guangxi Zhuangzu Zizhiqu, S China
Guimarães *92 B2 var.* Guimarães. Braga, N Portugal
Guinea *74 C4 var.* Guinée; *prev.* French Guinea, People's Revolutionary Republic of Guinea. *Country* W Africa

Guinea 74

Official name Republic of Guinea
Formation 1958
Capital Conakry
Population 7.4 million / 78 people per sq mile (30 people per sq km)
Total area 94,926 sq miles (245,860 sq km)
Languages French, Fulani, Malinke, Soussou
Religions Muslim 85%, Christian 8%, Traditional beliefs 7%
Ethnic mix Fila (Fulani) 30%, Malinke 30%, Soussou 15%, other 25%
Government Multiparty republic
Currency Guinea franc = 100 centimes
Literacy rate 38%
Calorie consumption 2,389 kilocalories

Guinea Basin *69 A5 undersea feature* E Atlantic Ocean
Guinea-Bissau *74 B4 Fr.* Guinée-Bissau, *Port.* Guiné-Bissau; *prev.* Portuguese Guinea. *Country* W Africa

Guinea-Bissau 74

Official name Republic of Guinea-Bissau
Formation 1974
Capital Bissau
Population 1.2 million / 111 people per sq mile (43 people per sq km)
Total area 10,857 sq miles (28,120 sq km)
Languages Portuguese, Creole, Balante
Religions Traditional beliefs 52%, Muslim 40%, Christian 8%
Ethnic mix Balante 30%, Fila (Fulani) 22%, Malinke 12%, other 36%
Government Multiparty republic
Currency Guinea peso = 100 centavos
Literacy rate 33.6%
Calorie consumption 2,556 kilocalories

Guinea, Gulf of *68 B4 Fr.* Golfe de Guinée. *Gulf* E Atlantic Ocean
Güiria *59 E1* Sucre, NE Venezuela
Guiyang *128 B6 var.* Kuei-Yang, Kuei-yang, Kueyang, Kweiyang; *prev.* Kweichu. Guizhou, S China
Guizhou *128 B6 var.* Guizhou Sheng, Kuei-chou, Kweichow, Qian. Admin. region *province* S China

Guizhou Sheng *see* Guizhou
Gujarāt *134 C4 var.* Gujerat. Admin. region *state* W India
Gujerat *see* Gujarāt
Gujrānwāla *134 D2* Punjab, NE Pakistan
Gujrāt *134 D2* Punjab, E Pakistan
Gulbarga *132 C1* Karnātaka, C India
Gulbene *106 D3 Ger.* Alt-Schwanenburg. Gulbene, NE Latvia
Gulfport *42 C3* Mississippi, S USA
Gulf, The *120 C4 var.* Persian Gulf, *Ar.* Khalīj al 'Arabī, *Per.* Khalīj-e Fars. *Gulf* SW Asia
Guliston *123 E2 Rus.* Gulistan. Sirdaryo Wiloyati, E Uzbekistan
Gulja *see* Yining
Gulkana *36 D3* Alaska, USA
Gulu *73 B6* N Uganda
Gulyantsi *104 C1* Pleven, N Bulgaria
Guma *see* Pishan
Gümülcine *see* Komotiní
Gümüljina *see* Komotiní
Gümüşane *see* Gümüşhane
Gümüşhane *117 E3 var.* Gümüşane, Gumushkhane. Gümüşhane, NE Turkey
Gumushkhane *see* Gümüşhane
Güney Doğu Toroslar *117 E4 mountain range* SE Turkey
Gunnbjørn Fjeld *82 D4 var.* Gunnbjörns Bjerge. *Mountain* C Greenland
Gunnbjörns Bjerge *see* Gunnbjørn Fjeld
Gunnedah *149 D6* New South Wales, SE Australia
Gunnison *44 C5* Colorado, C USA
Gurbantünggüt Shamo *126 B2 desert* W China
Gurgan *see* Gorgān
Guri, Embalse de *59 E2 reservoir* E Venezuela
Gurktaler Alpen *95 D7 mountain range* S Austria
Gürün *116 D3* Sivas, C Turkey
Gusau *75 G4* Zamfara, NW Nigeria
Gusev *106 B4 Ger.* Gumbinnen. Kaliningradskaya Oblast', W Russian Federation
Gushgy *122 D4 prev.* Kushka. Maryyskiy Velayat, S Turkmenistan
Gustavus *36 D4* Alaska, USA
Güstrow *94 C3* Mecklenburg-Vorpommern, NE Germany
Gütersloh *94 B4* Nordrhein-Westfalen, W Germany
Guwāhāti *135 G3 prev.* Gauhāti. Assam, NE India
Guyana *59 F3 prev.* British Guiana. *Country* N South America

Guyana 59

Official name Cooperative Republic of Guyana
Formation 1966
Capital Georgetown
Population 861,000 / 11 people per sq mile (4 people per sq km)
Total area 76,003 sq miles (196,850 sq km)
Languages English, English Creole, Hindi, Tamil, Amerindian languages
Religions Christian 57%, Hindu 33%, Muslim 9%, other 1%
Ethnic mix East Indian 52%, Black African 38%, other 10%
Government Multiparty republic
Currency Guyana dollar = 100 cents
Literacy rate 98%
Calorie consumption 2,384 kilocalories

Guyane *see* French Guiana
Guymon *49 E1* Oklahoma, C USA
Güzelyurt *see* Mórfou
Gvardeysk *106 A4 Ger.* Tapiau. Kaliningradskaya Oblast', W Russian Federation
Gwādar *134 A3 var.* Gwadur. Baluchistān, SW Pakistan

Gwadur *see* Gwādar
Gwalior *134 D3* Madhya Pradesh, C India
Gwanda *78 D3* Matabeleland South, SW Zimbabwe
Gwy *see* Wye
Gyangzê *126 C5* Xizang Zizhiqu, W China
Gyaring Co *126 C5 lake* W China
Gympie *149 E5* Queensland, E Australia
Gyomaendrőd *99 D7* Békés, SE Hungary
Gyöngyös *99 D6* Heves, NE Hungary
Győr *99 C6 Ger.* Raab; *Lat.* Arrabona. Győr-Moson-Sopron, NW Hungary
Gytheio *105 B6 var.* Githio; *prev.* Yíthion. Pelopónnisos, S Greece
Gyumri *117 F2 var.* Giumri, *Rus.* Kumayri; *prev.* Aleksandropol', Leninakan. W Armenia
Gyzylarbat *122 C2 prev.* Kizyl-Arvat. Balkanskiy Velayat, W Turkmenistan

H

Haabai *see* Ha'apai Group
Haacht *87 C6* Vlaams Brabant, C Belgium
Haaksbergen *86 E3* Overijssel, E Netherlands
Ha'apai Group *145 F4 var.* Haabai. *Island group* C Tonga
Haapsalu *106 D2 Ger.* Hapsal. Läänemaa, W Estonia
Haarlem *86 C3 prev.* Harlem. Noord-Holland, W Netherlands
Haast *151 B6* West Coast, South Island, NZ
Hachijō-jima *131 D6 var.* Hatizyô Zima. *Island* Izu-shotō, SE Japan
Hachinohe *130 D3* Aomori, Honshū, C Japan
Hadama *see* Nazrēt
Haddummati Atoll *see* Hadhdhunmathi Atoll
Hadejia *75 G3 river* N Nigeria
Hadejia *75 G4* Jigawa, N Nigeria
Hadera *119 A6 var.* Khadera. Haifa, C Israel
Hadhdhunmathi Atoll *132 A5 var.* Haddummati Atoll, Laamu Atoll. *Atoll* S Maldives
Ha Đông *136 D3 var.* Hadong. Ha Tây, N Vietnam
Hadong *see* Ha Đông
Ḩaḍramawt *121 C6 Eng.* Hadhramaut. *Mountain range* S Yemen
Haerbin *see* Harbin
Haerhpin *see* Harbin
Hafren *see* Severn
Hagåtña *160 B1 var.* Agana / Agaña. *Dependent territory capital* (Guam), NW Guam
Hagerstown *41 E4* Maryland, NE USA
Ha Giang *136 D3* Ha Giang, N Vietnam
Hagondange *90 D3* Moselle, NE France
Haguenau *90 E3* Bas-Rhin, NE France
Haicheng *128 D3* Liaoning, NE China
Haidarabad *see* Hyderābād
Haifa *see* Hefa
Haifong *see* Hai Phong
Haikou *128 C7 var.* Hai-k'ou, Hoihow, *Fr.* Hoï-Hao. Hainan, S China
Hai-k'ou *see* Haikou
Ḩā'il *120 B4 off.* Minṭaqah Ḩā'il. *Province* N Saudi Arabia
Hai-la-erh *see* Hailar
Hailar *127 F1 var.* Hai-la-erh; *prev.* Hulun. Nei Mongol Zizhiqu, N China
Hailuoto *84 D4 Swe.* Karlö. *Island* W Finland
Hainan *128 B7 var.* Hainan Sheng, Qiong. Admin. region *province* S China
Hainan Dao *128 C7 island* S China

Hainan Sheng *see* Hainan
Haines *36 D4* Alaska, USA
Hainichen *94 D4* Sachsen, E Germany
Hai Phong *136 D3 var.* Haifong, Haiphong. N Vietnam
Haiphong *see* Hai Phong
Haiti *54 D3* C West Indies

Haiti 54

Official name Republic of Haiti
Formation 1804
Capital Port-au-Prince
Population 8.2 million / 761 people per sq mile (298 people per sq km)
Total area 10,640 sq miles (27,560 sq km)
Languages French, French Creole
Religions Roman Catholic 80%, Protestant 16%, non-religious 1%, other 3%
Ethnic mix Black 95%, European-African 5%
Government Multiparty republic
Currency Gourde = 100 centimes
Literacy rate 45.8%
Calorie consumption 1,706 kilocalories

Haiya *72 C3* Red Sea, NE Sudan
Hajdúhadház *99 D6* Hajdú-Bihar, E Hungary
Hajîne *see* Abū Ḩardān
Hajnówka *98 E3 Ger.* Hermhausen. Podlaskie, NE Poland
Hakodate *130 D3* Hokkaidō, NE Japan
Ḩalab *118 B2 Eng.* Aleppo, *Fr.* Alep; *anc.* Beroea. Ḩalab, NW Syria
Ḩalāniyāt, Juzur al *137 D6 var.* Jazā'ir Bin Ghalfān, *Eng.* Kuria Muria Islands. *Island group* S Oman
Halberstadt *94 C4* Sachsen-Anhalt, C Germany
Halden *85 B6 prev.* Fredrikshald. Østfold, S Norway
Halfmoon Bay *151 A8 var.* Oban. Stewart Island, Southland, NZ
Halifax *39 F4* Nova Scotia, SE Canada
Halkida *see* Chalkída
Halle *87 B6 Fr.* Hal. Vlaams Brabant, C Belgium
Halle *94 C4 var.* Halle an der Saale. Sachsen-Anhalt, C Germany
Halle an der Saale *see* Halle
Halle-Neustadt *94 C4* Sachsen-Anhalt, C Germany
Halley *154 B2 UK research station* Antarctica
Hall Islands *142 B2 island group* C Micronesia
Halls Creek *146 C3* Western Australia
Halmahera, Pulau *139 F3 prev.* Djailolo, Gilolo, Jailolo. *Island* E Indonesia
Halmahera Sea *139 F4 Ind.* Laut Halmahera. *Sea* E Indonesia
Halmstad *85 B7* Halland, S Sweden
Hama *see* Ḩamāh
Hamada *131 B6* Shimane, Honshū, SW Japan
Hamadān *120 C3 anc.* Ecbatana. Hamadān, W Iran
Ḩamāh *118 B3 var.* Hama; *anc.* Epiphania, *Bibl.* Hamath. Ḩamāh, W Syria
Hamamatsu *131 D6 var.* Hamamatu. Shizuoka, Honshū, S Japan
Hamamatu *see* Hamamatsu
Hamar *85 B5 prev.* Storhammer. Hedmark, S Norway
Hamath *see* Ḩamāh
Hamburg *94 B3* Hamburg, N Germany
Ḩamḍ, Wādī al *136 A4 dry watercourse* W Saudi Arabia
Hämeenlinna *85 D5 Swe.* Tavastehus. Etelä-Suomi, S Finland
Hamersley Range *146 A4 mountain range* Western Australia

Hamhŭng 129 E3 C North Korea
Hami 126 C3 *var.* Ha-mi, *Uigh.*
Kumul, Qomul. Xinjiang Uygur
Zizhiqu, NW China
Ha-mi *see* Hami
Hamilton 42 C2 Alabama, S USA
Hamilton 38 D5 Ontario, S Canada
Hamilton 88 C4 S Scotland, UK
Hamilton 150 D3 Waikato, North
Island, NZ
Ḥamīm, Wād˹1 al 87 G2 river
NE Libya
Hamïs Musait *see* Khamīs Mushayt
Hamiton 42 A5 *dependent territory
capital* (Bermuda) C Bermuda
Hamm 94 B4 *var.* Hamm in
Westfalen. Nordrhein-Westfalen,
W Germany
Hammada du Drâa *see* Dra,
Hamada du
Hammamet, Golfe de 102 D3 *Ar.*
Khalīj al Ḥammāmāt. *Gulf*
NE Tunisia
Ḥammār, Hawr al 136 C3 lake
SE Iraq
Hamm in Westfalen *see* Hamm
Hampden 151 B7 Otago, South
Island, NZ
Hampstead 89 A7 SE England, UK
Hamrun 102 B5 C Malta
Hâncești *see* Hîncești
Handan 128 C4 *var.* Han-tan. Hebei,
E China
Haneda 130 A2 *international airport*
(Tōkyō) Tōkyō, Honshū, S Japan
HaNegev 119 A7 *Eng.* Negev. *Desert*
S Israel
Hanford 47 C6 California, W USA
Hangayn Nuruu 126 D2 *mountain
range* C Mongolia
Hang-chou *see* Hangzhou
Hangchow *see* Hangzhou
Hangö *see* Hanko
Hangzhou 128 D5 *var.* Hang-chou,
Hangchow. Zhejiang, SE China
Hania *see* Chaniá
Hanka, Lake *see* Khanka, Lake
Hanko 85 D6 *Swe.* Hangö. Etelä-
Suomi, SW Finland
Han-k'ou *see* Wuhan
Hankow *see* Wuhan
Hanmer Springs 151 C5
Canterbury, South Island, NZ
Hannibal 45 G4 Missouri, C USA
Hannover 94 B3 *Eng.* Hanover.
Niedersachsen, NW Germany
Hanöbukten 85 B7 *bay* S Sweden
Ha Nôi 136 D3 *Eng.* Hanoi, *Fr.* Ha
noï. *Country capital* (Vietnam)
N Vietnam
Hanoi *see* Ha Nôi
Han Shui 127 F4 *river* C China
Han-tan *see* Handan
Hantsavichy 107 B6 *Pol.*
Hancewicze, *Rus.* Gantsevichi.
Brestskaya Voblasts', SW Belarus
Hanyang *see* Wuhan
Hanzhong 128 B5 Shaanxi, C China
Hāora 135 F4 *prev.* Howrah. West
Bengal, NE India
Haparanda 84 D4 Norrbotten,
N Sweden
Haradok 107 E5 *Rus.* Gorodok.
Vitsyebskaya Voblasts', N Belarus
Haradzyets 107 B6 *Rus.* Gorodets.
Brestskaya Voblasts', SW Belarus
Haramachi 130 D4 Fukushima,
Honshū, E Japan
Harany 107 D5 *Rus.* Gorany.
Vitsyebskaya Voblasts', N Belarus
Harare 78 D3 *prev.* Salisbury.
Country capital (Zimbabwe)
Mashonaland East, NE Zimbabwe
Harbavichy 107 E6 *Rus.* Gorbovichi.
Mahilyowskaya Voblasts',
E Belarus
Harbel 74 C5 W Liberia
Harbin 129 E2 *var.* Haerbin, Ha-erh-
pin, Kharbin; *prev.* Haerhpin,
Pingkiang, Pinkiang.
Heilongjiang, NE China
Hardangerfjorden 85 A6 *fjord*
S Norway
Hardangervidda 85 A6 *plateau*
S Norway
Hardenberg 86 E3 Overijssel,
E Netherlands

Harelbeke 87 A6 *var.* Harlebeke.
West-Vlaanderen, W Belgium
Harem *see* Ḥārim
Haren 86 E2 Groningen,
NE Netherlands
Hārer 73 D5 E Ethiopia
Hargeisa *see* Hargeysa
Hargeysa 73 D5 *var.* Hargeisa.
Woqooyi Galbeed, NW Somalia
Hariana *see* Haryāna
Hari, Batang 138 B4 *prev.* Djambi.
River Sumatera, W Indonesia
Ḥārim 118 B2 *var.* Harem. Idlib,
W Syria
Harima-nada 131 B6 *sea* S Japan
Harīrūd *var.* Tedzhen, *Turkm.* Tejen.
River Afghanistan/Iran *see also*
Tedzhen
Harlan 45 F3 Iowa, C USA
Harlebeke *see* Harelbeke
Harlingen 86 D2 *Fris.* Harns.
Friesland, N Netherlands
Harlingen 49 G5 Texas, SW USA
Harlow 89 E6 E England, UK
Harney Basin 46 B4 *basin* Oregon,
NW USA
Härnösand 85 C5 *var.* Hernösand.
Västernorrland, C Sweden
Har Nuur 126 C2 *lake* NW Mongolia
Harper 74 D5 *var.* Cape Palmas.
NE Liberia
Harricana 38 D3 *river* Québec,
SE Canada
Harris 88 B3 *physical region*
NW Scotland, UK
Harrisburg 41 E4 *state capital*
Pennsylvania, NE USA
Harrisonburg 41 E4 Virginia,
NE USA
Harrison, Cape 39 F2 *headland*
Newfoundland and Labrador,
E Canada
Harris Ridge *see* Lomonosov Ridge
Harrogate 89 D5 N England, UK
Hârşova 108 D5 *prev.* Hîrşova.
Constanţa, SE Romania
Harstad 84 C2 Troms, N Norway
Hartford 41 G3 *state capital*
Connecticut, NE USA
Hartlepool 89 D5 N England, UK
Harunabad *see* Eslāmābād
Harwich 89 E6 E England, UK
Haryāna 134 D2 *var.* Hariana.
Admin. region *state* N India
Hasselt 87 C6 Limburg,
NE Belgium
Hassetché *see* Al Ḥasakah
Hastings 150 E4 Hawke's Bay,
North Island, NZ
Hastings 45 E4 Nebraska, C USA
Hastings 89 E7 SE England, UK
Haţeg 108 B4 *Ger.* Wallenthal, *Hung.*
Hátszeg; *prev.* Hatzeg, Hötzing.
Hunedoara, SW Romania
Hatizyô Zima *see* Hachijō-jima
Hattem 86 D3 Gelderland,
E Netherlands
Hatteras, Cape 43 G1 *headland*
North Carolina, SE USA
Hatteras Plain 35 D6 *undersea
feature* W Atlantic Ocean
Hattiesburg 42 C3 Mississippi, S USA
Hatton Bank *see* Hatton Ridge
Hatton Ridge 80 B2 *var.* Hatton
Bank. *Undersea feature* N Atlantic
Ocean
Hat Yai 137 C7 *var.* Ban Hat Yai.
Songkhla, SW Thailand
Haugesund 85 A6 Rogaland,
S Norway
Haukeligrend 85 A6 Telemark,
S Norway
Haukivesi 85 E5 *lake* SE Finland
Hauraki Gulf 150 D2 *gulf* North
Island, NZ
Hauroko, Lake 151 A7 *lake* South
Island, NZ
Haut Atlas 70 B3 *Eng.* High Atlas.
Mountain range C Morocco
Hautes Fagnes 87 D6 *Ger.* Hohes
Venn. *Mountain range* E Belgium
Haut Plateau du Dra *see* Dra,
Hamada du
Hauts Plateaux 70 D2 *plateau*
Algeria/Morocco
Hauzenberg 95 D6 Bayern,
SE Germany

Havana *see* La Habana
Havana 35 D6 Illinois, N USA
Havant 89 D7 S England, UK
Havelock 43 F1 North Carolina,
SE USA
Havelock North 150 E4 Hawke's
Bay, North Island, NZ
Haverfordwest 89 C6 SW Wales, UK
Havířov 99 C5 Ostravský Kraj,
E Czech Republic
Havre 44 C1 Montana, NW USA
Havre-St-Pierre 39 F3 Québec,
E Canada
Hawaii 47 B8 *Haw.* Hawai'i. *Island*
Hawaiian Islands, USA, C Pacific
Ocean
Hawaii 47 A8 *off.* State of Hawaii;
also known as Aloha State,
Paradise of the Pacific. *State* USA,
C Pacific Ocean
Hawaiian Islands 152 D2 *prev.*
Sandwich Islands. *Island group*
Hawaii, USA, C Pacific Ocean
Hawaiian Ridge 113 H4 *undersea
feature* N Pacific Ocean
Hawash *see* Āwash
Hawea, Lake 151 B6 *lake* South
Island, NZ
Hawera 150 D4 Taranaki, North
Island, NZ
Hawick 88 C4 SE Scotland, UK
Hawke Bay 150 E4 *bay* North
Island, NZ
Hawlēr *see* Arbīl
Hawthorne 47 C6 Nevada, W USA
Hay 149 C6 New South Wales,
SE Australia
Hayes 38 B2 *river* Manitoba,
C Canada
Hay River 37 E4 Northwest
Territories, W Canada
Hays 45 E5 Kansas, C USA
Haysyn 108 D3 *Rus.* Gaysin.
Vinnyts'ka Oblast', C Ukraine
Heard and McDonald Islands 141
B7 *Australian external territory*
S Indian Ocean
Hearst 38 C4 Ontario, S Canada
Heathrow 89 A8 *international airport*
(London)SE England, UK
Hebei 128 C4 *var.* Hebei Sheng,
Hopeh, Hopei, Ji; *prev.* Chihli.
Admin. region *province* E China
Hebei Sheng *see* Hebei
Hebron 119 A6 *var.* Al Khalīl,
El Khalil, *Heb.* Ḥevron; *anc.*
Kiriath-Arba. S West Bank
Hebrus *see* Maritsa
Heemskerk 86 C3 Noord-Holland,
W Netherlands
Heerde 86 D3 Gelderland,
E Netherlands
Heerenveen 86 D2 *Fris.* It
Hearrenfean. Friesland,
N Netherlands
Heerhugowaard 86 C2 Noord-
Holland, NW Netherlands
Heerlen 87 D6 Limburg,
SE Netherlands
Heerwegen *see* Polkowice
Hefa 119 A5 *var.* Haifa; *hist.* Caiffa,
Caiphas, *anc.* Sycaminum. Haifa,
N Israel
Hefa, Mifraz 119 A5 *Eng.* Bay of
Haifa. *Bay* N Israel
Hefei 128 D5 *var.* Hofei; *hist.*
Luchow. Anhui, E China
Hegang 129 E2 Heilongjiang,
NE China
Hei *see* Heilongjiang
Heide 94 B2 Schleswig-Holstein,
N Germany
Heidelberg 95 B5 Baden-
Württemberg, SW Germany
Heidenheim *see* Heidenheim an
der Brenz
Heidenheim an der Brenz 95 B6
var. Heidenheim. Baden-
Württemberg, S Germany
Heilbronn 95 B6 Baden-
Württemberg, SW Germany
Heilongjiang 128 D2 *var.* Hei,
Heilongjiang Sheng, Hei-lung-
chiang, Heilungkiang. Admin.
region *province* NE China
Heilongjiang Sheng *see*
Heilongjiang

Heiloo 86 C3 Noord-Holland,
NW Netherlands
Hei-lung-chiang *see* Heilongjiang
Heilungkiang *see* Heilongjiang
Heimdal 85 B5 Sør-Trøndelag,
S Norway
Hekimhan 116 D3 Malatya, C Turkey
Helena 44 B2 *state capital* Montana,
NW USA
Helensville 150 D2 Auckland,
North Island, NZ
Helgoland Bay *see* Helgoländer
Bucht
Helgoländer Bucht 94 A2 *var.*
Helgoland Bay, Heligoland Bight.
Bay NW Germany
Heligoland Bight *see* Helgoländer
Bucht
Heliopolis *see* Baalbek
Hellevoetsluis 86 B4 Zuid-Holland,
SW Netherlands
Hellín 93 E4 Castilla-La Mancha,
C Spain
Helmand, Daryā-ye *var.* Rūd-e
Hīrmand. *River* Afghanistan/Iran
see also Hīrmand, Rūd-e
Helmond 87 D5 Noord-Brabant,
S Netherlands
Helsingborg 85 B7 *prev.*
Hälsingborg. Skåne, S Sweden
Helsinki 85 D6 *Swe.* Helsingfors.
Country capital (Finland) Etelä-
Suomi, S Finland
Henan 128 C5 *var.* Henan Sheng,
Honan, Yu. Admin. region
province C China
Henan Sheng *see* Henan
Henderson 40 B5 Kentucky, S USA
Henderson 47 D7 Nevada, W USA
Henderson 49 H3 Texas, SW USA
Hengchow *see* Hengyang
Hengduan Shan 128 A5 *mountain
range* SW China
Hengelo 86 E3 Overijssel,
E Netherlands
Hengnan *see* Hengyang
Hengyang 128 C6 *var.* Hengnan,
Heng-yang; *prev.* Hengchow.
Hunan, S China
Heng-yang *see* Hengyang
Heniches'k 109 F4 *Rus.* Genichesk.
Khersons'ka Oblast', S Ukraine
Hennebont 90 A3 Morbihan,
NW France
Henzada 136 B4 Irrawaddy,
SW Myanmar
Herakleion *see* Irákleio
Herāt 122 D4 *var.* Herat; *anc.* Aria.
Herāt, W Afghanistan
Herat *see* Herāt
Heredia 53 E4 Heredia, C Costa
Rica
Hereford 49 E2 Texas, SW USA
Herford 94 B4 Nordrhein-
Westfalen, NW Germany
Herk-de-Stad 87 C6 Limburg,
NE Belgium
Hermansverk 85 A5 Sogn Og
Fjordane, S Norway
Hermhausen *see* Hajnówka
Hermiston 46 C2 Oregon, NW USA
Hermon, Mount 119 B5 *Ar.* Jabal
ash Shaykh. *Mountain* S Syria
Hermosillo 50 B2 Sonora,
NW Mexico
Hermoupolis *see* Ermoúpoli
Hernösand *see* Härnösand
Herrera del Duque 92 D3
Extremadura, W Spain
Herselt 87 C5 Antwerpen,
C Belgium
Herstal 87 D6 *Fr.* Héristal. Liège,
E Belgium
Hessen 95 B5 *cultural region*
C Germany
Ḥevron *see* Hebron
Heydebrech *see* Kędzierzyn-Kole
Heywood Islands 146 C3 *island
group* Western Australia
Hibbing 45 F1 Minnesota, N USA
Hidalgo del Parral 50 C2 *var.* Parral.
Chihuahua, N Mexico
Hida-sanmyaku 131 C5 *mountain
range* Honshū, S Japan
Hierro 70 A3 *var.* Ferro. *Island* Islas
Canarias, Spain, NE Atlantic
Ocean

High Plains *see* Great Plains
High Point *43 E1* North Carolina, SE USA
High Veld *see* Great Karoo
Hiiumaa *106 C2 Ger.* Dagden, *Swe.* Dagö. *Island* W Estonia
Hikurangi *150 D2* Northland, North Island, NZ
Hildesheim *94 B4* Niedersachsen, N Germany
Hilla *see* Al Ḩillah
Hillaby, Mount *55 G1 mountain* N Barbados
Hill Bank *52 C1* Orange Walk, N Belize
Hillegom *86 C3* Zuid-Holland, W Netherlands
Hilo *47 B8* Hawaii, USA, C Pacific Ocean
Hilton Head Island *43 E2* South Carolina, SE USA
Hilversum *86 C3* Noord-Holland, C Netherlands
Himalaya *see* Himalayas
Himalayas *135 E2 var.* Himalaya, *Chin.* Himalaya Shan. *Mountain range* S Asia
Himalaya Shan *see* Himalayas
Himeji *131 C6 var.* Himezi. Hyōgo, Honshū, SW Japan
Himezi *see* Himeji
Ḩimṣ *118 B4 var.* Homs; *anc.* Emesa. Ḩimṣ, C Syria
Hîncești *108 D4 var.* Hânceşti; *prev.* Kotovsk. C Moldova
Hinchinbrook Island *148 D3 island* Queensland, NE Australia
Hinds *151 C6* Canterbury, South Island, NZ
Hindu Kush *123 F4 Per.* Hendū Kosh. *Mountain range* Afghanistan/Pakistan
Hinesville *43 E3* Georgia, SE USA
Hinnøya *84 C3 island* C Norway
Hinson Bay *42 A5 bay* W Bermuda
Hios *see* Chíos
Hirosaki *130 D3* Aomori, Honshū, C Japan
Hiroshima *131 B6 var.* Hirosima. Hiroshima, Honshū, SW Japan
Hirosima *see* Hiroshima
Hirson *90 D3* Aisne, N France
Hispaniola *56 B1 island* Dominion Republic/Haiti
Hitachi *131 D5 var.* Hitati. Ibaraki, Honshū, S Japan
Hitati *see* Hitachi
Hitra *84 A4 prev.* Hitteren. *Island* S Norway
Hjälmaren *85 C6 Eng.* Lake Hjalmar. *Lake* C Sweden
Hjørring *85 B7* Nordjylland, N Denmark
Hkakabo Razi *136 B1 mountain* Myanmar/China
Hlobyne *109 F2 Rus.* Globino. Poltavs'ka Oblast', NE Ukraine
Hlukhiv *109 F1 Rus.* Glukhov. Sums'ka Oblast', NE Ukraine
Hlybokaye *107 D5 Rus.* Glubokoye. Vitsyebskaya Voblasts', N Belarus
Hoa Binh *136 D3* Hoa Binh, N Vietnam
Hoang Liên Sơn *136 D3 mountain range* N Vietnam
Hobart *149 C8 prev.* Hobarton, Hobart Town. *State capital* Tasmania, SE Australia
Hobbs *49 E3* New Mexico, SW USA
Hobro *85 A7* Nordjylland, N Denmark
Hô Chi Minh *137 E6 var.* Ho Chi Minh City; *prev.* Saigon. S Vietnam
Ho Chi Minh City *see* Hồ Chi Minh
Hódmezővásárhely *99 D7* Csongrád, SE Hungary
Hodna, Chott El *118 C4 var.* Chott el-Hodna, *Ar.* Shatt al-Hodna. *Salt lake* N Algeria
Hodonín *99 C5 Ger.* Göding. Brněnský Kraj, SE Czech Republic
Hoë Karoo *see* Great Karoo
Hof *95 C5* Bayern, SE Germany
Hofei *see* Hefei
Hōfu *131 B7* Yamaguchi, Honshū, SW Japan

Hofuf *see* Al Hufūf
Hogoley Islands *see* Chuuk Islands
Hohe Tauern *95 C7 mountain range* W Austria
Hohhot *127 F3 var.* Huhehot, Huhuohaote, *Mong.* Kukukhoto; *prev.* Kweisui, Kwesui. Nei Mongol Zizhiqu, N China
Hôi An *137 E5 prev.* Faifo. Quang Nam-Đa Nang, C Vietnam
Hoï-Hao *see* Haikou
Hoihow *see* Haikou
Hokianga Harbour *150 C2 inlet* SE Tasman Sea
Hokitika *151 B5* West Coast, South Island, NZ
Hokkaidō *130 C2 prev.* Ezo, Yeso, Yezo. *Island* NE Japan
Hola Prystan' *109 E4 Rus.* Golaya Pristan. Khersons'ka Oblast', S Ukraine
Holbrook *48 B2* Arizona, SW USA
Holetown *55 G1 prev.* Jamestown. W Barbados
Holguín *54 C2* Holguín, SE Cuba
Hollabrunn *95 E6* Niederösterreich, NE Austria
Hollandia *see* Jayapura
Holly Springs *42 C1* Mississippi, S USA
Holman *37 E3* Victoria Island, Northwest Territories, N Canada
Holmsund *84 D4* Västerbotten, N Sweden
Holon *119 A6 var.* Kholon. Tel Aviv, C Israel
Holovanivs'k *109 E3 Rus.* Golovanevsk. Kirovohrads'ka Oblast', C Ukraine
Holstebro *85 A7* Ringkøbing, W Denmark
Holsteinborg *see* Sisimiut
Holsteinsborg *see* Sisimiut
Holstenborg *see* Sisimiut
Holstensborg *see* Sisimiut
Holyhead *89 C5 Wel.* Caer Gybi. NW Wales, UK
Hombori *75 E3* Mopti, S Mali
Homs *see* Al Khums
Homs *see* Ḩimṣ
Homyel' *107 D7 Rus.* Gomel'. Homyel'skaya Voblasts', SE Belarus
Honan *see* Henan
Honan *see* Luoyang
Hondo *see* Honshū
Hondo *49 F4* Texas, SW USA
Honduras *52 C2 Country* Central America

Honduras 52

Official name Republic of Honduras
Formation 1838
Capital Tegucigalpa
Population 6.3 million / 150 people per sq mile (58 people per sq km)
Total area 43,200 sq miles (111,890 sq km)
Languages Spanish, Black Carib, English Creole
Religions Roman Catholic 97%, other (including Protestant) 3%
Ethnic mix Mestizo 90%, Black African 5%, Amerindian 4%, White 1%
Government Multiparty republic
Currency Lempira = 100 centavos
Literacy rate 70.7%
Calorie consumption 2,305 kilocalories

Honduras, Gulf of *52 C2 Sp.* Golfo de Honduras. *Gulf* W Caribbean Sea
Hønefoss *85 B6* Buskerud, S Norway
Honey Lake *47 B5 lake* California, W USA
Hon Gai *see* Hông Gai
Hongay *see* Hông Gai
Hông Gai *136 E3 var.* Hon Gai, Hongay. Quang Ninh, N Vietnam
Hong Kong *128 A1 Chin.* Xianggang. S China

Hong Kong Island *128 B2 Chin.* Xianggang. *Island* S China
Honiara *144 C3 country capital* (Solomon Islands) Guadalcanal, C Solomon Islands
Honjō *130 D4 var.* Honzyô. Akita, Honshū, C Japan
Honolulu *47 A8 admin capital* Oahu, Hawaii, USA, C Pacific Ocean
Honshū *131 E5 var.* Hondo, Honsyû. *Island* SW Japan
Honsyû *see* Honshū
Honzyô *see* Honjō
Hoogeveen *86 E2* Drenthe, NE Netherlands
Hoogezand-Sappemeer *86 E2* Groningen, NE Netherlands
Hoorn *86 C2* Noord-Holland, NW Netherlands
Hopa *117 F2* Artvin, NE Turkey
Hope *36 C3* British Columbia, SW Canada
Hopedale *39 F2* Newfoundland and Labrador, NE Canada
Hopeh *see* Hebei
Hopei *see* Hebei
Hopkinsville *40 B5* Kentucky, S USA
Horasan *117 F3* Erzurum, NE Turkey
Horizon Deep *152 D4 undersea feature* W Pacific Ocean
Horki *107 E6 Rus.* Gorki. Mahilyowskaya Voblasts', E Belarus
Horlivka *109 G3 Rom.* Adâncata, *Rus.* Gorlovka. Donets'ka Oblast', E Ukraine
Hormuz, Strait of *120 D4 var.* Strait of Ormuz, *Per.* Tangeh-ye Hormoz. *Strait* Iran/Oman
Hornos, Cabo de *65 C8 Eng.* Cape Horn. *Headland* S Chile
Hornsby *148 E1* New South Wales, SE Australia
Horodnya *109 E1 Rus.* Gorodnya. Chernihivs'ka Oblast', NE Ukraine
Horodyshche *109 E2 Rus.* Gorodishche. Cherkas'ka Oblast', C Ukraine
Horokok *108 B2 Pol.* Gródek Jagielloński, *Rus.* Gorodok, Gorodok Yagellonski. L'vivs'ka Oblast', NW Ukraine
Horoshiri-dake *130 D2 var.* Horosiri Dake. *Mountain* Hokkaidō, N Japan
Horosiri Dake *see* Horoshiri-dake
Horsburgh Atoll *132 A4 atoll* N Maldives
Horseshoe Bay *42 A5 bay* W Bermuda
Horseshoe Seamounts *80 A4 undersea feature* E Atlantic Ocean
Horsham *149 B7* Victoria, SE Australia
Horst *87 D5* Limburg, SE Netherlands
Horten *85 B6* Vestfold, S Norway
Horyn' *87 D7 Rus.* Goryn. *River* NW Ukraine
Hosingen *87 D7* Diekirch, NE Luxembourg
Hospitalet *see* L'Hospitalet de Llobregat
Hotan *126 B4 var.* Khotan, *Chin.* Ho-t'ien. Xinjiang Uygur Zizhiqu, NW China
Ho-t'ien *see* Hotan
Hoting *84 C4* Jämtland, C Sweden
Hot Springs *42 B1* Arkansas, C USA
Houayxay *136 C3 var.* Ban Houayxay, Ban Houei Sai. Bokèo, N Laos
Houghton *40 B1* Michigan, N USA
Houilles *91 B5* Yvelines, N France
Houlton *41 H1* Maine, NE USA
Houma *42 B3* Louisiana, S USA
Houston *49 H4* Texas, SW USA
Hovd *126 C2 var.* Khovd. Hovd, W Mongolia
Hove *89 E7* SE England, UK
Hoverla, Hora *108 C3 Rus.* Gora Goverla. *Mountain* W Ukraine
Hovsgol, Lake *see* Hövsgöl Nuur

Hövsgöl Nuur *126 D1 var.* Lake Hovsgol. *Lake* N Mongolia
Howar, Wâdi *72 A4 var.* Ouadi Howa. *River* Chad/Sudan *see also* Howa, Ouadi
Hoy *88 C2 island* N Scotland, UK
Hoyerswerda *94 D4* Sachsen, E Germany
Hradec Králové *99 B5 Ger.* Königgrätz. Hradecký Kraj, N Czech Republic
Hrandzichy *107 B5 Rus.* Grandichi. Hrodzyenskaya Voblasts', W Belarus
Hranice *99 C5 Ger.* Mährisch-Weisskirchen. Olomoucký Kraj, E Czech Republic
Hrebinka *109 E2 Rus.* Grebenka. Poltavs'ka Oblast', NE Ukraine
Hrodna *107 B5 Pol.* Grodno. Hrodzyenskaya Voblasts', W Belarus
Hsia-men *see* Xiamen
Hsiang-t'an *see* Xiangtan
Hsi Chiang *see* Xi Jiang
Hsing-k'ai Hu *see* Khanka, Lake
Hsining *see* Xining
Hsinking *see* Changchun
Hsin-yang *see* Xinyang
Hsu-chou *see* Xuzhou
Huacho *60 C4* Lima, W Peru
Hua Hin *see* Ban Hua Hin
Huaihua *128 C5* Hunan, S China
Huailai *128 C3 prev.* Shacheng. Hebei, E China
Huainan *128 D5 var.* Huai-nan, Hwainan. Anhui, E China
Huai-nan *see* Huainan
Huajuapan *51 F5 var.* Huajuapan de León. Oaxaca, SE Mexico
Huajuapan de León *see* Huajuapan
Hualapai Peak *48 A2 mountain* Arizona, SW USA
Huallaga, Río *60 C3 river* N Peru
Huambo *78 B2 Port.* Nova Lisboa. Huambo, C Angola
Huancavelica *60 D4* Huancavelica, SW Peru
Huancayo *60 D3* Junín, C Peru
Huang He *128 C4 var.* Yellow River. *River* C China
Huangshi *128 C5 var.* Huang-shih, Hwangshih. Hubei, C China
Huang-shih *see* Huangshi
Huanta *60 D4* Ayacucho, C Peru
Huánuco *60 C3* Huánuco, C Peru
Huaunui *61 F4* Oruro, W Bolivia
Huaral *60 C4* Lima, W Peru
Huarás *see* Huaraz
Huaraz *60 C3 var.* Huarás. Ancash, W Peru
Huarmey *60 C3* Ancash, W Peru
Huatabampo *50 C2* Sonora, NW Mexico
Hubli *124 B1* Karnātaka, SW India
Huddersfield *89 D5* N England, UK
Hudiksvall *85 C5* Gävleborg, C Sweden
Hudson Bay *37 G4 bay* NE Canada
Hudson Strait *37 H3 Fr.* Détroit d'Hudson. *Strait* Nunavut/Québec, NE Canada
Hudur *see* Xuddur
Huê *136 E4* Thua Thiên-Huê, C Vietnam
Huehuetenango *52 A2* Huehuetenango, W Guatemala
Huelva *92 C4 anc.* Onuba. Andalucía, SW Spain
Huesca *93 F2 anc.* Osca. Aragón, NE Spain
Huéscar *93 E4* Andalucía, S Spain
Hughenden *148 C3* Queensland, NE Australia
Hugo *49 G2* Oklahoma, C USA
Huhehot *see* Hohhot
Huhuohaote *see* Hohhot
Huíla Plateau *78 B2 plateau* S Angola
Huixtla *51 G5* Chiapas, SE Mexico
Hukui *see* Fukui
Hukuoka *see* Fukuoka
Hukusima *see* Fukushima
Hulingol *127 G2 prev.* Huolin Gol. Nei Mongol Zizhiqu, N China
Hull *see* Kingston upon Hull

Hull *38 D4* Québec, SE Canada

Hulst *87 B5* Zeeland, SW Netherlands

Hulun *see* Hailar

Hu-lun Ch'ih *see* Hulun Nur

Hulun Nur *127 F1 var.* Hu-lun Ch'ih; *prev.* Dalai Nor. *lake* NE China

Humaitá *62 D2* Amazonas, N Brazil

Humboldt River *47 C5 river* Nevada, W USA

Humphreys Peak *48 B1 mountain* Arizona, SW USA

Humpolec *99 B5 Ger.* Gumpolds, Humpoletz. Jihlavský Kraj, C Czech Republic

Hunan *128 C6 var.* Hunan Sheng, Xiang. Admin. region *province* S China

Hunan ShEng *see* Xiang

Hunedoara *108 B4 Ger.* Eisenmarkt, *Hung.* Vajdahunyad. Hunedoara, SW Romania

Hünfeld *95 B5* Hessen, C Germany

Hungary *99 C6 Ger.* Ungarn, *Hung.* Magyarország, *Rom.* Ungaria, *SCr.* Madarska, *Ukr.* Uhorshchyna; *prev.* Hungarian People's Republic. *Country* C Europe

---

Hungary 99

Official name Republic of Hungary
Formation 1918
Capital Budapest
Population 10 million / 280 people per sq mile (108 people per sq km)
Total area 35,652 sq miles (92,340 sq km)
Languages Hungarian
Religions Roman Catholic 64%, Calvinist 20%, non-religious 7%, Lutheran 4%, other 5%
Ethnic mix Magyar 90%, German 2%, Romany 1%, Slovak 1%, other 6%
Government Multiparty republic
Currency Forint = 100 filler
Literacy rate 99%
Calorie consumption 3,503 kilocalories

Hungary, Plain of *see* Great Hungarian Plain

Hunter Island *149 B8 island* Tasmania, SE Australia

Huntington *40 D4* West Virginia, NE USA

Huntington Beach *47 B8* California, W USA

Huntly *150 D3* Waikato, North Island, NZ

Huntsville *42 D1* Alabama, S USA

Huntsville *49 G3* Texas, SW USA

Hurghada *72 C2 var.* Al Ghurdaqah, Ghurdaqah. E Egypt

Huron *45 E3* South Dakota, N USA

Huron, Lake *40 D2 lake* Canada/USA

Hurukawa *see* Furukawa

Hurunui *151 C5 river* South Island, NZ

Húsavík *83 E4* Nordhurland Eystra, NE Iceland

Husum *94 B2* Schleswig-Holstein, N Germany

Hutchinson *45 F5* Kansas, C USA

Hutchinson Island *43 F4 island* Florida, SE USA

Huy *87 C6 Dut.* Hoei, Hoey. Liège, E Belgium

Huzi *see* Fuji

Hvannadalshnúkur *83 E5 mountain* S Iceland

Hvar *100 B4 It.* Lesina; *anc.* Pharus. *Island* S Croatia

Hwainan *see* Huainan

Hwange *78 D3 prev.* Wankie. Matabeleland North, W Zimbabwe

Hwangshih *see* Huangshi

Hyargas Nuur *126 C2 lake* NW Mongolia

Hyderābād *134 D5 var.* Haidarabad. Andhra Pradesh, C India

Hyderābād *134 B3 var.* Haidarabad. Sind, SE Pakistan

Hyères *91 D6* Var, SE France

Hyères, Îles d' *91 D6 island group* S France

Hypanis *see* Kuban'

Hyrcania *see* Gorgān

Hyvinkää *85 D5 Swe.* Hyvinge. Etelä-Suomi, S Finland

I

Ialomiţa *108 C5 river* SE Romania

Iaşi *108 D3 Ger.* Jassy. Iaşi, NE Romania

Ibadan *75 F5* Oyo, SW Nigeria

Ibagué *58 B3* Tolima, C Colombia

Ibar *100 D4 Alb.* Ibër. *River* C Yugoslavia

Ibarra *60 B1 var.* San Miguel de Ibarra. Imbabura, N Ecuador

Iberian Mountains *see* Ibérico, Sistema

Iberian Peninsula *80 B4 physical region* Portugal/Spain

Iberian Plain *80 B4 undersea feature* E Atlantic Ocean

Ibérico, Sistema *93 E2 var.* Cordillera Ibérica, *Eng.* Iberian Mountains. *Mountain range* NE Spain

Ibiza *see* Eivissa

Ibo *see* Sassandra

Ica *60 D4* Ica, SW Peru

Içá *see* Putumayo, Río

Icaria *see* Ikaría

Içá, Rio *62 C2 var.* Río Putumayo. *River* NW South America *see also* Putumayo, Río

Iceland *83 E4 Dan.* Island, *Icel.* Ísland. *Country* N Atlantic Ocean

---

Iceland 83

Official name Republic of Iceland
Formation 1944
Capital Reykjavik
Population 281,000 / 7 people per sq mile (3 people per sq km)
Total area 38,706 sq miles (100,250 sq km)
Languages Icelandic
Religions Evangelical Lutheran 93%, non-religious 6%, other Christian 1%
Ethnic mix Icelandic 98%, other 2%
Government Constitutional republic
Currency Icelandic króna = 100 aurar
Literacy rate 99%
Calorie consumption 3,058 kilocalories

Iceland Basin *80 B1 undersea feature* N Atlantic Ocean

Icelandic Plateau *see* Iceland Plateau

Iceland Plateau *172 B5 var.* Icelandic Plateau. *Undersea feature* S Greenland Sea

Iconium *see* Konya

Idabel *49 H2* Oklahoma, C USA

Idaho *46 D3 off.* State of Idaho; also known as Gem of the Mountains, Gem State. *State* NW USA

Idaho Falls *46 E3* Idaho, NW USA

Idensalmi *see* Iisalmi

Idfu *72 B2 var.* Edfu. SE Egypt

Ídhra *see* Ýdra

Idi Amin, Lac *see* Edward, Lake

Idîni *74 B2* Trarza, W Mauritania

Idlib *118 B3* Idlib, NW Syria

Idre *85 B5* Kopparberg, C Sweden

Iecava *106 C3* Bauska, S Latvia

Ieper *87 A6 Fr.* Ypres. West-Vlaanderen, W Belgium

Ierápetra *105 D8* Kríti, Greece, E Mediterranean Sea

Ierisós *see* Ierissós

Ierissós *104 C4 var.* Ierisós. Kentrikí Makedonía, N Greece

Iferouâne *75 G2* Agadez, N Niger

Ifôghas, Adrar des *75 E2 var.* Adrar des Iforas. *Mountain range* NE Mali

---

Igarka *114 D3* Krasnoyarskiy Kray, N Russian Federation

Iglesias *97 A5* Sardegna, Italy, C Mediterranean Sea

Igloolik *37 G2* Nunavut, N Canada

Igoumenítsa *104 A4* Ípeiros, W Greece

Iguaçu, Rio *63 E4 Sp.* Río Iguazú. *River* Argentina/Brazil *see also* Iguazú, Río

Iguaçu, Salto do *63 E4 Sp.* Cataratas del Iguazú; *prev.* Victoria Falls. *Waterfall* Argentina/Brazil *see also* Iguazú, Cataratas del

Iguala *51 E4 var.* Iguala de la Independencia. Guerrero, S Mexico

Iguala de la Independencia *see* Iguala

Iguidi, 'Erg *70 C3 var.* Erg Iguid. *Desert* Algeria/Mauritania

Ihavandiffulu Atoll *see* Ihavandippolhu Atoll

Ihavandippolhu Atoll *132 A3 var.* Ihavandiffulu Atoll. *Atoll* N Maldives

Ihosy *79 F4* Fianarantsoa, S Madagascar

Ijmuiden *86 C3* Noord-Holland, W Netherlands

Iisalmi *84 E4 var.* Idensalmi. Itä-Suomi, C Finland

IJssel *86 D3 var.* Yssel. *River* Netherlands/Germany

IJsselmeer *86 C2 prev.* Zuider Zee. *Lake* N Netherlands

IJsselmuiden *86 D3* Overijssel, E Netherlands

Ijzer *87 A6 river* W Belgium

Ikaría *105 D6 var.* Kariot, Nicaria, Nikaria; *anc.* Icaria. *Island* Dodekánisos, Greece, Aegean Sea

Ikela *77 D6* Equateur, C Dem. Rep. Congo (Zaire)

Iki *131 A7 island* SW Japan

Ilagan *139 E1* Luzon, N Philippines

Ilave *61 E4* Puno, S Peru

Iława *98 D3 Ger.* Deutsch-Eylau. Warmińsko-Mazurskie, NE Poland

Ilebo *77 C6 prev.* Port-Francqui. Kasai Occidental, W Dem. Rep. Congo (Zaire)

Île-de-France *90 C3 cultural region* N France

Îles de la Société *see* Société, Archipel de la

Îles Tubuai *see* Australes, Îles

Ilfracombe *89 C7* SW England, UK

Ilha Caviana *see* Caviana de Fora, Ilha

Ilha de Corvo *see* Corvo

Ilha de Madeira *see* Madeira

Ilha do Corvo *see* Corvo

Ilha do Faial *see* Faial

Ilha do Pico *see* Pico

Ilha do Porto Santo *see* Porto Santo

Ilha Graciosa *see* Graciosa

Ilhas dos Açores *see* Azores

Ilha Terceira *see* Terceira

Ílhavo *92 B2* Aveiro, N Portugal

Ili *112 C3 Kaz.* Ile, *Rus.* Reka Ili. *River* China/Kazakhstan

Iliamna Lake *36 C3 lake* Alaska, USA

Ilici *see* Elche

Iligan *139 E2 off.* Iligan City. Mindanao, S Philippines

Illapel *64 B4* Coquimbo, C Chile

Illichivs'k *109 E4 Rus.* Il'ichevsk. Odes'ka Oblast', SW Ukraine

Illicis *see* Elche

Illinois *40 A4 off.* State of Illinois; also known as Prairie State, Sucker State. *State* C USA

Illinois River *40 B4 river* Illinois, N USA

Ilo *61 E4* Moquegua, SW Peru

Iloilo *139 E2 off.* Iloilo City. Panay Island, C Philippines

Ilorin *75 F4* Kwara, W Nigeria

Îlots de Bass *see* Marotiri

Ilovlya *111 B6* Volgogradskaya Oblast', SW Russian Federation

Iluh *see* Batman

Il'yaly *122 C2 var.* Yylanly. Dashkhovuzskiy Velayat, N Turkmenistan

---

Imatra *85 E5* Etelä-Suomi, S Finland

Imbros *see* Gökçeada

İmişli *117 H3 Rus.* Imishli. C Azerbaijan

Imola *96 C3* Emilia-Romagna, N Italy

Imperatriz *63 F2* Maranhão, NE Brazil

Imperia *96 A3* Liguria, NW Italy

Impfondo *77 C5* La Likouala, NE Congo

Imphāl *135 H3* Manipur, NE India

Imroz Adası *see* Gökçeada

Inagua Islands *see* Great Inagua

Inagua Islands *see* Little Inagua

Inarijärvi *84 D2 Lapp.* Aanaarjävri, *Swe.* Enareträsk. *Lake* N Finland

Inawashiro-ko *131 D5 var.* Inawasiro Ko. *Lake* Honshū, C Japan

Inawasiro Ko *see* Inawashiro-ko

İncesu *116 D3* Kayseri, C Turkey

Inch'ŏn *129 E4 off.* Inch'ŏn-gwangyŏksi, *Jap.* Jinsen; *prev.* Chemulpo. NW South Korea

Incudine, Monte *91 E7 mountain* Corse, France, C Mediterranean Sea

Indefatigable Island *see* Santa Cruz, Isla

Independence *45 F4* Missouri, C USA

Independence Fjord *83 E1 fjord* N Greenland

Independence Mountains *46 C4 mountain range* Nevada, W USA

India *124 B3 var.* Indian Union, Union of India, *Hind.* Bhārat. *Country* S Asia

---

India 124

Official name Republic of India
Formation 1947
Capital New Delhi
Population 1 billion / 883 people per sq mile (341 people per sq km)
Total area 1,147,948 sq miles (2,973,190 sq km)
Languages Hindi, English, and 16 regional languages
Religions Hindu 83%, Muslim 11%, Christian 2%, Sikh 2%, other 2%
Ethnic mix Indo-Aryan 72%, Dravidian 25%, Mongoloid and other 3%
Government Multiparty republic
Currency Indian rupee = 100 paisa
Literacy rate 53.5%
Calorie consumption 2,395 kilocalories

Indiana *40 B4 off.* State of Indiana; also known as The Hoosier State. *State* N USA

Indianapolis *40 C4 state capital* Indiana, N USA

Indian Church *52 C1* Orange Walk, N Belize

Indian Desert *see* Thar Desert

Indianola *45 F4* Iowa, C USA

Indigirka *115 F2 river* NE Russian Federation

Indija *100 D3 Hung.* India; *prev.* Indjija. Serbia, N Yugoslavia

Indira Point *132 G3 headland* Andaman and Nicobar Islands, India, NE Indian Ocean

Indomed Fracture Zone *141 B6 tectonic feature* SW Indian Ocean

Indonesia *138 B4 Ind.* Republik Indonesia; *prev.* Dutch East Indies, Netherlands East Indies, United States of Indonesia. *Country* SE Asia

---

Indonesia 138

Official name Republic of Indonesia
Formation 1949
Capital Jakarta

Indonesia (continued)

Population 212 million / 303 people per sq mile (117 people per sq km)
Total area 699,447 sq miles (1,811,570 sq km)
Languages Bahasa Indonesia, Javanese, Madurese, Sundanese, Dutch
Religions Muslim 87%, Protestant 6%, Roman Catholic 3%, other 4%
Ethnic mix Javanese 45%, Sundanese 14%, Coastal Malays 8%, Madurese 8%, other 25%
Government Multiparty republic
Currency Rupiah = 100 sen
Literacy rate 85%
Calorie consumption 2,752 kilocalories

Indore 134 D4 Madhya Pradesh, C India
Indus 134 C2 *Chin.* Yindu He; *prev.* Yin-tu Ho. *River* S Asia
Indus Cone *see* Indus Fan
Indus Fan 112 C5 *var.* Indus Cone. *Undersea feature* N Arabian Sea
Indus, Mouths of the 134 B4 *delta* S Pakistan
Ínebolu 116 C2 Kastamonu, N Turkey
Ineu 108 A4 *Hung.* Borosjenő; *prev.* Ináu. Arad, W Romania
Infiernillo, Presa del 51 E4 *reservoir* S Mexico
Inglewood 46 D2 California, W USA
Ingolstadt 95 C6 Bayern, S Germany
Inhambane 79 E4 Inhambane, SE Mozambique
Inhulets' 109 F3 *Rus.* Ingulets. Dnipropetrovs'ka Oblast', E Ukraine
I-ning *see* Yining
Inis *see* Ennis
Inis Ceithleann *see* Enniskillen
Inn 95 C6 *river* C Europe
Innaanganeq 82 C1 *var.* Kap York. *Headland* NW Greenland
Inner Hebrides 88 B4 *island group* W Scotland, UK
Inner Islands 79 H1 *var.* Central Group. *Island group* NE Seychelles
Inner Mongolia 127 F3 *var.* Nei Mongol, *Eng.* Inner Mongolia, Inner Mongolian Autonomous Region; *prev.* Nei Monggol Zizhiqu. Admin. region *autonomous region* N China
Inner Mongolian Autonomous Region *see* Inner Mongolia
Innisfail 148 D3 Queensland, NE Australia
Inniskilling *see* Enniskillen
Innsbruch *see* Innsbruck
Innsbruck 95 C7 *var.* Innsbruch. Tirol, W Austria
Inoucdjouac *see* Inukjuak
Inowrocław 98 C3 *Ger.* Hohensalza; *prev.* Inowrazlaw. Kujawski-pomorskie, C Poland
I-n-Salah 70 D3 *var.* In Salah. C Algeria
In Salah *see* I-n-Salah
Insula *see* Lille
Inta 110 E3 Respublika Komi, NW Russian Federation
International Falls 45 F1 Minnesota, N USA
Inukjuak 38 D2 *var.* Inoucdjouac; *prev.* Port Harrison. Québec, NE Canada
Inuvik *see* Inuvik
Inuvik 36 D3 *var.* Inuuvik. *District capital* Northwest Territories, NW Canada
Invercargill 151 A7 Southland, South Island, NZ
Inverness 88 C3 N Scotland, UK
Investigator Ridge 141 D5 *undersea feature* E Indian Ocean
Investigator Strait 149 B7 *strait* South Australia
Inyangani 78 D3 *mountain* NE Zimbabwe

Ioánnina 104 A4 *var.* Janina, Yannina. Ípeiros, W Greece
Iola 45 F5 Kansas, C USA
Ionia Basin *see* Ionian Basin
Ionian Basin 80 D5 *var.* Ionia Basin. *Undersea feature* Ionian Sea, C Mediterranean Sea
Ionian Islands *see* Iónioi Nísoi
Ionian Sea 103 E3 *Gk.* Iónio Pélagos, *It.* Mar Ionio. *Sea* C Mediterranean Sea
Iónioi Nísoi 105 A5 *Eng.* Ionian Islands. *Island group* W Greece
Íos 105 D6 *var.* Nio. *Island* Kykládes, Greece, Aegean Sea
Íos 105 D6 Íos, Kykládes, Greece, Aegean Sea
Iowa 45 F3 *off.* State of Iowa; also known as The Hawkeye State. *State* C USA
Iowa City 45 G3 Iowa, C USA
Iowa Falls 45 G3 Iowa, C USA
Ipel' 99 C6 *var.* Ipoly, *Ger.* Eipel. *River* Hungary/Slovakia
Ipiales 58 A4 Nariño, SW Colombia
Ipoh 138 B3 Perak, Peninsular Malaysia
Ipoly 99 C6 *var.* Ipel', *Ger.* Eipel. *River* Hungary/Slovakia
Ippy 76 C4 Ouaka, C Central African Republic
Ipswich 89 E6 *hist.* Gipeswic. E England, UK
Ipswich 149 E5 Queensland, E Australia
Iqaluit 37 H3 *prev.* Frobisher Bay. Baffin Island, Nunavut, NE Canada
Iquique 64 B1 Tarapacá, N Chile
Iquitos 60 C1 Loreto, N Peru
Irákleio 105 D7 *var.* Herakleion, *Eng.* Candia; *prev.* Iráklion. Kríti, Greece, E Mediterranean Sea
Iráklion *see* Irákleio
Iran 120 C3 *prev.* Persia. *Country* SW Asia

Iran 120

Official name Islamic Republic of Iran
Formation 1906
Capital Tehran
Population 67.7 million / 107 people per sq mile (41 people per sq km)
Total area 631,659 sq miles (1,636,000 sq km)
Languages Farsi (Persian), Azerbaijani, Gilaki, Mazanderani, Kurdish, Baluchi
Religions Shi'a Muslim 95%, Sunni Muslim 4%, other 1%
Ethnic mix Persian 50%, Azeri 20%, Lur and Bakhtiari 10%, Kurd 8%, other 12%
Government Islamic republic
Currency Iranian rial = 100 dinars
Literacy rate 73.3%
Calorie consumption 2,860 kilocalories

Iranian Plateau 120 D3 *var.* Plateau of Iran. *plateau* N Iran
Iran, Plateau of *see* Iranian Plateau
Irapuato 51 E4 Guanajuato, C Mexico
Iraq 120 B3 *Ar.* 'Irāq. *Country* SW Asia

Iraq 120

Official name Republic of Iraq
Formation 1932
Capital Baghdad
Population 23 million / 137 people per sq mile (53 people per sq km)
Total area 168,868 sq miles (437,370 sq km)
Languages Arabic, Kurdish, Armenian, Assyrian
Religions Shi'a ithna Muslim 62%, Sunni Muslim 33%, other 5%
Ethnic mix Arab 79%, Kurdish 16%, Persian 3%, Turkoman 2%

Iraq (continued)

Government Single-party republic
Currency Iraqi dinar = 1,000 fils
Literacy rate 58%
Calorie consumption 2,121 kilocalories

Irbid 119 B5 Irbid, N Jordan
Irbil *see* Arbil
Ireland 80 C3 *Lat.* Hibernia. *Island* Ireland/UK
Ireland, Republic of 89 A5 *var.* Ireland, *Ir.* Éire. *Country* NW Europe

Ireland 89

Official name Republic of Ireland
Formation 1922
Capital Dublin
Population 3.7 million / 139 people per sq mile (54 people per sq km)
Total area 26,598 sq miles (68,890 sq km)
Languages English, Irish Gaelic
Religions Roman Catholic 88%, Anglican 3%, other and non-religious 9%
Ethnic mix Mostly Celtic with English minority
Government Multiparty republic
Currency Punt = 100 pence
Literacy rate 99%
Calorie consumption 3,847 kilocalories

Irian Barat *see* Irian Jaya
Irian Jaya 139 H4 *var.* Irian Barat, West Irian, West New Guinea, West Papua; *prev.* Dutch New Guinea, Netherlands New Guinea. Admin. region *province* E Indonesia
Irian, Teluk *see* Cenderawasih, Teluk
Iringa 73 C7 Iringa, C Tanzania
Iriomote-jima 130 A4 *island* Sakishima-shotō, SW Japan
Iriona 52 D2 Colón, NE Honduras
Irish Sea 89 C5 *Ir.* Muir Éireann. *Sea* C British Isles
Irkutsk 115 E4 Irkutskaya Oblast', S Russian Federation
Irminger Basin *see* Reykjanes Basin
Iroise 90 A3 *sea* NW France
Iron Mountain 40 B2 Michigan, N USA
Ironwood 40 B1 Michigan, N USA
Irrawaddy 136 B2 *var.* Ayeyarwady. *River* W Myanmar
Irrawaddy, Mouths of the 137 A5 *delta* SW Myanmar
Irtish *see* Irtysh
Irtysh 114 C4 *var.* Irtish, *Kaz.* Ertis. *River* C Asia
Irún 93 E1 País Vasco, N Spain
Iruña *see* Pamplona
Isabela, Isla 60 A5 *var.* Albemarle Island. *Island* Galapagos Islands, Ecuador, E Pacific Ocean
Isaccea 108 D4 Tulcea, E Romania
Isachsen 37 F1 Ellef Ringnes Island, Nunavut, N Canada
Ísafjördhur 83 E4 Vestfirdhir, NW Iceland
Isbarta *see* Isparta
Ise 131 C6 Mie, Honshū, SW Japan
Isère 91 D5 *var.* Æsernia. Molise, C Italy
Ise-wan 131 C6 *bay* S Japan
Isha Baydhabo *see* Baydhabo
Ishigaki-jima 130 A4 *var.* Isigaki Zima. *Island* Sakishima-shotō, SW Japan
Ishikari-wan 130 C2 *bay* Hokkaidō, NE Japan
Ishim 114 C4 *Kaz.* Esil. *River* Kazakhstan/Russian Federation
Ishim 114 C4 Tyumenskaya Oblast', C Russian Federation
Ishinomaki 130 D4 *var.* Isinomaki. Miyagi, Honshū, C Japan

Ishkoshim 123 F3 *Rus.* Ishkashim. S Tajikistan
Isigaki Zima *see* Ishigaki-jima
Isinomaki *see* Ishinomaki
Isiro 77 E5 Orientale, NE Dem. Rep. Congo (Zaire)
Iskăr *see* Iskŭr
İskenderun 116 D4 *Eng.* Alexandretta. Hatay, S Turkey
İskenderun Körfezi 118 A2 *Eng.* Gulf of Alexandretta. *Gulf* S Turkey
Iskŭr 104 C2 *var.* Iskăr. *River* NW Bulgaria
Iskŭr, Yazovir 104 B2 *prev.* Yazovir Stalin. *Reservoir* W Bulgaria
Isla Cristina 92 C4 Andalucía, S Spain
Isla Gran Malvina *see* West Falkalnd
Islāmābād 134 C1 *country capital* (Pakistan) Federal Capital Territory Islāmābād, NE Pakistan
I-n-Sâkâne, 'Erg 75 E2 *desert* N Mali
Islas de los Galápagos *see* Galapagos Islands
Islas Malvinas *see* Falkland Islands
Islay 88 B4 *island* SW Scotland, UK
Isle 91 B5 *river* W France
Isle of Man 89 B5 *UK crown dependency* NW Europe
Ismailia *see* Ismâ'ilîya
Ismâ'ilîya 72 B1 *var.* Ismailia. N Egypt
Ismid *see* İzmit
Isna 72 B2 *var.* Esna. SE Egypt
Isoka 78 D1 Northern, NE Zambia
Isola Grossa *see* Dugi Otok
Isola Lunga *see* Dugi Otok
Isole Lipari *see* Eolie, Isole
Ísparta 116 B4 *var.* Isbarta. Isparta, SW Turkey
İspir 117 E3 Erzurum, NE Turkey
Israel 119 A7 *var.* Medinat Israel, *Heb.* Yisrael, Yisra'el. *Country* SW Asia

Israel 119

Official name State of Israel
Formation 1948
Capital Jerusalem
Population 6.2 million / 790 people per sq mile (305 people per sq km)
Total area 7,849 sq miles (20,330 sq km)
Languages Hebrew, Arabic, Yiddish, German, Russian, Polish, Romanian
Religions Jewish 82%, Muslim (mainly Sunni) 14%, other (including Druze) 4%
Ethnic mix Jewish 82%, other (mostly Arab) 18%
Government Multiparty republic
Currency New Israeli shekel = 100 agorat
Literacy rate 95.4%
Calorie consumption 3,050 kilocalories

Issiq Köl *see* Issyk-Kul', Ozero
Issoire 91 C5 Puy-de-Dôme, C France
Issyk-Kul', Ozero 123 G2 *var.* Issiq Köl, *Kir.* Ysyk-Köl. *Lake* E Kyrgyzstan
İstanbul 116 B2 *Bul.* Tsarigrad, *Eng.* Istanbul; *prev.* Constantinople, *anc.* Byzantium. İstanbul, NW Turkey
İstanbul Boğazı 116 B2 *var.* Bosporus Thracius, *Eng.* Bosphorus, Bosporus, *Turk.* Karadeniz Boğazı. *Strait* NW Turkey
Istra 100 A3 *Eng.* Istria, *Ger.* Istrien. *Cultural region* NW Croatia
Istra 96 D2 *Eng.* Istria. *Peninsula* NW Croatia
Itabuna 63 G3 Bahia, E Brazil
Itagüí 58 B3 Antioquia, W Colombia
Itaipú, Represa de 63 E4 *reservoir* Brazil/Paraguay
Itaituba 63 E2 Pará, NE Brazil

Italy 96 C3 *It.* Italia, Republica
Italiana. *Country* S Europe

Italy 96

Official name Italian Republic
Formation 1871
Capital Rome
Population 57.3 million /
505 people per sq mile
(195 people per sq km)
Total area 113,536 sq miles
(294,060 sq km)
Languages Italian, German, French,
Rhaeto-Romanic, Sardinian
Religions Roman Catholic 83%,
other and non-religious 17%
Ethnic mix Italian 94%, Sardinian
2%, other 4%
Government Multiparty
republic
Currency Italian lira
= 100 centesimi
Literacy rate 98.3%
Calorie consumption 3,561
kilocalories

Italy 80 D4 Texas, SW USA
Iténez, Río *see* Guaporé, Rio
Ithaca 41 E3 New York, NE USA
Itoigawa 131 C5 Niigata, Honshū,
C Japan
Itseqqortoormiit *see*
Ittoqqortoormiit
Ittoqqortoormiit 83 E3 *var.*
Itseqqortoormiit, *Dan.*
Scoresbysund, *Eng.* Scoresby
Sound. C Greenland
Iturup, Ostrov 130 E1 *island*
Kuril'skiye Ostrova, SE Russian
Federation
Itzehoe 94 B2 Schleswig-Holstein,
N Germany
Ivalo 84 D2 *Lapp.* Avveel, Avvil.
Lappi, N Finland
Ivanava 107 B7 *Pol.* Janów, Janów
Poleski, *Rus.* Ivanovo. Brestskaya
Voblasts', SW Belarus
Ivanhoe 149 C6 New South Wales,
SE Australia
Ivano-Frankivs'k 108 C2 *Ger.*
Stanislau, *Pol.* Stanisławów, *Rus.*
Ivano-Frankovsk; *prev.* Stanislav.
Ivano-Frankivs'ka Oblast',
W Ukraine
Ivanovo 111 B5 Ivanovskaya
Oblast', W Russian Federation
Ivatsevichy 107 B6 *Pol.* Iwacewicze,
Rus. Ivantsevichi, Ivatsevichi.
Brestskaya Voblasts', SW Belarus
Ivigtut *see* Ivittuut
Ivittuut 82 B4 *var.* Ivigtut.
S Greenland
Iviza *see* Eivissa
Ivory Coast *see* Côte d'Ivoire
Ivujivik 38 D1 Québec, NE Canada
Iwaki 131 D5 Fukushima, Honshū,
N Japan
Iwakuni 131 B7 Yamaguchi,
Honshū, SW Japan
Iwanai 130 C2 Hokkaidō, NE Japan
Iwate 130 D3 Iwate, Honshū,
N Japan
Ixtapa 51 E5 Guerrero, S Mexico
Ixtepec 51 F5 Oaxaca, SE Mexico
Iyo-nada 131 B7 *sea* S Japan
Izabal, Lago de 52 B2 *prev.* Golfo
Dulce. *Lake* E Guatemala
Izad Khvāst 120 D3 Fārs, C Iran
Izegem 87 A6 *prev.* Iseghem. West-
Vlaanderen, W Belgium
Izhevsk 111 D5 *prev.* Ustinov.
Udmurtskaya Respublika,
NW Russian Federation
Izmayil 108 D4 *Rus.* Izmail.
Odes'ka Oblast', SW Ukraine
İzmir 116 A3 *prev.* Smyrna. İzmir,
W Turkey
İzmit 116 B2 *var.* Ismid; *anc.*
Astacus. Kocaeli, NW Turkey
İznik Gölü 116 B3 *lake* NW Turkey
Izu-hantō 131 D6 *peninsula* Honshū,
S Japan
Izu Shichito *see* Izu-shotō
Izu-shotō 131 D6 *var.* Izu Shichito.
Island group S Japan
Izvor 104 B2 Pernik, W Bulgaria

Izyaslav 108 C2 Khmel'nyts'ka
Oblast', W Ukraine
Izyum 109 G2 Kharkivs'ka Oblast',
E Ukraine

J

Jabal ash Shifā 120 A4 *desert*
NW Saudi Arabia
Jabalpur 135 E4 *prev.* Jubbulpore.
Madhya Pradesh, C India
Jabbūl, Sabkhat al 134 B2 *salt flat*
NW Syria
Jablah 118 A3 *var.* Jeble, *Fr.* Djéblé.
Al Lādhiqīyah, W Syria
Jaca 93 F1 Aragón, NE Spain
Jacaltenango 52 A2
Huehuetenango, W Guatemala
Jackson 42 B2 *state capital*
Mississippi, S USA
Jackson 43 H5 Missouri, C USA
Jackson 42 C1 Tennessee, S USA
Jackson Head 151 A6 *headland*
South Island, NZ
Jacksonville 43 E3 Florida, SE USA
Jacksonville 40 B4 Illinois, N USA
Jacksonville 43 F1 North Carolina,
SE USA
Jacksonville 49 G3 Texas, SW USA
Jacmel 54 D3 *var.* Jaquemel. S Haiti
Jacobābād 134 B3 Sind, SE Pakistan
Jaén 92 D4 Andalucía, SW Spain
Jaén 60 B2 Cajamarca, N Peru
Jaffna 132 D3 Northern Province,
N Sri Lanka
Jagannath *see* Puri
Jagdalpur 135 E5 Madhya Pradesh,
C India
Jagdaqi 127 G1 Nei Mongol
Zizhiqu, N China
Jagodina 100 D4 *prev.* Svetozarevo.
Serbia, C Yugoslavia
Jahra *see* Al Jahrā'
Jaipur 134 D3 *prev.* Jeypore.
Rājasthān, N India
Jaisalmer 134 C3 Rājasthān,
NW India
Jajce 100 B3 Federacija Bosna I
Hercegovina, W Bosnia and
Herzegovina
Jakarta 138 C5 *prev.* Djakarta, *Dut.*
Batavia. *Country capital*
(Indonesia) Jawa, C Indonesia
Jakobstad 84 D4 *Fin.* Pietarsaari.
Länsi-Suomi, W Finland
Jalālābād 123 F4 *var.* Jalalabad,
Jelalabad. Nangarhār,
E Afghanistan
Jalandhar 134 D2 *prev.* Jullundur.
Punjab, N India
Jalapa *see* Xalapa
Jalapa 52 D3 Nueva Segovia,
NW Nicaragua
Jalapa Enríquez *see* Xalapa
Jalpa 50 D4 Zacatecas, C Mexico
Jālū 71 G3 *var.* Jālā. NE Libya
Jaluit Atoll 144 D2 *var.* Jālwōj. *Atoll*
Ralik Chain, S Marshall Islands
Jālwōj *see* Jaluit Atoll
Jamaame 73 D6 *It.* Giamame; *prev.*
Margherita. Jubbada Hoose,
S Somalia
Jamaica 54 A4 *country* W West
Indies

Jamaica 54

Official name Jamaica
Formation 1962
Capital Kingston
Population 2.6 million /
622 people per sq mile
(240 people per sq km)
Total area 4,181 sq miles
(10,830 sq km)
Languages English, English
Creole
Religions Christian (Church of
God, Baptist, Anglican, other
Protestant) 55%, other and non-
religious 45%
Ethnic mix Black 75%, mixed 15%,
South Asian 5%, other 5%
Government Parliamentary
democracy

Jamaica (continued)

Currency Jamaican dollar
= 100 cents
Literacy rate 85.5%
Calorie consumption 2,607
kilocalories

Jamaica 56 A1 *island* W West Indies
Jamaica Channel 54 D3 *channel*
Haiti/Jamaica
Jamālpur 135 F3 Bihār, NE India
Jambi 138 B4 *var.* Telanaipura; *prev.*
Djambi. Sumatera, W Indonesia
James Bay 38 C3 *bay*
Ontario/Québec, E Canada
James River 45 E2 *river* North
Dakota/South Dakota, N USA
James River 41 E5 *river* Virginia,
NE USA
Jamestown 41 E3 New York,
NE USA
Jamestown 45 E2 North Dakota,
N USA
Jammu 134 D2 *prev.* Jummoo.
Jammu and Kashmir, NW India
Jammu and Kashmīr 134 D1
disputed region India/Pakistan
Jāmnagar 134 C4 *prev.* Navanagar.
Gujarāt, W India
Jamshedpur 135 F4 Bihār, NE India
Jamuna *see* Brahmaputra
Janaúba 63 F3 Minas Gerais,
SE Brazil
Janesville 40 B3 Wisconsin,
N USA
Janīn *see* Jenīn
Janina *see* Ioánnina
Jan Mayen 83 F4 *Norwegian
dependency* N Atlantic Ocean
Jánoshalma 99 C7 *SCr.* Jankovac.
Bács-Kiskun, S Hungary
Japan 130 C4 *var.* Nippon, *Jap.*
Nihon. *Country* E Asia

Japan 130

Official name Japan
Formation 1600
Capital Tokyo
Population 126.7 million /
872 people per sq mile
(337 people per sq km)
Total area 145,374 sq miles
(376,520 sq km)
Languages Japanese, Korean,
Chinese
Religions Shinto and Buddhist
76%, Buddhist 16%, other
(including Christian) 8%
Ethnic mix Japanese 99%, other
(mainly Korean) 1%
Government Constitutional
monarchy
Currency Yen = 100 sen
Literacy rate 99%
Calorie consumption 2,903
kilocalories

Japan, Sea of 130 A4 *var.* East Sea,
Rus. Yaponskoye More. *Sea*
NW Pacific Ocean
Japan Trench 125 F1 *undersea feature*
NW Pacific Ocean
Japiim 62 C2 *var.* Máncio Lima.
Acre, W Brazil
Japurá, Rio 62 C2 *var.* Río Caquetá,
Yapurá. *River* Brazil/Colombia *see
also* Caquetá, Río
Jaqué 53 G5 Darién, SE Panama
Jaquemel *see* Jacmel
Jarablos *see* Jarābulus
Jarābulus 118 C2 *var.* Jarablos,
Jerablus, *Fr.* Djérablous. Ḥalab,
N Syria
**Jardines de la Reina,
Archipiélago de los** 54 B2 *island
group* C Cuba
Jarocin 98 C4 Wielkopolskie,
C Poland
Jarosław 99 E5 *Ger.* Jaroslau, *Rus.*
Yaroslav. Podkarpackie,
SE Poland
Jarqŭrghon 123 E3 *Rus.*
Dzharkurgan. Surkhondaryo
Wiloyati, S Uzbekistan

Jarvis Island 145 G2 US
unincorporated territory C Pacific
Ocean
Jasło 99 D5 Podkarpackie,
SE Poland
Jastrzębie-Zdrój 99 C5 Śląskie,
S Poland
Jataí 63 E3 Goiás, C Brazil
Jativa *see* Xátiva
Jauf *see* Al Jawf
Jaunpiebalga 106 D3 Gulbene,
NE Latvia
Jaunpur 135 E3 Uttar Pradesh,
N India
Java 152 A3 *prev.* Djawa. *Island*
C Indonesia
Javalambre 93 E3 *mountain*
E Spain
Javari, Río 62 C2 *var.* Yavarí. *River*
Brazil/Peru
Java Sea 138 D4 *Ind.* Laut Jawa. *Sea*
W Indonesia
Java Trench 124 D5 *var.* Sunda
Trench. *Undersea feature* E Indian
Ocean
Jawhar 73 D6 *var.* Jowhar, *It.*
Giohar. Shabeellaha Dhexe,
S Somalia
Jaya, Puncak 139 G4 *prev.* Puntjak
Carstensz, Puntjak Sukarno.
Mountain Irian Jaya,
E Indonesia
Jayapura 139 H4 *var.* Djajapura,
Dut. Hollandia; *prev.* Kotabaru,
Sukarnapura. Irian Jaya,
E Indonesia
Jazā'ir Bin Ghalfān *see* Ḥalāniyāt,
Juzur al
Jazīrat Jarbah *see* Jerba, Île de
Jazīreh-ye Qeshm *see* Qeshm
Jaz Mūrīān, Hāmūn-e 120 E4 *lake*
SE Iran
Jebba 75 F4 Kwara, W Nigeria
Jebel esh Sharqi *see* Anti-Lebanon
Jebel Uweinat *see* 'Uwaynāt, Jabal
al
Jeble *see* Jablah
Jędrzejów 98 D4 *Ger.*
Endersdorf. Świętokrzyskie,
C Poland
Jefferson City 45 G5 *state capital*
Missouri, C USA
Jega 75 F4 Kebbi, NW Nigeria
Jehol *see* Chengde
Jēkabpils 106 D4 *Ger.* Jakobstadt.
Jēkabpils, S Latvia
Jelalabad *see* Jalālābād
Jelenia Góra 98 B4 *Ger.* Hirschberg,
Hirschberg im Riesengebirge,
Hirschberg in Riesengebirge,
Hirschberg in Schlesien.
Dolnośląskie, SW Poland
Jelgava 106 C3 *Ger.* Mitau. Jelgava,
C Latvia
Jemappes 87 B6 Hainaut,
S Belgium
Jember 138 D5 *prev.* Djember. Jawa,
C Indonesia
Jena 94 C4 Thüringen,
C Germany
Jenīn 119 A6 *var.* Janīn, Jinīn; *anc.*
Engannim. N West Bank
Jerablus *see* Jarābulus
Jerada 70 D2 NE Morocco
Jerba, Île de 71 F2 *var.* Djerba,
Jazīrat Jarbah. *Island* E Tunisia
Jérémie 54 D3 SW Haiti
Jerez *see* Jeréz de la Frontera
Jeréz de la Frontera 92 C5 *var.*
Jerez; *prev.* Xeres. Andalucía,
SW Spain
Jeréz de los Caballeros 92 C4
Extremadura, W Spain
Jericho 119 B6 *Ar.* Arīḥā, *Heb.*
Yeriḥo. E West Bank
Jerid, Chott el 87 E2 *var.* Shaṭṭ
al Jarīd. *salt lake* SW Tunisia
Jersey 89 D8 UK *dependent territory*
NW Europe
Jerusalem 103 H4 *Ar.* El Quds, *Heb.*
Yerushalayim; *anc.* Hierosolyma.
Country capital (Israel) Jerusalem,
NE Israel
Jerusalem 112 A4 Admin. region
district E Israel
Jesenice 95 D7 *Ger.* Assling.
NW Slovenia

Jessore 135 G4 Khulna, W Bangladesh
Jesús María 64 C3 Córdoba, C Argentina
Jhānsi 134 D3 Uttar Pradesh, N India
Jhelum 134 C2 Punjab, NE Pakistan
Ji see Hebei
Ji see Jilin
Jiangmen 128 C6 Guangdong, S China
Jiangsu 128 D4 var. Chiang-su, Jiangsu Sheng, Kiangsu, Su. Admin. region province E China
Jiangsu Sheng see Jiangsu
Jiangxi 128 C6 var. Chiang-hsi, Gan, Jiangxi Sheng, Kiangsi. Admin. region province S China
Jiangxi Sheng see Jiangxi
Jiaxing 128 D5 Zhejiang, SE China
Jiayi see Chiai
Jibuti see Djibouti
Jiddah 121 A5 Eng. Jedda. Makkah, W Saudi Arabia
Jih-k'a-tse see Xigazê
Jihlava 99 B5 Ger. Iglau, Pol. Iglawa. Jihlavský Kraj, C Czech Republic
Jilib 73 D6 It. Gelib. Jubbada Dhexe, S Somalia
Jilin 128 D3 var. Chi-lin, Girin, Ji, Jilin Sheng, Kirin. Admin. region province NE China
Jilin 129 E3 var. Chi-lin, Girin, Kirin; prev. Yungki, Yunki. Jilin, NE China
Jilin Sheng see Jilin
Jīma 73 C5 var. Jimma, It. Gimma. C Ethiopia
Jimbolia 108 A4 Ger. Hatzfeld, Hung. Zsombolya. Timiş, W Romania
Jiménez 50 D2 Chihuahua, N Mexico
Jimma see Jīma
Jimsar 126 C3 Xinjiang Uygur Zizhiqu, NW China
Jin see Shanxi
Jin see Tianjin Shi
Jinan 128 C4 var. Chinan, Chi-nan, Tsinan. Shandong, E China
Jingdezhen 128 C5 Jiangxi, S China
Jinghong 128 A6 var. Yunjinghong. Yunnan, SW China
Jinhua 128 D5 Zhejiang, SE China
Jinīn see Jenīn
Jining 127 F3 Shandong, E China
Jinja 73 C6 S Uganda
Jinotega 52 D3 Jinotega, NW Nicaragua
Jinotepe 52 D3 Carazo, SW Nicaragua
Jinsha Jiang 128 A5 river SW China
Jinzhou 128 D3 var. Chin-chou, Chinchow; prev. Chinhsien. Liaoning, NE China
Jisr ash Shadadi see Ash Shadādah
Jiu 108 B5 Ger. Schil, Schyl, Hung. Zsil, Zsily. River S Romania
Jiujiang 128 C5 Jiangxi, S China
Jixi 129 E2 Heilongjiang, NE China
Jīzān 121 B6 var. Qīzān. Jīzān, SW Saudi Arabia
Jizzakh 123 E2 Rus. Dzhizak. Jizzakh Wiloyati, C Uzbekistan
João Pessoa 63 G2 prev. Paraíba. State capital Paraíba, E Brazil
Jo'burg see Johannesburg
Jo-ch'iang see Ruoqiang
Jodhpur 134 C3 Rājasthān, NW India
Joensuu 85 E5 Itä-Suomi, E Finland
Jōetsu 131 C5 var. Zyôetu. Niigata, Honshū, C Japan
Johanna Island see Anjouan
Johannesburg 78 D4 var. Egoli, Erautini, Gauteng, abbrev. Jo'burg. Gauteng, NE South Africa
John Day River 46 C3 river Oregon, NW USA
John o'Groats 88 C2 N Scotland, UK
Johnston Atoll 143 E1 US unincorporated territory C Pacific Ocean
Johor Baharu see Johor Bahru

Johor Bahru 138 B3 var. Johor Baharu, Johore Bahru. Johor, Peninsular Malaysia
Johore Bahru see Johor Bahru
Johore Strait 138 A1 Mal. Selat Johor. Strait Malaysia/Singapore
Joinvile see Joinville
Joinville 63 E4 var. Joinvile. Santa Catarina, S Brazil
Jokkmokk 84 C3 Norrbotten, N Sweden
Joliet 40 B3 Illinois, N USA
Jonava 106 B4 Ger. Janow, Pol. Janów. Jonava, C Lithuania
Jonesboro 42 B1 Arkansas, C USA
Joniškis 106 C3 Ger. Janischken. Joniškis, N Lithuania
Jönköping 85 B7 Jönköping, S Sweden
Jonquière 39 E4 Québec, SE Canada
Joplin 45 F5 Missouri, C USA
Jordan 119 B5 Ar. Urdunn, Heb. HaYarden. River SW Asia
Jordan 119 B6 Ar. Al Mamlakah al Urduníyah al Hāshimīyah, Al Urdunn; prev. Transjordan. Country SW Asia

---

Jordan 119

Official name Hashemite Kingdom of Jordan
Formation 1946
Capital Amman
Population 6.7 million / 195 people per sq mile (75 people per sq km)
Total area 34,335 sq miles (88,930 sq km)
Languages Arabic
Religions Muslim (mainly Sunni) 92%, other (mostly Christian) 8%
Ethnic mix Arab 98% (Palestinian 40%), Armenian 1%, Circassian 1%
Government Constitutional monarchy
Currency Jordanian dinar = 1,000 fils
Literacy rate 87.2%
Calorie consumption 3,022 kilocalories

Jorhāt 135 H3 Assam, NE India
Jos 75 G4 Plateau, C Nigeria
Joseph Bonaparte Gulf 146 D2 gulf N Australia
Jos Plateau 75 G4 plateau C Nigeria
Jotunheimen 85 A5 mountain range S Norway
Joûnié 118 A4 var. Junīyah. W Lebanon
Joure 86 D2 Fris. De Jouwer. Friesland, N Netherlands
Joutseno 85 E5 Etelä-Suomi, S Finland
Jowhar see Jawhar
JStorm Thurmond Reservoir see Clark Hill Lake
Juan Aldama 50 D3 Zacatecas, C Mexico
Juan de Fuca, Strait of 46 A1 strait Canada/USA
Juan Fernández, Islas 57 A6 Eng. Juan Fernandez Islands. Island group W Chile
Juazeiro 63 G3 prev. Joazeiro. Bahia, E Brazil
Juazeiro do Norte 63 G2 Ceará, E Brazil
Juba 73 D6 Amh. Genalē Wenz, It. Guba, Som. Ganaane, Webi Jubba. River Ethiopia/Somalia
Juba 73 B5 var. Jūbā. Bahr el Gabel, S Sudan
Júcar 93 E3 var. Jucar. River C Spain
Juchitán 51 F5 var. Juchitán de Zaragosa. Oaxaca, SE Mexico
Juchitán de Zaragosa see Juchitán
Judayyidat Hāmir 120 B3 S Iraq
Judenburg 95 D7 Steiermark, C Austria
Juigalpa 52 D3 Chontales, S Nicaragua
Juiz de Fora 63 F4 Minas Gerais, SE Brazil
Jujuy see San Salvador de Jujuy

Jūlā see Jālū
Juliaca 61 E4 Puno, SE Peru
Juliana Top 59 G3 mountain C Suriname
Jumilla 93 E4 Murcia, SE Spain
Jumporn see Chumphon
Junction City 45 F4 Kansas, C USA
Juneau 36 D4 state capital Alaska, USA
Junín 64 C4 Buenos Aires, E Argentina
Junīyah see Joûnié
Junkseylon see Phuket
Jur 73 B5 river C Sudan
Jura 88 B4 island SW Scotland, UK
Jura 95 A7 canton NW Switzerland
Jura 90 D4 department E France
Jurbarkas 106 B4 Ger. Georgenburg, Jurburg. Jurbarkas, W Lithuania
Jūrmala 106 C3 Rīga, C Latvia
Juruá, Rio 62 C2 var. Río Yuruá. River Brazil/Peru
Juruena, Rio 62 D3 river W Brazil
Jutiapa 52 B2 Jutiapa, S Guatemala
Juticalpa 52 D2 Olancho, C Honduras
Juventud, Isla de la 54 A2 var. Isla de Pinos, Eng. Isle of Youth; prev. The Isle of the Pines. Island W Cuba
Južna Morava 101 E5 Ger. Südliche Morava. River SE Yugoslavia
Juzur Qarqannah see Kerkenah, Îles de
Jwaneng 78 C4 Southern, SE Botswana
Jylland 85 A7 Eng. Jutland. Peninsula W Denmark
Jyväskylä 85 D5 Länsi-Suomi, W Finland

K

K2 126 A4 Chin. Qogir Feng, Eng. Mount Godwin Austen. Mountain China/Pakistan
Kaafu Atoll see Male' Atoll
Kaaimanston 59 G3 Sipaliwini, N Suriname
Kaakhka 122 C3 var. Kaka. Akhalskiy Velayat, S Turkmenistan
Kaala see Caála
Kaamanen 84 D2 Lapp. Gámas. Lappi, N Finland
Kaapstad see Cape Town
Kaaresuvanto 84 C3 Lapp. Gárassavon. Lappi, N Finland
Kabale 73 B6 SW Uganda
Kabinda see Cabinda
Kabinda 77 D7 Kasai Oriental, SE Dem. Rep. Congo (Zaire)
Kābol see Kābul
Kabompo 78 C2 river W Zambia
Kābul 123 E4 var. Kabul, Per. Kābol. Country capital (Afghanistan). Kābul, E Afghanistan
Kabul see Kābul
Kabwe 78 D2 Central, C Zambia
Kachchh, Gulf of 134 B4 var. Gulf of Cutch, Gulf of Kutch. Gulf W India
Kachchh, Rann of 134 B4 var. Rann of Kachh, Rann of Kutch. Salt marsh India/Pakistan
Kachh, Rann of see Kachchh, Rann of
Kadan Kyun 137 B5 prev. King Island. Island Mergui Archipelago, S Myanmar
Kadavu 145 E4 prev. Kandavu. Island S Fiji
Kadoma 78 D3 prev. Gatooma. Mashonaland West, C Zimbabwe
Kadugli 72 B4 Southern Kordofan, S Sudan
Kaduna 75 G4 Kaduna, C Nigeria
Kadzhi-Say 123 G2 Kir. Kajisay. Issyk-Kul'skaya Oblast', NE Kyrgyzstan
Kaédi 74 C3 Gorgol, S Mauritania
Kaffa see Feodosiya
Kafue 78 D2 river C Zambia
Kafue 78 D2 Lusaka, SE Zambia
Kaga Bandoro 76 C4 prev. Fort-Crampel. Nana-Grébizi, C Central African Republic

Kâghet 74 D1 var. Karet. Physical region N Mauritania
Kagi see Chiai
Kagoshima 131 B8 var. Kagosima. Kagoshima, Kyūshū, SW Japan
Kagoshima-wan 131 A8 bay SW Japan
Kagosima see Kagoshima
Kahmard, Daryā-ye 123 E4 prev. Darya-i-Surkhab. River NE Afghanistan
Kahraman Maraş see Kahramanmaraş
Kahramanmaraş 116 C4 var. Kahraman Maraş, Maraş, Marash. Kahramanmaraş, S Turkey
Kaiapoi 151 C6 Canterbury, South Island, NZ
Kaifeng 128 C4 Henan, C China
Kai, Kepulauan 139 F4 prev. Kei Islands. Island group Maluku, SE Indonesia
Kaikohe 150 C2 Northland, North Island, NZ
Kaikoura 151 C5 Canterbury, South Island, NZ
Kaikoura Peninsula 151 C5 peninsula South Island, NZ
Kainji Lake see Kainji Reservoir
Kainji Reservoir 75 F4 var. Kainji Lake. Reservoir W Nigeria
Kaipara Harbour 150 C2 harbour North Island, NZ
Kairouan 71 E2 var. Al Qayrawān. E Tunisia
Kaisaria see Kayseri
Kaiserslautern 95 A5 Rheinland-Pfalz, SW Germany
Kaišiadorys 107 B5 Kaišiadorys, S Lithuania
Kaitaia 150 C2 Northland, North Island, NZ
Kajaani 84 E4 Swe. Kajana. Oulu, C Finland
Kaka see Kaakhka
Kake 36 D4 Kupreanof Island, Alaska, USA
Kakhovka 109 F4 Khersons'ka Oblast', S Ukraine
Kakhovs'ka Vodoskhovyshche 109 F4 Rus. Kakhovskoye Vodokhranilishche. Reservoir SE Ukraine
Kākināda 132 D1 prev. Cocanada. Andhra Pradesh, E India
Kaktovik 36 D2 Alaska, USA
Kalahari Desert 78 B4 desert Southern Africa
Kalamariá 104 B4 Kentrikí Makedonía, N Greece
Kalámata 105 B6 prev. Kalámai. Pelopónnisos, S Greece
Kalamazoo 40 C3 Michigan, N USA
Kalambaka see Kalampáka
Kálamos 105 C5 Attikí, C Greece
Kalampáka 104 B4 var. Kalambaka. Thessalía, C Greece
Kalanchak 109 F4 Khersons'ka Oblast', S Ukraine
Kalarash see Călăraşi
Kalasin 136 D4 var. Muang Kalasin. Kalasin, E Thailand
Kalāt 123 E5 Per. Qalāt. Zābul, S Afghanistan
Kalāt 134 B2 var. Kelat, Khelat. Baluchistān, SW Pakistan
Kalbarri 147 A5 Western Australia
Kalecik 116 C3 Ankara, N Turkey
Kalemie 77 E6 prev. Albertville. Shaba, SE Dem. Rep. Congo (Zaire)
Kale Sultanie see Çanakkale
Kalgan see Zhangjiakou
Kalgoorlie 147 B6 Western Australia
Kalima 77 D6 Maniema, E Dem. Rep. Congo (Zaire)
Kalimantan 138 D4 Eng. Indonesian Borneo. Geopolitical region Borneo, C Indonesia
Kálimnos see Kálymnos
Kaliningrad see Kaliningradskaya Oblast'
Kaliningrad 106 A4 Kaliningradskaya Oblast', W Russian Federation

Kaliningradskaya Oblast' 106 B4 var. Kaliningrad. Admin. region *province and enclave* W Russian Federation

Kalinkavichy 107 C7 Rus. Kalinkovichi. Homyel'skaya Voblasts', SE Belarus

Kalispell 44 B1 Montana, NW USA

Kalisz 98 C4 Ger. Kalisch, Rus. Kalish; anc. Calisia. Wielkopolskie, C Poland

Kalix 84 D4 Norrbotten, N Sweden

Kalixälven 84 D3 river N Sweden

Kallaste 106 E3 Ger. Krasnogor. Tartumaa, SE Estonia

Kallavesi 85 E5 lake SE Finland

Kalloní 105 D5 Lésvos, E Greece

Kalmar 85 C7 var. Calmar. Kalmar, S Sweden

Kalmthout 87 C5 Antwerpen, N Belgium

Kalpáki 104 A4 Ípeiros, W Greece

Kalpeni Island 132 B3 island Lakshadweep, India, N Indian Ocean

Kaluga 111 B5 Kaluzhskaya Oblast', W Russian Federation

Kalush 108 C2 Pol. Kałusz. Ivano-Frankivs'ka Oblast', W Ukraine

Kalutara 132 D4 Western Province, SW Sri Lanka

Kalvarija 107 B5 Pol. Kalwaria. Marijampolė, S Lithuania

Kalyān 134 C5 Mahārāshtra, W India

Kálymnos 105 D6 var. Kálimnos. *Island* Dodekánisos, Greece, Aegean Sea

Kama 110 D4 river NW Russian Federation

Kamarang 59 F3 W Guyana

Kamchatka see Kamchatka, Poluostrov

Kamchatka, Poluostrov 115 G3 Eng. Kamchatka. *Peninsula* E Russian Federation

Kamensk-Shakhtinskiy 111 B6 Rostovskaya Oblast', SW Russian Federation

Kamina 77 D7 Shaba, S Dem. Rep. Congo (Zaire)

Kamishli see Al Qāmishlī

Kamloops 37 E5 British Columbia, SW Canada

Kammu Seamount 152 C2 undersea feature N Pacific Ocean

Kampala 73 B6 country capital (Uganda) S Uganda

Kâmpóng Cham 137 D6 prev. Kompong Cham. Kâmpóng Cham, C Cambodia

Kâmpóng Chhnăng 137 D6 prev. Kompong. Kâmpóng Chhnăng, C Cambodia

Kâmpóng Saôm 137 D6 prev. Kompong Som, Sihanoukville. Kâmpóng Saôm, SW Cambodia

Kâmpóng Spoe 137 D6 prev. Kompong Speu. Kâmpóng Spœ, S Cambodia

Kâmpôt 137 D6 Kâmpôt, SW Cambodia

Kam"yanets'-Podil's'kyy 108 C3 Rus. Kamenets-Podol'skiy. Khmel'nyts'ka Oblast', W Ukraine

Kam"yanka-Dniprovs'ka 109 F3 Rus. Kamenka Dneprovskaya. Zaporiz'ka Oblast', SE Ukraine

Kamyshin 111 B6 Volgogradskaya Oblast', SW Russian Federation

Kanaky see New Caledonia

Kananga 77 D6 prev. Luluabourg. Kasai Occidental, S Dem. Rep. Congo (Zaire)

Kananur see Cannanore

Kanara see Karnātaka

Kanash 111 C5 Chuvashskaya Respublika, W Russian Federation

Kanazawa 131 C5 Ishikawa, Honshū, SW Japan

Kanbe 136 B4 Yangon, SW Myanmar

Kānchipuram 132 C2 prev. Conjeeveram. Tamil Nādu, SE India

Kandahār 123 E5 Per. Qandahār. Kandahār, S Afghanistan

Kandalakša see Kandalaksha

Kandalaksha 110 B2 var. Kandalakša, Fin. Kantalahti. Murmanskaya Oblast', NW Russian Federation

Kandangan 138 D4 Borneo, C Indonesia

Kandava 106 C3 Ger. Kandau. Tukums, W Latvia

Kandi 75 F4 N Benin

Kandy 132 D3 Central Province, C Sri Lanka

Kane Fracture Zone 66 B4 tectonic feature NW Atlantic Ocean

Kaneohe 47 A8 Haw. Kāne'ohe. Oahu, Hawaii, USA, C Pacific Ocean

Kangān 120 D4 Būshehr, S Iran

Kangaroo Island 149 A7 island South Australia

Kangertittivaq 83 E4 Dan. Scoresby Sund. *Fjord* E Greenland

Kangikajik 83 E4 var. Kap Brewster. *Headland* E Greenland

Kaniv 109 E2 Rus. Kanëv. Cherkas'ka Oblast', C Ukraine

Kanivs'ke Vodoskhovyshche 109 E2 Rus. Kanevskoye Vodokhranilishche. *Reservoir* C Ukraine

Kanjiža 100 D2 Ger. Altkanischa, Hung. Magyarkanizsa, Ókanizsa; prev. Stara Kanjiža. Serbia, N Yugoslavia

Kankaanpää 85 D5 Länsi-Suomi, W Finland

Kankakee 40 B3 Illinois, N USA

Kankan 74 D4 Haute-Guinée, E Guinea

Kannur see Cannanore

Kano 75 G4 Kano, N Nigeria

Kānpur 135 E3 Eng. Cawnpore. Uttar Pradesh, N India

Kansas 49 F1 off. State of Kansas; also known as Jayhawker State, Sunflower State. *State* C USA

Kansas 45 F5 Kansas, C USA

Kansas City 45 F4 Kansas, C USA

Kansas City 45 F4 Missouri, C USA

Kansas River 45 F5 river Kansas, C USA

Kansk 115 E4 Krasnoyarskiy Kray, S Russian Federation

Kansu see Gansu

Kantalahti see Kandalaksha

Kántanos 105 C7 Kríti, Greece, E Mediterranean Sea

Kantemirovka 111 B6 Voronezhskaya Oblast', W Russian Federation

Kanton 145 F3 var. Abariringa, Canton Island; prev. Mary Island. *Atoll* Phoenix Islands, C Kiribati

Kanye 78 C4 Southern, SE Botswana

Kaohsiung 128 D6 var. Gaoxiong, Jap. Takao, Takow. S Taiwan

Kaolack 74 B3 var. Kaolak. W Senegal

Kaolak see Kaolack

Kaolan see Lanzhou

Kaoma 78 C2 Western, W Zambia

Kap Brewster see Kangikajik

Kapelle 87 B5 Zeeland, SW Netherlands

Kapellen 87 C5 Antwerpen, N Belgium

Kap Farvel see Uummannarsuaq

Kapka, Massif du 76 C2 mountain range E Chad

Kaplangky, Plato 122 C2 ridge Turkmenistan/Uzbekistan

Kapoeta 73 C5 Eastern Equatoria, SE Sudan

Kaposvár 99 C7 Somogy, SW Hungary

Kappeln 94 B2 Schleswig-Holstein, N Germany

Kapstad see Cape Town

Kaptsevichy 107 C7 Rus. Koptsevichi. Homyel'skaya Voblasts', SE Belarus

Kapuas, Sungai 138 C4 prev. Kapoeas. *River* Borneo, C Indonesia

Kapuskasing 38 C4 Ontario, S Canada

Kapyl' 107 C6 Rus. Kopyl'. Minskaya Voblasts', C Belarus

Kap York see Innaanganeq

Kara-Balta 123 F2 Chuyskaya Oblast', N Kyrgyzstan

Karabil', Vozvyshennost' 122 D3 mountain range S Turkmenistan

Karabük 116 C2 Karabük NW Turkey

Karāchi 134 B3 Sind, SE Pakistan

Karadeniz see Black Sea

Karadeniz Boğazı see İstanbul Boğazı

Karaferiye see Véroia

Karaganda 114 C4 Kaz. Qaraghandy. Karaganda, C Kazakhstan

Karaginskiy, Ostrov 115 H2 island E Russian Federation

Karak see Al Karak

Kara-Kala 122 C3 var. Garrygala. Balkanskiy Velayat, W Turkmenistan

Karakax see Moyu

Karakılısse see Ağrı

Karakol 123 G2 prev. Przheval'sk. Issyk-Kul'skaya Oblast', NE Kyrgyzstan

Karakol 123 G2 var. Karakolka. Issyk-Kul'skaya Oblast', NE Kyrgyzstan

Karakolka see Karakol

Karakoram Range 134 D1 mountain range C Asia

Karaköse see Ağrı

Kara Kum see Garagumy

Kara Kum Canal see Garagumskiy Kanal

Karakumskiy Kanal see Garagumskiy Kanal

Karamai see Karamay

Karaman 116 C4 Karaman, S Turkey

Karamay 126 B2 var. Karamai, Kelamayi, prev. Chin. K'o-la-ma-i. Xinjiang Uygur Zizhiqu, NW China

Karamea Bight 151 B5 gulf South Island, NZ

Karapelit 104 E1 Rom. Stejarul. Dobrich, NE Bulgaria

Kara-Say 123 G2 Issyk-Kul'skaya Oblast', NE Kyrgyzstan

Karasburg 78 B4 Karas, S Namibia

Kara Sea see Karskoye More

Karatau 114 C5 Kaz. Qarataū. Zhambyl, S Kazakhstan

Karavás 105 B7 Kýthira, S Greece

Karbalā' 120 B3 var. Kerbala, Kerbela. S Iraq

Kardhítsa see Kardítsa

Kardítsa 105 B5 var. Kardhítsa. Thessalía, C Greece

Kärdla 106 C2 Ger. Kertel. Hiiumaa, W Estonia

Karet see Kâghet

Kargı 116 C2 Çorum, N Turkey

Kargilik see Yecheng

Kariba 78 D2 Mashonaland West, N Zimbabwe

Kariba, Lake 78 D3 reservoir Zambia/Zimbabwe

Karibib 78 B3 Erongo, C Namibia

Karies see Karyés

Karigasniemi 84 D2 Lapp. Garegasnjárga. Lappi, N Finland

Karimata, Selat 138 C4 strait W Indonesia

Karīmnagar 134 D5 Andhra Pradesh, C India

Karin 72 D4 Woqooyi Galbeed, N Somalia

Kariot see Ikaría

Káristos see Kárystos

Karkinits'ka Zatoka 109 E4 Rus. Karkinitskiy Zaliv. *Gulf* S Ukraine

Karkük see Kirkük

Karlovac 100 B3 Ger. Karlstadt, Hung. Károlyváros. Karlovac, C Croatia

Karlovy Vary 99 A5 Ger. Karlsbad; prev. Eng. Carlsbad. Karlovarský Kraj, W Czech Republic

Karlskrona 85 C7 Blekinge, S Sweden

Karlsruhe 95 B6 var. Carlsruhe. Baden-Württemberg, SW Germany

Karlstad 85 B6 Värmland, C Sweden

Karnāl 134 D2 Haryāna, N India

Karnātaka 132 C1 var. Kanara; prev. Maisur, Mysore. Admin. region *state* W India

Karnobat 104 D2 Burgas, E Bulgaria

Karnul see Kurnool

Karpaten see Carpathian Mountains

Kárpathos 105 E7 It. Scarpanto; anc. Carpathos, Carpathus. *Island* SE Greece

Kárpathos 105 E7 Kárpathos, SE Greece

Karpaty see Carpathian Mountains

Karpeníси 105 B5 prev. Karpenísion. Stereá Ellás, C Greece

Kars 117 F2 var. Qars. Kars, NE Turkey

Kārsava 106 D4 Ger. Karsau; prev. Rus. Korsovka. Ludza, E Latvia

Karskiye Vorota, Proliv 110 E2 Eng. Kara Strait. *Strait* N Russian Federation

Karskoye More 114 D2 Eng. Kara Sea. *Sea* Arctic Ocean

Karyés 104 C4 var. Karies. Ágion Óros, N Greece

Kárystos 105 C6 var. Káristos. Évvoia, C Greece

Kasai 77 C6 var. Cassai, Kassai. *River* Angola/Dem. Rep. Congo (Zaire)

Kasaji 77 D7 Shaba, S Dem. Rep. Congo (Zaire)

Kasama 78 D1 Northern, N Zambia

Kāsargod 132 B2 Kerala, SW India

Kāshān 120 C3 Eşfahān, C Iran

Kashi 126 A3 Chin. Kaxgar, K'o-shih, Uigh. Kashgar. Xinjiang Uygur Zizhiqu, NW China

Kasongo 77 D6 Maniema, E Dem. Rep. Congo (Zaire)

Kasongo-Lunda 77 C7 Bandundu, SW Dem. Rep. Congo (Zaire)

Kásos 105 D7 island S Greece

Kaspiysk 111 B8 Respublika Dagestan, SW Russian Federation

Kassai see Kasai

Kassala 72 C4 Kassala, E Sudan

Kassel 94 B4 prev. Cassel. Hessen, C Germany

Kasserine 71 E2 var. Al Qaṣrayn. W Tunisia

Kastamonu 116 C2 var. Castamoni, Kastamuni. Kastamonu, N Turkey

Kastamuni see Kastamonu

Kastaneá 104 B4 Kentrikí Makedonía, N Greece

Kastélli 105 C7 Kríti, Greece, E Mediterranean Sea

Kastoría 104 B4 Dytikí Makedonía, N Greece

Kástro 105 C6 Sífnos, Kykládes, Greece, Aegean Sea

Kastsyukovichy 107 E7 Rus. Kostyukovichi. Mahilyowskaya Voblasts', E Belarus

Kastsyukowka 107 D7 Rus. Kostyukovka. Homyel'skaya Voblasts', SE Belarus

Kasulu 73 B7 Kigoma, W Tanzania

Kasumiga-ura 131 D5 lake Honshū, S Japan

Katahdin, Mount 41 G1 mountain Maine, NE USA

Katalla 36 C3 Alaska, USA

Katana see Qaṭanā

Katanning 147 B7 Western Australia

Katawaz see Zarghūn Shahr

Katchall Island 133 F3 island Nicobar Islands, India, NE Indian Ocean

Katerini 104 B4 Kentrikí Makedonía, N Greece

Katha 136 B2 Sagaing, N Myanmar

Katherine 148 A2 Northern Territory, N Australia

Kathmandu 135 F3 prev. Kantipur. *Country capital* (Nepal) Central, C Nepal

Katikati 150 D3 Bay of Plenty, North Island, NZ

Katima Mulilo *78 C3* Caprivi, NE Namibia
Katiola *74 D4* C Côte d'Ivoire
Káto Achaïa *105 B5 var.* Kato Ahaia, Káto Akhaía. Dytikí Ellás, S Greece
Kato Ahaia *see* Káto Achaïa
Káto Akhaía *see* Káto Achaïa
Katoúna *105 A5* Dytikí Ellás, C Greece
Katowice *99 C5 Ger.* Kattowitz. Śląskie, S Poland
Katsina *75 G3* Katsina, N Nigeria
Kattaqürghon *123 E2 Rus.* Kattakurgan. Samarqand Wiloyati, C Uzbekistan
Kattavía *105 E7* Ródos, Dodekánisos, Greece, Aegean Sea
Kattegat *85 B7 Dan.* Kattegatt. *Strait* N Europe
Kauai *47 A7 Haw.* Kaua'i. *Island* Hawaiian Islands, Hawaii, USA, C Pacific Ocean
Kaufbeuren *95 C6* Bayern, S Germany
Kaunas *106 B4 Ger.* Kauen, *Pol.* Kowno; *prev.* Rus. Kovno. Kaunas, C Lithuania
Kavadarci *101 E6 Turk.* Kavadar. C FYR Macedonia
Kavajë *101 C6 It.* Cavaia, Kavaja. Tiranë, W Albania
Kavála *104 C3 prev.* Kaválla. Anatolikí Makedonía kai Thráki, NE Greece
Kāvali *132 D2* Andhra Pradesh, E India
Kavango *see* Cubango
Kavaratti Island *132 A3 island* Lakshadweep, India, N Indian Ocean
Kavarna *104 E2* Dobrich, NE Bulgaria
Kavengo *see* Cubango
Kavīr, Dasht-e *120 D3 var.* Great Salt Desert. *Salt pan* N Iran
Kavīr-e Lūt *see* Lūt, Dasht-e
Kawagoe *131 D5* Saitama, Honshū, S Japan
Kawasaki *130 A2* Kanagawa, Honshū, S Japan
Kawerau *150 E3* Bay of Plenty, North Island, NZ
Kaya *75 E3* C Burkina faso
Kayan *136 B4* Yangon, SW Myanmar
Kayan, Sungai *138 D3 prev.* Kajan. *River* Borneo, C Indonesia
Kayes *74 C3* Kayes, W Mali
Kayseri *116 D3 var.* Kaisaria; *anc.* Caesarea Mazaca, Mazaca. Kayseri, C Turkey
Kazach'ye *115 F2* Respublika Sakha (Yakutiya), NE Russian Federation
Kazakhskiy Melkosopochnik *114 C4 Eng.* Kazakh Uplands, Kirghiz Steppe, *Kaz.* Saryarqa. *Uplands* C Kazakhstan
Kazakhstan *114 B4 var.* Kazakstan, *Kaz.* Qazaqstan, Qazaqstan Respublikasy; *prev.* Kazakh Soviet Socialist Republic, *Rus.* Kazakhskaya SSR. *Country* C Asia

Kazakhstan 114

Official name Republic of Kazakhstan
Formation 1991
Capital Astana
Population 16.2 million / 15 people per sq mile (6 people per sq km)
Total area 1,049,150 sq miles (2,717,300 sq km)
Languages Kazakh, Russian, German
Religions Muslim (mainly Sunni) 47%, Russian Orthodox 15%, other 38%
Ethnic mix Kazakh 44%, Russian 36%, Ukranian 5%, German 4%, Uzbek and Tartar 2%, other 9%
Government Multiparty republic
Currency Tenge = 100 tein
Literacy rate 99%
Calorie consumption not available

Kazakh Uplands *see* Kazakhskiy Melkosopochnik
Kazan' *111 C5* Respublika Tatarstan, W Russian Federation
Kazanlŭk *104 D2 prev.* Kazanlik. Stara Zagora, C Bulgaria
Kazbegi *see* Kazbek
Kazbek *117 F1 var.* Kazbegi, *Geor.* Mqinvartsveri. *Mountain* N Georgia
Kāzerūn *120 D4* Fārs, S Iran
Kazvin *see* Qazvīn
Kéa *105 C6 prev.* Kéos, *anc.* Ceos. *Island* Kykládes, Greece, Aegean Sea
Kéa *105 C6* Kéa, Kykládes, Greece, Aegean Sea
Kea, Mauna *47 B8 mountain* Hawaii, USA, C Pacific Ocean
Kéamu *see* Aneityum
Kearney *45 E4* Nebraska, C USA
Keban Baraji *117 E3 reservoir* C Turkey
Kebkabiya *72 A4* Northern Darfur, W Sudan
Kebnekaise *84 C3 mountain* N Sweden
Kecskemét *99 D7* Bács-Kiskun, C Hungary
Kediri *138 D5* Jawa, C Indonesia
Kędzierzyn-Kole *99 C5 Ger.* Heydebrech. Opolskie, S Poland
Keelung *see* Chilung
Keetmanshoop *78 B4* Karas, S Namibia
Kefallinía *105 A5 var.* Kefallonía. *Island* Iónioi Nísoi, Greece, C Mediterranean Sea
Kefallonía *see* Kefallinía
Kefe *see* Feodosiya
Kehl *95 A6* Baden-Württemberg, SW Germany
Keila *106 D2 Ger.* Kegel. Harjumaa, NW Estonia
Keïta *75 F3* Tahoua, C Niger
Keitele *84 D4 lake* C Finland
Keith *149 B7* South Australia
Kёk-Art *123 G2 prev.* Alaykel', Alay-Kuu. Oshskaya Oblast', SW Kyrgyzstan
Kékes *99 C6 mountain* N Hungary
Kelamayi *see* Karamay
Kelang *see* Klang
Kelat *see* Kālat
Kelifskiy Uzboy *122 D3 salt marsh* E Turkmenistan
Kelkit Çayı *117 E3 river* N Turkey
Kelmė *106 B4* Kelmė, C Lithuania
Kélo *76 B4* Tandjilé, SW Chad
Kelowna *37 E5* British Columbia, SW Canada
Kelso *46 B2* Washington, NW USA
Keluang *138 B3 var.* Kluang. Johor, Peninsular Malaysia
Kem' *110 B3* Respublika Kareliya, NW Russian Federation
Kemah *117 E3* Erzincan, E Turkey
Kemaman *see* Cukai
Kemerovo *114 D4 prev.* Shcheglovsk. Kemerovskaya Oblast', C Russian Federation
Kemi *84 D4* Lappi, NW Finland
Kemijärvi *84 D3 Swe.* Kemiträsk. Lappi, N Finland
Kemijoki *84 D3 river* NW Finland
Kemin *123 G2 prev.* Bystrovka. Chuyskaya Oblast', N Kyrgyzstan
Kempele *84 D4* Oulu, C Finland
Kempten *95 B7* Bayern, S Germany
Kendal *89 D5* NW England, UK
Kendari *139 E4* Sulawesi, C Indonesia
Kenedy *49 G4* Texas, SW USA
Kenema *74 C4* SE Sierra Leone
Kёneurgench *122 C2 Turkm.* Köneürgench; *prev.* Kunya-Urgench. Dashkhovuzskiy Velayat, N Turkmenistan
Kenge *77 C6* Bandundu, SW Dem. Rep. Congo (Zaire)
Keng Tung *136 C3 var.* Kentung. Shan State, E Myanmar
Kénitra *70 C2 prev.* Port-Lyautey. NW Morocco
Kennett *45 H5* Missouri, C USA
Kennewick *46 C2* Washington, NW USA

Kenora *38 A3* Ontario, S Canada
Kenosha *40 B3* Wisconsin, N USA
Kentau *114 B5* Yuzhnyy Kazakhstan, S Kazakhstan
Kentucky *40 C5 off.* Commonwealth of Kentucky; also known as The Bluegrass State. *State* C USA
Kentucky Lake *40 B5 reservoir* Kentucky/Tennessee, S USA
Kentung *see* Keng Tung
Kenya *73 C6 Country* E Africa

Kenya 73

Official name Republic of Kenya
Formation 1963
Capital Nairobi
Population 30 million / 138 people per sq mile (53 people per sq km)
Total area 218,907 sq miles (566,970 sq km)
Languages Swahili, English, Kikuyu, Luo, Kalenjin
Religions Christian 60%, Traditional beliefs 25%, Muslim 6%, other 9%
Ethnic mix Kikuyu 21%, Luhya 14%, Luo 13%, Kalenjin 11%, other 41%
Government Multiparty republic
Currency Kenya shilling = 100 cents
Literacy rate 79.3%
Calorie consumption 2,075 kilocalories

Keokuk *45 G4* Iowa, C USA
Kępno *98 C4* Wielkopolskie, C Poland
Keppel Island *see* Niuatoputapu
Kepulauan Sangihe *see* Sangir, Kepulauan
Kerak *see* Al Karak
Kerala *132 C2 state* S India
Kerasunt *see* Giresun
Keratea *see* Keratéa
Keratéa *105 C6 var.* Keratea. Attikí, C Greece
Kerbala *see* Karbalā'
Kerbela *see* Karbalā'
Kerch *109 G5 Rus.* Kerch'. Respublika Krym, SE Ukraine
Kerchens'ka Protska *see* Kerch Strait
Kerchenskiy Proliv *see* Kerch Strait
Kerch Strait *109 G4 var.* Bosporus Cimmerius, Enikale Strait, *Rus.* Kerchenskiy Proliv, *Ukr.* Kerchens'ka Protska. *Strait* Black Sea/Sea of Azov
Kerguelen *141 C7 island* C French Southern and Antarctic Territories
Kerguelen Plateau *141 C7 undersea feature* S Indian Ocean
Kerí *105 A6* Zákynthos, Iónioi Nísoi, Greece, C Mediterranean Sea
Kerikeri *150 D2* Northland, North Island, NZ
Kerkenah, Îles de *102 D4 var.* Kerkenna Islands, *Ar.* Juzur Qarqannah. *Island group* E Tunisia
Kerkenna Islands *see* Kerkenah, Îles de
Kerki *122 D3* Lebapskiy Velayat, E Turkmenistan
Kérkira *see* Kérkyra
Kerkrade *87 D6* Limburg, SE Netherlands
Kerkuk *see* Kirkūk
Kérkyra *104 A4 var.* Kérkira, *Eng.* Corfu. *Island* Iónioi Nísoi, Greece, C Mediterranean Sea
Kermadec Islands *152 C4 island group* NZ, SW Pacific Ocean
Kermadec Trench *143 E4 undersea feature* SW Pacific Ocean
Kermān *120 D3 var.* Kirman; *anc.* Carmana. Kermān, C Iran
Kermānshāh *see* Bākhtarān
Kerrville *49 F4* Texas, SW USA
Kerulen *127 E2 Chin.* Herlen He, *Mong.* Herlen Gol. *River* China/Mongolia
Kerýneia *102 C5 var.* Girne, Kyrenia. N Cyprus

Kesennuma *130 D4* Miyagi, Honshū, C Japan
Keszthely *99 C7* Zala, SW Hungary
Ketchikan *36 D4* Revillagigedo Island, Alaska, USA
Kętrzyn *98 D2 Ger.* Rastenburg. Warmiusko-Mazurskie, NE Poland
Kettering *89 D6* C England, UK
Kettering *40 C4* Ohio, N USA
Keuruu *85 D5* Länsi-Suomi, W Finland
Keweenaw Peninsula *40 B1 peninsula* Michigan, N USA
Key Largo *43 F5* Key Largo, Florida, SE USA
Key West *43 E5* Florida Keys, Florida, SE USA
Khabarovsk *115 G4* Khabarovskiy Kray, SE Russian Federation
Khadera *see* Ḥadera
Khairpur *134 B3* Sind, SE Pakistan
Khalīj al 'Aqabah *see* Aqaba, Gulf of
Khalīj al 'Arabī *see* Gulf, The
Khalīj-e Fars *see* Gulf, The
Khalkidhikí *see* Chalkidikí
Khalkís *see* Chalkída
Khambhāt, Gulf of *134 C4 Eng.* Gulf of Cambay. *Gulf* W India
Khamīs Mushayt *121 B6 var.* Hamīs Musait. 'Asir, SW Saudi Arabia
Khānābād *123 E3* Kunduz, NE Afghanistan
Khān al Baghdādī *see* Al Baghdādī
Khandwa *134 D4* Madhya Pradesh, C India
Khanh *see* Soc Trăng
Khaniá *see* Chaniá
Khanka, Lake *129 E2 var.* Hsing-k'ai Hu, Lake Hanka, *Chin.* Xingkai Hu, *Rus.* Ozero Khanka. *Lake* China/Russian Federation
Khanthabouli *136 D4 prev.* Savannakhét. Savannakhét, S Laos
Khanty-Mansiysk *114 C3 prev.* Ostyako-Voguls'k. Khanty-Mansiyskiy Avtonomnyy Okrug, C Russian Federation
Khān Yūnis *119 A7 var.* Khān Yūnus. S Gaza Strip
Khān Yūnus *see* Khān Yūnis
Khanzi *see* Ghanzi
Kharagpur *135 F4* West Bengal, NE India
Kharbin *see* Harbin
Kharkiv *109 G2 Rus.* Khar'kov. Kharkivs'ka Oblast', NE Ukraine
Kharmanli *104 D3* Khaskovo, S Bulgaria
Khartoum *72 B4 var.* El Khartûm, Khartum. *Country capital* (Sudan) Khartoum, C Sudan
Khartum *see* Khartoum
Khasavyurt *111 B8* Respublika Dagestan, SW Russian Federation
Khāsh, Dasht-e *122 D5 Eng.* Khash Desert. *Desert* SW Afghanistan
Khashim Al Qirba *see* Khashm el Girba
Khashm al Qirbah *see* Khashm el Girba
Khashm el Girba *72 C4 var.* Khashim Al Qirba, Khashm al Qirbah. Kassala, E Sudan
Khaskovo *104 D3* Khaskovo, S Bulgaria
Khaydarkan *123 F2 var.* Khaydarken. Oshskaya Oblast', SW Kyrgyzstan
Khaydarken *see* Khaydarkan
Khelat *see* Kālat
Kherson *109 E4* Khersons'ka Oblast', S Ukraine
Kheta *115 E2 river* N Russian Federation
Khíos *see* Chíos
Khirbet el 'Aujā et Tahtā *119 E7 var.* 'Aujā et Tahtā. E West Bank
Khiwa *122 D2 Rus.* Khiva. Khorazm Wiloyati, W Uzbekistan
Khmel'nyts'kyy *108 C2 Rus.* Khmel'nitskiy; *prev.* Proskurov. Khmel'nyts'ka Oblast', W Ukraine
Khodasy *107 E6 Rus.* Khodosy. Mahilyowskaya Voblasts', E Belarus

Khodoriv 108 C2 Pol. Chodorów, Rus. Khodorov. L'vivs'ka Oblast', NW Ukraine
Khodzhent see Khŭjand
Khoi see Khvoy
Khojend see Khŭjand
Khokand see Qŭqon
Kholm 123 E3 var. Tashqurghan, Pash. Khulm. Balkh, N Afghanistan
Kholon see Holon
Khoms see Al Khums
Khong Sedone see Muang Khôngxédôn
Khon Kaen 136 D4 var. Muang Khon Kaen. Khon Kaen, E Thailand
Khor 115 G4 Khabarovskiy Kray, SE Russian Federation
Khorat see Nakhon Ratchasima
Khorugh 123 F3 Rus. Khorog. S Tajikistan
Khotan see Hotan
Khouribga 70 B2 C Morocco
Khovd see Hovd
Khowst 123 F4 Paktīā, E Afghanistan
Khoy see Khvoy
Khoyniki 107 D8 Rus. Khoyniki. Homyel'skaya Voblasts', SE Belarus
Khrebet Kolymskiy see Kolyma Range
Khrebet Kopetdag see Koppeh Dāgh
Khrebet Lomonosova see Lomonosov Ridge
Khudzhand see Khŭjand
Khŭjand 123 E2 var. Khodzhent, Khojend, Rus. Khudzhand; prev. Leninabad, Taj. Leninobod. N Tajikistan
Khulm see Kholm
Khulna 135 G4 Khulna, SW Bangladesh
Khums see Al Khums
Khust 108 B3 Cz. Chust, Husté, Hung. Huszt. Zakarpats'ka Oblast', W Ukraine
Khvoy 120 C2 var. Khoi, Khoy. Āžarbāyjān-e Bākhtarī, NW Iran
Khyber Pass 134 C1 var. Kowtal-e Khaybar. Pass Afghanistan/Pakistan
Kiangmai see Chiang Mai
Kiang-ning see Nanjing
Kiangsi see Jiangxi
Kiangsu see Jiangsu
Kiáto 105 B6 prev. Kiáton. Pelopónnisos, S Greece
Kiayi see Chiai
Kibangou 77 B6 Le Niari, SW Congo
Kibombo 77 D6 Maniema, E Dem. Rep. Congo (Zaire)
Kičevo 101 D6 SW FYR Macedonia
Kidderminster 89 D6 C England, UK
Kiel 98 B2 Schleswig-Holstein, N Germany
Kielce 98 D4 Rus. Keltsy. Świętokrzyskie, C Poland
Kieler Bucht 94 B2 bay N Germany
Kiev see Kyyiv
Kiffa 74 C3 Assaba, S Mauritania
Kigali 73 B6 country capital (Rwanda) C Rwanda
Kigoma 73 B7 Kigoma, W Tanzania
Kihnu 106 C2 var. Kihnu Saar, Ger. Kühnö. Island SW Estonia
Kihnu Saar see Kihnu
Kii-suidō 131 C7 strait S Japan
Kikinda 100 D3 Ger. Grosskikinda, Hung. Nagykikinda; prev. Velika Kikinda. Serbia, N Yugoslavia
Kikládhes see Kykládes
Kikwit 77 C6 Bandundu, W Dem. Rep. Congo (Zaire)
Kilien Mountains see Qilian Shan
Kilimane see Quelimane
Kilimanjaro 73 C7 var. Uhuru Peak. Mountain NE Tanzania
Kilimanjaro 69 E5 region E Tanzania
Kilingi-Nõmme 106 D3 Ger. Kurkund. Pärnumaa, SW Estonia
Kilis 116 D4 Kilis S Turkey
Kiliya 108 D4 Rom. Chilia-Nouă. Odes'ka Oblast', SW Ukraine

Kilkenny 89 B6 Ir. Cill Chainnigh. S Ireland
Kilkís 104 B3 Kentrikí Makedonía, N Greece
Killarney 89 A6 Ir. Cill Airne. SW Ireland
Killeen 49 G3 Texas, SW USA
Kilmain see Quelimane
Kilmarnock 88 C4 W Scotland, UK
Kilwa see Kilwa Kivinje
Kilwa Kivinje 73 C7 var. Kilwa. Lindi, SE Tanzania
Kimberley 78 C4 Northern Cape, C South Africa
Kimberley Plateau 146 C3 plateau Western Australia
Kimch'aek 129 E3 prev. Sŏngjin. E North Korea
Kinabalu, Gunung 138 D3 mountain East Malaysia
Kindersley 37 F5 Saskatchewan, S Canada
Kindia 74 C4 Guinée-Maritime, SW Guinea
Kindley Field 42 A4 air base E Bermuda
Kindu 77 D6 prev. Kindu-Port-Empain. Maniema, C Dem. Rep. Congo (Zaire)
Kineshma 111 C5 Ivanovskaya Oblast', W Russian Federation
King Island 149 B8 island Tasmania, SE Australia
Kingman 48 A1 Arizona, SW USA
Kingman Reef 145 E2 US territory C Pacific Ocean
Kingsford Smith 148 E2 international airport (Sydney) New South Wales, SE Australia
King's Lynn 89 E6 var. Bishop's Lynn, Kings Lynn, Lynn, Lynn Regis. E England, UK
King Sound 146 B3 sound Western Australia
Kingsport 43 E1 Tennessee, S USA
Kingston 54 B5 country capital (Jamaica) E Jamaica
Kingston 41 F3 New York, NE USA
Kingston 38 D5 Ontario, SE Canada
Kingston upon Hull 89 D5 var. Hull. E England, UK
Kingston upon Thames 89 A8 SE England, UK
Kingstown 55 H4 country capital (Saint Vincent and the Grenadines) Saint Vincent, Saint Vincent and the Grenadines
Kingsville 49 G5 Texas, SW USA
King William Island 37 F3 island Nunavut, N Canada Arctic Ocean
Kinrooi 87 D5 Limburg, NE Belgium
Kinshasa 77 B6 prev. Léopoldville. Country capital (Congo (Zaire)) Kinshasa, W Dem. Rep. Congo (Zaire)
Kintyre 88 B4 peninsula W Scotland, UK
Kinyeti 73 B5 mountain S Sudan
Kiparissía see Kyparissía
Kipili 73 B7 Rukwa, W Tanzania
Kipushi 77 D8 Shaba, SE Dem. Rep. Congo (Zaire)
Kirdzhali see Kŭrdzhali
Kirghiz Range 123 F2 Rus. Kirgizskiy Khrebet; prev. Alexander Range. Mountain range Kazakhstan/Kyrgyzstan
Kirghiz Steppe see Kazakhskiy Melkosopochnik
Kiriath-Arba see Hebron
Kiribati 145 F2 Country C Pacific Ocean

Kiribati 145

Official name Republic of Kiribati
Formation 1979
Capital Bairiki (Tarawa Atoll)
Population 84,000 / 306 people per sq mile (118 people per sq km)
Total area 274 sq miles (710 sq km)
Languages English, Micronesian dialect
Religions Roman Catholic 53%,

Kiribati (continued)

Kiribati Protestant Church 39%, other 8%
Ethnic mix Micronesian 98%, other 2%
Government Multiparty republic
Currency Australian dollar = 100 cents
Literacy rate 98%
Calorie consumption 2,651 kilocalories

Kırıkhan 116 D4 Hatay, S Turkey
Kırıkkale 116 C3 Kırıkkale, C Turkey
Kirin see Jilin
Kirinyaga 73 C6 prev. Mount Kenya. Volcano C Kenya
Kirishi 110 B4 var. Kirisi. Leningradskaya Oblast', NW Russian Federation
Kirisi see Kirishi
Kiritimati 145 G2 prev. Christmas Island. Atoll Line Islands, E Kiribati
Kirkenes 84 E2 var. Kirkkoniemi. Finnmark, N Norway
Kirkkoniemi see Kirkenes
Kirkland Lake 38 D4 Ontario, S Canada
Kırklareli 116 A2 prev. Kirk-Kilissa. Kırklareli, NW Turkey
Kirkpatrick, Mount 154 B3 mountain Antarctica
Kirksville 45 G4 Missouri, C USA
Kirkūk 120 B3 var. Karkūk, Kerkuk. N Iraq
Kirkwall 88 C2 NE Scotland, UK
Kirkwood 45 G4 Missouri, C USA
Kirman see Kermān
Kir Moab see Al Karak
Kirov 111 C5 prev. Vyatka. Kirovskaya Oblast', NW Russian Federation
Kirovo-Chepetsk 111 D5 Kirovskaya Oblast', NW Russian Federation
Kirovohrad 109 E3 Rus. Kirovograd; prev. Kirovo, Yelizavetgrad, Zinov'yevsk. Kirovohrads'ka Oblast', C Ukraine
Kırthar Range 134 B3 mountain range S Pakistan
Kirun' see Chilung
Kiruna 84 C3 Norrbotten, N Sweden
Kisangani 77 D5 prev. Stanleyville. Orientale, NE Dem. Rep. Congo (Zaire)
Kislovodsk 111 B7 Stavropol'skiy Kray, SW Russian Federation
Kismaayo 73 D6 var. Chisimayu, Kismayu, It. Chisimaio. Jubbada Hoose, S Somalia
Kismayu see Kismaayo
Kissidougou 74 C4 Guinée-Forestière, S Guinea
Kissimmee, Lake 43 E4 lake Florida, SE USA
Kisumu 73 C6 prev. Port Florence. Nyanza, W Kenya
Kisvárda 99 E6 Ger. Kleinwardein. Szabolcs-Szatmár-Bereg, E Hungary
Kita 74 D3 Kayes, W Mali
Kitakyūshū 131 A7 var. Kitakyûsyû. Fukuoka, Kyūshū, SW Japan
Kitakyûsyû see Kitakyūshū
Kitami 130 D2 Hokkaidō, NE Japan
Kitchener 38 C5 Ontario, S Canada
Kíthira see Kýthira
Kíthnos see Kýthnos
Kitimat 36 D4 British Columbia, SW Canada
Kitinen 84 D3 river N Finland
Kitob 123 E3 Rus. Kitab. Qashqadaryo Wiloyati, S Uzbekistan
Kitwe 78 D2 var. Kitwe-Nkana. Copperbelt, C Zambia
Kitwe-Nkana see Kitwe
Kitzbühler Alpen 95 C7 mountain range W Austria
Kivalina 36 C2 Alaska, USA
Kivalo 84 D3 ridge C Finland

Kivertsi 108 C1 Pol. Kiwerce, Rus. Kivertsy. Volyns'ka Oblast', NW Ukraine
Kivu, Lake 77 E6 Fr. Lac Kivu. Lake Rwanda/Dem. Rep. Congo (Zaire)
Kızıl Irmak 116 C3 river C Turkey
Kizil Kum see Kyzyl Kum
Kladno 99 A5 Středočesky Kraj, NW Czech Republic
Klagenfurt 95 D7 Slvn. Celovec. Kärnten, S Austria
Klaipėda 106 B3 Ger. Memel. Klaipėda, NW Lithuania
Klamath Falls 46 B4 Oregon, NW USA
Klamath Mountains 46 A4 mountain range California/Oregon, W USA
Klang 138 B3 var. Kelang; prev. Port Swettenham. Selangor, Peninsular Malaysia
Klarälven 85 B6 river Norway/Sweden
Klatovy 99 A5 Ger. Klattau. Plzeňský Kraj, W Czech Republic
Klazienaveen 86 E2 Drenthe, NE Netherlands
Klein Karas 78 B4 Karas, S Namibia
Kleisoúra 105 A5 Ípeiros, W Greece
Klerksdorp 78 D4 North-West, N South Africa
Klimavichy 107 E7 Rus. Klimovichi. Mahilyowskaya Voblasts', E Belarus
Klintsy 111 A5 Bryanskaya Oblast', W Russian Federation
Klisura 104 C2 Plovdiv, C Bulgaria
Ključ 100 B3 Federacija Bosna I Hercegovina, NW Bosnia and Herzegovina
Kłobuck 98 C4 Śląskie, S Poland
Klosters 95 B7 Graubünden, SE Switzerland
Kluang see Keluang
Kluczbork 98 C4 Ger. Kreuzburg, Kreuzburg in Oberschlesien. Opolskie, S Poland
Klyuchevskaya Sopka, Vulkan 115 H3 volcano E Russian Federation
Knin 100 A3 Šibenik-Knin, S Croatia
Knjaževac 100 E4 Serbia, E Yugoslavia
Knokke-Heist 87 A5 West-Vlaanderen, NW Belgium
Knoxville 42 D1 Tennessee, S USA
Knud Rasmussen Land 82 D1 physical region N Greenland
Kōbe 131 C6 Hyōgo, Honshū, SW Japan
København 85 B7 Eng. Copenhagen; anc. Hafnia. Country capital (Denmark) Sjælland, København, E Denmark
Kobenni 74 D3 Hodh el Gharbi, S Mauritania
Koblenz 95 A5 prev. Coblenz, Fr. Coblence, anc. Confluentes. Rheinland-Pfalz, W Germany
Kobryn 107 A6 Pol. Kobryn, Rus. Kobrin. Brestskaya Voblasts', SW Belarus
K'obulet'i 117 F2 W Georgia
Kočani 101 E6 NE FYR Macedonia
Kočevje 95 D8 Ger. Gottschee. S Slovenia
Koch Bihār 135 G3 West Bengal, NE India
Kōchi 131 B7 var. Kôti. Kōchi, Shikoku, SW Japan
Kochi see Cochin
Kochiu see Gejiu
Kodiak 36 C3 Kodiak Island, Alaska, USA
Kodiak Island 36 C3 island Alaska, USA
Koeln see Köln
Ko-erh-mu see Golmud
Koetai see Mahakam, Sungai
Koetaradja see Bandaaceh
Kōfu 131 D5 var. Kôhu. Yamanashi, Honshū, S Japan
Kogarah 148 E2 New South Wales, SE Australia
Kogon 122 D2 Rus. Kagan. Bukhoro Wiloyati, C Uzbekistan
Kohīma 135 H3 Nāgāland, E India

Koh I Noh *see* Büyükağrı Dağı
Kohtla-Järve 106 E2 Ida-Virumaa, NE Estonia
Kõhu *see* Kõfu
Kokand *see* Qŭqon
Kokkola 84 D4 *Swe.* Karleby; *prev.* Swe. Gamlakarleby. Länsi-Suomi, W Finland
Koko *see* Qinghai Hu
Koko 75 F4 Kebbi, W Nigeria
Kokomo 40 C4 Indiana, N USA
Koko Nor *see* Qinghai
Kokrines 36 C2 Alaska, USA
Kokshaal-Tau 123 G2 *Rus.* Khrebet Kakshaal-Too. China/Kyrgyzstan
Kokshetau 114 C4 *Kaz.* Kökshetaü; *prev.* Kokchetav. Severnyy Kazakhstan, N Kazakhstan
Koksijde 87 A5 West-Vlaanderen, W Belgium
Koksoak 38 D2 *river* Québec, E Canada
Kokstad 78 D5 KwaZulu/Natal, E South Africa
Kola *see* Kol'skiy Poluostrov
Kolaka 139 E4 Sulawesi, C Indonesia
Kolam *see* Quilon
K'o-la-ma-i *see* Karamay
Kola Peninsula *see* Kol'skiy Poluostrov
Kolari 84 D3 Lappi, NW Finland
Kolárovo 99 C6 *Ger.* Gúta; *prev.* Guta, *Hung.* Gúta. Nitriansky Kraj, SW Slovakia
Kolda 74 C3 S Senegal
Kolding 85 A7 Vejle, C Denmark
Kölen 81 E1 *Nor.* Kjølen. *Mountain range* Norway/Sweden
Kolguyev, Ostrov 110 C2 *island* NW Russian Federation
Kolhápur 132 B1 Mahárâshtra, SW India
Kolhumadulu Atoll 132 A5 *var.* Kolumadulu Atoll, Thaa Atoll. *Atoll* S Maldives
Kolín 99 B5 *Ger.* Kolin. Středočesky Kraj, C Czech Republic
Kolka 106 C2 Talsi, NW Latvia
Kolkasrags 106 C2 *prev. Eng.* Cape Domesnes. *Headland* NW Latvia
Kollam *see* Quilon
Köln 94 A4 *var.* Koeln, *Eng./Fr.* Cologne; *prev.* Cöln, *anc.* Colonia Agrippina, Oppidum Ubiorum. Nordrhein-Westfalen, W Germany
Koło 98 C3 Wielkopolskie, C Poland
Kołobrzeg 98 B2 *Ger.* Kolberg. Zachodniopomorskie, NW Poland
Kolokani 74 D3 Koulikoro, W Mali
Kolomna 111 B5 Moskovskaya Oblast', W Russian Federation
Kolomyya 108 C3 *Ger.* Kolomea. Ivano-Frankivs'ka Oblast', W Ukraine
Kolpa 100 A2 *Ger.* Kulpa, *SCr.* Kupa. *River* Croatia/Slovenia
Kolpino 110 B4 Leningradskaya Oblast', NW Russian Federation
Kólpos Ammóchostos 102 C5 *var.* Famagusta Bay, *bay* E Cyprus
Kol'skiy Poluostrov 110 C2 *Eng.* Kola Peninsula. *Peninsula* NW Russian Federation
Kolumadulu Atoll *see* Kolhumadulu Atoll
Kolwezi 77 D7 Shaba, S Dem. Rep. Congo (Zaire)
Kolyma 115 G2 *river* NE Russian Federation
Kolyma Range 113 G2 *var.* Khrebet Kolymskiy, *Eng.* Kolyma Range. *Mountain range* E Russian Federation
Komatsu 131 C5 *var.* Komatu. Ishikawa, Honshū, SW Japan
Komatu *see* Komatsu
Kommunizma Pik *see* Kommunizm, Qullai
Kommunizm, Qullai 123 F3 *var.* Qullai Garmo, *Eng.* Communism Peak, *Rus.* Kommunizma Pik; *prev.* Stalin Peak. *Mountain* E Tajikistan

Komoé 75 E4 *var.* Komoé Fleuve. *River* E Côte d'Ivoire
Komoé Fleuve *see* Komoé
Komotiní 104 D3 *var.* Gümüljina, *Turk.* Gümülcine. Anatolikí Makedonía kai Thráki, NE Greece
Komsomolets, Ostrov 115 E1 *island* Severnaya Zemlya, N Russian Federation
Komsomol'sk-na-Amure 115 G4 Khabarovskiy Kray, SE Russian Federation
Kondolovo 104 E3 Burgas, E Bulgaria
Kondopoga 110 B3 Respublika Kareliya, NW Russian Federation
Kondoz *see* Kunduz
Kondüz *see* Kunduz
Kong Christian IX Land 82 D4 *Eng.* King Christian IX Land. *Physical region* SE Greenland
Kong Frederik IX Land 82 C3 *Eng.* King Frederik IX Land. *Physical region* SW Greenland
Kong Frederik VIII Land 83 E2 *Eng.* King Frederik VIII Land. *Physical region* N Greenland
Kong Frederik VI Kyst 82 C4 *Eng.* King Frederik VI Coast. *Physical region* SE Greenland
Kong Karls Land 83 G2 *Eng.* King Charles Islands. *Island group* SE Svalbard
Kongo *see* Congo
Kongolo 77 D6 Shaba, E Dem. Rep. Congo (Zaire)
Kongor 73 B5 Jonglei, SE Sudan
Kong Oscar Fjord 83 E3 *fjord* E Greenland
Kongsberg 85 B6 Buskerud, S Norway
Kông, Tônle 137 E5 *Lao.* Xê Kong. *River* Cambodia/Laos
Konia *see* Konya
Konieh *see* Konya
Konin 98 C3 *Ger.* Kuhnau. Wielkopolskie, C Poland
Konispol 101 C7 *var.* Konispoli. Vlorë, S Albania
Konispoli *see* Konispol
Kónitsa 104 A4 Ípeiros, W Greece
Konitz *see* Chojnice
Konjic 100 C4 Federacija Bosna I Hercegovina, S Bosnia and Herzegovina
Konosha 110 C4 Arkhangel'skaya Oblast', NW Russian Federation
Konotop 109 F1 Sums'ka Oblast', NE Ukraine
Konstanz 95 B7 *var.* Constanz, *Eng.* Constance; *hist.* Kostnitz, *anc.* Constantia. Baden-Württemberg, S Germany
Konstanza *see* Constanţa
Konya 116 C4 *var.* Konieh; *prev.* Konia, *anc.* Iconium. Konya, C Turkey
Kopaonik 101 D5 *mountain range* S Yugoslavia
Koper 95 D8 *It.* Capodistria; *prev.* Kopar. SW Slovenia
Kopetdag Gershi 122 C3 *mountain range* Iran/Turkmenistan
Koppeh Dägh 120 D2 *var.* Khrebet Kopetdag. *Mountain range* Iran/Turkmenistan
Koprivnica 100 B2 *Ger.* Kopreinitz, *Hung.* Kaproncza. Koprivnica-Križevci, N Croatia
Korat *see* Nakhon Ratchasima
Korat Plateau 136 D4 *plateau* E Thailand
Korba 135 E4 Madhya Pradesh, C India
Korça *see* Korçë
Korçë 101 D6 *var.* Korça, *Gk.* Korytsa, *It.* Corriza; *prev.* Koritsa. Korçë, SE Albania
Korčula 100 B4 *It.* Curzola; *anc.* Corcyra Nigra. S Croatia
Korea Bay 127 G3 *bay* China/North Korea
Korea Strait 131 A7 *Jap.* Chōsen-kaikyō, *Kor.* Taehan-haehyŏp. *Channel* Japan/South Korea
Korhogo 74 D4 N Côte d'Ivoire

Korinthiakós Kólpos 105 B5 *Eng.* Gulf of Corinth; *anc.* Corinthiacus Sinus. *Gulf* C Greece
Kórinthos 105 B6 *Eng.* Corinth; *anc.* Corinthus. Pelopónnisos, S Greece
Koritsa *see* Korçë
Kōriyama 131 D5 Fukushima, Honshū, C Japan
Korla 126 C3 *Chin.* K'u-erh-lo. Xinjiang Uygur Zizhiqu, NW China
Körmend 99 B7 Vas, W Hungary
Koróni 105 B6 Pelopónnisos, S Greece
Koror *see* Oreor
Korosten' 108 D1 Zhytomyrs'ka Oblast', NW Ukraine
Koro Toro 76 C2 Borkou-Ennedi-Tibesti, N Chad
Kortrijk 87 A6 *Fr.* Courtrai. West-Vlaanderen, W Belgium
Koryak Range *see* Koryakskoye Nagor'ye
Koryakskiy Khrebet *see* Koryakskoye Nagor'ye
Koryakskoye Nagor'ye 115 H2 *var.* Koryakskiy Khrebet, *Eng.* Koryak Range. *Mountain range* NE Russian Federation
Koryazhma 110 C4 Arkhangel'skaya Oblast', NW Russian Federation
Korytsa *see* Korçë
Kos 105 E6 *It.* Coo; *anc.* Cos. *Island* Dodekánisos, Greece, Aegean Sea
Kos 105 E6 Kos, Dodekánisos, Greece, Aegean Sea
Kō-saki 131 A7 *headland* Nagasaki, Tsushima, SW Japan
Kościan 98 B4 *Ger.* Kosten. Wielkopolskie, C Poland
Koscian *see* Lubań
Kościerzyna 98 C2 Pomorskie, NW Poland
Kosciusko, Mount *see* Kosciuszko, Mount
Kosciuszko, Mount 149 C7 *prev.* Mount Kosciusko. *Mountain* New South Wales, SE Australia
Koshikijima-rettō 131 A8 *var.* Kosikizima Rettō. *Island group* SW Japan
Košice 99 D6 *Ger.* Kaschau, *Hung.* Kassa. Košický Kraj, E Slovakia
Kosikizima Rettō *see* Koshikijima-rettō
Koson 123 E3 *Rus.* Kasan. Qashqadaryo Wiloyati, S Uzbekistan
Kosovo 101 D5 *prev.* Autonomous Province of Kosovo and Metohija. *Region* S Yugoslavia
Kosovo Polje 101 D5 Serbia, S Yugoslavia
Kosovska Mitrovica 101 D5 *Alb.* Mitrovicë; *prev.* Mitrovica, Titova Mitrovica. Serbia, S Yugoslavia
Kosrae 144 C2 *prev.* Kusaie. *Island* Caroline Islands, E Micronesia
Kossou, Lac de 74 D5 *lake* C Côte d'Ivoire
Kostanay 130 C4 *var.* Kustanay, *Kaz.* Qostanay. Kostanay, N Kazakhstan
Kosten *see* Lubań
Kostenets 104 C2 *prev.* Georgi Dimitrov. Sofiya, W Bulgaria
Kostnitz *see* Konstanz
Kostroma 110 B4 Kostromskaya Oblast', NW Russian Federation
Kostyantynivka 109 G3 *Rus.* Konstantinovka. Donets'ka Oblast', SE Ukraine
Koszalin 98 B2 *Ger.* Köslin. Zachodniopomorskie, NW Poland
Kota 134 D3 *prev.* Kotah. Rájasthán, N India
Kota Baharu *see* Kota Bharu
Kota Bahru *see* Kota Bharu
Kotabaru *see* Jayapura
Kota Bharu 138 B3 *var.* Kota Baharu, Kota Bahru. Kelantan, Peninsular Malaysia
Kotabumi 138 B4 *prev.* Kotaboemi. Sumatera, W Indonesia
Kota Kinabalu 138 D3 *prev.* Jesselton. Sabah, East Malaysia

Kotel'nyy, Ostrov 115 E2 *island* Novosibirskiye Ostrova, N Russian Federation
Kôti *see* Kôchi
Kotka 85 E5 Kymi, S Finland
Kotlas 110 C4 Arkhangel'skaya Oblast', NW Russian Federation
Kotonu *see* Cotonou
Kotor 101 C5 *It.* Cattaro. Montenegro, SW Yugoslavia
Kotovs'k 108 D3 *Rus.* Kotovsk. Odes'ka Oblast', SW Ukraine
Kotovsk *see* Hîncești
Kotte *see* Sri Jayawardanapura
Kotto 76 D4 *river* Central African Republic/Dem. Rep. Congo (Zaire)
Kotuy 115 E2 *river* N Russian Federation
Koudougou 75 E4 C Burkina faso
Koulamoutou 77 B6 Ogooué-Lolo, C Gabon
Koulikoro 74 D3 Koulikoro, SW Mali
Koumra 76 C4 Moyen-Chari, S Chad
Kourou 59 H3 N French Guiana
Kousseir *see* Al Quşayr
Kousséri 76 B3 *prev.* Fort-Foureau. Extrême-Nord, NE Cameroon
Koutiala 74 D4 Sikasso, S Mali
Kouvola 85 E5 Kymi, S Finland
Kovel' 108 C1 *Pol.* Kowel. Volyns'ka Oblast', NW Ukraine
Kowloon 128 A2 *Chin.* Jiulong. Hong Kong, S China
Kowtal-e Barowghîl *see* Baroghil Pass
Kowtal-e Khaybar *see* Khyber Pass
Kozáni 104 B4 Dytikí Makedonía, N Greece
Kozara 100 B3 *mountain range* NW Bosnia and Herzegovina
Kozarska Dubica *see* Bosanska Dubica
Kozhikode *see* Calicut
Kōzu-shima 131 D6 *island* E Japan
Kozyatyn 108 D2 *Rus.* Kazatin. Vinnyts'ka Oblast', C Ukraine
Kpalimé 75 E5 *var.* Palimé. SW Togo
Krâchéh 137 D6 *prev.* Kratie. Krâchéh, E Cambodia
Kragujevac 100 D4 Serbia, C Yugoslavia
Kra, Isthmus of 137 B6 *isthmus* Malaysia/Thailand
Kraków 99 D5 *Eng.* Cracow, *Ger.* Krakau; *anc.* Cracovia. Małopolskie, S Poland
Krâlănh 137 D5 Siĕmréab, NW Cambodia
Kraljevo 100 D4 *prev.* Rankovićevo. Serbia, C Yugoslavia
Kramators'k 109 G3 *Rus.* Kramatorsk. Donets'ka Oblast', SE Ukraine
Kramfors 85 C5 Västernorrland, C Sweden
Kranéa 104 B4 Dytikí Makedonía, N Greece
Kranj 95 D7 *Ger.* Krainburg. NW Slovenia
Krāslava 106 D4 Krāslava, SE Latvia
Krasnaye 107 C5 *Rus.* Krasnoye. Minskaya Voblasts', C Belarus
Krasnoarmeysk 111 C6 Saratovskaya Oblast', W Russian Federation
Krasnodar 111 A7 *prev.* Ekaterinodar, Yekaterinodar. Krasnodarskiy Kray, SW Russian Federation
Krasnodon 109 H3 Luhans'ka Oblast', E Ukraine
Krasnohvardiys'ke 109 F4 *Rus.* Krasnogvardeyskoye. Respublika Krym, S Ukraine
Krasnokamensk 115 F4 Chitinskaya Oblast', S Russian Federation
Krasnokamsk 111 D5 Permskaya Oblast', W Russian Federation
Krasnoperekops'k 109 F4 *Rus.* Krasnoperekopsk. Respublika Krym, S Ukraine

Krasnovodskiy Zaliv 122 A2 *Turkm.*
Krasnowodsk Aylagy. *Lake gulf*
W Turkmenistan
Krasnoyarsk 114 D4 Krasnoyarskiy
Kray, S Russian Federation
Krasnystaw 98 E4 *Rus.* Krasnostav.
Lubelskie, E Poland
Krasnyy Kut 111 C6 Saratovskaya
Oblast', W Russian Federation
Krasnyy Luch 109 H3 *prev.*
Krindachovka. Luhans'ka Oblast',
E Ukraine
Krâvanh, Chuŏr Phnum 137 C6
Eng. Cardamom Mountains, *Fr.*
Chaîne des Cardamomes.
Mountain range W Cambodia
Krefeld 94 A4 Nordrhein-Westfalen,
W Germany
Kremenchuk 109 F2 *Rus.*
Kremenchug. Poltavs'ka Oblast',
NE Ukraine
Kremenchuts'ke Vodoskhovyshche
109 F2 Eng. Kremenchuk
Reservoir, *Rus.* Kremenchugskoye
Vodokhranilishche. *Reservoir*
C Ukraine
Kremenets' 108 C2 *Pol.*
Krzemieniec, *Rus.* Kremenets.
Ternopil's'ka Oblast', W Ukraine
Kreminna 109 G2 *Rus.*
Kremennaya. Luhans'ka Oblast',
E Ukraine
Kresena *see* Kresna
Kresna 104 C3 *var.* Kresena.
Blagoevgrad, SW Bulgaria
Kretikon Delagos *see* Kritikó
Pélagos
Kretinga 106 B3 *Ger.* Krottingen.
Kretinga, NW Lithuania
Krishna 132 C1 *prev.* Kistna. *River*
C India
Krishnagiri 132 C2 Tamil Nādu,
SE India
Kristiansand 85 A6 *var.*
Christiansand. Vest-Agder,
S Norway
Kristianstad 85 B7 Skåne,
S Sweden
Kristiansund 84 A4 *var.*
Christiansund. Møre og Romsdal,
S Norway
Kríti 105 C7 *Eng.* Crete. *Island*
Greece, Aegean Sea
Kritikó Pélagos 105 D7 *var.*
Kretikon Delagos, *Eng.* Sea of
Crete; *anc.* Mare Creticum. *Sea*
Greece, Aegean Sea
Križevci 100 B2 *Ger.* Kreuz, *Hung.*
Kőrös. Varaždin, N Croatia
Krk 100 A3 *It.* Veglia; *anc.* Curieta.
Island NW Croatia
Krolevets' 109 F1 *Rus.* Krolevets.
Sums'ka Oblast', NE Ukraine
Kronach 95 C5 Bayern, E Germany
Kroonstad 78 D4 Free State,
C South Africa
Kropotkin 111 A7 Krasnodarskiy
Kray, SW Russian Federation
Krosno 99 D5 *Ger.* Krossen.
Podkarpackie, SE Poland
Krosno Odrzańskie 98 B3 *Ger.*
Crossen, Kreisstadt. Lubuskie, W
Poland
Krško 95 E8 *Ger.* Gurkfeld; *prev.*
Videm-Krško. E Slovenia
Kruhlaye 107 D6 *Rus.* Krugloye.
Mahilyowskaya Voblasts',
E Belarus
Kruja *see* Krujë
Krujë 101 C6 *var.* Kruja, *It.* Croia.
Durrës, C Albania
Krummau *see* Český Krumlov
Krung Thep 137 C5 *var.* Krung
Thep Mahanakhon, *Eng.* Bangkok.
Country capital (Thailand)
Bangkok, C Thailand
Krung Thep, Ao 137 C5 *var.* Bight
of Bangkok. *Bay* S Thailand
Krung Thep Mahanakhon *see*
Krung Thep
Krupki 107 D6 *Rus.* Krupki.
Minskaya Voblasts', C Belarus
Krychaw 107 E7 *Rus.* Krichëv.
Mahilyowskaya Voblasts',
E Belarus
Krym *see* Crimea
Krymskaya Oblast' *see* Crimea

Kryms'ki Hory 109 F5 *mountain*
range S Ukraine
Kryms'kyy Pivostriv 109 F5
peninsula S Ukraine
Krynica 99 D5 *Ger.* Tannenhof.
Małopolskie, S Poland
Kryve Ozero 109 E3 Odes'ka
Oblast', SW Ukraine
Kryvyy Rih 109 F3 *Rus.* Krivoy
Rog. Dnipropetrovs'ka Oblast',
SE Ukraine
Ksar al Kabir *see* Ksar-el-Kebir
Ksar al Soule *see* Er-Rachidia
Ksar-el-Kebir 70 C2 *var.* Alcázar,
Ksar al Kabir, Ksar-el-Kébir, *Ar.*
Al-Kasr al-Kebir, Al-Qsar al-Kbir,
Sp. Alcazarquivir. NW Morocco
Ksar-el-Kébir *see* Ksar-el-Kebir
Kuala Dungun *see* Dungun
Kuala Lumpur 138 B3 *country*
capital (Malaysia) Kuala Lumpur,
Peninsular Malaysia
Kuala Terengganu 138 B3 *var.*
Kuala Trengganu. Terengganu,
Peninsular Malaysia
Kuala Trengganu *see* Kuala
Terengganu
Kuan 109 G5 *var.* Hypanis. *River*
SW Russian Federation
Kubango *see* Cubango
Kuching 138 C3 *prev.* Sarawak.
Sarawak, East Malaysia
Küchnay Darweyshān 122 D5
Helmand, S Afghanistan
Kuçova *see* Kuçovë
Kuçovë 101 C6 *var.* Kuçova; *prev.*
Qyteti Stalin. Berat, C Albania
Kudara *see* Ghüdara
Kudus 138 C5 *prev.* Koedoes. Jawa,
C Indonesia
Kuei-chou *see* Guizhou
Kuei-lin *see* Guilin
Kuei-Yang *see* Guiyang
Kueyang *see* Guiyang
Kugluktuk 53 E3 *var.* Qurlurtuuq
prev. Coppermine. Nunavut, NW
Canada
Kuhmo 84 E4 Oulu, E Finland
Kühnö *see* Kihnu
Kuibyshev *see* Kuybyshevskoye
Vodokhranilishche
Kuito 78 B2 *Port.* Silva Porto. Bié,
C Angola
Kuji 130 D3 *var.* Kuzi. Iwate,
Honshū, C Japan
Kükës 101 D5 *var.* Kukësi. Kükës,
NE Albania
Kukësi *see* Kükës
Kukong *see* Shaoguan
Kukukhoto *see* Hohhot
Kula Kangri 135 G3 *var.* Kulhakangri.
Mountain Bhutan/China
Kuldīga 106 B3 *Ger.* Goldingen.
Kuldiga, W Latvia
Kuldja *see* Yining
Kulhakangri *see* Kula Kangri
Kullorsuaq 82 D2 *var.*
Kuvdlorssuak. C Greenland
Kulmsee *see* Chełmża
Külob 123 F3 *Rus.* Kulyab.
SW Tajikistan
Kulu 116 C3 Konya, W Turkey
Kulunda Steppe 114 C4 *Kaz.*
Qulyndy Zhazyghy, *Rus.*
Kulundinskaya Ravnina.
Grassland Kazakhstan/Russian
Federation
Kum *see* Qom
Kuma 111 B7 *river* SW Russian
Federation
Kumamoto 131 A7 Kumamoto,
Kyūshū, SW Japan
Kumanovo 101 E5 *Turk.* Kumanova.
N FYR Macedonia
Kumasi 75 E5 *prev.* Coomassie.
C Ghana
Kumayri *see* Gyumri
Kumba 77 A5 Sud-Ouest,
W Cameroon

Kumertau 111 D6 Respublika
Bashkortostan, W Russian
Federation
Kumo 75 G4 Gombe, E Nigeria
Kumon Range 136 B2 *mountain*
range N Myanmar
Kumul *see* Hami
Kunashiri *see* Kunashir, Ostrov
Kunashir, Ostrov 130 E1 *var.*
Kunashiri. *Island* Kuril'skiye
Ostrova, SE Russian Federation
Kunda 106 E2 Lääne-Virumaa,
NE Estonia
Kunduz 123 E3 *var.* Kondoz,
Kundūz, Qondūz, *Per.* Kondūz.
Kunduz, NE Afghanistan
Kuneitra *see* Al Qunayţirah
Kunene *see* Cunene
Kungsbacka 85 B7 Halland,
S Sweden
Kungur 111 D5 Permskaya Oblast',
NW Russian Federation
Kunlun Mountains *see* Kunlun Shan
Kunlun Shan 126 B4 *Eng.* Kunlun
Mountains. *Mountain range*
NW China
Kunming 128 B6 *var.* K'un-ming;
prev. Yunnan. Yunnan, SW China
K'un-ming *see* Kunming
Kununurra 146 D3 Western
Australia
Kuopio 85 E5 Itä-Suomi, C Finland
Kupang 139 E5 *prev.* Koepang.
Timor, C Indonesia
Kup"yans'k 109 G2 *Rus.* Kupyansk.
Kharkivs'ka Oblast', E Ukraine
Kura 117 H3 *Az.* Kür, *Geor.* Mtkvari,
Turk. Kura Nehri. *River* SW Asia
Kurashiki 131 B6 *var.* Kurasiki.
Okayama, Honshū, SW Japan
Kurasiki *see* Kurashiki
Kurdistan 117 F4 *cultural region*
SW Asia
Kŭrdzhali 104 D3 *var.* Kirdzhali.
Kŭrdzhali, S Bulgaria
Kure 131 B7 Hiroshima, Honshū,
SW Japan
Küre Dağları 116 C2 *mountain range*
N Turkey
Kuressaare 106 C2 *Ger.* Arensburg;
prev. Kingissepp. Saaremaa,
W Estonia
Kureyka 112 D2 *river* N Russian
Federation
Kuria Muria Islands *see* Ḩalāniyāt,
Juzur al
Kurile Islands *see* Kuril'skiye
Ostrova
Kurile-Kamchatka Depression *see*
Kurile Trench
Kurile Trench 113 F3 *var.* Kurile-
Kamchatka Depression. *Undersea*
feature NW Pacific Ocean
Kuril'sk 130 E1 Kuril'skiye Ostrova,
Sakhalinskaya Oblast', SE Russian
Federation
Kuril'skiye Ostrova 115 H4 *Eng.*
Kurile Islands. *Island group*
SE Russian Federation
Ku-ring-gai 148 E1 New South
Wales, SE Australia
Kurnool 132 C1 *var.* Karnul. Andhra
Pradesh, S India
Kursk 111 A6 Kurskaya Oblast',
W Russian Federation
Kuršumlija 101 D5 Serbia,
S Yugoslavia
Kuruktag 126 C3 *mountain range*
NW China
Kurume 131 A7 Fukuoka, Kyūshū,
SW Japan
Kurupukari 59 F3 C Guyana
Kurzeme 106 B3 *Eng.* Courland,
Ger. Kurland. *Former province*
W Latvia
Kushiro 130 D2 *var.* Kusiro.
Hokkaidō, NE Japan
Kusiro *see* Kushiro
Kuskokwim Mountains 36 C3
mountain range Alaska, USA
Kuźnica 98 E2 Podlaskie, NE
Poland
Kustanay *see* Kostanay
Küstence *see* Constanţa
Küstendje *see* Constanţa
Kütahya 116 B3 *prev.* Kutaia.
Kütahya, W Turkey

Kutai *see* Mahakam, Sungai
K'ut'aisi 117 F2 W Georgia
Küt al 'Amārah *see* Al Küt
Kut al Imara *see* Al Küt
Kutaradja *see* Bandaaceh
Kutaraja *see* Bandaaceh
Kutch, Gulf of *see* Kachchh, Gulf
of
Kutch, Rann of *see* Kachchh, Rann
of
Kutina 100 B3 Sisak-Moslavina,
NE Croatia
Kutno 98 C3 Łódzkie, C Poland
Kuujjuaq 39 E2 *prev.* Fort-Chimo.
Québec, E Canada
Kuusamo 84 E3 Oulu, E Finland
Kuvango *see* Cubango
Kuvdlorssuaq *see* Kullorsuaq
Kuwait 120 C4 *var.* Dawlat
al Kuwait, Koweit, Kuwait.
Country SW Asia

Kuwait 120

Official name State of Kuwait	
Formation 1961	
Capital Kuwait City	
Population 2 million / 291 people per sq mile (112 people per sq km)	
Total area 6880 sq miles (17,820 sq km)	
Languages Arabic, English	
Religions Muslim (mainly Sunni) 92%, Christian 6%, other 2%	
Ethnic mix Kuwaiti 45%, other Arab 35%, South Asian 9%, Iranian 4%, other 7%	
Government Constitutional monarchy	
Currency Kuwaiti dinar = 1,000 fils	
Literacy rate 80.4%	
Calorie consumption 2,523 kilocalories	

Kuwait *see* Al Kuwayt
Kuwait City *see* Al Kuwayt
Kuwajleen *see* Kwajalein Atoll
Kuwayt 120 C3 E Iraq
Kuybyshev Reservoir *see*
Kuybyshevskoye
Vodokhranilishche
Kuybyshevskoye
Vodokhranilishche 111 C5 *var.*
Kuibyshev, *Eng.* Kuybyshev
Reservoir. *Reservoir* W Russian
Federation
Kuytun 126 B2 Xinjiang Uygur
Zizhiqu, NW China
Kuzi *see* Kuji
Kuznetsk 111 B6 Penzenskaya
Oblast', W Russian Federation
Kvaløya 84 C2 *island* N Norway
Kvarnbergsvattnet 84 B4 *var.*
Frostviken. *Lake* N Sweden
Kvarner 100 A3 *var.* Carnaro, *It.*
Quarnero. *Gulf* W Croatia
Kvitøya 83 G1 *island* NE Svalbard
Kwajalein Atoll 144 C1 *var.*
Kuwajleen. *Atoll* Ralik Chain,
C Marshall Islands
Kwando *see* Cuando
Kwangchow *see* Guangzhou
Kwangju 129 E4 *off.* Kwangju-
gwangyŏksi, *var.* Guangju,
Kwangchu, *Jap.* Kōshū. SW South
Korea
Kwango 77 C7 *Port.* Cuango. *River*
Angola/Dem. Rep. Congo (Zaire)
see also Cuango
Kwango *see* Cuango
Kwangsi *see* Guangxi Zhuangzu
Zizhiqu
Kwangsi Chuang Autonomous
Region *see* Guangxi Zhuangzu
Zizhiqu
Kwangtung *see* Guangdong
Kwangyuan *see* Guangyuan
Kwanza *see* Cuanza
Kweichow *see* Guizhou
Kweichu *see* Guiyang
Kweilin *see* Guilín
Kweisui *see* Hohhot
Kweiyang *see* Guiyang
Kwekwe 78 D3 *prev.* Que Que.
Midlands, C Zimbabwe
Kwesui *see* Hohhot

Kwidzyń *98 C2 Ger.* Marienwerder. Pomorskie, N Poland
Kwigillingok *36 C3* Alaska, USA
Kwilu *77 C6 river* W Dem. Rep. Congo (Zaire)
Kwito *see* Cuito
Kyabé *76 C4* Moyen-Chari, S Chad
Kyaikkami *137 B5 prev.* Amherst. Mon State, S Myanmar
Kyaiklat *136 B4* Irrawaddy, SW Myanmar
Kyaikto *136 B4* Mon State, S Myanmar
Kyakhta *115 E5* Respublika Buryatiya, S Russian Federation
Kyaukse *136 B3* Mandalay, C Myanmar
Kyjov *99 C5 Ger.* Gaya. Brněnský Kraj, SE Czech Republic
Kykládes *105 D6 var.* Kikládhes, *Eng.* Cyclades. *Island group* SE Greece
Kými *105 C5 prev.* Kími. Évvoia, C Greece
Kyōto *131 C6* Kyōto, Honshū, SW Japan
Kyparissía *105 B6 var.* Kiparissía. Pelopónnisos, S Greece
Kyrá Panagía *105 C5 island* Vóreioi Sporádes, Greece, Aegean Sea
Kyrenia *see* Kerýneia
Kyrgyzstan *123 F2 var.* Kirghizia; *prev.* Kirgizskaya SSR, Kirghiz SSR, Republic of Kyrgyzstan. *Country* C Asia

Kyrgyzstan 123

Official name Kyrgyz Republic
Formation 1991
Capital Bishkek
Population 4.7 million / 61 people per sq mile (24 people per sq km)
Total area 76,640 sq miles (198,500 sq km)
Languages Kyrgyz, Russian
Religions Muslim 65%, other (mainly Russian Orthodox) 35%
Ethnic mix Kyrgyz 57%, Russian 19%, Uzbek 13%, Tartar 2%, Ukranian 2%, other 7%
Government Multiparty republic
Currency Som = 100 teen
Literacy rate 97%
Calorie consumption not available

Kýthira *105 C7 var.* Kíthira, *It.* Cerigo; *Lat.* Cythera. *Island* S Greece
Kýthnos *105 C6 var.* Kíthnos, Thermiá, *It.* Termia; *anc.* Cythnos. *Island* Kykládes, Greece, Aegean Sea
Kýthnos *105 C6* Kýthnos, Kykládes, Greece, Aegean Sea
Kythréa *102 C5* N Cyprus
Kyūshū *131 B7 var.* Kyûsyû. *Island* SW Japan
Kyushu-Palau Ridge *125 F3 var.* Kyusyu-Palau Ridge. *Undersea feature* W Pacific Ocean
Kyustendil *104 B2 anc.* Pautalia. Kyustendil, W Bulgaria
Kyûsyû *see* Kyūshū
Kyusyu-Palau Ridge *see* Kyushu-Palau Ridge
Kyyiv *109 E2 Eng.* Kiev, *Rus.* Kiyev. *Country capital* (Ukraine) Kyyivs'ka Oblast', N Ukraine
Kyyivs'ke Vodoskhovyshche *109 E1 Eng.* Kiev Reservoir, *Rus.* Kiyevskoye Vodokhranilishche. *Reservoir* N Ukraine
Kyzyl *114 D4* Respublika Tyva, C Russian Federation
Kyzyl Kum *122 D2 var.* Kizil Kum, Qizil Qum, Qizilqum. *Desert* Kazakhstan/Uzbekistan
Kyzylorda *114 B5 var.* Kzyl-orda, Qizil Orda, *Kaz.* Qyzylorda; *prev.* Perovsk. Kyzylorda, S Kazakhstan
Kyzyl-Suu *123 G2 prev.* Pokrovka. Issyk-Kul'skaya Oblast', NE Kyrgyzstan
Kyzyl-orda *see* Kyzylorda

L

La Algaba *92 C4* Andalucía, S Spain
Laamu Atoll *see* Hadhdhunmathi Atoll
Laarne *87 B5* Oost-Vlaanderen, NW Belgium
La Asunción *59 E1* Nueva Esparta, NE Venezuela
Laâyoune *70 B3 var.* Aaiún. *Dependent territory capital* (Western Sahara) NW Western Sahara
la Baule-Escoublac *90 A4* Loire-Atlantique, NW France
Labé *74 C4* Moyenne-Guinée, NW Guinea
La Blanquilla *see* Blanquilla, Isla
Laborec *99 E5 Hung.* Laborca. *River* E Slovakia
Labrador *39 F2 cultural region* Newfoundland and Labrador, SW Canada
Labrador Basin *34 E3 var.* Labrador Sea Basin. *Undersea feature* Labrador Sea
Labrador Sea *82 A4 sea* NW Atlantic Ocean
Labrador Sea Basin *see* Labrador Basin
Labutta *137 A5* Irrawaddy, SW Myanmar
Laç *101 C6 var.* Laci. Lezhë, C Albania
La Calera *64 B4* Valparaíso, C Chile
La Carolina *92 D4* Andalucía, S Spain
Laccadive Islands *see* Lakshadweep
La Ceiba *52 D2* Atlántida, N Honduras
Lachanás *104 B3* Kentrikí Makedonía, N Greece
La Chaux-de-Fonds *95 A7* Neuchâtel, W Switzerland
Lachlan River *149 C6 river* New South Wales, SE Australia
Laci *see* Laç
la Ciotat *91 D6 anc.* Citharista. Bouches-du-Rhône, SE France
La Concepción *58 C7* Zulia, NW Venezuela
La Concepción *53 E5 var.* Concepción. Chiriquí, W Panama
La Condamine *91 C8* NW Andorra
Laconia *41 G2* New Hampshire, NE USA
La Crosse *40 A2* Wisconsin, N USA
La Cruz *52 D4* Guanacaste, NW Costa Rica
Lacus Asphaltites *see* Dead Sea
Ladoga, Lake *see* Ladozhskoye Ozero
Ladozhskoye Ozero *110 B3 Eng.* Lake Ladoga, *Fin.* Laatokka. *Lake* NW Russian Federation
Ladysmith *40 B2* Wisconsin, N USA
Lae *144 B3* Morobe, W PNG
La Esperanza *52 C2* Intibucá, SW Honduras
Lafayette *40 C4* Indiana, N USA
Lafayette *42 B3* Louisiana, S USA
La Fé *54 A2* Pinar del Río, W Cuba
Lafia *75 G4* Nassarawa, C Nigeria
la Flèche *90 B4* Sarthe, NW France
Lagdo, Lac de *76 B4 lake* N Cameroon
Laghouat *70 D2* N Algeria
Lago dos Gansos *see* Goose Lake
Lago General Carrera *see* Buenos Aires, Lago
Lago Nyassa *see* Nyasa, Lake
Lago Pampa Aullagas *see* Poopó, Lago
Lagos *92 B5 anc.* Lacobriga. Faro, S Portugal
Lagos *75 F5* Lagos, SW Nigeria
Lagos de Moreno *51 E4* Jalisco, SW Mexico
Lagouira *70 A4* SW Western Sahara
La Grande *44 C3* Oregon, NW USA
La Guaira *66 B4* Distrito Federal, N Venezuela
Laguna Merín *see* Mirim Lagoon
Lagunas *64 B1* Tarapacá, N Chile
Lagunillas *61 G4* Santa Cruz, SE Bolivia

La Habana *54 B2 var.* Havana. *Country capital* (Cuba) Ciudad de La Habana, W Cuba
Lahat *138 B4* Sumatera, W Indonesia
La Haye *see* 's-Gravenhage
Laholm *85 B7* Halland, S Sweden
Lahore *134 D2* Punjab, NE Pakistan
Lahr *95 A6* Baden-Württemberg, S Germany
Lahti *85 D5 Swe.* Lahtis. Etelä-Suomi, S Finland
Laï *76 B4 prev.* Behagle, De Behagle. Tandjilé, S Chad
Lai Châu *136 D3* Lai Châu, N Vietnam
Laila *see* Laylá
La Junta *44 D5* Colorado, C USA
Lake Charles *42 A3* Louisiana, S USA
Lake City *43 E3* Florida, SE USA
Lake District *89 C5 physical region* NW England, UK
Lake Havasu City *48 A2* Arizona, SW USA
Lake Jackson *49 H4* Texas, SW USA
Lakeland *43 E4* Florida, SE USA
Lakeside *47 C8* California, W USA
Lakewood *44 D4* Colorado, C USA
Lakhnau *see* Lucknow
Lakonikós Kólpos *105 B7 gulf* S Greece
Laksely *84 D2* Finnmark, N Norway
Lakshadweep *132 A3 Eng.* Laccadive Islands. *Island group* India, N Indian Ocean
la Laon *see* Laon
Lalibela *72 C4* N Ethiopia
La Libertad *52 B1* Petén, N Guatemala
La Ligua *64 B4* Valparaíso, C Chile
Lalín *92 C1* Galicia, NW Spain
Lalitpur *135 F3* Central, C Nepal
La Louvière *87 B6* Hainaut, S Belgium
La Maçana *see* La Massana
la Maddalena *96 A4* Sardegna, Italy, C Mediterranean Sea
la Manche *see* English Channel
Lamar *44 D5* Colorado, C USA
La Marmora, Punta *97 A5 mountain* Sardegna, Italy, C Mediterranean Sea
La Massana *91 A8 var.* La Maçana. W Andorra
Lambaréné *77 A6* Moyen-Ogooué, W Gabon
Lamego *92 C2* Viseu, N Portugal
Lamesa *49 E3* Texas, SW USA
Lamezia *97 D6* Calabria, SE Italy
Lamía *105 B5* Stereá Ellás, C Greece
Lamoni *45 F4* Iowa, C USA
Lampang *136 C4 var.* Muang Lampang. Lampang, NW Thailand
Lámpeia *105 B6* Dytikí Ellás, S Greece
Lanbi Kyun *137 B6 prev.* Sullivan Island. *Island* Mergui Archipelago, S Myanmar
Lancang Jiang *see* Mekong
Lancaster *47 C7* California, W USA
Lancaster *89 D5* NW England, UK
Lancaster *41 F4* Pennsylvania, NE USA
Lancaster Sound *37 F2 sound* Nunavut, N Canada
Lan-chou *see* Lanzhou
Lan-chow *see* Lanzhou
Landen *87 C6* Vlaams Brabant, C Belgium
Lander *44 C3* Wyoming, C USA
Landerneau *90 A3* Finistère, NW France
Landes *91 B5 department* SW France
Land's End *89 B8 headland* SW England, UK
Landshut *95 C6* Bayern, SE Germany
Langar *123 E2 Rus.* Lyangar. Nawoiy Wiloyati, C Uzbekistan
Langfang *128 D4* Hebei, E China
Langkawi, Pulau *137 B7 island* Peninsular Malaysia

Langres *90 D4* Haute-Marne, N France
Langsa *138 A3* Sumatera, W Indonesia
Lang Shan *127 E3 mountain range* N China
Lang Son *136 D3 var.* Langson. Lang Son, N Vietnam
Langson *see* Lang Son
Lang Suan *137 B6* Chumphon, SW Thailand
Languedoc *91 C6 cultural region* S France
Länkäran *117 H3 Rus.* Lenkoran'. S Azerbaijan
Lansing *40 C3 state capital* Michigan, N USA
Lanta, Ko *137 B7 island* S Thailand
Lantau Island *128 A2 Cant.* Tai Yue Shan, *Chin.* Landao. *Island* Hong Kong, S China
Lan-ts'ang Chiang *see* Mekong
Lanzarote *70 B3 island* Islas Canarias, Spain, NE Atlantic Ocean
Lanzhou *128 B4 var.* Lan-chou, Lanchow, Lan-chow; *prev.* Kaolan. Gansu, C China
Lao Cai *136 D3* Lao Cai, N Vietnam
Laojunmiao *see* Yumen
Laon *90 D3 var.* la Laon; *anc.* Laudunum. Aisne, N France
La Orchila, Isla *58 D1 island* N Venezuela
La Oroya *60 C3* Junín, C Peru
Laos *136 D4 Country* SE Asia

Laos 136

Official name Lao People's Democratic Republic
Formation 1953
Capital Vientiane
Population 5.4 million / 61 people per sq mile (23 people per sq km)
Total area 89,111 sq miles (230,800 sq km)
Languages Lao, Miao, Yao
Religions Buddhist 85%, other (including Animist) 15%
Ethnic mix Lao Loum 56%, Lao Theung 34%, Lao Soung 9%, other 1%
Government Single-party republic
Currency New kip = 100 cents
Literacy rate 58.6%
Calorie consumption 2,259 kilocalories

La Palma *70 A3 island* Islas Canarias, Spain, NE Atlantic Ocean
La Palma *53 G5* Darién, SE Panama
La Paz *61 F4 var.* La Paz de Ayacucho. *Country capital* (Bolivia-legislative and administrative capital) La Paz, W Bolivia
La Paz *50 B3* Baja California Sur, NW Mexico
La Paz, Bahía de *50 B3 bay* W Mexico
La Paz de Ayacucho *see* La Paz
La Perouse Strait *130 D1 Jap.* Sōya-kaikyō, *Rus.* Proliv Laperuza. *Strait* Japan/Russian Federation
Lápithos *102 C5* NW Cyprus
Lapland *84 D3 Fin.* Lappi, *Swe.* Lappland. *Cultural region* N Europe
La Plata *64 D4* Buenos Aires, E Argentina
Lappeenranta *85 E5 Swe.* Villmanstrand. Etelä-Suomi, S Finland
Lappi *see* Lapland
Lappland *see* Lapland
Lapta *see* Lápithos
Laptev Sea *see* Laptevykh, More
Laptevykh, More *115 E2 Eng.* Laptev Sea. *Sea* Arctic Ocean
Lapua *85 D5 Swe.* Lappo. Länsi-Suomi, W Finland
La Puebla *see* Sa Pobla
Łapy *98 E3* Podlaskie
La Quiaca *64 C2* Jujuy, N Argentina

L'Aquila 96 C4 var. Aquila, Aquila degli Abruzzo. Abruzzo, C Italy
Laracha 92 B1 Galicia, NW Spain
Laramie 44 C4 Wyoming, C USA
Laramie Mountains 44 C3 mountain range Wyoming, C USA
Laredo 93 E1 Cantabria, N Spain
Laredo 49 F5 Texas, SW USA
Largo 43 E4 Florida, SE USA
Largo, Cayo 54 B2 island W Cuba
Lario see Como, Lago di
La Rioja 93 E2 La Rioja, NW Argentina
Lárisa 104 B4 var. Larissa. Thessalía, C Greece
Larissa see Lárisa
Lārkāna 134 B3 var. Larkhana. Sind, SE Pakistan
Larkhana see Lārkāna
Lárnaka 102 C5 var. Larnaca, Larnax. SE Cyprus
Larnax see Lárnaka
la Rochelle 90 B4 anc. Rupella. Charente-Maritime, W France
la Roche-sur-Yon 90 B4 prev. Bourbon Vendée, Napoléon-Vendée. Vendée, NW France
La Roda 93 E3 Castilla-La Mancha, C Spain
La Romana 55 E3 E Dominican Republic
Larvotto 91 C8 N Monaco
La-sa see Lhasa
Las Cabezas de San Juan 92 C5 Andalucía, S Spain
Las Cruces 48 D3 New Mexico, SW USA
La See d'Urgel 93 G1 var. La Seu d'Urgell, Seo de Urgel. Cataluña, NE Spain
La Serena 64 B3 Coquimbo, C Chile
La Seu d'Urgell see La See d'Urgel
la Seyne-sur-Mer 91 D6 Var, SE France
Lashio 136 B3 Shan State, E Myanmar
Lashkar Gāh 122 D5 var. Lash-Kar-Gar'. Helmand, S Afghanistan
Lash-Kar-Gar' see Lashkar Gāh
La Sila 97 D6 mountain range SW Italy
La Sirena 52 D3 Región Autónoma Atlántico Sur, E Nicaragua
Łask 98 C4 Łódzkie, C Poland
Las Lomitas 64 D2 Formosa, N Argentina
La Solana 93 E4 Castilla-La Mancha, C Spain
Las Palmas de Gran Canaria 70 A3 Gran Canaria, Islas Canarias, Spain, NE Atlantic Ocean
La Spezia 96 B3 Liguria, NW Italy
Lassa see Lhasa
Las Tablas 53 F5 Los Santos, S Panama
Las Tunas 54 C2 var. Victoria de las Tunas. Las Tunas, E Cuba
Las Vegas 47 D7 Nevada, W USA
Latacunga 60 B1 Cotopaxi, C Ecuador
la Teste 91 B5 Gironde, SW France
Latina 97 C5 prev. Littoria. Lazio, C Italy
La Tortuga, Isla 59 E1 var. Isla Tortuga. Island N Venezuela
La Tuque 39 E4 Québec, SE Canada
Latvia 106 C3 Ger. Lettland, Latv. Latvija,Latvijas Republika; prev. Latvian SSR, Rus. Latviyskaya SSR. Country NE Europe

Latvia 106

Official name Republic of Latvia
Formation 1991
Capital Riga
Population 2.4 million / 96 people per sq mile (37 people per sq km)
Total area 24,938 sq miles (64,589 sq km)
Languages Latvian, Russian
Religions Evangelical Lutheran 85%, other Christian 15%
Ethnic mix Latvian 52%, Russian34%,

Latvia (continued)

Belorussian 5%, Ukranian 4%, other 5%
Government Multiparty republic
Currency Lat = 100 santimi
Literacy rate 99%
Calorie consumption not available

Laudunum see Laon
Lauenburg see Lębork
Lauenburg in Pommern see Lębork
Lau Group 145 E4 island group E Fiji
Launceston 149 C8 Tasmania, SE Australia
La Unión 93 F4 Murcia, SE Spain
La Unión 52 C2 Olancho, C Honduras
Laurel 42 C3 Mississippi, S USA
Laurel 44 C2 Montana, NW USA
Laurentian Highlands see Laurentian Mountains
Laurentian Mountains 39 E3 var. Laurentian Highlands, Fr. Les Laurentides. Plateau Newfoundland and Labrador/Québec, Canada
Lauria 97 D6 Basilicata, S Italy
Laurinburg 43 F1 North Carolina, SE USA
Lauru see Choiseul
Lausanne 95 A7 It. Losanna. Vaud, SW Switzerland
Laut Banda see Banda Sea
Laut, Pulau 138 D4 prev. Laoet. Island Borneo, C Indonesia
Laval 90 B3 Mayenne, NW France
Laval 38 D4 Québec, SE Canada
La Vega 55 E3 var. Concepción de la Vega. C Dominican Republic
La Vila Jojosa see Villajoyosa
Lávrio 105 C6 prev. Lávrion. Attikí, C Greece
Lawrence 41 G3 Massachusetts, NE USA
Lawrenceburg 42 C1 Tennessee, S USA
Lawton 49 F2 Oklahoma, C USA
La Yarada 61 E4 Tacna, SW Peru
Laylá 121 C5 var. Laila. Ar Riyāḍ, C Saudi Arabia
Lazarev Sea 154 B1 sea Antarctica
Lázaro Cárdenas 51 E5 Michoacán de Ocampo, SW Mexico
Læsø 85 B7 island N Denmark
Leamhcán see Lucan
Leamington 38 C5 Ontario, S Canada
Lebak 139 E3 Mindanao, S Philippines
Lebanon 118 A4 Ar. Al Lubnān, Fr. Liban. Country SW Asia

Lebanon 118

Official name Republic of Lebanon
Formation 1944
Capital Beirut
Population 3.3 million / 835 people per sq mile (323 people per sq km)
Total area 3,949 sq miles (10,230 sq km)
Languages Arabic, French, Armenian
Religions Muslim (mainly Shi'a) 70%, Christian (mainly Maronite) 30%
Ethnic mix Arab 93% (Lebanese 83%, Palestinian 10%), other 7%
Government Multiparty republic
Currency Lebanese pound = 100 piastres
Literacy rate 84.4%
Calorie consumption 3,317 kilocalories

Lebanon 45 G5 Missouri, C USA
Lebanon 41 G2 New Hampshire, NE USA
Lebanon 46 B3 Oregon, NW USA
Lebap 122 D2 Lebapskiy Velayat, NE Turkmenistan

Lebedyn 109 F2 Rus. Lebedin. Sums'ka Oblast', NE Ukraine
Lębork 98 C2 var. Lebórk, Ger. Lauenburg, Lauenburg in Pommern. Pomorskie, N Poland
Lebrija 92 C5 Andalucía, S Spain
Lebu 65 A5 Bío Bío, C Chile
le Cannet 91 D6 Alpes-Maritimes, SE France
Le Cap see Cap-Haïtien
Lecce 97 E6 Puglia, SE Italy
Lechaná 105 B6 var. Lehena, Lekhainá. Dytikí Ellás, S Greece
Leduc 37 E5 Alberta, SW Canada
Leech Lake 45 F2 lake Minnesota, N USA
Leeds 89 D5 N England, UK
Leek 86 E2 Groningen, NE Netherlands
Leer 94 A3 Niedersachsen, NW Germany
Leeuwarden 86 D1 Fris. Ljouwert. Friesland, N Netherlands
Leeuwin, Cape 142 A5 headland Western Australia
Leeward Islands 55 G3 island group E West Indies
Leeward Islands see Sotavento, Ilhas de
Lefkáda 105 A5 It. Santa Maura; prev. Levkás, anc. Leucas. Island Iónioi Nísoi, Greece, C Mediterranean Sea
Lefkáda 105 A5 prev. Levkás. Iónioi Nísoi, Greece, C Mediterranean Sea
Lefká Óri 105 C7 mountain range Kríti, Greece, E Mediterranean Sea
Lefkímmi 105 A5 var. Levkímmi. Kérkyra, Iónioi Nísoi, Greece, C Mediterranean Sea
Legaspi 139 E2 off. Legaspi City. Luzon, N Philippines
Legnica 98 B4 Ger. Liegnitz. Dolnośląskie
le Havre 90 B3 Eng. Havre; prev. le Havre-de-Grâce. Seine-Maritime, N France
Leicester 89 D6 Lat. Batae Coritanorum. C England, UK
Leiden 86 B3 prev. Leyden, anc. Lugdunum Batavorum. Zuid-Holland, W Netherlands
Leie 90 D2 Fr. Lys. River Belgium/France
Leinster 89 B6 Ir. Cúige Laighean. Cultural region E Ireland
Leipsoí 105 E6 island Dodekánisos, Greece, Aegean Sea
Leipzig 94 C4 Pol. Lipsk; hist. Leipsic, anc. Lipsia. Sachsen, E Germany
Leiria 92 B3 anc. Collipo. Leiria, C Portugal
Leirvik 85 A6 Hordaland, S Norway
Lek 86 C4 river SW Netherlands
Lekhainá see Lechaná
Lekhchevo 104 C2 Montana, NW Bulgaria
Leksand 85 C5 Kopparberg, C Sweden
Lelystad 86 D3 Flevoland, C Netherlands
le Mans 90 B3 Sarthe, NW France
Lemesós 102 C5 var. Limassol. SW Cyprus
Lena 115 F3 river NE Russian Federation
Lena Tablemount 141 B7 undersea feature S Indian Ocean
Len Dao 128 C8 island S Spratly Islands
Lengshuitan 128 C6 Hunan, S China
Leninabad see Khŭjand
Leninakan see Gyumri
Lenine 109 G5 Rus. Lenino. Respublika Krym, S Ukraine
Leningrad see Sankt-Peterburg
Leningradskaya 154 B4 Russian research station Antarctica
Leninobod see Khŭjand

Leninpol' 123 F2 Talasskaya Oblast', NW Kyrgyzstan
Lenti 99 B7 Zala, SW Hungary
Leoben 95 E7 Steiermark, C Austria
León 51 E4 var. León de los Aldamas. Guanajuato, C Mexico
León 92 D1 Castilla-León, NW Spain
León 52 C3 León, NW Nicaragua
León de los Aldamas see León
Leonídi 105 B6 Pelopónnisos, S Greece
Lepe 92 C4 Andalucía, S Spain
le Portel 90 C2 Pas-de-Calais, N France
le Puy 91 C5 prev. le Puy-en-Velay, hist. Anicium, Podium Anicensis. Haute-Loire, C France
Léré 76 B4 Mayo-Kébbi, SW Chad
Lerma 92 D2 Castilla-León, N Spain
Léros 105 D6 island Dodekánisos, Greece, Aegean Sea
Lerrnayin Gharabakh see Nagornyy Karabakh
Lerwick 88 D1 NE Scotland, UK
Lesbos see Lésvos
Les Cayes see Cayes
Les Gonaïves see Gonaïves
Lesh see Lezhë
Leshan 128 B5 Sichuan, C China
les Herbiers 90 B4 Vendée, NW France
Leshi see Lezhë
Leskovac 101 E5 Serbia, SE Yugoslavia
Les Laurentides see Laurentian Highlands
Lesotho 78 D4 prev. Basutoland. Country S Africa

Lesotho 78

Official name Kingdom of Lesotho
Formation 1966
Capital Maseru
Population 2.2 million / 188 people per sq mile (72 people per sq km)
Total area 11,718 sq miles (30,350 sq km)
Languages English, Sesotho, Zulu
Religions Christian 90%, Traditional beliefs 10%
Ethnic mix Basotho 97%, European and Asian 3%
Government Constitutional monarchy
Currency Loti = 100 lisente
Literacy rate 82.3%
Calorie consumption 2,201 kilocalories

les Sables-d'Olonne 90 B4 Vendée, NW France
Lesser Antarctica 154 A3 var. West Antarctica. Physical region Antarctica
Lesser Antilles 55 G4 island group E West Indies
Lesser Caucasus 117 F2 Rus. Malyy Kavkaz. Mountain range SW Asia
Lesser Sunda Islands see Nusa Tenggara
Lésvos 116 A3 anc. Lesbos. Island E Greece
Leszno 98 B4 Ger. Lissa. Wielkopolskie, C Poland
Lethbridge 37 E5 Alberta, SW Canada
Lethem 59 F3 S Guyana
Leti, Kepulauan 139 F5 island group E Indonesia
Letpadan 136 B4 Pegu, SW Myanmar
Letsôk-aw Kyun 137 B6 var. Letsutan Island; prev. Domel Island. Island Mergui Archipelago, S Myanmar
Letsutan Island see Letsôk-aw Kyun
Leuven 87 C6 Fr. Louvain, Ger. Löwen. Vlaams Brabant, C Belgium
Leuze see Leuze-en-Hainaut

Leuze-en-Hainaut 87 B6 var. Leuze. Hainaut, SW Belgium
Levanger 84 B4 Nord-Trøndelag, C Norway
Levelland 49 E2 Texas, SW USA
Leverkusen 94 A4 Nordrhein-Westfalen, W Germany
Levice 99 C6 Ger. Lewentz, Lewenz, Hung. Léva. Nitriansky Kraj, SW Slovakia
Levin 150 D4 Manawatu-Wanganui, North Island, NZ
Levkímmi see Lefkímmi
Lewis, Isle of 88 B2 island NW Scotland, UK
Lewis Range 44 B1 mountain range Montana, NW USA
Lewiston 46 C2 Idaho, NW USA
Lewiston 41 G2 Maine, NE USA
Lewistown 44 C1 Montana, NW USA
Lexington 40 C5 Kentucky, S USA
Lexington 45 E4 Nebraska, C USA
Leyte 139 F2 island C Philippines
Leżajsk 99 E5 Podkarpackie, SE Poland
Lezha see Lezhë
Lezhë 101 C6 var. Lezha; prev. Lesh, Leshi. Lezhë, NW Albania
Lhasa 126 C5 var. La-sa, Lassa. Xizang Zizhiqu, W China
Lhaviyani Atoll see Faadhippolhu Atoll
Lhazê 126 C5 Xizang Zizhiqu, W China
L'Hospitalet de Llobregat 93 G2 var. Hospitalet. Cataluña, NE Spain
Liancourt Rocks 131 A5 Jap. Takeshima, Kor. Tok-Do. Island group Japan/South Korea
Lianyungang 128 D4 var. Xinpu. Jiangsu, E China
Liao see Liaoning
Liaodong Wan 127 G3 Eng. Gulf of Lantung, Gulf of Liaotung. Gulf NE China
Liao He 125 E1 river NE China
Liaoning 128 D3 var. Liao, Liaoning Sheng, Shengking; hist. Fengtien, Shenking. Admin. region province NE China
Liaoyuan 129 E3 var. Dongliao, Shuang-liao, Jap. Chengchiatun. Jilin, NE China
Liard see Fort Liard
Liban, Jebel 118 B4 Ar. Jabal al Gharbt, Jabal Lubnān, Eng. Mount Lebanon. Mountain range C Lebanon
Libby 44 A1 Montana, NW USA
Liberal 45 E5 Kansas, C USA
Liberec 98 B4 Ger. Reichenberg. Liberecký Kraj, N Czech Republic
Liberia 74 C5 Country W Africa

Liberia 74

Official name Republic of Liberia
Formation 1847
Capital Monrovia
Population 3.2 million / 86 people per sq mile (33 people per sq km)
Total area 37,189 sq miles (96,320 sq km)
Languages English, Kpelle, Vai, Bassa, Kru, Grebo, Kissi, Gola, Loma
Religions Christian 68%, Traditional beliefs 18%, Muslim 14%
Ethnic mix Indigenous tribes (16 main groups) 95%, Americo-Liberians 5%
Government Multiparty republic
Currency Liberian dollar = 100 cents
Literacy rate 38.3%
Calorie consumption 1,640 kilocalories

Liberia 52 D4 Guanacaste, NW Costa Rica
Libian Desert see Libyan Desert
Libourne 91 B5 Gironde, SW France

Libreville 77 A5 country capital (Gabon) Estuaire, NW Gabon
Libya 71 F3 Ar. Al Jamāhīrīyah al 'Arabīyah al Lībīyah ash Sha'bīyah al Ishtirākīyah; prev. Libyan Arab Republic. Country N Africa

Libya 71

Official name Great Socialist People's Libyan Arab Jamahariyah
Formation 1951
Capital Tripoli/Benghazi
Population 5.6 million / 8 people per sq mile (3 people per sq km)
Total area 679,358 sq miles (1,759,540 sq km)
Languages Arabic, Tuareg
Religions Muslim (mainly Sunni) 97%, other 3%
Ethnic mix Arab and Berber 95%, other 5%
Government Single-party state
Currency Libyan dinar = 1,000 dirhams
Literacy rate 76.5%
Calorie consumption 3,308 kilocalories

Libyan Desert 71 H4 var. Libian Desert, Ar. Aş Şahrā' al Lībīyah. Desert N Africa
Libyan Plateau 103 F4 var. Aḍ Ḍiffah. Plateau Egypt/Libya
Lichtenfels 95 C5 Bayern, SE Germany
Lichtenvoorde 86 E4 Gelderland, E Netherlands
Lichuan 128 C5 Hubei, C China
Lida 107 B5 Rus. Lida. Hrodzyenskaya Voblasts', W Belarus
Lidköping 85 B6 Västra Götaland, S Sweden
Lidoríki 105 B5 prev. Lidhorikion, Lidokhorikion. Stereá Ellás, C Greece
Lidzbark Warmiński 98 D2 Ger. Heilsberg. Warmińsko-Mazurskie, NE Poland
Liechtenstein 94 D1 Country C Europe

Liechtenstein 94

Official name Principality of Liechtenstein
Formation 1719
Capital Vaduz
Population 32,000/ 508 people per sq mile (200 people per sq km)
Total area 62 sq miles (160 sq km)
Languages German, Alemannish dialect, Italian
Religions Roman Catholic 81%, Protestant 7%, other 12%
Ethnic mix Liectensteiner 63%, Swiss 15%, German 9%, other 13%
Government Constitutional monarchy
Currency Swiss franc = 100 centimes
Literacy rate 99%
Calorie consumption not available

Liège 87 D6 Dut. Luik, Ger. Lüttich. Liège, E Belgium
Lienz 95 D7 Tirol, W Austria
Liepāja 106 B3 Ger. Libau. Liepāja, W Latvia
Liezen 95 D7 Steiermark, C Austria
Liffey 89 B6 river E Ireland
Lifou 144 D5 island Îles Loyauté, E New Caledonia
Liger see Loire
Ligure, Appennino 96 A2 Eng. Ligurian Mountains. Mountain range NW Italy
Ligurian Sea 96 A3 Fr. Mer Ligurienne, It. Mar Ligure. Sea N Mediterranean Sea
Lihue 47 A7 Haw. Lihu'e. Kauai, Hawaii, USA, C Pacific Ocean

Lihula 106 D2 Ger. Leal. Läänemaa, W Estonia
Likasi 77 D7 prev. Jadotville. Shaba, SE Dem. Rep. Congo (Zaire)
Liknes 85 A6 Vest-Agder, S Norway
Lille 90 C2 var. l'Isle, Dut. Rijssel, Flem. Ryssel; prev. Lisle, anc. Insula. Nord, N France
Lillehammer 85 B5 Oppland, S Norway
Lillestrøm 85 B6 Akershus, S Norway
Lilongwe 79 E2 country capital (Malawi) Central, W Malawi
Lima 60 C4 country capital (Peru) Lima, W Peru
Limanowa 99 D5 Małopolskie, S Poland
Limassol see Lemesós
Limerick 89 A6 Ir. Luimneach. SW Ireland
Límnos 103 F3 anc. Lemnos. Island E Greece
Limoges 91 C5 anc. Augustoritum Lemovicensium, Lemovices. Haute-Vienne, C France
Limón 53 E4 var. Puerto Limón. Limón, E Costa Rica
Limón 52 D2 Colón, NE Honduras
Limousin 91 C5 cultural region C France
Limoux 91 C6 Aude, S France
Limpopo 78 D3 var. Crocodile. River S Africa
Linares 92 D4 Andalucía, S Spain
Linares 64 B4 Maule, C Chile
Linares 51 E3 Nuevo León, NE Mexico
Linchuan 128 D5 var. Fuzhou. Jiangxi, S China
Lincoln 89 D5 anc. Lindum, Lindum Colonia. E England, UK
Lincoln 45 F4 state capital Nebraska, C USA
Lincoln 41 H2 Maine, NE USA
Lincoln Sea 34 D2 sea Arctic Ocean
Linden 59 F3 E Guyana
Líndhos see Líndos
Lindi 73 D8 Lindi, SE Tanzania
Líndos 105 E7 var. Líndhos. Ródos, Dodekánisos, Greece, Aegean Sea
Line Islands 145 G3 island group E Kiribati
Lingeh see Bandar-e Langeh
Lingen 94 A3 var. Lingen an der Ems. Niedersachsen, NW Germany
Lingen an der Ems see Lingen
Lingga, Kepulauan 138 B4 island group W Indonesia
Linköping 85 C6 Östergötland, S Sweden
Linz 95 D6 anc. Lentia. Oberösterreich, N Austria
Lion, Golfe du 91 C7 Eng. Gulf of Lion, Gulf of Lions; anc. Sinus Gallicus. Gulf S France
Lipari Islands see Eolie, Isole
Lipari, Isola 97 D6 island Isole Eolie, S Italy
Lipetsk 111 B5 Lipetskaya Oblast', W Russian Federation
Lipno 98 C3 Kujawsko-pomorskie, C Poland
Lipova 108 A4 Hung. Lippa. Arad, W Romania
Liqeni i Ohrit see Ohrid, Lake
Lira 73 B6 N Uganda
Lisala 77 C5 Equateur, N Dem. Rep. Congo (Zaire)
Lisboa 92 B4 Eng. Lisbon; anc. Felicitas Julia, Olisipo. Country capital (Portugal) Lisboa, W Portugal
Lisbon see Lisboa
Lisieux 90 B3 anc. Noviomagus. Calvados, N France
Liski 111 B6 prev. Georgiu-Dezh. Voronezhskaya Oblast', W Russian Federation
Lisle see Lille
l'Isle see Lille
Lismore 149 E5 Victoria, SE Australia
Lisse 86 C3 Zuid-Holland, W Netherlands

Litang 128 A5 Sichuan, C China
Lītani, Nahr el 135 B5 var. Nahr al Litant. River C Lebanon
Lithgow 149 D6 New South Wales, SE Australia
Lithuania 106 B4 Ger. Litauen, Lith. Lietuva, Pol. Litwa, Rus. Litva; prev. Lithuanian SSR, Rus. Litovskaya SSR. Country NE Europe

Lithuania 106

Official name Republic of Lithuania
Formation 1991
Capital Vilnius
Population 3.7 million / 147 people per sq mile (57 people per sq km)
Total area 25,174 sq miles (65,200 sq km)
Languages Lithuanian, Russian
Religions Roman Catholic 87%, Russian Orthodox 10%, other 3%
Ethnic mix Lithuanian 80%, Russian 9%, Polish 7%, other 4%
Government Multiparty republic
Currency Litas = 100 centas
Literacy rate 99%
Calorie consumption not available

Litóchoro 104 B4 var. Litohoro, Litókhoron. Kentrikí Makedonía, N Greece
Litohoro see Litóchoro
Litókhoron see Litóchoro
Little Alföld 99 C6 Ger. Kleines Ungarisches Tiefland, Hung. Kisalföld, Slvk. Podunajská Rovina. Plain Hungary/Slovakia
Little Andaman 133 F2 island Andaman Islands, India, NE Indian Ocean
Little Barrier Island 150 D2 island N NZ
Little Bay 93 H5 bay S Gibraltar
Little Cayman 54 B3 island E Cayman Islands
Little Falls 45 F2 Minnesota, N USA
Littlefield 49 E2 Texas, SW USA
Little Inagua 54 D2 var. Inagua Islands. Island S Bahamas
Little Minch, The 88 B3 strait NW Scotland, UK
Little Missouri River 44 D2 river NW USA
Little Nicobar 133 G3 island Nicobar Islands, India, NE Indian Ocean
Little Rock 42 B1 state capital Arkansas, C USA
Little Saint Bernard Pass 91 D5 Fr. Col du Petit St-Bernard, It. Colle di Piccolo San Bernardo. Pass France/Italy
Little Sound 42 A5 bay Bermuda, NW Atlantic Ocean
Littleton 44 D4 Colorado, C USA
Liu-chou see Liuzhou
Liuchow see Liuzhou
Liuzhou 128 C6 var. Liu-chou, Liuchow. Guangxi Zhuangzu Zizhiqu, S China
Livanátes 105 B5 prev. Livanátai. Stereá Ellás, C Greece
Līvāni 106 D4 Ger. Lievenhof. Preiļi, SE Latvia
Liverpool 148 D2 New South Wales, SE Australia
Liverpool 39 F5 Nova Scotia, SE Canada
Liverpool 89 C5 NW England, UK
Livingston 44 B2 Montana, NW USA
Livingstone 78 C3 var. Maramba. Southern, S Zambia
Livingston 49 H3 Texas, SW USA
Livingstone Mountains 151 A7 mountain range South Island, NZ
Livno 100 B4 Federacija Bosna I Hercegovina, SW Bosnia and Herzegovina
Livojoki 84 D4 river C Finland
Livonia 40 D3 Michigan, N USA

Livorno 96 B3 *Eng.* Leghorn. Toscana, C Italy

Lixoúri 105 A5 *prev.* Lixoúrion. Kefalliniá, Iónioi Nísoi, Greece, C Mediterranean Sea

Ljubljana 95 D7 *Ger.* Laibach, *It.* Lubiana; *anc.* Aemona, Emona. *Country capital* (Slovenia) C Slovenia

Ljungby 85 B7 Kronoberg, S Sweden

Ljusdal 85 C5 Gävleborg, C Sweden

Ljusnan 85 C5 *river* C Sweden

Llanelli 89 C6 *prev.* Llanelly. SW Wales, UK

Llanes 92 D1 Asturias, N Spain

Llanos 58 D2 *physical region* Colombia/Venezuela

Lleida 93 F2 *Cast.* Lérida; *anc.* Ilerda. Cataluña, NE Spain

Lluchmayor *see* Llucmajor

Llucmajor 93 G3 *var.* Lluchmayor. Mallorca, Spain, W Mediterranean Sea

Loaita Island 128 C8 *island* W Spratly Islands

Loanda *see* Luanda

Lobatse 78 C4 *var.* Lobatsi. Kgatleng, SE Botswana

Lobatsi *see* Lobatse

Löbau 94 D4 Sachsen, E Germany

Lobito 78 B2 Benguela, W Angola

Lob Nor *see* Lop Nur

Loburi *see* Lop Buri

Locarno 95 B8 *Ger.* Luggarus. Ticino, S Switzerland

Lochem 86 E3 Gelderland, E Netherlands

Lockport 41 E3 New York, NE USA

Lodja 77 D6 Kasai Oriental, C Dem. Rep. Congo (Zaire)

Lodwar 73 C6 Rift Valley, NW Kenya

Łódź 98 D4 *Rus.* Lodz. Łódzkie, C Poland

Loei 136 C4 *var.* Loey, Muang Loei. Loei, C Thailand

Loey *see* Loei

Lofoten 84 B3 *var.* Lofoten Islands. *Island group* C Norway

Lofoten Islands *see* Lofoten

Logan 44 B3 Utah, W USA

Logan, Mount 36 D3 *mountain* Yukon Territory, W Canada

Logroño 93 E1 *anc.* Vareia, *Lat.* Juliobriga. La Rioja, N Spain

Loibl Pass 95 D7 *Ger.* Loiblpass, *Slvn.* Ljubelj. *Pass* Austria/Slovenia

Loi-Kaw 136 B4 Kayah State, C Myanmar

Loire 90 B4 *var.* Liger. *River* C France

Loja 60 B2 Loja, S Ecuador

Lokitaung 73 C5 Rift Valley, NW Kenya

Lokoja 75 G4 Kogi, C Nigeria

Loksa 106 E2 *Ger.* Loxa. Harjumaa, NW Estonia

Lolland 85 B8 *prev.* Laaland. *Island* S Denmark

Lom 104 C1 *prev.* Lom-Palanka. Montana, NW Bulgaria

Lomami 77 D6 *river* C Dem. Rep. Congo (Zaire)

Lomas 60 D4 Arequipa, SW Peru

Lomas de Zamora 64 D4 Buenos Aires, E Argentina

Lombardia 96 B2 *cultural region* N Italy

Lombok, Pulau 138 D5 *island* Nusa Tenggara, C Indonesia

Lomé 75 F5 *country capital* (Togo) S Togo

Lomela 77 D6 Kasai Oriental, C Dem. Rep. Congo (Zaire)

Lommel 87 C5 Limburg, N Belgium

Lomond, Loch 88 B4 *lake* C Scotland, UK

Lomonosov Ridge 155 B3 *var.* Harris Ridge, *Rus.* Khrebet Lomnosova. *Undersea feature* Arctic Ocean

Lompoc 47 B7 California, W USA

Lom Sak 136 C4 *var.* Muang Lom Sak. Phetchabun, C Thailand

Łomża 98 D3 *off.* Województwo Łomżyńskie, *Rus.* Lomzha. Podlaskie, NE Poland

Loncoche 65 B5 Araucanía, C Chile

London 89 A7 *anc.* Augusta, *Lat.* Londinium. *Country capital* (UK) SE England, UK

London 40 C5 Kentucky, S USA

London 38 C5 Ontario, S Canada

Londonderry 88 B4 *var.* Derry, *Ir.* Doire. NW Northern Ireland, UK

Londonderry, Cape 146 C2 *headland* Western Australia

Londrina 63 E4 Paraná, S Brazil

Longa, Proliv 115 G1 *Eng.* Long Strait. *Strait* NE Russian Federation

Long Bay 43 F2 *bay* North Carolina/South Carolina, E USA

Long Beach 47 C7 California, W USA

Longford 89 B5 *Ir.* An Longfort. C Ireland

Long Island 54 D2 *island* C Bahamas

Long Island 41 G4 *island* New York, NE USA

Long Island *see* Bermuda

Longlac 38 C3 Ontario, S Canada

Longmont 44 D4 Colorado, C USA

Longreach 148 C4 Queensland, E Australia

Long Strait *see* Longa, Proliv

Longview 49 H3 Texas, SW USA

Longview 46 B2 Washington, NW USA

Long Xuyên 137 D6 *var.* Longxuyen. An Giang, S Vietnam

Longxuyen *see* Long Xuyên

Longyan 128 D6 Fujian, SE China

Longyearbyen 83 G2 *dependent territory capital* (Svalbard) Spitsbergen, W Svalbard

Lons-le-Saunier 90 D4 *anc.* Ledo Salinarius. Jura, E France

Lop Buri 137 C5 *var.* Loburi. Lop Buri, C Thailand

Lop Nor *see* Lop Nur

Lop Nur 126 C3 *var.* Lob Nor, Lop Nor, Lo-pu Po. *Seasonal lake* NW China

Loppersum 86 E1 Groningen, NE Netherlands

Lo-pu Po *see* Lop Nur

Lorca 93 E4 *Ar.* Lurka; *anc.* Eliocroca, *Lat.* Illur co. Murcia, S Spain

Lord Howe Island 142 C4 *island* E Australia

Lord Howe Rise 142 C4 *undersea feature* SW Pacific Ocean

Loreto 50 B3 Baja California Sur, W Mexico

Lorient 90 A3 *prev.* l'Orient. Morbihan, NW France

Lorn, Firth of 88 B4 *inlet* W Scotland, UK

Loro Sae *see* East Timor

Lörrach 95 A7 Baden-Württemberg, S Germany

Lorraine 90 D3 *cultural region* NE France

Los Alamos 48 C1 New Mexico, SW USA

Los Amates 52 B2 Izabal, E Guatemala

Los Angeles 47 C7 California, W USA

Los Ángeles 65 B5 Bío Bío, C Chile

Lošinj 100 A3 *Ger.* Lussin, *It.* Lussino. *Island* W Croatia

Los Mochis 50 C3 Sinaloa, C Mexico

Los Roques, Islas 58 D1 *island group* N Venezuela

Los Testigos, Isla 55 G5 *island* NE Venezuela

Lost River Range 46 D3 *mountain range* Idaho, C USA

Lot 91 B5 *cultural region* C France

Lot 91 B5 *river* S France

Lotagipi Swamp 73 C5 *wetland* Kenya/Sudan

Louangnamtha 136 C3 *var.* Luong Nam Tha. Louang Namtha, N Laos

Louangphabang 124 D3 *var.* Louangphrabang, Luang Prabang. Louangphabang, N Laos

Louangphrabang *see* Louangphabang

Loudéac 90 A3 Côtes d'Armor, NW France

Loudi 128 C5 Hunan, S China

Louga 74 B3 NW Senegal

Louisiade Archipelago 144 B4 *island group* SE PNG

Louisiana 42 A2 *off.* State of Louisiana; also known as Creole State, Pelican State. *State* S USA

Louisville 40 C5 Kentucky, S USA

Louisville Ridge 143 E4 *undersea feature* S Pacific Ocean

Loup River 45 E4 *river* Nebraska, C USA

Lourdes 91 B6 Hautes-Pyrénées, S France

Louth 89 E5 E England, UK

Loutrá 104 C4 Kentrikí Makedonía, N Greece

Lóuva 78 C1 Lunda Norte, NE Angola

Louvain-la Neuve 87 C6 Wallon Brabant, C Belgium

Louviers 90 C3 Eure, N France

Lovech 104 C2 Lovech, N Bulgaria

Loveland 44 D4 Colorado, C USA

Lovosice 98 A4 *Ger.* Lobositz. Ústecký Kraj, NW Czech Republic

Lowell 41 G3 Massachusetts, NE USA

Lower California *see* Baja California

Lower Hutt 151 D5 Wellington, North Island, NZ

Lower Lough Erne 89 A5 *lake* SW Northern Ireland, UK

Lower Red Lake 45 F1 *lake* Minnesota, N USA

Lower Tunguska *see* Nizhnyaya Tunguska

Lowestoft 89 E6 E England, UK

Lo-yang *see* Luoyang

Loyauté, Îles 144 D5 *island group* S New Caledonia

Loyew 107 D8 *Rus.* Loyev. Homyel'skaya Voblasts', SE Belarus

Loznica 100 C3 Serbia, W Yugoslavia

Lu *see* Shandong

Lualaba 77 D6 *Fr.* Loualaba. *River* SE Dem. Rep. Congo (Zaire)

Luanda 78 A1 *var.* Loanda, *Port.* São Paulo de Loanda. *Country capital* (Angola) Luanda, NW Angola

Luang Prabang *see* Louangphabang

Luang, Thale 137 C7 *lagoon* S Thailand

Luangua, Rio *see* Luangwa

Luangwa 73 B8 *var.* Aruângua, Rio Luangua. *River* Mozambique/Zambia

Luanshya 78 D2 Copperbelt, C Zambia

Luarca 92 C1 Asturias, N Spain

Lubaczów 99 E5 *var.* Lúbaczów. Podkarpackie, SE Poland

Lubań 98 B4 *var.* Koscian, *Ger.* Kosten. Dolnośląskie, SW Poland

Lubānas Ezers *see* Lubāns

Lubango 78 B2 *Port.* Sá da Bandeira. Huíla, SW Angola

Lubāns 106 D4 *var.* Lubānas Ezers. *Lake* E Latvia

Lubao 77 D6 Kasai Oriental, C Dem. Rep. Congo (Zaire)

Lübben 94 D4 Brandenburg, E Germany

Lübbenau 94 D4 Brandenburg, E Germany

Lubbock 49 E2 Texas, SW USA

Lübeck 94 C2 Schleswig-Holstein, N Germany

Lubelska, Wyżyna 98 E4 *plateau* SE Poland

Lubin 98 B4 *Ger.* Lüben. Dolnośląskie, W Poland

Lublin 98 E4 *Rus.* Lyublin. Lubelskie, E Poland

Lubliniec 98 C4 Śląskie, S Poland

Lubny 109 F2 Poltavs'ka Oblast', NE Ukraine

Lubsko 98 B4 *Ger.* Sommerfeld. Lubuskie, W Poland

Lubumbashi 77 E8 *prev.* Élisabethville. Shaba, SE Dem. Rep. Congo (Zaire)

Lubutu 77 D6 Maniema, E Dem. Rep. Congo (Zaire)

Lucan 89 B5 *Ir.* Leamhcán. E Ireland

Lucano, Appennino 97 D5 *Eng.* Lucanian Mountains. *Mountain range* S Italy

Lucapa 78 C1 *var.* Lukapa. Lunda Norte, NE Angola

Lucca 96 B3 *anc.* Luca. Toscana, C Italy

Lucea 54 A4 W Jamaica

Lucena 139 E1 *off.* Lucena City. Luzon, N Philippines

Lucena 92 D4 Andalucía, S Spain

Lučenec 99 D6 *Ger.* Losontz, *Hung.* Losonc. Banskobystrický Kraj, C Slovakia

Luchow *see* Hefei

Lucknow 135 E3 *var.* Lakhnau. Uttar Pradesh, N India

Lüda *see* Dalian

Luda Kamchiya 104 D2 *river* E Bulgaria

Lüderitz 78 B4 *prev.* Angra Pequena. Karas, SW Namibia

Ludhiāna 134 D2 Punjab, N India

Ludington 40 C2 Michigan, N USA

Luduş 108 B4 *Ger.* Ludasch, *Hung.* Marosludas. Mureş, C Romania

Ludvika 85 C6 Kopparberg, C Sweden

Ludwigslust 94 C3 Mecklenburg-Vorpommern, N Germany

Ludwigsburg 95 B6 Baden-Württemberg, SW Germany

Ludwigsfelde 94 D3 Brandenburg, NE Germany

Ludwigshafen 95 B5 *var.* Ludwigshafen am Rhein. Rheinland-Pfalz, W Germany

Ludwigshafen am Rhein *see* Ludwigshafen

Ludza 106 D4 *Ger.* Ludsan. Ludza, E Latvia

Luebo 77 C6 Kasai Occidental, SW Dem. Rep. Congo (Zaire)

Luena 78 C2 *var.* Lwena, *Port.* Luso. Moxico, E Angola

Lufira 77 E7 *river* SE Dem. Rep. Congo (Zaire)

Lufkin 49 H3 Texas, SW USA

Luga 110 A4 Leningradskaya Oblast', NW Russian Federation

Lugano 95 B8 *Ger.* Lauis. Ticino, S Switzerland

Lugenda, Rio 79 E2 *river* N Mozambique

Lugo 92 C1 *anc.* Lugus Augusti. Galicia, NW Spain

Lugoj 108 A4 *Ger.* Lugosch, *Hung.* Lugos. Timiş, W Romania

Luhans'k 109 H3 *Rus.* Lugansk; *prev.* Voroshilovgrad. Luhans'ka Oblast', E Ukraine

Luimneach *see* Limerick

Lukapa *see* Lucapa

Lukenie 77 C6 *river* C Dem. Rep. Congo (Zaire)

Lukovit 104 C2 Lovech, NW Bulgaria

Łuków 98 E4 *Ger.* Bogendorf. Lubelskie, E Poland

Lukuga 77 D7 *river* SE Dem. Rep. Congo (Zaire)

Luleå 84 D4 Norrbotten, N Sweden

Luleälven 84 C3 *river* N Sweden

Lulonga 77 C5 *river* NW Dem. Rep. Congo (Zaire)

Lulua 77 D7 *river* S Dem. Rep. Congo (Zaire)

Lumbo 79 F2 Nampula, NE Mozambique

Lumsden 151 A7 Southland, South Island, NZ

Lund 85 B7 Skåne, S Sweden

Lüneburg 94 C3 Niedersachsen,
N Germany
Lungkiang see Qiqihar
Lungué-Bungo 78 C2 var.
Lungwebungu. River
Angola/Zambia see also
Lungwebungu
Lungwebungu see Lungué-Bungo
Luninyets 107 B7 Pol. Łuniniec,
Rus. Luninets. Brestskaya
Voblasts', SW Belarus
Lunteren 86 D4 Gelderland,
C Netherlands
Luong Nam Tha see
Louangnamtha
Luoyang 128 C4 var. Honan,
Lo-yang. Henan, C China
Lúrio 79 F2 Nampula,
NE Mozambique
Lúrio, Rio 79 E2 river
NE Mozambique
Lusaka 78 D2 country capital
(Zambia) Lusaka, SE Zambia
Lushnja see Lushnjë
Lushnjë 101 C6 var. Lushnja. Fier,
C Albania
Luso see Luena
Lüt, Dasht-e 120 D3 var. Kavīr-e
Lūt. Desert E Iran
Luton 89 D6 SE England, UK
Łutselk'e 37 F4 prev. Snowdrift.
Northwest Territories, W Canada
Luts'k 108 C1 Pol. Łuck, Rus. Lutsk.
Volyns'ka Oblast', NW Ukraine
Lutzow-Holm Bay see Lützow
Holmbukta
Lützow Holmbukta 154 C2 var.
Lutzow-Holm Bay. Bay Antarctica
Luuq 73 D6 It. Lugh Ganana. Gedo,
SW Somalia
Luvua 77 D7 river SE Dem. Rep.
Congo (Zaire)
Luwego 73 C8 river S Tanzania
Luxembourg 87 D8 var.
Lëtzebuerg, Luxemburg. Country
NW Europe

Luxembourg 87

Official name Grand Duchy of
Luxembourg
Formation 1867
Capital Luxembourg
Population 431,000/ 432 people per
sq mile (165 people per sq km)
Total area 998 sq miles
(2,586 sq km)
Languages French, German,
Letzeburghish
Religions Roman Catholic 97%,
other 3%
Ethnic mix Luxembourger 72%,
Portuguese 9%, Italian 5%,
other 14%
Government Constitutional
monarchy
Currency Franc = 100 centimes
Literacy rate 99%
Calorie consumption 3,681
kilocalories

Luxembourg 87 D8 country capital
(Luxembourg) Luxembourg,
S Luxembourg
Luxor 72 B2 Ar. Al Uqşur. E Egypt
Luza 110 C4 Kirovskaya Oblast',
NW Russian Federation
Luz, Costa de la 92 C5 coastal region
SW Spain
Luzern 95 B7 Fr. Lucerne, It.
Lucerna. Luzern, C Switzerland
Luzon 139 E1 island N Philippines
Luzon Strait 125 E3 strait
Philippines/Taiwan
L'viv 108 B2 Ger. Lemberg, Pol.
Lwów, Rus. L'vov. L'vivs'ka
Oblast', W Ukraine
Lwena see Luena
Lyakhavichy 107 B6 Rus.
Lyakhovichi. Brestskaya Voblasts',
SW Belarus
Lycksele 84 C4 Västerbotten,
N Sweden
Lycopolis see Asyût
Lyel'chytsy 107 C7 Rus. Lel'chitsy.
Homyel'skaya Voblasts',
SE Belarus

Lyepyel' 107 D5 Rus. Lepel'.
Vitsyebskaya Voblasts', N Belarus
Lyme Bay 89 C7 bay S England, UK
Lynchburg 41 E5 Virginia, NE USA
Lynn Regis see King's Lynn
Lyon 91 D5 Eng. Lyons; anc.
Lugdunum. Rhône, E France
Lyozna 107 E6 Rus. Liozno.
Vitsyebskaya Voblasts',
NE Belarus
Lypovets' 108 D2 Rus. Lipovets.
Vinnyts'ka Oblast', C Ukraine
Lysychans'k 109 H3 Rus.
Lisichansk. Luhans'ka Oblast',
E Ukraine
Lyttelton 151 C6 Canterbury, South
Island, NZ
Lyubotyn 109 G2 Rus. Lyubotin.
Kharkivs'ka Oblast', E Ukraine
Lyulyakovo 104 E2 prev. Keremitlik.
Burgas, E Bulgaria
Lyusina 107 B6 Rus. Lyusino.
Brestskaya Voblasts', SW Belarus

M

Ma'ān 119 B7 Ma'ān, SW Jordan
Maardu 106 D2 Ger. Maart.
Harjumaa, NW Estonia
Ma'aret-en-Nu'man see Ma'arrat
an Nu'mān
Ma'arrat an Nu'mān 118 B3 var.
Ma'aret-en-Nu'man, Fr. Maarret
enn Naamâne. Idlib, NW Syria
Maarret enn Naamâne see Ma'arrat
an Nu'mān
Maaseik 87 D5 prev. Maeseyck.
Limburg, NE Belgium
Maastricht 87 D6 var. Maestricht;
anc. Traietum ad Mosam,
Traiectum Tungorum. Limburg,
SE Netherlands
Macao 129 C6 Chin. Aomen, Port.
Macao. S China
Macapá 63 E1 state capital Amapá,
N Brazil
Macassar see Ujungpandang
MacCluer Gulf see Berau, Teluk
Macdonnell Ranges 146 D4
mountain range Northern Territory,
C Australia
Macedonia, FYR 101 D6 var.
Macedonia, Mac. Makedonija,
abbrev. FYR Macedonia, FYROM.
Country SE Europe

Macedonia 101

Official name Former Yugoslav
Republic of Macedonia
Formation 1991
Capital Skopje
Population 2 million / 201 people
per sq mile (78 people per sq km)
Total area 9,929 sq miles
(25,715 sq km)
Languages Macedonian, Serbian,
Croatian
Religions Christian 80%,
Muslim 20%
Ethnic mix Macedonian 67%,
Albanian 23%, Turkish 4%,
other 6%
Government Multiparty republic
Currency Macedonian denar
= 100 deni
Literacy rate 94%
Calorie consumption
not available

Maceió 63 G3 state capital Alagoas,
E Brazil
Machachi 60 B1 Pichincha,
C Ecuador
Machala 60 B2 El Oro, SW Ecuador
Machanga 79 E3 Sofala,
E Mozambique
Machilīpatnam 132 D1 var. Bandar
Masulipatnam. Andhra Pradesh,
E India
Machiques 58 C2 Zulia,
NW Venezuela
Macías Nguema Biyogo see Bioco,
Isla de
Măcin 108 D5 Tulcea, SE Romania
Macizo de las Guayanas see
Guiana Highlands

Mackay 148 D4 Queensland,
NE Australia
Mackay, Lake 146 C4 salt lake
Northern Territory/Western
Australia
Mackenzie 37 E3 river Northwest
Territories, NW Canada
Mackenzie Bay 154 D3 bay
Antarctica
Mackenzie Mountains 36 D3
mountain range Northwest
Territories, NW Canada
Macleod, Lake 146 A4 lake Western
Australia
Macomb 40 A4 Illinois, N USA
Macomer 97 A5 Sardegna, Italy,
C Mediterranean Sea
Macon 42 D2 Georgia, SE USA
Macon 45 G4 Missouri, C USA
Mâcon 91 D5 anc. Matisco, Matisco
Ædourum. Saône-et-Loire,
C France
Macquarie Ridge 154 C5 undersea
feature SW Pacific Ocean
Macuspana 51 G4 Tabasco,
SE Mexico
Ma'dabā 119 B6 var. Mādabā,
Madeba; anc. Medeba. 'Ammān,
NW Jordan
Madagascar 79 F3 Malg.
Madagasikara; prev. Malagasy
Republic. Country W Indian
Ocean

Madagascar 79

Official name Republic of
Madagascar
Formation 1960
Capital Antananarivo
Population 16 million / 71 people
per sq mile (27 people per sq km)
Total area 224,532 sq miles
(581,540 sq km)
Languages French, Malagasy
Religions Traditional beliefs 52%,
Christian 41%, Muslim 7%
Ethnic mix Merina 26%,
Betsimisaraka 15%, other 59%
Government Multiparty republic
Currency Malagasy franc
= 100 centimes
Literacy rate 47%
Calorie consumption 2,135
kilocalories

Madagascar 79 F3 island W Indian
Ocean
Madagascar Basin 69 E7 undersea
feature W Indian Ocean
Madagascar Plateau 69 E7 var.
Madagascar Ridge, Madagascar
Rise, Rus. Madagaskarskiy
Khrebet. Undersea feature
W Indian Ocean
Madagascar Ridge see Madagascar
Plateau
Madagascar Rise see Madagascar
Plateau
Madagaskarskiy Khrebet see
Madagascar Plateau
Madang 144 B3 Madang, N PNG
Madanīyīn see Médenine
Made 86 C4 Noord-Brabant,
S Netherlands
Madeba see Ma'dabā
Madeira 70 A2 var. Ilha de Madeira.
Island Portugal, NE Atlantic
Spain
Madeira 70 A2 var. Madeira, Port.
Arquipélago da Madeira. Island
group Portugal, NE Atlantic Ocean
Madeira Plain 66 C3 undersea feature
E Atlantic Ocean
Madeira, Rio 62 D2 Sp. Río Madera.
River Bolivia/Brazil see also
Madera, Río
Madeleine, Îles de la 39 F4 Eng.
Magdalen Islands. Island group
Québec, E Canada
Madera 47 B6 California, W USA
Madhya Pradesh 135 E4 prev.
Central Provinces and Berar.
Admin. region state C India
Madīnat ath Thawrah 118 C2 var.
Ath Thawrah. Ar Raqqah, N Syria
Asia

Madison 40 B3 state capital
Wisconsin, N USA
Madison 45 F3 South Dakota, N USA
Madiun 138 D5 prev. Madioen.
Jawa, C Indonesia
Madona 106 D4 Ger. Modohn.
Madona, E Latvia
Madras see Tamil Nādu
Madras see Chennai
Madre de Dios 56 B4 off.
Departamento de Madre de Dios.
Department E Peru
Madre de Dios, Río 61 E3 river
Bolivia/Peru
Madre del Sur, Sierra 51 E5
mountain range S Mexico
Madre, Laguna 51 F3 lagoon
NE Mexico
Madre, Laguna 49 G5 lake Texas,
SW USA
Madre Occidental, Sierra 50 C3 var.
Western Sierra Madre. Mountain
range C Mexico
Madre Oriental, Sierra 51 E3 var.
Eastern Sierra Madre. Mountain
range C Mexico
Madrid 92 D3 country capital (Spain)
Madrid, C Spain
Madurai 132 C3 prev. Madura,
Mathurai. Tamil Nādu, S India
Madura, Pulau 138 D5 prev.
Madoera. Island C Indonesia
Maebashi 131 D5 var. Maebasi,
Mayebashi. Gunma, Honshū,
S Japan
Maebasi see Maebashi
Mae Nam Khong see Mekong
Mae Nam Nan 136 C4 river
NW Thailand
Mae Nam Yom 136 C4 river
W Thailand
Maestricht see Maastricht
Maéwo 144 D4 prev. Aurora. Island
C Vanuatu
Mafia 73 D7 island E Tanzania
Mafraq see Al Mafraq
Magadan 115 G3 Magadanskaya
Oblast', E Russian Federation
Magangué 58 B2 Bolívar,
N Colombia
Magdalena 56 A2 off. Departamento
del Magdalena. Province
N Colombia
Magdalena 61 F3 Beni, N Bolivia
Magdalena 50 B1 Sonora,
NW Mexico
Magdalena, Isla 53 B8 island
W Mexico
Magdalena, Río 58 B2 river
C Colombia
Magdeburg 94 C3 Sachsen-Anhalt,
C Germany
Magelang 138 C5 Jawa, C Indonesia
Magellan, Strait of 65 B8 Sp.
Estrecho de Magallanes. Strait
Argentina/Chile
Magerøy see Magerøya
Magerøya 84 D1 var. Magerøy.
Island N Norway
Maggiore, Lake 96 B1 It. Lago
Maggiore. Lake Italy/Switzerland
Maglaj 100 C3 Federacija Bosna I
Hercegovina, N Bosnia and
Herzegovina
Maglie 97 E6 Puglia, SE Italy
Magna 44 B4 Utah, W USA
Magnesia see Manisa
Magnitogorsk 114 B4
Chelyabinskaya Oblast',
C Russian Federation
Magta' Lahjar 74 C3 var. Magta
Lahjar, Magta' Lahjar, Magtá
Lahjar. Brakna, SW Mauritania
Magway see Magwe
Magwe 136 A3 var. Magway.
Magwe, W Myanmar
Mahajanga 79 F2 var. Majunga.
Mahajanga, NW Madagascar
Mahakam, Sungai 138 D4 var.
Koetai, Kutai. River Borneo,
C Indonesia
Mahalapye 78 D3 var. Mahalatswe.
Central, SE Botswana
Mahalatswe see Mahalapye
Mahān 120 D3 Kermān, E Iran
Mahānadi 135 F4 river E India
Mahārāshtra 134 D5 state W India

Mahbés *see* El Mahbas
Mahbūbnagar *134 D5* Andhra Pradesh, C India
Mahdia *71 F2 var.* Al Mahdīyah, Mehdia. NE Tunisia
Mahé *79 H1 island* Inner Islands, NE Seychelles
Mahia Peninsula *150 E4 peninsula* North Island, NZ
Mahilyow *107 D6 Rus.* Mogilëv. Mahilyowskaya Voblasts', E Belarus
Mahmūd-e 'Erāqī *see* Mahmūd-e Rāqī
Mahmūd-e Rāqī *123 E4 var.* Mahmūd-e 'Erāqī. Kāpīsā, NE Afghanistan
Mahón *93 H3 Cat.* Maó, *Eng.* Port Mahon; *anc.* Portus Magonis. Menorca, Spain, W Mediterranean Sea
Maicao *58 C1* La Guajira, N Colombia
Mai Ceu *see* Maych'ew
Mai Chio *see* Maych'ew
Maidstone *89 E7* SE England, UK
Maiduguri *75 H4* Borno, NE Nigeria
Maimāna *see* Meymaneh
Main *95 B5 river* C Germany
Mai-Ndombe, Lac *77 C6 prev.* Lac Léopold II. *Lake* W Dem. Rep. Congo (Zaire)
Maine *41 G2 off.* State of Maine; also known as Lumber State, Pine Tree State. *State* NE USA
Maine *90 B3 cultural region* NW France
Maine, Gulf of *41 H2 gulf* NE USA
Main Island *see* Bermuda
Mainland *88 C2 island* Orkney, N Scotland, UK
Mainland *88 D1 island* Shetland, NE Scotland, UK
Mainz *95 B5 Fr.* Mayence. Rheinland-Pfalz, SW Germany
Maio *74 A3 var.* Mayo. *Island* Ilhas de Sotavento, SE Cape Verde
Maisur *see* Karnātaka
Maisur *see* Mysore
Maizhokunggar *126 C5* Xizang Zizhiqu, W China
Maíz, Islas del *53 E3 var.* Corn Islands. *Island group* SE Nicaragua
Mājro *see* Majuro Atoll
Majunga *see* Mahajanga
Majuro Atoll *144 D2 var.* Mājro. *Atoll* Ratak Chain, SE Marshall Islands
Makale *see* Mek'elē
Makarov Basin *155 B3 undersea feature* Arctic Ocean
Makarska *100 B4 It.* Macarsca. Split-Dalmacija, SE Croatia
Makasar *see* Ujungpandang
Makassar *see* Ujungpandang
Makassar Strait *138 C4 Ind.* Selat Makasar. *Strait* C Indonesia
Makay *79 F3 var.* Massif du Makay. *Mountain range* SW Madagascar
Makeni *74 C4* S Sierra Leone
Makhachkala *114 A4 prev.* Petrovsk-Port. Respublika Dagestan, SW Russian Federation
Makin *144 D2 prev.* Pitt Island. *Atoll* Tungaru, W Kiribati
Makira *see* San Cristobal
Makiyivka *109 G3 Rus.* Makeyevka; *prev.* Dmitriyevsk. Donets'ka Oblast', E Ukraine
Makkah *121 A5 Eng.* Mecca. Makkah, W Saudi Arabia
Makkovik *39 F2* Newfoundland and Labrador, NE Canada
Makó *99 D7 Rom.* Macău. Csongrád, SE Hungary
Makoua *77 B5* Cuvette, C Congo
Makran Coast *120 E4 coastal region* SE Iran
Makrany *107 A6 Rus.* Mokrany. Brestskaya Voblasts', SW Belarus
Mākū *120 B2* Āzarbāyjān-e Bākhtarī, NW Iran
Makurdi *75 G4* Benue, C Nigeria
Mala *see* Malaita
Malabār Coast *132 B3 coast* SW India

Malabo *77 A5 prev.* Santa Isabel. *Country capital* (Equatorial Guinea) Isla de Bioco, NW Equatorial Guinea
Malacca *see* Melaka
Malacca, Strait of *138 B3 Ind.* Selat Malaka. *Strait* Indonesia/Malaysia
Malacky *99 C6 Hung.* Malacka. Bratislavský Kraj, W Slovakia
Maladzyechna *107 C5 Pol.* Molodeczno, *Rus.* Molodechno. Minskaya Voblasts', C Belarus
Málaga *92 D5 anc.* Malaca. Andalucía, S Spain
Malagarasi River *73 B7 river* W Tanzania
Malaita *144 C3 var.* Mala. *Island* N Solomon Islands
Malakal *73 B5* Upper Nile, S Sudan
Malakula *see* Malekula
Malang *138 D5* Jawa, C Indonesia
Malange *see* Malanje
Malanje *78 B1 var.* Malange. Malanje, NW Angola
Mälaren *85 C6 lake* C Sweden
Malatya *117 E4 anc.* Melitene. Malatya, SE Turkey
Mala Vyska *109 E3 Rus.* Malaya Viska. Kirovohrads'ka Oblast', S Ukraine
Malawi *79 E1 prev.* Nyasaland, Nyasaland Protectorate. *Country* S Africa

Malawi 79

Official name Republic of Malawi
Formation 1964
Capital Lilongwe
Population 11 million / 300 people per sq mile (116 people per sq km)
Total area 36,324 sq miles (94,080 sq km)
Languages English, Chewa, Lomwe
Religions Protestant 55%, Roman Catholic 20%, Muslim 20%, other 5%
Ethnic mix Maravi 55%, Lomwe 17%, Yao 13%, other 15%
Government Multiparty republic
Currency Malawi kwacha = 100 tambala
Literacy rate 57.7%
Calorie consumption 1,825 kilocalories

Malawi, Lake *see* Nyasa, Lake
Malay Peninsula *124 D4 peninsula* Malaysia/Thailand
Malaysia *138 B3 var.* Federation of Malaysia; *prev.* the separate territories of Federation of Malaya, Sarawak and Sabah (North Borneo) and Singapore. *Country* SE Asia

Malaysia 138

Official name Federation of Malaysia
Formation 1963
Capital Kuala Lumpur
Population 22.2 million / 175 people per sq mile (68 people per sq km)
Total area 126,853 sq miles (328,550 sq km)
Languages English, Bahara Malay
Religions Muslim 53%, Buddhist 19%, Chinese faiths 12%, other 16%
Ethnic mix Malay 47%, Chinese 32%, Indigenous tribes 12%, other 9%
Government Federal constitutional monarchy
Currency Ringgit = 100 cents
Literacy rate 85.7%
Calorie consumption 2,888 kilocalories

Malaysia, Federation of *see* Malaysia

Malbork *98 C2 Ger.* Marienburg, Marienburg in Westpreussen. Pomorskie, N Poland
Malchin *94 C3* Mecklenburg-Vorpommern, N Germany
Malden *45 H5* Missouri, C USA
Malden Island *145 G3 prev.* Independence Island. *Atoll* E Kiribati
Maldives *132 A4 Country* N Indian Ocean

Maldives 132

Official name Republic of Maldives
Formation 1965
Capital Malé
Population 286,000 / 2,469 people per sq mile (953 people per sq km)
Total area 116 sq miles (300 sq km)
Languages Dhivehi (Maldivian), Sinhala, Tamil
Religions Sunni Muslim 100%
Ethnic mix Maldivian 99%, other 1%
Government Republic
Currency Rufiyaa (Maldivian rupee) = 100 laari
Literacy rate 95.7%
Calorie consumption 2,580 kilocalories

Male' *132 B4* Male' Atoll, C Maldives
Male' Atoll *132 B4 var.* Kaafu Atoll. *Atoll* C Maldives
Malekula *144 D4 var.* Malakula; *prev.* Mallicolo. *Island* W Vanuatu
Malesína *105 C5* Stereá Ellás, E Greece
Malheur Lake *46 C3 lake* Oregon, NW USA
Mali *75 E3 Fr.* République du Mali; *prev.* French Sudan, Sudanese Republic. *Country* W Africa

Mali 75

Official name Republic of Mali
Formation 1960
Capital Bamako
Population 11.2 million / 24 people per sq mile (9 people per sq km)
Total area 471,115 sq miles (1,220,190 sq km)
Languages French, Bambara, Fulani, Senufo, Soninké
Religions Muslim (mainly Sunni) 80%, Traditional beliefs 18%, other 2%
Ethnic mix Mande 50%, Peul 17%, Voltaic 12%, Songhai 6%, other 15%
Government Multiparty republic
Currency CFA franc = 100 centimes
Literacy rate 35.5%
Calorie consumption 2,278 kilocalories

Malik, Wadi al *see* Milk, Wadi el
Mali Kyun *137 B5 var.* Tavoy Island. *Island* Mergui Archipelago, S Myanmar
Malindi *73 D7* Coast, SE Kenya
Malko Tŭrnovo *104 E3* Burgas, E Bulgaria
Mallaig *88 B3* N Scotland, UK
Mallicolo *see* Malekula
Mallorca *93 G3 Eng.* Majorca; *anc.* Baleares Major. *Island* Islas Baleares, Spain, W Mediterranean Sea
Malmberget *84 C3* Norrbotten, N Sweden
Malmédy *87 D6* Liège, E Belgium
Malmö *85 B7* Skåne, S Sweden
Maloelap *see* Maloelap Atoll
Maloelap Atoll *144 D1 var.* Majoelap. *Atoll* E Marshall Islands
Małopolska *98 D4 plateau* S Poland

Malozemel'skaya Tundra *110 D3 physical region* NW Russian Federation
Malta *97 C8 Country* C Mediterranean Sea

Malta 97

Official name Republic of Malta
Formation 1964
Capital Valetta
Population 389,000 / 3,148 people per sq mile (1,216 people per sq km)
Total area 124 sq miles (320 sq km)
Languages Maltese, English
Religions Roman Catholic 98%, other and non-religious 2%
Ethnic mix Maltese (mixed Arab, Sicilian, Norman, Spanish, Italian, English) 98%, other 2%
Government Multiparty republic
Currency Maltese lira = 100 cents
Literacy rate 91%
Calorie consumption 3,486 kilocalories

Malta *97 C8 island* Malta, C Mediterranean Sea
Malta *44 C1* Montana, NW USA
Malta *106 D4* Rēzekne, SE Latvia
Malta Channel *97 C8 It.* Canale di Malta. *Strait* Italy/Malta
Maluku *139 F4 Dut.* Molukken, *Eng.* Moluccas; *prev.* Spice Islands. *Island group* E Indonesia
Malung *85 B6* Kopparberg, C Sweden
Malyn *108 D2 Rus.* Malin. Zhytomyrs'ka Oblast', N Ukraine
Mamberamo, Sungai *139 H4 river* Irian Jaya, E Indonesia
Mambij *see* Manbij
Mamonovo *106 A4 Ger.* Heiligenbeil. Kaliningradskaya Oblast', W Russian Federation
Mamoré, Rio *61 F3 river* Bolivia/Brazil
Mamou *74 C4* Moyenne-Guinée, W Guinea
Mamoudzou *79 F2 dependent territory capital* (Mayotte) C Mayotte
Mamuno *78 C3* Ghanzi, W Botswana
Manacor *93 G3* Mallorca, Spain, W Mediterranean Sea
Manado *139 F3 prev.* Menado. Sulawesi, C Indonesia
Managua *52 D3 country capital* (Nicaragua) Managua, W Nicaragua
Managua, Lago de *52 C3 var.* Xolotlán. *Lake* W Nicaragua
Manakara *79 G4* Fianarantsoa, SE Madagascar
Manama *see* Al Manāmah
Mananjary *79 G3* Fianarantsoa, SE Madagascar
Manapouri, Lake *151 A7 lake* South Island, NZ
Manar *see* Mannar
Manas, Gora *123 E2 mountain* Kyrgyzstan/Uzbekistan
Manaus *62 D2 prev.* Manáos. *State capital* Amazonas, NW Brazil
Manavgat *116 B4* Antalya, SW Turkey
Manbij *118 C2 var.* Mambij, *Fr.* Membidj. Ḥalab, N Syria
Manchester *89 D5 Lat.* Mancunium. NW England, UK
Manchester *41 G3* New Hampshire, NE USA
Man-chou-li *see* Manzhouli
Manchuria *125 E1 cultural region* NE China
Máncio Lima *see* Japiim
Mand *see* Mand, Rūd-e
Mandalay *136 B3* Mandalay, C Myanmar
Mandan *45 E2* North Dakota, N USA
Mandeville *54 B5* C Jamaica
Mándra *105 C6* Attikí, C Greece

Mand, Rūd-e *120 D4 var.* Mand.
River S Iran
Mandurah *147 A6* Western
Australia
Manduria *97 E5* Puglia, SE Italy
Mandya *132 C2* Karnātaka, C India
Manfredonia *97 D5* Puglia, SE Italy
Mangai *77 C6* Bandundu, W Dem.
Rep. Congo (Zaire)
Mangaia *145 G5 island group* S Cook
Islands
Mangalia *108 D5 anc.* Callatis.
Constanţa, SE Romania
Mangalmé *76 C3* Guéra, SE Chad
Mangalore *132 B2* Karnātaka,
W India
Mangaung *see* Bloemfontein
Mango *see* Sansanné-Mango
Mangoky *79 F3 river*
. W Madagascar
Manhattan *45 F4* Kansas, C USA
Manicouagan, Réservoir *38 D3 lake*
Québec, E Canada
Manihiki *145 G4 atoll* N Cook
Islands
Manihiki Plateau *143 E3 undersea
feature* C Pacific Ocean
Maniitsoq *82 C3 var.* Manîtsoq,
Dan. Sukkertoppen. S Greenland
Manila *139 E1 off.* City of Manila.
Country capital (Philippines)
Luzon, N Philippines
Manisa *116 A3 var.* Manissa; *prev.*
Saruhan, *anc.* Magnesia. Manisa,
W Turkey
Manissa *see* Manisa
Manitoba *37 F5 province* S Canada
Manitoba, Lake *37 F5 lake*
Manitoba, S Canada
Manitoulin Island *38 C4 island*
Ontario, S Canada
Manîtsoq *see* Maniitsoq
Manizales *58 B3* Caldas,
W Colombia
Manjimup *147 A7* Western
Australia
Mankato *45 F3* Minnesota, N USA
Manlleu *93 G2* Cataluña, NE Spain
Manly *148 E1* New South Wales,
SE Australia
Manmād *134 C5* Mahārāshtra,
W India
Mannar *132 C3 var.* Manar.
Northern Province, NW Sri Lanka
Mannar, Gulf of *132 C3 gulf*
India/Sri Lanka
Mannheim *95 B5* Baden-
Württemberg, SW Germany
Manono *77 E7* Shabo, SE Dem. Rep.
Congo (Zaire)
Manosque *91 D6* Alpes-de-Haute-
Provence, SE France
Manra *145 F3 prev.* Sydney Island.
Atoll Phoenix Islands, C Kiribati
Mansa *78 D2 prev.* Fort Rosebery.
Luapula, N Zambia
Mansel Island *37 G3 island*
Nunavut, NE Canada
Mansfield *40 D4* Ohio, N USA
Manta *60 A2* Manabí, W Ecuador
Manteca *47 B6* California, W USA
Mantova *96 B2 Eng.* Mantua, *Fr.*
Mantoue. Lombardia, NW Italy
Manuae *145 G4 island* S Cook Islands
Manurewa *150 D3 var.* Manukau.
Auckland, North Island, NZ
Manzanares *93 E3* Castilla-La
Mancha, C Spain
Manzanillo *50 D4* Colima,
SW Mexico
Manzanillo *54 C3* Granma, E Cuba
Manzhouli *127 F1 var.* Man-chou-li.
Nei Mongol Zizhiqu, N China
Mao *76 B3* Kanem, W Chad
Maoke, Pegunungan *139 H4 Dut.*
Sneeuw-gebergte, *Eng.* Snow
Mountains. *Mountain range* Irian
Jaya, E Indonesia
Maoming *128 C6* Guangdong,
S China
Mapmaker Seamounts *125 H2
undersea feature* N Pacific Ocean
Maputo *78 D4 prev.* Lourenço
Marques. *Country capital*
(Mozambique) Maputo,
S Mozambique
Marabá *63 F2* Pará, NE Brazil

Maracaibo *58 C1* Zulia,
NW Venezuela
Maracaibo, Lago de *58 C2 var.* Lake
Maracaibo. *Inlet* NW Venezuela
Maracaibo, Lake *see* Maracaibo,
Lago de
Maracay *58 D2* Aragua,
N Venezuela
Marada *see* Marādah
Marādah *71 G3 var.* Marada.
N Libya
Maradi *75 G3* Maradi, S Niger
Maragha *see* Marāgheh
Marāgheh *120 C2 var.* Maragha.
Āžarbāyjān-e Khāvarī, NW Iran
Marajó, Baía de *63 F1 bay* N Brazil
Marajó, Ilha de *63 E1 island*
N Brazil
Marakesh *see* Marrakech
Maramba *see* Livingstone
Maranhão *63 F2 off.* Estado do
Maranhão. *State* E Brazil
Marañón, Río *60 B2 river* N Peru
Maraş *see* Kahramanmaraş
Marash *see* Kahramanmaraş
Marathon *38 C4* Ontario, S Canada
Marathónas *105 C5 prev.* Marathón.
Attikí, C Greece
Marbella *92 D5* Andalucía,
S Spain
Marble Bar *146 B4* Western
Australia
Marburg an der Lahn *94 B4 hist.*
Marburg. Hessen, W Germany
March *see* Morava
Marche *91 C5 cultural region*
C France
Marche *96 C3 cultural region*
E Italy
Marche-en-Famenne *87 C7*
Luxembourg, SE Belgium
Marchena, Isla *60 B5 var.* Bindloe
Island. *Island* Galapagos Islands,
Ecuador, E Pacific Ocean
Mar Chiquita, Laguna *64 C3 lake*
C Argentina
Marcounda *see* Markounda
Mardān *134 C1* North-West Frontier
Province, N Pakistan
Mar del Plata *65 D5* Buenos Aires,
E Argentina
Mardin *117 E4* Mardin, SE Turkey
Maré *144 D5 island* Îles Loyauté,
E New Caledonia
Marea Neagră *see* Black Sea
Mare Creticum *see* Kritikó Pélagos
Mareeba *148 D3* Queensland,
NE Australia
Margarita, Isla de *59 E1 island*
N Venezuela
Margate *89 E7 prev.* Mergate.
SE England, UK
Marghita *108 B3 Hung.* Margitta.
Bihor, NW Romania
Marhanets' *109 F3 Rus.* Marganets.
Dnipropetrovs'ka Oblast',
E Ukraine
María Cleofas, Isla *50 C4 island*
C Mexico
Maria Island *149 C8 island*
Tasmania, SE Australia
María Madre, Isla *50 C4 island*
C Mexico
María Magdalena, Isla *50 C4 island*
C Mexico
Mariana Trench *125 G4 undersea
feature* W Pacific Ocean
Mariánské Lázně *99 A5 Ger.*
Marienbad. Karlovarský Kraj,
W Czech Republic
Marías, Islas *50 C4 island group*
C Mexico
Maribor *95 E7 Ger.* Marburg.
NE Slovenia
Marica *see* Maritsa
Maridi *73 B5* Western Equatoria,
SW Sudan
Marie Byrd Land *154 A3 physical
region* Antarctica
Marie-Galante *55 G4 var.* Ceyre to
the Caribs. *Island* SE
Guadeloupe
Mariental *78 B4* Hardap,
SW Namibia
Mariestad *85 B6* Västra Götaland,
S Sweden
Marietta *42 D2* Georgia, SE USA

Marijampolė *106 B4 prev.*
Kapsukas. Marijampolė,
S Lithuania
Marília *63 E4* São Paulo, S Brazil
Marín *92 B1* Galicia, NW Spain
Mar''ina Horka *107 C6 Rus.*
Mar'ina Gorka. Minskaya
Voblasts', C Belarus
Maringá *63 E4* Paraná, S Brazil
Marion *45 G3* Iowa, C USA
Marion *40 D4* Ohio, N USA
Marion, Lake *43 E2 reservoir* South
Carolina, SE USA
Mariscal Estigarribia *64 D2*
Boquerón, NW Paraguay
Maritsa *104 D3 var.* Marica, *Gk.*
Évros, *Turk.* Meriç; *anc.* Hebrus.
River SW Europe *see also*
Évros/Meriç
Maritzburg *see* Pietermaritzburg
Mariupol' *109 G4 prev.* Zhdanov.
Donets'ka Oblast', SE Ukraine
Marka *73 D6 var.* Merca.
Shabeellaha Hoose, S Somalia
Markham, Mount *154 B4 mountain*
Antarctica
Markounda *76 C4 var.* Marcounda.
Ouham, NW Central African
Republic
Marktredwitz *95 C5* Bayern,
E Germany
Marmande *91 B5 anc.* Marmanda.
Lot-et-Garonne, SW France
Marmara Denizi *116 A2 Eng.* Sea of
Marmara. *Sea* NW Turkey
Marmara, Sea of *see* Marmara
Denizi
Marmaris *116 A4* Muğla,
SW Turkey
Marne *90 C3 cultural region*
N France
Marne *90 D3 river* N France
Maro *76 C4* Moyen-Chari, S Chad
Maroantsetra *79 G2* Toamasina,
NE Madagascar
Maromokotro *79 G2 mountain*
N Madagascar
Maroni River *59 G3 Dut.*
Marowijne. *River* French
Guiana/Suriname
Maros *see* Mureş
Marosch *see* Mureş
Marotiri *145 C4 var.* Îlots de Bass,
Morotiri. *Island group* Îles
Australes, SW French Polynesia
Maroua *76 B3* Extrême-Nord,
N Cameroon
Marquesas Fracture Zone *153 E3
tectonic feature* E Pacific Ocean
Marquesas Islands *153 E3 island
group* N French Polynesia
Marquette *40 B1* Michigan, N USA
Marrakech *70 C2 var.* Marakesh,
Eng. Marrakesh; *prev.* Morocco.
W Morocco
Marrakesh *see* Marrakech
Marrawah *149 C8* Tasmania,
SE Australia
Marree *149 B5* South Australia
Marsá al Burayqah *71 G3 var.*
Al Burayqah. N Libya
Marsabit *73 C6* Eastern, N Kenya
Marsala *97 B7 anc.* Lilybaeum.
Sicilia, Italy, C Mediterranean Sea
Marsberg *94 B4* Nordrhein-
Westfalen, W Germany
Marseille *91 D6 Eng.* Marseilles;
anc. Massilia. Bouches-du-Rhône,
SE France
Marshall *45 F2* Minnesota, N USA
Marshall *49 H2* Texas, SW USA
Marshall Islands *144 C1 Country*
W Pacific Ocean

Marshall Islands 144

Official name Republic of the
Marshall Islands
Formation 1986
Capital Delap district
Population 51,000 /
728 people per sq mile
(281 people per sq km)
Total area 70 sq miles (181 sq km)
Languages Marshallese, English,
Japanese, German

Marshall Islands (continued)

Religions Protestant 80%,Roman
Catholic 15%, other 5%
Ethnic mix Micronesian 97%,
other 3%
Government Republic
Currency US dollar = 100 cents
Literacy rate 91%
Calorie consumption
not available

Marshall Seamounts *125 H3
undersea feature* SW Pacific Ocean
Marsh Harbour *54 C1* Great Abaco,
W Bahamas
Martaban *136 B4 var.* Moktama.
Mon State, S Myanmar
Martha's Vineyard *41 G3 island*
Massachusetts, NE USA
Martigues *91 D6* Bouches-du-
Rhône, SE France
Martin *99 C5 Ger.* Sankt Martin,
Hung. Turócszentmárton; *prev.*
Turčiansky Svätý Martin. Žilinský
Kraj, N Slovakia
Martinique *55 G4 French overseas
department* E West Indies
Martinique Channel *see*
Martinique Passage
Martinique Passage *55 G4 var.*
Dominica Channel, Martinique
Channel. *Channel*
Dominica/Martinique
Marton *150 D4* Manawatu-
Wanganui, North Island, NZ
Martos *92 D4* Andalucía, S Spain
Marungu *77 E7 mountain range*
SE Dem. Rep. Congo (Zaire)
Mary *122 D3 prev.* Merv. Maryyskiy
Velayat, S Turkmenistan
Maryborough *see* Portlaoise
Maryborough *148 D4* Queensland,
E Australia
Mary Island *see* Kanton
Maryland *41 E5 off.* State of
Maryland; also known as America
in Miniature, Cockade State, Free
State, Old Line State. *State* NE USA
Maryland *42 D1* Tennessee, S USA
Maryville *45 F4* Missouri, C USA
Masai Steppe *73 C7 grassland*
NW Tanzania
Masaka *73 B6* SW Uganda
Masallı *117 H3 Rus.* Masally.
S Azerbaijan
Masasi *73 C8* Mtwara, SE Tanzania
Masawa *see* Massawa
Masaya *52 D3* Masaya,
W Nicaragua
Mascarene Basin *141 B5 undersea
feature* W Indian Ocean
Mascarene Islands *79 H4 island
group* W Indian Ocean
Mascarene Plain *141 B5 undersea
feature* W Indian Ocean
Mascarene Plateau *141 B5 undersea
feature* W Indian Ocean
Maseru *78 D4 country capital*
(Lesotho) W Lesotho
Mashhad *120 E2 var.* Meshed.
Khorāsān, NE Iran
Mas-ha *119 D7* W Bank
Masindi *73 B6* W Uganda
Masīra *see* Maşīrah, Jazīrat
Masira, Gulf of *see* Maşīrah, Khalīj
Maşīrah, Jazīrat *121 E5 var.* Masīra.
Island E Oman
Maşīrah, Khalīj *121 E5 var.* Gulf of
Masira. *Bay* E Oman
Masis *see* Büyükağrı Dağı
Maskat *see* Masqaţ
Mason City *45 F3* Iowa, C USA
Masqaţ *121 E5 var.* Maskat, *Eng.*
Muscat. *Country capital* (Oman)
NE Oman
Massa *96 B3* Toscana, C Italy
Massachusetts *41 G3 off.*
Commonwealth of Massachusetts;
also known as Bay State, Old Bay
State, Old Colony State. *State*
NE USA
Massawa *72 C4 var.* Masawa, *Amh.*
Mits'iwa. E Eritrea
Massenya *76 B3* Chari-Baguirmi,
SW Chad

Massif Central 91 C5 *plateau*
C France
Massif du Makay *see* Makay
Massoukou *see* Franceville
Masterton 151 D5 Wellington,
North Island, NZ
Masty 107 B5 *Rus.* Mosty.
Hrodzyenskaya Voblasts',
W Belarus
Masuda 131 B6 Shimane, Honshū,
SW Japan
Masuku *see* Franceville
Masvingo 78 D3 *prev.* Fort Victoria,
Nyanda, Victoria. Masvingo,
SE Zimbabwe
Masyāf 118 B3 *Fr.* Misiaf. Ḥamāh,
C Syria
Matadi 77 B6 Bas-Zaïre, W Dem.
Rep. Congo (Zaire)
Matagalpa 52 D3 Matagalpa,
C Nicaragua
Matale 132 D3 Central Province,
C Sri Lanka
Matam 74 C3 NE Senegal
Matamata 150 D3 Waikato, North
Island, NZ
Matamoros 50 D3 Coahuila de
Zaragoza, NE Mexico
Matamoros 51 E2 Tamaulipas,
C Mexico
Matane 39 E4 Québec, SE Canada
Matanzas 54 B2 Matanzas, NW Cuba
Matara 132 D4 Southern Province,
S Sri Lanka
Mataram 138 D5 Pulau Lombok,
C Indonesia
Mataró 93 G2 *anc.* Illuro. Cataluña,
E Spain
Mataura 151 B7 *river* South Island,
NZ
Mataura 151 B7 Southland, South
Island, NZ
Mata Uta *see* Matā'utu
Matā'utu 145 E4 *var.* Mata Uta.
Dependent territory capital (Wallis
and Futuna) Île Uvea, Wallis and
Futuna
Matera 97 E5 Basilicata, S Italy
Matías Romero 51 F5 Oaxaca,
SE Mexico
Mato Grosso 63 E4 *prev.* Vila Bela
da Santissima Trindade. Mato
Grosso, W Brazil
Mato Grosso do Sul 63 E4 *off.*
Estado de Mato Grosso do Sul.
State S Brazil
Mato Grosso, Planalto de 56 C4
plateau C Brazil
Matosinhos 92 B2 *prev.* Matozinhos.
Porto, NW Portugal
Matsue 131 B6 *var.* Matsuye, Matue.
Shimane, Honshū, SW Japan
Matsumoto 131 C5 *var.* Matumoto.
Nagano, Honshū, S Japan
Matsuyama 131 B7 *var.* Matuyama.
Ehime, Shikoku, SW Japan
Matsuye *see* Matsue
Matterhorn 95 A8 *It.* Monte
Cervino. *Mountain*
Italy/Switzerland *see also*
Cervino, Monte
Matthews Ridge 59 F2 N Guyana
Matthew Town 54 D2 Great Inagua,
S Bahamas
Matucana 60 C4 Lima, W Peru
Matue *see* Matsue
Matumoto *see* Matsumoto
Maturín 59 E2 Monagas,
NE Venezuela
Matuyama *see* Matsuyama
Mau 135 E3 *var.* Maunāth Bhanjan.
Uttar Pradesh, N India
Maui 47 B8 *island* Hawaii, USA,
C Pacific Ocean
Maulmain *see* Moulmein
Maun 78 C3 Ngamiland, C Botswana
Maunāth Bhanjan *see* Mau
Mauren 94 E1 NE Liechtenstein
Mauritania 74 C2 *Ar.* Mūrītānīyah.
Country W Africa

Mauritania 74

Official name Islamic Republic of
Mauritania
Formation 1960

Mauritania (continued)

Capital Nouakchott
Population 2.7 million / 7 people
per sq mile (3 people per sq km)
Total area 395,953 sq miles
(1,025,520 sq km)
Languages Hassaniyah Arabic,
French, Wolof
Religions Muslim (Maliki) 100%
Ethnic mix Maur 30%, Black 30%,
mixed 40%
Government Multiparty republic
Currency Ouguiya = 5 khoums
Literacy rate 38.4%
Calorie consumption 2,685
kilocalories

Mauritius 79 H3 *Fr.* Maurice.
Country W Indian Ocean

Mauritius 79

Official name Mauritius
Formation 1968
Capital Port Louis
Population 1.2 million /
1,671 people per sq mile
(645 people per sq km)
Total area 718 sq miles
(1,860 sq km)
Languages English, French, French
Creole, Hindi, Urdu, Tamil, Chinese
Religions Hindu 52%, Roman
Catholic 26%, Muslim 17%,
Protestant 2%, other 3%
Ethnic mix Creole 55%,
South Asian 40%, Chinese 3%,
other 2%
Government Multiparty republic
Currency Mauritian rupee
= 100 cents
Literacy rate 83%
Calorie consumption 2,690
kilocalories

Mauritius 141 B5 *island* W Indian
Ocean
Mawlamyine *see* Moulmein
Mawson 154 D2 *Australian research
station* Antarctica
Maya 52 B1 *river* E Russian
Federation
Mayadin *see* Al Mayādīn
Mayaguana 54 D2 *island*
SE Bahamas
Mayaguana Passage 54 D2 *passage*
SE Bahamas
Mayagüez 55 F3 W Puerto Rico
Mayamey 120 D2 Semnān, N Iran
Maya Mountains 52 B2 *Sp.*
Montañas Mayas. *Mountain range*
Belize/Guatemala
Maych'ew 72 C4 *var.* Mai Chio, *It.*
Mai Ceu. N Ethiopia
Maydān Shahr 123 E4 Wardag,
E Afghanistan
Mayebashi *see* Maebashi
Mayfield 151 B6 Canterbury, South
Island, NZ
Maykop 111 A7 Respublika
Adygeya, SW Russian Federation
Maymana *see* Meymaneh
Maymyo 136 B3 Mandalay,
C Myanmar
Mayo *see* Maio
Mayor Island 150 D3 *island*
NE NZ
Mayor Pablo Lagerenza *see*
Capitán Pablo Lagerenza
Mayotte 79 F2 *French territorial
collectivity* E Africa
May Pen 54 B5 C Jamaica
Mazabuka 78 D2 Southern,
S Zambia
Mazaca *see* Kayseri
Mazār-e Sharīf 123 E3 *var.* Mazār-i
Sharif. Balkh, N Afghanistan
Mazār-i Sharif *see* Mazār-e Sharīf
Mazatlán 50 D3 Sinaloa, C Mexico
Mažeikiai 106 B3 Mažeikiai,
NW Lithuania
Mazirbe 106 C2 Talsi, NW Latvia
Mazra'a *see* Al Mazra'ah
Mazury 98 D3 *physical region*
NE Poland

Mazyr 107 C7 *Rus.* Mozyr'.
Homyel'skaya Voblasts',
SE Belarus
Mbabane 78 D4 *country capital*
(Swaziland) NW Swaziland
Mbacké *see* Mbaké
M'Baiki *see* Mbaïki
Mbaïki 77 C5 *var.* M'Baiki. Lobaye,
SW Central African Republic
Mbaké 74 B3 *var.* Mbacké.
W Senegal
Mbala 78 D1 *prev.* Abercorn.
Northern, NE Zambia
Mbale 73 C6 E Uganda
Mbandaka 77 C5 *prev.*
Coquilhatville. Equateur,
NW Dem. Rep. Congo (Zaire)
M'Banza Congo 78 B1 *var.* Mbanza
Congo; *prev.* São Salvador, São
Salvador do Congo. Zaire,
NW Angola
Mbanza-Ngungu 77 B6 Bas-Zaïre,
W Dem. Rep. Congo (Zaire)
Mbarara 73 B6 SW Uganda
Mbé 76 B4 Nord, N Cameroon
Mbeya 73 C7 Mbeya, SW Tanzania
Mbomou *see* Bomu
M'Bomu *see* Bomu
Mbour 74 B3 W Senegal
Mbuji-Mayi 77 D7 *prev.* Bakwanga.
Kasai Oriental, S Dem. Rep.
Congo (Zaire)
McAlester 49 G2 Oklahoma, C USA
McAllen 49 G5 Texas, SW USA
McCamey 49 E3 Texas, SW USA
McClintock Channel 37 F2 *channel*
Nunavut, N Canada
McComb 42 B3 Mississippi, S USA
McCook 45 E4 Nebraska, C USA
McKean Island 145 E3 *island*
Phoenix Islands, C Kiribati
McKinley, Mount 36 C3 *var.* Denali.
Mountain Alaska, USA
McKinley Park 36 C3 Alaska, USA
McMinnville 46 B3 Oregon,
NW USA
McMurdo Base 154 B4 *US research
station* Antarctica
McPherson *see* Fort McPherson
McPherson 45 E5 Kansas, C USA
Mdantsane 78 D5 Eastern Cape,
SE South Africa
Mead, Lake 47 D6 *reservoir*
Arizona/Nevada, W USA
Mecca *see* Makkah
Mechelen 87 C5 *Eng.* Mechlin, *Fr.*
Malines. Antwerpen, C Belgium
Mecklenburger Bucht 94 C2 *bay*
N Germany
Mecsek 99 C7 *mountain range*
SW Hungary
Medan 138 B3 Sumatera,
E Indonesia
Medeba *see* Ma'dabā
Medellín 58 B3 Antioquia,
NW Colombia
Médenine 71 F2 *var.* Madanīyīn.
SE Tunisia
Medford 46 B4 Oregon, NW USA
Medgidia 108 D5 Constanța,
SE Romania
Mediaş 108 B4 *Ger.* Mediasch,
Hung. Medgyes. Sibiu, C Romania
Medicine Hat 37 F5 Alberta,
SW Canada
Medinaceli 93 E2 Castilla-León,
N Spain
Medina del Campo 92 D2 Castilla-
León, N Spain
Mediterranean Sea 102 D3 *Fr.* Mer
Méditerranée. Sea
Africa/Asia/Europe
Médoc 91 B5 *cultural region*
SW France
Medvezh'yegorsk 110 B3
Respublika Kareliya, NW Russian
Federation
Meekatharra 147 B5 Western
Australia
Meemu Atoll *see* Mulaku Atoll
Meerssen 87 D6 *var.* Mersen.
Limburg, SE Netherlands
Meerut 134 D2 Uttar Pradesh,
N India
Mehdia *see* Mahdia
Meheso *see* Mī'ēso
Me Hka *see* Nmai Hka

Mehrīz 120 D3 Yazd, C Iran
Mehtar Lām *see* Mehtarlām
Mehtarlām 123 F4 *var.* Mehtar Lām,
Meterlam, Methariam,
Metharlam. Laghmān,
E Afghanistan
Meiktila 136 B3 Mandalay,
C Myanmar
Mejillones 64 B2 Antofagasta,
N Chile
Mek'elē 72 C4 *var.* Makale.
N Ethiopia
Mékhé 74 B3 NW Senegal
Mekong 124 D3 *var.* Lan-ts'ang
Chiang, *Cam.* Mékôngk, *Chin.*
Lancang Jiang, *Lao.* Mènam
Khong, *Th.* Mae Nam Khong, *Tib.*
Dza Chu, *Vtn.* Sông Tiên Giang.
River SE Asia
Mékôngk *see* Mekong
Mekong, Mouths of the 137 E6
delta S Vietnam
Melaka 138 B3 *var.* Malacca.
Melaka, Peninsular Malaysia
Melanesia 144 D3 *island group*
W Pacific Ocean
Melanesian Basin 142 C2 *undersea
feature* W Pacific Ocean
Melbourne 149 C7 *state capital*
Victoria, SE Australia
Melbourne 43 E4 Florida, SE USA
Melghir, Chott 71 E2 *var.* Chott
Melrhir. *Salt lake* E Algeria
Melilla 80 B5 *anc.* Rusaddir,
Russadir. Melilla, Spain, N Africa
Melilla 70 D2 *enclave* Spain,
N Africa
Melita 37 F5 Manitoba, S Canada
Melitopol' 109 F4 Zaporiz'ka
Oblast', SE Ukraine
Melle 87 B5 Oost-Vlaanderen,
NW Belgium
Mellerud 85 B6 Västra Götaland,
S Sweden
Mellieha 102 B5 E Malta
Mellizo Sur, Cerro 65 A7 *mountain*
S Chile
Melo 64 E4 Cerro Largo,
NE Uruguay
Melsungen 94 B4 Hessen,
C Germany
Melun 90 C3 *anc.* Melodunum.
Seine-et-Marne, N France
Melville Island 146 D2 *island*
Northern Territory, N Australia
Melville Island 37 E2 *island* Parry
Islands, Northwest
Territories/Nunavut, NW Canada
Melville, Lake 39 F2 *lake*
Newfoundland and Labrador,
E Canada
Melville Peninsula 37 G3 *peninsula*
Northwest Territories, NE Canada
Membidj *see* Manbij
Memmingen 95 B6 Bayern,
S Germany
Memphis 42 C1 Tennessee, S USA
Ménaka 75 F3 Goa, E Mali
Menaldum 86 D1 *Fris.* Menaam.
Friesland, N Netherlands
Mènam Khong *see* Mekong
Mendaña Fracture Zone 153 F4
tectonic feature E Pacific Ocean
Mende 91 C5 *anc.* Mimatum.
Lozère, S France
Mendeleyev Ridge 155 B2 *undersea
feature* Arctic Ocean
Mendocino Fracture Zone 152 D2
tectonic feature NE Pacific Ocean
Mendoza 64 B4 Mendoza,
W Argentina
Menemen 116 A3 İzmir, W Turkey
Menengiyn Tal 127 F2 *plain*
E Mongolia
Menongue 78 B2 *var.* Vila Serpa
Pinto, *Port.* Serpa Pinto. Cuando
Cubango, C Angola
Menorca 93 H3 *Eng.* Minorca; *anc.*
Balearis Minor. *Island* Islas
Baleares, Spain, W Mediterranean
Sea
Mentawai, Kepulauan 138 A4
island group W Indonesia
Meppel 86 D2 Drenthe,
NE Netherlands
Merano 96 C1 *Ger.* Meran. Trentino-
Alto Adige, N Italy
Merca *see* Marka

Mercedes *see* Villa Mercedes
Mercedes *64 D3* Corrientes,
　NE Argentina
Mercedes *64 D4* Soriano,
　SW Uruguay
Meredith, Lake *49 E1 reservoir*
　Texas, SW USA
Merefa *109 G2* Kharkivs´ka Oblast´,
　E Ukraine
Mergui *137 B6* Tenasserim,
　S Myanmar
Mergui Archipelago *137 B6 island*
　group S Myanmar
Meriç *see* Maritsa
Mérida *92 C4 anc.* Augusta Emerita.
　Extremadura, W Spain
Mérida *58 C2* Mérida, W Venezuela
Mérida *51 H3* Yucatán, SW Mexico
Meridian *42 C2* Mississippi, S USA
Mérignac *91 B5* Gironde,
　SW France
Merkinė *107 B5* Varėna, S Lithuania
Merowe *72 B3 desert* W Sudan
Merredin *147 B6* Western Australia
Mersen *see* Meerssen
Mersey *89 D5 river* NW England,
　UK
Mersin *116 C4* İçel, S Turkey
Mērsrags *106 C3* Talsi, NW Latvia
Meru *73 C6* Eastern, C Kenya
Merzifon *116 D2* Amasya,
　N Turkey
Merzig *95 A5* Saarland,
　SW Germany
Mesa *48 B2* Arizona, SW USA
Meshed *see* Mashhad
Mesopotamia *57 C5 var.*
　Mesopotamia Argentina. *Physical*
　region NE Argentina
Mesopotamia Argentina *see*
　Mesopotamia
Messalo, Rio *79 E2 var.* Mualo.
　River NE Mozambique
Messana *see* Messina
Messene *see* Messina
Messina *97 D7 var.* Messana,
　Messene; *anc.* Zancle. Sicilia, Italy,
　C Mediterranean Sea
Messina *78 D3* Northern, NE South
　Africa
Messina, Stretto di *97 D7 Eng.*
　Strait of Messina. *Strait* SW Italy
Messíni *105 B6* Pelopónnisos,
　S Greece
Mestghanem *see* Mostaganem
Mestia *117 F1 var.* Mestiya.
　N Georgia
Mestiya *see* Mestia
Mestre *96 C2* Veneto, NE Italy
Meta *56 B2 off.* Departamento del
　Meta. *Province* C Colombia
Metairie *42 B3* Louisiana, S USA
Metán *64 C2* Salta, N Argentina
Metapán *52 B2* Santa Ana,
　NW El Salvador
Meta, Río *58 D3 river*
　Colombia/Venezuela
Meterlam *see* Mehtarlām
Methariam *see* Mehtarlām
Metharlam *see* Mehtarlām
Metković *100 B4* Dubrovnik-
　Neretva, SE Croatia
Métsovo *104 B4 prev.* Métsovon.
　Ípeiros, C Greece
Metz *90 D3 anc.* Divodurum
　Mediomatricum, Mediomatrica,
　Metis. Moselle, NE France
Meulaboh *138 A3* Sumatera,
　W Indonesia
Meuse *87 C6 Dut.* Maas. *River*
　W Europe *see also* Maas
Meuse *90 D3 department*
　NE France
Mexcala, Río *see* Balsas, Río
Mexicali *50 A1* Baja California,
　NW Mexico
Mexico *50 C3 var.* Méjico, México,
　Sp. Estados Unidos Mexicanos.
　Country N Central America

Mexico 50

Official name United States of
　Mexico
Formation 1836
Capital Mexico City

Mexico (continued)

Population 99 million /
134 people per sq mile
(52 people per sq km)
Total area 736,945 sq miles
(1,908,690 sq km)
Languages Spanish, Nahuatl,
Maya, Zapotec, Mixtec, Otomí,
Totonac
Religions Roman Catholic 95%,
Protestant 1%, other 4%
Ethnic mix Mestizo 55%,
Indigenous Indian 20%,
European 16%, other 9%
Government Multiparty
republic
Currency Mexican peso
= 100 centavos
Literacy rate 90%
Calorie consumption 3,146
kilocalories

Mexico *45 G4* Missouri, C USA
México *51 E4 var.* Ciudad de
　México, *Eng.* Mexico City.
　Country capital (Mexico) México,
　C Mexico
Mexico City *see* México
Mexico, Gulf of *51 F2 Sp.* Golfo de
　México. *Gulf* W Atlantic Ocean
Meyadine *see* Al Mayādīn
Meymaneh *122 D3 var.* Maimāna,
　Maymana. Fāryāb,
　NW Afghanistan
Mezen´ *110 D3 river* NW Russian
　Federation
Mezőtúr *99 D7* Jász-Nagykun-
　Szolnok, E Hungary
Mġarr *102 A5* Gozo, N Malta
Miahuatlán *51 F5 var.* Miahuatlán
　de Porfirio Díaz. Oaxaca,
　SE Mexico
Miahuatlán de Porfirio Díaz *see*
　Miahuatlán
Miami *43 F5* Florida, SE USA
Miami *49 G1* Oklahoma, C USA
Miami Beach *43 F5* Florida,
　SE USA
Miāneh *120 C2 var.* Miyāneh.
　Āzarbāyjān-e Khāvarī, NW Iran
Mianyang *128 B5* Sichuan, C China
Miastko *98 C2 Ger.* Rummelsburg
　in Pommern. Pomorskie,
　N Poland
Mi Chai *see* Nong Khai
Michalovce *99 E5 Ger.* Grossmichel,
　Hung. Nagymihály. Košický Kraj,
　E Slovakia
Michigan *40 C1 off.* State of
　Michigan; also known as Great
　Lakes State, Lake State, Wolverine
　State. *State* N USA
Michigan, Lake *40 C2 lake* N USA
Michurinsk *111 B5*
　Tambovskaya Oblast´, W Russian
　Federation
Micoud *55 F2* SE Saint Lucia
Micronesia *144 B1 Country*
　W Pacific Ocean

Micronesia 144

Official name Federated States of
　Micronesia
Formation 1986
Capital Palikir (Pohnpei island)
Population 111,500 / 411 people per
　sq mile (159 people per sq km)
Total area 271 sq miles (702 sq km)
Languages English, Trukese,
　Pohnpeian, Mortlockese, Losrean
Religions Roman Catholic 50%,
　Protestant 48%, other 2%
Ethnic mix Micronesian 99%,
　other 1%
Government Republic
Currency US dollar = 100 cents
Literacy rate 89%
Calorie consumption
　not available

Micronesia *144 C1 island group*
　W Pacific Ocean
Mid-Atlantic Cordillera *see* Mid-
　Atlantic Ridge

Mid-Atlantic Ridge *66 C3 var.* Mid-
　Atlantic Cordillera, Mid-Atlantic
　Rise, Mid-Atlantic Swell. *Undersea*
　feature Atlantic Ocean
Mid-Atlantic Rise *see* Mid-Atlantic
　Ridge
Mid-Atlantic Swell *see* Mid-
　Atlantic Ridge
Middelburg *87 B5* Zeeland,
　SW Netherlands
Middelharnis *86 B4* Zuid-Holland,
　SW Netherlands
Middelkerke *87 A5* West-
　Vlaanderen, W Belgium
Middle America Trench *35 B7*
　undersea feature E Pacific Ocean
Middle Andaman *133 F2 island*
　Andaman Islands, India,
　NE Indian Ocean
Middlesboro *40 C5* Kentucky, S USA
Middlesbrough *89 D5* N England,
　UK
Middletown *41 F4* New Jersey,
　NE USA
Middletown *41 F3* New York,
　NE USA
Mid-Indian Basin *141 C5 undersea*
　feature N Indian Ocean
Mid-Indian Ridge *141 C5 var.*
　Central Indian Ridge. *Undersea*
　feature C Indian Ocean
Midland *40 C3* Michigan, N USA
Midland *38 D3* Ontario, S Canada
Midland *49 E3* Texas, SW USA
Mid-Pacific Mountains *152 C2 var.*
　Mid-Pacific Seamounts. *Undersea*
　feature NW Pacific Ocean
Mid-Pacific Seamounts *see* Mid-
　Pacific Mountains
Midway Islands *152 D2 US territory*
　C Pacific Ocean
Miechów *99 D5* Małopolskie,
　S Poland
Międzyrzec Podlaski *98 E3*
　Lubelskie, E Poland
Międzyrzecz *98 B3 Ger.* Meseritz.
　Lubuskie, W Poland
Mielec *99 D5* Podkarpackie,
　SE Poland
Miercurea-Ciuc *108 C4 Ger.*
　Szeklerburg, *Hung.* Csíkszereda.
　Harghita, C Romania
Mieres del Camino *see* Mieres del
　Camino
Mieres del Camino *108 D1 var.*
　Mieres del Camín. Asturias,
　NW Spain
Mieresch *see* Mureş
Mī´ēso *73 D5 var.* Meheso, Miesso.
　C Ethiopia
Miesso *see* Mī´ēso
Miguel Asua *50 D3 var.* Miguel
　Auza. Zacatecas, C Mexico
Miguel Auza *see* Miguel Asua
Mijdrecht *86 C3* Utrecht,
　C Netherlands
Mikashevichy *107 C7 Pol.*
　Mikaszewicze, *Rus.* Mikashevichi.
　Brestskaya Voblasts´, SW Belarus
Mikhaylovka *111 B6*
　Volgogradskaya Oblast´,
　SW Russian Federation
Míkonos *see* Mýkonos
Mikre *104 C2* Lovech, N Bulgaria
Mikun´ *110 D4* Respublika Komi,
　NW Russian Federation
Mikuni-sanmyaku *131 D5 mountain*
　range Honshū, N Japan
Mikura-jima *131 D6 island* E Japan
Milagro *60 B2* Guayas, SW Ecuador
Milan *see* Milano
Milange *79 E2* Zambézia,
　NE Mozambique
Milano *96 B2 Eng.* Milan, *Ger.*
　Mailand; *anc.* Mediolanum.
　Lombardia, N Italy
Milas *116 A4* Muğla, SW Turkey
Milashavichy *107 C7 Rus.*
　Milashevichi. Homyel´skaya
　Voblasts´, SE Belarus
Mildura *149 C6* Victoria,
　SE Australia
Mile *see* Mili Atoll
Miles *149 D5* Queensland,
　E Australia
Miles City *44 C2* Montana,
　NW USA

Milford Haven *89 C6 prev.* Milford.
　SW Wales, UK
Milford Sound *151 A6 inlet* South
　Island, NZ
Milford Sound *151 A6* Southland,
　South Island, NZ
Mili Atoll *144 D2 var.* Mile. *Atoll*
　Ratak Chain, SE Marshall Islands
Mil´kovo *115 H3* Kamchatskaya
　Oblast´, E Russian Federation
Milk River *44 C1 river* Montana,
　NW USA
Milk River *37 E5* Alberta,
　SW Canada
Milk, Wadi el *88 B4 var.* Wadi
　al Malik. *River* C Sudan
Milledgeville *43 E2* Georgia,
　SE USA
Mille Lacs Lake *45 F2 lake*
　Minnesota, N USA
Millennium Island *160 C8 prev.*
　Caroline Island, Thornton Island.
　Atoll Line Islands, E Kiribati
Millerovo *111 B6* Rostovskaya
　Oblast´, SW Russian Federation
Mílos *105 C7 island* Kykládes,
　Greece, Aegean Sea
Mílos *105 C6* Milos, Kykládes,
　Greece, Aegean Sea
Milton *151 B7* Otago, South Island,
　NZ
Milton Keynes *89 D6* SE England,
　UK
Milwaukee *40 B3* Wisconsin,
　N USA
Min *see* Fujian
Mīnā´ Qābūs *140 B3* NE Oman
Minas Gerais *63 F3 off.* Estado de
　Minas Gerais. *State* E Brazil
Minatitlán *51 F4* Veracruz-Llave,
　E Mexico
Minbu *136 A3* Magwe,
　W Myanmar
Minch, The *88 B3 var.* North Minch.
　Strait NW Scotland, UK
Mindanao *139 F2 island*
　S Philippines
Mindanao Sea *see* Bohol Sea
Mindelheim *95 C6* Bayern,
　S Germany
Mindello *see* Mindelo
Mindelo *74 A2 var.* Mindello; *prev.*
　Porto Grande. São Vicente,
　N Cape Verde
Minden *94 B4 var.* Minthun.
　Nordrhein-Westfalen,
　NW Germany
Mindoro *139 E2 island*
　N Philippines
Mindoro Strait *139 E2 strait*
　W Philippines
Mineral Wells *49 F2* Texas,
　SW USA
Mingäçevir *117 G2 Rus.*
　Mingechaur, Mingechevir.
　C Azerbaijan
Mingāora *134 C1 var.* Mingora,
　Mongora. North-West Frontier
　Province, N Pakistan
Mingora *see* Mingāora
Minho *92 B2 former province*
　N Portugal
Minho, Rio *92 B2 Sp.* Miño. *river*
　Portugal/Spain *see also* Miño
Minicoy Island *132 B3 island*
　SW India
Minius *see* Miño
Minna *75 G4* Niger, C Nigeria
Minneapolis *45 F2* Minnesota,
　N USA
Minnesota *45 F2 off.* State of
　Minnesota; also known as Gopher
　State, New England of the West,
　North Star State. *State* N USA
Miño *92 B2 var.* Mino, Minius, *Port.*
　Rio Minho. *River* Portugal/Spain
　see also Minho, Rio
Mino *see* Miño
Minot *45 E1* North Dakota, N USA
Minsk *107 C6 country capital*
　(Belarus) Minskaya Voblasts´,
　C Belarus
Minskaya Wzvyshsha *107 C6*
　mountain range C Belarus
Minsk Mazowiecki *98 D3 var.*
　Nowo-Minsk. Mazowieckie, C
　Poland

Minto, Lac *38 D2 lake* Québec, C Canada
Minya *see* El Minya
Miraflores *50 C3* Baja California Sur, N W Mexico
Miranda de Ebro *93 E1* La Rioja, N Spain
Miri *138 D3* Sarawak, East Malaysia
Mirim Lagoon *63 E5 var.* Lake Mirim, *Sp.* Laguna Merín. *Lagoon* Brazil/Uruguay
Mirim, Lake *see* Mirim Lagoon
Mírina *see* Mýrina
Mīrjāveh *120 E4* Sīstān va Balūchestān, SE Iran
Mirny *154 C3 Russian research station* Antarctica
Mirnyy *115 F3* Respublika Sakha (Yakutiya), NE Russian Federation
Mīrpur Khās *134 B3* Sind, SE Pakistan
Mirtóo Pélagos *105 C6 Eng.* Mirtoan Sea; *anc.* Myrtoum Mare. *Sea* S Greece
Miskito Coast *see* Mosquito Coast
Miskitos, Cayos *53 E2 island group* NE Nicaragua
Miskolc *99 D6* Borsod-Abaúj-Zemplén, NE Hungary
Misool, Pulau *139 F4 island* Maluku, E Indonesia
Miṣrātah *71 F2 var.* Misurata. NW Libya
Mission *49 G5* Texas, SW USA
Mississippi *42 B2 off.* State of Mississippi; also known as Bayou State, Magnolia State. *State* SE USA
Mississippi Delta *42 B4 delta* Louisiana, S USA
Mississippi River *35 C6 river* C USA
Missoula *44 B1* Montana, NW USA
Missouri *45 F5 off.* State of Missouri; also known as Bullion State, Show Me State. *State* C USA
Missouri River *45 E3 river* C USA
Mistassini, Lac *38 D3 lake* Québec, SE Canada
Mistelbach an der Zaya *95 E6* Niederösterreich, NE Austria
Misti, Volcán *61 E4 mountain* S Peru
Misurata *see* Miṣrātah
Mitchell *149 D5* Queensland, E Australia
Mitchell *45 E3* South Dakota, N USA
Mitchell, Mount *43 E1 mountain* North Carolina, SE USA
Mitchell River *148 C2 river* Queensland, NE Australia
Mi Tho *see* My Tho
Mitilíni *see* Mytilíni
Mito *131 D5* Ibaraki, Honshū, S Japan
Mits'iwa *see* Massawa
Mitspe Ramon *see* Mizpé Ramon
Mitú *58 C4* Vaupés, SE Colombia
Mitumba, Monts *77 E7 var.* Chaîne des Mitumba, Mitumba Range. *Mountain range* E Dem. Rep. Congo (Zaire)
Mitumba Range *see* Mitumba, Monts
Miyako *130 D4* Iwate, Honshū, C Japan
Miyako-jima *131 D6 island* Sakishima-shotō, SW Japan
Miyakonojō *131 B8 var.* Miyakonzyô. Miyazaki, Kyūshū, SW Japan
Miyakonzyô *see* Miyakonojō
Miyāneh *see* Miāneh
Miyazaki *131 B8* Miyazaki, Kyūshū, SW Japan
Mizil *108 C5* Prahova, SE Romania
Miziya *104 C1* Vratsa, NW Bulgaria
Mizpé Ramon *119 A7 var.* Mitspe Ramon, Southern, S Israel
Mjosa *85 B6 var.* Mjøsen. *Lake* S Norway
Mjøsen *see* Mjøsa
Mladenovac *100 D4* Serbia, C Yugoslavia
Mława *98 D3* Mazowieckie, C Poland
Mljet *101 B5 It.* Meleda; *anc.* Melita. *Island* S Croatia

Mmabatho *78 C4* North-West, N South Africa
Moab *44 B5* Utah, W USA
Moab, Kir of *see* Al Karak
Moa Island *148 C1 island* Queensland, NE Australia
Moanda *77 B6 var.* Mouanda. Haut-Ogooué, SE Gabon
Moba *77 E7* Shaba, E Dem. Rep. Congo (Zaire)
Mobay *see* Montego Bay
Mobaye *77 C5* Basse-Kotto, S Central African Republic
Moberly *45 G4* Missouri, C USA
Mobile *42 C3* Alabama, S USA
Mobutu Sese Seko, Lac *see* Albert, Lake
Mochudi *78 C4* Kgatleng, SE Botswana
Mocímboa da Praia *79 F2 var.* Vila de Mocímboa da Praia. Cabo Delgado, N Mozambique
Môco *78 B2 var.* Morro de Môco. *Mountain* W Angola
Mocoa *58 A4* Putumayo, SW Colombia
Mocuba *79 E3* Zambézia, NE Mozambique
Modena *96 B3 anc.* Mutina. Emilia-Romagna, N Italy
Modesto *47 B6* California, W USA
Modica *97 C7 anc.* Motyca. Sicilia, Italy, C Mediterranean Sea
Modriča *100 C3* Republika Srpska, N Bosnia and Herzegovina
Moe *149 C7* Victoria, SE Australia
Moero, Lac *see* Mweru, Lake
Mogadishu *see* Muqdisho
Mogilno *98 C3* Kujawski-pomorskie, C Poland
Mohammedia *70 C2 prev.* Fédala. NW Morocco
Mohave, Lake *44 A4 reservoir* Arizona/Nevada, W USA
Mohawk River *41 F3 river* New York, NE USA
Mohéli *79 F2 var.* Mwali, Mohilla, Mohila, *Fr.* Moili. *Island* S Comoros
Mohila *see* Mohéli
Mohilla *see* Mohéli
Mohns Ridge *83 F3 undersea feature* Greenland Sea/Norwegian Sea
Moho *61 E4* Puno, SW Peru
Mohoro *73 C7* Pwani, E Tanzania
Mohyliv-Podil's'kyy *108 D3 Rus.* Mogilev-Podol'skiy. Vinnyts'ka Oblast', C Ukraine
Moi *85 A6* Rogaland, S Norway
Moili *see* Mohéli
Mo i Rana *84 C3* Nordland, C Norway
Mõisaküla *106 D3 Ger.* Moiseküll. Viljandimaa, S Estonia
Moissac *91 B6* Tarn-et-Garonne, S France
Mojácar *93 E5* Andalucía, S Spain
Mojave Desert *47 D7 plain* California, W USA
Moktama *see* Martaban
Mol *87 C5 prev.* Moll. Antwerpen, N Belgium
Moldavia *see* Moldova
Moldavian SSR/Moldavskaya SSR *see* Moldova
Molde *85 A5* Møre og Romsdal, S Norway
Moldo-Too, Khrebet *123 G2 prev.* Khrebet Moldotau. *Mountain range* C Kyrgyzstan
Moldova *108 D3 var.* Moldavia; *prev.* Moldavian SSR, *Rus.* Moldavskaya SSR. *Country* SE Europe

Moldova 108

Official name Republic of Moldova
Formation 1991
Capital Chisinau
Population 4.4 million / 338 people per sq mile (131 people per sq km)
Total area 13,000 sq miles (33,700 sq km)
Languages Romanian, Moldovan

Moldova (continued)

Religions Roman Orthodox 98%, Jewish 1%, other 1%
Ethnic mix Moldovan 65%, Ukrainian 14%, Russian 13%, Gagauz 4%, other 4%
Government Multiparty republic
Currency Moldovan leu = 100 bani
Literacy rate 98.3%
Calorie consumption not available

Moldova Nouă *108 A4 Ger.* Neumoldowa, *Hung.* Újmoldova. Caraş-Severin, SW Romania
Moldoveanul *see* Vârful Moldoveanu
Molfetta *97 E5* Puglia, SE Italy
Mollendo *61 E4* Arequipa, SW Peru
Mölndal *85 B7* Västra Götaland, S Sweden
Molochans'k *109 G4 Rus.* Molochansk. Zaporiz'ka Oblast', SE Ukraine
Molodezhnaya *154 C2 Russian research station* Antarctica
Molokai *47 B8 Haw.* Moloka'i. *Island* Hawaii, USA, C Pacific Ocean
Molokai Fracture Zone *153 E2 tectonic feature* NE Pacific Ocean
Molopo *78 C4 seasonal river* Botswana/South Africa
Mólos *105 B5* Stereá Ellás, C Greece
Moluccas *see* Maluku
Molucca Sea *139 F4 Ind.* Laut Maluku. *Sea* E Indonesia
Mombasa *73 D7 international airport* Coast, SE Kenya
Mombasa *73 D7* Coast, SE Kenya
Mombetsu *see* Monbetsu
Momchilgrad *104 D3 prev.* Mastanli. Kŭrdzhali, S Bulgaria
Møn *85 B8 prev.* Möen. *Island* SE Denmark
Monaco *91 E6 Country* W Europe

Monaco 91

Official name Principality of Monaco
Formation 1861
Capital Monaco
Population 32,000 / 42,503 people per sq mile (16,410 people per sq km)
Total area 0.75 sq miles (1.95 sq km)
Languages French, Italian, Monégasque, English
Religions Roman Catholic, 89%, Protestant 6%, other 5%
Ethnic mix French 47%, Monégasque 16%, Italian 16%, other 21%
Government Constitutional monarchy
Currency French franc = 100 centimes
Literacy rate 99%
Calorie consumption not available

Monaco *91 C7 var.* Monaco-Ville; *anc.* Monoecus. *Country capital* (Monaco) S Monaco
Monaco, Port de *91 C8 bay* S Monaco
Monaco-Ville *see* Monaco
Monahans *49 E3* Texas, SW USA
Mona, Isla *55 E3 island* W Puerto Rico
Mona Passage *55 E3 Sp.* Canal de la Mona. *Channel* Dominican Republic/Puerto Rico
Monbetsu *130 D2 var.* Mombetsu, Monbetu. Hokkaidō, NE Japan
Monbetu *see* Monbetsu
Moncalieri *96 A2* Piemonte, NW Italy
Monchegorsk *110 C2* Murmanskaya Oblast', NW Russian Federation
Monclova *50 D2* Coahuila de Zaragoza, NE Mexico

Moncton *39 F4* New Brunswick, SE Canada
Mondovì *96 A2* Piemonte, NW Italy
Monfalcone *96 D2* Friuli-Venezia Giulia, NE Italy
Monforte *92 C1* Galicia, NW Spain
Mongo *76 C3* Guéra, C Chad
Mongolia *126 C2 Mong.* Mongol Uls. *Country* E Asia

Mongolia 126

Official name Mongolia
Formation 1924
Capital Ulan Bator
Population 2.7 million / 4 people per sq mile (2 people per sq km)
Total area 604,247 sq miles (1,565,000 sq km)
Languages Khalka Mongol, Turkic, Chinese, Russian
Religions Predominantly Tibetan Buddhist, with a Muslim minority
Ethnic mix Mongol 90%, Kazakh 4%, Chinese 2%, Russian 2%, other 2%
Government Multiparty republic
Currency Tugrik (togrog) = 100 möngös
Literacy rate 84%
Calorie consumption 1,899 kilocalories

Mongolia, Plateau of *124 D1 plateau* E Mongolia
Mongora *see* Mingãora
Mongu *78 C2* Western, W Zambia
Monkchester *see* Newcastle upon Tyne
Monkey Bay *79 E2* Southern, SE Malawi
Monkey River *see* Monkey River Town
Monkey River Town *52 C2 var.* Monkey River. Toledo, SE Belize
Monoecus *see* Monaco
Mono Lake *47 C6 lake* California, W USA
Monóvar *93 F4* País Valenciano, E Spain
Monroe *42 B2* Louisiana, S USA
Monrovia *74 C5 country capital* (Liberia) W Liberia
Mons *87 B6 Dut.* Bergen. Hainaut, S Belgium
Monselice *96 C2* Veneto, NE Italy
Montagnes Rocheuses *see* Rocky Mountains
Montana *44 B1 off.* State of Montana; also known as Mountain State, Treasure State. *State* NW USA
Montana *104 C2 prev.* Ferdinand, Mikhaylovgrad. Montana, NW Bulgaria
Montargis *90 C4* Loiret, C France
Montauban *91 B6* Tarn-et-Garonne, S France
Montbéliard *90 D4* Doubs, E France
Mont Cenis, Col du *91 D5 pass* E France
Mont-de-Marsan *91 B6* Landes, SW France
Monteagudo *61 G4* Chuquisaca, S Bolivia
Monte-Carlo *91 C8* NE Monaco
Monte Caseros *64 D3* Corrientes, NE Argentina
Monte Cristi *54 D3 var.* San Fernando de Monte Cristi. NW Dominican Republic
Montegiardino *96 E2* SE San Marino
Montego Bay *54 A4 var.* Mobay. W Jamaica
Montélimar *91 D5 anc.* Acunum Acusio, Montilium Adhemari. Drôme, E France
Montemorelos *51 E3* Nuevo León, NE Mexico
Montenegro *101 C5 Serb.* Crna Gora. Admin. region *republic* SW Yugoslavia
Monte Patria *64 B3* Coquimbo, N Chile

Monterey *see* Monterrey
Monterey 47 *B6* California, W USA
Monterey Bay 47 *A6 bay* California,
W USA
Montería 58 *B2* Córdoba,
NW Colombia
Montero 61 *G4* Santa Cruz,
C Bolivia
Monterrey 51 *E3 var.* Monterey.
Nuevo León, NE Mexico
Montes Claros 63 *F3* Minas Gerais,
SE Brazil
Montevideo 64 *D4 country capital*
(Uruguay) Montevideo,
S Uruguay
Montevideo 45 *F2* Minnesota,
N USA
Montgenèvre, Col de 91 *D5 pass*
France/Italy
Montgomery 42 *D2 state capital*
Alabama, S USA
Monthey 95 *A7* Valais,
SW Switzerland
Montluçon 90 *C4* Allier, C France
Montoro 92 *D4* Andalucía,
S Spain
Montpelier 41 *G2 state capital*
Vermont, NE USA
Montpellier 91 *C6* Hérault,
S France
Montréal 39 *E4 Eng.* Montreal.
Québec, SE Canada
Montrose 44 *C5* Colorado, C USA
Montrose 88 *D3* E Scotland, UK
Montserrat 55 *G3 var.* Emerald Isle.
UK dependent territory E West
Indies
Monywa 136 *B3* Sagaing,
C Myanmar
Monza 96 *B2* Lombardia, N Italy
Monze 78 *D2* Southern, S Zambia
Monzón 93 *F2* Aragón, NE Spain
Moonie 149 *D5* Queensland,
E Australia
Moora 147 *A6* Western Australia
Moore 49 *G1* Oklahoma, C USA
Moore, Lake 147 *B6 lake* Western
Australia
Moorhead 45 *F2* Minnesota,
N USA
Moose 38 *C3 river* Ontario,
S Canada
Moosehead Lake 41 *G1 lake* Maine,
NE USA
Moosonee 38 *C3* Ontario,
SE Canada
Mopti 75 *E3* Mopti, C Mali
Moquegua 61 *E4* Moquegua,
SE Peru
Mora 85 *C5* Kopparberg, C Sweden
Morales 52 *C2* Izabal, E Guatemala
Morant Bay 54 *B5* E Jamaica
Moratalla 93 *E4* Murcia, SE Spain
Morava 99 *C5 var.* March. *River*
C Europe *see also* March
Morava *see* Velika Morava
Moravia 99 *B5* Iowa, C USA
Moray Firth 88 *C3 inlet* N Scotland,
UK
Morea *see* Pelopónnisos
Moreau River 44 *D2 river* South
Dakota, N USA
Moree 149 *D5* New South Wales,
SE Australia
Morelia 51 *E4* Michoacán de
Ocampo, S Mexico
Morena, Sierra 92 *C4 mountain
range* S Spain
Moreni 108 *C5* Dâmbovița,
S Romania
Mórfou 102 *C5* W Cyprus
Morgan City 42 *B3* Louisiana, S USA
Morghāb, Daryā-ye 122 *D3 var.*
Murgab, Murghab, *Turkm.*
Murgap Deryasy. *River*
Afghanistan/Turkmenistan *see
also* Murgab
Morioka 130 *D4* Iwate, Honshū,
C Japan
Morlaix 90 *A3* Finistère, NW France
Mornington Abyssal Plain 167 *A7
undersea feature* SE Pacific Ocean
Mornington Island 148 *B2 island*
Wellesley Islands, Queensland,
N Australia
Morocco 70 *B3 Ar.* Al Mamlakah.
Country N Africa

Official name Kingdom of
Morocco
Formation 1956
Capital Rabat
Population 28.4 million /
165 people per sq mile
(64 people per sq km)
Total area 172,316 sq miles
(446,300 sq km)
Languages Arabic, Berber
(Shluh, Tamazight, Riffian),
French, Spanish
Religions Muslim 98%, other 2%
Ethnic mix Arab and Berber 99%,
European 1%
Government Constititional
monarchy
Currency Moroccan dirham
= 100 centimes
Literacy rate 45.9%
Calorie consumption 2,984
kilocalories

Morocco *see* Marrakech
Morogoro 73 *C7* Morogoro,
E Tanzania
Moro Gulf 139 *E3 gulf* S Philippines
Morón 54 *C2* Ciego de Ávila,
C Cuba
Mörön 126 *D2* Hövsgöl,
N Mongolia
Morondava 79 *F3* Toliara,
W Madagascar
Moroni 79 *F2 country capital*
(Comoros) Grande Comore,
NW Comoros
Morotai, Pulau 139 *F3 island*
Maluku, E Indonesia
Morotiri *see* Marotiri
Morrinsville 150 *D3* Waikato,
North Island, NZ
Morris 45 *F2* Minnesota, N USA
Morris Jesup, Kap 83 *E1 headland*
N Greenland
Morro de Môco *see* Môco
Morvan 90 *D4 physical region*
C France
Moscow *see* Moskva
Moscow 46 *C2* Idaho, NW USA
Mosel 95 *A5 Fr.* Moselle. *River*
W Europe *see also* Moselle
Moselle 87 *E8 Ger.* Mosel. *River*
W Europe *see also* Mosel
Moselle 90 *D3 department*
NE France
Mosgiel 151 *B7* Otago, South
Island, NZ
Moshi 73 *C7* Kilimanjaro,
NE Tanzania
Mosjøen 84 *B4* Nordland,
C Norway
Moskva 111 *B5 Eng.* Moscow.
Country capital (Russian
Federation) Gorod Moskva,
W Russian Federation
Moskva 123 *E3 Rus.* Moskovskiy;
prev. Chubek. SW Tajikistan
Mosonmagyaróvár 99 *C6 Ger.*
Wieselburg-Ungarisch-Altenburg;
prev. Moson and Magyaróvár, *Ger.*
Wieselburg and Ungarisch-
Altenburg. Győr-Moson-Sopron,
NW Hungary
Mosquito Coast 53 *E3 var.* Miskito
Coast. *Coastal region* E Nicaragua
Mosquitos, Golfo de los 53 *F4 Eng.*
Mosquito Gulf. *Gulf* N Panama
Moss 85 *B6* Østfold, S Norway
Mosselbaai 78 *C5 var.* Mosselbai,
Eng. Mossel Bay. Western Cape,
SW South Africa
Mossendjo 77 *B6* Le Niari,
SW Congo
Mossoró 63 *G2* Rio Grande do
Norte, NE Brazil
Most 98 *A4 Ger.* Brüx. Ústecký Kraj,
NW Czech Republic
Mosta 102 *B5 var.* Musta. C Malta
Mostaganem 70 *D2 var.*
Mestghanem. NW Algeria
Mostar 100 *C4* Federacija Bosna I
Hercegovina, S Bosnia and
Herzegovina
Mosul *see* Al Mawşil

Mota del Cuervo 93 *E3* Castilla-La
Mancha, C Spain
Motagua, Río 52 *B2 river*
Guatemala/Honduras
Motril 92 *D5* Andalucía, S Spain
Motru 108 *B4* Gorj, SW Romania
Motueka 151 *C5* Tasman, South
Island, NZ
Motul 51 *H3 var.* Motul de Felipe
Carrillo Puerto. Yucatán,
SE Mexico
Motul de Felipe Carrillo Puerto *see*
Motul
Mouanda *see* Moanda
Mouhoun *see* Black Volta
Mouila 77 *A6* Ngounié, C Gabon
Mould Bay 37 *E2* Prince Patrick
Island, Northwest
Territories/Nunavut, N Canada
Moulins 90 *C4* Allier, C France
Moulmein 136 *B4 var.* Maulmain,
Mawlamyine. Mon State,
S Myanmar
Moundou 76 *B4* Logone-Occidental,
SW Chad
Moŭng Roessei 137 *D5*
Bătdâmbâng, W Cambodia
Moun Hou *see* Black Volta
Mountain Home 42 *B1* Arkansas,
C USA
Mount Ara *see* Büyükağrı Dağı
Mount Cook 151 *B6* Canterbury,
South Island, NZ
Mount Desert Island 41 *H2 island*
Maine, NE USA
Mount Fuji *see* Fuji-san
Mount Gambier 149 *B7* South
Australia
Mount Isa 148 *B3* Queensland,
C Australia
Mount Magnet 147 *B5* Western
Australia
Mount Pleasant 45 *G4* Iowa, C USA
Mount Pleasant 40 *C3* Michigan,
N USA
Mount Vernon 40 *B5* Illinois,
N USA
Mount Vernon 46 *B1* Washington,
NW USA
Mourdi, Dépression du 76 *C2 desert
lowland* Chad/Sudan
Mouscron 87 *A6 Dut.* Moeskroen.
Hainaut, W Belgium
Mouse River *see* Souris River
Moussoro 76 *B3* Kanem, W Chad
Moyen Atlas 70 *C2 Eng.* Middle
Atlas. *Mountain range* N Morocco
Moyobamba 60 *B2* San Martín,
NW Peru
Moyu 126 *B3 var.* Karakax. Xinjiang
Uygur Zizhiqu, NW China
Moynkum, Peski 123 *F1 Kaz.*
Moyynqum. *Desert* S Kazakhstan
Mozambique 79 *E3 prev.* People's
Republic of Mozambique,
Portuguese East Africa. *Country*
S Africa

Official name Republic of
Mozambique
Formation 1975
Capital Maputo
Population 19.7 million /
65 people per sq mile
(25 people per sq km)
Total area 302,737 sq miles
(784,090 sq km)
Languages Portuguese, Makua,
Tsonga, Sena, Lomwe
Religions Traditional beliefs 60%,
Christian 30%, Muslim 10%
Ethnic mix Makua-Lomwe 47%,
Thonga 23%, Malawi 12%,
other 18%
Government Multiparty republic
Currency Metical = 100 centavos
Literacy rate 40.5%
Calorie consumption 1,680
kilocalories

Mozambique Basin *see* Natal Basin
Mozambique Channel 79 *E3 Fr.*
Canal de Mozambique, *Mal.*
Lakandranon' i Mozambika. *Strait*
W Indian Ocean

Mozambique Plateau 69 *D7 var.*
Mozambique Rise. *Undersea
feature* SW Indian Ocean
Mozambique Rise *see*
Mozambique Plateau
Mpama 77 *B6 river* C Congo
Mpika 78 *D2* Northern, NE Zambia
Mqinvartsveri *see* Kazbek
Mragowo 98 *D2 Ger.* Sensburg.
Olsztyn, NE Poland
Mtwara 73 *D8* Mtwara, SE Tanzania
Mualo *see* Messalo, Rio
Muang Chiang Rai *see* Chiang Rai
Muang Kalasin *see* Kalasin
Muang Không 137 *D5* Champasak,
S Laos
Muang Khôngxédôn 137 *D5 var.*
Khong Sedone. Salavan, S Laos
Muang Khon Kaen *see* Khon Kaen
Muang Lampang *see* Lampang
Muang Loei *see* Loei
Muang Lom Sak *see* Lom Sak
Muang Nakhon Sawan *see*
Nakhon Sawan
Muang Namo 136 *C3* Oudômxai,
N Laos
Muang Nan *see* Nan
Muang Phalan 136 *D4 var.* Muang
Phalane. Savannakhét, S Laos
Muang Phalane *see* Muang Phalan
Muang Phayao *see* Phayao
Muang Phitsanulok *see*
Phitsanulok
Muang Phrae *see* Phrae
Muang Roi Et *see* Roi Et
Muang Sakon Nakhon *see* Sakon
Nakhon
Muang Samut Prakan *see* Samut
Prakan
Muang Sing 136 *C3* Louang
Namtha, N Laos
Muang Ubon *see* Ubon Ratchathani
Muar 138 *B3 var.* Bandar Maharani.
Johor, Peninsular Malaysia
Mucojo 79 *F2* Cabo Delgado,
N Mozambique
Mudanjiang 129 *E3 var.* Mu-tan-
chiang. Heilongjiang, NE China
Mudon 137 *B5* Mon State,
S Myanmar
Muenchen *see* Munich
Muenster *see* Münster
Mufulira 78 *D2* Copperbelt,
C Zambia
Mughla *see* Muğla
Muğla 116 *A4 var.* Mughla. Muğla,
SW Turkey
Müh, Sabkhat al 134 *C3 lake*
C Syria
Muir Éireann *see* Irish Sea
Muisne 60 *A1* Esmeraldas,
NW Ecuador
Mukacheve 108 *B3 Hung.* Munkács,
Rus. Mukachevo. Zakarpats'ka
Oblast', W Ukraine
Mukalla *see* Al Mukallā
Mula 93 *E4* Murcia, SE Spain
Mulaku Atoll 132 *B4 var.* Meemu
Atoll. *Atoll* C Maldives
Muleshoe 49 *E2* Texas, SW USA
Mulhacén 93 *E5 var.* Cerro de
Mulhacén. *Mountain* S Spain
Mulhouse 90 *E4 Ger.* Mülhausen.
Haut-Rhin, NE France
Muller, Pegunungan 138 *D4 Dut.*
Müller-gerbergte. *Mountain range*
Borneo, C Indonesia
Müllheim 95 *A6* Baden-
Württemberg, SW Germany
Mull, Isle of 88 *B4 island*
W Scotland, UK
Mulongo 77 *D7* Shaba, SE Dem.
Rep. Congo (Zaire)
Multán 134 *C2* Punjab, E Pakistan
Mumbai 134 *C5 prev.* Bombay.
Mahārāshtra, W India
Munamägi *see* Suur Munamägi
Münchberg 95 *C5* Bayern,
E Germany
Muncie 40 *C4* Indiana, N USA
Mungbere 77 *E5* Orientale,
NE Dem. Rep. Congo (Zaire)
Mu Nggava *see* Rennell
Munich 80 *D4 var.* Muenchen,
Bayern, SE Germany
Munkhafaḍ al Qaṭṭārah *see*
Qaṭṭāra, Monkhafad el

Munster 89 A6 Ir. Cúige Mumhan.
Cultural region S Ireland
Münster 94 A4 var. Muenster,
Münster in Westfalen. Nordrhein-
Westfalen, W Germany
Münster in Westfalen *see* Münster
Muong Xiang Ngeun 136 C4 var.
Xieng Ngeun. Louangphabang,
N Laos
Muonio 84 D3 Lappi, N Finland
Muonioälv 84 D3 river
Finland/Sweden
Muqāt 119 C5 Al Mafraq, E Jordan
Muqdisho 73 D6 Eng. Mogadishu,
It. Mogadiscio. *Country capital*
(Somalia) Banaadir, S Somalia
Mur 95 E7 SCr. Mura. *River*
C Europe
Muradiye 117 F3 Van, E Turkey
Murapara *see* Murupara
Murata 96 E2 S San Marino
Murchison River 147 A5 river
Western Australia
Murcia 93 E4 cultural region
SE Spain
Murcia 93 F4 Murcia, SE Spain
Mureş 108 A4 var. Maros, Mureşul,
Ger. Marosch, Mieresch. *River*
Hungary/Romania *see also* Maros
Mureşul *see* Mureş
Murfreesboro 42 D1 Tennessee,
S USA
Murgab 122 D3 prev. Murgap.
Maryyskiy Velayat,
S Turkmenistan
Murgab 122 D3 var. Murghab, Pash.
Daryā-ye Morghāb, Turkm.
Murgap Deryasy. *River*
Afghanistan/Turkmenistan *see
also* Morghāb, Daryā-ye
Murgap *see* Murgab
Murgap Deryasy *see* Morghāb,
Daryā-ye/Murgab
Murghab *see* Morghāb, Daryá-
ye/Murgab
Murghob 123 F3 Rus. Murgab.
SE Tajikistan
Murgon 149 E5 Queensland,
E Australia
Müritz 94 C3 var. Müritzee. *Lake*
NE Germany
Müritzee *see* Müritz
Murmansk 110 C2 Murmanskaya
Oblast', NW Russian Federation
Murmashi 110 C2 Murmanskaya
Oblast', NW Russian Federation
Murom 111 B5 Vladimirskaya
Oblast', W Russian Federation
Muroran 130 D3 Hokkaidō,
NE Japan
Muros 92 B1 Galicia, NW Spain
Murray Fracture Zone 153 E2
tectonic feature NE Pacific Ocean
Murray Range *see* Murray Ridge
Murray Ridge 112 C5 var. Murray
Range. *Undersea feature* N Arabian
Sea
Murray River 149 B6 river
SE Australia
Murrumbidgee River 149 C6 river
New South Wales, SE Australia
Murska Sobota 95 E7 Ger. Olsnitz.
NE Slovenia
Murupara 150 E3 var. Murapara.
Bay of Plenty, North Island, NZ
Murviedro *see* Sagunto
Murwāra 135 E4 Madhya Pradesh,
N India
Murwillumbah 149 E5 New South
Wales, SE Australia
Murzuq, Idhān 71 F4 var. Edeyin
Murzuq. *Desert* SW Libya
Mürzzuschlag 95 E7 Steiermark,
E Austria
Muş 117 F3 var. Mush. Muş, E Turkey
Mûsa, Gebel 72 C2 mountain
NE Egypt
Musala 104 B3 mountain W Bulgaria
Muscat *see* Masqaţ
Muscatine 45 G3 Iowa, C USA
Musgrave Ranges 147 D5 mountain
range South Australia
Mush *see* Muş
Muskegon 40 C3 Michigan, N USA
Muskogee 49 G1 Oklahoma,
C USA
Musoma 73 C6 Mara, N Tanzania
Musta *see* Mosta

Musters, Lago 65 B6 lake
S Argentina
Muswellbrook 149 D6 New South
Wales, SE Australia
Mut 116 C4 İçel, S Turkey
Mu-tan-chiang *see* Mudanjiang
Mutare 78 D3 var. Mutari; prev.
Umtali. Manicaland, E Zimbabwe
Mutari *see* Mutare
Mutsu-wan 130 D3 bay N Japan
Muttonbird Islands 151 A8 island
group SW NZ
Mu Us Shamo 127 E3 var. Ordos
Desert. *Desert* N China
Muy Muy 52 D3 Matagalpa,
C Nicaragua
Mŭynoq 122 C1 Rus. Muynak.
Qoraqalpoghiston Respublikasi,
NW Uzbekistan
Mužlja 100 D3 Hung. Felsőmuzslya;
prev. Gornja Mužlja. Serbia,
N Yugoslavia
Mwali *see* Mohéli
Mwanza 73 B6 Mwanza,
NW Tanzania
Mweka 77 C6 Kasai Occidental,
C Dem. Rep. Congo (Zaire)
Mwene-Ditu 77 D7 Kasai Oriental,
S Dem. Rep. Congo (Zaire)
Mweru, Lake 77 D7 var. Lac Moero.
Lake Congo (Zaire)/Zambia
Mweru Wantipa, Lake 77 E7 lake
N Zambia
Myadzyel 107 C5 Pol. Miadzioł
Nowy, Rus. Mjadel'. Minskaya
Voblasts', N Belarus
Myanmar 136 A3 var. Burma.
Country SE Asia

Myanmar (Burma) 136

Official name Union of Myanmar
Formation 1948
Capital Yangon (Rangoon)
Population 45.6 million /
180 people per sq mile
(69 people per sq km)
Total area 253,876 sq miles
(657,540 sq km)
Languages Burmese, Karen, Shan,
Chin, Kachin, Mon, Palaung, Wa
Religions Buddhist 87%, Christian
6%, Muslim 4%, Hindu 1%,
other 2%
Ethnic mix Burman (Bamah) 68%,
Shan 9%, Karen 6%, other 17%
Government Military regime
Currency Kyat = 100 pyas
Literacy rate 83.6%
Calorie consumption 2,598
kilocalories

Myanaung 136 B4 Irrawaddy,
SW Myanmar
Myaungmya 136 A4 Irrawaddy,
SW Myanmar
Myerkulavichy 107 D7 Rus.
Merkulovichi. Homyel'skaya
Voblasts', SE Belarus
Myingyan 136 B3 Mandalay,
C Myanmar
Myitkyina 136 B2 Kachin State,
N Myanmar
Mykolayiv 109 E4 Rus.
Nikolayev. Mykolayivs'ka Oblast',
S Ukraine
Mýkonos 105 C6 var. Míkonos. Island
Kykládes, Greece, Aegean Sea
Myrhorod 109 F2 Rus. Mirgorod.
Poltavs'ka Oblast', NE Ukraine
Mýrina 104 D4 var. Mírina. Límnos,
SE Greece
Myrtle Beach 43 F2 South Carolina,
SE USA
Mýrtos 105 D8 Kríti, Greece,
E Mediterranean Sea
Myślibórz 98 B3
Zachodniopomorskie, NW Poland
Mysore 132 C2 var. Maisur.
Karnātaka, W India
Mysore *see* Karnātaka
My Tho 137 E6 var. Mi Tho. Tiên
Giang, S Vietnam
Mytilene *see* Mytilíni
Mytilíni 105 D5 var. Mitilíni; anc.
Mytilene. Lésvos, E Greece
Mzuzu 79 E2 Northern, N Malawi

N

Naberezhnyye Chelny 111 D5 prev.
Brezhnev. Respublika Tatarstan,
W Russian Federation
Nablus 119 A6 var. Nābulus, Heb.
Shekhem; anc. Neapolis, Bibl.
Shechem. N West Bank
Nābulus *see* Nablus
Nacala 79 F2 Nampula,
NE Mozambique
Nacogdoches 49 H3 Texas, SW USA
Nada *see* Danzhou
Nadi 145 E4 prev. Nandi. Viti Levu,
W Fiji
Nadur 102 A5 Gozo, N Malta
Nadvirna 108 C3 Pol. Nadwórna,
Rus. Nadvornaya. Ivano-
Frankivs'ka Oblast', W Ukraine
Nadvoitsy 110 B3 Respublika
Kareliya, NW Russian Federation
Nadym 114 C3 Yamalo-Nenetskiy
Avtonomnyy Okrug, N Russian
Federation
Náfpaktos 105 B5 var.`Návpaktos.
Dytikí Ellás, C Greece
Náfplio 105 B6 prev. Návplion.
Pelopónnisos, S Greece
Naga 139 E2 off. Naga City; prev.
Nueva Caceres. Luzon,
N Philippines
Nagano 131 C5 Nagano, Honshū,
S Japan
Nagaoka 131 D5 Niigata, Honshū,
C Japan
Nagara Pathom *see* Nakhon
Pathom
Nagara Sridharmaraj *see* Nakhon
Si Thammarat
Nagara Svarga *see* Nakhon Sawan
Nagasaki 131 A7 Nagasaki,
Kyūshū, SW Japan
Nagato 131 A7 Yamaguchi, Honshū,
SW Japan
Nāgercoil 132 C3 Tamil Nādu,
SE India
**Nagorno-Karabakhskaya
Avtonomnaya Oblast** *see*
Nagornyy Karabakh
Nagornyy Karabakh 117 G3 var.
Nagorno-Karabakhskaya
Avtonomnaya Oblast , Arm.
Lernnayin Gharabakh, Az. Dağliq
Qarabağ. Former autonomous region
SW Azerbaijan
Nagoya 131 C6 Aichi, Honshū,
SW Japan
Nāgpur 134 D4 Mahārāshtra,
C India
Nagqu 126 C5 Chin. Na-ch'ii; prev.
Hei-ho. Xizang Zizhiqu, W China
Nagykálló 99 E6 Szabolcs-Szatmár-
Bereg, E Hungary
Nagykanizsa 99 C7 Ger.
Grosskanizsa. Zala, SW Hungary
Nagykőrös 99 D7 Pest, C Hungary
Nagyszentmiklós *see* Sânnicolau
Mare
Naha 130 A3 Okinawa, Okinawa,
SW Japan
Nahariya *see* Nahariyya
Nahariyya 119 A5 var. Nahariya.
Northern, N Israel
Nahr al'Aşī *see* Orantes
Nahr al Litant *see* Līţani, Nahr el
Nahr an Nīl *see* Nile
Nahr el Aassi *see* Orantes
Nahuel Huapi, Lago 65 B5 lake
W Argentina
Na'īn 120 D3 Eşfahān, C Iran
Nain 39 F2 Newfoundland and
Labrador, NE Canada
Nairobi 69 E5 country capital
(Kenya) Nairobi Area, S Kenya
Nairobi 73 C6 international airport
Nairobi Area, S Kenya
Najaf *see* An Najaf
Najima *see* Fukuoka
Najin 129 E3 NE North Korea
Najrān 121 B6 var. Abā as Su'ūd.
Najrān, S Saudi Arabia
Nakambé *see* White Volta
Nakamura 131 B7 Kōchi, Shikoku,
SW Japan
Nakatsugawa 131 C6 var.
Nakatugawa. Gifu, Honshū,
SW Japan

Nakatugawa *see* Nakatsugawa
Nakhodka 115 G5 Primorskiy Kray,
SE Russian Federation
Nakhon Pathom 137 C5 var. Nagara
Pathom, Nakorn Pathom. Nakhon
Pathom, W Thailand
Nakhon Ratchasima 137 C5 var.
Khorat, Korat. Nakhon
Ratchasima, E Thailand
Nakhon Sawan 137 C5 var. Muang
Nakhon Sawan, Nagara Svarga.
Nakhon Sawan, W Thailand
Nakhon Si Thammarat 137 C7 var.
Nagara Sridharmaraj, Nakhon
Sithamnaraj. Nakhon Si
Thammarat, SW Thailand
Nakhon Sithamnaraj *see* Nakhon
Si Thammarat
Nakorn Pathom *see* Nakhon
Pathom
Nakuru 73 C6 Rift Valley,
SW Kenya
Nal'chik 111 B8 Kabardino-
Balkarskaya Respublika, SW
Russian Federation
Nālūt 71 F2 NW Libya
Namakan Lake 40 A1 lake
Canada/USA
Namangan 123 F2 Namangan
Wiloyati, E Uzbekistan
Nambala 78 D2 Central, C Zambia
Nam Co 126 C5 lake W China
Nam Đinh 136 D3 Nam Ha,
N Vietnam
Namib Desert 78 B3 desert
W Namibia
Namibe 78 A2 Port. Moçâmedes,
Mossâmedes. Namibe,
SW Angola
Namibia 78 B3 var. South West
Africa, Afr. Suidwes-Afrika, Ger.
Deutsch-Südwestafrika; prev.
German Southwest Africa, South-
West Africa. Country S Africa

Namibia 78

Official name Republic of Namibia
Formation 1990
Capital Windhoek
Population 1.7 million /
5 people per sq mile
(2 people per sq km)
Total area 317,872 sq miles
(823,290 sq km)
Languages English, Ovambo,
Kavango, Bergdama, German
Religions Christian 90%, other 10%
Ethnic mix Ovambo 50%,, Kavango
9%, Herero 8%, Damara 8%,
other 25%
Government Multiparty republic
Currency Namibian dollar
= 100 cents,
South African rand
= 100 cents
Literacy rate 79.8%
Calorie consumption 2,134
kilocalories

Namo *see* Namu Atoll
Nam Ou 136 C3 river N Laos
Nampa 46 D3 Idaho, NW USA
Nampula 79 E2 Nampula,
NE Mozambique
Namsos 84 B4 Nord-Trøndelag,
C Norway
Nam Tha 136 C4 river N Laos
Namu Atoll 144 D2 var. Namo.
Atoll Ralik Chain, C Marshall
Islands
Namur 87 C6 Dut. Namen. Namur,
SE Belgium
Namyit Island 128 C8 island
S Spratly Islands
Nan 136 C4 var. Muang Nan. Nan,
NW Thailand
Nanaimo 36 D5 Vancouver Island,
British Columbia, SW Canada
Nanchang 128 C5 var. Nan-ch'ang,
Nanch'ang-hsien. Jiangxi, S China
Nanch'ang-hsien *see* Nanchang
Nan-ching *see* Nanjing
Nancy 90 D3 Meurthe-et-Moselle,
NE France
Nandaime 52 D3 Granada,
SW Nicaragua

Nānded 134 D5 Mahārāshtra, C India

Nandyāl 132 C1 Andhra Pradesh, E India

Nanjing 128 D5 var. Nan-ching, Nanking; prev. Chianning, Chian-ning, Kiang-ning. Jiangsu, E China

Nanking see Nanjing

Nanning 128 B6 var. Nan-ning; prev. Yung-ning. Guangxi Zhuangzu Zizhiqu, S China

Nan-ning see Nanning

Nanortalik 82 C5 S Greenland

Nanpan Jiang 136 D2 river S China

Nanping 128 D6 var. Nan-p'ing; prev. Yenping. Fujian, SE China

Nanseí-Shotô 130 A2 var. Ryukyu Islands. Island group SW Japan

Nansei Syotô Trench see Ryukyu Trench

Nansen Basin 155 C4 undersea feature Arctic Ocean

Nansen Cordillera 155 B3 var. Arctic-Mid Oceanic Ridge, Nansen Ridge. Undersea feature Arctic Ocean

Nansen Ridge see Nansen Cordillera

Nanterre 90 D1 Hauts-de-Seine, N France

Nantes 90 B4 Bret. Naoned; anc. Condivincum, Namnetes. Loire-Atlantique, NW France

Nantucket Island 41 G3 island Massachusetts, NE USA

Nanumaga 145 E3 var. Nanumanga. Atoll NW Tuvalu

Nanumanga see Nanumaga

Nanumea Atoll 145 E3 atoll NW Tuvalu

Nanyang 128 C5 var. Nan-yang. Henan, C China

Napa 47 B6 California, W USA

Napier 150 E4 Hawke's Bay, North Island, NZ

Naples 80 D5 anc. Neapolis. Campania, S Italy

Naples 43 E5 Florida, SE USA

Napo 56 A3 province NE Ecuador

Napo, Río 60 C1 river Ecuador/Peru

Naracoorte 149 B7 South Australia

Naradhivas see Narathiwat

Narathiwat 137 C7 var. Naradhivas. Narathiwat, SW Thailand

Narbada see Narmada

Narbonne 91 C6 anc. Narbo Martius. Aude, S France

Narborough Island see Fernandina, Isla

Nares Abyssal Plain see Nares Plain

Nares Plain 35 E6 var. Nares Abyssal Plain. Undersea feature NW Atlantic Ocean

Nares Strait 82 D1 Dan. Nares Stræde. Strait Canada/Greenland

Narew 98 E3 river E Poland

Narmada 124 B3 var. Narbada. River C India

Narowlya 107 C8 Rus. Narovlya. Homyel'skaya Voblasts', SE Belarus

Närpes 85 D5 Fin. Närpiö. Länsi-Suomi, W Finland

Narrabri 149 D6 New South Wales, SE Australia

Narrogin 147 B6 Western Australia

Narva 106 E2 prev. Narova. River Estonia/Russian Federation

Narva 106 E2 Ida-Virumaa, NE Estonia

Narva Bay 106 E2 Est. Narva Laht, Ger. Narwa-Bucht, Rus. Narvskiy Zaliv. Bay Estonia/Russian Federation

Narva Reservoir 106 E2 Est. Narva Veehoidla, Rus. Narvskoye Vodokhranilishche. Reservoir Estonia/Russian Federation

Narvik 84 C3 Nordland, C Norway

Nar'yan-Mar 110 D3 prev. Beloshchel'ye, Dzerzhinskiy. Nenetskiy Avtonomnyy Okrug, NW Russian Federation

Naryn 123 G2 Narynskaya Oblast', C Kyrgyzstan

Nāsāud 108 B3 Ger. Nussdorf, Hung. Naszód. Bistriţa-Năsăud, N Romania

Nase see Naze

Nāshik 134 C5 prev. Nāsik. Mahārāshtra, W India

Nashua 41 G3 New Hampshire, NE USA

Nashville 42 C1 state capital Tennessee, S USA

Näsijärvi 85 D5 lake SW Finland

Nāsiri see Ahvāz

Nasiriya see An Nāşirīyah

Nassau 54 C1 country capital (Bahamas) New Providence, N Bahamas

Nasser, Lake 72 B3 var. Buhayrat Nasir, Buhayrat Nāşir, Buheiret Nâşir. Lake Egypt/Sudan

Nata 78 C3 Central, NE Botswana

Natal 63 G2 Rio Grande do Norte, E Brazil

Natal Basin 141 A6 var. Mozambique Basin. Undersea feature W Indian Ocean

Natanya see Netanya

Natchez 42 B3 Mississippi, S USA

Natchitoches 42 A2 Louisiana, S USA

Nathanya see Netanya

Natitingou 75 F4 NW Benin

Natsrat see Nazerat

Natuna Islands 124 D4 island group W Indonesia

Naturaliste Plateau 141 E6 undersea feature E Indian Ocean

Naugard see Nowogard

Naujamiestis 106 C4 Panevėžys, C Lithuania

Nauru 144 D2 prev. Pleasant Island. Country W Pacific Ocean

Nauru 144

Official name	Republic of Nauru
Formation	1968
Capital	No official capital
Population	11,500 / 1,381 people per sq mile (548 people per sq km)
Total area	8.2 sq miles (21.2 sq km)
Languages	Nauruan, English, Kiribati, Chinese, Tuvaluan
Religions	Christian 95%, other 5%
Ethnic mix	Nauruan 62%, other Pacific islanders 25%, Chinese and Vietnamese 8%, European 5%
Government	Parliamentary democracy
Currency	Australian dollar = 100 cents
Literacy rate	99%
Calorie consumption	not available

Nauta 60 C2 Loreto, N Peru

Navahrudak 107 C6 Pol. Nowogródek, Rus. Novogrudok. Hrodzyenskaya Voblasts', W Belarus

Navapolatsk 107 D5 Rus. Novopolotsk. Vitsyebskaya Voblasts', N Belarus

Navarra 93 E2 cultural region N Spain

Navassa Island 54 C3 US unincorporated territory C West Indies

Navojoa 50 C2 Sonora, NW Mexico

Navolat see Navolato

Navolato 66 D4 var. Navolat. Sinaloa, C Mexico

Návpaktos see Náfpaktos

Nawabashah see Nawābshāh

Nawābshāh 134 B3 var. Nawabashah. Sind, S Pakistan

Nawoiy 123 E2 Rus. Navoi. Nawoiy Wiloyati, C Uzbekistan

Naxçıvan 117 G3 Rus. Nakhichevan'. SW Azerbaijan

Náxos 105 D6 var. Naxos. Náxos, Kykládes, Greece, Aegean Sea

Náxos 105 D6 island Kykládes, Greece, Aegean Sea

Nayoro 130 D2 Hokkaidō, NE Japan

Nazca 60 D4 Ica, S Peru

Nazca Ridge 57 A5 undersea feature E Pacific Ocean

Naze 130 B3 var. Nase. Kagoshima, Amami-ōshima, SW Japan

Nazerat 119 A5 var. Natsrat, Ar. En Nazira, Eng. Nazareth. Northern, N Israel

Nazilli 116 A4 Aydın, SW Turkey

Nazrēt 73 C5 var. Adama, Hadama. C Ethiopia

N'Dalatando 78 B1 Port. Salazar, Vila Salazar. Cuanza Norte, NW Angola

Ndélé 76 C4 Bamingui-Bangoran, N Central African Republic

Ndendé 77 B6 Ngounié, S Gabon

Ndindi 77 A6 Nyanga, S Gabon

Ndjamena 76 B3 var. N'Djamena; prev. Fort-Lamy. Country capital (Chad) Chari-Baguirmi, W Chad

Ndjolé 77 A5 Moyen-Ogooué, W Gabon

Ndola 78 D2 Copperbelt, C Zambia

Neagh, Lough 89 B5 lake E Northern Ireland, UK

Néa Moudanía 104 C4 var. Néa Moudhaniá. Kentrikí Makedonía, N Greece

Néa Moudhaniá see Néa Moudanía

Neápoli 104 B4 prev. Neápolis. Dytikí Makedonía, N Greece

Neápoli 105 D8 Kríti, Greece, E Mediterranean Sea

Neápoli 105 C7 Pelopónnisos, S Greece

Neapolis see Nablus

Near Islands 36 A2 island group Aleutian Islands, Alaska, USA

Néa Zíchni 104 C3 var. Néa Zíchni; prev. Néa Zíkhna. Kentrikí Makedonía, NE Greece

Néa Zíkhna see Néa Zíchni

Néa Zíkhni see Néa Zíchni

Nebaj 52 B2 Quiché, W Guatemala

Nebitdag 122 B2 Balkanskiy Velayat, W Turkmenistan

Neblina, Pico da 62 C1 mountain NW Brazil

Nebraska 44 D4 off. State of Nebraska; also known as Blackwater State, Cornhusker State, Tree Planters State. State C USA

Nebraska City 45 F4 Nebraska, C USA

Neches River 49 H3 river Texas, SW USA

Neckar 95 B6 river SW Germany

Necochea 65 D5 Buenos Aires, E Argentina

Neder Rijn 86 D4 Eng. Lower Rhine. River C Netherlands

Nederweert 87 D5 Limburg, SE Netherlands

Neede 86 E3 Gelderland, E Netherlands

Neerpelt 87 D5 Limburg, NE Belgium

Neftekamsk 111 D5 Respublika Bashkortostan, W Russian Federation

Negēlē 73 D5 var. Negelli, It. Neghelli. C Ethiopia

Negelli see Negēlē

Neghelli see Negēlē

Negomane 79 E2 var. Negomano. Cabo Delgado, N Mozambique

Negomano see Negomane

Negombo 132 C3 Western Province, SW Sri Lanka

Negotin 100 E4 Serbia, E Yugoslavia

Negra, Punta 60 A3 headland NW Peru

Negreşti-Oaş 108 B3 Hung. Avasfelsőfalu; prev. Negreşti. Satu Mare, NE Romania

Negro, Río 65 C5 river E Argentina

Negro, Rio 62 D1 river N South America

Negro, Río 64 D4 river Brazil/Uruguay

Negros 139 E2 island C Philippines

Nehbandān 120 E3 Khorāsān, E Iran

Neijiang 128 B5 Sichuan, C China

Nei Monggol Zizhiqu see Inner Mongolia

Nei Mongol see Inner Mongolia

Neiva 58 B3 Huila, S Colombia

Nellore 132 D2 Andhra Pradesh, E India

Nelson 37 G4 river Manitoba, C Canada

Nelson 151 C5 Nelson, South Island, NZ

Néma 74 D3 Hodh ech Chargui, SE Mauritania

Neman 106 A4 Bel. Nyoman, Ger. Memel, Lith. Nemunas, Pol. Niemen, Rus. Neman. River NE Europe

Neman 106 B4 Ger. Ragnit. Kaliningradskaya Oblast', W Russian Federation

Neméa 105 B6 Pelopónnisos, S Greece

Nemours 90 C3 Seine-et-Marne, N France

Nemuro 130 E2 Hokkaidō, NE Japan

Neochóri 105 B5 Dytikí Ellás, C Greece

Nepal 135 E3 Country S Asia

Nepal 135

Official name	Kingdom of Nepal
Formation	1769
Capital	Kathmandu
Population	24 million / 452 people per sq mile (175 people per sq km)
Total area	52,818 sq miles (136,800 sq km)
Languages	Nepali, Maithili, Bhojpuri
Religions	Hindu 90%, Buddhist 4%, Muslim 3%, Christian 1%, other 2%
Ethnic mix	Nepalese 58%, Bihari 19%, Tamang 6%, other 17%
Government	Constitutional monarchy
Currency	Nepalese rupee = 100 paisa
Literacy rate	38%
Calorie consumption	1,957 kilocalories

Nereta 106 C4 Aizkraukle, S Latvia

Neretva 100 C4 river Bosnia and Herzegovina/Croatia

Neringa 106 A3 Ger. Nidden; prev. Nida. Neringa, SW Lithuania

Neris 107 C5 Bel. Viliya, Pol. Wilia; prev. Pol. Wilja. River Belarus/Lithuania

Nerva 92 C4 Andalucía, S Spain

Neryungri 115 F4 Respublika Sakha (Yakutiya), NE Russian Federation

Neskaupstadhur 83 E5 Austurland, E Iceland

Ness, Loch 88 C3 lake N Scotland, UK

Néstos 104 C3 Bul. Mesta, Turk. Kara Su. River Bulgaria/Greece see also Mesta

Netanya 119 A6 var. Natanya, Nathanya. Central, C Israel

Netherlands 86 C3 var. Holland, Dut. Koninkrijk der Nederlanden, Nederland. Country NW Europe

Netherlands 86

Official name	Kingdom of the Netherlands
Formation	1815
Capital	Amsterdam, The Hague
Population	15.8 million / 1,206 people per sq mile (466 people per sq km)
Total area	13,096 sq miles (33,920 sq km)
Languages	Dutch, Frisian
Religions	Roman Catholic 36%, Protestant 27%, Muslim 3%, other 34%
Ethnic mix	Dutch 96%, other 4%
Government	Constitutional monarchy

Netherlands (continued)

Currency Netherlands guilden (guilder) or florin = 100 cents
Literacy rate 99%
Calorie consumption 3,222 kilocalories

Netherlands Antilles *55 E5 prev.* Dutch West Indies. *Dutch autonomous region* S Caribbean Sea
Netherlands New Guinea *see* Irian Jaya
Nettilling Lake *37 G3 lake* Baffin Island, Nunavut, N Canada
Neubrandenburg *94 D3* Mecklenburg-Vorpommern, NE Germany
Neuchâtel *95 A7 Ger.* Neuenburg. Neuchâtel, W Switzerland
Neuchâtel, Lac de *A7 Ger.* Neuenburger See. *Lake* W Switzerland
Neufchâteau *87 D8* Luxembourg, SE Belgium
Neumünster *94 B2* Schleswig-Holstein, N Germany
Neunkirchen *95 A5* Saarland, SW Germany
Neuquén *65 B5* Neuquén, SE Argentina
Neuruppin *94 C3* Brandenburg, NE Germany
Neusalz an der Oder *see* Nowa Sól
Neusiedler See *95 E6 Hung.* Fertő. *Lake* Austria/Hungary
Neustadt an der Weinstrasse *95 B5 prev.* Neustadt an der Haardt, *hist.* Niewenstat, *anc.* Nova Civitas. Rheinland-Pfalz, SW Germany
Neustrelitz *94 D3* Mecklenburg-Vorpommern, NE Germany
Neu-Ulm *95 B6* Bayern, S Germany
Neuwied *95 A5* Rheinland-Pfalz, W Germany
Neuzen *see* Terneuzen
Nevada *47 C5 off.* State of Nevada; also known as Battle Born State, Sagebrush State, Silver State. *State* W USA
Nevada, Sierra *92 D5 mountain range* S Spain
Nevers *90 C4 anc.* Noviodunum. Nièvre, C France
Neves *76 E2* São Tomé, S Sao Tome and Príncipe
Nevinnomyssk *111 B7* Stavropol'skiy Kray, SW Russian Federation
Nevşehir *116 C3 var.* Nevsehir. Nevşehir, C Turkey
Nevsehir *see* Nevşehir
Newala *73 C8* Mtwara, SE Tanzania
New Albany *40 C5* Indiana, N USA
New Amsterdam *59 G3* E Guyana
Newark *41 F4* New Jersey, NE USA
New Bedford *41 G3* Massachusetts, NE USA
Newberg *46 B3* Oregon, NW USA
New Bern *43 F1* North Carolina, SE USA
New Braunfels *49 G4* Texas, SW USA
Newbridge *89 B6 Ir.* An Droichead Nua. C Ireland
New Britain *144 B3 island* E PNG
New Brunswick *39 F4 Fr.* Nouveau-Brunswick. *Province* SE Canada
New Caledonia *144 D4 var.* Kanaky, *Fr.* Nouvelle-Calédonie. *French overseas territory* SW Pacific Ocean
New Caledonia *144 C5 island* SW Pacific Ocean
New Caledonia Basin *142 C4 undersea feature* W Pacific Ocean
Newcastle *see* Newcastle upon Tyne
Newcastle *149 D6* New South Wales, SE Australia
Newcastle upon Tyne *88 D4 var.* Newcastle; *hist.* Monkchester, *Lat.* Pons Aelii. NE England, UK
New Delhi *134 D3 country capital* (India) Delhi, N India

Newfoundland *39 G3 Fr.* Terre-Neuve. *Island* Newfoundland, SE Canada
Newfoundland *39 F2 Fr.* Terre Neuve. *Province* SE Canada
Newfoundland Basin *66 B3 undersea feature* NW Atlantic Ocean
New Georgia Islands *144 C3 island group* NW Solomon Islands
New Glasgow *39 F4* Nova Scotia, SE Canada
New Goa *see* Panaji
New Guinea *144 A3 Dut.* Nieuw Guinea, *Ind.* Irian. *Island* Indonesia/PNG
New Hampshire *41 F2 off.* State of New Hampshire; also known as The Granite State. *State* NE USA
New Haven *41 G3* Connecticut, NE USA
New Iberia *42 B3* Louisiana, S USA
New Ireland *144 C3 island* NE PNG
New Jersey *41 F4 off.* State of New Jersey; also known as The Garden State. *State* NE USA
Newman *146 B4* Western Australia
Newmarket *89 E6* E England, UK
New Mexico *48 C2 off.* State of New Mexico; also known as Land of Enchantment, Sunshine State. *State* SW USA
New Orleans *42 B3* Louisiana, S USA
New Plymouth *150 C4* Taranaki, North Island, NZ
Newport *40 C4* Kentucky, S USA
Newport *89 D7* S England, UK
Newport *89 C7* SE Wales, UK
Newport *41 G2* Vermont, NE USA
Newport News *41 F5* Virginia, NE USA
New Providence *54 C1 island* N Bahamas
Newquay *89 C7* SW England, UK
Newry *89 B5 Ir.* An tIúr. SE Northern Ireland, UK
New Sarum *see* Salisbury
New Siberian Islands *see* Novosibirskiye Ostrova
New South Wales *149 C6 state* SE Australia
Newton *45 G3* Iowa, C USA
Newtownabbey *89 B5 Ir.* Baile na Mainistreach. E Northern Ireland, UK
New Ulm *45 F2* Minnesota, N USA
New York *41 F4* New York, NE USA
New York *41 F3 state* NE USA
New Zealand *150 A4 abbrev.* NZ. *Country* SW Pacific Ocean

New Zealand 150

Official name Dominion of New Zealand
Formation 1947
Capital Wellington
Population 4 million /38 people per sq mile (15 people per sq km)
Total area 103,730 sq miles (268,680 sq km)
Languages English, Maori
Religions Protestant 47%, non-religious 16%, Roman Catholic 15%, other 22%
Ethnic mix European 82%, Maori 9%, Pacific Islanders 3%, other 6%
Government Parliamentary democracy
Currency New Zealand dollar = 100 cents
Literacy rate 99%
Calorie consumption 3,669 kilocalories

Neyveli *132 C2* Tamil Nādu, SE India
Ngangzê Co *126 B5 lake* W China
Ngaoundéré *76 B4 var.* N'Gaoundéré. Adamaoua, N Cameroon
N'Giva *78 B3 var.* Ondjiva, *Port.* Vila Pereira de Eça. Cunene, S Angola
Ngo *77 B6* Plateaux, SE Congo

Ngoko *77 B5 river* Cameroon/Congo
Ngourti *75 H3* Diffa, E Niger
Nguigmi *75 H3 var.* N'Guigmi. Diffa, SE Niger
Nguru *75 G3* Yobe, NE Nigeria
Nha Trang *137 E6* Khanh Hoa, S Vietnam
Niagara Falls *40 D3 waterfall* Canada/USA
Niagara Falls *41 E3* New York, NE USA
Niagara Falls *38 D5* Ontario, S Canada
Niamey *75 F3 country capital* (Niger) Niamey, SW Niger
Niangay, Lac *75 E3 lake* E Mali
Nia-Nia *77 E5* Orientale, NE Dem. Rep. Congo (Zaire)
Nias, Pulau *138 A3 island* W Indonesia
Nicaragua *52 D3 Country* Central America

Nicaragua 52

Official name Republic of Nicaragua
Formation 1838
Capital Managua
Population 5 million / 111 people per sq mile (43 people per sq km)
Total area 45,849 sq miles (118,750 sq km)
Languages Spanish, English Creole, Miskito
Religions Roman Catholic 95%, other 5%
Ethnic mix Mestizo 69%, White 14%, Black 8%, other 9%
Government Multiparty republic
Currency Córdoba oro = 100 pence
Literacy rate 63.4%
Calorie consumption 2,293 kilocalories

Nicaragua, Lago de *52 D4 var.* Cocibolca, Gran Lago, *Eng.* Lake Nicaragua. *Lake* S Nicaragua
Nicaragua, Lake *see* Nicaragua, Lago de
Nicaria *see* Ikaría
Nice *91 D6 It.* Nizza; *anc.* Nicaea. Alpes-Maritimes, SE France
Nicephorium *see* Ar Raqqah
Nicholas II Land *see* Severnaya Zemlya
Nicholls Town *54 C1* Andros Island, NW Bahamas
Nicobar Islands *124 B4 island group* India, E Indian Ocean
Nicosia *102 C5 Gk.* Lefkosía, *Turk.* Lefkoşa. *Country capital* (Cyprus) C Cyprus
Nicoya *52 D4* Guanacaste, W Costa Rica
Nicoya, Golfo de *52 D5 gulf* W Costa Rica
Nicoya, Península de *52 D4 peninsula* W Costa Rica
Nidzica *98 D3 Ger.* Niedenburg. Warmińsko-Mazurskie, NE Poland
Niedere Tauern *99 A6 mountain range* C Austria
Nieuw Amsterdam *59 G3* Commewijne, NE Suriname
Nieuw-Bergen *86 D4* Limburg, SE Netherlands
Nieuwegein *86 C4* Utrecht, C Netherlands
Nieuw Nickerie *59 G3* Nickerie, NW Suriname
Niğde *116 C4* Niğde, C Turkey
Niger *75 F3 Country* W Africa

Niger 75

Official name Republic of Niger
Formation 1960
Capital Niamey
Population 10.7 million / 22 people per sq mile (8 people per sq km)
Total area 489,072 sq miles (1,266,700 sq km)

Niger (continued)

Languages French, Hausa, Djerma
Religions Muslim 85%, Traditional beliefs 14%, Christian 1%
Ethnic mix Hausa 54%, Djerma and Songhai 21%, Fulani 10%, Tuareg 9%, other 6%
Government Multiparty republic
Currency CFA franc = 100 centimes
Literacy rate 14.3%
Calorie consumption 2,257 kilocalories

Niger *75 F4 river* W Africa
Nigeria *75 F4 Country* W Africa

Nigeria 75

Official name Federal Republic of Nigeria
Formation 1960
Capital Abuja
Population 112 million / 317 people per sq mile (122 people per sq km)
Total area 351,648 sq miles (910,770 sq km)
Languages English, Hausa, Yoruba, Ibo
Religions Muslim 50%, Christian 40%, Traditional beliefs 10%
Ethnic mix Hausa 21%, Yoruba 21%, Ibo 18%, Fulani 11%, other 29%
Government Multiparty republic
Currency Naira = 100 kobo
Literacy rate 59.5%
Calorie consumption 2,124 kilocalories

Niger, Mouths of the *75 F5 delta* S Nigeria
Nihon *see* Japan
Niigata *131 D5* Niigata, Honshū, C Japan
Niihama *131 B7* Ehime, Shikoku, SW Japan
Niihau *47 A7 island* Hawaii, USA, C Pacific Ocean
Nii-jima *131 D6 island* E Japan
Nijkerk *86 D3* Gelderland, C Netherlands
Nijlen *87 C5* Antwerpen, N Belgium
Nijmegen *86 D4 Ger.* Nimwegen; *anc.* Noviomagus. Gelderland, SE Netherlands
Nikaria *see* Ikaría
Nikel' *110 C2* Murmanskaya Oblast', NW Russian Federation
Nikiniki *139 E5* Timor, S Indonesia
Nikopol' *109 F3* Pleven, N Bulgaria
Nikšić *101 C5* Montenegro, SW Yugoslavia
Nikumaroro *145 E3 prev.* Gardner Island, Kemins Island. *Atoll* Phoenix Islands, C Kiribati
Nikunau *145 E3 var.* Nukunau; *prev.* Byron Island. *Atoll* Tungaru, W Kiribati
Nile *68 D3 Ar.* Nahr an Nīl. *River* N Africa
Nile *72 B2 former province* NW Uganda
Nile Delta *72 B1 delta* N Egypt
Nîmes *91 C6 anc.* Nemausus, Nismes. Gard, S France
Nine Degree Channel *132 B3 channel* India/Maldives
Ninetyeast Ridge *141 D5 undersea feature* E Indian Ocean
Ninety Mile Beach *150 C1 beach* North Island, NZ
Ningbo *128 D5 var.* Ning-po, Yin-hsien; *prev.* Ninghsien. Zhejiang, SE China
Ninghsien *see* Ningbo
Ning-po *see* Ningbo
Ningxia *128 B4 off.* Ningxia Huizu Zizhiqu, *var.* Ning-hsia, Ningsia, *Eng.* Ningsia Hui, Ningsia Hui Autonomous Region. Admin. region *autonomous region* N China

Ningxia Huizu Zizhiqu *see* Ningxia
Nio *see* Íos
Niobrara River *45 E3 river* Nebraska/Wyoming, C USA
Nioro *74 D3 var.* Nioro du Sahel. Kayes, W Mali
Nioro du Sahel *see* Nioro
Niort *90 B4* Deux-Sèvres, W France
Nipigon *38 B4* Ontario, S Canada
Nipigon, Lake *38 B3 lake* Ontario, S Canada
Nippon *see* Japan
Niš *101 E5 Eng.* Nish, *Ger.* Nisch; *anc.* Naissus. Serbia, SE Yugoslavia
Nişab *120 B4* Al Ḩudūd ash Shamālīyah, N Saudi Arabia
Nisibin *see* Nusaybin
Nisiros *see* Nísyros
Nisko *98 E4* Podkarpackie, SE Poland
Nísyros *105 E7 var.* Nisiros. *Island* Dodekánisos, Greece, Aegean Sea
Nitra *99 C6 Ger.* Neutra, *Hung.* Nyitra. *River* W Slovakia
Nitra *99 C6 Ger.* Neutra, *Hung.* Nyitra. Nitriansky Kraj, SW Slovakia
Niuatobutabu *see* Niuatoputapu
Niuatoputapu *145 E4 var.* Niuatobutabu; *prev.* Keppel Island. *Island* N Tonga
Niue *145 F4 self-governing territory in free association with NZ* S Pacific Ocean
Niulakita *145 E3 var.* Nurakita. *Atoll* S Tuvalu
Niutao *145 E3 atoll* NW Tuvalu
Nivernais *90 C4 cultural region* C France
Nizāmābād *134 D5* Andhra Pradesh, C India
Nizhnekamsk *111 C5* Respublika Tatarstan, W Russian Federation
Nizhnevartovsk *114 D3* Khanty-Mansiyskiy Avtonomnyy Okrug, C Russian Federation
Nizhniy Novgorod *111 C5 prev.* Gor'kiy. Nizhegorodskaya Oblast', W Russian Federation
Nizhniy Odes *110 D4* Respublika Komi, NW Russian Federation
Nizhnyaya Tunguska *115 E3 Eng.* Lower Tunguska. *River* N Russian Federation
Nizhyn *109 E1 Rus.* Nezhin. Chernihivs'ka Oblast', NE Ukraine
Njazidja *see* Grande Comore
Njombe *73 C8* Iringa, S Tanzania
Nkayi *77 B6 prev.* Jacob. La Bouenza, S Congo
Nkongsamba *76 A4 var.* N'Kongsamba. Littoral, W Cameroon
Nmai Hka *136 B2 var.* Me Hka. *River* N Myanmar
Nobeoka *131 B7* Miyazaki, Kyūshū, SW Japan
Noboribetsu *130 D3 var.* Noboribetu. Hokkaidō, NE Japan
Noboribetu *see* Noboribetsu
Nogales *48 B3* Arizona, SW USA
Nogales *50 B1* Sonora, NW Mexico
Nogal Valley *see* Dooxo Nugaaleed
Nokia *85 D5* Länsi-Suomi, W Finland
Nokou *76 B3* Kanem, W Chad
Nola *77 B5* Sangha-Mbaéré, SW Central African Republic
Nolinsk *111 C5* Kirovskaya Oblast', NW Russian Federation
Nongkaya *see* Nong Khai
Nong Khai *136 C4 var.* Mi Chai, Nongkaya. Nong Khai, E Thailand
Nonouti *144 D2 prev.* Sydenham Island. *Atoll* Tungaru, W Kiribati
Noord-Beveland *86 B4 var.* North Beveland. *Island* SW Netherlands
Noordwijk aan Zee *86 C3* Zuid-Holland, W Netherlands
Nora *85 C6* Örebro, C Sweden
Norak *123 E3 Rus.* Nurek. W Tajikistan

Nord *83 F1* N Greenland
Nordaustlandet *83 G1 island* NE Svalbard
Norden *94 A3* Niedersachsen, NW Germany
Norderstedt *94 B3* Schleswig-Holstein, N Germany
Nordfriesische Inseln *see* North Frisian Islands
Nordhausen *94 C4* Thüringen, C Germany
Nordhorn *94 A3* Niedersachsen, NW Germany
Nordkapp *84 D1 Eng.* North Cape. *Headland* N Norway
Norfolk *45 E3* Nebraska, C USA
Norfolk *41 F5* Virginia, NE USA
Norfolk Island *142 D4 Australian external territory* SW Pacific Ocean
Norfolk Ridge *142 D4 undersea feature* W Pacific Ocean
Norias *49 G5* Texas, SW USA
Noril'sk *114 D3* Taymyrskiy (Dolgano-Nenetskiy) Avtonomnyy Okrug, N Russian Federation
Norman *49 G1* Oklahoma, USA
Normandie *90 B3 Eng.* Normandy. *Cultural region* N France
Normandy *see* Normandie
Normanton *148 C3* Queensland, NE Australia
Norrköping *85 C6* Östergötland, S Sweden
Norrtälje *85 C6* Stockholm, C Sweden
Norseman *147 B6* Western Australia
North Albanian Alps *101 C5 Alb.* Bjeshkët e Namuna, *SCr.* Prokletije. *Mountain range* Albania/Yugoslavia
Northallerton *89 D5* N England, UK
Northam *147 A6* Western Australia
North America *34 continent*
Northampton *89 D6* C England, UK
North Andaman *133 F2 island* Andaman Islands, India, NE Indian Ocean
North Australian Basin *141 E5 Fr.* Bassin Nord de l' Australie. *Undersea feature* E Indian Ocean
North Bay *38 D4* Ontario, S Canada
North Beveland *see* Noord-Beveland
North Cape *66 D1 headland* New Ireland, NE PNG
North Cape *150 C1 headland* North Island, NZ
North Cape *see* Nordkapp
North Carolina *43 E1 off.* State of North Carolina; also known as Old North State, Tar Heel State, Turpentine State. *State* SE USA
North Channel *40 D2 lake channel* Canada/USA
North Charleston *43 F2* South Carolina, SE USA
North Dakota *44 D2 off.* State of North Dakota; also known as Flickertail State, Peace Garden State, Sioux State. *State* N USA
Northeast Providence Channel *54 C1 channel* N Bahamas
Northeim *94 B4* Niedersachsen, C Germany
Northern Cook Islands *145 F4 island group* N Cook Islands
Northern Cyprus, Turkish Republic of *102 D5 disputed region* N Cyprus
Northern Dvina *see* Severnaya Dvina
Northern Ireland *88 B4 var.* The Six Counties. *Political division* UK
Northern Mariana Islands *142 B1 US commonwealth territory* W Pacific Ocean
Northern Sporades *see* Vóreioi Sporádes
Northern Territory *144 A5 territory* N Australia
North European Plain *81 E3 plain* N Europe
Northfield *45 F2* Minnesota, N USA
North Fiji Basin *142 D3 undersea feature* N Coral Sea

North Frisian Islands *94 B2 var.* Nordfriesische Inseln. *Island group* N Germany
North Huvadhu Atoll *132 B5 var.* Gaafu Alifu Atoll. *Atoll* S Maldives
North Island *150 B2 island* N NZ
North Korea *129 E3 Kor.* Chosŏn-minjujuŭi-inmin-kanghwaguk. *Country* E Asia

North Korea 129

Official name Democratic People's Republic of Korea
Formation 1948
Capital Pyongyang
Population 24 million / 516 people per sq mile (199 people per sq km)
Total area 46,490 sq miles (120,410 sq km)
Languages Korean, Chinese
Religions Non-religious 68%, Traditional beliefs 16%, Ch'ondogyo 14%, Buddhist 2%, Ethnic mix Korean 100%
Government Single-party republic
Currency N Korean won = 100 chon
Literacy rate 95%
Calorie consumption 2,833 kilocalories

North Little Rock *42 B1* Arkansas, C USA
North Minch *see* Minch, The
North Mole *93 G4 harbour wall* NW Gibraltar
North Platte *45 E4* Nebraska, C USA
North Platte River *44 D4 river* C USA
North Pole *155 B3 pole* Arctic Ocean
North Saskatchewan *37 F5 river* Alberta/Saskatchewan, S Canada
North Sea *C3 Dan.* Nordsøen, *Dut.* Noordzee, *Fr.* Mer du Nord, *Ger.* Nordsee, *Nor.* Nordsjøen; *prev.* German Ocean, *Lat.* Mare Germanicum. *Sea* NW Europe
North Siberian Lowland *see* Severo-Sibirskaya Nizmennost'
North Siberian Plain *see* Severo-Sibirskaya Nizmennost'
North Taranaki Bight *150 C3 gulf* North Island, NZ
North Uist *88 B3 island* NW Scotland, UK
Northwest Atlantic Mid-Ocean Canyon *34 E4 undersea feature* N Atlantic Ocean
North West Highlands *88 C3 mountain range* N Scotland, UK
Northwest Pacific Basin *113 G4 undersea feature* NW Pacific Ocean
Northwest Providence Channel *54 C1 channel* N Bahamas
Northwest Territories *37 E3 Fr.* Territoires du Nord-Ouest. *Territory* NW Canada (the eastern part is now the territory of Nunavut)
Northwind Plain *155 B2 undersea feature* Arctic Ocean
Norton Sound *36 C2 inlet* Alaska, USA
Norway *85 A5 Nor.* Norge. *Country* N Europe

Norway 85

Official name Kingdom of Norway
Formation 1905
Capital Oslo
Population 4.5 million / 38 people per sq mile (15 people per sq km)
Total area 118,467 sq miles (306,830 sq km)
Languages Norwegian, Lappish
Religions Evangelical Lutheran 89%, Roman Catholic 1%, other and non-religious 10%

Norway (continued)

Ethnic mix Norwegian 95%, Lapp 1%, other 4%
Government Constitutional monarchy
Currency Norwegian krone = 100 ore
Literacy rate 99%
Calorie consumption 3,244 kilocalories

Norwegian Basin *83 F4 undersea feature* NW Norwegian Sea
Norwegian Sea *83 F4 Nor.* Norske Havet. *Sea* NE Atlantic Ocean
Norwich *89 E6* E England, UK
Noshiro *130 D4 var.* Nosiro; *prev.* Noshirominato. Akita, Honshū, C Japan
Noshirominato *see* Noshiro
Nosiro *see* Noshiro
Nosivka *109 E1 Rus.* Nosovka. Chernihivs'ka Oblast', NE Ukraine
Noşratābād *120 E3* Sīstān va Balūchestān, E Iran
Nossob *78 C4 river* E Namibia
Noteć *98 C3 Ger.* Netze. *River* NW Poland
Nóties Sporádes *see* Dodekánisos
Nottingham *89 D6* C England, UK
Nouâdhibou *74 B2 prev.* Port-Étienne. Dakhlet Nouâdhibou, W Mauritania
Nouakchott *74 B2 country capital* (Mauritania) Nouakchott District, SW Mauritania
Nouméa *144 C5 dependent territory capital* (New Caledonia) Province Sud, S New Caledonia
Nouvelle-Calédonie *see* New Caledonia
Nova Gorica *95 D8* W Slovenia
Nova Gradiška *100 C3 Ger.* Neugradisk, *Hung.* Újgradiska. Brod-Posavina, NE Croatia
Nova Iguaçu *63 F4* Rio de Janeiro, SE Brazil
Novara *96 B2 anc.* Novaria. Piemonte, NW Italy
Nova Scotia *39 F4 Fr.* Nouvelle Écosse. *Province* SE Canada
Nova Scotia *35 E5 physical region* SE Canada
Novaya Sibir', Ostrov *115 F1 island* Novosibirskiye Ostrova, NE Russian Federation
Novaya Zemlya *110 D1 island group* N Russian Federation
Novaya Zemlya Trench *see* East Novaya Zemlya Trench
Novgorod *110 B4* Novgorodskaya Oblast', W Russian Federation
Novi Grad *see* Bosanski Novi
Novi Iskŭr *104 C2* Sofiya-Grad, W Bulgaria
Novi Pazar *101 D5 Turk.* Yenipazar. Shumen, NE Bulgaria
Novi Sad *100 D3 Ger.* Neusatz, *Hung.* Újvidék. Serbia, N Yugoslavia
Novoazovs'k *109 G4 Rus.* Novoazovsk. Donets'ka Oblast', E Ukraine
Novocheboksarsk *111 C5* Chuvashskaya Respublika, W Russian Federation
Novocherkassk *111 B7* Rostovskaya Oblast', SW Russian Federation
Novodvinsk *110 C3* Arkhangel'skaya Oblast', NW Russian Federation
Novohrad-Volyns'kyy *108 D2 Rus.* Novograd-Volynskiy. Zhytomyrs'ka Oblast', N Ukraine
Novokazalinsk *see* Ayteke Bi
Novokuznetsk *114 D4 prev.* Stalinsk. Kemerovskaya Oblast', S Russian Federation
Novolazarevskaya *154 C2 Russian research station* Antarctica
Novo Mesto *95 E8 Ger.* Rudolfswert; *prev. Ger.* Neustadtl. SE Slovenia
Novomoskovs'k *109 F3 Rus.* Novomoskovsk. Dnipropetrovs'ka Oblast', E Ukraine

Novomoskovsk 111 B5 Tul'skaya Oblast', W Russian Federation
Novorossiysk 111 A7 Krasnodarskiy Kray, SW Russian Federation
Novoshakhtinsk 111 B6 Rostovskaya Oblast', SW Russian Federation
Novosibirsk 114 D4 Novosibirskaya Oblast', C Russian Federation
Novosibirskiye Ostrova 115 F1 *Eng.* New Siberian Islands. *Island group* N Russian Federation
Novotroitsk 111 D6 Orenburgskaya Oblast', W Russian Federation
Novotroyits'ke 109 F4 *Rus.* Novotroitskoye. Khersons'ka Oblast', S Ukraine
Novovolyns'k 108 C1 *Rus.* Novovolynsk. Volyns'ka Oblast', NW Ukraine
Novy Dvor 107 B6 *Rus.* Novyy Dvor. Hrodzyenskaya Voblasts', W Belarus
Novyy Buh 109 E3 *Rus.* Novyy Bug. Mykolayivs'ka Oblast', S Ukraine
Novyy Uzen' *see* Zhanaözen
Nowa Sól 98 B4 *var.* Nowasól, *Ger.* Neusalz an der Oder. Lubuskie, W Poland
Nowogard *see* Nowogard
Nowo-Minsk *see* Miusk Mazowiecki
Nowy Dwór Mazowiecki 98 D3 Mazowieckie, C Poland
Nowy Sącz 99 D5 *Ger.* Neu Sandec. Małopolskie, S Poland
Nowy Tomyśl 98 B3 *var.* Nowy Tomysl. Wielkopolskie, C Poland
Noyon 90 C3 Oise, N France
Nsanje 79 E3 Southern, S Malawi
Nsawam 75 E5 SE Ghana
Ntomba, Lac 77 C6 *var.* Lac Tumba. *Lake* NW Dem. Rep. Congo (Zaire)
Nubian Desert 72 B3 *desert* NE Sudan
Nu'eima 119 E7 E West Bank
Nueva Gerona 54 B2 Isla de la Juventud, S Cuba
Nueva Rosita 50 D2 Coahuila de Zaragoza, NE Mexico
Nuevitas 54 C2 Camagüey, E Cuba
Nuevo, Bajo 53 G1 *island* NW Colombia
Nuevo Casas Grandes 50 C1 Chihuahua, N Mexico
Nuevo, Golfo 65 C6 *gulf* S Argentina
Nuevo Laredo 51 E2 Tamaulipas, NE Mexico
Nui Atoll 145 E3 *atoll* W Tuvalu
Nûk *see* Nuuk
Nuku'alofa 145 E5 *country capital* (Tonga) Tongatapu, S Tonga
Nukufetau Atoll 145 E3 *atoll* C Tuvalu
Nukulaelae Atoll 145 E3 *var.* Nukulailai. *Atoll* E Tuvalu
Nukulailai *see* Nukulaelae Atoll
Nukunau *see* Nikunau
Nukunonu Atoll 145 E3 *island* C Tokelau
Nukus 122 C2 Qoraqalpoghiston Respublikasi, W Uzbekistan
Nullarbor Plain 147 C6 *plateau* South Australia/Western Australia
Nunap Isua 98 B5 *var* Uummannarsuaq, *Dan.* Kap Farvel, *Eng.* Cape Farewell. *Headland* S Greenland
Nunavut 37 I3 *territory* N Canada
Nuneaton 89 D6 C England, UK
Nunivak Island 36 B2 *island* Alaska, USA
Nunspeet 86 D3 Gelderland, E Netherlands
Nuoro 97 A5 Sardegna, Italy, C Mediterranean Sea
Nuquí 58 A3 Chocó, W Colombia
Nurakita *see* Niulakita

Nuremberg *see* Nürnberg
Nurmes 84 E4 Itä-Suomi, E Finland
Nürnberg 95 C5 *Eng.* Nuremberg. Bayern, S Germany
Nurota 123 E2 *Rus.* Nurata. Nawoiy Wiloyati, C Uzbekistan
Nusa Tenggara 139 E5 *Eng.* Lesser Sunda Islands. East Timor / C Indonesia
Nusaybin 117 F4 *var.* Nisibin. Manisa, SE Turkey
Nuuk 82 C4 *var.* Nûk, *Dan.* Godthaab, Godthåb. *Dependent territory capital* (Greenland) SW Greenland
Nyagan' 114 C3 Khanty-Mansiyskiy Avtonomnyy Okrug, N Russian Federation
Nyainqêntanglha Shan 126 C5 *mountain range* W China
Nyala 72 A4 Southern Darfur, W Sudan
Nyamapanda 78 D3 Mashonaland East, NE Zimbabwe
Nyamtumbo 73 C8 Ruvuma, S Tanzania
Nyandoma 110 C4 Arkhangel'skaya Oblast', NW Russian Federation
Nyantakara 73 B7 Kagera, NW Tanzania
Nyasa, Lake 79 E2 *var.* Lake Malawi; *prev.* Lago Nyassa. *Lake* E Africa
Nyasvizh 107 C6 *Pol.* Nieśwież, *Rus.* Nesvizh. Minskaya Voblasts', C Belarus
Nyaunglebin 136 B4 Pegu, SW Myanmar
Nyeri 73 C6 Central, C Kenya
Nyima 126 C5 Xizang Zizhiqu, W China
Nyíregyháza 99 D6 Szabolcs-Szatmár-Bereg, NE Hungary
Nykøbing 85 B8 Storstrøm, SE Denmark
Nyköping 85 C6 Södermanland, S Sweden
Nylstroom 78 D4 Northern, NE South Africa
Nyngan 149 D6 New South Wales, SE Australia
Nyurba 115 F3 Republika Sakha (Yakutiya), NE Russian Federation
Nyzhn'ohirs'kyy 109 F4 *Rus.* Nizhnegorskiy. Respublika Krym, S Ukraine
Nzega 73 C7 Tabora, C Tanzania
Nzérékoré 74 D4 Guinée-Forestière, SE Guinea
Nzwani *see* Anjouan

O

Oahu 47 A7 *Haw.* O'ahu. *Island* Hawaii, USA, C Pacific Ocean
Oak Harbor 46 B1 Washington, NW USA
Oakland 47 B6 California, W USA
Oamaru 151 B7 Otago, South Island, NZ
Oaxaca 51 F5 *var.* Oaxaca de Juárez; *prev.* Antequera. Oaxaca, SE Mexico
Oaxaca de Juárez *see* Oaxaca
Ob' 112 C2 *river* C Russian Federation
Obal' 107 D5 *Rus.* Obol'. Vitsyebskaya Voblasts', N Belarus
Oban *see* Halfmoon Bay
Oban 88 C4 W Scotland, UK
Obando *see* Puerto Inírida
Obeliai 106 C4 Rokiškis, NE Lithuania
Oberhollabrunn *see* Tulln
Ob, Gulf of *see* Obskaya Guba
Obihiro 130 D2 Hokkaidō, NE Japan
Obo 76 D4 Haut-Mbomou, E Central African Republic
Obock 72 D4 E Djibouti
Oborniki 98 C3 Wielkopolskie, C Poland
Obskaya Guba 114 D3 *Eng.* Gulf of Ob'. *Gulf* N Russian Federation
Ob' Tablemount 141 B7 *undersea feature* S Indian Ocean

Ocala 43 E4 Florida, SE USA
Ocaña 92 D3 Castilla-La Mancha, C Spain
Ocaña 58 B2 Norte de Santander, N Colombia
O Carballiño 108 C1 *var* Carballiño. Gallicia, NW Spain
Occidental, Cordillera 61 E4 *mountain range* W South America
Occidental, Cordillera 58 B2 *mountain range* W Colombia
Occidental, Cordillera 60 D4 *mountain range* W Peru
Ocean Falls 36 D5 British Columbia, SW Canada
Ocean Island *see* Banaba
Oceanside 47 C8 California, W USA
Ochakiv 109 E4 *Rus.* Ochakov. Mykolayivs'ka Oblast', S Ukraine
Och'amch'ire 117 E2 *Rus.* Ochamchira. W Georgia
Ocho Rios 54 B4 C Jamaica
Ochrida, Lake *see* Ohrid, Lake
Ocotal 52 D3 Nueva Segovia, NW Nicaragua
Ocozocuautla 51 G5 Chiapas, SE Mexico
Ocú 53 F5 Herrera, S Panama
Ōdate 130 D3 Akita, Honshū, C Japan
Oddur *see* Xuddur
Ödemiş 116 A4 İzmir, SW Turkey
Odense 85 B7 Fyn, C Denmark
Oder 98 B3 *Cz./Pol.* Odra. *River* C Europe
Oderhaff *see* Szczeciński, Zalew
Odesa 109 E4 *Rus.* Odessa. Odes'ka Oblast', SW Ukraine
Odessa 49 E3 Texas, SW USA
Odienné 74 D4 NW Côte d'Ivoire
Ôdôngk 137 D6 Kâmpóng Spoe, S Cambodia
Odoorn 86 E2 Drenthe, NE Netherlands
Of 117 E2 Trabzon, NE Turkey
Ofanto 97 D5 *river* S Italy
Offenbach 95 B5 *var.* Offenbach am Main. Hessen, W Germany
Offenbach am Main *see* Offenbach
Offenburg 95 B6 Baden-Württemberg, SW Germany
Ogaden 73 D5 *Som.* Ogaadeen. *Plateau* Ethiopia/Somalia
Ōgaki 131 C6 Gifu, Honshū, SW Japan
Ogallala 44 D4 Nebraska, C USA
Ogbomosho 75 F4 Oyo, W Nigeria
Ogden 44 B4 Utah, W USA
Ogdensburg 41 F2 New York, NE USA
Ogulin 100 A3 Karlovac, NW Croatia
Ohio 40 C4 *off.* State of Ohio; also known as The Buckeye State. *State* N USA
Ohio River 40 C4 *river* N USA
Ohrid 101 D6 *Turk.* Ochrida, Ohri. SW FYR Macedonia
Ohrid, Lake 101 D6 *var.* Lake Ochrida, Alb. Liqeni i Ohrit, *Mac.* Ohridsko Ezero. *Lake* Albania/FYR Macedonia
Ohridsko Ezero *see* Ohrid, Lake
Ohura 150 D3 Manawatu-Wanganui, North Island, NZ
Oirschot 87 C5 Noord-Brabant, S Netherlands
Oise 90 C4 *river* N France
Oistins 55 G2 S Barbados
Ōita 131 B7 Ōita, Kyūshū, SW Japan
Ojinaga 50 D2 Chihuahua, N Mexico
Ojos del Salado, Cerro 64 B3 *mountain* W Argentina
Okaihau 150 C2 Northland, North Island, NZ
Okāra 134 C2 Punjab, E Pakistan
Okavanggo *see* Cubango
Okavango *see* Cubango
Okavango 78 C3 *district* NW Namibia
Okavango Delta 78 C3 *wetland* N Botswana
Okayama 131 B6 Okayama, Honshū, SW Japan

Okazaki 131 C6 Aichi, Honshū, C Japan
Okeechobee, Lake 43 E4 *lake* Florida, SE USA
Okefenokee Swamp 43 E3 *wetland* Georgia, SE USA
Okhotsk 115 G3 Khabarovskiy Kray, E Russian Federation
Okhotskoye More 115 G3 *sea* NW Pacific Ocean
Okhotsk, Sea of 113 F3 *sea* NW Pacific Ocean
Okhtyrka 109 F2 *Rus.* Akhtyrka. Sums'ka Oblast', NE Ukraine
Oki-guntō *see* Oki-shotō
Okinawa 130 A3 *island* SW Japan
Okinawa-shotō 130 A3 *island group* SW Japan
Oki-shotō 131 B6 *var.* Oki-guntō. *Island group* SW Japan
Oklahoma 49 F2 *off.* State of Oklahoma; also known as The Sooner State. *State* C USA
Oklahoma City 49 G1 *state capital* Oklahoma, C USA
Okmulgee 49 G1 Oklahoma, C USA
Oko, Wadi 72 C3 *river* NE Sudan
Oktyabr'skiy 111 D6 Volgogradskaya Oblast', SW Russian Federation
Oktyabr'skoy Revolyutsii, Ostrov 115 E2 *Eng.* October Revolution Island. *Island* Severnaya Zemlya, N Russian Federation
Okulovka *see* Uglovka
Okushiri-tō 130 C3 *var.* Okusiri Tô. *Island* NE Japan
Okusiri Tô *see* Okushiri-tō
Öland 85 C7 *island* S Sweden
Olavarría 65 D5 Buenos Aires, E Argentina
Oława 98 C4 *Ger.* Ohlau. Dolnośląskie, SW Poland
Olbia 97 A5 *prev.* Terranova Pausania. Sardegna, Italy, C Mediterranean Sea
Oldebroek 86 D3 Gelderland, E Netherlands
Oldenburg 94 B3 Niedersachsen, NW Germany
Oldenburg 94 C2 Schleswig-Holstein, N Germany
Oldenzaal 86 E3 Overijssel, E Netherlands
Old Harbour 54 B5 C Jamaica
Olëkma 115 F4 *river* C Russian Federation
Olëkminsk 115 F3 Respublika Sakha (Yakutiya), NE Russian Federation
Oleksandrivka 109 E3 *Rus.* Aleksandrovka. Kirovohrads'ka Oblast', C Ukraine
Oleksandriya 109 F3 *Rus.* Aleksandriya. Kirovohrads'ka Oblast', C Ukraine
Olenegorsk 110 C2 Murmanskaya Oblast', NW Russian Federation
Olenëk 115 E3 Respublika Sakha (Yakutiya), NE Russian Federation
Olenëk 115 E3 *river* NE Russian Federation
Oléron, Île d' 91 A5 *island* W France
Olevs'k 108 D1 *Rus.* Olevsk. Zhytomyrs'ka Oblast', N Ukraine
Ölgiy 126 C2 Bayan-Ölgiy, W Mongolia
Olhão 92 B5 Faro, S Portugal
Olifa 78 B3 Kunene, NW Namibia
Ólimbos *see* Ólympos
Olimpo *see* Fuerte Olimpo
Oliva 93 F4 País Valenciano, E Spain
Olivet 90 C4 Loiret, C France
Olmaliq 123 E2 *Rus.* Almalyk. Toshkent Wiloyati, E Uzbekistan
Olomouc 99 C5 *Ger.* Olmütz, *Pol.* Ołomuniec. Olomoucký Kraj, E Czech Republic
Olonets 110 B3 Respublika Kareliya, NW Russian Federation
Olovyannaya 115 F4 Chitinskaya Oblast', S Russian Federation
Olpe 94 B4 Nordrhein-Westfalen, W Germany

Olsztyn *98 D2 Ger.* Allenstein. Warmińsko-Mazurskie, NE Poland
Olt *108 B5 var.* Oltul, *Ger.* Alt. *River* S Romania
Olteniţa *108 C5 prev. Eng.* Oltenitsa, *anc.* Constantiola. Călăraşi, SE Romania
Oltul *see* Olt
Olvera *92 D5* Andalucía, S Spain
Olympia *46 B2 state capital* Washington, NW USA
Olympic Mountains *46 A2 mountain range* Washington, NW USA
Ólympos *104 B4 var.* Ólimbos, *Eng.* Mount Olympus. *Mountain* N Greece
Olympus, Mount *see* Ólympos
Omagh *89 B5 Ir.* An Ómaigh. W Northern Ireland, UK
Omaha *45 F4* Nebraska, C USA
Oman *121 D6 Ar.* Salṭanat 'Umān; *prev.* Muscat and Oman. *Country* SW Asia

---

Oman 121

Official name Sultanate of Oman
Formation 1951
Capital Muscat
Population 2.5 million / 30 people per sq mile (12 people per sq km)
Total area 82,030 sq miles (212,460 sq km)
Languages Arabic, Baluchi
Religions Ibadhi Muslim 75%, other Muslim and Hindu 25%
Ethnic mix Arab 75%, Baluchi 15%, other 10%
Government Monarchy with Consultative Council
Currency Omani rial = 1,000 baizas
Literacy rate 67%
Calorie consumption 3,013 kilocalories

Oman, Gulf of *120 E4 Ar.* Khalīj 'Umān. *Gulf* N Arabian Sea
Omboué *77 A6* Ogooué-Maritime, W Gabon
Omdurman *72 B4 var.* Umm Durmān. Khartoum, C Sudan
Ometepe, Isla de *52 D4 island* S Nicaragua
Ommen *86 E3* Overijssel, E Netherlands
Omsk *114 C4* Omskaya Oblast', C Russian Federation
Ōmuta *131 A7* Fukuoka, Kyūshū, SW Japan
Onda *93 F3* País Valenciano, E Spain
Ondjiva *see* N'Giva
Öndörhaan *127 E2* Hentiy, E Mongolia
Onega *110 B4 river* NW Russian Federation
Onega *110 C3* Arkhangel'skaya Oblast', NW Russian Federation
Onega, Lake *see* Onezhskoye Ozero
Onex *95 A7* Genève, SW Switzerland
Onezhskoye Ozero *110 B4 Eng.* Lake Onega. *Lake* NW Russian Federation
Ongole *132 D1* Andhra Pradesh, E India
Onitsha *75 G5* Anambra, S Nigeria
Onon Gol *127 E2 river* N Mongolia
Ononte *see* Orantes
Onslow *146 A4* Western Australia
Onslow Bay *43 F1 bay* North Carolina, E USA
Ontario *38 B3 province* S Canada
Ontario, Lake *41 E3 lake* Canada/USA
Onteniente *see* Ontinyent
Ontinyent *93 F4 var.* Onteniente. País Valenciano, E Spain
Ontong Java Rise *125 H4 undersea feature* W Pacific Ocean
Oostakker *87 B5* Oost-Vlaanderen, NW Belgium

Oostburg *87 B5* Zeeland, SW Netherlands
Oostende *87 A5 Eng.* Ostend, *Fr.* Ostende. West-Vlaanderen, NW Belgium
Oosterbeek *86 D4* Gelderland, SE Netherlands
Oosterhout *86 C4* Noord-Brabant, S Netherlands
Opatija *100 A2 It.* Abbazia. Primorje-Gorski Kotar, NW Croatia
Opava *99 C5 Ger.* Troppau. Ostravský Kraj, E Czech Republic
Opelika *42 D2* Alabama, S USA
Opelousas *42 B3* Louisiana, S USA
Opmeer *86 C2* Noord-Holland, NW Netherlands
Opochka *110 A4* Pskovskaya Oblast', W Russian Federation
Opole *98 C4 Ger.* Oppeln. Opolskie, S Poland
Opotiki *150 E3* Bay of Plenty, North Island, NZ
Oppidum Ubiorum *see* Köln
Oqtosh *123 E2 Rus.* Aktash. Samarqand Wiloyati, C Uzbekistan
Oradea *108 B3 prev.* Oradea Mare, *Ger.* Grosswardein, *Hung.* Nagyvárad. Bihor, NW Romania
Orahovac *101 D5 Alb.* Rahovec. Serbia, S Yugoslavia
Oran *70 D2 var.* Ouahran, Wahran. NW Algeria
Orange *91 D6 anc.* Arausio. Vaucluse, SE France
Orange *149 D6* New South Wales, SE Australia
Orangeburg *43 E2* South Carolina, SE USA
Orange Cone *see* Orange Fan
Orange Fan *69 C7 var.* Orange Cone. *Undersea feature* SW Indian Ocean
Orange Mouth *see* Oranjemund
Orangemund *see* Oranjemund
Orange River *78 B4 Afr.* Oranjerivier. *River* S Africa
Orange Walk *52 C1* Orange Walk, N Belize
Oranienburg *94 D3* Brandenburg, NE Germany
Oranjemund *78 B4 var.* Orangemund; *prev.* Orange Mouth. Karas, SW Namibia
Oranjestad *55 E5 dependent territory capital* (Aruba) W Aruba
Orantes *118 B3 var.* Ononte, *Ar.* Nahr el Aassi, Nahr al 'Aṣī. *River* SW Asia
Oraviţa *108 A4 Ger.* Orawitza, *Hung.* Oravicabánya. Caraş-Severin, SW Romania
Orbetello *96 B4* Toscana, C Italy
Orcadas *154 A1 Argentinian research station* South Orkney Islands, Antarctica
Orchard Homes *44 B1* Montana, NW USA
Ordino *91 A8* NW Andorra
Ordos Desert *see* Mu Us Shamo
Ordu *116 D2 anc.* Cotyora. Ordu, N Turkey
Ordzhonikidze *109 F3* Dnipropetrovs'ka Oblast', E Ukraine
Orealla *59 G3* E Guyana
Örebro *85 C6* Örebro, C Sweden
Oregon *46 B3 off.* State of Oregon; also known as Beaver State, Sunset State, Valentine State, Webfoot State. *State* NW USA
Oregon City *46 B3* Oregon, NW USA
Orël *111 B5* Orlovskaya Oblast', W Russian Federation
Orem *44 B4* Utah, W USA
Orenburg *111 D6 prev.* Chkalov. Orenburgskaya Oblast', W Russian Federation
Orense *see* Ourense
Oreor *144 A2 var.* Koror. *Country capital* (Palau) Oreor, N Palau
Orestiáda *104 D3 prev.* Orestiás. Anatolikí Makedonía kai Thráki, NE Greece
Organ Peak *48 D3 mountain* New Mexico, SW USA

Orgeyev *see* Orhei
Orhei *108 D3 var.* Orheiu, *Rus.* Orgeyev. N Moldova
Orheiu *see* Orhei
Oriental, Cordillera *60 D3 mountain range* Bolivia/Peru
Oriental, Cordillera *61 F4 mountain range* C Bolivia
Oriental, Cordillera *58 B3 mountain range* C Colombia
Orihuela *93 F4* País Valenciano, E Spain
Orikhiv *109 G3 Rus.* Orekhov. Zaporiz'ka Oblast', SE Ukraine
Orinoco, Río *59 E2 river* Colombia/Venezuela
Orissa *135 F4 state* NE India
Orissaare *106 C2 Ger.* Orissaar. Saaremaa, W Estonia
Oristano *97 A5* Sardegna, Italy, C Mediterranean Sea
Orito *58 A4* Putumayo, SW Colombia
Orizaba, Volcán Pico de *35 C7 var.* Citlaltépetl. *Mountain* S Mexico
Orkney *see* Orkney Islands
Orkney Islands *88 C2 var.* Orkney, Orkneys. *Island group* N Scotland, UK
Orkneys *see* Orkney Islands
Orlando *43 E4* Florida, SE USA
Orléanais *90 C4 cultural region* C France
Orléans *90 C4 anc.* Aurelianum. Loiret, C France
Orléansville *see* Chlef
Orly *90 E2 international airport* (Paris) Essonne, N France
Orlya *107 B6 Rus.* Orlya. Hrodzyenskaya Voblasts', W Belarus
Ormuz, Strait of *see* Hormuz, Strait of
Örnsköldsvik *85 C5* Västernorrland, C Sweden
Oromocto *39 F4* New Brunswick, SE Canada
Orona *145 F3 prev.* Hull Island. *Atoll* Phoenix Islands, C Kiribati
Orosirá Rodhópis *see* Rhodope Mountains
Orpington *89 B8* SE England, UK
Orsha *107 E6 Rus.* Orsha. Vitsyebskaya Voblasts', NE Belarus
Orsk *114 B4* Orenburgskaya Oblast', W Russian Federation
Orşova *108 A4 Ger.* Orschowa, *Hung.* Orsova. Mehedinţi, SW Romania
Orthez *91 B6* Pyrénées-Atlantiques, SW France
Ortona *96 D4* Abruzzo, C Italy
Oruba *see* Aruba
Oruro *61 F4* Oruro, W Bolivia
Ōsaka *131 C6 hist.* Naniwa. Ōsaka, Honshū, SW Japan
Osa, Península de *53 E5 peninsula* S Costa Rica
Osborn Plateau *141 D5 undersea feature* E Indian Ocean
Osh *123 F2* Oshskaya Oblast', SW Kyrgyzstan
Oshawa *38 D5* Ontario, SE Canada
Oshikango *78 B3* Ohangwena, N Namibia
Ō-shima *131 D6 island* S Japan
Oshkosh *40 B2* Wisconsin, N USA
Osijek *100 C3 prev.* Osiek, Osjek, *Ger.* Esseg, *Hung.* Eszék. Osijek-Baranja, E Croatia
Oskaloosa *45 G4* Iowa, C USA
Oskarshamn *85 C7* Kalmar, S Sweden
Oskil *109 G2 Rus.* Oskol. *River* Russian Federation/Ukraine
Oslo *85 B6 prev.* Christiania, Kristiania. *Country capital* (Norway) Oslo, S Norway
Osmaniye *116 D4* Osmaniye, admin. region *province* S Turkey
Osnabrück *94 A3* Niedersachsen, NW Germany
Osogov Mountains *120 B3 var.* Osogovske Planine, Osogovski Planina, *Mac.* Osogovski Planini. *mountain range* Bulgaria/FYR, Macedonia

Osogovske Planine/Osogovski Planina/Osogovski Planini *see* Osogov Mountains
Osorno *65 B5* Los Lagos, C Chile
Oss *86 D4* Noord-Brabant, S Netherlands
Ossa, Serra d' *92 C4 mountain range* SE Portugal
Ossora *115 H2* Koryakskiy Avtonomnyy Okrug, E Russian Federation
Ostend *see* Oostende
Ostende *see* Oostende
Oster *109 E1* Chernihivs'ka Oblast', N Ukraine
Östersund *85 C5* Jämtland, C Sweden
Ostfriesische Inseln *94 A3 Eng.* East Frisian Islands. *Island group* NW Germany
Ostiglia *96 C2* Lombardia, N Italy
Ostrava *99 C5* Ostravský Kraj, E Czech Republic
Ostróda *98 D3 Ger.* Osterode. Osterode in Ostpreussen. Warmińsko-Mazurskie, NE Poland
Ostrołęka *98 D3 Ger.* Wiesenhof, *Rus.* Ostrolenka. Mazowieckie, C Poland
Ostrov *110 A4 Latv.* Austrava. Karlovarský Kraj, W Czech Republic
Ostrovets *see* Ostrowiec Świętokrzyski
Ostrów *see* Ostrów Wielkopolski
Ostrowiec *see* Ostrowiec Świętokrzyski
Ostrowiec Świętokrzyski *98 D4 var.* Ostrowiec, *Rus.* Ostrovets. Świętokrzyskie, C Poland
Ostrów Mazowiecka *98 D3 var.* Ostrów Mazowiecki. Mazowieckie, C Poland
Ostrów Mazowiecki *see* Ostrów Mazowiecka
Ostrowo *see* Ostrów Wielkopolski
Ostrów Wielkopolski *98 C4 var.* Ostrów, *Ger.* Ostrowo. Wielkopolskie, C Poland
Osum *see* Osumit, Lumi i
Ōsumi-shotō *131 A8 island group* SW Japan
Osumit, Lumi i *101 D7 var.* Osum. *River* SE Albania
Osuna *92 D4* Andalucía, S Spain
Oswego *41 F2* New York, NE USA
Otago Peninsula *151 B7 peninsula* South Island, NZ
Otaki *150 D4* Wellington, North Island, NZ
Otaru *130 C2* Hokkaidō, NE Japan
Otavalo *60 B1* Imbabura, N Ecuador
Otavi *78 B3* Otjozondjupa, N Namibia
Oţelu Roşu *108 B4 Ger.* Ferdinandsberg, *Hung.* Nándorhgy. Caras-Severin, SW Romania
Otepää *106 D3 Ger.* Odenpäh. Valgamaa, SE Estonia
Oti *75 E4 river* W Africa
Otira *151 C6* West Coast, South Island, NZ
Otjiwarongo *78 B3* Otjozondjupa, N Namibia
Otorohanga *150 D3* Waikato, North Island, NZ
Otranto, Strait of *101 C6 It.* Canale d'Otranto. *Strait* Albania/Italy
Otrokovice *99 C5 Ger.* Otrokowitz. Zlínský Kraj, E Czech Republic
Ōtsu *131 C6 var.* Ôtu. Shiga, Honshū, SW Japan
Ottawa *41 F4* Outaouais. Admin. region *river* Ontario/Québec, SE Canada
Ottawa *38 D5 country capital* (Canada) Ontario, SE Canada
Ottawa *40 B3* Illinois, N USA
Ottawa *45 F5* Kansas, C USA
Ottawa Islands *38 C1 island group* Northwest Territories, C Canada
Ottignies *87 C6* Wallon Brabant, C Belgium
Ottumwa *45 G4* Iowa, C USA
Ôtu *see* Ōtsu

Ouachita Mountains *42 A1*
mountain range
Arkansas/Oklahoma, C USA
Ouachita River *42 B2 river*
Arkansas/Louisiana, C USA
Ouadi Howa *see* Howar, Wâdi
Ouagadougou *75 E4 var.*
Wagadugu. *Country capital*
(Burkina Faso) C Burkina Faso
Ouahigouya *75 E3* NW Burkina
faso
Ouahran *see* Oran
Oualata *see* Oualâta
Oualâta *74 D3 var.* Oualata. Hodh
ech Chargui, SE Mauritania
Ouanary *59 H3* E French Guiana
Ouanda Djallé *76 D4* Vakaga,
NE Central African Republic
Ouarâne *74 D2 desert* C Mauritania
Ouargla *71 E2 var.* Wargla.
NE Algeria
Ouarzazate *70 C3* S Morocco
Oubangui *see* Ubangi
Oubangui-Chari *see* Central
African Republic
Ouessant, Île d' *90 A3 Eng.* Ushant.
Island NW France
Ouésso *77 B5* La Sangha,
NW Congo
Oujda *70 D2 Ar.* Oudjda, Ujda.
NE Morocco
Oujeft *74 C2* Adrar, C Mauritania
Oulu *84 D4 Swe.* Uleåborg. Oulu,
C Finland
Oulujärvi *84 D4 Swe.* Uleträsk. *Lake*
C Finland
Oulujoki *84 D4 Swe.* Uleälv. *River*
C Finland
Ounasjoki *84 D3 river* N Finland
Ounianga Kébir *76 C2* Borkou-
Ennedi-Tibesti, N Chad
Oup *see* Auob
Oupeye *87 D6* Liège, E Belgium
Our *87 D6 river* NW Europe
Ourense *92 C1 var. Cast.* Orense;
Lat. Aurium. Galicia, NW Spain
Ourique *92 B4* Beja, S Portugal
Ourthe *87 D7 river* E Belgium
Ouse *89 D5 river* N England, UK
Outer Hebrides *88 B3 var.* Western
Isles. *Island group* NW Scotland,
UK
Outer Islands *79 G1 island group*
SW Seychelles
Outes *92 B1* Galicia, NW Spain
Ouvéa *144 D5 island* Îles Loyauté,
NE New Caledonia
Ouyen *149 C6* Victoria, SE Australia
Ovalle *64 B3* Coquimbo, N Chile
Ovar *92 B2* Aveiro, N Portugal
Overflakkee *86 B4 island*
SW Netherlands
Overijse *87 C6* Vlaams Brabant,
C Belgium
Oviedo *92 C1 anc.* Asturias.
Asturias, NW Spain
Ovruch *108 D1* Zhytomyrs'ka
Oblast', N Ukraine
Owando *77 B5 prev.* Fort-Rousset.
Cuvette, C Congo
Owase *131 C6* Mie, Honshū,
SW Japan
Owatonna *45 F3* Minnesota, N USA
Owen Fracture Zone *140 B4 tectonic
feature* W Arabian Sea
Owen, Mount *151 C5 mountain*
South Island, NZ
Owensboro *40 B5* Kentucky, S USA
Owen Stanley Range *144 B3*
mountain range S PNG
Owerri *75 G5* Imo, S Nigeria
Owo *75 F5* Ondo, SW Nigeria
Owyhee River *46 C4 river*
Idaho/Oregon, NW USA
Oxford *89 D6 Lat.* Oxonia.
S England, UK
Oxford *151 C6* Canterbury, South
Island, NZ
Oxkutzcab *51 H4* Yucatán,
SE Mexico
Oxnard *47 B7* California, W USA
Oyama *131 D5* Tochigi, Honshū,
S Japan
Oyem *77 B5* Woleu-Ntem, N Gabon
Oyo *77 B6* Cuvette, C Congo
Oyo *75 F4* Oyo, W Nigeria
Ozark *42 D3* Alabama, S USA

Ozark Plateau *45 G5 plain*
Arkansas/Missouri, C USA
Ozarks, Lake of the *45 F5 reservoir*
Missouri, C USA
Ozbourn Seamount *152 D4*
undersea feature W Pacific Ocean
Ózd *99 D6* Borsod-Abaúj-Zemplén,
NE Hungary
Ozero Khanka *see* Khanka, Lake
Ozero Ubsu-Nur *see* Uvs Nuur
Ozieri *97 A5* Sardegna, Italy,
C Mediterranean Sea

P

Paamiut *82 B4 var.* Pâmiut, *Dan.*
Frederikshåb. S Greenland
Pa-an *136 B4* Karen State, S Myanmar
Pabianice *98 C4* Lodz, C Poland
Pabna *135 G4* Rajshahi,
W Bangladesh
Pachuca *51 E4 var.* Pachuca de Soto.
Hidalgo, C Mexico
Pachuca de Soto *see* Pachuca
Pacific-Antarctic Ridge *154 B5*
undersea feature S Pacific Ocean
Pacific Ocean *152 D3 ocean*
Padalung *see* Phatthalung
Padang *138 B4* Sumatera,
W Indonesia
Paderborn *94 B4* Nordrhein-
Westfalen, NW Germany
Padma *see* Brahmaputra
Padova *96 C2 Eng.* Padua; *anc.*
Patavium. Veneto, NE Italy
Padre Island *49 G5 island* Texas,
SW USA
Padua *see* Padova
Paducah *40 B5* Kentucky, S USA
Paeroa *150 D3* Waikato, North
Island, NZ
Páfos *102 C5 var.* Paphos. W Cyprus
Pag *100 A3 It.* Pago. *Island* Zadar
SW Croatia
Page *48 B1* Arizona, SW USA
Pago Pago *145 F4 dependent territory
capital* (American Samoa) Tuituila,
W American Samoa
Pahiatua *150 D4* Manawatu-
Wanganui, North Island, NZ
Pahsien *see* Chongqing
Paide *106 D2 Ger.* Weissenstein.
Järvamaa, N Estonia
Paihia *150 D2* Northland, North
Island, NZ
Päijänne *85 D5 lake* S Finland
Paine, Cerro *65 A7 mountain* S Chile
Painted Desert *48 B1 desert*
Arizona, SW USA
Paisley *88 C4* W Scotland, UK
País Valenciano *93 F3 cultural region*
NE Spain
País Vasco *93 E1 cultural region*
N Spain
Paita *60 B3* Piura, NW Peru
Pakanbaru *see* Pekanbaru
Pakaraima Mountains *59 E3 var.*
Serra Pacaraim, Sierra Pacaraima.
Mountain range N South America
Pakistan *134 A2 var.* Islami
Jamhuriya e Pakistan. *Country* S Asia

Pakistan 134

Official name Islamic Republic of
Pakistan
Formation 1947
Capital Islamabad
Population 156.5 million /
526 people per sq mile
(203 people per sq km)
Total area 297,636 sq miles
(770,880 sq km)
Languages Urdu, Punjabi, Sindhi
Religions Sunni Muslim 77%,
Shi'a Muslim 29%, Hindu 2%,
Christian 1%
Ethnic mix Punjabi 50%, Sindhi
15%, Pashto 15%, Mohajir 8%,
other 12%
Government Multiparty republic
Currency Pakistani rupee
= 100 paisa
Literacy rate 41%
Calorie consumption 2,315
kilocalories

Paknam *see* Samut Prakan
Pakokku *136 A3* Magwe,
C Myanmar
Pak Phanang *137 C7 var.* Ban Pak
Phanang. Nakhon Si Thammarat,
SW Thailand
Pakruojis *106 C4* Pakruojis,
N Lithuania
Paks *99 C7* Tolna, S Hungary
Paksé *see* Pakxé
Pakxé *137 D5 var.* Paksé.
Champasak, S Laos
Palafrugell *93 G2* Cataluña,
NE Spain
Palagruža *101 B5 It.* Pelagosa. *Island*
SW Croatia
Palaiá Epídavros *105 C6*
Pelopónnisos, S Greece
Palaiseau *90 D2* Essonne,
N France
Palamós *93 G2* Cataluña, NE Spain
Palamuse *106 E2 Ger.* Sankt-
Bartholomäi. Jõgevamaa,
E Estonia
Pālanpur *134 C4* Gujarāt, W India
Palapye *78 D3* Central,
SE Botswana
Palau *144 A2 var.* Belau. *Country*
W Pacific Ocean

Palau 144

Official name Republic of Palau
Formation 1994
Capital Koror
Population 18,500 million /
94 people per sq mile
(36 people per sq km)
Total area 196 sq miles
(508 sq km)
Languages Belauan (Palauan),
English, Japanese
Religions Roman Catholic 66%,
Modekngei 34%
Ethnic mix Polynesian 96%,
other 4%
Government Multiparty republic
Currency US dollar = 100 cents
Literacy rate 92%
Calorie consumption
not available

Palawan *139 E2 island*
W Philippines
Palawan Passage *138 D2 passage*
W Philippines
Paldiski *106 D2 prev.* Baltiski, *Eng.*
Baltic Port, *Ger.* Baltischport.
Harjumaa, NW Estonia
Palembang *138 B4* Sumatera,
W Indonesia
Palencia *92 D2 anc.* Palantia,
Pallantia. Castilla-León,
NW Spain
Palermo *97 C7 Fr.* Palerme; *anc.*
Panhormus, Panormus. Sicilia,
Italy, C Mediterranean Sea
Pāli *134 C3* Rājasthān, N India
Palikir *144 C2 country capital*
(Micronesia) Pohnpei,
E Micronesia
Palimé *see* Kpalimé
Palioúri, Akrotírio *104 C4 var.*
Akra Kanestron. *Headland*
NE Greece
Palk Strait *132 C3 strait* India/Sri
Lanka
Palliser, Cape *151 D5 headland*
North Island, NZ
Palma *93 G3 var.* Palma de
Mallorca. Mallorca, Spain,
W Mediterranean Sea
Palma del Río *92 D4* Andalucía,
S Spain
Palma de Mallorca *see* Palma
Palmar Sur *53 E5* Puntarenas,
SE Costa Rica
Palma Soriano *54 C3* Santiago de
Cuba, E Cuba
Palm Beach *148 E1* New South
Wales, SE Australia
Palmer *154 A2 US research station*
Antarctica
Palmer Land *154 A3 physical region*
Antarctica
Palmerston *145 F4 island* S Cook
Islands

Palmerston North *150 D4*
Manawatu-Wanganui, North
Island, NZ
Palmi *97 D7* Calabria, SW Italy
Palmira *58 B3* Valle del Cauca,
W Colombia
Palm Springs *47 D7* California,
W USA
Palmyra *see* Tudmur
Palmyra Atoll *145 G2 US privately
owned unincorporated territory*
C Pacific Ocean
Palo Alto *47 B6* California, W USA
Palu *139 E4 prev.* Paloe. Sulawesi,
C Indonesia
Pamiers *91 B6* Ariège, S France
Pamir *var.* Daryā-ye Pāmīr, *Taj.*
Dar″yoi Pomir. *River*
Afghanistan/Tajikistan *see also*
Pāmīr, Daryā-ye
Pamirs *123 F3 Pash.* Daryā-ye
Pāmīr, *Rus.* Pamir. *Mountain range*
C Asia
Pâmiut *see* Paamiut
Pamlico Sound *43 G1 sound* North
Carolina, SE USA
Pampa *49 E1* Texas, SW USA
Pampas *64 C4 plain* C Argentina
Pamplona *59 E1* Norte de
Santander, N Colombia
Pamplona *58 C2* Norte de
Santander, N Colombia
Panaji *132 B1 var.* Pangim, Panjim,
New Goa. Goa, W India
Panama *53 G5 Country* Central
America

Panama 53

Official name Republic of Panama
Formation 1903
Capital Panama City
Population 3 million /
99 people per sq mile
(38 people per sq km)
Total area 29,339 sq miles
(75,990 sq km)
Languages Spanish, English
Creole, Amerindian languages,
Chibchan
Religions Roman Catholic 93%,
other 7%
Ethnic mix Mestizo 60%, White
14%, Black 12%, Amerindian 8%,
Asian 4%, other 2%
Government Multiparty republic
Currency Balboa = 100 centesimos
Literacy rate 91%
Calorie consumption 2,242
kilocalories

Panamá *53 G4 var.* Ciudad de
Panamá, *Eng.* Panama City.
Country capital (Panama) Panamá,
C Panama
Panama Basin *35 C8 undersea feature*
E Pacific Ocean
Panama Canal *53 F4 canal* E Panama
Panama City *see* Panamá
Panama City *42 D3* Florida, SE USA
Panamá, Golfo de *53 G5 var.* Gulf
of Panama. *Gulf* S Panama
Panama, Gulf of *see* Panamá, Golfo
de
Panama, Isthmus of *see* Panamá,
Istmo de
Panamá, Istmo de *53 G4 Eng.*
Isthmus of Panama; *prev.* Isthmus
of Darien. *Isthmus* E Panama
Panay Island *139 E2 island*
C Philippines
Pančevo *100 D3 Ger.* Pantschowa,
Hung. Pancsova. Serbia,
N Yugoslavia
Paneas *see* Bāniyās
Panevėžys *106 C4* Panevėžys,
C Lithuania
Pangim *see* Panaji
Pangkalpinang *138 C4* Pulau
Bangka, W Indonesia
Pang-Nga *see* Phang-Nga
Panjim *see* Panaji
Pánormos *105 C7* Kríti, Greece,
E Mediterranean Sea
Pantanal *63 E3 var.* Pantanalmato-
Grossense. *Swamp* SW Brazil

Pantanalmato-Grossense *see* Pantanal
Pantelleria, Isola di *97 B7 island* SW Italy
Pánuco *51 E3* Veracruz-Llave, E Mexico
Pao-chi *see* Baoji
Paoki *see* Baoji
Paola *102 B5* E Malta
Pao-shan *see* Baoshan
Pao-t'ou *see* Baotou
Paotow *see* Baotou
Papagayo, Golfo de *52 C4 gulf* NW Costa Rica
Papakura *150 D3* Auckland, North Island, NZ
Papantla *51 F4 var.* Papantla de Olarte. Veracruz-Llave, E Mexico
Papantla de Olarte *see* Papantla
Papeete *145 H4 dependent territory capital* (French Polynesia) Tahiti, W French Polynesia
Paphos *see* Páfos
Papilė *106 B3* Akmenė, NW Lithuania
Papillion *45 F4* Nebraska, C USA
Papua, Gulf of *144 B3 gulf* S PNG
Papua New Guinea *144 B3 prev.* Territory of Papua and New Guinea, *abbrev.* PNG. Country NW Melanesia

Papua New Guinea 144

Official name Independent State of Papua New Guinea
Formation 1975
Capital Port Moresby
Population 4.8 million / 27 people per sq mile (10 people per sq km)
Total area 174,849 sq miles (452,860 sq km)
Languages English, Pidgin English, Papuan, c.750 native languages
Religions Christian 62%, Traditional beliefs 34%, other 4%
Ethnic mix Papuan 85%, other 15%
Government Parliamentary democracy
Currency Kina = 100 toea
Literacy rate 73.7%
Calorie consumption 2,613 kilocalories

Papuk *100 C3 mountain range* NE Croatia
Pará *63 E2 off.* Estado do Pará. *State* NE Brazil
Pará *see* Belém
Paracel Islands *125 E3 disputed territory* SE Asia
Paracín *100 D4* Serbia, C Yugoslavia
Paragua, Río *59 E3 river* SE Venezuela
Paraguay *64 D2 var.* Río Paraguay. *River* C South America
Paraguay *64 C2 country* C South America

Paraguay 64

Official name Republic of Paraguay
Formation 1811
Capital Asunción
Population 5.5 million / 36 people per sq mile (14 people per sq km)
Total area 153,397 sq miles (397,300 sq km)
Languages Spanish, Guaraní
Religions Roman Catholic 90%, other 10%
Ethnic mix Mestizo 90%, Amerindian 2%, other 8%
Government Multiparty republic
Currency Guaraní = 100 centimos
Literacy rate 92.4%
Calorie consumption 2,670 kilocalories

Paraguay, Río *see* Paraguay

Paraíba *63 G2 off.* Estado da Paraíba; *prev.* Parahiba, Parahyba. *State* E Brazil
Parakou *75 F4* C Benin
Paramaribo *59 G3 country capital* (Suriname) Paramaribo, N Suriname
Paramushir, Ostrov *115 H3 island* SE Russian Federation
Paraná *63 E5 off.* Estado do Paraná. *State* S Brazil
Paraná *57 C4 var.* Alto Paraná. *River* C South America
Paraná *63 E4* Entre Ríos, E Argentina
Paranéstio *104 C3* Anatolikí Makedonía kai Thráki, NE Greece
Paraparaumu *151 D5* Wellington, North Island, NZ
Parchim *94 C3* Mecklenburg-Vorpommern, N Germany
Parczew *98 E4* Lubelskie, E Poland
Pardubice *99 B5 Ger.* Pardubitz. Pardubický Kraj, C Czech Republic
Parechcha *107 B5 Rus.* Porech'ye. Hrodzyenskaya Voblasts', NE Belarus
Parecis, Chapada dos *62 D3 var.* Serra dos Parecis. *Mountain range* W Brazil
Parepare *139 E4* Sulawesi, C Indonesia
Párga *105 A5* Ípeiros, W Greece
Paria, Golfo de *see* Paria, Gulf of
Paria, Gulf of *59 E1 var.* Golfo de Paria. *Gulf* Trinidad and Tobago/Venezuela
Parika *59 F2* NE Guyana
Paris *90 D1 anc.* Lutetia, Lutetia Parisiorum, Parisii. *Country capital* (France) Paris, N France
Paris *49 G2* Texas, SW USA
Parkersburg *40 D4* West Virginia, NE USA
Parkes *149 D6* New South Wales, SE Australia
Parma *96 B2* Emilia-Romagna, N Italy
Parnahyba *see* Parnaíba
Parnaíba *63 F2 var.* Parnahyba. Piauí, E Brazil
Pärnu *106 D2 Ger.* Pernau, *Latv.* Pērnava; *prev.* Rus. Pernov. Pärnumaa, SW Estonia
Pärnu *106 D2 var.* Parnu Jõgi, *Ger.* Pernau. *River* SW Estonia
Pärnu-Jaagupi *106 D2 Ger.* Sankt-Jakobi. Pärnumaa, SW Estonia
Parnu Jõgi *see* Pärnu
Pärnu Laht *106 D2 Ger.* Pernauer Bucht. *Bay* SW Estonia
Páros *105 C6 island* Kykládes, Greece, Aegean Sea
Páros *105 D6* Páros, Kykládes, Greece, Aegean Sea
Parral *see* Hidalgo del Parral
Parral *64 B4* Maule, C Chile
Parramatta *148 D1* New South Wales, SE Australia
Parras *50 D3 var.* Parras de la Fuente. Coahuila de Zaragoza, NE Mexico
Parras de la Fuente *see* Parras
Parsons *45 F5* Kansas, C USA
Pasadena *47 C7* California, W USA
Pasadena *49 H4* Texas, SW USA
Paşcani *108 C3 Hung.* Páskán. Iaşi, NE Romania
Pasco *46 C2* Washington, NW USA
Pas de Calais *see* Dover, Strait of
Pasewalk *94 D3* Mecklenburg-Vorpommern, NE Germany
Pasinler *117 F3* Erzurum, NE Turkey
Pasłęk *98 D2 Ger.* Preußisch Holland. Warmińsko-Mazurskie, NE Poland
Pasni *134 A3* Baluchistán, SW Pakistan
Paso de Indios *65 B6* Chubut, S Argentina
Passau *95 D6* Bayern, SE Germany
Passo del Brennero *see* Brenner Pass
Passo Fundo *63 E5* Rio Grande do Sul, S Brazil

Pastavy *107 C5 Pol.* Postawy, *Rus.* Postavy. Vitsyebskaya Voblasts', NW Belarus
Pastaza, Río *60 B2 river* Ecuador/Peru
Pasto *58 A4* Nariño, SW Colombia
Pasvalys *106 C4* Pasvalys, N Lithuania
Patagonia *57 B7 physical region* Argentina/Chile
Patalung *see* Phatthalung
Patani *see* Pattani
Patavium *see* Padova
Patea *150 D4* Taranaki, North Island, NZ
Paterson *41 F3* New Jersey, NE USA
Pathein *see* Bassein
Pátmos *105 D6 island* Dodekánisos, Greece, Aegean Sea
Patna *135 F3 var.* Azimabad. Bihār, N India
Patnos *117 F3* Ağrı, E Turkey
Patos, Lagoa dos *63 E5 lagoon* S Brazil
Pátra *105 B5 Eng.* Patras; *prev.* Pátrai. Dytikí Ellás, S Greece
Pattani *137 C7 var.* Patani. Pattani, SW Thailand
Pattaya *137 C5* Chon Buri, S Thailand
Patuca, Río *52 D2 river* E Honduras
Pau *91 B6* Pyrénées-Atlantiques, SW France
Paulatuk *37 E3* Northwest Territories, NW Canada
Paungde *136 B4* Pegu, C Myanmar
Pavia *96 B2 anc.* Ticinum. Lombardia, N Italy
Pāvilosta *106 B3* Liepāja, W Latvia
Pavlikeni *104 D2* Veliko Tūrnovo, N Bulgaria
Pavlodar *114 C4* Pavlodar, NE Kazakhstan
Pavlohrad *109 G3 Rus.* Pavlograd. Dnipropetrovs'ka Oblast', E Ukraine
Pawn *136 B3 river* C Myanmar
Paxoí *105 A5 island* Iónioi Nísoi, Greece, C Mediterranean Sea
Payo Obispo *see* Chetumal
Paysandú *64 D4* Paysandú, W Uruguay
Pazar *117 E2* Rize, NE Turkey
Pazardzhik *104 C3 prev.* Tatar Pazardzhik. Pazardzhik, C Bulgaria
Pearl River *42 B3 river* Louisiana/Mississippi, S USA
Pearsall *49 F4* Texas, SW USA
Peć *101 D5 Alb.* Pejë, *Turk.* Ipek. Serbia, S Yugoslavia
Pechora *110 D3 river* NW Russian Federation
Pechora *110 D3* Respublika Komi, NW Russian Federation
Pechorskoye More *110 D2 Eng.* Pechora Sea. *Sea* NW Russian Federation
Pecos *49 E3* Texas, SW USA
Pecos River *49 E3 river* New Mexico/Texas, SW USA
Pécs *99 C7 Ger.* Fünfkirchen; *Lat.* Sopianae. Baranya, SW Hungary
Pedra Lume *74 A3* Sal, NE Cape Verde
Pedro Cays *54 C3 island group* S Jamaica
Pedro Juan Caballero *64 D2* Amambay, E Paraguay
Peer *87 D5* Limburg, NE Belgium
Pegasus Bay *151 C6 bay* South Island, NZ
Pegu *136 B4 var.* Bago. Pegu, SW Myanmar
Pehuajó *64 C4* Buenos Aires, E Argentina
Pei-ching *see* Beijing
Peine *94 B3* Niedersachsen, C Germany
Pei-p'ing *see* Beijing
Peipus, Lake *83 Est.* Peipsi Järv, *Ger.* Peipus-See, *Rus.* Chudskoye Ozero. *Lake* Estonia/Russian Federation
Peiraiás *105 C6 prev.* Piraiévs, *Eng.* Piraeus. Attikí, C Greece

Pèk *136 D4 var.* Xieng Khouang; *prev.* Xiangkhoang. Xiangkhoang, N Laos
Pekalongan *138 C4* Jawa, C Indonesia
Pekanbaru *138 B3 var.* Pakanbaru. Sumatera, W Indonesia
Pekin *40 B4* Illinois, N USA
Peking *see* Beijing
Pelagie, Isole *97 B8 island group* SW Italy
Pelly Bay *37 G3* Nunavut, N Canada
Peloponnese *see* Pelopónnisos
Peloponnesus *see* Pelopónnisos
Pelopónnisos *105 B6 var.* Morea, *Eng.* Peloponnese; *anc.* Peloponnesus. *Peninsula* S Greece
Pematangsiantar *138 B3* Sumatera, W Indonesia
Pemba *79 F2 prev.* Port Amelia, Porto Amélia. Cabo Delgado, NE Mozambique
Pemba *73 D7 island* E Tanzania
Pembroke *38 D4* Ontario, SE Canada
Penang *see* George Town
Penang *see* Pinang, Pulau
Penas, Golfo de *65 A7 gulf* S Chile
Penderma *see* Bandırma
Pendleton *46 C3* Oregon, NW USA
Pend Oreille, Lake *46 D2 lake* Idaho, NW USA
Peneius *see* Pineiós
Peng-pu *see* Bengbu
Peniche *92 B3* Leiria, W Portugal
Péninsule de la Gaspésie *see* Gaspé, Péninsule de
Pennine Alps *95 A8 Fr.* Alpes Pennines, *It.* Alpi Pennine; *Lat.* Alpes Penninae. *Mountain range* Italy/Switzerland
Pennine Chain *see* Pennines
Pennines *89 D5 var.* Pennine Chain. *Mountain range* N England, UK
Pennsylvania *40 D3 off.* Commonwealth of Pennsylvania; *also known as* The Keystone State. *State* NE USA
Penobscot River *41 G2 river* Maine, NE USA
Penong *149 A6* South Australia
Penonomé *53 F5* Coclé, C Panama
Penrhyn *145 G3 atoll* N Cook Islands
Penrhyn Basin *143 F3 undersea feature* C Pacific Ocean
Penrith *148 D1* New South Wales, SE Australia
Penrith *89 D5* NW England, UK
Pensacola *42 C3* Florida, SE USA
Pentecost *144 D4 Fr.* Pentecôte. *Island* C Vanuatu
Penza *111 C6* Penzenskaya Oblast', W Russian Federation
Penzance *89 C7* SW England, UK
Peoria *40 B4* Illinois, N USA
Perchtoldsdorf *95 E6* Niederösterreich, NE Austria
Percival Lakes *146 C4 lakes* Western Australia
Perdido, Monte *93 F1 mountain* NE Spain
Perece Vela Basin *see* West Mariana Basin
Pereira *58 B3* Risaralda, W Colombia
Pergamino *64 C4* Buenos Aires, E Argentina
Périgueux *91 C5 anc.* Vesuna. Dordogne, SW France
Perito Moreno *65 B6* Santa Cruz, S Argentina
Perlas, Archipiélago de las *53 G5 Eng.* Pearl Islands. *Island group* SE Panama
Perlas, Laguna de *53 E3 Eng.* Pearl Lagoon. *Lagoon* E Nicaragua
Perleberg *94 C3* Brandenburg, N Germany
Perm' *114 C3 prev.* Molotov. Permskaya Oblast', NW Russian Federation
Pernambuco *63 G2 off.* Estado de Pernambuco. *State* E Brazil
Pernambuco Abyssal Plain *see* Pernambuco Plain

Pernambuco Plain 67 C5 var.
Pernambuco Abyssal Plain.
Undersea feature E Atlantic Ocean
Pernau see Pärnu
Pernik 104 B2 prev. Dimitrovo.
Pernik, W Bulgaria
Perote 51 F4 Veracruz-Llave,
E Mexico
Perovsk see Kyzylorda
Perpignan 91 C6 Pyrénées-
Orientales, S France
Perryton 49 F1 Texas, SW USA
Perryville 45 H5 Missouri, C USA
Persian Gulf see Gulf, The
Perth 147 A6 state capital Western
Australia
Perth 88 C4 C Scotland, UK
Perth Basin 141 E6 undersea feature
SE Indian Ocean
Peru 60 C3 Country W South America

Peru 60

Official name Republic of Peru
Formation 1824
Capital Lima
Population 27.9 million /
52 people per sq mile
(20 people per sq km)
Total area 494,208 sq miles
(1,280,000 sq km)
Languages Spanish, Quechua,
Aymará
Religions Roman Catholic 95%,
other 5%
Ethnic mix Amerindian 54%,
Mestizo 32%, White 12%, other 2%
Government Multiparty republic
Currency New sol = 100 centimos
Literacy rate 88.7%
Calorie consumption 1,882
kilocalories

Peru see Beru
Peru Basin 67 A5 undersea feature
E Pacific Ocean
Peru-Chile Trench 56 A4 undersea
feature E Pacific Ocean
Perugia 96 C4 Fr. Pérouse; anc.
Perusia. Umbria, C Italy
Péruwelz 87 B6 Hainaut,
SW Belgium
Pervomays'k 109 E3 prev.
Ol'viopol'. Mykolayivs'ka Oblast',
S Ukraine
Pervyy Kuril'skiy Proliv 115 H3
strait E Russian Federation
Pesaro 96 C3 anc. Pisaurum.
Marche, C Italy
Pescara 96 D4 anc. Aternum, Ostia
Aterni. Abruzzo, C Italy
Peshāwar 134 C1 North-West
Frontier Province, N Pakistan
Peshkopi 101 C4 var. Peshkopia,
Peshkopija. Dibër, NE Albania
Peshkopia see Peshkopi
Peshkopija see Peshkopi
Peski Karakumy see Garagumy
Pessac 91 B5 Gironde, SW France
Petach-Tikva see Petaḥ Tiqwa
Petaḥ Tiqwa see Petaḥ Tiqwa
Petaḥ Tiqwa 119 A6 var. Petach-
Tikva, Petah Tiqva, Petakh Tikva.
Tel Aviv, C Israel
Petakh Tikva see Petaḥ Tiqwa
Pétange 87 D8 Luxembourg,
SW Luxembourg
Petchaburi see Phetchaburi
Peterborough 89 E6 prev.
Medeshamstede. E England, UK
Peterborough 38 D3 Ontario,
SE Canada
Peterborough 149 B6 South
Australia
Peterhead 88 D3 NE Scotland, UK
Peter I Island 154 A3 Norwegian
dependency Antarctica
Petermann Bjerg 83 E3 mountain
C Greenland
Petersburg 41 E5 Virginia, NE USA
Peters Mine 59 F3 var. Peter's Mine.
N Guyana
Peto 51 H4 Yucatán, SE Mexico
Petoskey 40 C2 Michigan, N USA
Petra see Wādī Mūsā
Petrich 104 C3 Blagoevgrad,
SW Bulgaria

Petrinja 100 B3 Sisak-Moslavina,
C Croatia
Petrodvorets 110 A4 Fin. Pietarhovi.
Leningradskaya Oblast',
NW Russian Federation
Petrograd see Sankt-Peterburg
Petropavlovsk 114 C4 Kaz.
Petropavl. Severnyy Kazakhstan,
N Kazakhstan
Petropavlovsk-Kamchatskiy 115
H3 Kamchatskaya Oblast',
E Russian Federation
Petroşani 108 B4 var. Petroşeni, Ger.
Petroschen, Hung. Petrozsény.
Hunedoara, W Romania
Petroschen see Petroşani
Petroşeni see Petroşani
Petrozavodsk 114 B2 Fin. Petroskoi.
Respublika Kareliya, NW Russian
Federation
Petrozsény see Petroşani
Pevek 115 G1 Chukotskiy
Avtonomnyy Okrug, NE Russian
Federation
Pezinok 99 C6 Ger. Bösing, Hung.
Bazin. Bratislavský Kraj,
W Slovakia
Pforzheim 95 B6 Baden-
Württemberg, SW Germany
Pfungstadt 95 B5 Hessen,
W Germany
Phangan, Ko 137 C6 island
SW Thailand
Phang-Nga 137 B7 var. Pang-Nga,
Phangnga. Phangnga,
SW Thailand
Phangnga see Phang-Nga
Phanom Dang Raek see Dângrêk,
Chuŏr Phnum
Phanom Dong Rak see Dângrêk,
Chuŏr Phnum
Phan Rang see Phan Rang-Thap
Cham
Phan Rang-Thap Cham 137 E6 var.
Phanrang, Phan Rang, Phan Rang
Thap Cham. Ninh Thuận,
S Vietnam
Phan Thiết 137 E6 Bình Thuận,
S Vietnam
Pharnacia see Giresun
Phatthalung 137 C7 var. Padalung,
Patalung. Phatthalung,
SW Thailand
Phayao 136 C4 var. Muang Phayao.
Phayao, NW Thailand
Phenix City 42 D2 Alabama,
S USA
Phet Buri see Phetchaburi
Phetchaburi 137 C5 var. Bejraburi,
Petchaburi, Phet Buri.
Phetchaburi, SW Thailand
Philadelphia see 'Ammān
Philadelphia 41 F4 Pennsylvania,
NE USA
Philippine Basin 125 F3 undersea
feature W Pacific Ocean
Philippines 139 E1 Country SE Asia

Philippines 139

Official name Republic of the
Philippines
Formation 1946
Capital Manila
Population 76 million /
660 people per sq mile
(255 people per sq km)
Total area 115,123 sq miles
(298,170 sq km)
Languages Filipino, English,
Cebuano
Religions Roman Catholic 83%,
Protestant 9%, Muslim 5%,
other 3%
Ethnic mix Malay 50%, Indonesian
and Polynesian 30%, other 20%
Government Multiparty
republic
Currency Peso = 100 centavos
Literacy rate 94.6%
Calorie consumption 2,257
kilocalories

Philippines 139 E1 island group
W Pacific Ocean
Philippine Sea 125 F3 sea W Pacific
Ocean

Philippine Trench 142 A1 undersea
feature W Philippine Sea
Phitsanulok 136 C4 var. Bisnulok,
Muang Phitsanulok, Pitsanulok.
Phitsanulok, C Thailand
Phlórina see Flórina
Phnom Penh see Phnum Penh
Phnum Penh 137 D6 var. Phnom
Penh. Country capital (Cambodia)
Phnum Penh, S Cambodia
Phoenix 48 B2 state capital Arizona,
SW USA
Phoenix Islands 145 E3 island group
C Kiribati
Phôngsali 136 C3 var. Phong Saly.
Phôngsali, N Laos
Phong Saly see Phôngsali
Phrae 136 C4 var. Muang Phrae,
Prae. Phrae, NW Thailand
Phra Nakhon Si Ayutthaya see
Ayutthaya
Phra Thong, Ko 137 B6 island
SW Thailand
Phuket 137 B7 var. Bhuket, Puket,
Mal. Ujung Salang; prev.
Junkseylon, Salang. Phuket,
SW Thailand
Phuket, Ko 137 B7 island
SW Thailand
Phumĭ Kâmpóng Trâbêk 137 D5
Kâmpóng Chhnăng, C Cambodia
Phumĭ Sâmraông 137 D5 Poŭthĭsăt,
NW Cambodia
Phu Vinh see Tra Vinh
Piacenza 96 B2 Fr. Paisance; anc.
Placentia. Emilia-Romagna,
N Italy
Piatra-Neamţ 108 C4 Hung.
Karácsonkő. Neamţ, NE Romania
Piauí 63 F2 off. Estado do Piauí;
prev. Piauhy. State E Brazil
Picardie 90 C3 Eng. Picardy.
Cultural region N France
Pichilemu 64 B4 Libertador, C Chile
Pico 92 A5 var. Ilha do Pico. Island
Azores, Portugal, NE Atlantic
Ocean
Picos 63 F2 Piauí, E Brazil
Picton 151 C5 Marlborough, South
Island, NZ
Piedras Negras 51 E2 var. Ciudad
Porfirio Díaz. Coahuila de
Zaragoza, NE Mexico
Pielinen 84 E4 var. Pielisjärvi. Lake
E Finland
Pielisjärvi see Pielinen
Piemonte 96 A2 Eng. Piedmont.
Cultural region NW Italy
Pierre 45 E3 state capital South
Dakota, N USA
Piešťany 99 C6 Ger. Pistyan, Hung.
Pöstyén. Trnavský Kraj,
W Slovakia
Pietermaritzburg 78 C5 var.
Maritzburg. KwaZulu/Natal,
E South Africa
Pietersburg 78 D4 Northern,
NE South Africa
Pigs, Bay of see Cochinos, Bahía de
Pijijiapán 51 G5 Chiapas,
SE Mexico
Pikes Peak 44 C5 mountain
Colorado, C USA
Pikeville 40 D5 Kentucky, S USA
Pikinni see Bikini Atoll
Piła 98 B3 Ger. Schneidemühl.
Wielkopolskie, C Poland
Pilar 64 D3 var. Villa del Pilar.
Ñeembucú, S Paraguay
Pilcomayo 57 C5 river C South
America
Pilos see Pýlos
Pinang see George Town
Pinang, Pulau 138 B3 var. Penang,
Pinang; prev. Prince of Wales
Island. Island Peninsular Malaysia
Pinar del Río 54 A2 Pinar del Río,
W Cuba
Píndhos see Píndos
Píndhos Óros see Píndos
Pindus Mountains see Píndos
Pine Bluff 42 B2 Arkansas, C USA
Pine Creek 146 D2 Northern
Territory, N Australia

Pinega 110 C3 river NW Russian
Federation
Pineiós 104 B4 var. Piniós; anc.
Peneius. River C Greece
Pineland 49 H3 Texas, SW USA
Pines, The Isle of the see Juventud,
Isla de la
Pingdingshan 128 C4 Henan,
C China
Pingkiang see Harbin
Ping, Mae Nam 136 B4 river
W Thailand
Piniós see Pineiós
Pinkiang see Harbin
Pínnes, Akrotírio 104 C4 headland
N Greece
Pinos, Isla de see Juventud, Isla de
la
Pinotepa Nacional 51 F5 var.
Santiago Pinotepa Nacional.
Oaxaca, SE Mexico
Pinsk 107 B7 Pol. Pińsk. SW Belarus
Pinta, Isla 60 A5 var. Abingdon.
Island Galapagos Islands,
Ecuador, E Pacific Ocean
Piombino 96 B3 Toscana, C Italy
Pioneer Mountains 46 D3 mountain
range Montana, N USA
Pionerskiy 106 A4 Ger. Neukuhren.
Kaliningradskaya Oblast',
W Russian Federation
Piotrków Trybunalski 98 D4 Ger.
Petrikau, Rus. Petrokov. Łódzkie,
C Poland
Piraeus see Peiraías
Pírgos see Pýrgos
Piripiri 63 F2 Piauí, E Brazil
Pirna 94 D4 Sachsen, E Germany
Pirot 101 E5 Serbia, SE Yugoslavia
Pisa 96 B3 var. Pisae. Toscana,
C Italy
Pisae see Pisa
Pisco 60 D4 Ica, SW Peru
Písek 99 A5 Budějovicky Kraj,
S Czech Republic
Pishan 126 A3 var. Guma. Xinjiang
Uygur Zizhiqu, NW China
Pishpek see Bishkek
Pistoia 96 B3 anc. Pistoria, Pistoriæ.
Toscana, C Italy
Pisz 98 D3 Ger. Johannisburg.
Warminsko-Mazurskie,
NE Poland
Pita 74 C4 Moyenne-Guinée,
NW Guinea
Pitalito 58 B4 Huila, S Colombia
Pitcairn Island 143 G4 island
S Pitcairn Islands
Pitcairn Islands 143 G4 UK
dependent territory C Pacific Ocean
Piteå 84 D4 Norrbotten, N Sweden
Piteşti 108 B5 Argeş, S Romania
Pitsanulok see Phitsanulok
Pittsburg 45 F5 Kansas, C USA
Pittsburgh 41 E4 Pennsylvania,
NE USA
Pittsfield 41 F3 Massachusetts,
NE USA
Piura 60 B2 Piura, NW Peru
Pivdennyy Buh 109 E3 Rus.
Yuzhnyy Bug. River S Ukraine
Placetas 54 B2 Villa Clara, C Cuba
Plainview 49 E2 Texas, SW USA
Planeta Rica 58 B2 Córdoba,
NW Colombia
Planken 94 E1 C Liechtenstein
Plano 49 G2 Texas, SW USA
Plasencia 92 C3 Extremadura,
W Spain
Plata, Río de la 64 D4 var. River
Plate. Estuary Argentina/Uruguay
Plateau du Bemaraha see Bemaraha
Platinum 36 C3 Alaska, USA
Plattensee see Balaton
Platte River 45 E4 river Nebraska,
C USA
Plattsburgh 41 F2 New York,
NE USA
Plauen 95 C5 var. Plauen im
Vogtland. Sachsen, E Germany
Plauen im Vogtland see Plauen
Pļaviņas 106 D4 Ger.
Stockmannshof. Aizkraukle,
S Latvia
Plây Cu 137 E5 var. Pleiku. Gia Lai,
C Vietnam
Pleiku see Plây Cu

Plenty, Bay of 150 E3 *bay* North Island, NZ
Plérin 90 A3 Côtes d'Armor, NW France
Plesetsk 110 C3 Arkhangel'skaya Oblast', NW Russian Federation
Pleszew 98 C4 Wielkopolskie, C Poland
Pleven 104 C2 *prev.* Plevna. Pleven, N Bulgaria
Pljevlja 100 C4 *prev.* Plevlja, Plevlje. Montenegro, N Yugoslavia
Ploče 100 B4 *It.* Plocce; *prev.* Kardeljevo. Dubrovnik-Neretva, SE Croatia
Płock 98 D3 Ger. Plozk. Mazowieckie, C Poland
Plöcken Pass 95 C7 Ger. Plöckenpass, *It.* Passo di Monte Croce Carnico. *Pass* SW Austria
Ploieşti 108 C5 *prev.* Ploeşti. Prahova, SE Romania
Plomári 105 D5 *prev.* Plomárion. Lésvos, E Greece
Płońsk 98 D3 Mazowieckie, C Poland
Plovdiv 104 C3 *prev.* Eumolpias, *anc.* Evmolpia, Philippopolis, *Lat.* Trimontium. Plovdiv, C Bulgaria
Plungė 106 B3 Plungė, W Lithuania
Plyeshchanitsy 107 D5 *Rus.* Pleshchenitsy. Minskaya Voblasts', N Belarus
Plymouth 55 G3 *dependent territory capital* (Montserrat) SW Montserrat
Plymouth 89 C7 SW England, UK
Plzeň 99 A5 Ger. Pilsen, *Pol.* Pilzno. Plzeňský Kraj, W Czech Republic
Po 80 D4 *river* N Italy
Pobeda Peak *see* Pobedy, Pik
Pobedy, Pik 126 B3 *var.* Pobeda Peak, *Chin.* Tomur Feng. *Mountain* China/Kyrgyzstan *see also* Tomur Feng
Pocahontas 42 B1 Arkansas, C USA
Pocatello 46 E4 Idaho, NW USA
Pochinok 111 A5 Smolenskaya Oblast', W Russian Federation
Pocking 95 D6 Bayern, SE Germany
Poděbrady 99 B5 Ger. Podiebrad. Středočeský Kraj, C Czech Republic
Podgorica 101 C5 *prev.* Titograd. Montenegro, SW Yugoslavia
Podil's'ka Vysochyna 108 D3 *Rus.* Podol'skaya Vozvyshennost'. *Mountain range* SW Ukraine
Podkarpackie admin. region *province* SE Poland
Podol'sk 111 B5 Moskovskaya Oblast', W Russian Federation
Podravska Slatina *see* Slatina.
Podujevo 101 D5 Serbia, S Yugoslavia
Po, Foci del 96 C2 *var.* Bocche del Po. *River* NE Italy
Pogradec 101 D6 *var.* Pogradeci. Korçë, SE Albania
Pogradeci *see* Pogradec
Pohnpei 144 C2 *prev.* Ponape Ascension Island. *Island* E Micronesia
Poinsett, Cape 154 D4 *headland* Antarctica
Pointe-à-Pitre 55 G3 Grande Terre, C Guadeloupe
Pointe-Noire 77 B6 Le Kouilou, S Congo
Point Lay 36 C2 Alaska, USA
Poitiers 90 B4 *prev.* Poictiers, *anc.* Limonum. Vienne, W France
Poitou 90 B4 *cultural region* W France
Pokhara 135 E3 Western, C Nepal
Pokrovs'ke 109 G3 *Rus.* Pokrovskoye. Dnipropetrovs'ka Oblast', E Ukraine
Pola de Lena 92 D1 Asturias, N Spain
Poland 98 D4 *var.* Polish Republic, *Pol.* Polska, Rzeczpospolita Polska; *prev. Pol.* Polska Rzeczpospolita Ludowa, Polish People's Republic. *Country* C Europe

Poland 98

Official name Republic of Poland
Formation 1918
Capital Warsaw
Population 38.8 million / 330 people per sq mile (127 people per sq km)
Total area 117,552 sq miles (304,460 sq km)
Languages Polish
Religions Roman Catholic 93%, Eastern Orthodox 2%, other and non-religious 5%
Ethnic mix Polish 98%, other 2%
Government Multiparty republic
Currency Zloty = 100 groszy
Literacy rate 99%
Calorie consumption 3,301 kilocalories

Poland 81 E3 Kiritimati, E Kiribati
Polatli 116 C3 Ankara, C Turkey
Polatsk 107 D5 *Rus.* Polotsk. Vitsyebskaya Voblasts', N Belarus
Pol-e Khomri 123 E4 *var.* Pul-i-Khumri. Baghlān, NE Afghanistan
Poli *see* Pólis
Polikastro *see* Polýkastro
Políkastron *see* Polýkastro
Polikrayshte 104 D2 Veliko Tŭrnovo, N Bulgaria
Pólis 102 C5 *var.* Poli. W Cyprus
Polkowice 98 B4 Ger. Heerwegen. Dolnośląskie, SW Poland
Pollença 93 G3 *var.* Pollensa. Mallorca, Spain, W Mediterranean Sea
Pollensa *see* Pollença
Polohy 109 G3 *Rus.* Pologi. Zaporiz'ka Oblast', SE Ukraine
Polonne 108 D2 *Rus.* Polonnoye. Khmel'nyts'ka Oblast', NW Ukraine
Polsko Kosovo 104 D2 Ruse, N Bulgaria
Poltava 109 F2 Poltavs'ka Oblast', NE Ukraine
Põlva 106 E3 Ger. Põlwe. Põlvamaa, SE Estonia
Polyarnyy 110 C2 Murmanskaya Oblast', NW Russian Federation
Polýkastro 104 B3 *var.* Polikastro; *prev.* Políkastron. Kentrikí Makedonía, N Greece
Polynesia 143 F4 *island group* C Pacific Ocean
Pomeranian Bay 94 D2 Ger. Pommersche Bucht, *Pol.* Zatoka Pomorska. *Bay* Germany/Poland
Pomorskiy Proliv 110 D2 *strait* NW Russian Federation
Pompano Beach 43 F5 Florida, SE USA
Ponca City 49 G1 Oklahoma, C USA
Ponce 55 F3 C Puerto Rico
Pondicherry 132 C2 *var.* Puducherri, *Fr.* Pondichéry. Pondicherry, SE India
Pondichéry *see* Pondicherry
Ponferrada 92 C1 Castilla-León, NW Spain
Poniatowa 98 E4 Lublin, E Poland
Pons Aelii *see* Newcastle upon Tyne
Ponta Delgada 92 B5 São Miguel, Azores, Portugal, NE Atlantic Ocean
Ponta Grossa 63 E4 Paraná, S Brazil
Pontarlier 90 D2 Doubs, E France
Ponteareas 92 B2 Galicia, NW Spain
Ponte da Barca 92 B2 Viana do Castelo, N Portugal
Pontevedra 92 B1 *anc.* Pons Vetus. Galicia, NW Spain
Pontiac 40 D3 Michigan, N USA
Pontianak 138 C4 Borneo, C Indonesia
Pontivy 90 A3 Morbihan, NW France
Pontoise 90 C3 *anc.* Briva Isarae, Cergy-Pontoise, Pontisarae. Val-d'Oise, N France
Ponziane, Isole 97 C5 *island* C Italy

Poole 89 D7 S England, UK
Poopó, Lago 61 F4 *var.* Lago Pampa Aullagas. *Lake* W Bolivia
Popayán 58 B4 Cauca, SW Colombia
Poperinge 87 A6 West-Vlaanderen, W Belgium
Poplar Bluff 45 G5 Missouri, C USA
Popocatépetl 51 E4 *volcano* S Mexico
Poprad 99 D5 Ger. Deutschendorf, *Hung.* Poprád. Prešovský Kraj, E Slovakia
Poprad 99 D5 Ger. Popper, *Hung.* Poprád. *River* Poland/Slovakia
Porbandar 134 B4 Gujarāt, W India
Porcupine Plain 80 B3 *undersea feature* E Atlantic Ocean
Pordenone 96 C2 *anc.* Portenau. Friuli-Venezia Giulia, NE Italy
Poreč 100 A2 *It.* Parenzo. Istra, NW Croatia
Pori 85 D5 *Swe.* Björneborg. Länsi-Suomi, W Finland
Porirua 151 D5 Wellington, North Island, NZ
Porkhov 110 A4 Pskovskaya Oblast', W Russian Federation
Porlamar 59 E1 Nueva Esparta, NE Venezuela
Póros 105 A5 Kefallinía, Iónioi Nísoi, Greece, C Mediterranean Sea
Póros 105 C6 Póros, S Greece
Porsangen 84 D2 *fjord* N Norway
Porsgrunn 85 B6 Telemark, S Norway
Portachuelo 61 G4 Santa Cruz, C Bolivia
Portadown 89 B5 *Ir.* Port An Dúnáin. S Northern Ireland, UK
Portalegre 92 C3 *anc.* Ammaia, Amoea. Portalegre, E Portugal
Port Alexander 36 D4 Baranof Island, Alaska, USA
Port Alfred 78 D5 Eastern Cape, S South Africa
Port An Dúnáin *see* Portadown
Port Angeles 46 B1 Washington, NW USA
Port Antonio 54 B5 NE Jamaica
Port Arthur 49 H4 Texas, SW USA
Port Augusta 149 B6 South Australia
Port-au-Prince 54 D3 *country capital* (Haiti) C Haiti
Port-au-Prince 35 D7 *international airport* E Haiti
Port Blair 133 F2 Andaman and Nicobar Islands, SE India
Port Charlotte 43 E4 Florida, SE USA
Port d'Envalira 91 B8 E Andorra
Port Douglas 148 D3 Queensland, NE Australia
Port Elizabeth 78 C5 Eastern Cape, S South Africa
Porterville 47 C7 California, W USA
Port-Gentil 77 A6 Ogooué-Maritime, W Gabon
Port Harcourt 75 G5 Rivers, S Nigeria
Port Hardy 36 D5 Vancouver Island, British Columbia, SW Canada
Port Harrison *see* Inukjuak
Port Hedland 146 B4 Western Australia
Port Huron 40 D3 Michigan, N USA
Portimão 92 B4 *var.* Vila Nova de Portimão. Faro, S Portugal
Port Jackson 148 E1 *harbour* New South Wales, SE Australia
Port Láirge *see* Waterford
Portland 41 G2 Maine, NE USA
Portland 46 B3 Oregon, NW USA
Portland 49 G4 Texas, SW USA
Portland 149 B7 Victoria, SE Australia
Portland Bight 54 B5 *bay* S Jamaica
Portlaoighise *see* Portlaoise
Portlaoise 89 B6 *Ir.* Portlaoighise; *prev.* Maryborough. C Ireland
Port Lavaca 49 G4 Texas, SW USA
Port Lincoln 149 A6 South Australia

Port Louis 79 H3 *country capital* (Mauritius) NW Mauritius
Port Macquarie 149 E6 New South Wales, SE Australia
Portmore 54 B5 C Jamaica
Port Moresby 144 B3 *country capital* (PNG) Central/National Capital District, SW PNG
Port Musgrave 149 B9 *bay* Queensland, N Australia
Port Natal *see* Durban
Porto 92 B2 Eng. Oporto; *anc.* Portus Cale. Porto, NW Portugal
Porto Alegre 63 E5 *var.* Pôrto Alegre. *State capital* Rio Grande do Sul, S Brazil
Porto Alegre 76 E2 São Tomé, S Sao Tome and Principe
Porto Bello *see* Portobelo
Portobelo 53 G4 *var.* Porto Bello, Puerto Bello. Colón, N Panama
Port O'Connor 49 G4 Texas, SW USA
Porto Edda *see* Sarandë
Portoferraio 96 B4 Toscana, C Italy
Port-of-Spain 55 H5 *country capital* (Trinidad and Tobago) Trinidad, Trinidad and Tobago
Porto Grande *see* Mindelo
Portogruaro 96 C2 Veneto, NE Italy
Porto-Novo 75 F5 *country capital* (Benin) S Benin
Porto Santo 70 A2 *var.* Ilha do Porto Santo. *Island* Madeira, Portugal, NE Atlantic Ocean
Porto Torres 97 A5 Sardegna, Italy, C Mediterranean Sea
Porto Velho 62 D2 *var.* Velho. *State capital* Rondônia, W Brazil
Portoviejo 60 A2 *var.* Puertoviejo. Manabí, W Ecuador
Port Pirie 149 B6 South Australia
Port Said 72 B1 *Ar.* Bûr Sa'îd. N Egypt
Portsmouth 41 G3 New Hampshire, NE USA
Portsmouth 40 D4 Ohio, N USA
Portsmouth 89 D7 S England, UK
Portsmouth 41 F5 Virginia, NE USA
Port Stanley *see* Stanley
Port Sudan 72 C3 Red Sea, NE Sudan
Port Swettenham *see* Klang
Port Talbot 89 C7 S Wales, UK
Portugal 92 B3 *Country* SW Europe

Portugal 92

Official name Republic of Portugal
Formation 1140
Capital Lisbon
Population 10 million / 279 people per sq mile (108 people per sq km)
Total area 35,501 sq miles (91,950 sq km)
Languages Portuguese
Religions Roman Catholic 97%, Protestant 1%, other 2%
Ethnic mix Portuguese 99%, African 1%
Government Multiparty republic
Currency Portuguese escudo = 100 centavos
Literacy rate 90.8%
Calorie consumption 3,634 kilocalories

Portuguese Timor *see* East Timor
Port-Vila 144 D4 *var.* Vila. *Country capital* (Vanuatu) Éfaté, C Vanuatu
Porvenir 65 B8 Magallanes, S Chile
Porvenir 61 E3 Pando, NW Bolivia
Porvoo 85 E6 *Swe.* Borgå. Etelä-Suomi, S Finland
Posadas 64 D3 Misiones, NE Argentina
Poschega *see* Požega
Posterholt 87 D5 Limburg, SE Netherlands
Postojna 95 D8 Ger. Adelsberg, *It.* Postumia. SW Slovenia
Potamós 105 C7 Antikýthira, S Greece
Potenza 97 D5 *anc.* Potentia. Basilicata, S Italy

P'ot'i 117 F2 W Georgia
Potiskum 75 G4 Yobe, NE Nigeria
Potomac River 41 E5 river NE USA
Potosí 61 F4 Potosí, S Bolivia
Potsdam 94 D3 Brandenburg, NE Germany
Potwar Plateau 134 C2 plateau NE Pakistan
Poŭthisǎt 137 D6 prev. Pursat. Poŭthǐsǎt, W Cambodia
Po Valley 96 C2 It. Valle del Po. Valley N Italy
Považská Bystrica 99 C5 Ger. Waagbistritz, Hung. Vágbesztercze. Trenčiansky Kraj, W Slovakia
Poverty Bay 150 E4 inlet North Island, NZ
Póvoa de Varzim 92 B2 Porto, NW Portugal
Powder River 44 D2 river Montana/Wyoming, NW USA
Powell 44 C2 Wyoming, C USA
Powell, Lake 44 B5 lake Utah, W USA
Požarevac 100 D4 Ger. Passarowitz. Serbia, NE Yugoslavia
Poza Rica 51 F4 var. Poza Rica de Hidalgo. Veracruz-Llave, E Mexico
Poza Rica de Hidalgo see Poza Rica
Požega 100 D4 prev. Slavonska Požega. Ger. Poschega, Hung. Pozsega. Požega-Slavonija, NE Croatia
Pozsega see Požega
Poznań 98 C3 Ger. Posen, Posnania. Wielkopolskie, C Poland
Pozoblanco 92 D4 Andalucía, S Spain
Pozzallo 97 C8 Sicilia, Italy, C Mediterranean Sea
Prachatice 99 A5 Ger. Prachatitz. Budějovický Kraj, S Czech Republic
Prado del Ganso see Goose Green
Prae see Phrae
Prague 80 D3 Oklahoma, C USA
Praha 99 A5 Eng. Prague, Ger. Prag, Pol. Praga. Country capital (Czech Republic) Středočeský Kraj, NW Czech Republic
Praia 74 A3 country capital (Cape Verde) Santiago, S Cape Verde
Prato 96 B3 Toscana, C Italy
Pratt 45 E5 Kansas, C USA
Prattville 42 D2 Alabama, S USA
Pravda 104 D1 prev. Dogrular. Silistra, NE Bulgaria
Pravia 92 C1 Asturias, N Spain
Prenzlau 94 D3 Brandenburg, NE Germany
Přerov 99 C5 Ger. Prerau. Olomoucký Kraj, E Czech Republic
Presa de la Amistad see Amistad Reservoir
Preschau see Prešov
Prescott 48 B2 Arizona, SW USA
Prešovo 101 D5 Serbia, SE Yugoslavia
Presidente Epitácio 63 E4 São Paulo, S Brazil
Prešov 99 D5 var. Preschau, Ger. Eperies, Hung. Eperjes. Prešouský Kraj, E Slovakia
Prespa, Lake 101 D6 Alb. Liqen i Prespës, Gk. Límni Megáli Préspa, Limni Prespa, Mac. Prespansko Ezero, Serb. Prespansko Jezero. Lake SE Europe
Presque Isle 41 H1 Maine, NE USA
Preston 89 D5 NW England, UK
Prestwick 88 C4 W Scotland, UK
Pretoria 78 D4 var. Epitoli, Tshwane. Country capital (South Africa-administrative capital) Gauteng, NE South Africa
Préveza 105 A5 Ípeiros, W Greece
Pribilof Islands 36 A3 island group Alaska, USA
Priboj 100 C4 Serbia, W Yugoslavia
Price 44 B4 Utah, W USA
Prichard 42 C3 Alabama, S USA
Priekulė 106 B3 Ger. Prökuls. Gargždai, W Lithuania
Prienai 107 B5 Pol. Preny. Prienai, S Lithuania

Prieska 78 C4 Northern Cape, C South Africa
Prijedor 100 B3 Republika Srpska, NW Bosnia and Herzegovina
Prijepolje 100 D4 Serbia, W Yugoslavia
Prilep 101 D6 Turk. Perlepe. S FYR Macedonia
Primorsk 106 A4 Ger. Fischhausen. Kaliningradskaya Oblast', W Russian Federation
Primorsko 104 E2 prev. Keupriya. Burgas, E Bulgaria
Prince Albert 37 F5 Saskatchewan, S Canada
Prince Edward Island 39 F4 Fr. Île-du Prince-Édouard. Province SE Canada
Prince Edward Islands 69 E8 island group S South Africa
Prince George 37 E5 British Columbia, SW Canada
Prince of Wales Island 37 F2 island Queen Elizabeth Islands, Nunavut, NW Canada
Prince of Wales Island 148 B1 island Queensland, E Australia
Prince Patrick Island 37 E2 island Parry Islands, Northwest Territories, NW Canada
Prince Rupert 36 D4 British Columbia, SW Canada
Prince's Island see Príncipe
Princess Charlotte Bay 148 C2 bay Queensland, NE Australia
Princess Elizabeth Land 154 C3 physical region Antarctica
Príncipe 77 A5 var. Príncipe Island, Eng. Prince's Island. Island N Sao Tome and Principe
Príncipe Island see Príncipe
Prinzapolka 53 E3 Región Autónoma Atlántico Norte, NE Nicaragua
Pripet 107 C7 Bel. Prypyats', Ukr. Pryp''yat'. River Belarus/Ukraine
Pripet Marshes 107 B7 wetland Belarus/Ukraine
Priština 101 D5 Alb. Prishtinë. Serbia, S Yugoslavia
Privas 91 D5 Ardèche, E France
Prizren 101 D5 Alb. Prizreni. Serbia, S Yugoslavia
Probolinggo 138 D5 Jawa, C Indonesia
Progreso 51 H3 Yucatán, SE Mexico
Prokhladnyy 111 B8 Kabardino-Balkarskaya Respublika, SW Russian Federation
Prokuplje 101 D5 Serbia, SE Yugoslavia
Prome 136 B4 var. Pyè. Pegu, C Myanmar
Promyshlennyy 110 E3 Respublika Komi, NW Russian Federation
Prostějov 99 C5 Ger. Prossnitz, Pol. Prościejów. Olomoucký Kraj, E Czech Republic
Provence 91 D6 cultural region SE France
Providence see Fort Providence
Providence 41 G3 state capital Rhode Island, NE USA
Providencia, Isla de 53 F3 island NW Colombia
Provideniya 172 B1 Chukotskiy Avtonomnyy Okrug, NE Russian Federation
Provo 44 B4 Utah, W USA
Prudhoe Bay 36 D2 Alaska, USA
Prusa see Bursa
Pruszków 98 D3 Ger. Kaltdorf. Mazowieckie, C Poland
Prut 108 D4 Ger. Pruth. River E Europe
Pruzhany 107 B6 Pol. Prużana. Brestskaya Voblasts', SW Belarus
Prydz Bay 154 D3 bay Antarctica
Pryluky 109 F2 Rus. Priluki. Chernihivs'ka Oblast', NE Ukraine
Prymors'k 109 G4 Rus. Primorsk; prev. Primorskoye. Zaporiz'ka Oblast', SE Ukraine
Przemyśl 99 E5 Rus. Peremyshl. Podkarpackie, SE Poland
Psará 105 D5 island E Greece

Psël 109 F2 river Russian Federation/Ukraine
Pskov 114 B2 Ger. Pleskau, Latv. Pleskava. Pskovskaya Oblast', W Russian Federation
Pskov, Lake E3 Est. Pihkva Järv, Ger. Pleskauer See, Rus. Pskovskoye Ozero. Lake Estonia/Russian Federation
Ptsich 107 C7 Rus. Ptich'. River SE Belarus
Ptsich 107 C7 Rus. Ptich'. Homyel'skaya Voblasts', SE Belarus
Ptuj 95 E7 Ger. Pettau; anc. Poetovio. NE Slovenia
Pucallpa 60 C3 Ucayali, C Peru
Puck 98 C2 Pomorskie, N Poland
Pudasjärvi 84 D4 Oulu, C Finland
Puducherri see Pondicherry
Puebla 51 F4 var. Puebla de Zaragoza. Puebla, S Mexico
Puebla de Zaragoza see Puebla
Pueblo 44 D5 Colorado, C USA
Puerto Acosta 61 E4 La Paz, W Bolivia
Puerto Aisén 65 B6 Aisén, S Chile
Puerto Ángel 51 F5 Oaxaca, SE Mexico
Puerto Argentino see Stanley
Puerto Ayacucho 58 D3 Amazonas, SW Venezuela
Puerto Baquerizo Moreno 60 B5 var. Baquerizo Moreno. Galapagos Islands, Ecuador, E Pacific Ocean
Puerto Barrios 52 C2 Izabal, E Guatemala
Puerto Bello see Portobelo
Puerto Berrío 58 B2 Antioquia, C Colombia
Puerto Cabello 58 D1 Carabobo, N Venezuela
Puerto Cabezas 53 E2 var. Bilwi. Región Autónoma Atlántico Norte, NE Nicaragua
Puerto Carreño 58 D3 Vichada, E Colombia
Puerto Cortés 52 C2 Cortés, NW Honduras
Puerto Cumarebo 58 C1 Falcón, N Venezuela
Puerto Deseado 65 C7 Santa Cruz, SE Argentina
Puerto Escondido 51 F5 Oaxaca, SE Mexico
Puerto Francisco de Orellana 60 B1 var. Coca. Napo, N Ecuador
Puerto Gallegos see Río Gallegos
Puerto Inírida 58 D3 var. Obando. Guainía, E Colombia
Puerto La Cruz 59 E1 Anzoátegui, NE Venezuela
Puerto Lempira 53 E2 Gracias a Dios, E Honduras
Puerto Limón see Limón
Puertollano 92 D4 Castilla-La Mancha, C Spain
Puerto López 58 C1 La Guajira, N Colombia
Puerto Maldonado 61 E3 Madre de Dios, E Peru
Puerto México see Coatzacoalcos
Puerto Montt 65 B5 Los Lagos, C Chile
Puerto Natales 65 B7 Magallanes, S Chile
Puerto Obaldía 53 H5 San Blas, NE Panama
Puerto Plata 55 E3 var. San Felipe de Puerto Plata. N Dominican Republic
Puerto Princesa 139 E2 off. Puerto Princesa City. Palawan, W Philippines
Puerto Rico 55 F3 off. Commonwealth of Puerto Rico; prev. Porto Rico. US commonwealth territory C West Indies
Puerto Rico 56 B1 island E West Indies
Puerto Rico Trench 56 B1 undersea feature NE Caribbean Sea
Puerto San José see San José
Puerto San Julián 65 B7 var. San Julián. Santa Cruz, SE Argentina
Puerto Suárez 61 H4 Santa Cruz, E Bolivia

Puerto Vallarta 50 D4 Jalisco, SW Mexico
Puerto Varas 65 B5 Los Lagos, C Chile
Puerto Viejo 53 E4 Heredia, NE Costa Rica
Puertoviejo see Portoviejo
Puget Sound 46 B1 sound Washington, NW USA
Puglia 97 E5 Eng. Apulia. Cultural region SE Italy
Pukaki, Lake 151 B6 lake South Island, NZ
Pukekohe 150 D3 Auckland, North Island, NZ
Puket see Phuket
Pukhavichy 107 C6 Rus. Pukhovichi. Minskaya Voblasts', C Belarus
Pula 100 A3 It. Pola; prev. Pulj. Istra, NW Croatia
Pulaski 40 D5 Virginia, NE USA
Pulau Butung see Buton, Pulau
Puławy 98 D4 Ger. Neu Amerika. Lublin, E Poland
Pul-i-Khumri see Pol-e Khomrī
Pullman 46 C2 Washington, NW USA
Pułtusk 98 D3 Mazowieckie, C Poland
Puná, Isla 60 A2 island SW Ecuador
Pune 134 C5 prev. Poona. Mahārāshtra, W India
Punjab 134 C2 prev. West Punjab, Western Punjab. Province E Pakistan
Puno 61 E4 Puno, SE Peru
Punta Alta 65 C5 Buenos Aires, E Argentina
Punta Arenas 65 B8 prev. Magallanes. Magallanes, S Chile
Punta Gorda 53 E4 Región Autónoma Atlántico Sur, SE Nicaragua
Punta Gorda 52 C2 Toledo, SE Belize
Puntarenas 52 D4 Puntarenas, W Costa Rica
Punto Fijo 58 C1 Falcón, N Venezuela
Pupuya, Nevado 61 E4 mountain W Bolivia
Puri 135 F5 var. Jagannath. Orissa, E India
Puriramya see Buriram
Purmerend 86 C3 Noord-Holland, C Netherlands
Purus, Río 62 C2 Sp. Río Purús. River Brazil/Peru
Pusan 129 E4 off. Pusan-gwangyŏksi, var. Busan, Jap. Fusan. SE South Korea
Püspökladány 99 D6 Hajdú-Bihar, E Hungary
Putorana Mountains see Putorana, Plato
Putorana, Plato 114 D3 var. Gory Putorana, Eng. Putorana Mountains. Mountain range N Russian Federation
Puttalam 132 C3 North Western Province, W Sri Lanka
Puttgarden 94 C2 Schleswig-Holstein, N Germany
Putumayo, Río 58 B5 var. Rio Içá. River North South America see also Içá, Rio
Putumayo, Río see Içá, Rio
Puurmani 106 D2 Ger. Talkhof. Jõgevamaa, E Estonia
Pyatigorsk 111 B7 Stavropol'skiy Kray, SW Russian Federation
P"yatykhatky 109 F3 Rus. Pyatikhatki. Dnipropetrovs'ka Oblast', E Ukraine
Pyè see Prome
Pyetrykaw 107 C7 Rus. Petrikov. Homyel'skaya Voblasts', SE Belarus
Pyinmana 136 B4 Mandalay, C Myanmar
Pýlos 105 B6 var. Pilos. Pelopónnisos, S Greece
P'yŏngyang 129 E4 var. P'yŏngyang-si, Eng. Pyongyang. Country capital (North Korea) SW North Korea
P'yŏngyang-si see P'yŏngyang

Pyramid Lake *47 C5 lake* Nevada, W USA
Pyrenees *102 B2 Fr.* Pyrénées, *Sp.* Pirineos; *anc.* Pyrenaei Montes. *Mountain range* SW Europe
Pýrgos *105 B6 var.* Pírgos. Dytikí Ellás, S Greece
Pyryatyn *109 E2 Rus.* Piryatin. Poltavs'ka Oblast', NE Ukraine
Pyrzyce *98 E3 Ger.* Pyritz. Zachodniopomorskie, NW Poland
Pyu *136 B4* Pegu, C Myanmar
Pyuntaza *136 B4* Pegu, SW Myanmar

Q

Qā' al Jafr *119 C7 lake* S Jordan
Qaanaaq *82 D1 var.* Qânâq, *Dan.* Thule. N Greenland
Qabātiya *119 E6* N West Bank
Qābis *see* Gabès
Qacentina *see* Constantine
Qafsah *see* Gafsa
Qagan Us *see* Dulan
Qahremānshahr *see* Bākhtarān
Qaidam Pendi *126 C4 basin* C China
Qal'aikhum *123 F3 Rus.* Kalaikhum. S Tajikistan
Qal'at Bīshah *121 B5 'Asīr,* SW Saudi Arabia
Qalqīlya *119 D6* N West Bank
Qamdo *126 D5* Xizang Zizhiqu, W China
Qamishly *see* Al Qāmishlī
Qânâq *see* Qaanaaq
Qaqortoq *82 C4 Dan.* Julianehåb. S Greenland
Qara Qum *see* Garagumy
Qarkilik *see* Ruoqiang
Qarokŭl *123 F3 Rus.* Karakul'. E Tajikistan
Qars *see* Kars
Qarshi *123 E3 Rus.* Karshi; *prev.* Bek-Budi. Qashqadaryo Wiloyati, S Uzbekistan
Qasigiannguit *see* Qasigiannguit
Qasigiannguit *82 C3 var.* Qasigianguit, *Dan.* Christianshåb. C Greenland
Qasr Farâfra *72 B2* W Egypt
Qaṭanā *119 B5 var.* Katana. Dimashq, S Syria
Qatar *120 C4 Ar.* Dawlat Qaṭar. *Country* SW Asia

Qatar 120

Official name State of Qatar
Formation 1971
Capital Doha
Population 699,000 / 165 people per sq mile (64 people per sq km)
Total area 4,247 sq miles (11,000 sq km)
Languages Arabic
Religions Sunni Muslim 86%, Hindu 10%, Christian 4%
Ethnic mix Arab 40%, Pakistani 18%, Indian 18%, Iranian 10%, other 14%
Government Absolute monarchy
Currency Qatar riyal = 100 dirhams
Literacy rate 80%
Calorie consumption not available

Qattara Depression *see* Qaṭṭâra, Monkhafad el
Qaṭṭâra, Monkhafad el *88 A1 var.* Munkhafaḍ al Qaṭṭârah, *Eng.* Qattara Depression. *Desert* NW Egypt
Qazimämmäd *117 H3 Rus.* Kazi Magomed. SE Azerbaijan
Qazvin *120 C2 var.* Kazvin. Qazvin, N Iran
Qena *72 B2 var.* Qinā; *anc.* Caene, Caenepolis. E Egypt
Qeqertarssuaq *see* Qeqertarsuaq
Qeqertarsuaq *82 C3 var.* Qeqertarssuaq, *Dan.* Godhavn. S Greenland
Qeqertarsuaq *82 C3 island* W Greenland

Qeqertarsuup Tunua *82 C3 Dan.* Disko Bugt. *Inlet* W Greenland
Qerveh *see* Qorveh
Qeshm *120 D4 var.* Jazīreh-ye Qeshm, Qeshm Island. *Island* S Iran
Qeshm Island *see* Qeshm
Qian *see* Guizhou
Qilian Shan *126 D3 var.* Kilien Mountains. *Mountain range* N China
Qimusseriarsuaq *82 C2 Dan.* Melville Bugt, *Eng.* Melville Bay. *Bay* NW Greenland
Qinā *see* Qena
Qing *see* Qinghai
Qingdao *128 D4 var.* Ching-Tao, Ch'ing-tao, Tsingtao, Tsintao, *Ger.* Tsingtau. Shandong, E China
Qinghai *126 C4 var.* Chinghai, Koko Nor, Qing, Qinghai Sheng, Tsinghai. Admin. region *province* C China
Qinghai Hu *126 D4 var.* Ch'ing Hai, Tsing Hai, *Mong.* Koko Nor. *lake* C China
Qinghai Sheng *see* Qinghai
Qingzang Gaoyuan *126 B4 var.* Xizang Gaoyuan, *Eng.* Plateau of Tibet. *Plateau* W China
Qinhuangdao *128 D3* Hebei, E China
Qinzhou *128 B6* Guangxi Zhuangzu Zizhiqu, S China
Qiong *see* Hainan
Qiqihar *128 D2 var.* Ch'i-ch'i-haerh, Tsitsihar; *prev.* Lungkiang. Heilongjiang, NE China
Qira *126 B4* Xinjiang Uygur Zizhiqu, NW China
Qitai *126 C3* Xinjiang Uygur Zizhiqu, NW China
Qīzān *see* Jīzān
Qizil Orda *see* Kyzylorda
Qizil Qum *see* Kyzyl Kum
Qizilrabot *123 G3 Rus.* Kyzylrabot. SE Tajikistan
Qom *120 C3 var.* Kum, Qum, Qom, N Iran
Qomul *see* Hami
Qonduz *see* Kunduz
Qorveh *120 C3 var.* Qerveh, Qurveh. Kordestān, W Iran
Qostanay *see* Kostanay
Qoubaïyât *118 B4 var.* Al Qubayyāt. N Lebanon
Qoussantîna *see* Constantine
Quang Ngai *137 E5 var.* Quangngai, Quang Nghia. Quang Ngai, C Vietnam
Quangngai *see* Quang Ngai
Quang Nghia *see* Quang Ngai
Quanzhou *128 D6 var.* Ch'uanchou, Tsinkiang; *prev.* Tsinchiang. Fujian, SE China
Quanzhou *128 C6* Guangxi Zhuangzu Zizhiqu, S China
Qu'Appelle *37 F5 river* Saskatchewan, S Canada
Quarles, Pegunungan *139 E4 mountain range* Sulawesi, C Indonesia
Quarnero *see* Kvarner
Quartu Sant' Elena *97 A6* Sardegna, Italy, C Mediterranean Sea
Quba *117 H2 Rus.* Kuba. N Azerbaijan
Qubba *see* Ba'qūbah
Québec *39 E4 var.* Quebec. Québec, SE Canada
Quebec *38 D3 var.* Québec. Admin. region *province* SE Canada
Queen Charlotte Islands *36 C5 Fr.* Îles de la Reine-Charlotte. *Island group* British Columbia, SW Canada
Queen Charlotte Sound *36 C5 sea area* British Columbia, W Canada
Queen Elizabeth Islands *37 F2 Fr.* Îles de la Reine-Élisabeth. *Island group* Northwest Territories/Nunavut, N Canada
Queensland *148 B4 state* N Australia
Queenstown *78 D5* Eastern Cape, S South Africa
Queenstown *151 B7* Otago, South Island, NZ

Quelimane *79 E3 var.* Kilimane, Kilmain, Quilimane. Zambézia, NE Mozambique
Quepos *53 E4* Puntarenas, S Costa Rica
Querétaro *51 E4* Querétaro de Arteaga, C Mexico
Quesada *53 E4 var.* Ciudad Quesada, San Carlos. Alajuela, N Costa Rica
Quetta *134 B2* Baluchistān, SW Pakistan
Quetzalcoalco *see* Coatzacoalcos
Quetzaltenango *see* Quezaltenango
Quezaltenango *52 A2 var.* Quetzaltenango. Quezaltenango, W Guatemala
Quibdó *58 A3* Chocó, W Colombia
Quilimane *see* Quelimane
Quillabamba *60 D3* Cusco, C Peru
Quilon *132 C3 var.* Kolam, Kollam. Kerala, SW India
Quimper *90 A3 anc.* Quimper Corentin. Finistère, NW France
Quimperlé *90 A3* Finistère, NW France
Quincy *40 A4* Illinois, N USA
Qui Nhon *see* Quy Nhon
Quissico *79 E4* Inhambane, S Mozambique
Quito *60 B1 country capital* (Ecuador) Pichincha, N Ecuador
Qullai Garmo *see* Kommunizm, Qullai
Qum *see* Qom
Qunaytra *see* Al Qunayṭirah
Qŭqon *123 F2 var.* Khokand, *Rus.* Kokand. Farghona Wiloyati, E Uzbekistan
Qurein *see* Al Kuwayt
Qŭrghonteppa *123 E3 Rus.* Kurgan-Tyube. SW Tajikistan
Qurlurtuuq *see* Kugluktuk
Qurveh *see* Qorveh
Quşayr *see* Al Quşayr
Quy Nhơn *137 E5 var.* Quinhon, Qui Nhon. Bình Đinh, C Vietnam
Qyteti Stalin *see* Kuçovë
Qyzylorda *see* Kyzylorda

R

Raab *100 B1 Hung.* Rába. *River* Austria/Hungary *see also* Rába
Raahe *84 D4 Swe.* Brahestad. Oulu, W Finland
Raalte *86 D3* Overijssel, E Netherlands
Raamsdonksveer *86 C4* Noord-Brabant, S Netherlands
Raasiku *106 D2 Ger.* Rasik. Harjumaa, NW Estonia
Rába *99 B7 Ger.* Raab. *River* Austria/Hungary *see also* Raab
Rabat *70 C2 var.* al Dar al Baida. *Country capital* (Morocco) NW Morocco
Rabat *see* Victoria
Rabat *102 B5* W Malta
Rabbah Ammon *see* 'Ammān
Rabbath Ammon *see* 'Ammān
Rabinal *52 B2* Baja Verapaz, C Guatemala
Rabka *99 D5* Małopolskie, S Poland
Rābnița *see* Rîbnița
Rabyānah, Ramlat *71 G4 var.* Rebiana Sand Sea, ṣaḥrâ' Rabyanāh. *Desert* SE Libya
Race, Cape *39 H3 headland* Newfoundland, Newfoundland and Labrador, E Canada
Rach Gia *137 D6* Kiên Giang, S Vietnam
Rach Gia, Vinh *137 D6 bay* S Vietnam
Racine *40 B3* Wisconsin, N USA
Rădăuți *108 C3 Ger.* Radautz, *Hung.* Rádóc. Suceava, N Romania
Radom *98 D4* Mazowieckie, C Poland
Radomsko *98 D4 Rus.* Novoradomsk. Łódzkie, C Poland
Radomyshl' *108 D2* Zhytomyrs'ka Oblast', N Ukraine
Radoviš *101 E6 prev.* Radovište. E FYR Macedonia

Radviliškis *106 B4* Radviliškis, N Lithuania
Radzyń Podlaski *98 E4* Lubelskie, E Poland
Rae-Edzo *see* Edzo
Raetihi *150 D4* Manawatu-Wanganui, North Island, NZ
Rafa *see* Rafah
Rafaela *64 C3* Santa Fe, E Argentina
Rafah *119 A7 var.* Rafa, Rafaḥ, *Heb.* Rafiaḥ, Raphiah. SW Gaza Strip
Rafaḥ *see* Rafah
Rafḥah *120 B4* Al Ḥudūd ash Shamālīyah, N Saudi Arabia
Rafiaḥ *see* Rafah
Raga *73 A5* Western Bahr el Ghazal, SW Sudan
Ragged Island Range *54 C2 island group* S Bahamas
Ragusa *97 C7* Sicilia, Italy, C Mediterranean Sea
Rahachow *107 D7 Rus.* Rogachëv. Homyel'skaya Voblasts', SE Belarus
Rahaeng *see* Tak
Rahaṭ, Ḥarrat *121 B5 lavaflow* W Saudi Arabia
Rahīmyār Khān *134 C3* Punjab, SE Pakistan
Raiatea *145 G4 island* Îles Sous le Vent, W French Polynesia
Rāichūr *132 C1* Karnātaka, C India
Rainier, Mount *34 A4 volcano* Washington, NW USA
Rainy Lake *38 A4 lake* Canada/USA
Raipur *135 E4* Madhya Pradesh, C India
Rājahmundry *135 E5* Andhra Pradesh, E India
Rajang *see* Rajang, Batang
Rajang, Batang *138 D3 var.* Rajang. *River* East Malaysia
Rājapālaiyam *132 C3* Tamil Nādu, SE India
Rājasthān *134 C3 state* NW India
Rājkot *134 C4* Gujarāt, W India
Rāj Nāndgaon *135 E4* Madhya Pradesh, C India
Rajshahi *135 G3 prev.* Rampur Boalia. Rajshahi, W Bangladesh
Rakahanga *145 F3 atoll* N Cook Islands
Rakaia *151 B6 river* South Island, NZ
Rakka *see* Ar Raqqah
Rakke *106 E2* Lääne-Virumaa, NE Estonia
Rakvere *106 E2 Ger.* Wesenberg. Lääne-Virumaa, N Estonia
Ralik Chain *144 D1 island group* Ralik Chain, W Marshall Islands
Ramadi *see* Ar Ramādī
Ramlat Ahl Wahībah *see* Wahībah, Ramlat Āl
Ramlat Al Wahaybah *see* Wahībah, Ramlat Āl
Râmnicu Sărat *108 C4 prev.* Râmnicul-Sărat, Rîmnicu-Sărat. Buzău, E Romania
Râmnicu Vâlcea *108 B4 prev.* Rîmnicu Vîlcea. Vâlcea, C Romania
Ramree Island *136 A4 island* W Myanmar
Ramtha *see* Ar Ramthā
Rancagua *64 B4* Libertador, C Chile
Rānchi *135 F4* Bihār, N India
Randers *85 B7* Århus, C Denmark
Rangiora *151 C6* Canterbury, South Island, NZ
Rangitikei *150 D4 river* North Island, NZ
Rangoon *see* Yangon
Rangpur *135 G3* Rajshahi, N Bangladesh
Rankin Inlet *37 G3* Nunavut, C Canada
Ranong *137 B6* Ranong, SW Thailand
Rapa Nui *see* Easter Island
Raphiah *see* Rafah
Rapid City *44 D3* South Dakota, N USA
Räpina *106 E3 Ger.* Rappin. Põlvamaa, SE Estonia

Rapla 106 D2 Ger. Rappel.
Raplamaa, NW Estonia
Rarotonga 145 G5 island S Cook
Islands, C Pacific Ocean
Ras al 'Ain see Ra's al 'Ayn
Ra's al 'Ayn 118 D1 var. Ras al 'Ain.
Al Ḥasakah, N Syria
Ra's an Naqb 119 B7 Ma'ān,
S Jordan
Raseiniai 106 B4 Raseiniai,
C Lithuania
Ras Hafun see Xaafuun, Raas
Rasht 120 C2 var. Resht. Gīlān,
NW Iran
Râşnov 108 C4 prev. Rîşno,
Rozsnyó, Hung. Barcarozsnyó.
Braşov, C Romania
Ratak Chain 144 D1 island group
Ratak Chain, E Marshall Islands
Ratan 85 C5 Jämtland, C Sweden
Rat Buri see Ratchaburi
Ratchaburi 137 C5 var. Rat Buri.
Ratchaburi, W Thailand
Rastenburg see Kętrzyn
Rat Islands 36 A2 island group
Aleutian Islands, Alaska, USA
Ratlām 134 D4 prev. Rutlam.
Madhya Pradesh, C India
Ratnapura 132 D4 Sabaragamuwa
Province, S Sri Lanka
Raton 48 D1 New Mexico, SW USA
Rättvik 85 C5 Kopparberg,
C Sweden
Raudhatain see Ar Rawḍatayn
Raufarhöfn 83 E4 Nordhurland
Eystra, NE Iceland
Raukawa see Cook Strait
Raukumara Range 150 E3 mountain
range North Island, NZ
Raŭlakela 151 F4 var Raurkela, prev.
Rourkela. Orissa, E India
Rauma 85 D5 Swe. Raumo. Länsi-
Suomi, W Finland
Raurkela see Raulakela
Ravenna 96 C3 Emilia-Romagna,
N Italy
Rāvi 134 C2 river India/Pakistan
Rāwalpindi 134 C1 Punjab,
NE Pakistan
Rawa Mazowiecka 98 D4 Łódzkie,
C Poland
Rawicz 98 C4 Ger. Rawitsch.
Wielkopolskie, C Poland
Rawlins 44 C3 Wyoming, C USA
Rawson 65 C6 Chubut,
SE Argentina
Rayak 118 B4 var. Rayaq, Riyāq.
E Lebanon
Rayaq see Rayak
Rayleigh 43 F1 state capital North
Carolina, SE USA
Rayong 137 C5 Rayong,
S Thailand
Razāzah, Buḥayrat ar 120 B3 var.
Baḥr al Milḥ. Lake C Iraq
Razgrad 104 D2 Razgrad,
N Bulgaria
Razim, Lacul 108 D5 prev. Lacul
Razelm. Lagoon NW Black Sea
Reading 41 F4 Pennsylvania,
NE USA
Reading 89 D7 S England, UK
Realicó 64 C4 La Pampa,
C Argentina
Reăng Kesei 137 D5 Bătdâmbâng,
W Cambodia
Rebecca, Lake 147 C6 lake Western
Australia
Rebiana Sand Sea see Rabyanāh,
Ramlat
Rebun-tō 130 C2 island NE Japan
Rechytsa 107 D7 Rus. Rechitsa.
Brestskaya Voblasts', SW Belarus
Recife 63 G2 prev. Pernambuco.
State capital Pernambuco,
E Brazil
Recklinghausen 94 A4 Nordrhein-
Westfalen, W Germany
Recogne 87 C7 Luxembourg,
SE Belgium
Reconquista 64 D3 Santa Fe,
C Argentina
Red Deer 37 E5 Alberta,
SW Canada
Redding 47 B5 California, W USA
Redon 90 B4 Ille-et-Vilaine,
NW France

Red River 136 C2 var. Yuan, Chin.
Yuan Jiang, Vtn. Sông Hồng Hà.
River China/Vietnam
Red River 45 E1 river Canada/USA
Red River 42 B3 river Louisiana,
S USA
Red River 35 C6 river S USA
Red Sea 72 C3 anc. Sinus Arabicus.
Sea Africa/Asia
Red Wing 45 G2 Minnesota, N USA
Reefton 151 C5 West Coast, South
Island, NZ
Reese River 47 C5 river Nevada,
W USA
Refahiye 117 E3 Erzincan, C Turkey
Regensburg 95 C6 Eng. Ratisbon,
Fr. Ratisbonne; hist. Ratisbona,
anc. Castra Regina, Reginum.
Bayern, SE Germany
Regenstauf 95 C6 Bayern,
SE Germany
Reggane 70 D3 C Algeria
Reggio see Reggio nell' Emilia
Reggio Calabria see Reggio di
Calabria
Reggio di Calabria 97 D7 var.
Reggio Calabria, Gk. Rhegion; anc.
Regium, Rhegium. Calabria,
SW Italy
Reggio Emilia see Reggio nell'
Emilia
Reggio nell' Emilia 96 B2 var.
Reggio Emilia, abbrev. Reggio; anc.
Regium Lepidum. Emilia-
Romagna, N Italy
Reghin 108 C4 Ger. Sächsisch-Reen,
Hung. Szászrégen; prev. Reghinul
Săsesc, Ger. Sächsisch-Regen.
Mureş, C Romania
Regina 37 F5 Saskatchewan,
S Canada
Registan see Rīgestān
Regium see Reggio di Calabria
Regium Lepidum see Reggio nell'
Emilia
Rehoboth see Rehovot
Rehoboth 78 B3 Hardap,
C Namibia
Reḥovot 119 A6 var. Rehoboth,
Rehovoth, Rekhovot. Central,
C Israel
Rehovoth see Rehovot
Reid 147 D6 Western Australia
Reikjavik see Reykjavík
Ré, Île de 90 A4 island W France
Reims 90 D3 Eng. Rheims; anc.
Durocortorum, Remi. Marne,
N France
Reindeer Lake 37 F4 lake
Manitoba/Saskatchewan,
C Canada
Reinga, Cape 150 C1 headland North
Island, NZ
Reinosa 92 D1 Cantabria, N Spain
Rekhovot see Rehovot
Reliance 37 F4 Northwest
Territories, C Canada
Rendina see Rentína
Rendsburg 94 B2 Schleswig-
Holstein, N Germany
Rengat 138 B4 Sumatera,
W Indonesia
Reni 108 D4 Odes'ka Oblast',
SW Ukraine
Rennell 144 C4 var. Mu Nggava.
Island S Solomon Islands
Rennes 90 B3 Bret. Roazon; anc.
Condate. Ille-et-Vilaine,
NW France
Reno 47 C5 Nevada, W USA
Renqiu 128 C4 Hebei, E China
Rentína 105 B5 var. Rendina.
Thessalía, C Greece
Republika Srpska Admin. region
republic Bosnia and Herzegovina
République Centrafricaine see
Central African Republic
Repulse Bay 37 G3 Nunavut,
N Canada
Resht see Rasht
Resistencia 64 D3 Chaco,
NE Argentina
Reşiţa 108 A4 Ger. Reschitza, Hung.
Resicabánya. Caraş-Severin,
W Romania
Resolute 37 F2 Cornwallis Island,
Nunavut, N Canada

Resolution Island 39 E1 island
Northwest Territories, NE Canada
Resolution Island 151 A7 island
SW NZ
Réunion 79 H4 off. La Réunion.
French overseas department
W Indian Ocean
Réunion 141 B5 island W Indian
Ocean
Reus 93 F2 Cataluña, E Spain
Reutlingen 95 B6 Baden-
Württemberg, S Germany
Reuver 87 D5 Limburg,
SE Netherlands
Revillagigedo Islands see
Revillagigedo, Islas
Revillagigedo, Islas 50 B5 Eng.
Revillagigedo Islands. Island group
W Mexico
Rexburg 46 E3 Idaho, NW USA
Reyes 61 F3 Beni, NW Bolivia
Rey, Isla del 53 G5 island
Archipiélago de las Perlas,
SE Panama
Reykjanes Basin 82 C5 var.
Irminger Basin. Undersea feature
N Atlantic Ocean
Reykjanes Ridge 80 A1 undersea
feature N Atlantic Ocean
Reykjavík 83 E5 var. Reikjavik.
Country capital (Iceland)
Höfudhborgarsvaedhi, W Iceland
Reynosa 51 E2 Tamaulipas,
C Mexico
Rezé 90 A4 Loire-Atlantique,
NW France
Rēzekne 106 D4 Ger. Rositten; prev.
Rus. Rezhitsa. Rēzekne, SE Latvia
Rezovo 104 E3 Turk. Rezve. Burgas,
E Bulgaria
Rhegion see Reggio di Calabria
Rhegium see Reggio di Calabria
Rhein see Rhine
Rheine 94 A3 var. Rheine in
Westfalen. Nordrhein-Westfalen,
NW Germany
Rheine in Westfalen see Rheine
Rheinisches Schiefergebirge 95 A5
var. Rhine State Uplands, Eng.
Rhenish Slate Mountains.
Mountain range W Germany
Rhenish Slate Mountains see
Rheinisches Schiefergebirge
Rhine 80 D4 Dut. Rijn, Fr. Rhin, Ger.
Rhein. River W Europe
Rhinelander 40 B2 Wisconsin,
N USA
Rhine State Uplands see
Rheinisches Schiefergebirge
Rho 96 B2 Lombardia, N Italy
Rhode Island 41 G3 off. State of
Rhode Island and Providence
Plantations; also known as Little
Rhody, Ocean State. State NE USA
Rhodes see Ródos
Rhodope Mountains 104 C3 var.
Rodhópi Óri, Bul. Rhodope
Planina, Rodopi, Gk. Orosirá
Rodhópis, Turk. Dospad Dagh.
Mountain range Bulgaria/Greece
Rhodope Planina see Rhodope
Mountains
Rhodos see Ródos
Rhône 80 C4 river
France/Switzerland
Rhône 91 D6 department E France
Rhum 88 B3 var. Rum. Island
W Scotland, UK
Ribble 89 D5 river NW England, UK
Ribeira 92 B1 Galicia, NW Spain
Ribeirão Preto 63 F4 São Paulo,
S Brazil
Riberalta 61 F2 Beni, N Bolivia
Rîbniţa 108 D3 var. Râbniţa, Rus.
Rybnitsa. NE Moldova
Rice Lake 40 A2 Wisconsin, N USA
Richard Toll 74 B3 N Senegal
Richfield 44 B4 Utah, W USA
Richland 46 C2 Washington,
NW USA
Richmond 41 E5 state capital
Virginia, NE USA
Richmond 40 C5 Kentucky, S USA
Richmond 151 C5 Tasman, South
Island, NZ
Richmond Range 151 C5 mountain
range South Island, NZ

Ricobayo, Embalse de 92 C2
reservoir NW Spain
Ridgecrest 47 C7 California, W USA
Ried see Ried im Innkreis
Ried im Innkreis 95 D6 var. Ried.
Oberösterreich, NW Austria
Riemst 87 D6 Limburg, NE Belgium
Riesa 94 D4 Sachsen, E Germany
Rift Valley see Great Rift Valley
Rīga 106 C3 Eng. Riga. Country
capital (Latvia) Rīga, C Latvia
Riga, Gulf of 106 C3 Est. Liivi Laht,
Ger. Rigaer Bucht, Latv. Rīgas
Jūras Līcis, Rus. Rizhskiy Zaliv;
prev. Est. Riia Laht. Gulf
Estonia/Latvia
Rīgān 120 E4 Kermān, SE Iran
Rīgestān 122 D5 var. Registan.
Desert region S Afghanistan
Riihimäki 85 D5 Etelä-Suomi,
S Finland
Rijeka 100 A2 Ger. Sankt Veit am
Flaum, It. Fiume, Slvn. Reka; anc.
Tarsatica. Primorje-Gorski Kotar,
NW Croatia
Rijssel see Lille
Rijssen 86 E3 Overijssel,
E Netherlands
Rimah, Wādī ar 120 B4 var. Wādī ar
Rummah. Dry watercourse C Saudi
Arabia
Rimini 96 C3 anc. Ariminum.
Emilia-Romagna, N Italy
Rimouski 39 E4 Québec,
SE Canada
Ringebu 85 B5 Oppland,
S Norway
Ringkøbing Fjord 85 A7 fjord
W Denmark
Ringvassøya 84 C2 island N Norway
Rio see Rio de Janeiro
Riobamba 60 B1 Chimborazo,
C Ecuador
Rio Branco 56 B3 state capital Acre,
W Brazil
Río Bravo 51 E2 Tamaulipas,
C Mexico
Río Cuarto 64 C4 Córdoba,
C Argentina
Rio de Janeiro 63 F4 var. Rio. State
capital Rio de Janeiro, SE Brazil
Río Gallegos 65 B7 var. Gallegos,
Puerto Gallegos. Santa Cruz,
S Argentina
Rio Grande 63 E5 var. São Pedro do
Rio Grande do Sul. Rio Grande do
Sul, S Brazil
Río Grande 50 D3 Zacatecas,
C Mexico
Rio Grande do Norte 63 G2 off.
Estado do Rio Grande do Norte.
State E Brazil
Rio Grande do Sul 63 E5 off. Estado
do Rio Grande do Sul. State
S Brazil
Rio Grande Plateau see Rio Grande
Rise
Rio Grande Rise 57 E6 var. Rio
Grande Plateau. Undersea feature
SW Atlantic Ocean
Ríohacha 58 B1 La Guajira,
N Colombia
Río Lagartos 51 H3 Yucatán,
SE Mexico
Riom 91 C5 anc. Ricomagus. Puy-
de-Dôme, C France
Río San Juan 53 E4 department
S Nicaragua
Rioverde see Río Verde
Río Verde 51 E4 var. Rioverde. San
Luis Potosí, C Mexico
Ripoll 93 G2 Cataluña, NE Spain
Rishiri-tō 130 C2 var. Risiri Tô.
Island NE Japan
Risiri Tô see Rishiri-tō
Risti 106 D2 Ger. Kreuz. Läänemaa,
W Estonia
Rivas 52 D4 Rivas, SW Nicaragua
Rivera 64 D3 Rivera, NE
Uruguay
River Falls 40 A2 Wisconsin,
N USA
River Plate see Plata, Río de la
Riverside 47 C7 California, W USA
Riverton 151 A7 Southland, South
Island, NZ
Riverton 44 C3 Wyoming, C USA

Rivière-du-Loup *39 E4* Québec, SE Canada
Rivne *108 C2 Pol.* Równe, *Rus.* Rovno. Rivnens'ka Oblast', NW Ukraine
Rivoli *96 A2* Piemonte, NW Italy
Riyadh *see* Ar Riyāḍ
Riyāq *see* Rayak
Rize *117 E2* Rize, NE Turkey
Rizhao *128 D4* Shandong, E China
Rkiz *74 C3* Trarza, W Mauritania
Road Town *55 F3 dependent territory capital* (British Virgin Islands) Tortola, C British Virgin Islands
Roanne *91 C5 anc.* Rodunma. Loire, E France
Roanoke *41 E5* Virginia, NE USA
Roanoke River *43 F1 river* North Carolina/Virginia, SE USA
Roatán *52 C2 var.* Coxen Hole, Coxin Hole. Islas de la Bahía, N Honduras
Robbie Ridge *143 E3 undersea feature* W Pacific Ocean
Robert Williams *see* Caála
Robinson Range *147 B5 mountain range* Western Australia
Robson, Mount *37 E5 mountain* British Columbia, SW Canada
Robstown *49 G4* Texas, SW USA
Roca Partida, Isla *50 B5 island* W Mexico
Rocas, Atol das *63 G2 island* E Brazil
Rochefort *90 B4 var.* Rochefort sur Mer. Charente-Maritime, W France
Rochefort *87 C7* Namur, SE Belgium
Rochefort sur Mer *see* Rochefort
Rochester *45 G3* Minnesota, N USA
Rochester *41 G2* New Hampshire, NE USA
Rochester *41 E3* New York, NE USA
Rockall Bank *80 B2 undersea feature* N Atlantic Ocean
Rockall Trough *80 B2 undersea feature* N Atlantic Ocean
Rockdale *148 E2* New South Wales, SE Australia
Rockford *40 B3* Illinois, N USA
Rockhampton *148 D4* Queensland, E Australia
Rock Hill *43 E1* South Carolina, SE USA
Rockies *see* Rocky Mountains
Rockingham *147 A6* Western Australia
Rock Island *40 B3* Illinois, N USA
Rock Sound *54 C1* Eleuthera Island, C Bahamas
Rock Springs *44 C3* Wyoming, C USA
Rockstone *59 F3* C Guyana
Rocky Mount *43 F1* North Carolina, SE USA
Rocky Mountains *34 B4 var.* Rockies, *Fr.* Montagnes Rocheuses. *Mountain range* Canada/USA
Roden *86 E2* Drenthe, NE Netherlands
Rodez *91 C5 anc.* Segodunum. Aveyron, S France
Rodhópi Óri *see* Rhodope Mountains
Ródhos *see* Ródos
Rodi *see* Ródos
Rodopi *see* Rhodope Mountains
Ródos *105 E7 var.* Ródhos, *Eng.* Rhodes, *It.* Rodi; *anc.* Rhodos. Island Dodekánisos, Greece, Aegean Sea
Roermond *87 D5* Limburg, SE Netherlands
Roeselare *87 A6 Fr.* Roulers; *prev.* Rousselaere. West-Vlaanderen, W Belgium
Rogatica *100 C4* Republika Srpska, SE Bosnia and Herzegovina
Rogers *42 A1* Arkansas, C USA
Roger Simpson Island *see* Abemama
Roi Ed *see* Roi Et
Roi Et *137 D5 var.* Muang Roi Et, Roi Ed. Roi Et, E Thailand

Roja *106 C2* Talsi, NW Latvia
Rokiškis *106 C4* Rokiškis, NE Lithuania
Rokycany *99 A5 Ger.* Rokytzan. Plzeňský Kraj, W Czech Republic
Rokytzan *see* Rokycany
Rólas, Ilha das *76 E2 island* S Sao Tome and Principe
Rolla *45 G5* Missouri, C USA
Roma *96 C4 Eng.* Rome. *Country capital* (Italy) Lazio, C Italy
Roma *149 D5* Queensland, E Australia
Roman *108 C4 Hung.* Románvásár. Neamț, NE Romania
Roman *104 C2* Vratsa, NW Bulgaria
Romania *108 B4 Bul.* Rumŭniya, *Ger.* Rumänien, *Hung.* Románia, *Rom.* România, *SCr.* Rumunjska, *Ukr.* Rumuniya; *prev.* Republica Socialistă România, Roumania, Rumania, Socialist Republic of Romania, *Rom.* Romînia. *Country* SE Europe

Romania 108

Official name Romania
Formation 1878
Capital Bucharest
Population 22.3 million / 251 people per sq mile (97 people per sq km)
Total area 88,934 sq miles (230,340 sq km)
Languages Romanian, Hungarian, German
Religions Romanian Orthodox 87%, Roman Catholic 5%, other 8%
Ethnic mix Romanian 89%, Magyar 9%, Romany 1%, other 1%
Government Multiparty republic
Currency Leu = 100 bani
Literacy rate 97.8%
Calorie consumption 3,051 kilocalories

Rome *see* Roma
Rome *42 D2* Georgia, SE USA
Romny *109 F2* Sums'ka Oblast', NE Ukraine
Rømø *85 A7 Ger.* Röm. *Island* SW Denmark
Roncador, Serra do *56 D4 mountain range* C Brazil
Ronda *92 D5* Andalucía, S Spain
Rondônia *62 D3 off.* Estado de Rondônia; *prev.* Território de Rondônia. *State* W Brazil
Rondonópolis *63 E3* Mato Grosso, W Brazil
Rongelap Atoll *144 D1 var.* Rōñļap. Atoll Ralik Chain, NW Marshall Islands
Rōngu *106 D3 Ger.* Ringen. Tartumaa, SE Estonia
Rōñļap *see* Rongelap Atoll
Rønne *85 B8* Bornholm, E Denmark
Ronne Ice Shelf *154 A3 ice shelf* Antarctica
Roosendaal *87 C5* Noord-Brabant, S Netherlands
Roosevelt Island *154 B4 island* Antarctica
Roraima *62 D1 off.* Estado de Roraima; *prev.* Território de Rio Branco, Território de Roraima. *State* N Brazil
Roraima, Mount *59 E3 mountain* N South America
Røros *85 B5* Sør-Trøndelag, S Norway
Rosa, Lake *54 D2 lake* Great Inagua, S Bahamas
Rosario *64 D2* San Pedro, C Paraguay
Rosario *64 D4* Santa Fe, C Argentina
Rosarito *50 A1* Baja California, NW Mexico
Roscommon *40 C2* Michigan, N USA
Roseau *55 G4 prev.* Charlotte Town. *Country capital* (Dominica) SW Dominica
Roseburg *46 B4* Oregon, NW USA

Rosenberg *49 G4* Texas, SW USA
Rosengarten *94 B3* Niedersachsen, N Germany
Rosenheim *95 C6* Bayern, S Germany
Rosia *93 H5* W Gibraltar
Rosia Bay *93 H5 bay* SW Gibraltar
Roşiori de Vede *108 B5* Teleorman, S Romania
Roslavl' *111 A5* Smolenskaya Oblast', W Russian Federation
Rosmalen *86 C4* Noord-Brabant, S Netherlands
Ross *151 B6* West Coast, South Island, NZ
Rossano *97 E6 anc.* Roscianum. Calabria, SW Italy
Ross Ice Shelf *154 B4 ice shelf* Antarctica
Rosso *74 B3* Trarza, SW Mauritania
Rossosh' *111 B6* Voronezhskaya Oblast', W Russian Federation
Ross Sea *154 B4 sea* Antarctica
Rostak *see* Ar Rustāq
Rostock *94 C2* Mecklenburg-Vorpommern, NE Germany
Rostov *see* Rostov-na-Donu
Rostov-na-Donu *111 B7 var.* Rostov, *Eng.* Rostov-on-Don. Rostovskaya Oblast', SW Russian Federation
Rostov-on-Don *see* Rostov-na-Donu
Roswell *48 D2* New Mexico, SW USA
Rota *144 B1 island* S Northern Mariana Islands
Rothera *154 A2 UK research station* Antarctica
Rotorua *150 D3* Bay of Plenty, North Island, NZ
Rotorua, Lake *150 D3 lake* North Island, NZ
Rotterdam *86 C4* Zuid-Holland, SW Netherlands
Rottweil *95 B6* Baden-Württemberg, S Germany
Rotuma *145 E4 island* NW Fiji
Roubaix *90 C2* Nord, N France
Rouen *90 C3 anc.* Rotomagus. Seine-Maritime, N France
Round Rock *49 G3* Texas, SW USA
Rourkela *see* Rāulakela
Roussillon *91 C6 cultural region* S France
Rouyn-Noranda *38 D4* Québec, SE Canada
Rovaniemi *84 D3* Lappi, N Finland
Rovigo *96 C2* Veneto, NE Italy
Rovinj *100 A3 It.* Rovigno. Istra, NW Croatia
Rovuma, Rio *79 F2 var.* Ruvuma. *River* Mozambique/Tanzania *see also* Ruvuma
Rovuma, Rio *see* Ruvuma
Roxas City *139 E2* Panay Island, C Philippines
Royale, Isle *40 B1 island* Michigan, N USA
Royan *91 B5* Charente-Maritime, W France
Rozdol'ne *109 F4 Rus.* Razdolnoye. Respublika Krym, S Ukraine
Rožňava *99 D6 Ger.* Rosenau, *Hung.* Rozsnyó. Košický Kraj, E Slovakia
Ruapehu, Mount *150 D4 mountain* North Island, NZ
Ruapuke Island *151 B8 island* SW NZ
Ruatoria *150 E3* Gisborne, North Island, NZ
Ruawai *150 D2* Northland, North Island, NZ
Rubizhne *109 H3 Rus.* Rubezhnoye. Luhans'ka Oblast', E Ukraine
Ruby Mountains *47 D5 mountain range* Nevada, W USA
Rucava *106 B3* Liepāja, SW Latvia
Rūd-e Hirmand *see* Helmand, Daryā-ye
Rūdiškės *107 B5* Trakai, S Lithuania
Rudnik *104 E2* Varna, E Bulgaria
Rudny *see* Rudnyy
Rudnyy *114 C4 var.* Rudny. Kostanay, N Kazakhstan
Rudolf, Lake *see* Turkana, Lake

Rudolfswert *see* Novo Mesto
Rudzyensk *107 C6 Rus.* Rudensk. Minskaya Voblasts', C Belarus
Rufiji *73 C7 river* E Tanzania
Rufino *64 C4* Santa Fe, C Argentina
Rugāji *106 D4* Balvi, E Latvia
Rügen *94 D2 headland* NE Germany
Ruggell *94 E1* N Liechtenstein
Ruhnu *106 C2 var.* Ruhnu Saar, *Swe.* Runö. Island SW Estonia
Ruhnu Saar *see* Ruhnu
Rūjiena *106 D3 Est.* Ruhja, *Ger.* Rujen. Valmiera, N Latvia
Rukwa, Lake *73 B7 lake* SE Tanzania
Rum *see* Rhum
Ruma *100 D3* Serbia, N Yugoslavia
Rumadiya *see* Ar Ramādī
Rumbek *73 B5* El Buhayrat, S Sudan
Rum Cay *54 D2 island* C Bahamas
Rumia *98 C2* Pomorskie, N Poland
Rummah, Wādī ar *see* Rimah, Wādī ar
Runanga *151 B5* West Coast, South Island, NZ
Runaway Bay *54 B4* C Jamaica
Rundu *78 C3 var.* Runtu. Okavango, NE Namibia
Runö *see* Ruhnu
Runtu *see* Rundu
Ruoqiang *126 C3 var.* Jo-ch'iang, *Uigh.* Charkhlik, Charkhliq, Qarkilik. Xinjiang Uygur Zizhiqu, NW China
Rupea *108 C4 Ger.* Reps, *Hung.* Kőhalom; *prev.* Cohalm. Brașov, C Romania
Rupel *87 B5 river* N Belgium
Rupert, Rivière de *38 D3 river* Québec, C Canada
Ruschuk *see* Ruse
Rusçuk *see* Ruse
Ruse *104 D1 var.* Ruschuk, Rustchuk, *Turk.* Rusçuk. Ruse, N Bulgaria
Rus Krymskaya ASSR *see* Crimea
Russellville *42 A1* Arkansas, C USA
Russian Federation *112 D2 var.* Russia, *Latv.* Krievija, *Rus.* Rossiyskaya Federatsiya. *Country* Asia/Europe

Russian Federation 112

Official name Russian Federation
Formation 1991
Capital Moscow
Population 147 million / 22 people per sq mile (9 people per sq km)
Total area 6,592,812 sq miles (17,075,400 sq km)
Languages Russian
Religions Russian Orthodox 75%, other 25%
Ethnic mix Russian 82%, Tatar 4%, Ukranian 3%, Chuvash 1%, other 10%
Government Multiparty republic
Currency Rouble = 100 kopeks
Literacy rate 99%
Calorie consumption not available

Rustaq *see* Ar Rustāq
Rust'avi *117 G2* SE Georgia
Rustchuk *see* Ruse
Ruston *42 B2* Louisiana, S USA
Rutanzige I M, Lake *see* Edward, Lake
Rutba *see* Ar Ruṭbah
Rutland *41 F2* Vermont, NE USA
Rutog *126 A4 var.* Rutok. Xizang Zizhiqu, W China
Rutok *see* Rutog
Ruvuma *69 C5 var.* Rio Rovuma. *River* Mozambique/Tanzania *see also* Rovuma, Rio
Ruvuma *see* Rovuma, Rio
Ruwenzori *77 E5 mountain range* Uganda/Dem. Rep. Congo (Zaire)
Ruzhany *107 B6 Rus.* Ruzhany. Brestskaya Voblasts', SW Belarus

Ružomberok *99 C5 Ger.* Rosenberg, *Hung.* Rózsahegy. Žilinsky Kraj, N Slovakia
Rwanda *73 B6 prev.* Ruanda. *Country* C Africa

Rwanda 73

Official name Republic of Rwanda
Formation 1982
Capital Kigali
Population 7.7 million / 799 people per sq mile (309 people per sq km)
Total area 9,633 sq miles (24,950 sq km)
Languages French, Rwandan, Kiswahili, English
Religions Roman Catholic 65%, Protestant 9%, Muslim 1%, other 25%
Ethnic mix Hutu 90%, Tutsi 8%, other (including Twa) 2%
Government Multiparty republic
Currency Rwanda franc = 100 centimes
Literacy rate 63%
Calorie consumption 1,821 kilocalories

Ryazan' *111 B5* Ryazanskaya Oblast', W Russian Federation
Rybinsk *110 B4 prev.* Andropov. Yaroslavskaya Oblast', W Russian Federation
Rybnik *99 C5* Śląskie, S Poland
Rybnitsa *see* Rîbniţa
Ryde *148 E1* New South Wales, SE Australia
Ryki *98 D4* Lublin, E Poland
Rypin *98 C3* Kujawsko-pomorskie, C Poland
Ryssel *see* Lille
Rysy *99 C5 mountain* S Poland
Ryukyu Islands *125 E3 island group* SW Japan
Ryukyu Trench *125 F3 var.* Nansei Syotō Trench. *Undersea feature* S East China Sea
Rzeszów *99 E5* Podkarpackie, SE Poland
Rzhev *110 B4* Tverskaya Oblast', W Russian Federation

S

Saale *94 C4 river* C Germany
Saalfeld *95 C5 var.* Saalfeld an der Saale. Thüringen, C Germany
Saalfeld an der Saale *see* Saalfeld
Saarbrücken *95 A6 Fr.* Sarrebruck. Saarland, SW Germany
Säare *106 C2 var.* Sjar. Saaremaa, W Estonia
Saaremaa *106 C2 Ger.* Oesel, Ösel; *prev.* Saare. *Island* W Estonia
Saariselkä *84 D2 Lapp.* Suoločielgi. Lappi, N Finland
Sab' Ābār *118 C4 var.* Sab'a Biyar, Sa'b Bi'ār. Ḩimş, C Syria
Sab'a Biyar *see* Sab' Ābār
Šabac *100 D3* Serbia, W Yugoslavia
Sabadell *93 G2* Cataluña, E Spain
Sabah *138 D3 cultural region* Borneo, SE Asia
Sabanalarga *58 B1* Atlántico, N Colombia
Sabaneta *58 C1* Falcón, N Venezuela
Sab'atayn, Ramlat as *121 C6 desert* C Yemen
Sabaya *61 F4* Oruro, S Bolivia
Sa'b Bi'ār *see* Sab' Ābār
Şāberī, Hāmūn-e *var.* Daryācheh-ye Hāmūn, Daryācheh-ye Sīstān. *Lake* Afghanistan/Iran *see also* Sīstān, Daryācheh-ye
Sabhā *71 F3* C Libya
Sabi, Rio *see* Save, Rio
Sabinas *51 E2* Coahuila de Zaragoza, NE Mexico
Sabinas Hidalgo *51 E2* Nuevo León, NE Mexico
Sabine River *49 H3 river* Louisiana/Texas, SW USA
Sabkha *see* As Sabkhah

Sable, Cape *43 E5 headland* Florida, SE USA
Sable Island *39 G4 island* Nova Scotia, SE Canada
Şabyā *121 B6* Jīzān, SW Saudi Arabia
Sabzawar *see* Sabzevār
Sabzevār *120 D2 var.* Sabzawar. Khorāsān, NE Iran
Sachsen *94 D4 Eng.* Saxony, *Fr.* Saxe. *State* E Germany
Sachs Harbour *37 E2* Banks Island, Northwest Territories, N Canada
Sacramento *47 B5 state capital* California, W USA
Sacramento Mountains *48 D2 mountain range* New Mexico, SW USA
Sacramento River *47 B5 river* California, W USA
Sacramento Valley *47 B5 valley* California, W USA
Şa'dah *121 B6* NW Yemen
Sado *131 C5 var.* Sadoga-shima. *Island* C Japan
Sadoga-shima *see* Sado
Safad *see* Zefat
Safed *see* Zefat
Säffle *85 B6* Värmland, C Sweden
Safford *48 C3* Arizona, SW USA
Safi *70 B2* W Morocco
Safīd Kūh, Selseleh-ye *122 D4 Eng.* Paropamisus Range. *Mountain range* W Afghanistan
Sagaing *136 B3* Sagaing, C Myanmar
Sagami-nada *131 D6 inlet* SW Japan
Sagan *see* Żagań
Sāgar *134 D4 prev.* Saugor. Madhya Pradesh, C India
Saghez *see* Saqqez
Saginaw *40 C3* Michigan, N USA
Saginaw Bay *40 D2 lake bay* Michigan, N USA
Sagua la Grande *54 B2* Villa Clara, C Cuba
Sagunt *see* Sagunto
Sagunto *93 F3 var.* Sagunt, *Ar.* Murviedro; *anc.* Saguntum. País Valenciano, E Spain
Saguntum *see* Sagunto
Sahara *68 B3 desert* Libya/Algeria
Sahara el Gharbîya *72 B2 var.* Aş Şaḥrā' al Gharbīyah, *Eng.* Western Desert. *Desert* C Egypt
Saharan Atlas *see* Atlas Saharien
Sahel *74 D3 physical region* C Africa
Sāḩilīyah, Jibāl as *118 B3 mountain range* NW Syria
Sāhīwāl *134 C2 prev.* Montgomery. Punjab, E Pakistan
ṣaḥrā' Rabyanāh *see* Rabyanāh, Ramlat
Saïda *119 A5 var.* Şaydā, Sayida; *anc.* Sidon. W Lebanon
Saidpur *135 G3 var.* Syedpur. Rajshahi, NW Bangladesh
Saigon *see* Hô Chi Minh
Sai Hun *see* Syr Darya
Saimaa *85 E5 lake* SE Finland
St Albans *89 E6 anc.* Verulamium. E England, UK
Saint Albans *40 D5* West Virginia, NE USA
St Andrews *88 C4* E Scotland, UK
Saint Anna Trough *see* Svyataya Anna Trough
St.Ann's Bay *54 B4* C Jamaica
St.Anthony *39 G3* Newfoundland, Newfoundland and Labrador, SE Canada
Saint Augustine *43 E3* Florida, SE USA
St Austell *89 C7* SW England, UK
St-Brieuc *90 A3* Côtes d'Armor, NW France
St. Catharines *38 D5* Ontario, S Canada
St-Chamond *91 D5* Loire, E France
St.Clair, Lake *40 D3 Fr.* Lac à L'Eau Claire. *Lake* Canada/USA
St-Claude *91 D5 anc.* Condate. Jura, E France
Saint Cloud *45 F2* Minnesota, N USA
St Croix *55 F3 island* S Virgin Islands (US)

Saint Croix River *40 A2 river* Minnesota/Wisconsin, N USA
St David's Island *42 B5 island* E Bermuda
St-Denis *79 G4 dependent territory capital* (Réunion) NW Réunion
St-Dié *90 E4* Vosges, NE France
St-Egrève *91 D5* Isère, E France
Saintes *91 B5 anc.* Mediolanum. Charente-Maritime, W France
St-Étienne *91 D5* Loire, E France
St-Flour *91 C5* Cantal, C France
Saint Gall *see* Sankt Gallen
St-Gaudens *91 B6* Haute-Garonne, S France
St George *42 B4* N Bermuda
Saint George *149 D5* Queensland, E Australia
Saint George *44 A5* Utah, W USA
St.George's *55 G5 country capital* (Grenada) SW Grenada
St-Georges *59 H3* E French Guiana
St-Georges *39 E4* Québec, SE Canada
St George's Channel *89 B6 channel* Ireland/Wales, UK
St George's Island *42 B4 island* E Bermuda
Saint Helena *69 B6 UK dependent territory* C Atlantic Ocean
St.Helena Bay *78 B5 bay* SW South Africa
St Helier *89 D8 dependent territory capital* (Jersey) S Jersey, Channel Islands
Saint Ignace *40 C2* Michigan, N USA
St-Jean, Lac *39 E4 lake* Québec, SE Canada
Saint Joe River *46 D2 river* Idaho, NW USA
Saint John *41 H1 river* Canada/USA
Saint John *39 F4* New Brunswick, SE Canada
St John's *55 G3 country capital* (Antigua and Barbuda) Antigua, Antigua and Barbuda
St.John's *39 H3* Newfoundland, Newfoundland and Labrador, E Canada
Saint Joseph *45 F4* Missouri, C USA
St Julian's *102 B5* N Malta
St Kilda *88 A3 island* NW Scotland, UK
Saint Kitts and Nevis *55 F3 var.* Saint Christopher-Nevis. *Country* E West Indies

Saint Kitts & Nevis 55

Official name Federation of Saint Christopher and Nevis
Formation 1983
Capital Basseterre
Population 41,000 / 289 people per sq mile (111 people per sq km)
Total area 139 sq miles (360 sq km)
Languages English, English Creole
Religions Anglican 33%, Methodist 29%, Roman Catholic 7%, other 31%
Ethnic mix Black 95%, mixed 5%
Government Parliamentary democracy
Currency Eastern Caribbean dollar = 100 cents
Literacy rate 90%
Calorie consumption 2,419 kilocalories

St-Laurent-du-Maroni *59 H3 var.* St-Laurent. NW French Guiana
St.Lawrence *39 E4 Fr.* Fleuve St-Laurent. *River* Canada/USA
St.Lawrence, Gulf of *39 F3 gulf* NW Atlantic Ocean
Saint Lawrence Island *36 B2 island* Alaska, USA
St-Lô *90 B3 anc.* Briovera, Laudus. Manche, N France
St-Louis *90 E4* Haut-Rhin, NE France
Saint Louis *45 G4* Missouri, C USA
Saint Louis *74 B3* NW Senegal

Saint Lucia *55 E1 country* SE West Indies

Saint Lucia 55

Official name Saint Lucia
Formation 1979
Capital Castries
Population 152,000 / 641 people per sq mile (248 people per sq km)
Total area 235 sq miles (610 sq km)
Languages English, French Creole
Religions Roman Catholic 90%, other 10%
Ethnic mix Black 90%, African-European 6%, South Asian 4%
Government Parliamentary democracy
Currency Eastern Caribbean dollar = 100 cents
Literacy rate 82%
Calorie consumption 2,588 kilocalories

Saint Lucia Channel *55 H4 channel* Martinique/Saint Lucia
St-Malo *90 B3* Ille-et-Vilaine, NW France
St-Malo, Golfe de *90 A3 gulf* NW France
St Matthew's Island *see* Zadetkyi Kyun
St.Matthias Group *144 B3 island group* NE PNG
St-Maur-des-Fossés *90 E2* Val-de-Marne, N France
St.Moritz *95 B7 Ger.* Sankt Moritz, *Rmsch.* San Murezzan. Graubünden, SE Switzerland
St-Nazaire *90 A4* Loire-Atlantique, NW France
St-Omer *90 C2* Pas-de-Calais, N France
Saint Paul *45 F2 state capital* Minnesota, N USA
St-Paul, Île *141 C6 var.* St.Paul Island. *Island* NE French Southern and Antarctic Territories
St Peter Port *89 D8 dependent territory capital* (Guernsey) C Guernsey, Channel Islands
Saint Petersburg *see* Sankt-Peterburg
Saint Petersburg *43 E4* Florida, SE USA
St-Pierre and Miquelon *35 E5 Fr.* Îles St-Pierre et Miquelon. *French territorial collectivity* NE North America
St-Quentin *90 C3* Aisne, N France
Saint Vincent *55 G4 island* N Saint Vincent and the Grenadines
Saint Vincent and the Grenadines *55 H4 country* SE West Indies

Saint Vincent & The Grenadines 55

Official name Saint Vincent and the Grenadines
Formation 1979
Capital Kingston
Population 111,000 / 846 people per sq mile (327 people per sq km)
Total area 131 sq miles (340 sq km)
Languages English, English Creole
Religions Anglican 42%, Methodist 20%, Roman Catholic 19%, other 19%
Ethnic mix Black 82%, mixed 14%, White 3%, South Asian 1%
Government Parliamentary democracy
Currency Eastern Caribbean dollar = 100 cents
Literacy rate 82%
Calorie consumption 2,347 kilocalories

Saint Vincent Passage *55 H4 passage* Saint Lucia/Saint Vincent and the Grenadines

Saipan 142 B1 *island country capital*
(Northern Mariana Islands)
S Northern Mariana Islands
Sajama, Nevado 61 F4 *mountain*
W Bolivia
Sajószentpéter 99 D6 Borsod-
Abaúj-Zemplén, NE Hungary
Sakākah 120 B4 Al Jawf, NW Saudi
Arabia
Sakakawea, Lake 44 D1 *reservoir*
North Dakota, N USA
Sakata 130 D4 Yamagata, Honshū,
C Japan
Sakhalin *see* Sakhalin, Ostrov
Sakhalin, Ostrov 115 G4 *var.*
Sakhalin. *Island* SE Russian
Federation
Sakhon Nakhon *see* Sakon Nakhon
Şäki 117 G2 *Rus.* Sheki; *prev.*
Nukha. NW Azerbaijan
Sakishima-shotō 130 A3 *var.*
Sakisima Syotō. *Island group*
SW Japan
Sakisima Syotō *see* Sakishima-shotō
Sakiz *see* Saqqez
Sakiz-Adasi *see* Chíos
Sakon Nakhon 136 D4 *var.* Muang
Sakon Nakhon, Sakhon Nakhon.
Sakon Nakhon, E Thailand
Saky 109 F5 *Rus.* Saki. Respublika
Krym, S Ukraine
Sal 74 A3 *island* Ilhas de Barlavento,
NE Cape Verde
Sala 85 C6 Västmanland, C Sweden
Salacgrīva 106 C3 *Est.* Salatsi.
Limbaži, N Latvia
Sala Consilina 97 D5 Campania,
S Italy
Salado, Río 64 C3 *river* C Argentina
Salado, Río 62 D5 *river*
E Argentina
Şalālah 121 D6 SW Oman
Salamá 52 B2 Baja Verapaz,
C Guatemala
Salamanca 92 D2 *anc.* Helmantica,
Salmantica. Castilla-León,
NW Spain
Salamanca 64 B4 Coquimbo, C Chile
Salamīyah 118 B3 *var.* As
Salamīyah. Ḩamāh, W Syria
Salang *see* Phuket
Salantai 106 B3 Kretinga,
NW Lithuania
Salavan 137 D5 *var.* Saravan,
Saravane. Salavan, S Laos
Salavat 111 D6 Respublika
Bashkortostan, W Russian
Federation
Sala y Gomez 153 F4 *island* Chile,
E Pacific Ocean
Sala y Gomez Fracture Zone *see*
Sala y Gomez Ridge
Sala y Gomez Ridge 153 G4 *var.*
Sala y Gomez Fracture Zone.
Tectonic feature SE Pacific Ocean
Šalčininkai 107 C5 Šalčininkai,
SE Lithuania
Saldus 106 B3 *Ger.* Frauenburg.
Saldus, W Latvia
Sale 149 C7 Victoria, SE Australia
Salé 70 C2 NW Morocco
Salekhard 114 D3 *prev.* Obdorsk.
Yamalo-Nenetskiy Avtonomnyy
Okrug, N Russian Federation
Salem 46 B3 *state capital* Oregon,
NW USA
Salem 132 C2 Tamil Nādu, SE India
Salerno 97 D5 *anc.* Salernum.
Campania, S Italy
Salerno, Golfo di 97 C5 *Eng.* Gulf
of Salerno. *Gulf* S Italy
Salihorsk 107 C7 *Rus.* Soligorsk.
Minskaya Voblasts', S Belarus
Salima 79 E2 Central, C Malawi
Salina 45 E5 Kansas, C USA
Salina Cruz 51 F5 Oaxaca,
SE Mexico
Salinas 47 B6 California, W USA
Salinas 60 A2 Guayas, W Ecuador
Salisbury 89 D7 *var.* New Sarum.
S England, UK
Sallyana *see* Salyan
Salmon River 46 D3 *river* Idaho,
NW USA
Salmon River Mountains 46 D3
mountain range Idaho, NW USA
Salo 85 D6 Länsi-Suomi, W
Finland

Salon-de-Provence 91 D6 Bouches-
du-Rhône, SE France
Salonta 108 A3 Hung.
Nagyszalonta. Bihor, W Romania
Sal'sk 111 B7 Rostovskaya Oblast',
SW Russian Federation
Salt *see* As Salṭ
Salta 64 C2 Salta, NW Argentina
Saltash 89 C7 SW England, UK
Saltillo 51 E3 Coahuila de
Zaragoza, NE Mexico
Salt Lake City 44 B4 *state capital*
Utah, W USA
Salto 64 D4 Salto, N Uruguay
Salton Sea 47 D8 *lake* California,
W USA
Salvador 63 G3 *prev.* São Salvador.
Bahia, E Brazil
Salween 124 C2 *Bur.* Thanlwin,
Chin. Nu Chiang, Nu Jiang. *River*
SE Asia
Salyan 135 E3 *var.* Sallyana. Mid
Western, W Nepal
Salzburg 95 D6 *anc.* Juvavum.
Salzburg, N Austria
Salzgitter 94 C3 *prev.* Watenstedt-
Salzgitter. Niedersachsen,
C Germany
Salzwedel 94 C3 Sachsen-Anhalt,
N Germany
Šamac *see* Bosanski Šamac
Samakhixai 137 E5 *var.* Attapu,
Attopeu. Attapu, S Laos
Samalayuca 50 C1 Chihuahua,
N Mexico
Samar 139 F2 *island* C Philippines
Samara 114 B3 *prev.* Kuybyshev.
Samarskaya Oblast', W Russian
Federation
Samarang *see* Semarang
Samarinda 138 D4 Borneo,
C Indonesia
Samarqand 123 E2 *Rus.* Samarkand.
Samarqand Wiloyati,
C Uzbekistan
Samawa *see* As Samāwah
Sambalpur 135 F4 Orissa, E India
Sambava 79 G2 Antsiraňana,
NE Madagascar
Sambir 108 B2 *Rus.* Sambor.
L'vivs'ka Oblast', NW Ukraine
Sambre 90 D2 *river* Belgium/France
Samfya 78 D2 Luapula, N Zambia
Saminatal 94 E2 *valley*
Austria/Liechtenstein
Samnān *see* Semnān
Sam Neua *see* Xam Nua
Samoa 145 E4 *var.* Sāmoa; *prev.*
Western Samoa. *Country*
W Polynesia

Samoa 145

Official name Independent State
of Samoa
Formation 1962
Capital Apia
Population 180,000 / 165 people
per sq mile (64 people per sq km)
Total area 1,092 sq miles
(2,830 sq km)
Languages Samoan, English
Religions Christian 100%
Ethnic mix Polynesian 90%,
Euronesian 9%, other 1%
Government Parliamentary state
Currency Tala = 100 sene
Literacy rate 98%
Calorie consumption 2,828
kilocalories

Samoa Basin 143 E3 *undersea feature*
W Pacific Ocean
Samobor 100 A2 Zagreb, N Croatia
Sámos 105 E6 *prev.* Limín Vathéos.
Sámos, Dodekánisos, Greece,
Aegean Sea
Sámos 105 E6 *island* Dodekánisos,
Greece, Aegean Sea
Samosch *see* Someş
Samothráki 104 C4 *anc.*
Samothrace. *Island* NE Greece
Samothráki 104 C4 Samothráki,
NE Greece
Sampit 138 C4 Borneo, C Indonesia
Samsun 116 D2 *anc.* Amisus.
Samsun, N Turkey

Samtredia 117 F2 W Georgia
Samui, Ko 137 C6 *island*
SW Thailand
Samut Prakan 137 C5 *var.* Muang
Samut Prakan, Paknam. Samut
Prakan, C Thailand
San 99 E5 *river* SE Poland
San 74 D3 Ségou, C Mali
Şan'ā' 121 B6 Eng. Sana. *Country
capital* (Yemen) W Yemen
Sana 100 B3 *river* NW Bosnia and
Herzegovina
Sana *see* Şan'ā'
Sanae 154 B2 *South African research
station* Antarctica
Sanaga 77 B5 *river* C Cameroon
San Ambrosio, Isla 57 A5 *Eng.* San
Ambrosio Island. *Island* W Chile
Sanandaj 120 C3 *prev.* Sinneh.
Kordestān, W Iran
San Andrés, Isla de 53 F3 *island*
NW Colombia
San Andrés Tuxtla 51 F4 *var.* Tuxtla.
Veracruz-Llave, E Mexico
San Angelo 49 F3 Texas, SW USA
San Antonio 49 F4 Texas, SW USA
San Antonio 52 B2 Toledo, S Belize
San Antonio 64 B4 Valparaíso,
C Chile
San Antonio Oeste 65 C5 Río
Negro, E Argentina
San Antonio River 49 G4 *river*
Texas, SW USA
Sanāw 121 C6 *var.* Sanaw.
NE Yemen
San Benedicto, Isla 50 B4 *island*
W Mexico
San Benito 52 B1 Petén,
N Guatemala
San Benito 49 G5 Texas, SW USA
San Bernardino 47 C7 California,
W USA
San Blas 50 C3 Sinaloa, C Mexico
San Blas, Cape 42 D3 *headland*
Florida, SE USA
San Blas, Cordillera de 53 G4
mountain range NE Panama
San Carlos *see* Quesada
San Carlos 48 B2 Arizona, SW USA
San Carlos 52 D4 Río San Juan,
S Nicaragua
San Carlos de Bariloche 65 B5 Río
Negro, SW Argentina
San Carlos del Zulia 58 C2 Zulia,
W Venezuela
San Clemente Island 47 B8 *island*
Channel Islands, California,
W USA
San Cristobal 144 C4 *var.* Makira.
Island SE Solomon Islands
San Cristóbal 58 C2 San Cristóbal de
Las Casas
San Cristóbal 58 C2 Táchira,
W Venezuela
San Cristóbal de Las Casas 51 G5
var. San Cristóbal. Chiapas,
SE Mexico
San Cristóbal, Isla 60 B5 *var.*
Chatham Island. *Island*
Galapagos Islands, Ecuador,
E Pacific Ocean
Sancti Spíritus 54 B2 Sancti
Spíritus, C Cuba
Sandakan 138 D3 Sabah, East
Malaysia
Sandanski 104 C3 *prev.* Sveti Vrach.
Blagoevgrad, SW Bulgaria
Sanday 88 D2 *island* NE Scotland,
UK
Sanders 48 C2 Arizona, SW USA
Sand Hills 44 D3 *mountain range*
Nebraska, C USA
San Diego 47 C8 California, W USA
Sandnes 85 A6 Rogaland,
S Norway
Sandomierz 98 D4 *Rus.* Sandomir.
Świętokrzyskie, C Poland
Sandoway 136 A4 Arakan State,
W Myanmar
Sandpoint 46 C1 Idaho, NW USA
Sand Springs 49 G1 Oklahoma,
C USA
Sandusky 40 D3 Ohio, N USA
Sandvika 85 A6 Akershus,
S Norway
Sandviken 85 C6 Gävleborg,
C Sweden

Sandy Bay 93 H5 *bay* E Gibraltar
Sandy City 44 B4 Utah, W USA
Sandy Lake 38 B3 *lake* Ontario,
C Canada
San Esteban 52 D2 Olancho,
C Honduras
San Felipe 58 D1 Yaracuy,
NW Venezuela
San Felipe de Puerto Plata *see*
Puerto Plata
San Félix, Isla 57 A5 *Eng.* San Felix
Island. *Island* W Chile
San Fernando 92 C5 *prev.* Isla de
León. Andalucía, S Spain
San Fernando 58 D2 *var.* San
Fernando de Apure. Apure,
C Venezuela
San Fernando 46 D1 California,
W USA
San Fernando 55 H5 Trinidad,
Trinidad and Tobago
San Fernando de Apure *see* San
Fernando
**San Fernando del Valle de
Catamarca** 64 C3 *var.* Catamarca.
Catamarca, NW Argentina
San Fernando de Monte Cristi *see*
Monte Cristi
San Francisco 47 B6 California,
W USA
San Francisco del Oro 50 C2
Chihuahua, N Mexico
San Francisco de Macorís 55 E3
C Dominican Republic
San Gabriel 60 B1 Carchi,
N Ecuador
San Gabriel Mountains 46 E1
mountain range California, W USA
Sangir, Kepulauan 139 F3 *var.*
Kepulauan Sangihe. *Island group*
N Indonesia
Sāngli 132 B1 Mahārāshtra,
W India
Sangmélima 77 B5 Sud,
S Cameroon
Sangre de Cristo Mountains 48 D1
mountain range Colorado/New
Mexico, C USA
San Ignacio 52 B1 *prev.* Cayo,
El Cayo. Cayo, W Belize
San Ignacio 50 B2 Baja California
Sur, W Mexico
San Ignacio 61 F3 Beni, N Bolivia
San Joaquin Valley 47 B7 *valley*
California, W USA
San Jorge, Golfo 65 C6 *var.* Gulf of
San Jorge. *Gulf* S Argentina
San Jorge, Gulf of *see* San Jorge,
Golfo
San José *see* San José del Guaviare
San Jose 47 B6 California, W USA
San José 52 B3 *var.* Puerto San José.
Escuintla, S Guatemala
San José 61 G3 *var.* San José de
Chiquitos. Santa Cruz, E Bolivia
San José 53 E4 *country capital* (Costa
Rica) San José, C Costa Rica
San José de Chiquitos *see* San José
San José de Cúcuta *see* Cúcuta
San José del Guaviare 58 C4 *var.*
San José. Guaviare, S Colombia
San Juan 55 F3 *dependent territory
capital* (Puerto Rico) NE Puerto
Rico
San Juan *see* San Juan de los
Morros
San Juan 64 B4 San Juan,
W Argentina
San Juan Bautista 64 D3 Misiones,
S Paraguay
San Juan Bautista Tuxtepec *see*
Tuxtepec
San Juan de Alicante 93 F4 País
Valenciano, E Spain
San Juan del Norte 53 E4 *var.*
Greytown. Río San Juan,
SE Nicaragua
San Juan de los Morros 58 D2 *var.*
San Juan. Guárico, N Venezuela
San Juanito, Isla 50 C4 *island*
C Mexico
San Juan Mountains 48 D1
mountain range Colorado,
C USA
San Juan River 48 C1 *river*
Colorado/Utah, W USA
San Julián *see* Puerto San Julián

235

Sankt Gallen 95 B7 var. St.Gallen, Eng. Saint Gall, Fr. St-Gall. Sankt Gallen, NW Switzerland
Sankt-Peterburg 110 B4 prev. Leningrad, Petrograd, Eng. Saint Petersburg, Fin. Pietari. Leningradskaya Oblast', NW Russian Federation
Sankt Pölten 95 E6 Niederösterreich, N Austria
Sankuru 77 D6 river C Dem. Rep. Congo (Zaire)
Şanlıurfa 117 E4 prev. Sanli Urfa, Urfa, anc. Edessa. Şanlıurfa, S Turkey
San Lorenzo 60 A1 Esmeraldas, N Ecuador
San Lorenzo 61 G5 Tarija, S Bolivia
San Lorenzo, Isla 60 C4 island W Peru
Sanlúcar de Barrameda 92 C5 Andalucía, S Spain
San Luis 50 A1 var. San Luis Colorado. Sonora, NW Mexico
San Luis 52 B2 Petén, NE Guatemala
San Luis 64 C4 San Luis, C Argentina
San Luis Obispo 47 B7 California, W USA
San Luis Potosí 51 E3 San Luis Potosí, C Mexico
San Luis Río Colorado see San Luis
San Marcos 52 A2 San Marcos, W Guatemala
San Marcos 49 G4 Texas, SW USA
San Marino 96 D1 Country S Europe

San Marino 96

Official name Republic of San Marino
Formation AD 301
Capital San Marino
Population 26,000 / 1,115 people per sq mile (431 people per sq km)
Total area 24 sq miles (61 sq km)
Languages Italian
Religions Roman Catholic 93%, other and non-religious 7%
Ethnic mix Sanmaranesi 95%, other 5%
Government Multiparty republic
Currency Lira = 100 centesimi
Literacy rate 96%
Calorie consumption 3,561 kilocalories

San Marino 96 E1 country capital (San Marino) C San Marino
San Martín 154 A2 Argentinian research station Antarctica
San Mateo 59 E2 Anzoátegui, NE Venezuela
San Matías 61 H3 Santa Cruz, E Bolivia
San Matías, Golfo 65 C5 var. Gulf of San Matías. Gulf E Argentina
San Matías, Gulf of see San Matías, Golfo
Sanmenxia 128 C4 var. Shan Xian. Henan, C China
Sânnicolăuş Mare see Sânnicolau Mare
San Miguel 50 D2 Coahuila de Zaragoza, N Mexico
San Miguel 52 C3 San Miguel, SE El Salvador
San Miguel de Ibarra see Ibarra
San Miguel de Tucumán 64 C3 var. Tucumán. Tucumán, N Argentina
San Miguelito 53 G4 Panamá, C Panama
San Miguel, Río 61 G3 river E Bolivia
Sannär see Sennar
Sânnicolaul-Mare see Sânnicolau Mare
Sânnicolau Mare 108 A4 var. Sânnicolaul-Mare, Hung. Nagyszentmiklós; prev. Sânnicläuş Mare, Sînnicolau Mare. Timiş, W Romania
Sanok 99 E5 Podkarpackie, SE Poland
San Pablo 61 F5 Potosí, S Bolivia

San Pedro 50 D3 var. San Pedro de las Colonias. Coahuila de Zaragoza, NE Mexico
San Pedro 52 C1 Corozal, NE Belize
San-Pédro 74 D5 S Côte d'Ivoire
San Pedro de la Cueva 50 C2 Sonora, NW Mexico
San Pedro de las Colonias see San Pedro
San Pedro de Lloc 60 B3 La Libertad, NW Peru
San Pedro Mártir, Sierra 50 A1 mountain range NW Mexico
San Pedro Sula 52 C2 Cortés, NW Honduras
San Rafael 64 B4 Mendoza, W Argentina
San Rafael Mountains 47 C7 mountain range California, W USA
San Ramón de la Nueva Orán 64 C2 Salta, N Argentina
San Remo 96 A3 Liguria, NW Italy
San Salvador 52 B3 country capital (El Salvador) San Salvador, SW El Salvador
San Salvador de Jujuy 64 C2 var. Jujuy. Jujuy, N Argentina
San Salvador, Isla 60 A4 prev. Watlings Island. Island E Bahamas
Sansanné-Mango 75 E4 var. Mango. N Togo
Sansepolcro 96 C3 Toscana, C Italy
San Severo 97 D5 Puglia, SE Italy
Santa Ana 61 F3 Beni, N Bolivia
Santa Ana 46 D2 California, W USA
Santa Ana 52 B3 Santa Ana, NW El Salvador
Santa Ana Mountains 46 E2 mountain range California, W USA
Santa Barbara 47 C7 California, W USA
Santa Barbara 50 C2 Chihuahua, N Mexico
Santa Catalina Island 47 B8 island Channel Islands, California, W USA
Santa Catarina 63 E5 off. Estado de Santa Catarina. State S Brazil
Santa Clara 54 B2 Villa Clara, C Cuba
Santa Clarita 46 D1 California, W USA
Santa Comba 92 B1 Galicia, NW Spain
Santa Cruz 61 G4 var. Santa Cruz de la Sierra. Santa Cruz, C Bolivia
Santa Cruz 47 B6 California, W USA
Santa Cruz 76 E2 São Tomé, C Sao Tome and Principe
Santa Cruz Barillas see Barillas
Santa Cruz de la Sierra see Santa Cruz
Santa Cruz del Quiché 52 B2 Quiché, W Guatemala
Santa Cruz de Tenerife 70 A3 Tenerife, Islas Canarias, Spain, NE Atlantic Ocean
Santa Cruz, Isla 60 B5 var. Indefatigable Island, Isla Chávez. Island Galapagos Islands, Ecuador, E Pacific Ocean
Santa Cruz Islands 144 D3 island group E Solomon Islands
Santa Cruz, Río 65 B7 river S Argentina
Santa Elena 52 B1 Cayo, W Belize
Santa Fe 48 D1 state capital New Mexico, SW USA
Santa Fe 64 C4 Santa Fe, C Argentina
Santa Genoveva 50 B3 mountain W Mexico
Santa Isabel 144 C3 var. Bughotu. Island N Solomon Islands
Santa Lucia Range 47 B7 mountain range California, W USA
Santa Margarita, Isla 50 B3 island W Mexico
Santa Maria 92 A5 island Azores, Portugal, NE Atlantic Ocean
Santa Maria 47 B7 California, W USA
Santa Maria 63 E5 Rio Grande do Sul, S Brazil
Santa María, Isla 60 A5 var. Isla Floreana, Charles Island. Island Galapagos Islands, Ecuador, E Pacific Ocean

Santa Marta 58 B1 Magdalena, N Colombia
Santa Monica 46 D1 California, W USA
Santana 76 E2 São Tomé, S Sao Tome and Principe
Santander 92 D1 Cantabria, N Spain
Santanilla, Islas 53 E1 Eng. Swan Islands. Island NE Honduras
Santarém 92 B3 anc. Scalabis. Santarém, W Portugal
Santarém 63 E2 Pará, N Brazil
Santa Rosa see Santa Rosa de Copán
Santa Rosa 47 B6 California, W USA
Santa Rosa 64 C4 La Pampa, C Argentina
Santa Rosa de Copán 52 C2 var. Santa Rosa. Copán, W Honduras
Santa Rosa Island 47 B8 island California, W USA
Sant Carles de la Rápida see Sant Carles de la Ràpita
Sant Carles de la Ràpita 93 F3 var. Sant Carles de la Rápida. Cataluña, NE Spain
Santiago 64 B4 var. Gran Santiago. Country capital (Chile) Santiago, C Chile
Santiago 92 B1 var. Santiago de Compostela, Eng. Compostella; anc. Campus Stellae. Galicia, NW Spain
Santiago 55 E3 var. Santiago de los Caballeros. N Dominican Republic
Santiago 74 A3 var. São Tiago. Island Ilhas de Sotavento, S Cape Verde
Santiago see Santiago de Cuba
Santiago 53 F5 Veraguas, S Panama
Santiago de Compostela see Santiago
Santiago de Cuba 54 C3 var. Santiago. Santiago de Cuba, E Cuba
Santiago de Guayaquil see Guayaquil
Santiago del Estero 64 C3 Santiago del Estero, C Argentina
Santiago de los Caballeros see Santiago
Santiago Pinotepa Nacional see Pinotepa Nacional
Santiago, Río 60 B2 river N Peru
Santi Quaranta see Sarandë
Santissima Trinidad see Chilung
Sant Julià de Lòria 91 A8 SW Andorra
Santo see Espiritu Santo
Santo Antão 74 A2 island Ilhas de Barlavento, N Cape Verde
Santo António 76 E1 Príncipe, N Sao Tome and Principe
Santo Domingo 54 D3 prev. Ciudad Trujillo. Country capital (Dominican Republic) SE Dominican Republic
Santo Domingo de los Colorados 60 B1 Pichincha, NW Ecuador
Santo Domingo Tehuantepec see Tehuantepec
Santos 63 F4 São Paulo, S Brazil
Santos Plateau 57 D5 undersea feature SW Atlantic Ocean
Santo Tomé 64 D3 Corrientes, NE Argentina
San Valentín, Cerro 65 A6 mountain S Chile
San Vicente 52 C3 San Vicente, C El Salvador
São Francisco, Rio 63 F3 river E Brazil
Sao Hill 73 C7 Iringa, S Tanzania
São João da Madeira 92 B2 Aveiro, N Portugal
São Jorge 92 A5 island Azores, Portugal, NE Atlantic Ocean
São Luís 63 F2 state capital Maranhão, NE Brazil
São Mandol see São Manuel, Rio
São Manuel, Rio 63 E3 var. São Mandol, Teles Pirés. River C Brazil
São Marcos, Baía de 63 F1 bay N Brazil

São Miguel 92 A5 island Azores, Portugal, NE Atlantic Ocean
Saona, Isla 55 E3 island SE Dominican Republic
Saône 91 D5 river E France
São Nicolau 74 A3 Eng. Saint Nicholas. Island Ilhas de Barlavento, N Cape Verde
São Paulo 63 E4 off. Estado de São Paulo. State S Brazil
São Paulo 63 E4 state capital São Paulo, S Brazil
São Paulo de Loanda see Luanda
São Pedro do Rio Grande do Sul see Rio Grande
São Roque, Cabo de 63 G2 headland E Brazil
São Salvador see M'Banza Congo
São Salvador do Congo see M'Banza Congo
São Tiago see Santiago
São Tomé 76 E2 Eng. Saint Thomas. Island S Sao Tome and Principe
São Tomé 77 A5 country capital (Sao Tome and Principe) São Tomé, S Sao Tome and Principe
Sao Tome and Principe 76 D1 Country E Atlantic Ocean

Sao Tome & Principe 76

Official name Democratic Republic of São Tomé and Prínfcipe
Formation 1975
Capital São Tomé
Population 142,000 / 383 people per sq mile (148 people per sq km)
Total area 370 sq miles (960 sq km)
Languages Portuguese, Portuguese Creole
Religions Roman Catholic 90%, other Christian 10%
Ethnic mix Black 90%, Portuguese and Creole 10%
Government Multiparty republic
Currency Dobra = 100 centimos
Literacy rate 75%
Calorie consumption 2,129 kilocalories

São Tomé, Pico de 76 D2 mountain São Tomé, S Sao Tome and Principe
São Vicente, Cabo de 92 B5 Eng. Cape Saint Vincent, Port. Cabo de São Vicente. Headland S Portugal
São Vincente 74 A3 Eng. Saint Vincent. Island Ilhas de Barlavento, N Cape Verde
Sápai see Sápes
Sapele 75 F5 Delta, S Nigeria
Sápes 104 D3 var. Sápai. Anatolikí Makedonía kai Thráki, NE Greece
Sapir see Sappir
Sa Pobla 93 G3 var. La Puebla. Mallorca, Spain, W Mediterranean Sea
Sappir 119 B7 var. Sapir. Southern, S Israel
Sapporo 130 D2 Hokkaidō, NE Japan
Sapri 97 D6 Campania, S Italy
Sapulpa 49 G1 Oklahoma, C USA
Saqqez 120 C2 var. Saghez, Sakiz, Saqqiz. Kordestän, NW Iran
Saqqiz see Saqqez
Sara Buri 137 C5 var. Saraburi. Saraburi, C Thailand
Saragt see Serakhs
Saraguro 60 B2 Loja, S Ecuador
Sarajevo 100 C4 country capital (Bosnia and Herzegovina). Federacija Bosna I Hercegovina, SE Bosnia and Herzegovina
Sarakhs 120 E2 Khorāsān, NE Iran
Saraktash 111 D6 Orenburgskaya Oblast', W Russian Federation
Saran' 114 C4 Kaz. Saran. Karaganda, C Kazakhstan
Saranda see Sarandë
Sarandë 101 C7 var. Saranda, It. Porto Edda; prev. Santi Quaranta. Vlorë, S Albania
Saransk 111 C5 Respublika Mordoviya, W Russian Federation
Sarasota 43 E4 Florida, SE USA

Saratov 114 B3 Saratovskaya
Oblast', W Russian Federation
Saravan see Salavan
Saravane see Salavan
Sarawak 138 D3 cultural region
Borneo, SE Asia
**Sarawak and Sabah (North
Borneo) and Singapore** see
Malaysia
Sarcelles 90 D1 Val-d'Oise, N
France
Sardegna 97 A5 Eng. Sardinia.
Island Italy, C Mediterranean Sea
Sardinia see Sardegna
Sarera, Teluk see Cenderawasih,
Teluk
Sargasso Sea 66 B4 sea W Atlantic
Ocean
Sargodha 134 C2 Punjab,
NE Pakistan
Sarh 76 C4 prev. Fort-Archambault.
Moyen-Chari, S Chad
Sārī 120 D2 var. Sari, Sāri.
Māzandarān, N Iran
Saría 105 E7 island SE Greece
Sarıkamış 117 F3 Kars, NE Turkey
Sarikol Range 123 G3 Rus.
Sarykol'skiy Khrebet. Mountain
range China/Tajikistan
Sark 89 D8 Fr. Sercq. Island Channel
Islands
Şarkışla 116 D3 Sivas, C Turkey
Sarmiento 65 B6 Chubut,
S Argentina
Sarnia 38 C5 Ontario, S Canada
Sarny 108 C1 Rivnens'ka Oblast',
NW Ukraine
Sarochyna 107 D5 Rus. Sorochino.
Vitsyebskaya Voblasts', N Belarus
Sarpsborg 85 B6 Østfold,
S Norway
Sartène 91 E7 Corse, France,
C Mediterranean Sea
Sarthe 90 B4 cultural region
N France
Sárti 104 C4 Kentrikí Makedonía,
N Greece
Saruhan see Manisa
Saryesik-Atyrau, Peski 123 G1
desert E Kazakhstan
Sary-Tash 123 F2 Oshskaya Oblast',
SW Kyrgyzstan
Sasebo 131 A7 Nagasaki, Kyūshū,
SW Japan
Saskatchewan 37 F5 river
Manitoba/Saskatchewan,
C Canada
Saskatchewan 37 F5 province
SW Canada
Saskatoon 37 F5 Saskatchewan,
S Canada
Sasovo 111 B5 Ryazanskaya Oblast',
W Russian Federation
Sassandra 74 D5 var. Ibo,
Sassandra Fleuve. River
S Côte d'Ivoire
Sassandra 74 D5 S Côte d'Ivoire
Sassandra Fleuve see Sassandra
Sassari 97 A5 Sardegna, Italy,
C Mediterranean Sea
Sassenheim 86 C3 Zuid-Holland,
W Netherlands
Sassnitz 94 D2 Mecklenburg-
Vorpommern, NE Germany
Sátoraljaújhely 99 D6 Borsod-
Abaúj-Zemplén, NE Hungary
Sātpura Range 134 D4 mountain
range C India
Satsunan-shotō 130 A3 var. Satunan
Syotō. Island group SW Japan
Sattanen 84 D3 Lappi, NE Finland
Satu Mare 108 B3 Ger. Sathmar,
Hung. Szatmárrnémeti. Satu Mare,
NW Romania
Satunan Syotō see Satsunan-shotō
Saudi Arabia 121 B5 Ar.
Al 'Arabīyah as Su'ūdīyah,
Al Mamlakah al 'Arabīyah as
Su'ūdīyah. Country SW Asia

Saudi Arabia 121

Official name Kingdom of Saudi
Arabia
Formation 1932
Capital Riyadh

Saudi Arabia (continued)

Population 21.6 million / 26 people
per sq mile (10 people per sq km)
Total area 829,995 sq miles
(2,149,690 sq km)
Languages Arabic
Religions Sunni Muslim 85%,
Shi'a Muslim 15%
Ethnic mix Arab 90%,
Afroasian 10%
Government Absolute monarchy
Currency Saudi riyal = 100 malalah
Literacy rate 73.4%
Calorie consumption 2,735
kilocalories

Sauer see Sûre
Saulkrasti 106 C3 Rīga, C Latvia
Sault Sainte Marie 40 C1 Michigan,
N USA
Sault Ste.Marie 38 C4 Ontario,
S Canada
Saumur 90 B4 Maine-et-Loire,
NW France
Saurimo 78 C1 Port. Henrique de
Carvalho, Vila Henrique de
Carvalho. Lunda Sul,
NE Angola
Sava 100 B3 Eng. Save, Ger. Sau,
Hung. Száva. River SE Europe
Sava 107 E6 Rus. Sava.
Mahilyowskaya Voblasts',
E Belarus
Savá 52 D2 Colón, N Honduras
Savai'i 145 E4 island NW Samoa
Savannah 43 E2 Georgia, SE USA
Savannah River 43 E2 river
Georgia/South Carolina, SE USA
Savanna-La-Mar 54 A5 W Jamaica
Save, Rio 79 E3 var. Rio Sabi. River
Mozambique/Zimbabwe
Saverne 90 E3 var. Zabern; anc. Tres
Tabernae. Bas-Rhin, NE France
Savigliano 96 A2 Piemonte,
NW Italy
Savigsivik see Savissivik
Savinski see Savinskiy
Savinskiy 110 C3 var. Savinski.
Arkhangel'skaya Oblast',
NW Russian Federation
Savissivik 82 D1 var. Savigsivik.
N Greenland
Savoie 91 D5 cultural region
E France
Savona 96 A2 Liguria, NW Italy
Savu Sea 139 E5 Ind. Laut Sawu.
Sea S Indonesia
Sawakin see Suakin
Sawdirī see Sodiri
Sawhāj see Sohāg
Şawqirah 121 D6 var. Suqrah.
S Oman
Sayanskiy Khrebet 112 D3
mountain range S Russian
Federation
Sayat 122 D3 Lebapskiy Velayat,
E Turkmenistan
Sayaxché 52 B2 Petén,
N Guatemala
Şaydā see Saïda
Sayhūt 121 D6 E Yemen
Sayida see Saïda
Saynshand 127 E2 Dornogovĭ,
SE Mongolia
Sayre 41 E3 Pennsylvania,
NE USA
Say'ūn 121 C6 var. Saywūn.
C Yemen
Saywūn see Say'ūn
Scandinavia 66 D2 geophysical region
NW Europe
Scarborough 89 D5 N England,
UK
Schaan 94 E1 W Liechtenstein
Schaerbeek 87 C6 Brussels,
C Belgium
Schaffhausen 95 B7 Fr. Schaffhouse.
Schaffhausen, N Switzerland
Schagen 86 C2 Noord-Holland,
NW Netherlands
Schebschi Mountains see Shebshi
Mountains
Scheessel 94 B3 Niedersachsen,
NW Germany
Schefferville 39 E2 Québec,
E Canada

Scheldt 87 B5 Dut. Schelde, Fr.
Escaut. River W Europe
Schell Creek Range 47 D5 mountain
range Nevada, W USA
Schenectady 41 F3 New York,
NE USA
Schertz 49 G4 Texas, SW USA
Schiermonnikoog 86 D1 Fris.
Skiermûntseach. Island
Waddeneilanden, N Netherlands
Schijndel 86 D4 Noord-Brabant,
S Netherlands
Schiltigheim 90 E3 Bas-Rhin,
NE France
Schleswig 94 B2 Schleswig-
Holstein, N Germany
Schleswig-Holstein 94 B2 cultural
region N Germany
Schönebeck 94 C4 Sachsen-Anhalt,
C Germany
Schooten see Schoten
Schoten 87 C5 var. Schooten.
Antwerpen, N Belgium
Schouwen 86 B4 island
SW Netherlands
Schwabenalb see Schwäbische Alb
Schwäbische Alb 95 B6 var.
Schwabenalb, Eng. Swabian Jura.
Mountain range S Germany
Schwandorf 95 C5 Bayern,
SE Germany
Schwarzwald 95 B6 Eng. Black
Forest. Mountain range
SW Germany
Schwaz 95 C7 Tirol, W Austria
Schweinfurt 95 B5 Bayern,
SE Germany
Schwerin 94 C3 Mecklenburg-
Vorpommern, N Germany
Schwiz see Schwyz
Schwyz 95 B7 var. Schwiz. Schwyz,
C Switzerland
Scilly, Isles of 89 B8 island group
SW England, UK
Scio see Chíos
Scoresby Sound see
Ittoqqortoormiit
Scoresbysund see Ittoqqortoormiit
Scotia Sea 67 C8 sea SW Atlantic
Ocean
Scotland 88 C3 national region UK
Scott Base 154 B4 NZ research station
Antarctica
Scott Island 154 B5 island Antarctica
Scottsbluff 44 D3 Nebraska, C USA
Scottsboro 42 D1 Alabama, S USA
Scottsdale 48 B2 Arizona, SW USA
Scranton 41 F3 Pennsylvania,
NE USA
Scupi see Skopje
Scutari see Shkodër
Scutari, Lake 101 C5 Alb. Liqeni i
Shkodrës, SCr. Skadarsko Jezero.
Lake Albania/Yugoslavia
Scyros see Skýros
Searcy 42 B1 Arkansas, C USA
Seattle 46 B2 Washington, NW USA
Sébaco 52 D3 Matagalpa,
W Nicaragua
Sebastián Vizcaíno, Bahía 50 A2
bay NW Mexico
Sechura, Bahía de 60 A3 bay
NW Peru
Secunderābād 134 D5 var.
Sikandarabad. Andhra Pradesh,
C India
Sedan 90 D3 Ardennes, N France
Seddon 151 D5 Marlborough, South
Island, NZ
Seddonville 151 C5 West Coast,
South Island, NZ
Sédhiou 74 B3 SW Senegal
Sedona 48 B2 Arizona, SW USA
Seesen 94 B4 Niedersachsen,
C Germany
Segestica see Sisak
Segezha 110 B3 Respublika
Kareliya, NW Russian Federation
Ségou 74 D3 var. Segu. Ségou,
C Mali
Segovia 92 D2 Castilla-León,
C Spain
Segoviao Wangkí see Coco, Río
Segu see Ségou
Séguédine 75 H2 Agadez, NE Niger
Seguin 49 G4 Texas, SW USA
Segura 93 E4 river S Spain

Seinäjoki 85 D5 Swe. Östermyra.
Länsi-Suomi, W Finland
Seine 90 D1 river N France
Seine, Baie de la 90 B3 bay
N France
Sekondi see Sekondi-Takoradi
Sekondi-Takoradi 75 E5 var.
Sekondi. S Ghana
Selat Balabac see Balabac Strait
Selenga 127 E1 Mong. Selenge
Mörön. River Mongolia/Russian
Federation
Sélestat 90 E4 Ger. Schlettstadt. Bas-
Rhin, NE France
Selfoss 83 E5 Sudhurland,
SW Iceland
Sélibabi 74 C3 var. Sélibaby.
Guidimaka, S Mauritania
Sélibaby see Sélibabi
Selma 47 C6 California, W USA
Selway River 46 D2 river Idaho,
NW USA
Selwyn Range 148 B3 mountain
range Queensland, C Australia
Selzaete see Zelzate
Semarang 138 C5 var. Samarang.
Jawa, C Indonesia
Sembé 77 B5 La Sangha,
NW Congo
Semey see Semipalatinsk
Seminole 49 E3 Texas, SW USA
Seminole, Lake 42 D3 reservoir
Florida/Georgia, SE USA
Semipalatinsk 114 D4 Kaz. Semey.
Vostochnyy kazakhstan,
E Kazakhstan
Semnān 120 D3 var. Samnān.
Semnān, N Iran
Semois 87 D8 river SE Belgium
Sendai 131 A8 Kagoshima, Kyūshū,
SW Japan
Sendai 130 D4 Miyagi, Honshū,
C Japan
Sendai-wan 130 D4 bay E Japan
Senec 99 C6 Ger. Wartberg, Hung.
Szenc; prev. Szempcz. Bratislavský
Kraj, W Slovakia
Senegal 74 C3 Fr. Sénégal. River
W Africa
Senegal 74 B3 Fr. Sénégal. Country
W Africa

Senegal 74

Official name Republic of Senegal
Formation 1960
Capital Dakar
Population 9.5 million /
128 people per sq mile
(49 people per sq km)
Total area 74,335 sq miles
(192,530 sq km)
Languages French, Wolof, Fulani,
Serer, Diola, Malinke, Soninke,
Arabic
Religions Muslim 90%, Christian
(mainly Roman Catholic) 5%,
Traditional beliefs 5%
Ethnic mix Wolof 36%, Fulani 17%,
Serer 17%, other 30%
Government Multiparty republic
Currency CFA franc
= 100 centimes
Literacy rate 34.6%
Calorie consumption 2,262
kilocalories

Senftenberg 94 D4 Brandenburg,
E Germany
Senica 99 C6 Ger. Senitz, Hung.
Szenice. Trnavský Kraj,
W Slovakia
Senj 100 A3 Ger. Zengg, It. Segna;
anc. Senia. Lika-Senj, NW Croatia
Senja 84 C2 prev. Senjen. Island
N Norway
Senkaku-shotō 130 A3 island group
SW Japan
Senlis 90 C3 Oise, N France
Sennar 72 C4 var. Sannār. Sinnar,
C Sudan
Sens 90 C3 anc. Agendicum,
Senones. Yonne, C France
Sên, Stœng 137 D5 river
C Cambodia
Senta 100 D3 Hung. Zenta. Serbia,
N Yugoslavia

237

Seo de Urgel *see* La See d'Urgel
Seoul *see* Sŏul
Sept-Îles *39 E3* Québec, SE Canada
Seraing *87 D6* Liège, E Belgium
Serakhs *122 D3 var.* Saragt.
Akhalskiy Velayat,
S Turkmenistan
Seram, Pulau *139 F4 var.* Serang,
Eng. Ceram. *Island* Maluku,
E Indonesia
Serang *see* Seram, Pulau
Serang *138 C5* Jawa, C Indonesia
Serasan, Selat *138 C3 strait*
Indonesia/Malaysia
Serbia *100 D4 Ger.* Serbien, *Serb.*
Srbija. Admin. region *republic*
Yugoslavia
Serdica *see* Sofiya
Seremban *138 B3* Negeri Sembilan,
Peninsular Malaysia
Serenje *78 D2* Central, E Zambia
Seres *see* Sérres
Seret *see* Siret
Sereth *see* Siret
Sérifos *105 C6 anc.* Seriphos. *Island*
Kykládes, Greece, Aegean Sea
Serov *113 C3* Sverdlovskaya
Oblast', C Russian Federation
Serowe *78 D3* Central, SE Botswana
Serpa Pinto *see* Menongue
Serpent's Mouth, The *59 F2 Sp.*
Boca de la Serpiente. *Strait*
Trinidad and Tobago/Venezuela
Serpukhov *111 B5* Moskovskaya
Oblast', W Russian Federation
Serra dos Parecis *see* Parecis,
Chapada dos
Sérrai *see* Sérres
Serrana, Cayo de *53 F2 island group*
NW Colombia
Serranilla, Cayo de *53 F2 island
group* NW Colombia
Serra Pacaraim *see* Pakaraima
Mountains
Serra Tumucumaque *see* Tumuc
Humac Mountains
Serravalle *96 E1* N San Marino
Sérres *104 C3 var.* Seres; *prev.* Sérrai.
Kentrikí Makedonía, NE Greece
Sert *see* Siirt
Sesto San Giovanni *96 B2*
Lombardia, N Italy
Sesvete *100 B2* Zagreb, N Croatia
Setabis *see* Xátiva
Sète *91 C6 prev.* Cette. Hérault,
S France
Setesdal *85 A6 valley* S Norway
Sétif *71 E2 var.* Stif. N Algeria
Setté Cama *77 A6* Ogooué-
Maritime, SW Gabon
Setúbal *92 B4 Eng.* Saint Ubes, Saint
Yves. Setúbal, W Portugal
Setúbal, Baía de *92 B4 bay*
W Portugal
Seul, Lac *38 B3 lake* Ontario,
S Canada
Sevan *117 G2* C Armenia
Sevana Lich *117 G3 Eng.* Lake
Sevan, *Rus.* Ozero Sevan. *Lake*
E Armenia
Sevastopol' *109 F5 Eng.* Sebastopol.
Respublika Krym, S Ukraine
Severn *89 D6 Wel.* Hafren. *River*
England/Wales, UK
Severn *38 B2 river* Ontario,
S Canada
Severnaya Dvina *110 C4 var.*
Northern Dvina. *River*
NW Russian Federation
Severnaya Zemlya *115 E2 var.*
Nicholas II Land. *Island group*
N Russian Federation
Severnyy *110 E3* Respublika Komi,
NW Russian Federation
Severodvinsk *110 C3 prev.* Molotov,
Sudostroy. Arkhangel'skaya
Oblast', NW Russian Federation
Severomorsk *110 C2* Murmanskaya
Oblast', NW Russian
Federation
Severo-Sibirskaya Nizmennost'
115 E2 var. North Siberian Plain,
Eng. North Siberian Lowland.
Lowlands N Russian Federation
Severskiy Donets *see* Donets
Sevier Lake *44 A4 lake* Utah,
W USA

Sevilla *92 C4 Eng.* Seville; *anc.*
Hispalis. Andalucía, SW Spain
Seville *see* Sevilla
Sevlievo *104 D2* Gabrovo, N Bulgaria
Seychelles *79 G1 Country* W Indian
Ocean

Seychelles 79

Official name Republic of the
Seychelles
Formation 1976
Capital Victoria
Population 79,000/
758 people per sq mile
(293 people per sq km)
Total area 108 sq miles
(280 sq km)
Languages Seselwa
(French Creole), English, French
Religions Roman Catholic 90%,
Anglican 8%, other 2%
Ethnic mix Seychellois (mixed
Asian, African, and European) 100%
Government Multiparty republic
Currency Seychelles rupee
= 100 cents
Literacy rate 84%
Calorie consumption 2,287
kilocalories

Seydhisfjördhur *83 E5* Austurland,
É Iceland
Seydi *122 D2 prev.* Neftezavodsk.
Lebapskiy Velayat,
E Turkmenistan
Seyhan *see* Adana
Sfákia *105 C8* Kríti, Greece,
E Mediterranean Sea
Sfântu Gheorghe *108 C4 Ger.* Sankt-
Georgen, *Hung.* Sepsiszentgyörgy;
prev. Şepsi-Sângeorz, Sfîntu
Gheorghe. Covasna, C Romania
Sfax *71 F2 Ar.* Şafāqis. E Tunisia
's-Gravenhage *86 B4 var.* Den Haag,
Eng. The Hague, *Fr.* La Haye.
Country capital (Netherlands-seat
of government) Zuid-Holland,
W Netherlands
's-Gravenzande *86 B4* Zuid-
Holland, W Netherlands
Shaan *see* Shaanxi
Shaanxi *128 B5 var.* Shaan, Shaanxi
Sheng, Shan-hsi, Shenshi, Shensi.
Admin. region *province* C China
Shaanxi Sheng *see* Shaanxi
Shache *126 A3 var.* Yarkant.
Xinjiang Uygur Zizhiqu,
NW China
Shackleton Ice Shelf *154 D3 ice
shelf* Antarctica
Shaddādī *see* Ash Shadādāh
Shāhābād *see* Eslāmābād
Shahjahanabad *see* Delhi
Shahr-e Kord *120 C3 var.* Shahr
Kord. Chahār Maḥall va
Bakhtīārī, C Iran
Shahr Kord *see* Shahr-e Kord
Shāhrūd *120 D2 prev.* Emāmrūd,
Emāmshahr. Semnān, N Iran
Shandī *see* Shendi
Shandong *128 D4 var.* Lu,
Shandong Sheng, Shantung.
Admin. region *province* E China
Shandong Sheng *see* Shandong
Shanghai *128 D5 var.* Shang-hai.
Shanghai Shi, E China
Shang-hai *see* Shanghai
Shangrao *128 D5* Jiangxi, S China
Shan-hsi *see* Shaanxi
Shan-hsi *see* Shanxi
Shannon *89 A6 Ir.* An tSionainn.
River W Ireland
Shan Plateau *136 B3 plateau*
E Myanmar
Shansi *see* Shanxi
Shantarskiye Ostrova *115 G3 Eng.*
Shantar Islands. *Island group*
E Russian Federation
Shantou *128 D6 var.* Shan-t'ou,
Swatow. Guangdong, S China
Shantung *see* Shandong
Shanxi *128 C4 var.* Jin, Shan-hsi,
Shansi, Shanxi Sheng. Admin.
region *province* C China
Shan Xian *see* Sanmenxia
Shanxi Sheng *see* Shanxi

Shaoguan *128 C6 var.* Shao-kuan,
Cant. Kukong; *prev.* Ch'u-chiang.
Guangdong, S China
Shao-kuan *see* Shaoguan
Shaqrā *see* Shuqrah
Shaqrā' *120 B4* Ar Riyāḍ, C Saudi
Arabia
Shar *130 D5 var.* Charsk.
Vostochnyy Kazakhstan,
E Kazakhstan
Shari *see* Chari
Shari *130 D2* Hokkaidō,
NE Japan
Shark Bay *147 A5 bay* Western
Australia
Shashe *78 D3 var.* Shashi. *River*
Botswana/Zimbabwe
Shashi *see* Shashe
Shatskiy Rise *125 G1 undersea
feature* N Pacific Ocean
Shatt al-Hodna *see* Hodna, Chott
El
Shaṭṭ al Jarīd *see* Jerid, Chott el
Shawnee *49 G1* Oklahoma, C USA
Shchadryn *107 D7 Rus.* Shchedrin.
Homyel'skaya Voblasts',
SE Belarus
Shchëkino *111 B5* Tul'skaya Oblast',
W Russian Federation
Shchors *109 E1* Chernihivs'ka
Oblast', N Ukraine
Shchuchinsk *114 C4 prev.*
Shchuchye. Severnyy kazakhstan,
N Kazakhstan
Shchuchyn *107 B5 Pol.* Szczuczyn
Nowogródzki, *Rus.* Shchuchin.
Hrodzyenskaya Voblasts',
W Belarus
Shebekino *111 A6* Belgorodskaya
Oblast', W Russian Federation
Shebeli *73 D5 Amh.* Wabē Shebelē
Wenz, *It.* Scebeli, *Som.* Webi
Shabeelle. *River* Ethiopia/Somalia
Sheberghān *123 E3 var.* Shibarghān,
Shiberghan, Shiberghān. Jowzjān,
N Afghanistan
Sheboygan *40 B2* Wisconsin,
N USA
Shebshi Mountains *76 A4 var.*
Schebschi Mountains. *Mountain
range* E Nigeria
Shechem *see* Nablus
Shedadi *see* Ash Shadādāh
Sheffield *89 D5* N England, UK
Shekhem *see* Nablus
Shelby *44 B1* Montana, NW USA
Sheldon *45 F3* Iowa, C USA
Shelekhov Gulf *see* Shelikhova,
Zaliv
Shelikhova, Zaliv *115 G2 Eng.*
Shelekhov Gulf. *Gulf* E Russian
Federation
Shendi *72 C4 var.* Shandī. River
Nile, NE Sudan
Shengking *see* Liaoning
Shenking *see* Liaoning
Shenshi *see* Shaanxi
Shensi *see* Shaanxi
Shenyang *128 D3 Chin.* Shen-yang,
Eng. Moukden, Mukden; *prev.*
Fengtien. Liaoning, NE China
Shepetivka *108 D2 Rus.*
Shepetovka. Khmel'nyts'ka
Oblast', NW Ukraine
Shepparton *149 C7* Victoria,
SE Australia
Sherbrooke *39 E4* Quebec,
SE Canada
Shereik *72 C3* River Nile, N Sudan
Sheridan *44 C2* Wyoming, C USA
Sherman *49 G2* Texas, SW USA
's-Hertogenbosch *86 C4 Fr.* Bois-le-
Duc, *Ger.* Herzogenbusch. Noord-
Brabant, S Netherlands
Shetland Islands *88 D1 island group*
NE Scotland, UK
Shibarghān *see* Sheberghān
Shiberghan *see* Sheberghān
Shibetsu *130 D2 var.* Sibetu.
Hokkaidō, NE Japan
Shibh Jazīrat Sīnā' *see* Sinai
Shibushi-wan *131 B8 bay* SW Japan
Shigatse *see* Xigazê
Shih-chia-chuang *see* Shijiazhuang
Shihezi *126 C2* Xinjiang Uygur
Zizhiqu, NW China
Shihmen *see* Shijiazhuang

Shijiazhuang *128 C4 var.* Shih-chia-
chuang; *prev.* Shihmen. Hebei,
E China
Shikārpur *134 B3* Sind, S Pakistan
Shikoku *131 C7 var.* Sikoku. *Island*
SW Japan
Shikoku Basin *125 F2 var.* Sikoku
Basin. *Undersea feature*
N Philippine Sea
Shikotan, Ostrov *130 E2 Jap.*
Shikotan-tō. *Island* NE Russian
Federation
Shilabo *73 D5* E Ethiopia
Shiliguri *135 F3 prev.* Siliguri. West
Bengal, NE India
Shilka *115 F4 river* S Russian
Federation
Shimbir Berris *see* Shimbiris
Shimbiris *72 E4 var.* Shimbir Berris.
Mountain N Somalia
Shimoga *132 C2* Karnātaka, W India
Shimonoseki *131 A7 var.*
Simonoseki; *hist.* Akamagaseki,
Bakan. Yamaguchi, Honshū,
SW Japan
Shinano-gawa *131 C5 var.* Sinano
Gawa. *River* Honshū, C Japan
Shīndand *122 D4* Farāh,
W Afghanistan
Shingū *131 C6 var.* Singū.
Wakayama, Honshū, SW Japan
Shinjō *130 D4 var.* Sinzyô.
Yamagata, Honshū, C Japan
Shinyanga *73 C7* Shinyanga,
NW Tanzania
Shiprock *48 C1* New Mexico,
SW USA
Shīrāz *120 D4 var.* Shīrāz. Fārs,
S Iran
Shivpuri *134 D3* Madhya Pradesh,
C India
Shizugawa *130 D4* Miyagi, Honshū,
NE Japan
Shizuoka *131 D6 var.* Sizuoka.
Shizuoka, Honshū, S Japan
Shklow *107 D6 Rus.* Shklov.
Mahilyowskaya Voblasts',
E Belarus
Shkodër *101 C5 var.* Shkodra, *It.*
Scutari, *SCr.* Skadar. Shkodër,
NW Albania
Shkodra *see* Shkodër
Shkubinit, Lumi i *101 C6 var.*
Shkumbî, Shkumbin. *River*
C Albania
Shkumbî *see* Shkubinit, Lumi i
Shkumbin *see* Shkubinit, Lumi i
Sholāpur *see* Solāpur
Shostka *109 F1* Sums'ka Oblast',
NE Ukraine
Show Low *48 B2* Arizona, SW USA
Shpola *109 E3* Cherkas'ka Oblast',
N Ukraine
Shreveport *42 A2* Louisiana, S USA
Shrewsbury *89 D6 hist.*
Scrobesbyrig'. W England, UK
Shu *114 C5 Kaz.* Shū. Zhambyl,
SE Kazakhstan
Shuang-liao *see* Liaoyuan
Shumagin Islands *36 B3 island
group* Alaska, USA
Shumen *104 D2* Shumen,
NE Bulgaria
Shumilina *107 E5 Rus.* Shumilino.
Vitsyebskaya Voblasts', NE Belarus
Shuqrah *121 B7 var.* Shaqrā.
SW Yemen
Shwebo *136 B3* Sagaing, C Myanmar
Shyichy *107 C7 Rus.* Shiichi.
Homyel'skaya Voblasts',
SE Belarus
Shymkent *114 B5 prev.* Chimkent.
Yuzhnyy Kazakhstan,
S Kazakhstan
Shyshchytsy *107 C6 Rus.*
Shishchitsy. Minskaya Voblasts',
C Belarus
Si *see* Syr Darya
Siam, Gulf of *see* Thailand, Gulf of
Sian *see* Xi'an
Siang *see* Brahmaputra
Siangtan *see* Xiangtan
Šiauliai *106 B4 Ger.* Schaulen.
Šiauliai, N Lithuania
Sibay *111 D6* Respublika
Bashkortostan, W Russian
Federation

Šibenik 116 B4 It. Sebenico. Šibenik-Knin, S Croatia
Siberia see Sibir'
Siberut, Pulau 138 A4 prev. Siberoet. Island Kepulauan Mentawai, W Indonesia
Sibetu see Shibetsu
Sibi 134 B2 Baluchistãn, SW Pakistan
Sibir' 115 E3 var. Siberia. Physical region NE Russian Federation
Sibiti 77 B6 La Lékoumou, S Congo
Sibiu 108 B4 Ger. Hermannstadt, Hung. Nagyszeben. Sibiu, C Romania
Sibolga 138 B3 Sumatera, W Indonesia
Sibu 138 D3 Sarawak, East Malaysia
Sibut 76 C4 prev. Fort-Sibut. Kémo, S Central African Republic
Sibuyan Sea 139 E2 sea C Philippines
Sichon 137 C6 var. Ban Sichon, Si Chon. Nakhon Si Thammarat, SW Thailand
Sichuan 128 B5 var. Chuan, Sichuan Sheng, Ssu-ch'uan, Szechuan, Szechwan. Admin. region province C China
Sichuan Pendi 128 B5 depression C China
Sichuan Sheng see Sichuan
Sicilia 97 C7 Eng. Sicily; anc. Trinacria. Island Italy, C Mediterranean Sea
Sicilian Channel see Sicily, Strait of
Sicily see Sicilia
Sicily, Strait of 97 B7 var. Sicilian Channel. Strait C Mediterranean Sea
Sicuani 61 E4 Cusco, S Peru
Sidári 104 A4 Kérkyra, Iónio Nísoi, Greece, C Mediterranean Sea
Sidas 138 C4 Borneo, C Indonesia
Siderno 97 D7 Calabria, SW Italy
Sîdi Barrâni 72 A1 NW Egypt
Sidi Bel Abbès 70 D2 var. Sidi bel Abbès, Sidi-Bel-Abbès. NW Algeria
Sidirókastro 104 C3 prev. Sidhirókastron. Kentrikí Makedonía, NE Greece
Sidley, Mount 154 B4 mountain Antarctica
Sidney 44 D1 Montana, NW USA
Sidney 44 D4 Nebraska, C USA
Sidney 40 C4 Ohio, N USA
Sidon see Saïda
Sidra see Surt
Siedlce 98 E3 Eng. Sedlez, Rus. Sesdlets. Mazowieckie, C Poland
Siegen 94 B4 Nordrhein-Westfalen, W Germany
Siemiatycze 98 E3 Podlaskie
Siena 96 B3 Fr. Sienne; anc. Saena Julia. Toscana, C Italy
Sieradz 98 C4 Łódzkie, C Poland
Sierpc 98 D3 Mazowieckie, C Poland
Sierra de Soconusco see Sierra Madre
Sierra Leone 74 C4 Country W Africa

Sierra Leone 74

Official name Republic of Sierra Leone
Formation 1961
Capital Freetown
Population 5 million / 177 people per sq mile (68 people per sq km)
Total area 27,652 sq miles (71,620 sq km)
Languages English, Mende, Temne, Krio
Religions Traditional beliefs 52%, Muslim 40%, Christian 8%
Ethnic mix Mende 35%, Temne 32%, Limba 8%, Kuranko 4%, other 21%
Government Multiparty republic
Currency Leone = 100 cents
Literacy rate 33.3%
Calorie consumption 1,694 kilocalories

Sierra Leone Basin 66 C4 undersea feature E Atlantic Ocean
Sierra Leone Ridge see Sierra Leone Rise
Sierra Leone Rise 66 C4 var. Sierra Leone Ridge, Sierra Leone Schwelle. Undersea feature E Atlantic Ocean
Sierra Leone Schwelle see Sierra Leone Rise
Sierra Madre 52 B2 var. Sierra de Soconusco. Mountain range Guatemala/Mexico
Sierra Madre see Madre Occidental, Sierra
Sierra Nevada 47 C6 mountain range W USA
Sierra Pacaraima see Pakaraima Mountains
Sierra Vieja 48 D3 mountain range Texas, SW USA
Sierra Vista 48 B3 Arizona, SW USA
Sífnos 105 C6 anc. Siphnos. Island Kykládes, Greece, Aegean Sea
Sigli 138 A3 Sumatera, W Indonesia
Siglufjördhur 83 E4 Nordhurland Vestra, N Iceland
Signal Peak 48 A2 mountain Arizona, SW USA
Signan see Xi'an
Signy 154 A2 UK research station South Orkney Islands, Antarctica
Siguatepeque 52 C2 Comayagua, W Honduras
Siguiri 74 D4 Haute-Guinée, NE Guinea
Siilinjärvi 84 E4 Itä-Suomi, C Finland
Siirt 117 F4 var. Sert; anc. Tigranocerta. Siirt, SE Turkey
Sikandarabad see Secunderãbãd
Sikasso 74 D4 Sikasso, S Mali
Sikeston 45 H5 Missouri, C USA
Sikhote-Alin', Khrebet 115 G4 mountain range SE Russian Federation
Siking see Xi'an
Siklós 99 C7 Baranya, SW Hungary
Sikoku see Shikoku
Sikoku Basin see Shikoku Basin
Šilalė 106 B4 Šilalė, W Lithuania
Silchar 135 G3 Assam, NE India
Silesia 98 B4 physical region SW Poland
Silifke 116 C4 anc. Seleucia. İçel, S Turkey
Siling Co 126 C5 lake W China
Silinhot see Xilinhot
Silistra 104 E1 var. Silistria; anc. Durostorum. Silistra, NE Bulgaria
Silistria see Silistra
Sillamäe 106 E2 Ger. Sillamäggi. Ida-Virumaa, NE Estonia
Šilutė 106 B4 Ger. Heydekrug. Šilutė, W Lithuania
Silvan 117 E4 Diyarbakır, SE Turkey
Silverek 117 E4 Şanlıurfa, SE Turkey
Simanggang see Sri Aman
Simanichy 107 C7 Rus. Simonichi. Homyel'skaya Voblasts', SE Belarus
Simav 116 B3 Kütahya, W Turkey
Simav Çayı 116 A3 river NW Turkey
Simeto 97 C7 river Sicilia, Italy, C Mediterranean Sea
Simeulue, Pulau 138 A3 island NW Indonesia
Simferopol' 109 F5 Respublika Krym, S Ukraine
Simitli 104 C3 Blagoevgrad, SW Bulgaria
Şimleu Silvaniei 108 B3 Hung. Szilágysomlyó; prev. Şimlăul Silvaniei, Şimleul Silvaniei. Sãlaj, NW Romania
Simonoseki see Shimonoseki
Simpelveld 87 D6 Limburg, SE Netherlands
Simplon Pass 95 B8 pass S Switzerland
Simpson see Fort Simpson
Simpson Desert 148 B4 desert Northern Territory/South Australia

Sīnā' see Sinai
Sinai 72 C2 var. Sinai Peninsula, Ar. Shibh Jazīrat Sīnā', Sīnā'. Physical region NE Egypt
Sinaia 108 C4 Prahova, SE Romania
Sinai Peninsula see Sinai
Sinano Gawa see Shinano-gawa
Sincelejo 58 B2 Sucre, NW Colombia
Sind 134 B3 var. Sindh. Admin. region province SE Pakistan
Sindelfingen 95 B6 Baden-Württemberg, SW Germany
Sindh see Sind
Sindi 106 D2 Ger. Zintenhof. Pärnumaa, SW Estonia
Sines 92 B4 Setúbal, S Portugal
Singan see Xi'an
Singapore 138 A1 Country SE Asia

Singapore 138

Official name Republic of Singapore
Formation 1965
Capital Singapore
Population 3.6 million / 15,285 people per sq mile (5,902 people per sq km)
Total area 236 sq miles (610 sq km)
Languages Malay, English, Mandarin Chinese, Tamil
Religions Buddhist and Daoist 53%, Muslim 16%, Hindu 4%, Christian 1%, other 26%
Ethnic mix Chinese 78%, Malay 14%, Indian 6%, other 2%
Government Multiparty republic
Currency Singapore dollar = 100 cents
Literacy rate 91.4%
Calorie consumption 3,128 kilocalories

Singapore 138 B3 country capital (Singapore) S Singapore
Singen 95 B6 Baden-Württemberg, S Germany
Singida 73 C7 Singida, C Tanzania
Singkang 139 E4 Sulawesi, C Indonesia
Singkawang 138 C3 Borneo, C Indonesia
Singora see Songkhla
Singū see Shingū
Sining see Xining
Siniscola 97 A5 Sardegna, Italy, C Mediterranean Sea
Sinj 100 B4 Split-Dalmacija, SE Croatia
Sinkiang see Xinjiang Uygur Zizhiqu
Sinkiang Uighur Autonomous Region see Xinjiang Uygur Zizhiqu
Sinnamarie see Sinnamary
Sinnamary 59 H3 var. Sinnamarie. N French Guiana
Sînnicolau Mare see Sânnicolau Mare
Sinoie, Lacul 108 D5 prev. Lacul Sinoe. Lagoon SE Romania
Sinop 116 D2 anc. Sinope. Sinop, N Turkey
Sinsheim 95 B6 Baden-Württemberg, SW Germany
Sint Maarten 55 G3 Eng. Saint Martin. Island N Netherlands Antilles
Sint-Michielsgestel 86 C4 Noord-Brabant, S Netherlands
Sint-Niklaas 87 B5 Fr. Saint-Nicolas. Oost-Vlaanderen, N Belgium
Sint-Pieters-Leeuw 87 B6 Vlaams Brabant, C Belgium
Sintra 92 B3 prev. Cintra. Lisboa, W Portugal
Sinujiif 73 E5 Nugaal, NE Somalia
Sinus Aelaniticus see Aqaba, Gulf of
Sinyang see Xinyang
Sinzyô see Shinjõ
Sion 95 A7 Ger. Sitten; anc. Sedunum. Valais, SW Switzerland
Sioux City 45 F3 Iowa, C USA

Sioux Falls 45 F3 South Dakota, N USA
Siping 128 D3 var. Ssu-p'ing, Szeping; prev. Ssu-p'ing-chieh. Jilin, NE China
Siple, Mount 154 A4 mountain Siple Island, Antarctica
Siquirres 53 E4 Limón, E Costa Rica
Siracusa 97 D7 Eng. Syracuse. Sicilia, Italy, C Mediterranean Sea
Sir Darya see Syr Darya
Sir Edward Pellew Group 148 B2 island group Northern Territory, NE Australia
Siret 108 C3 var. Siretul, Ger. Sereth, Rus. Seret, Ukr. Siret. River Romania/Ukraine
Siret see Seret
Siretul see Siret
Sirikit Reservoir 136 C4 lake N Thailand
Sīrjān 120 D3 prev. Sa'īdãbãd. Kermãn, S Iran
Sirna see Sýrna
Şırnak 117 F4 Şırnak, SE Turkey
Síros see Sýros
Sirte see Surt
Sirte, Gulf of see Surt, Khalīj
Sisak 100 B3 var. Siscia, Ger. Sissek, Hung. Sziszek; anc. Segestica. Sisak-Moslavina, C Croatia
Siscia see Sisak
Sisimiut 82 C3 var. Holsteinborg, Holsteinsborg, Holstenborg, Holstensborg. S Greenland
Sissek see Sisak
Sistema Penibético see Béticos, Sistemas
Siteía 105 D8 var. Sitía. Kríti, Greece, E Mediterranean Sea
Sitges 93 G2 Cataluña, NE Spain
Sitía see Siteía
Sittang 136 B4 var. Sittoung. River S Myanmar
Sittard 87 D5 Limburg, SE Netherlands
Sittoung see Sittang
Sittwe 136 A3 var. Akyab. Arakan State, W Myanmar
Siuna 52 D3 Región Autónoma Atlántico Norte, NE Nicaragua
Siut see Asyūṭ
Sivas 116 D3 anc. Sebastia, Sebaste. Sivas, C Turkey
Sivers'kyy Donets' see Donets
Siwa 72 A2 var. Sīwah. NW Egypt
Sīwah see Siwa
Six-Fours-les-Plages 91 D6 Var, SE France
Siyäzän 117 H2 Rus. Siazan'. NE Azerbaijan
Sizuoka see Shizuoka
Sjar see Sääre
Sjælland B8 Eng. Zealand, Ger. Seeland. Island E Denmark
Sjenica 101 D5 Turk. Seniça. Serbia, SW Yugoslavia
Skadar see Shkodër
Skagerak see Skagerrak
Skagerrak 85 A6 var. Skagerak. Channel N Europe
Skagit River 46 B1 river Washington, NW USA
Skalka 84 C3 lake N Sweden
Skarżysko-Kamienna 98 D4 Świętokrzyskie, C Poland
Skaudvilė 106 B4 Tauragė, SW Lithuania
Skegness 89 E6 E England, UK
Skellefteå 84 D4 Västerbotten, N Sweden
Skellefteälven 84 C4 river N Sweden
Ski 85 B6 Akershus, S Norway
Skíathos 105 C5 Skíathos, Vóreioi Sporádes, Greece, Aegean Sea
Skidal' 107 B5 Rus. Skidel'. Hrodzyenskaya Voblasts', W Belarus
Skierniewice 98 D3 Łódzkie, C Poland
Skiftet 106 C1 Fin. Kihti. Strait Gulf of Bothnia/Gulf of Finland
Skíros see Skýros
Skópelos 105 C5 Skópelos, Vóreioi Sporádes, Greece, Aegean Sea

Skopje 101 D6 var. Üsküb, Turk.
Úsküp; prev. Skoplje, anc. Scupi.
Country capital (FYR Macedonia)
N FYR Macedonia
Skoplje see Skopje
Skovorodino 115 F4 Amurskaya
Oblast', SE Russian Federation
Skuodas 106 B3 Ger. Schoden, Pol.
Szkudy. Skuodas, NW Lithuania
Skye, Isle of 88 B3 island
NW Scotland, UK
Skýros 105 C5 var. Skíros. Skýros,
Vóreioi Sporádes, Greece, Aegean
Sea
Skýros 105 C5 var. Skíros; anc.
Scyros. Island Vóreioi Sporádes,
Greece, Aegean Sea
Slagelse 85 B7 Vestsjælland,
E Denmark
Slatina 108 B5 Olt, S Romania
Slatina 100 C3 Hung. Szlatina, prev.
Podravska Slatina. Virovitica-
Podravina, NE Croatia
Slavonska Požega see Požega
Slavonski Brod 100 C3 Ger. Brod,
Hung. Bród; prev. Brod, Brod na
Savi. Brod-Posavina, NE Croatia
Slavuta 108 C2 Khmel'nyts'ka
Oblast', NW Ukraine
Slawharad 107 E7 Rus. Slavgorod.
Mahilyowskaya Voblasts',
E Belarus
Sławno 98 C2
Zachodniopomorskie, NW Poland
Sléibhte Chill Mhantáin see
Wicklow Mountains
Slēmānī see As Sulaymānīyah
Sliema 102 B5 N Malta
Sligeach see Sligo
Sligo 89 A5 Ir. Sligeach. NW Ireland
Sliven 104 D2 var. Slivno. Sliven,
C Bulgaria
Slivnitsa 104 B2 Sofiya, W Bulgaria
Slivno see Sliven
Slobozia 108 C5 Ialomiţa,
SE Romania
Slonim 107 B6 Pol. Słonim, Rus.
Slonim. Hrodzyenskaya Voblasts',
W Belarus
Slovakia 99 C6 Ger. Slowakei, Hung.
Szlovákia, Slvk. Slovensko.
Country C Europe

Slovakia 99

Official name Slovak Republic
Formation 1993
Capital Bratislava
Population 5.4 million /
285 people per sq mile
(110 people per sq km)
Total area 18,932 sq miles
(49,036 sq km)
Languages Slovak, Hungarian,
Czech
Religions Roman Catholic 60%,
Atheist 10%, Protestant 8%,
Orthodox 4%, other 18%
Ethnic mix Slovak 85%,
Hungarian 9%, Czech 1%, other 5%
Government Multiparty
republic
Currency Koruna = 100 halierov
Literacy rate 99%
Calorie consumption 3,156
kilocalories

Slovak Ore Mountains see
Slovenské rudohorie
Slovenia 95 D8 Ger. Slowenien,
Slvn. Slovenija. Country SE Europe

Slovenia 95

Official name Republic of Slovenia
Formation 1991
Capital Ljubljana
Population 2 million / 256 people
per sq mile (99 people per sq km)
Total area 7820 sq miles
(20,250 sq km)
Languages Slovene, Serbian,
Croatian
Religions Roman Catholic 94%,
Orthodox Catholic 2%, Muslim 1%,
other 3%

Slovenia (continued)

Ethnic mix Slovene 88%,
Croat 3%, Serb 2%, Bosnian 1%,
other 6%
Government Multiparty republic
Currency Tolar = 100 stotins
Literacy rate 99%
Calorie consumption
not available

Slovenské rudohorie 99 D6 Eng.
Slovak Ore Mountains, Ger.
Slowakisches Erzgebirge,
Ungarisches Erzgebirge. Mountain
range C Slovakia
Slov"yans'k 109 G3 Rus. Slavyansk.
Donets'ka Oblast', E Ukraine
Slowakisches Erzgebirge see
Slovenské rudohorie
Słubice 98 B3 Ger. Frankfurt.
Lubuskie, W Poland
Sluch 108 D1 river NW Ukraine
Słupsk 98 C2 Ger. Stolp. Pomorskie,
N Poland
Slutsk 107 C6 Rus. Slutsk.
Minskaya Voblasts', S Belarus
Smallwood Reservoir 39 F2 lake
Newfoundland and Labrador,
S Canada
Smara 70 B3 var. Es Semara.
N Western Sahara
Smarhon' 107 C5 Pol. Smorgonie,
Rus. Smorgon'. Hrodzyenskaya
Voblasts', W Belarus
Smederevo 100 D4 Ger. Semendria.
Serbia, N Yugoslavia
Smederevska Palanka 100 D4
Serbia, C Yugoslavia
Smila 109 E2 Rus. Smela.
Cherkas'ka Oblast', C Ukraine
Smiltene 106 D3 Ger. Smilten.
Valka, N Latvia
Smøla 84 A4 island W Norway
Smolensk 111 A5 Smolenskaya
Oblast', W Russian Federation
Snake 34 B4 river Yukon Territory,
NW Canada
Snake River 46 C3 river NW USA
Snake River Plain 46 D4 plain
Idaho, NW USA
Sneek 86 D2 Friesland,
N Netherlands
Sněžka 98 B4 Ger. Schneekoppe.
Mountain N Czech Republic
Śniardwy, Jezioro 114 D2 Ger.
Spirdingsee. Lake NE Poland
Snina 99 E5 Hung. Szinna.
Prešovský Kraj, E Slovakia
Snowdonia 89 C6 mountain range
NW Wales, UK
Snyder 49 F3 Texas, SW USA
Sobradinho, Represa de 63 F2 var.
Barragem de Sobradinho.
Reservoir E Brazil
Sochi 111 A7 Krasnodarskiy Kray,
SW Russian Federation
Société, Archipel de la 145 G4 var.
Archipel de Tahiti, Îles de la
Société, Eng. Society Islands.
Island group W French Polynesia
Society Islands see Société,
Archipel de la
Socorro 48 D2 New Mexico,
SW USA
Socorro, Isla 50 B5 island W Mexico
Socotra see Suquţrā
Soc Trăng 137 D6 var. Khanh. Soc
Trăng, S Vietnam
Socuéllamos 93 E3 Castilla-La
Mancha, C Spain
Sodankylä 84 D3 Lappi, N Finland
Sodari see Sodiri
Söderhamn 85 C5 Gävleborg,
C Sweden
Södertälje 85 C6 Stockholm,
C Sweden
Sodiri 72 B4 var. Sawdirī, Sodari.
Northern Kordofan, C Sudan
Sofia see Sofiya
Sofiya 104 C2 var. Sophia, Eng.
Sofia; Lat. Serdica. Country capital
(Bulgaria) Sofiya-Grad,
W Bulgaria
Sogamoso 58 B3 Boyacá,
C Colombia

Sognefjorden 85 A5 fjord NE North
Sea
Sohâg 72 B2 var. Sawhāj, Suliag.
C Egypt
Sohar see Şuhār
Sohm Plain 66 B3 undersea feature
NW Atlantic Ocean
Sohrau see Żory
Sokal' 108 C2 Rus. Sokal. L'vivs'ka
Oblast', NW Ukraine
Söke 116 A4 Aydın, SW Turkey
Sokhumi 117 E1 Rus. Sukhumi.
NW Georgia
Sokodé 75 F4 C Togo
Sokol 110 C4 Vologodskaya Oblast',
NW Russian Federation
Sokółka 98 E3 Białystok,
NE Poland
Sokolov 99 A5 Ger. Falkenau an der
Eger; prev. Falknov nad Ohří.
Karlovarský Kraj, W Czech
Republic
Sokone 74 B3 W Senegal
Sokoto 75 F4 river NW Nigeria
Sokoto 75 F3 NW Nigeria
Sokotra see Suquţrā
Solāpur 124 B3 var. Sholāpur.
Mahārāshtra, W India
Solca 108 C3 Ger. Solka. Suceava,
N Romania
Sol, Costa del 92 D5 coastal region
S Spain
Soldeu 91 B7 NE Andorra
Solec Kujawski 98 C3 Kujawski-
pomorskie, C Poland
Soledad, Isla see East Falkland
Soledad 58 B1 Anzoátegui,
NE Venezuela
Solikamsk 114 C3 Permskaya
Oblast', NW Russian Federation
Sol'-Iletsk 111 D6 Orenburgskaya
Oblast', W Russian
Federation
Solingen 94 A4 Nordrhein-
Westfalen, W Germany
Sollentuna 85 C6 Stockholm,
C Sweden
Solok 138 B4 Sumatera,
W Indonesia
Solomon Islands 144 C3 prev.
British Solomon Islands
Protectorate. Country W Pacific
Ocean
Solomon Islands 144 C3 island
group PNG/Solomon Islands

Solomon Islands 144

Official name Solomon Islands
Formation 1978
Capital Honiara
Population 444,000 / 41 people per
sq mile (16 people per sq km)
Total area 10,806 sq miles
(27,990 sq km)
Languages English, Pidgin English,
Melanesian Pidgin
Religions Anglican 34%, Roman
Catholic 19%, South Seas
Evangelical Church 17%, Methodist
11%, other 19%
Ethnic mix Melanesian 94%,
other 6%
Government Parliamentary
democracy
Currency Solomon Islands dollar
= 100 cents
Literacy rate 62%
Calorie consumption 2,173
kilocalories

Solomon Sea 144 B3 sea W Pacific
Ocean
Soltau 94 B3 Niedersachsen,
NW Germany
Sol'tsy 110 A4 Novgorodskaya
Oblast', W Russian
Federation
Solwezi 78 D2 North Western,
NW Zambia
Sōma 130 D4 Fukushima, Honshū,
C Japan
Somalia 73 D5 Som. Jamuuriyada
Demuqraadiga Soomaaliyeed,
Soomaaliya; prev. Italian
Somaliland, Somaliland
Protectorate. Country E Africa

Somalia 73

Official name Somali Democratic
Republic
Formation 1960
Capital Mogadishu
Population 10 million / 42 people
per sq mile (16 people per sq km)
Total area 242,215 sq miles
(627,340 sq km)
Languages Arabic, Somali,
English, Italian
Religions Sunni Muslim 98%,
other 2%
Ethnic mix Somali 85%, other 15%
Government Transitional
Currency Somali shilling
= 100 cents
Literacy rate 24%
Calorie consumption 1,499
kilocalories

Somali Basin 69 E5 undersea feature
W Indian Ocean
Sombor 100 C3 Hung. Zombor.
Serbia, NW Yugoslavia
Someren 87 D5 Noord-Brabant,
SE Netherlands
Somerset 42 A5 var. Somerset
Village. W Bermuda
Somerset 40 C5 Kentucky, S USA
Somerset Island 37 F2 island Queen
Elizabeth Islands, Nunavut,
NW Canada
Somerset Island 42 A5 island
W Bermuda
Somerset Village see Somerset
Somers Islands see Bermuda
Somerton 48 A2 Arizona, SW USA
Someş 108 B3 var. Somesch,
Someşul, Szamos, Ger. Samosch.
River Hungary/Romania
Somesch see Someş
Someşul see Someş
Somme 90 C2 river N France
Somotillo 52 C3 Chinandega,
NW Nicaragua
Somoto 52 D3 Madriz,
NW Nicaragua
Songea 73 C8 Ruvuma, S Tanzania
Sông Hông Hà see Red River
Songkhla 137 C7 var. Songkla, Mal.
Singora. Songkhla, SW Thailand
Songkla see Songkhla
Sông Srepok see Srêpôk, Tônle
Sông Tiên Giang see Mekong
Sonoran Desert 48 A3 var. Desierto
de Altar. Desert Mexico/USA see
also Altar, Desierto de
Sonsonate 52 B3 Sonsonate,
W El Salvador
Soochow see Suzhou
Sop Hao 136 D3 Houaphan, N Laos
Sophia see Sofiya
Sopot 98 C2 Ger. Zoppot. Plovdiv, C
Bulgaria
Sopron 99 B6 Ger. Ödenburg. Győr-
Moson-Sopron, NW Hungary
Sorgues 91 D6 Vaucluse, SE France
Sorgun 116 D3 Yozgat, C Turkey
Soria 93 E2 Castilla-León, N Spain
Soroca 108 D3 Rus. Soroki.
N Moldova
Sorong 139 F4 Irian Jaya,
E Indonesia
Sørøy see Sørøya
Sørøya 84 C2 var. Sørøy. Island
N Norway
Sortavala 110 B3 Respublika
Kareliya, NW Russian Federation
Sotavento, Ilhas de 74 A3 var.
Leeward Islands. Island group
S Cape Verde
Sotkamo 84 E4 Oulu, C Finland
Souanké 77 B5 La Sangha,
NW Congo
Soueida see As Suwaydā'
Soufli 104 D3 prev. Souflion.
Anatolikí Makedonía kai Thráki,
NE Greece
Soufrière 55 F2 volcano S Dominica
Soukhné see As Sukhnah
Sŏul 129 E4 off. Sŏul-t'ŭkpyŏlsi,
Eng. Seoul, Jap. Keijō; prev.
Kyŏngsŏng. Country capital (South
Korea) NW South Korea

Soûr 119 A5 var. Şūr; anc. Tyre.
SW Lebanon
Souris River 45 E1 var. Mouse
River. River Canada/USA
Sourpi 105 B5 Thessalía, C Greece
Sousse 71 F2 var. Sûsah. NE Tunisia
South Africa 78 C4 Afr. Suid-Afrika.
Country S Africa

South Africa 78

Official name Republic of South
Africa
Formation 1934
Capital Pretoria
Population 40.4 million /
86 people per sq mile
(33 people per sq km)
Total area 471,443 sq miles
(1,221,040 sq km)
Languages Afrikaans, English,
11 African languages
Religions Protestant 39%, Roman
Catholic 8%, other 53%
Ethnic mix Zulu 23%, other Black
38%, White 16%, Mixed 10%,
other 13%
Government Multiparty republic
Currency Rand = 100 cents
Literacy rate 84%
Calorie consumption 2,695
kilocalories

South America 56 continent
Southampton 89 D7 hist. Hamwih,
Lat. Clausentum. S England, UK
Southampton Island 37 G3 island
Nunavut, NE Canada
South Andaman 133 F2 island
Andaman Islands, India,
NE Indian Ocean
South Australia 149 A5 state
S Australia
South Australian Basin 142 B5
undersea feature SW Indian Ocean
South Bend 40 C3 Indiana, N USA
South Beveland see Zuid-Beveland
South Bruny Island 149 C8 island
Tasmania, SE Australia
South Carolina 43 E2 off. State of
South Carolina; also known as
The Palmetto State. State SE USA
South Carpathians see Carpaţii
Meridionali
South China Basin 125 E4 undersea
feature SE South China Sea
South China Sea 124 D4 Chin. Nan
Hai, Ind. Laut Cina Selatan, Vtn.
Biên Đông. Sea SE Asia
South Dakota 44 D2 off. State of
South Dakota; also known as The
Coyote State, Sunshine State. State
N USA
Southeast Indian Ridge 141 D7
undersea feature Indian
Ocean/Pacific Ocean
Southeast Pacific Basin 153 E5 var.
Belling Hausen Mulde. Undersea
feature SE Pacific Ocean
South East Point 149 C7 headland
Victoria, S Australia
Southend-on-Sea 89 E6 E England,
UK
Southern Alps 151 B6 mountain
range South Island, NZ
Southern Cook Islands 145 F4
island group S Cook Islands
Southern Cross 147 B6 Western
Australia
Southern Indian Lake 37 F4 lake
Manitoba, C Canada
Southern Ocean 67 B7 ocean
Southern Uplands 88 C4 mountain
range S Scotland, UK
South Fiji Basin 142 D4 undersea
feature S Pacific Ocean
South Geomagnetic Pole 154 B3
pole Antarctica
South Georgia 57 D8 island South
Georgia and the South
Sandwich Islands, SW Atlantic
Ocean
South Goulburn Island 146 E2
island Northern Territory,
N Australia
South Huvadhu Atoll 132 A5 var.
Gaafu Dhaalu Atoll. Atoll
S Maldives

South Indian Basin 141 D7 undersea
feature Indian Ocean/Pacific
Ocean
South Island 151 C6 island S NZ
South Korea 129 E4 Kor. Taehan
Min'guk. Country E Asia

South Korea 129

Official name Republic of Korea
Formation 1948
Capital Seoul
Population 46.8 million /
1,228 people per sq mile
(474 people per sq km)
Total area 38,119 sq miles
(98,730 sq km)
Languages Korean, Chinese
Religions Mahayana
Buddhist 47%, Protestant 38%,
Roman Catholic 11%,
Confucian 3%, other 1%
Ethnic mix Korean 100%
Government Multiparty republic
Currency Korean won = 100 chon
Literacy rate 97.2%
Calorie consumption 3,285
kilocalories

South Lake Tahoe 47 C5 California,
W USA
South Orkney Islands 154 A2 island
group Antarctica
South Ossetia 117 F2 former
autonomous region SW Georgia
South Pacific Basin see Southwest
Pacific Basin
South Platte River 44 D4 river
Colorado/Nebraska, C USA
South Pole 154 B3 pole Antarctica
South Sandwich Islands 57 D8
island group SE South Georgia and
South Sandwich Islands
South Sandwich Trench 57 E8
undersea feature SW Atlantic Ocean
South Shetland Islands 154 A2
island group Antarctica
South Shields 88 D4 NE England,
UK
South Sioux City 45 F3 Nebraska,
C USA
South Taranaki Bight 150 C4 bight
SE Tasman Sea
South Tasmania Plateau see
Tasman Plateau
South Uist 88 B3 island
NW Scotland, UK
South West Cape 151 A8 headland
Stewart Island, NZ
Southwest Indian Ocean Ridge see
Southwest Indian Ridge
Southwest Indian Ridge 141 B6 var.
Southwest Indian Ocean Ridge.
Undersea feature SW Indian Ocean
Southwest Pacific Basin 143 E4 var.
South Pacific Basin. Undersea
feature SE Pacific Ocean
Sovereign Base Area 102 C5 UK
military installation E Cyprus
Sovereign Base Area 102 C5 UK
military installation S Cyprus
Soweto 78 D4 Gauteng, NE South
Africa
Spain 92 D3 Sp. España; anc.
Hispania, Iberia, Lat. Hispana.
Country SW Europe

Spain 92

Official name Kingdom of Spain
Formation 1492
Capital Madrid
Population 39.6 million /
205 people per sq mile
(79 people per sq km)
Total area 192,833 sq miles
(499,440 sq km)
Languages Spanish, Catalan,
Galician
Religions Roman Catholic 96%,
other 4%
Ethnic mix Castilian Spanish 72%,
Catalan 17%, Galician 6%,
other 5%
Government Constitutional
monarchy

Spain (continued)

Currency Spanish peseta
= 100 centimos
Literacy rate 97.2%
Calorie consumption 3,708
kilocalories

Spanish Town 54 B5 hist. St.Iago de
la Vega. C Jamaica
Sparks 47 C5 Nevada, W USA
Spartanburg 43 E1 South Carolina,
SE USA
Spárti 105 B6 Eng. Sparta.
Pelopónnisos, S Greece
Spearfish 44 D2 South Dakota,
N USA
Speightstown 55 G1 NW Barbados
Spencer 45 F3 Iowa, C USA
Spencer Gulf 149 B6 gulf South
Australia
Spey 88 C3 river NE Scotland, UK
Spiess Seamount 67 C7 undersea
feature S Atlantic Ocean
Spijkenisse 86 B4 Zuid-Holland,
SW Netherlands
Spíli 105 C8 Kríti, Greece,
E Mediterranean Sea
Spīn Būldak 123 E5 Kandahār,
S Afghanistan
Spirdingsee see Śniardwg, Jezioro
Spitsbergen 83 F2 island
NW Svalbard
Split 100 B4 It. Spalato. Split-
Dalmacija, S Croatia
Špoģi 106 D4 Daugvapils, SE Latvia
Spokane 46 C2 Washington,
NW USA
Spratly Islands 138 B2 Chin.
Nansha Qundao. Disputed territory
SE Asia
Spree 94 D4 river E Germany
Springfield 40 B4 state capital
Illinois, N USA
Springfield 43 G5 Massachusetts,
NE USA
Springfield 45 G5 Missouri, C USA
Springfield 40 C4 Ohio, N USA
Springfield 46 B3 Oregon,
NW USA
Spring Garden 59 F2 NE Guyana
Spring Hill 43 E4 Florida,
SE USA
Springs Junction 151 C5 West
Coast, South Island, NZ
Springsure 148 D4 Queensland,
E Australia
Spruce Knob 41 E4 mountain West
Virginia, NE USA
Srbinje see Foča
Srbobran see Donji Vakuf
Srebrenica 100 C4 Republika
Srpska, E Bosnia and
Herzegovina
Sredets 104 E2 prev. Grudovo.
Burgas, E Bulgaria
Sredets 104 D2 prev. Syulemeshlii.
Stara Zagora, C Bulgaria
Srednerusskaya Vozvyshennost'
109 G1 Eng. Central Russian
Upland. Mountain range
W Russian Federation
Srednesibirskoye Ploskogor'ye 114
D3 var. Central Siberian Uplands,
Eng. Central Siberian Plateau.
Mountain range N Russian
Federation
Sremska Mitrovica 100 C3 prev.
Mitrovica, Ger. Mitrowitz. Serbia,
NW Yugoslavia
Srêpôk, Tônle 137 E5 var.
Sông Srepok. River
Cambodia/Vietnam
Sri Aman 138 C3 var. Bandar Sri
Aman, Simanggang. Borneo, East
Malaysia
Sri Jayawardanapura 132 D3 var.
Sri Jayawardenapura; prev.
Kotte. Western Province, W Sri
Lanka
Sri Jayawardenepura see Sri
Jayawardanapura
Srīkākulam 135 F5 Andhra
Pradesh, E India
Sri Lanka 132 D3 prev. Ceylon.
Country S Asia

Sri Lanka 132

Official name Democratic Socialist
Republic of Sri Lanka
Formation 1948
Capital Colombo
Population 18.6 million /
752 people per sq mile
(290 people per sq km)
Total area 24,996 sq miles
(64,740 sq km)
Languages Sinhalese, Tamil,
English
Religions Buddhist 70%, Hindu
15%, Christian 8%, Muslim 7%
Ethnic mix Sinhala 74%, Tamil 18%,
Moor 7%, other 1%
Government Multiparty republic
Currency Sri Lanka rupee
= 100 cents
Literacy rate 90.7%
Calorie consumption 2,273
kilocalories

Srpska, Republika 100 B3 Admin.
region republic NE Bosnia and
Herzegovina
Srinagarind Reservoir 137 C5 lake
W Thailand
Ssu-ch'uan see Sichuan
Ssu-p'ing see Siping
Ssu-p'ing-chieh see Siping
Stabroek 87 B5 Antwerpen,
N Belgium
Stade 94 B3 Niedersachsen,
NW Germany
Stadskanaal 86 E2 Groningen,
NE Netherlands
Stafford 89 D6 C England, UK
Staicele 106 D3 Limbaži, N Latvia
Stakhanov 109 H3 Luhans'ka
Oblast', E Ukraine
Stalinabad see Dushanbe
Stalingrad see Volgograd
Stalinobod see Dushanbe
Stalin Peak see Kommunizm,
Qullai
Stalowa Wola 98 E4 Podkarpackie,
SE Poland
Stamford 41 F3 Connecticut, NE USA
Stampalia see Astypálaia
Stanley 65 D7 var. Port Stanley,
Puerto Argentino. Dependent
territory capital (Falkland Islands)
East Falkland, Falkland Islands
Stanovoy Khrebet 113 E3 mountain
range SE Russian Federation
Stanthorpe 149 D5 Queensland,
E Australia
Staphorst 86 D2 Overijssel,
E Netherlands
Stara Pazova 100 D3 Ger. Altpasua,
Hung. Ópazova. Serbia,
N Yugoslavia
Stara Zagora 104 D2 Lat. Augusta
Trajana. Stara Zagora, C Bulgaria
Starbuck Island 145 G3 prev.
Volunteer Island. Island E Kiribati
Stargard Szczeciński 98 B3 Ger.
Stargard in Pommern.
Zachodniopomorskie, NW Poland
Starobil's'k 109 H2 Rus. Starobel'sk.
Luhans'ka Oblast',
E Ukraine
Starobin 107 C7 Rus. Starobin.
Minskaya Voblasts', S Belarus
Starogard Pomorskiei 98 C2 Ger.
Preussisch-Stargard. Pomorskie,
N Poland
Starokostyantyniv 108 D2 Rus.
Starokonstantinov. Khmel'nyts'ka
Oblast', NW Ukraine
Starominskaya 111 A7
Krasnodarskiy Kray, SW Russian
Federation
Staryya Darohi 107 C6 Rus. Staryye
Dorogi. Minskaya Voblasts',
S Belarus
Staryy Oskol 111 B6 Belgorodskaya
Oblast', W Russian Federation
State College 41 E4 Pennsylvania,
NE USA
Statesboro 43 E2 Georgia, SE USA
Staunton 41 E5 Virginia, NE USA

Stavanger 85 A6 Rogaland,
S Norway
Stavers Island *see* Vostok Island
Stavropol' 111 B7 *prev.*
Voroshilovsk. Stavropol'skiy Kray,
SW Russian Federation
Steamboat Springs 44 C4 Colorado,
C USA
Steenwijk 86 D2 Overijssel,
N Netherlands
Steier *see* Steyr
Steinkjer 84 B4 Nord-Trøndelag,
C Norway
Stendal 94 C3 Sachsen-Anhalt,
C Germany
Stephenville 49 F3 Texas, SW USA
Sterling 44 C4 Colorado, C USA
Sterling 40 B3 Illinois, N USA
Sterlitamak 114 B3 Respublika
Bashkortostan, W Russian
Federation
Stettiner Haff *see* Szczeciński,
Zalew
Stevenage 89 E6 E England, UK
Stevens Point 40 B2 Wisconsin,
N USA
Stewart Island 151 A8 *island* S NZ
Steyr 95 D6 *var.* Steier.
Oberösterreich, N Austria
St-Gall *see* Sankt Gallen
StGallen *see* Sankt Gallen
Stif *see* Sétif
Stillwater 49 G1 Oklahoma, C USA
Stirling 88 C4 C Scotland, UK
Stjørdal 84 B4 Nord-Trøndelag,
C Norway
St-Laurent *see* St-Laurent-du-
Maroni
Stockach 95 B6 Baden-
Württemberg, S Germany
Stockholm 85 C6 *country capital*
(Sweden) Stockholm, C Sweden
Stockton 47 B6 California, W USA
Stockton Plateau 49 E4 *plain* Texas,
SW USA
Stœng Trêng 137 D5 *prev.* Stung
Treng. Stœng Trêng,
NE Cambodia
Stoke *see* Stoke-on-Trent
Stoke-on-Trent 89 D6 *var.* Stoke.
C England, UK
Stómio 104 B4 Thessalía, C Greece
Stony Tunguska 112 D2 *river*
C Russian Federation
Store Bælt *see* Storebælt
Storebælt 85 B8 *var.* Store Bælt, *Eng.*
Great Belt, Storebelt. *Channel*
Baltic Sea/Kattegat
Storebelt *see* Storebælt
Støren 85 B5 Sør-Trøndelag,
S Norway
Storfjorden 83 G2 *fjord* S Norway
Stornoway 88 B2 NW Scotland,
UK
Storsjön 85 B5 *lake* C Sweden
Storuman 84 C4 *lake* N Sweden
Storuman 84 C4 Västerbotten,
N Sweden
Stowbtsy 107 C6 *Pol.* Stolbce, *Rus.*
Stolbtsy. Minskaya Voblasts',
C Belarus
St.Paul Island *see* St-Paul, Île
St-Pierre and Miquelon 39 G4 *Fr.*
Îles St-Pierre et Miquelon. *French
territorial collectivity* NE North
America
Strabane 89 B5 *Ir.* An Srath Bán.
W Northern Ireland, UK
Strakonice 99 A5 *Ger.* Strakonitz.
Budějovický Kraj, S Czech
Republic
Stralsund 94 D2 Mecklenburg-
Vorpommern, NE Germany
Stranraer 89 C5 S Scotland,
UK
Strasbourg 90 E3 *Ger.* Strassburg;
anc. Argentoratum. Bas-Rhin,
NE France
Strǎşeni 108 D3 *var.* Strasheny.
C Moldova
Strasheny *see* Strǎşeni
Stratford 150 D4 Taranaki, North
Island, NZ

Strathfield 148 E2 New South
Wales, SE Australia
Straubing 95 C6 Bayern,
SE Germany
Strehaia 108 B5 Mehedinţi,
SW Romania
Strelka 114 D4 Krasnoyarskiy Kray,
C Russian Federation
Strofilia *see* Strofyliá
Strofyliá 105 C5 *var.* Strofilia.
Évvoia, C Greece
Stromboli, Isola 97 D6 *island* Isole
Eolie, S Italy
Stromeferry 88 C3 N Scotland, UK
Strömstad 85 B6 Västra Götaland,
S Sweden
Strömsund 84 C4 Jämtland,
C Sweden
Struga 101 D6 SW FYR Macedonia
Strumica 101 E6 E FYR Macedonia
Strumyani 104 C3 Blagoevgrad,
SW Bulgaria
Strymónas 104 C3 *Bul.* Struma.
River Bulgaria/Greece *see also*
Struma
Stryy 108 B2 L'vivs'ka Oblast',
NW Ukraine
Studholme 151 B6 Canterbury,
South Island, NZ
Sturgis 44 D3 South Dakota, N USA
Stuttgart 95 B6 Baden-
Württemberg, SW Germany
Stykkishólmur 83 E4 Vesturland,
W Iceland
Styr 108 C1 *Rus.* Styr'. *River*
Belarus/Ukraine
Su *see* Jiangsu
Suakin 72 C3 *var.* Sawakin. Red Sea,
NE Sudan
Subačius 106 C4 Kupiškis,
NE Lithuania
Subaykhān 118 E3 Dayr az Zawr,
E Syria
Subotica 100 D2 *Ger.* Maria-
Theresiopel, *Hung.* Szabadka.
Serbia, N Yugoslavia
Suceava 108 C3 *Ger.* Suczawa,
Hung. Szucsava. Suceava,
NE Romania
Su-chou *see* Suzhou
Suchow *see* Xuzhou
Sucre 61 F4 *hist.* Chuquisaca, La
Plata. *Country capital* (Bolivia-legal
capital) Chuquisaca, S Bolivia
Sudan 72 A4 *Ar.* Jumhuriyat as-
Sudan; *prev.* Anglo-Egyptian
Sudan. *country* N Africa

Sudbury 38 C4 Ontario, S Canada
Sudd 73 B5 *swamp region*
S Sudan
Sudeten 98 B4 *var.* Sudetes, Sudetic
Mountains, *Cz./Pol.* Sudety.
Mountain range Czech
Republic/Poland
Sudetes *see* Sudeten
Sudetic Mountains *see* Sudeten
Sudety *see* Sudeten

Südkarpaten *see* Carpaţii
Meridionali
Sue 73 B5 *river* S Sudan
Sueca 93 F3 País Valenciano,
E Spain
Sue Wood Bay 42 B5 *bay*
W Bermuda
Suez 72 B1 *Ar.* As Suways,
El Suweis. NE Egypt
Suez Canal 72 B1 *Ar.* Qanât as
Suways. *Canal* NE Egypt
Suez, Gulf of 72 B2 *Ar.* Khalīj as
Suways. *Gulf* NE Egypt
Suğla Gölü 116 C4 *lake* SW Turkey
Şuḩār 121 D5 *var.* Sohar. N Oman
Sühbaatar 127 E1 Selenge,
N Mongolia
Suhl 95 C5 Thüringen, C Germany
Suixi 128 C6 Guangdong,
S China
Sujāwal 134 B3 Sind, SE Pakistan
Sukabumi 138 C5 *prev.* Soekaboemi.
Jawa, C Indonesia
Sukagawa 131 D5 Fukushima,
Honshū, C Japan
Sukarnapura *see* Jayapura
Sukhne *see* As Sukhnah
Sukhona 110 C4 *var.* Tot'ma. *River*
NW Russian Federation
Sukkertoppen *see* Maniitsoq
Sukkur 134 B3 Sind, SE Pakistan
Sukumo 131 B7 Kōchi, Shikoku,
SW Japan
Sulaimaniya *see* As Sulaymānīyah
Sulaimān Range 134 C2 *mountain
range* C Pakistan
Sula, Kepulauan 139 E4 *island
group* C Indonesia
Sulawesi 139 E4 *Eng.* Celebes.
Island C Indonesia
Sulechów 98 B3 *Ger.* Züllichau.
Lubuskie, W Poland
Suliag *see* Sohâg
Sullana 60 B2 Piura, NW Peru
Sulphur Springs 49 G2 Texas,
SW USA
Sulu Archipelago 139 E3 *island
group* SW Philippines
Sulu Sea 139 E2 *Ind.* Laut Sulu. *Sea*
SW Philippines
Sulyukta 123 E2 *Kir.* Sülüktü.
Oshkshaya Oblast', SW
Kyrgyzstan
Sumatera 137 B8 *Eng.* Sumatra.
Island W Indonesia
Sumatra *see* Sumatera
Sumba, Pulau 139 E5 *Eng.*
Sandalwood Island; *prev.* Soemba.
Island Nusa Tenggara,
C Indonesia
Sumba, Selat 139 E5 *strait* Nusa
Tenggara, S Indonesia
Sumbawanga 73 B7 Rukwa,
W Tanzania
Sumbe 78 B2 *prev.* N'Gunza, *Port.*
Novo Redondo. Cuanza Sul,
W Angola
Sumeih 73 B5 Southern Darfur,
S Sudan
Summer Lake 46 B4 *lake* Oregon,
NW USA
Summit 93 H5 *mountain*
C Gibraltar
Sumqayıt 117 H2 *Rus.* Sumgait.
E Azerbaijan
Sumy 109 F2 Sums'ka Oblast',
NE Ukraine
Sunbury 149 C7 Victoria,
SE Australia
Sunda Islands *see* Greater Sunda
Islands
Sunda, Selat 138 B5 *strait*
Jawa/Sumatera, SW Indonesia
Sunda Trench *see* Java Trench
Sunderland 88 D4 *var.* Wearmouth.
NE England, UK
Sundsvall 85 C5 Västernorrland,
C Sweden
Sungaipenuh 138 B4 *prev.*
Soengaipenoeh. Sumatera,
W Indonesia
Sunnyvale 47 A6 California,
W USA

Suntar 115 F3 Respublika Sakha
(Yakutiya), NE Russian
Federation
Sunyani 75 E5 W Ghana
Suomussalmi 84 E4 Oulu,
E Finland
Suŏng 137 D6 Kâmpóng Cham,
C Cambodia
Suoyarvi 110 B3 Respublika
Kareliya, NW Russian Federation
Supe 60 C3 Lima, W Peru
Superior 40 A1 Wisconsin, N USA
Superior, Lake 40 B1 *Fr.* Lac
Supérieur. *Lake* Canada/USA
Suqrah *see* Şawqirah
Suquţrā 121 C7 *var.* Sokotra, *Eng.*
Socotra. *Island* SE Yemen
Şūr *see* Soûr
Şūr 121 E5 NE Oman
Surabaya 138 D5 *prev.* Soerabaja,
Surabaja. Jawa, C Indonesia
Surakarta 138 C5 *Eng.* Solo; *prev.*
Soerakarta. Jawa, S Indonesia
Šurany 99 C6 *Hung.* Nagysurány.
Nitriansky Kraj, SW Slovakia
Sūrat 134 C4 Gujarāt, W India
Suratdhani *see* Surat Thani
Surat Thani 137 C6 *var.* Suratdhani.
Surat Thani, SW Thailand
Surazh 107 E5 *Rus.* Surazh.
Vitsyebskaya Voblasts',
NE Belarus
Surdulica 101 E5 Serbia,
SE Yugoslavia
Sûre 87 D7 *var.* Sauer. *River*
W Europe *see also* Sauer
Surendranagar 134 C4 Gujarāt,
W India
Surfers Paradise 149 E5
Queensland, E Australia
Surgut 114 D3 Khanty-Mansiyskiy
Avtonomnyy Okrug, C Russian
Federation
Surin 137 D5 Surin, E Thailand
Surinam *see* Suriname
Suriname 59 G3 *var.* Surinam; *prev.*
Dutch Guiana, Netherlands
Guiana. *Country* N S America

Surkhob 123 F3 *river* C Tajikistan
Surt 71 G2 *var.* Sidra, Sirte.
N Libya
Surt, Khalīj 71 F2 *Eng.* Gulf of
Sidra, Gulf of Sirti, Sidra. *Gulf*
N Libya
Surtsey 83 E5 *island* S Iceland
Suruga-wan 131 D6 *bay* SE Japan
Susa 96 A2 Piemonte, NE Italy
Sūsah *see* Sousse
Susanville 47 B5 California,
W USA
Susitna 36 C3 Alaska, USA
Susteren 87 D5 Limburg,
SE Netherlands
Susuman 115 G3 Magadanskaya
Oblast', E Russian Federation
Sutherland 148 E2 New South
Wales, SE Australia
Sutlej 134 C2 *river* India/Pakistan

Suur Munamägi *106 D3 var.*
Munamägi, *Ger.* Eier-Berg.
Mountain SE Estonia
Suur Väin *106 C2 Ger.* Grosser
Sund. *Strait* W Estonia
Suva *145 E4 country capital* (Fiji) Viti
Levu, W Fiji
Suwałki *98 E2 Lith.* Suvalkai, *Rus.*
Suvalki. Podlaskie, NE Poland
Şuwār *see* Aş Şuwār
Suweida *see* As Suwaydā'
Suzhou *128 D5 var.* Soochow, Su-
chou, Suchow; *prev.* Wuhsien.
Jiangsu, E China
Svalbard *83 E1 Norwegian*
dependency Arctic Ocean
Svartisen *84 C3 glacier* C Norway
Svay Riĕng *137 D6* Svay Riĕng,
S Cambodia
Sveg *85 B5* Jämtland,
C Sweden
Svenstavik *85 C5* Jämtland,
C Sweden
Svetlograd *111 B7* Stavropol'skiy
Kray, SW Russian Federation
Svilengrad *104 D3 prev.* Mustafa-
Pasha. Haskovo, S Bulgaria
Svitlovods'k *109 F3 Rus.*
Svetlovodsk. Kirovohrads'ka
Oblast', C Ukraine
Svobodnyy *115 G4* Amurskaya
Oblast', SE Russian Federation
Svyataya Anna Trough *172 C4 var.*
Saint Anna Trough. *Undersea*
feature N Kara Sea
Svyetlahorsk *107 D7 Rus.*
Svetlogorsk. Homyel'skaya
Voblasts', SE Belarus
Swabian Jura *see* Schwäbische Alb
Swakopmund *78 B3* Erongo,
W Namibia
Swansea *89 C7 Wel.* Abertawe.
S Wales, UK
Swarzędz *98 C3* Wielkopolskie,
C Poland
Swatow *see* Shantou
Swaziland *78 D4 Country* S Africa

Swaziland 78

Official name Kingdom of
Swaziland
Formation 1968
Capital Mbabane
Population 1 million / 152 people
per sq mile (59 people per sq km)
Total area 6,640 sq miles
(17,200 sq km)
Languages Siswati, English, Zulu
Religions Christian 60%,
Traditional beliefs 40%
Ethnic mix Swazi 95%, other 5%
Government Executive monarchy
Currency Lilangeni = 100 cents
Literacy rate 77.5%
Calorie consumption 2,706
kilocalories

Sweden *84 B4 Swe.* Sverige. *Country*
N Europe

Sweden 84

Official name Kingdom of Sweden
Formation 1809
Capital Stockholm
Population 8.9 million /
56 people per sq mile
(22 people per sq km)
Total area 158,926 sq miles
(411,620 sq km)
Languages Swedish, Finnish,
Lappish
Religions Evangelical Lutheran
89%, Roman Catholic 2%,
other 9%
Ethnic mix Swedish 91%, Finnish
and Lapp 3%, other European 6%
Government Constitutional
monarchy
Currency Swedish krona
= 100 ore
Literacy rate 99%
Calorie consumption 2,972
kilocalories

Swed Ormsö *see* Vormsi
Sweetwater *49 F3* Texas,
SW USA
Świdnica *98 B4 Ger.* Schweidnitz.
Wałbrzych, SW Poland
Świdwin *98 B2 Ger.* Schivelbein.
Zachodniopomorskie, NW Poland
Świebodzice *98 B4 Ger.* Freiburg in
Schlesien, Swiebodzice.
Wałbrzych, SW Poland
Świebodzin *98 B3 Ger.* Schwiebus.
Lubuskie, W Poland
Świecie *98 C3 Ger.* Schwertberg.
Kujawsko-pomorskie,
C Poland
Swindon *89 D7* S England, UK
Świnoujście *98 B2 Ger.*
Swinemünde.
Zachodniopomorskie, NW Poland
Switzerland *95 A7 Fr.* La Suisse,
Ger. Schweiz, *It.* Svizzera; *anc.*
Helvetia. *Country* C Europe

Switzerland 95

Official name Swiss
Confederation
Formation 1291
Capital Berne
Population 7.4 million /
482 people per sq mile
(186 people per sq km)
Total area 15,355 sq miles
(39,770 sq km)
Languages German, French,
Italian, Swiss German, Romansch
Religions Roman Catholic 46%,
Protestant 40%, other 14%
Ethnic mix German 65%, French
18%, Italian 10%, Romansh 1%,
other 6%
Government Federal republic
Currency Swiss franc
= 100 centimes
Literacy rate 99%
Calorie consumption 3,379
kilocalories

Sycaminum *see* Hefa
Sydney *148 D1 state capital* New
South Wales, SE Australia
Sydney *39 G4* Cape Breton Island,
Nova Scotia, SE Canada
Syedpur *see* Saidpur
Syemyezhava *107 C6 Rus.*
Semezhevo. Minskaya Voblasts',
C Belarus
Syene *see* Aswân
Syeverodonets'k *109 H3 Rus.*
Severodonetsk. Luhans'ka
Oblast', E Ukraine
Syktyvkar *110 D4 prev.* Ust'-
Sysol'sk. Respublika Komi,
NW Russian Federation
Sylhet *135 G3* Chittagong,
NE Bangladesh
Synel'nykove *109 G3*
Dnipropetrovs'ka Oblast',
E Ukraine
Syowa *154 C2 Japanese research*
station Antarctica
Syracuse *41 E3* New York, NE USA
Syrdariya *see* Syr Darya
Syr Darya *114 B4 var.* Sai Hun, Sir
Darya, Syrdarya, *Kaz.* Syrdariya,
Rus. Syrdar'ya, *Uzb.* Sirdaryo; *anc.*
Jaxartes. *River* C Asia
Syria *118 B3 var.* Siria, Syrie, *Ar.* Al-
Jumhūrīyah al-'Arabīyah as-
Sūrīyah, Sūrīya. *Country* SW Asia

Syria 118

Official name Syrian Arab
Republic
Formation 1946
Capital Damascus
Population 16 million /
227 people per sq mile
(87 people per sq km)
Total area 71,065 sq miles
(184,060 sq km)
Languages Arabic, French,
Kurdish

Syria 118 (continued)

Religions Sunni Muslim 74%,
other Muslim 16%,
Christian 10%
Ethnic mix Arab 89%,
Kurdish 6%, Armenian, Turkmen,
Circassian 2%, other 3%
Government Single-party republic
Currency Syrian pound
= 100 piastres
Literacy rate 71.6%
Calorie consumption 3,175
kilocalories

Syrian Desert *119 D5 Ar.*
Al Hamad, Bādiyat ash Shām.
Desert SW Asia
Sýrna *105 E7 var.* Sirna. *Island*
Kykládes, Greece, Aegean Sea
Sýros *105 C6 var.* Síros. *Island*
Kykládes, Greece, Aegean Sea
Syvash, Zatoka *109 F4 Rus.* Zaliv
Syvash. *Inlet* S Ukraine
Syzran' *111 C6* Samarskaya Oblast',
W Russian Federation
Szamos *see* Someş
Szamotuły *98 B3* Wielkopolskie,
C Poland
Szczecin *98 B3 Eng./Ger.* Stettin.
Zachodniopomorskie, NW Poland
Szczecinek *98 B2 Ger.* Neustettin.
Zachodniopomorskie, NW Poland
Szczeciński, Zalew *98 A2 var.*
Stettiner Haff, *Ger.* Oderhaff. *Bay*
Germany/Poland
Szczytno *98 D3 Ger.* Ortelsburg.
Olsztyn, NE Poland
Szechuan *see* Sichuan
Szechwan *see* Sichuan
Szeged *99 D7 Ger.* Szegedin, *Rom.*
Seghedin. Csongrád, SE Hungary
Székesfehérvár *99 C6 Ger.*
Stuhlweissenberg; *anc.* Alba
Regia. Fejér, W Hungary
Szekszárd *99 C7* Tolna, S Hungary
Szczentamás *see* Srbobran
Szeping *see* Siping
Sziszek *see* Sisak
Szlatina *see* Slatina
Szolnok *99 D6* Jász-Nagykun-
Szolnok, C Hungary
Szombathely *99 B6 Ger.*
Steinamanger; *anc.* Sabaria,
Savaria. Vas, W Hungary
Szprotawa *98 B4 Ger.* Sprottau.
Lubuskie, W Poland

T

Table Rock Lake *49 G1 reservoir*
Arkansas/Missouri, C USA
Tábor *99 B5* Budějovický Kraj,
S Czech Republic
Tabora *73 B7* Tabora, W Tanzania
Tabrīz *120 C2 var.* Tebriz; *anc.*
Tauris. Āzarbāyjān-e Khāvarī,
NW Iran
Tabuaeran *145 G2 prev.* Fanning
Island. *Atoll* Line Islands,
E Kiribati
Tabūk *120 A4* Tabūk, NW Saudi
Arabia
Täby *85 C6* Stockholm, C Sweden
Tachov *99 A5 Ger.* Tachau. Plzeňský
Kraj, W Czech Republic
Tacloban *139 F2 off.* Tacloban City.
Leyte, C Philippines
Tacna *61 E4* Tacna, SE Peru
Tacoma *46 B2* Washington,
NW USA
Tacuarembó *64 D4 prev.* San
Fructuoso. Tacuarembó,
C Uruguay
Tademaït, Plateau du *70 D3 plateau*
C Algeria
Tadmor *see* Tudmur
Tadmur *see* Tudmur
Tādpatri *132 C2* Andhra Pradesh,
E India
Taegu *129 E4 off.* Taegu-
gwangyŏksi, *var.* Daegu, *Jap.*
Taikyū. SE South Korea

Taejŏn *129 E4 off.* Taejŏn-
gwangyŏksi, *Jap.* Taiden. C South
Korea
Tafassâsset, Ténéré du *75 G2 desert*
N Niger
Tafila *see* Aţ Ţafīlah
Taganrog *111 A7* Rostovskaya
Oblast', SW Russian Federation
Taganrog, Gulf of *109 G4 Rus.*
Taganrogskiy Zaliv, *Ukr.*
Tahanroz'ka Zatoka. *Gulf* Russian
Federation/Ukraine
Taguatinga *63 F3* Tocantins,
C Brazil
Tagus *92 C3 Port.* Rio Tejo, *Sp.* Río
Tajo. *River* Portugal/Spain
Tagus Plain *80 A4 undersea feature*
E Atlantic Ocean
Tahat *71 E4 mountain* SE Algeria
Tahiti *145 H4 island* Îles du Vent,
W French Polynesia
Tahlequah *49 G1* Oklahoma, C USA
Tahoe, Lake *47 B5 lake*
California/Nevada, W USA
Tahoua *75 F3* Tahoua, W Niger
T'aichung *128 D6 Jap.* Taichū; *prev.*
Taiwan. C Taiwan
Taieri *151 B7 river* South Island, NZ
Taihape *150 D4* Manawatu-
Wanganui, North Island, NZ
Tailem Bend *149 B7* South Australia
T'ainan *128 D6 Jap.* Tainan; *prev.*
Dainan. S Taiwan
T'aipei *128 D6 Jap.* Taihoku; *prev.*
Daihoku. *Country capital* (Taiwan)
N Taiwan
Taiping *138 B3* Perak, Peninsular
Malaysia
Taiwan *128 D6 var.* Formosa,
Formo'sa. *Country* E Asia

Taiwan 128

Official name Republic of China
(Taiwan)
Formation 1949
Capital Taipei
Population 22 million /
1,756 people per sq mile
(678 people per sq km)
Total area 12,455 sq miles
(32,260 sq km)
Languages Mandarin Chinese,
Amoy Chinese, Hakka Chinese
Religions Buddhist, Confucian,
Taoist 93%, Christian 5%, other 2%
Ethnic mix Indigenous Chinese
84%, Mainland Chinese 14%,
Aborigine 2%
Government Multiparty republic
Currency Taiwan dollar
= 100 cents
Literacy rate 94%
Calorie consumption
not available

T'aiwan Haihsia *see* Taiwan Strait
Taiwan Haixia *see* Taiwan Strait
Taiwan Strait *128 D6 var.* Formosa
Strait, *Chin.* T'aiwan Haihsia,
Taiwan Haixia. *Strait*
China/Taiwan
Taiyuan *128 C4 prev.* T'ai-yuan,
T'ai-yüan, Yangku. Shanxi,
C China
Ta'izz *121 B7* SW Yemen
Tajikistan *123 E3 Rus.* Tadzhikistan,
Taj. Jumhurii Tojikiston; *prev.* Tajik
S.S.R. *Country* C Asia

Tajikistan 123

Official name Republic of Tajikistan
Formation 1991
Capital Dushanbe
Population 6.2 million /
112 people per sq mile
(43 people per sq km)
Total area 55,251 sq miles
(143,100 sq km)
Languages Tajik, Russian
Religions Sunni Muslim 80%,
Shi'a Muslim 5%, other 15%

Tajikistan (continued)

Ethnic mix Tajik 62%,
Uzbek 24%, Russian 4%,
Tatar 2%, other 8%
Government Multiparty republic
Currency Tajik rouble
= 100 kopeks
Literacy rate 99%
Calorie consumption
not available

Tak 136 C4 var. Rahaeng. Tak,
W Thailand
Takao see Kaohsiung
Takaoka 131 C5 Toyama, Honshū,
SW Japan
Takapuna 150 D2 Auckland, North
Island, NZ
Takhiatosh 122 C2 Rus. Takhiatash.
Qoraqalpoghiston Respublikasi,
W Uzbekistan
Takhtakŭpir 122 D1 Rus.
Takhtakupyr. Qoraqalpoghiston
Respublikasi, NW
Uzbekistan
Takikawa 130 D2 Hokkaidō,
NE Japan
Takla Makan Desert see
Taklimakan Shamo
Taklimakan Shamo 126 B3 Eng.
Takla Makan Desert. Desert
NW China
Takow see Kaohsiung
Takutea 145 G4 island S Cook
Islands
Talachyn 107 D6 Rus. Tolochin.
Vitsyebskaya Voblasts',
NE Belarus
Talamanca, Cordillera de 53 E5
mountain range S Costa Rica
Talara 60 B2 Piura, NW Peru
Talas 123 F2 Talasskaya Oblast',
NW Kyrgyzstan
Talaud, Kepulauan 139 F3 island
group E Indonesia
Talavera de la Reina 92 D3 anc.
Caesarobriga, Talabriga. Castilla-
La Mancha, C Spain
Talca 64 B4 Maule, C Chile
Talcahuano 65 B5 Bío Bío, C Chile
Taldykorgan 114 C5 Kaz.
Taldyqorghan; prev. Taldy-
Kurgan. Almaty, SE Kazakhstan
Taldy-Kurgan/Taldyqorghan see
Taldykorgan
Ta-lien see Dalian
Taliq-an see Tāloqān
Tal'ka 107 C6 Rus. Tal'ka. Minskaya
Voblasts', C Belarus
Tallahassee 42 D3 prev. Muskogean.
State capital Florida, SE USA
Tall al Abyaḍ see At Tall al Abyaḍ
Tallinn 106 D2 Ger. Reval, Rus.
Tallin; prev. Revel. Country capital
(Estonia) Harjumaa, NW Estonia
Tall Kalakh 118 B4 var. Tell Kalakh.
Ḥimṣ, C Syria
Tallulah 42 B2 Louisiana, S USA
Talnakh 114 D3 Taymyrskiy
(Dolgano-Nenetskiy)
Avtonomnyy Okrug, N Russian
Federation
Tal'ne 109 E3 Rus. Tal'noye.
Cherkas'ka Oblast', C Ukraine
Taloga 49 F1 Oklahoma, C USA
Tāloqān 123 E3 var. Taliq-an.
Takhār, NE Afghanistan
Talsi 106 C3 Ger. Talsen. Talsi,
NW Latvia
Taltal 62 B2 Antofagasta, N Chile
Talvik 84 D2 Finnmark,
N Norway
Tamabo, Banjaran 138 D3 mountain
range East Malaysia
Tamale 75 E4 C Ghana
Tamana 145 E3 prev. Rotcher Island.
Atoll Tungaru, W Kiribati
Tamanrasset 71 E4 var. Tamenghest.
S Algeria
Tamar 89 C7 river SW England, UK
Tamar see Tudmur
Tamatave see Toamasina

Tamazunchale 51 E4 San Luis
Potosí, C Mexico
Tambacounda 74 C3 SE Senegal
Tambov 111 B6 Tambovskaya
Oblast', W Russian Federation
Tambura 73 B5 Western Equatoria,
SW Sudan
Tamchaket see Tâmchekkeṭ
Tâmchekkeṭ 74 C3 var. Tamchaket.
Hodh el Gharbi, S Mauritania
Tamenghest see Tamanrasset
Tamiahua, Laguna de 51 F4 lagoon
E Mexico
Tamil Nādu 132 C3 prev. Madras.
State SE India
Tam Ky 137 E5 Quang Nam-Đa
Nāng, C Vietnam
Tampa 43 E4 Florida, SE USA
Tampa Bay 43 E4 bay Florida,
SE USA
Tampere 85 D5 Swe. Tammerfors.
Länsi-Suomi, W Finland
Tampico 51 E3 Tamaulipas,
C Mexico
Tamworth 149 D6 New South
Wales, SE Australia
Tana 84 D2 var. Tenojoki, Fin. Teno,
Lapp. Dealnu. River
Finland/Norway see also Teno
Tana 84 D2 Finnmark, N Norway
Tanabe 131 C7 Wakayama, Honshū,
SW Japan
T'ana Hāyk' 72 C4 Eng. Lake Tana.
Lake NW Ethiopia
Tanais see Don
Tanami Desert 146 D3 desert
Northern Territory, N Australia
Ţāndārei 108 D5 Ialomiţa,
SE Romania
Tandil 65 D5 Buenos Aires,
E Argentina
Tanega-shima 131 B8 island Nansei-
shotō, SW Japan
Tane Range 136 B4 Bur. Tanen
Taunggyi. Mountain range
W Thailand
Tanezrouft 70 D4 desert
Algeria/Mali
Ţanf, Jabal aṭ 118 D4 mountain
SE Syria
Tanga 69 E5 Tanga, E Tanzania
Tanga 73 C7 region E Tanzania
Tangeh-ye Hormoz see Hormuz,
Strait of
Tanger 70 C2 var. Tangiers, Tangier,
Fr./Ger. Tangerk, Sp. Tánger; anc.
Tingis. NW Morocco
Tangerk see Tanger
Tanggula Shan 126 C4 var. Dangla,
Tangla Range. Mountain range
W China
Tangier see Tanger
Tangiers see Tanger
Tangla Range see Tanggula Shan
Tangra Yumco 126 B5 var. Tangro
Tso. Lake W China
Tangro Tso see Tangra Yumco
Tangshan 128 D3 var. T'ang-shan.
Hebei, E China
T'ang-shan see Tangshan
Tanimbar, Kepulauan 139 F5 island
group Maluku, E Indonesia
Tanna 144 D4 island S Vanuatu
Tannenhof see Krynica
Tan-Tan 70 B3 SW Morocco
Tan-tung see Dandong
Tanzania 73 C7 Swa. Jamhuri ya
Muungano wa Tanzania;
prev. German East Africa,
Tanganyika and Zanzibar.
Country E Africa

Tanzania 73

Official name United Republic of
Tanzania
Formation 1961
Capital Dodoma
Population 33.5 million /
98 people per sq mile
(38 people per sq km)

Tanzania (continued)

Total area 342,100 sq miles
(886,040 sq km)
Languages English, Swahili,
Sukuma
Religions Muslim 33%, Christian
33%, Traditional beliefs 30%,
other 4%
Ethnic mix 120 small ethnic Bantu
groups 99%, other 1%
Government Multiparty republic
Currency Tanzanian shilling
= 100 cents
Literacy rate 71.6%
Calorie consumption 2,018
kilocalories

Taoudenit see Taoudenni
Taoudenni 75 E2 var. Taoudenit.
Tombouctou, N Mali
Tapa 106 E2 Ger. Taps. Lääne-
Virumaa, NE Estonia
Tapachula 51 G5 Chiapas,
SE Mexico
Tapajós, Rio 63 E2 var. Tapajóz.
River NW Brazil
Tapajóz see Tapajós, Rio
Ţarābulus 71 F2 var. Ţarābulus
al Gharb, Eng. Tripoli.Country
capital (Libya) NW Libya
Ţarābulus see Tripoli
Ţarābulus al Gharb see Ţarābulus
Ţarābulus ash Shām see Tripoli
Taraclia 108 D4 Rus. Tarakliya.
S Moldova
Taranaki, Mount 150 C4 var.
Egmont, Mount. Mountain North
Island, NZ
Tarancón 93 E3 Castilla-La Mancha,
C Spain
Taranto 97 E5 var. Tarentum. Puglia,
SE Italy
Taranto, Golfo di 97 E6 Eng. Gulf of
Taranto. Gulf S Italy
Tarapoto 60 C2 San Martín,
N Peru
Tarare 91 D5 Rhône, E France
Tarascon 91 D6 Bouches-du-Rhône,
SE France
Tarawa 144 D2 atoll Tungaru,
W Kiribati
Taraz 114 C5 prev. Aulie Ata,
Auliye-Ata, Dzhambul, Zhambyl.
Zhambyl, S Kazakhstan
Tarazona 93 E2 Aragón, NE Spain
Tarbes 91 B6 anc. Bigorra. Hautes-
Pyrénées, S France
Tarcoola 149 A6 South Australia
Taree 149 D6 New South Wales,
SE Australia
Tarentum see Taranto
Târgovişte 108 C5 prev. Tîrgovişte.
Dâmboviţa, S Romania
Târgu Jiu 108 B4 prev. Tîrgu Jiu.
Gorj, W Romania
Târgu Mureş 108 B4 prev. Oşorhei,
Tîrgu Mures, Ger. Neumarkt,
Hung. Marosvásárhely. Mureş,
C Romania
Târgu-Neamţ 108 C3 var. Târgul-
Neamţ; prev. Tîrgu-Neamţ.
Neamţ, NE Romania
Târgu Ocna 108 C4 Hung.
Aknavásár; prev. Tîrgu Ocna.
Bacău, E Romania
Târgu Secuiesc 108 C4 Ger.
Neumarkt, Szekler Neumarkt,
Hung. Kezdivásárhely; prev.
Chezdi-Oşorheiu, Tîrgul-
Săcuiesc, Tîrgu Secuiesc. Covasna,
E Romania
Tarija 61 G5 Tarija, S Bolivia
Tarīm 121 C6 C Yemen
Tarim Basin 124 C2 basin
NW China
Tarim He 126 B3 river NW China
Tarma 60 C3 Junín, C Peru
Tarn 91 C6 cultural region S France
Tarn 91 C6 river S France
Tarnobrzeg 98 D4 Podkarpackie,
SE Poland

Tarnów 99 D5 Małopolskie,
S Poland
Tarragona 93 G2 anc. Tarraco.
Cataluña, E Spain
Tàrrega 93 F2 var. Tarrega.
Cataluña, NE Spain
Tarsus 116 C4 İçel, S Turkey
Tartu 106 D3 Ger. Dorpat; prev. Rus.
Yurev, Yur'yev. Tartumaa,
SE Estonia
Ţarţūs 118 A3 Fr. Tartouss; anc.
Tortosa. Tarţūs, W Syria
Ta Ru Tao, Ko 137 B7 island
S Thailand
Tarvisio 96 D2 Friuli-Venezia
Giulia, NE Italy
Tashi Chho Dzong see Thimphu
Tashkent see Toshkent
Tash-Kumyr 123 F2 Kir. Tash-
Kömür. Dzhalal-Abadskaya
Oblast', W Kyrgyzstan
Tashqurghan see Kholm
Tasikmalaya 138 C5 prev.
Tasikmalaja. Jawa, C Indonesia
Tasman Basin 142 C5 var. East
Australian Basin. Undersea feature
S Tasman Sea
Tasman Bay 151 C5 inlet South
Island, NZ
Tasmania 149 B8 prev. Van
Diemen's Land. State SE Australia
Tasmania 152 B4 island SE Australia
Tasman Plateau 142 C5 var. South
Tasmania Plateau. Undersea feature
SW Tasman Sea
Tasman Sea 142 C5 sea SW Pacific
Ocean
Tassili-n-Ajjer 71 E4 plateau
E Algeria
Tatabánya 99 C6 Komárom-
Esztergom, NW Hungary
Tathlīth 121 B5 'Asīr, S Saudi
Arabia
Tatra Mountains 99 D5 Ger. Tatra,
Hung. Tátra, Pol./Slvk. Tatry.
Mountain range Poland/Slovakia
Ta-t'ung see Datong
Tatvan 117 F3 Bitlis, SE Turkey
Ta'ū 145 F4 var. Tau. Island Manua
Islands, E American Samoa
Tau see Ta'ū
Taukum, Peski 123 G1 desert
SE Kazakhstan
Taumarunui 150 D4 Manawatu-
Wanganui, North Island, NZ
Taungdwingyi 136 B3 Magwe,
C Myanmar
Taunggyi 136 B3 Shan State,
C Myanmar
Taunton 89 C7 SW England, UK
Taupo 150 D3 Waikato, North
Island, NZ
Taupo, Lake 150 D3 lake North
Island, NZ
Taurage 106 B4 Taurage, SW Lithuania
Tauranga 150 D3 Bay of Plenty,
North Island, NZ
Tauris see Tabriz
Tavas 116 B4 Denizli, SW Turkey
Tavira 92 C5 Faro, S Portugal
Tavoy 137 B5 var. Dawei.
Tenasserim, S Myanmar
Tavoy Island see Mali Kyun
Tawakoni, Lake 49 G2 reservoir
Texas, SW USA
Tawau 138 D3 Sabah, East Malaysia
Ţawkar see Tokar
Tawzar see Tozeur
Taxco 51 E4 var. Taxco de Alarcón.
Guerrero, S Mexico
Taxco de Alarcón see Taxco
Tay 88 C3 river C Scotland, UK
Taylor 49 G3 Texas, SW USA
Taymā' 120 A4 Tabūk, NW Saudi
Arabia
Taymyr, Ozero 115 E2 lake
N Russian Federation
Taymyr, Poluostrov 115 E2
peninsula N Russian
Federation
Taz 114 D3 river N Russian
Federation

T'bilisi 117 G2 *Eng.* Tiflis. *Country capital* (Georgia) SE Georgia
T'bilisi 112 B4 *international airport* S Georgia
Tchien *see* Zwedru
Tchongking *see* Chongqing
Tczew 98 C2 *Ger.* Dirschau. Pomorskie, N Poland
Te Anau 151 A7 Southland, South Island, NZ
Te Anau, Lake 151 A7 *lake* South Island, NZ
Teapa 51 G4 Tabasco, SE Mexico
Teate *see* Chieti
Tebingtinggi 138 B3 Sumatera, N Indonesia
Tebriz *see* Tabrīz
Techirghiol 108 D5 Constanța, SE Romania
Tecomán 50 D4 Colima, SW Mexico
Tecpan 51 E5 *var.* Tecpan de Galeana. Guerrero, S Mexico
Tecpan de Galeana *see* Tecpan
Tecuci 108 C4 Galați, E Romania
Tedzhen 122 C3 *Turkm.* Tejen. Akhalskiy Velayat, S Turkmenistan
Tedzhen *see* Harīrūd
Tees 89 D5 *river* N England, UK
Tefé 62 D2 Amazonas, N Brazil
Tegal 138 C4 Jawa, C Indonesia
Tegelen 87 D5 Limburg, SE Netherlands
Tegucigalpa 52 C3 *country capital* (Honduras) Francisco Morazán, SW Honduras
Teheran *see* Tehrān
Tehrān 120 C3 *var.* Teheran. *Country capital* (Iran) Tehrān, N Iran
Tehuacán 51 F4 Puebla, S Mexico
Tehuantepec 51 F5 *var.* Santo Domingo Tehuantepec. Oaxaca, SE Mexico
Tehuantepec, Golfo de 51 F5 *var.* Gulf of Tehuantepec. *Gulf* S Mexico
Tehuantepec, Gulf of *see* Tehuantepec, Golfo de
Tehuantepec, Isthmus of *see* Tehuantepec, Istmo de
Tehuantepec, Istmo de 51 F5 *var.* Isthmus of Tehuantepec. *Isthmus* SE Mexico
Tejen *see* Harīrūd
Te Kao 150 C1 Northland, North Island, NZ
Tekax 51 H4 *var.* Tekax de Álvaro Obregón. Yucatán, SE Mexico
Tekax de Álvaro Obregón *see* Tekax
Tekeli 114 C5 Almaty, SE Kazakhstan
Tekirdağ 116 A2 *It.* Rodosto; *anc.* Bisanthe, Raidestos, Rhaedestus. Tekirdağ, NW Turkey
Te Kuiti 150 D3 Waikato, North Island, NZ
Tela 52 C2 Atlántida, NW Honduras
Telanaipura *see* Jambi
Tel Aviv-Jaffa *see* Tel Aviv-Yafo
Tel Aviv-Yafo 119 A6 *var.* Tel Aviv-Jaffa. Tel Aviv, C Israel
Teles Pirés *see* São Manuel, Rio
Telish 104 C2 *prev.* Azizie. Pleven, NW Bulgaria
Tell Abiad *see* At Tall al Abyaḍ
Tell Abyad *see* At Tall al Abyaḍ
Tell Kalakh *see* Tall Kalakh
Tell Shedadi *see* Ash Shadādah
Telšiai 106 B3 *Ger.* Telschen. Telšiai, NW Lithuania
Teluk Irian *see* Cenderawasih, Teluk
Teluk Serera *see* Cenderawasih, Teluk
Temerin 100 D3 Serbia, N Yugoslavia
Temirtau 114 C4 *prev.* Samarandskaya, Samarandskoye. Karaganda, C Kazakhstan
Tempio Pausania 97 A5 Sardegna, Italy, C Mediterranean Sea

Temple 49 G3 Texas, SW USA
Temuco 65 B5 Araucanía, C Chile
Temuka 151 B6 Canterbury, South Island, NZ
Tenasserim 137 B6 Tenasserim, S Myanmar
Ténenkou 74 D3 Mopti, C Mali
Ténéré 75 G3 *physical region* C Niger
Tenerife 70 A3 *island* Islas Canarias, Spain, NE Atlantic Ocean
Tengger Shamo 127 E3 *desert* N China
Tengréla 74 D4 *var.* Tingréla. N Côte d'Ivoire
Tenkodogo 75 E4 S Burkina faso
Tennant Creek 148 A3 Northern Territory, C Australia
Tennessee 42 C1 *off.* State of Tennessee; also known as The Volunteer State. *State* SE USA
Tennessee River 42 C1 *river* S USA
Teno *see* Tana
Tenojoki *see* Tana
Tepelena *see* Tepelenë
Tepelenë 101 C7 *var.* Tepelena, *It.* Tepeleni. Gjirokastër, S Albania
Tepeleni *see* Tepelenë
Tepic 50 D4 Nayarit, C Mexico
Teplice 98 A4 *Ger.* Teplitz; *prev.* Teplice-Šanov, Teplitz-Schönau. Ústecký Kraj, NW Czech Republic
Tequila 50 D4 Jalisco, SW Mexico
Teraina 145 G2 *prev.* Washington Island. *Atoll* Line Islands, E Kiribati
Teramo 96 C4 *anc.* Interamna. Abruzzo, C Italy
Tercan 117 E3 Erzincan, NE Turkey
Terceira 92 A5 *var.* Ilha Terceira. *Island* Azores, Portugal, NE Atlantic Ocean
Teresina 63 F2 *var.* Therezina. *State capital* Piauí, NE Brazil
Termia *see* Kýthnos
Términos, Laguna de 51 G4 *lagoon* SE Mexico
Termiz 123 E3 *Rus.* Termez. Surkhondaryo Wiloyati, S Uzbekistan
Termoli 96 D4 Molise, C Italy
Terneuzen 87 B5 *var.* Neuzen. Zeeland, SW Netherlands
Terni 96 C4 *anc.* Interamna Nahars. Umbria, C Italy
Ternopil' 108 C2 *Pol.* Tarnopol, *Rus.* Ternopol'. Ternopil's'ka Oblast', W Ukraine
Terracina 97 C5 Lazio, C Italy
Terrassa 93 G2 *Cast.* Tarrasa. Cataluña, E Spain
Terre Adélie 154 C4 *disputed region* SE Antarctica
Terre Haute 40 B4 Indiana, N USA
Territoire du Yukon *see* Yukon Territory
Terschelling 86 C1 *Fris.* Skylge. *Island* Waddeneilanden, N Netherlands
Teruel 93 F3 *anc.* Turba. Aragón, E Spain
Tervel 104 E1 *prev.* Kurtbunar, *Rom.* Curtbunar. Dobrich, NE Bulgaria
Tervueren *see* Tervuren
Tervuren 87 C6 *var.* Tervueren. Vlaams Brabant, C Belgium
Teseney 72 C4 *var.* Tessenei. W Eritrea
Tessalit 75 E2 Kidal, NE Mali
Tessaoua 75 G3 Maradi, S Niger
Tessenderlo 87 C5 Limburg, NE Belgium
Tessenei *see* Teseney
Testigos, Islas los 59 E1 *island group* N Venezuela
Tete 79 E2 Tete, NW Mozambique
Teterow 94 C3 Mecklenburg-Vorpommern, NE Germany
Tétouan 70 C2 *var.* Tetouan, Tetuán. N Morocco

Tetuán *see* Tétouan
Tevere 96 C4 *Eng.* Tiber. *River* C Italy
Teverya 119 B5 *var.* Tiberias, Tverya. Northern, N Israel
Te Waewae Bay 151 A7 *bay* South Island, NZ
Texarkana 42 A2 Arkansas, C USA
Texarkana 49 H2 Texas, SW USA
Texas 49 F3 *off.* State of Texas; also known as The Lone Star State. *State* S USA
Texas City 49 H4 Texas, SW USA
Texel 86 C2 *island* Waddeneilanden, NW Netherlands
Texoma, Lake 49 G2 *reservoir* Oklahoma/Texas, C USA
Teziutlán 51 F4 Puebla, S Mexico
Thaa Atoll *see* Kolhumadulu Atoll
Thai Binh 136 D3 Thai Binh, N Vietnam
Thailand 137 C5 *Th.* Prathet Thai; *prev.* Siam. *Country* SE Asia

Thailand 137

Official name Kingdom of Thailand
Formation 1782
Capital Bangkok
Population 61.4 million / 311 people per sq mile (120 people per sq km)
Total area 197,254 sq miles (510,890 sq km)
Languages Thai, Chinese, Malay, Khmer, Mon, Karen, Miao
Religions Theravada Buddhist 95%, Muslim 3%, other 2%
Ethnic mix Thai 80%, Chinese 12%, Malay 4%, Khmer and other 4%
Government Constitutional monarchy
Currency Baht = 100 stangs
Literacy rate 94.7%
Calorie consumption 2,432 kilocalories

Thailand, Gulf of 137 C6 *var.* Gulf of Siam, *Th.* Ao Thai, *Vtn.* Vinh Thai Lan. *Gulf* SE Asia
Thai Nguyên 136 D3 Bắc Thai, N Vietnam
Thakhèk 136 D4 *prev.* Muang Khammouan. Khammouan, C Laos
Thamarid *see* Thamarīt
Thamarīt 121 D6 *var.* Thamarīd, Thumrayt. SW Oman
Thames 89 B8 *river* S England, UK
Thames 150 D3 Waikato, North Island, NZ
Thanh Hoa 136 D3 Vinh Phu, N Vietnam
Thanintari Taungdan *see* Bilauktaung Range
Thar Desert 134 C3 *var.* Great Indian Desert, Indian Desert. *Desert* India/Pakistan
Tharthār, Buḩayrat ath 120 B3 *lake* C Iraq
Thásos 104 C4 *island* E Greece
Thásos 104 C4 Thásos, E Greece
Thaton 136 B4 Mon State, S Myanmar
Thayetmyo 136 A4 Magwe, C Myanmar
The Crane 55 H2 *var.* Crane. S Barbados
The Dalles 46 B3 Oregon, NW USA
The Flatts Village *see* Flatts Village
The Hague *see* 's-Gravenhage
Theodosia *see* Feodosiya
The Pas 37 F5 Manitoba, C Canada
Therezina *see* Teresina
Thérma 105 D6 Ikaría, Dodekánisos, Greece, Aegean Sea
Thermaïkós Kólpos 104 B4 *Eng.* Thermaic Gulf; *anc.* Thermaicus Sinus. *Gulf* N Greece
Thermiá *see* Kýthnos
Thérmo 105 B5 Dytikí Ellás, C Greece

The Rock 93 H4 E Gibraltar
The Six Counties *see* Northern Ireland
Thessaloníki 104 C3 *Eng.* Salonica, Salonika, *SCr.* Solun, *Turk.* Selânik. Kentrikí Makedonía, N Greece
The Valley 55 G3 *dependent territory capital* (Anguilla) E Anguilla
The Village 49 G1 Oklahoma, C USA
Thiamis *see* Thýamis
Thibet *see* Xizang Zizhiqu
Thief River Falls 45 F1 Minnesota, N USA
Thienen *see* Tienen
Thiers 91 C5 Puy-de-Dôme, C France
Thiès 74 B3 W Senegal
Thimbu *see* Thimphu
Thimphu 135 G3 *var.* Thimbu; *prev.* Tashi Chho Dzong. *Country capital* (Bhutan) W Bhutan
Thionville 90 D3 *Ger.* Diedenhofen. Moselle, NE France
Thíra 105 D7 *prev.* Santorin, Santoríni, *anc.* Thera. Kykládes, Greece, Aegean Sea
Thíra 105 D7 Thíra, Kykládes, Greece, Aegean Sea
Thiruvanathapuram *see* Trivandrum
Thitu Island 128 C8 *island* NW Spratly Islands
Tholen 86 B4 *island* SW Netherlands
Thomasville 42 D3 Georgia, SE USA
Thompson 37 F4 Manitoba, C Canada
Thonon-les-Bains 91 D5 Haute-Savoie, E France
Thorlákshöfn 83 E5 Sudhurland, SW Iceland
Thornton Island *see* Millennium Island
Thouars 90 B4 Deux-Sèvres, W France
Thracian Sea 104 D4 *Gk.* Thrakikó Pélagos; *anc.* Thracium Mare. *Sea* Greece/Turkey
Three Kings Islands 150 C1 *island group* N NZ
Thrissur *see* Trichūr
Thuin 87 B7 Hainaut, S Belgium
Thule *see* Qaanaaq
Thumrayt *see* Thamarīt
Thun 95 A7 *Fr.* Thoune. Bern, W Switzerland
Thunder Bay 38 B4 Ontario, S Canada
Thuner See 95 A7 *lake* C Switzerland
Thung Song 137 C7 *var.* Cha Mai. Nakhon Si Thammarat, SW Thailand
Thurso 88 C2 N Scotland, UK
Thýamis 104 A4 *var.* Thiamis. *River* W Greece
Tianjin 128 D4 *var.* Tientsin. Tianjin Shi, E China
Tianjin *see* Tianjin Shi
Tianjin Shi 128 D4 *var.* Jin, Tianjin, T'ien-ching, Tientsin. Admin. region *municipality* E China
Tianshui 128 B4 Gansu, C China
Tiba *see* Chiba
Tiberias *see* Teverya
Tiberias, Lake 119 B5 *var.* Chinnereth, Sea of Bahr Tabariya, Sea of Galilee, *Ar.* Bahrat Tabariya, *Heb.* Yam Kinneret. *Lake* N Israel
Tibesti 76 C2 *var.* Tibesti Massif, *Ar.* Tībistī. *Mountain range* N Africa
Tibesti Massif *see* Tibesti
Tibet *see* Xizang Zizhiqu
Tibetan Autonomous Region *see* Xizang Zizhiqu
Tibet, Plateau of *see* Qingzang Gaoyuan
Tībistī *see* Tibesti

Tibnī *see* At Tibnī
Tiburón, Isla *50 B2 var.* Isla del Tiburón.
Tiburón, Isla del *see* Tiburón, Isla
Tîchît *74 D2 var.* Tichitt. Tagant, C Mauritania
Tichitt *see* Tîchît
Ticul *51 H3* Yucatán, SE Mexico
Tidjikdja *see* Tidjikja
Tidjikja *74 C2 var.* Tidjikdja; *prev.* Fort-Cappolani. Tagant, C Mauritania
T'ien-ching *see* Tianjin Shi
Tienen *87 C6 var.* Thienen, *Fr.* Tirlemont. Vlaams Brabant, C Belgium
Tien Shan *126 B3 Chin.* Thian Shan, Tian Shan, T'ien Shan, *Rus.* Tyan'-Shan'. *Mountain range* C Asia
Tientsin *see* Tianjin Shi
Tierp *85 C6* Uppsala, C Sweden
Tierra del Fuego *65 B8 off.* Provincia de la Tierra del Fuego. Admin. region *province* S Argentina
Tierra del Fuego *57 B8 island* Argentina/Chile
Tifton *42 D3* Georgia, SE USA
Tifu *139 F4* Pulau Buru, E Indonesia
Tighina *108 D4 Rus.* Bendery; *prev.* Bender. E Moldova
Tigranocerta *see* Siirt
Tigris *120 B2 Ar.* Dijlah, *Turk.* Dicle. *River* Iraq/Turkey
Tiguentourine *71 E3* E Algeria
Ti-hua *see* Ürümqi
Tihwa *see* Ürümqi
Tijuana *50 A1* Baja California, NW Mexico
Tikhoretsk *111 A7* Krasnodarskiy Kray, SW Russian Federation
Tikhvin *110 B4* Leningradskaya Oblast', NW Russian Federation
Tiki Basin *143 G3 undersea feature* S Pacific Ocean
Tiksi *115 F2* Respublika Sakha (Yakutiya), NE Russian Federation
Tilburg *86 C4* Noord-Brabant, S Netherlands
Tilimsen *see* Tlemcen
Tillabéri *75 F3 var.* Tillabéry. Tillabéri, W Niger
Tillabéry *see* Tillabéri
Tílos *105 E7 island* Dodekánisos, Greece, Aegean Sea
Timanskiy Kryazh *110 D3 Eng.* Timan Ridge. *Ridge* NW Russian Federation
Timaru *151 B6* Canterbury, South Island, NZ
Timbaki *see* Tympáki
Timbákion *see* Tympáki
Timbedgha *74 D3 var.* Timbédra. Hodh ech Chargui, SE Mauritania
Timbédra *see* Timbedgha
Timbuktu *see* Tombouctou
Timiş *108 A4 river* W Romania
Timişoara *108 A4 Ger.* Temeschwar, Temeswar, *Hung.* Temesvár; *prev.* Temeschburg. Timiş, W Romania
Timmins *38 C4* Ontario, S Canada
Timor *125 F5 island* Nusa Tenggara, East Timor/Indonesia
Timor Timur *see* East Timor
Timor Sea *125 F5 sea* E Indian Ocean
Timor Trench *see* Timor Trough
Timor Trough *125 F5 var.* Timor Trench. *Undersea feature* NE Timor Sea
Timrå *85 C5* Västernorrland, C Sweden
Tindouf *70 D3* W Algeria
Tineo *92 C1* Asturias, N Spain
Tingis I MM *see* Tanger
Tingo María *60 C3* Huánuco, C Peru
Tingréla *see* Tengréla
Tinhosa Grande *76 E2 island* N Sao Tome and Principe
Tinhosa Pequena *76 E1 island* N Sao Tome and Principe

Tinian *144 B1 island* S Northern Mariana Islands
Tínos *105 D6 anc.* Tenos. *Island* Kykládes, Greece, Aegean Sea
Tínos *105 D6* Tínos, Kykládes, Greece, Aegean Sea
Tip *101 E6* Irian Jaya, E Indonesia
Tipitapa *52 D3* Managua, W Nicaragua
Tip Top Mountain *38 C4 mountain* Ontario, S Canada
Tirana *see* Tiranë
Tiranë *101 C6 var.* Tirana. *Country capital* (Albania) Tiranë, C Albania
Tiraspol *108 D4 Rus.* Tiraspol'. E Moldova
Tiree *88 B3 island* W Scotland, UK
Tîrgu-Neamţ *see* Târgu-Neamţ
Tirlemont *see* Tienen
Tírnavos *see* Týrnavos
Tirol *95 C7 cultural region* Austria/Italy
Tiruchchirāppalli *132 C3 prev.* Trichinopoly. Tamil Nādu, SE India
Tiruppattūr *132 C2* Tamil Nādu, SE India
Tisza *103 F1 Ger.* Theiss, *Rom./Slvn./SCr.* Tisa, *Rus.* Tissa, *Ukr.* Tysa. *River* SE Europe *see also* Tisa
Tiszakécske *99 D7* Bács-Kiskun, C Hungary
Titano, Monte *96 E1 mountain* C San Marino
Titicaca, Lake *61 E4 lake* Bolivia/Peru
Titose *see* Chitose
Titu *108 C5* Dâmboviţa, S Romania
Titule *77 D5* Orientale, N Dem. Rep. Congo (Zaire)
Tiverton *89 C7* SW England, UK
Tivoli *96 C4 anc.* Tibur. Lazio, C Italy
Tizimín *51 H3* Yucatán, SE Mexico
Tizi Ouzou *71 E1 var.* Tizi-Ouzou. N Algeria
Tiznit *70 B3* SW Morocco
Tlaquepaque *50 D4* Jalisco, C Mexico
Tlascala *see* Tlaxcala
Tlaxcala *51 F4 var.* Tlascala, Tlaxcala de Xicohténcatl. Tlaxcala, C Mexico
Tlaxcala de Xicohténcatl *see* Tlaxcala
Tlemcen *70 D2 var.* Tilimsen, Tlemsen. NW Algeria
Tlemsen *see* Tlemcen
Toamasina *79 G3 var.* Tamatave. Toamasina, E Madagascar
Toba, Danau *138 B3 lake* Sumatera, W Indonesia
Tobago *55 H5 island* NE Trinidad and Tobago
Tobol *114 C4 Kaz.* Tobyl. *River* Kazakhstan/Russian Federation
Tobol'sk *114 C3* Tyumenskaya Oblast', C Russian Federation
Tocantins *63 E3 off.* Estado do Tocantins. *State* C Brazil
Tocantins, Rio *63 F2 river* N Brazil
Tocoa *52 D2* Colón, N Honduras
Tocopilla *64 B2* Antofagasta, N Chile
Todi *96 C4* Umbria, C Italy
Todos os Santos, Baía de *63 G3 bay* E Brazil
Toetoes Bay *151 B8 bay* South Island, NZ
Tofua *145 E4 island* Ha'apai Group, C Tonga
Togo *75 E4* French Togoland. *Country* W Africa

Togo 75

Official name Togolese Republic
Formation 1960
Capital Lomé
Population 4.6 million / 219 people per sq mile (85 peopleper sq km)

Togo (continued)

Total area 20,999 sq miles (54,390 sq km)
Languages French, Ewe, Kabye, Gurma
Religions Traditional beliefs 50%, Christian 35%, Muslim 15%
Ethnic mix Ewe 43%, Kabye 26%, Gurma 16%, other 15%
Government Multiparty republic
Currency CFA franc = 100 centimes
Literacy rate 53.2%
Calorie consumption 2,242 kilocalories

Tokanui *151 B7* Southland, South Island, NZ
Tokar *72 C3 var.* Ţawkar. Red Sea, NE Sudan
Tokat *116 D3* Tokat, N Turkey
Tokelau *145 E3 NZ overseas territory* W Polynesia
Tokio *see* Tōkyō
Tokmak *123 G2 Kir.* Tokmok. Chuyskaya Oblast', N Kyrgyzstan
Tokmak *109 G4 var.* Velykyy Tokmak. Zaporiz'ka Oblast', SE Ukraine
Tokoroa *150 D3* Waikato, North Island, NZ
Tokounou *74 C4* Haute-Guinée, C Guinea
Tokushima *131 C6 var.* Tokusima. Tokushima, Shikoku, SW Japan
Tokusima *see* Tokushima
Tōkyō *130 A1 var.* Tokio. *Country capital* (Japan) Tōkyō, Honshū, S Japan
Tōkyō Bay *130 A2 bay* SW Japan
Toledo *92 D3 anc.* Toletum. Castilla-La Mancha, C Spain
Toledo *40 D3* Ohio, N USA
Toledo Bend Reservoir *49 G3 reservoir* Louisiana/Texas, SW USA
Toliara *79 F4 var.* Toliary; *prev.* Tuléar. Toliara, SW Madagascar
Toliary *see* Toliara
Tolmin *95 D7 Ger.* Tolmein, *It.* Tolmino. W Slovenia
Tolna *99 C7 Ger.* Tolnau. Tolna, S Hungary
Tolosa *93 E1* País Vasco, N Spain
Toluca *51 E4 var.* Toluca de Lerdo. México, S Mexico
Toluca de Lerdo *see* Toluca
Tol'yatti *111 C6 prev.* Stavropol'. Samarskaya Oblast', W Russian Federation
Tomah *40 B2* Wisconsin, N USA
Tomakomai *130 D2* Hokkaidō, NE Japan
Tomar *92 B3* Santarém, W Portugal
Tomaschow *see* Tomaszów Mazowiecki
Tomaszów *see* Tomaszów Mazowiecki
Tomaszów Lubelski *98 E4 Ger.* Tomaschow. Lubelskie, E Poland
Tomaszów Mazowiecka *see* Tomaszów Mazowiecki
Tomaszów Mazowiecki *98 D4 var.* Tomaszów Mazowiecka; *prev.* Tomaszów, Ger. Tomaschow. Łódzkie, C Poland
Tombigbee River *42 C3 river* Alabama/Mississippi, S USA
Tombouctou *75 E3 Eng.* Timbuktu. Tombouctou, N Mali
Tombua *78 A2 Port.* Porto Alexandre. Namibe, SW Angola
Tomelloso *93 E3* Castilla-La Mancha, C Spain
Tomini, Gulf of *139 E4 var.* Teluk Tomini; *prev.* Teluk Gorontalo. *Bay* Sulawesi, C Indonesia
Tomini, Teluk *see* Tomini, Gulf of
Tomsk *114 D4* Tomskaya Oblast', C Russian Federation
Tomur Feng *see* Pobedy, Pik

Tonga *145 E4 var.* Friendly Islands. *Country* SW Pacific Ocean

Tonga 145

Official name Kingdom of Tonga
Formation 1970
Capital Nuku'alofa
Population 98,000 / 353 people per sq mile (136 people per sq km)
Total area 278 sq miles (720 sq km)
Languages Tongan, English
Religions Free Wesleyan 64%, Roman Catholic 15%, Other 21%
Ethnic mix Polynesian 99%, other Pacific groups and European 1%
Government Constitutional monarchy
Currency Pa'anga (Tongan dollar) = 100 seniti
Literacy rate 99%
Calorie consumption 2,946 kilocalories

Tongatapu *145 E5 island* Tongatapu Group, S Tonga
Tonga Trench *143 E3 undersea feature* S Pacific Ocean
Tongchuan *128 C4* Shaanxi, C China
Tongeren *87 D6 Fr.* Tongres. Limburg, NE Belgium
Tongking, Gulf of *128 B7 Chin.* Beibu Wan, *Vtn.* Vinh Băc Bô. *Gulf* China/Vietnam
Tongliao *127 G2* Nei Mongol Zizhiqu, N China
Tongshan *see* Xuzhou
Tongtian He *126 C4 river* C China
Tonj *73 B5* Warab, SW Sudan
Tônlé Sap *137 D5 Eng.* Great Lake. *Lake* W Cambodia
Tonopah *47 C6* Nevada, W USA
Tonyezh *107 C7 Rus.* Tonezh. Homyel'skaya Voblasts', SE Belarus
Tooele *44 B4* Utah, W USA
Toowoomba *149 E5* Queensland, E Australia
Topeka *45 F4 state capital* Kansas, C USA
Topliţa *108 C3 Ger.* Töplitz, *Hung.* Maroshévíz; *prev.* Topliţa Română, *Hung.* Oláh-Toplicza, Toplicza. Harghita, C Romania
Topoľčany *99 C6 Hung.* Nagytapolcsány. Nitriansky Kraj, SW Slovakia
Topolovgrad *104 D3 prev.* Kavakli. Khaskovo, S Bulgaria
Top Springs Roadhouse *146 D3* Northern Territory, N Australia
Torez *109 H3* Donets'ka Oblast', SE Ukraine
Torgau *94 D4* Sachsen, E Germany
Torhout *87 A5* West-Vlaanderen, W Belgium
Torino *96 A2 Eng.* Turin. Piemonte, NW Italy
Tornacum *see* Tournai
Torneälven *see* Tornionjoki
Torneträsk *84 C3 lake* N Sweden
Tornio *84 D4 Swe.* Torneå. Lappi, NW Finland
Torniojoki *see* Tornionjoki
Tornionjoki *84 D3 var.* Torniojoki, *Swe.* Torneälven. *River* Finland/Sweden
Toro *92 D2* Castilla-León, N Spain
Toronto *38 D5* Ontario, S Canada
Toros Dağları *116 C4 Eng.* Taurus Mountains. *Mountain range* S Turkey
Torquay *89 C7* SW England, UK
Torrance *46 C2* California, W USA
Torre, Alto da *92 B3 mountain* C Portugal
Torre del Greco *97 D5* Campania, S Italy
Torrejón de Ardoz *93 E3* Madrid, C Spain
Torrelavega *92 D1* Cantabria, N Spain

Torrens, Lake *149 A6 salt lake* South Australia
Torrent *see* Torrente
Torrent de l'Horta *see* Torrente
Torrente *93 F3 var.* Torrent, Torrent de l'Horta. País Valenciano, E Spain
Torreón *50 D3* Coahuila de Zaragoza, NE Mexico
Torres Strait *148 C1 strait* Australia/PNG
Torres Vedras *92 B3* Lisboa, C Portugal
Torrington *44 D3* Wyoming, C USA
Tórshavn *83 F5 Dan.* Thorshavn. *Dependent territory capital* (Faeroe Islands) N Faeroe Islands
Tortoise Islands *see* Galapagos Islands
Tortosa *93 F2 anc.* Dertosa. Cataluña, E Spain
Tortue, Montagne *59 H3 mountain range* C French Guiana
Tortuga, Isla *see* La Tortuga, Isla
Toruń *98 C3 Ger.* Thorn. Kujawskie-pomorskie, C Poland
Tõrva *106 D3 Ger.* Törwa. Valgamaa, S Estonia
Torzhok *110 B4* Tverskaya Oblast', W Russian Federation
Tosa-wan *131 B7 bay* SW Japan
Toscana *96 B3 Eng.* Tuscany. *Cultural region* C Italy
Toscano, Archipelago *96 B4 Eng.* Tuscan Archipelago. *Island group* C Italy
Toshkent *123 E2 Eng./Rus.* Tashkent. *Country capital* (Uzbekistan) Toshkent Wiloyati, E Uzbekistan
Totana *93 E4* Murcia, SE Spain
Tot'ma *see* Sukhona
Totness *59 G3* Coronie, N Suriname
Tottori *131 B6* Tottori, Honshū, SW Japan
Touâjîl *74 C2* Tiris Zemmour, N Mauritania
Touggourt *71 E2* NE Algeria
Toukoto *74 C3* Kayes, W Mali
Toul *90 D3* Meurthe-et-Moselle, NE France
Toulon *91 D6 anc.* Telo Martius, Tilio Martius. Var, SE France
Toulouse *91 B6 anc.* Tolosa. Haute-Garonne, S France
Toungoo *136 B4* Pegu, C Myanmar
Touraine *90 B4 cultural region* C France
Tourcoing *90 C2* Nord, N France
Tournai *87 A6 var.* Tournay, *Dut.* Doornik; *anc.* Tornacum. Hainaut, SW Belgium
Tournay *see* Tournai
Tours *90 B4 anc.* Caesarodunum, Turoni. Indre-et-Loire, C France
Tovarkovskiy *111 B5* Tul'skaya Oblast', W Russian Federation
Tower Island *see* Genovesa, Isla
Townsville *148 D3* Queensland, NE Australia
Towraghoudî *122 D4* Herãt, NW Afghanistan
Towson *41 F4* Maryland, NE USA
Towuti, Danau *139 E4 Dut.* Towoeti Meer. Lake Sulawesi, C Indonesia
Toyama *131 C5* Toyama, Honshū, SW Japan
Toyama-wan *131 B5 bay* W Japan
Toyota *131 C6* Aichi, Honshū, SW Japan
Tozeur *71 E2 var.* Tawzar. W Tunisia
Trâblous *see* Tripoli
Trabzon *117 E2 Eng.* Trebizond; *anc.* Trapezus. Trabzon, NE Turkey
Traiectum Tungorum *see* Maastricht
Traietum ad Mosam *see* Maastricht
Traiskirchen *95 E6* Niederösterreich, NE Austria
Trakai *107 C5 Ger.* Traken, *Pol.* Troki. Trakai, SE Lithuania
Tralee *89 A6 Ir.* Trá Lí. SW Ireland
Trá Lí *see* Tralee

Tralles *see* Aydın
Trang *137 C7* Trang, S Thailand
Transantarctic Mountains *154 B3 mountain range* Antarctica
Transsylvanische Alpen *see* Carpaţii Meridionali
Transylvania *108 B4 Eng.* Ardeal, Transilvania, *Ger.* Siebenbürgen, *Hung.* Erdély. *Cultural region* NW Romania
Transylvanian Alps *see* Carpaţii Meridionali
Trapani *97 B7 anc.* Drepanum. Sicilia, Italy, C Mediterranean Sea
Trâpeăng Vêng *137 D5* Kâmpóng Thum, C Cambodia
Traralgon *149 C7* Victoria, SE Australia
Trasimeno, Lago *C4 Eng.* Lake of Perugia, *Ger.* Trasimenischersee. *Lake* C Italy
Traverse City *40 C2* Michigan, N USA
Tra Vinh *137 D6 var.* Phu Vinh. Tra Vinh, S Vietnam
Travis, Lake *49 F3 reservoir* Texas, SW USA
Travnik *100 C4* Federacija Bosna I Hercegovina, C Bosnia and Herzegovina
Trbovlje *95 E7 Ger.* Trifail. C Slovenia
Třebíč *99 B5 Ger.* Trebitsch. Jihlavský Kraj, C Czech Republic
Trebinje *101 C5* Republika Srpska, S Bosnia and Herzegovina
Trebišov *99 D6 Hung.* Tőketerebes. Košický Kraj, E Slovakia
Trélazé *90 B4* Maine-et-Loire, NW France
Trelew *65 C6* Chubut, SE Argentina
Tremelo *87 C5* Vlaams Brabant, C Belgium
Trenčín *99 C5 Ger.* Trentschin, *Hung.* Trencsén. Trenčiansky Kraj, W Slovakia
Trenque Lauquen *64 C4* Buenos Aires, E Argentina
Trento *96 C2 Eng.* Trent, *Ger.* Trient; *anc.*Tridentum. Trentino-Alto Adige, N Italy
Trenton *41 F4 state capital* New Jersey, NE USA
Tres Arroyos *65 D5* Buenos Aires, E Argentina
Treskavica *100 C4 mountain range* SE Bosnia and Herzegovina
Tres Tabernae *see* Saverne
Treviso *96 C2 anc.* Tarvisium. Veneto, NE Italy
Trichūr *132 C3 var.* Thrissur. Kerala, SW India
Trier *95 A5 Eng.* Treves, *Fr.* Trèves; *anc.* Augusta Treverorum. Rheinland-Pfalz, SW Germany
Triesen *94 E2* SW Liechtenstein
Triesenberg *94 E2* SW Liechtenstein
Trieste *96 D2 Slvn.* Trst. Friuli-Venezia Giulia, NE Italy
Tríkala *104 B4 prev.* Trikkala. Thessalía, C Greece
Trincomalee *132 D3 var.* Trinkomali. Eastern Province, NE Sri Lanka
Trindade, Ilha da *67 C5 island* Brazil, W Atlantic Ocean
Trinidad *55 H5 island* C Trinidad and Tobago
Trinidad *61 F3* Beni, N Bolivia
Trinidad *44 D5* Colorado, C USA
Trinidad *64 D4* Flores, S Uruguay
Trinidad and Tobago *55 H5 Country* SE West Indies

Trinidad & Tobago *55*

Official name Republic of Trinidad and Tobago
Formation 1962
Capital Port-of-Spain
Population 1.3 million / 656 people per sq mile (253 people per sq km)

Trinidad & Tobago (continued)
Total area 1981 sq miles (5,130 sq km)
Languages English, English Creole
Religions Christian 58%, Hindu 30%, Muslim 8%, other 4%
Ethnic mix Asian 40%, Black 40%, Mixed 19%, White and Chinese 1%
Government Multiparty republic
Currency Trinidad and Tobago dollar = 100 cents
Literacy rate 97.8%
Calorie consumption 2,585 kilocalories

Trinité, Montagnes de la *59 H3 mountain range* C French Guiana
Trinity River *49 G3 river* Texas, SW USA
Trinkomali *see* Trincomalee
Tripoli *118 B4 var.* Tarãbulus, Ţarãbulus ash Shãm, Trãblous; *anc.* Tripolis. N Lebanon
Tripoli *see* Ţarãbulus
Trípoli *105 B6 prev.* Trípolis. Pelopónnisos, S Greece
Tripolis *see* Tripoli
Tristan da Cunha *69 B7 dependency of Saint Helena* SE Atlantic Ocean
Triton Island *128 B7 island* S Paracel Islands
Trivandrum *132 C3 var.* Thiruvanathapuram. Kerala, SW India
Trnava *99 C6 Ger.* Tyrnau, *Hung.* Nagyszombat. Trnavský Kraj, W Slovakia
Trogir *100 B4 It.* Traù. Split-Dalmacija, S Croatia
Troglav *100 B4 mountain* Bosnia and Herzegovina/Croatia
Trois-Rivières *39 E4* Québec, SE Canada
Trollhättan *85 B6* Västra Götaland, S Sweden
Tromsø *84 C2 Fin.* Tromssa. Troms, N Norway
Trondheim *84 B4 Ger.* Drontheim; *prev.* Nidaros, Trondhjem. Sør-Trøndelag, S Norway
Trondheimsfjorden *84 B4 fjord* S Norway
Troódos *102 C5 var.* Troodos Mountains. *Mountain range* C Cyprus
Troodos Mountains *see* Troódos
Troy *42 D3* Alabama, S USA
Troy *41 F3* New York, NE USA
Troyan *104 C2* Lovech, N Bulgaria
Troyes *90 D3 anc.* Augustobona Tricassium. Aube, N France
Trstenik *100 E4* Serbia, C Yugoslavia
Trujillo *52 D2* Colón, NE Honduras
Trujillo *93 C3* Extremadura, W Spain
Trujillo *60 B3* La Libertad, NW Peru
Truk Islands *see* Chuuk Islands
Trŭn *104 B2* Pernik, W Bulgaria
Truro *39 F4* Nova Scotia, SE Canada
Truro *89 C7* SW England, UK
Trzcianka *98 B3 Ger.* Schönlanke. Wielkopolskie, C Poland
Trzebnica *98 C4 Ger.* Trebnitz. Dolnośląskie, SW Poland
Tsalka *117 F2* S Georgia
Tsamkong *see* Zhanjiang
Tsangpo *see* Brahmaputra
Tsarevo *104 E2 prev.* Michurin. Burgas, E Bulgaria
Tsaritsyn *see* Volgograd
Tsefat *see* Zefat
Tsetserleg *126 D2* Arhangay, C Mongolia
Tsevat *see* Zefat
Tshela *77 B6* Bas-Zaïre, W Dem. Rep. Congo (Zaire)
Tshikapa *77 C7* Kasai Occidental, SW Dem. Rep. Congo (Zaire)

Tshuapa *77 D6 river* C Dem. Rep. Congo (Zaire)
Tshwane *see* Pretoria
Tsinan *see* Jinan
Tsing Hai *see* Qinghai Hu
Tsingtao *see* Qingdao
Tsingtau *see* Qingdao
Tsinkiang *see* Quanzhou
Tsintao *see* Qingdao
Tsitsihar *see* Qiqihar
Tsu *131 C6 var.* Tu. Mie, Honshū, SW Japan
Tsugaru-kaikyō *130 C3 strait* N Japan
Tsumeb *78 B3* Otjikoto, N Namibia
Tsuruga *131 C6 var.* Turuga. Fukui, Honshū, SW Japan
Tsuruoka *130 D4 var.* Turuoka. Yamagata, Honshū, C Japan
Tsushima *131 A7 var.* Tsushima-tō, Tusima. *Island group* SW Japan
Tsushima-tō *see* Tsushima
Tsyerakhowka *107 D8 Rus.* Terekhovka. Homyel'skaya Voblasts', SE Belarus
Tsyurupyns'k *109 E4 Rus.* Tsyurupinsk. Khersons'ka Oblast', S Ukraine
Tu *see* Tsu
Tuamotu Fracture Zone *143 H3 tectonic feature* E Pacific Ocean
Tuamotu, Îles *145 H4 var.* Archipel des Tuamotu, Dangerous Archipelago, Tuamotu Islands. *Island group* N French Polynesia
Tuamotu Islands *see* Tuamotu, Îles
Tuapi *53 E2* Región Autónoma Atlántico Norte, NE Nicaragua
Tuapse *111 A7* Krasnodarskiy Kray, SW Russian Federation
Tuba City *48 B1* Arizona, SW USA
Tubbergen *86 E3* Overijssel, E Netherlands
Tubize *87 B6 Dut.* Tubeke. Wallon Brabant, C Belgium
Tubmanburg *74 C5* NW Liberia
Ţubruq *71 H2 Eng.* Tobruk, *It.* Tobruch. NE Libya
Tubuai Islands *see* Australes, Îles
Tucker's Town *42 B5* E Bermuda
Tucson *48 B3* Arizona, SW USA
Tucumán *see* San Miguel de Tucumán
Tucumcari *49 E2* New Mexico, SW USA
Tucupita *59 E2* Delta Amacuro, NE Venezuela
Tucuruí, Represa de *63 F2 reservoir* NE Brazil
Tudela *93 E2 Basq.* Tutera; *anc.* Tutela. Navarra, N Spain
Tudmur *118 C3 var.* Tadmur, Tamar, *Gk.* Palmyra; *Bibl.* Tadmor. Ḥimş, C Syria
Tuguegarao *139 E1* Luzon, N Philippines
Tuktoyaktuk *37 E3* Northwest Territories, NW Canada
Tukums *106 C3 Ger.* Tuckum. Tukums, W Latvia
Tula *111 B5* Tul'skaya Oblast', W Russian Federation
Tulancingo *51 E4* Hidalgo, C Mexico
Tulare Lake Bed *47 C7 salt flat* California, W USA
Tulcán *60 B1* Carchi, N Ecuador
Tulcea *108 D5* Tulcea, E Romania
Tul'chyn *108 D3 Rus.* Tul'chin. Vinnyts'ka Oblast', C Ukraine
Tuléar *see* Toliara
Tulia *49 E2* Texas, SW USA
Tulle *91 C5 anc.* Tutela. Corrèze, C France
Tulln *95 E6 var.* Oberhollabrunn. Niederösterreich, NE Austria
Tully *148 D3* Queensland, NE Australia
Tulsa *49 G1* Oklahoma, C USA
Tuluá *58 B3* Valle del Cauca, W Colombia

Tulun *115 E4* Irkutskaya Oblast',
S Russian Federation
Tumaco *58 A4* Nariño,
SW Colombia
Tumba, Lac *see* Ntomba, Lac
Tumbes *60 A2* Tumbes, NW Peru
Tumkūr *132 C2* Karnātaka,
W India
Tumuc Humac Mountains *63 E1*
var. Serra Tumucumaque.
Mountain range N South America
Tunduru *73 C8* Ruvuma, S Tanzania
Tundzha *104 D3 Turk.* Tunca Nehri.
River Bulgaria / Turkey *see also*
Tunca Nehri
Tungabhadra Reservoir *132 C2 lake*
S India
Tungaru *145 E2 prev.* Gilbert
Islands. *Island group* W Kiribati
T'ung-shan *see* Xuzhou
Tungsten *36 D4* Northwest
Territories, W Canada
Tung-t'ing Hu *see* Dongting Hu
Tunis *71 E1 var.* Tūnis. *Country
capital* (Tunisia) NE Tunisia
Tūnis *see* Tunis
Tunis, Golfe de *102 D3 Ar.* Khalīj
Tūnis. *Gulf* NE Tunisia
Tunisia *71 F2 Ar.* Al Jumhūrīyah at
Tūnisīyah, *Fr.* République
Tunisienne. *Country* N Africa

Tunisia 71

Official name Republic of Tunisia
Formation 1956
Capital Tunis
Population 9.6 million /
160 people per sq mile
(62 people per sq km)
Total area 59,984 sq miles
(155,360 sq km)
Languages Arabic, French
Religions Muslim 98%,
Christian 1%, Jewish 1%
Ethnic mix Arab and Berber 98%,
European 1%, other 1%
Government Multiparty republic
Currency Tunisian dinar
= 1,000 millimes
Literacy rate 67%
Calorie consumption 3,330
kilocalories

Tunja *58 B3* Boyacá, C Colombia
Tuong Buong *see* T,ong Ð,ong
Tupelo *42 C2* Mississippi, S USA
Tupiza *61 G5* Potosí, S Bolivia
Turabah *121 B5* Makkah, W Saudi
Arabia
Turangi *150 D4* Waikato, North
Island, NZ
Turan Lowland *122 C2 var.* Turan
Plain, *Kaz.* Turan Oypaty, *Rus.*
Turanskaya Nizmennost', *Turk.*
Turan Pesligi, *Uzb.* Turon
Pasttekisligi. *Plain* C Asia
Turan Oypaty *see* Turan
Lowland
Turan Pesligi *see* Turan Lowland
Turan Plain *see* Turan Lowland
Turanskaya Nizmennost' *see* Turan
Lowland
Ţurayf *120 A3* Al Ḩudūd ash
Shamālīyah, NW Saudi Arabia
Turbat *134 A3* Baluchistān,
SW Pakistan
Turda *108 B4 Ger.* Thorenburg,
Hung. Torda. Cluj, NW
Romania
Turek *98 C3* Wielkopolskie, C
Poland
Turfan *see* Turpan
Turin *see* Torino
Turkana, Lake *89 C6 var.* Lake
Rudolph. *Lake* N Kenya
**Turkish Republic of Northern
Cyprus** *102 D5 Ger.* Dependent
territory, disputed territory.
Cyprus
Turkestan *114 B5 Kaz.* Türkistan.
Yuzhnyy Kazakhstan,
S Kazakhstan

Turkey *116 B3 Turk.* Türkiye
Cumhuriyeti. *Country* SW Asia

Turkey 116

Official name Republic of Turkey
Formation 1923
Capital Ankara
Population 66.6 million /
224 people per sq mile
(87 people per sq km)
Total area 297,154 sq miles
(769,630 sq km)
Languages Turkish, Kurdish,
Arabic, Circassian, Armenian,
Greek, Georgian
Religions Muslim (mainly Sunni)
99%, other 1%
Ethnic mix Turkish 70%, Kurdish
20%, Arab 2%, other 8%
Government Multiparty republic
Currency Turkish lira = 100 krural
Literacy rate 83.2%
Calorie consumption 3,429
kilocalories

Turkmenbashi *122 B2 prev.*
Krasnovodsk. Balkanskiy Velayat,
W Turkmenistan
Turkmenistan *122 B2 prev.*
Turkmenskaya Soviet Socialist
Republic. *Country* C Asia

Turkmenistan 122

Official name Turkmenistan
Formation 1991
Capital Ashgabat
Population 4.5 million /
24 people per sq mile
(9 people per sq km)
Total area 188,455 sq miles
(488,100 sq km)
Languages Turkmen, Uzbek,
Russian
Religions Sunni Muslim 87%,
Eastern Orthodox 11%, other 2%
Ethnic mix Turkmen 72%,
Russian 9%, Uzbek 9%, other 1%
Government Multiparty republic
Currency Manat = 100 tenge
Literacy rate 98%
Calorie consumption
not available

Turkmenskiy Zaliv *122 B2 Turkm.*
Türkmen Aylagy. *Lake gulf*
W Turkmenistan
Turks and Caicos Islands *55 E2 UK
dependent territory* N West Indies
Turlock *47 B6* California, W USA
Turnagain, Cape *150 D4 headland*
North Island, NZ
Turnhout *87 C5* Antwerpen,
N Belgium
Turnov *98 B4 Ger.* Turnau.
Liberecký Kraj, N Czech Republic
Turnu Măgurele *108 B5 var.* Turnu-
Măgurele. Teleorman, S Romania
Turon Pasttekisligi *see* Turan
Lowland
Turpan *126 C3 var.* Turfan. Xinjiang
Uygur Zizhiqu, NW China
Turpan Pendi *126 C3 Eng.* Turpan
Depression. *Depression* NW China
Türtkül *122 D2 Rus.* Turtkul'; *prev.*
Petroaleksandrovsk.
Qoraqalpoghiston Respublikasi,
W Uzbekistan
Turuga *see* Tsuruga
Turuoka *see* Tsuruoka
Tuscaloosa *42 C2* Alabama, S USA
Tusima *see* Tsushima
Tuticorin *132 C3* Tamil Nādu,
SE India
Tutrakan *104 D1* Silistra,
NE Bulgaria
Tutuila *145 F4 island* W American
Samoa
Tuvalu *145 E3 prev.* Ellice Islands.
Country SW Pacific Ocean
Ţuwayq, Jabal *121 C5 mountain
range* C Saudi Arabia

Tuvalu 145

Official name Tuvalu
Formation 1978
Capital Fongafale, on
Funafuti Atoll
Population 11,100 / 1,106 people
per sq mile (427 people per sq km)
Total area 10 sq miles (26 sq km)
Languages English, Tuvaluan,
Kiribati
Religions Church of Tuvalu 97%,
Seventh Day Adventist 1%,
Baha'i 1%, other 1%
Ethnic mix Polynesian 95%,
other 5%
Government Constitutional
monarchy
Currency Australian dollar and
Tuvaluan dollar = 100 cents
Literacy rate 95%
Calorie consumption
not available

Tuxpán *51 F4 var.* Tuxpán de
Rodríguez Cano. Veracruz-Llave,
E Mexico
Tuxpan *50 D4* Jalisco, C Mexico
Tuxpan *50 D4* Nayarit, C Mexico
Tuxpán de Rodríguez Cano *see*
Tuxpán
Tuxtepec *51 F4 var.* San Juan
Bautista Tuxtepec. Oaxaca,
S Mexico
Tuxtla *51 G5 var.* Tuxtla Gutiérrez.
Chiapas, SE Mexico
Tuxtla *see* San Andrés Tuxtla
Tuxtla Gutiérrez *see* Tuxtla
Tuy Hoa *137 E5* Phu Yên,
S Vietnam
Tuz Gölü *116 C3 lake* C Turkey
Tuzla *100 C3* Federacija Bosna I
Hercegovina, NE Bosnia and
Herzegovina
Tver' *110 B4 prev.* Kalinin.
Tverskaya Oblast', W Russian
Federation
Tverya *see* Teverya
Twin Falls *46 D4* Idaho, NW USA
Tychy *99 D5 Ger.* Tichau. Śląskie,
S Poland
Tyler *49 G3* Texas, SW USA
Tympáki *105 C8 var.* Timbaki; *prev.*
Timbákion. Kríti, Greece,
E Mediterranean Sea
Tynda *115 F4* Amurskaya Oblast',
SE Russian Federation
Tyne *88 D4 river* N England, UK
Tyōsi *see* Chōshi
Tyre *see* Soûr
Týrnavos *104 B4 var.* Tírnavos.
Thessalía, C Greece
Tyrrhenian Sea *97 B6 It.* Mare
Tirreno. *Sea* N Mediterranean Sea
Tyumen' *114 C3* Tyumenskaya
Oblast', C Russian Federation
Tyup *123 G2 Kir.* Tüp. Issyk-
Kul'skaya Oblast', NE
Kyrgyzstan
Tywyn *89 C6* W Wales, UK
Tzekung *see* Zigong
T,ong Ð,ong *136 D4 var.* Tuong
Buong. Nghệ An, N Vietnam

U

Uanle Uen *see* Wanlaweyn
Uaupés, Rio *see* Vaupés, Río
Ubangi *77 C5 Fr.* Oubangui. *River*
C Africa
Ubangi-Shari *see* Central African
Republic
Ube *131 B7* Yamaguchi, Honshū,
SW Japan
Ubeda *93 E4* Andalucía, S Spain
Uberaba *63 F4* Minas Gerais,
SE Brazil
Uberlândia *63 F4* Minas Gerais,
SE Brazil
Ubol Rajadhani *see* Ubon
Ratchathani
Ubol Ratchathani *see* Ubon
Ratchathani

Ubon Ratchathani *137 D5 var.*
Muang Ubon, Ubol Rajadhani,
Ubol Ratchathani, Udon
Ratchathani. Ubon Ratchathani,
E Thailand
Ubrique *92 D5* Andalucía, S Spain
Ucayali, Río *60 D3 river* C Peru
Uchiura-wan *130 D3 bay*
NW Pacific Ocean
Uchquduq *122 D2 Rus.* Uchkuduk.
Nawoiy Wiloyati, N Uzbekistan
Uchtagan, Peski *122 C2 Turkm.*
Uchtagan Gumy. *Desert*
NW Turkmenistan
Udaipur *134 C3 prev.* Oodeypore.
Rājasthān, N India
Uddevalla *85 B6* Västra Götaland,
S Sweden
Udine *96 D2 anc.* Utina. Friuli-
Venezia Giulia, NE Italy
Udintsev Fracture Zone *154 A5
tectonic feature* S Pacific Ocean
Udipi *see* Udupi
Udon Ratchathani *see* Ubon
Ratchathani
Udon Thani *136 C4 var.* Ban Mak
Khaeng, Udorndhani. Udon
Thani, N Thailand
Udorndhani *see* Udon Thani
Udupi *132 B2 var.* Udipi. Karnātaka,
SW India
Uele *77 D5 var.* Welle. *River*
NE Dem. Rep. Congo (Zaire)
Uelzen *94 C3* Niedersachsen,
N Germany
Ufa *111 D6* Respublika
Bashkortostan, W Russian
Federation
Ugāle *106 C2* Ventspils, NW
Latvia
Uganda *73 B6 Country* E Africa

Uganda 73

Official name Republic of
Uganda
Formation 1962
Capital Kampala
Population 21.8 million /
283 people per sq mile
(109 people per sq km)
Total area 77,046 sq miles
(199,550 sq km)
Languages English, Swahili,
Luganda
Religions Roman Catholic 38%,
Protestant 33%, Traditional beliefs
13%, Muslim (mainly Sunni) 5%,
other 11%
Ethnic mix African 99%, other 1%
Government Multiparty republic
Currency New Uganda shilling
= 100 cents
Literacy rate 64%
Calorie consumption 2,159
kilocalories

Uglovka *110 B4 var.* Okulovka.
Novgorodskaya Oblast',
W Russian Federation
Uhuru Peak *see* Kilimanjaro
Uíge *78 B1 Port.* Carmona, Vila
Marechal Carmona. Uíge,
NW Angola
Uinta Mountains *44 B4 mountain
range* Utah, W USA
Uitenhage *78 C5* Eastern Cape,
S South Africa
Uithoorn *86 C3* Noord-Holland,
C Netherlands
Ujelang Atoll *144 C1 var.* Wujlān.
Atoll Ralik Chain, W Marshall
Islands
Ujungpandang *139 E4 var.*
Macassar, Makassar; *prev.*
Makasar. Sulawesi, C Indonesia
Ujung Salang *see* Phuket
Ukhta *114 C3* Respublika Komi,
NW Russian Federation
Ukiah *47 B5* California, W
USA
Ukmergė *106 C4 Pol.* Wiłkomierz.
Ukmergė, C Lithuania

Ukraine *108 C2 Ukr.* Ukrayina; *prev.* Ukrainian Soviet Socialist Republic, Ukrainskaya S.S.R. *Country* SE Europe

Ukraine 108

Official name Ukraine
Formation 1991
Capital Kiev
Population 50.7 million / 218 people per sq mile (84 people per sq km)
Total area 223,090 sq miles (603,700 sq km)
Languages Ukrainian, Russian, Tartar
Religions Ukrainian Autonomous and Autocephalous Orthodox, with Roman Catholic (Uniate), Protestant and Jewish minorities
Ethnic mix Ukrainian 73%, Russian 22%, other 4%, Jewish 1%
Government Multiparty republic
Currency Hryvnia = 100 kopiykas
Literacy rate 99%
Calorie consumption not available

Ulaanbaatar *127 E2 Eng.* Ulan Bator. *Country capital* (Mongolia) Töv, C Mongolia
Ulaangom *126 C2 Uvs,* NW Mongolia
Ulan Bator *see* Ulaanbaatar
Ulanhad *see* Chifeng
Ulan-Ude *115 E4 prev.* Verkhneudinsk. Respublika Buryatiya, S Russian Federation
Ulft *86 E4* Gelderland, E Netherlands
Ullapool *88 C3* N Scotland, UK
Ulm *95 B6* Baden-Württemberg, S Germany
Ulsan *129 E4 Jap.* Urusan. SE South Korea
Ulster *89 B5 cultural region* N Ireland
Ulungur Hu *126 B2 lake* NW China
Uluru *147 D5 var.* Ayers Rock. *Rocky outcrop* Northern Territory, C Australia
Ulyanivka *109 E3 Rus.* Ul'yanovka. Kirovohrads'ka Oblast', C Ukraine
Ul'yanovsk *111 C5 prev.* Simbirsk. Ul'yanovskaya Oblast', W Russian Federation
Uman' *109 E3 Rus.* Uman. Cherkas'ka Oblast', C Ukraine
Umán *51 H3* Yucatán, SE Mexico
Umanak *see* Uummannaq
Umanaq *see* Uummannaq
Umbro-Marchigiano, Appennino *96 C3 Eng.* Umbrian-Machigian Mountains. *Mountain range* C Italy
Umeå *84 C4* Västerbotten, N Sweden
Umeälven *84 C4 river* N Sweden
Umiat *36 D2* Alaska, USA
Umm Buru *72 A4* Western Darfur, W Sudan
Umm Durmān *see* Omdurman
Umm Ruwaba *72 C4 var.* Umm Ruwābah, Um Ruwāba. Northern Kordofan, C Sudan
Umm Ruwābah *see* Umm Ruwaba
Umnak Island *36 A3 island* Aleutian Islands, Alaska, USA
Um Ruwāba *see* Umm Ruwaba
Umtali *see* Mutare
Umtata *78 D5* Eastern Cape, SE South Africa
Una *100 B3 river* Bosnia and Herzegovina/Croatia
Unac *100 B3 river* W Bosnia and Herzegovina
Unalaska Island *36 A3 island* Aleutian Islands, Alaska, USA
'Unayzah *120 B4 var.* Anaiza. Al Qaṣīm, C Saudi Arabia
Uncía *61 F4* Potosí, C Bolivia

Uncompahgre Peak *44 B5 mountain* Colorado, C USA
Ungarisches Erzgebirge *see* Slovenské rudohorie
Ungava Bay *39 E1 bay* Québec, E Canada
Ungava, Péninsule d' *38 D1 peninsula* Québec, SE Canada
Ungheni *108 D3 Rus.* Ungeny. W Moldova
Unimak Island *36 B3 island* Aleutian Islands, Alaska, USA
Union *43 E1* South Carolina, SE USA
Union City Tennessee, S USA
United Arab Emirates *121 C5 Ar.* Al Imārāt al 'Arabīyah al Muttaḥidah, *abbrev.* UAE; *prev.* Trucial States. *Country* SW Asia

United Arab Emirates 121

Official name United Arab Emirates
Formation 1971
Capital Abu Dhabi
Population 2.4 million / 74 people per sq mile (29 people per sq km)
Total area 32,278 sq miles (83,600 sq km)
Languages Arabic, Persian, English, Indian and Pakistani languages
Religions Muslim 96%, other 4%
Ethnic mix Asian 50%, Emirian 19%, other Arab 23%, other 8%
Government Federation of monarchs
Currency UAE dirham = 100 fils
Literacy rate 74.8%
Calorie consumption 3,384 kilocalories

United Kingdom *89 B5 abbrev.* UK. *Country* NW Europe

United Kingdom 89

Official name United Kingdom of Great Britain and Northern Ireland
Formation 1707
Capital London
Population 58.8 million / 630 people per sq mile (243 people per sq km)
Total area 93,281 sq miles (241,600 sq km)
Languages English, Welsh, Scottish
Religions Protestant 52%, Roman Catholic 9%, Muslim 3%, other 36%
Ethnic mix English 80%, Scottish 10%, Northern Irish 4%, Welsh 2%, other 4%
Government Constitutional monarchy
Currency Pound sterling = 100 pence
Literacy rate 99%
Calorie consumption 3,317 kilocalories

United States of America *35 B5 var.* America, The States, *abbrev.* U.S., USA. *Country*

United States of America 35

Official name United States of America
Formation 1787
Capital Washington DC
Population 278.4 million / 79 people per sq mile (30 people per sq km)
Total area 3,539,224 sq miles (9,166,600 sq km)

United States of America (continued)

Languages English, Spanish, Italian, German, French, Polish, Chinese, Greek
Religions Protestant 61%, Roman Catholic 25%, Jewish 2%, other 12%
Ethnic mix White (including Hispanic) 84%, Black 12%, Chinese 1%, Amerindian 1%, other 2%
Government Multiparty republic
Currency US dollar = 100 cents
Literacy rate 99%
Calorie consumption 3,732 kilocalories

Unst *88 D1 island* NE Scotland, UK
Ünye *116 D2* Ordu, W Turkey
Upala *52 D4* Alajuela, NW Costa Rica
Upata *59 E2* Bolívar, E Venezuela
Upemba, Lac *77 D7 lake* SE Dem. Rep. Congo (Zaire)
Upernavik *82 C2 var.* Upernivik. C Greenland
Upernivik *see* Upernavik
Upington *78 C4* Northern Cape, W South Africa
Upolu *145 F4 island* SE Samoa
Upper Klamath Lake *46 A4 lake* Oregon, NW USA
Upper Lough Erne *89 A5 lake* SW Northern Ireland, UK
Upper Red Lake *45 F1 lake* Minnesota, N USA
Uppsala *85 C6* Uppsala, C Sweden
Ural *112 B3 Kaz.* Zayyq. *River* Kazakhstan/Russian Federation
Ural Mountains *see* Ural'skiye Gory
Ural'sk *114 B3 Kaz.* Oral. Zapadnyy Kazakhstan, NW Kazakhstan
Ural'skiye Gory *114 C3 var.* Ural'skiy Khrebet, *Eng.* Ural Mountains. *Mountain range* Kazakhstan/Russian Federation
Ural'skiy Khrebet *see* Ural'skiye Gory
Uraricoera *62 D1* Roraima, N Brazil
Urbandale *45 F3* Iowa, C USA
Uren' *111 C5* Nizhegorodskaya Oblast', W Russian Federation
Urganch *122 D2 Rus.* Urgench; *prev.* Novo-Urgench. Khorazm Wiloyati, W Uzbekistan
Urgut *123 E3* Samarqand Wiloyati, C Uzbekistan
Uroševac *101 D5 Alb.* Ferizaj. Serbia, S Yugoslavia
Uroteppa *123 E2 Rus.* Ura-Tyube. NW Tajikistan
Uruapan *51 E4 var.* Uruapan del Progreso. Michoacán de Ocampo, SW Mexico
Uruapan del Progreso *see* Uruapan
Uruguai, Rio *see* Uruguay
Uruguay *64 D4 prev.* La Banda Oriental. *Country* E South America

Uruguay 64

Official name Eastern Republic of Uruguay
Formation 1828
Capital Montevideo
Population 3.3 million / 49 people per sq mile (19 people per sq km)
Total area 67,494 sq miles (174,810 sq km)
Languages Spanish
Religions Roman Catholic 66%, non-religious 30%, other 4%
Ethnic mix White 90%, other 10%
Government Multiparty republic
Currency Uruguayan peso = 100 centimos
Literacy rate 97.5%
Calorie consumption 2,750 kilocalories

Uruguay *64 D3 var.* Rio Uruguai, Río Uruguay. *River* E South America
Uruguay, Río *see* Uruguay
Urumchi *see* Ürümqi
Urumqi *see* Ürümqi
Ürümqi *126 C3 var.* Tihwa, Urumchi, Urumqi, Urumtsi, Wu-lu-k'o-mu-shi, Wu-lu-mu-ch'i; *prev.* Ti-hua. *Autonomous region capital* Xinjiang Uygur Zizhiqu, NW China
Urumtsi *see* Ürümqi
Urup, Ostrov *115 H4 island* Kuril'skiye Ostrova, SE Russian Federation
Urziceni *108 C5* Ialomiţa, SE Romania
Usa *110 E3 river* NW Russian Federation
Uşak *116 B3 prev.* Ushak. Uşak, W Turkey
Ushuaia *65 B8* Tierra del Fuego, S Argentina
Usinsk *110 E3* Respublika Komi, NW Russian Federation
Úsküb *see* Skopje
Üsküp *see* Skopje
Usmas Ezers *106 B3 lake* NW Latvia
Usol'ye-Sibirskoye *115 E4* Irkutskaya Oblast', C Russian Federation
Ussel *91 C5* Corrèze, C France
Ussuriysk *115 G5 prev.* Nikol'sk, Nikol'sk-Ussuriyskiy, Voroshilov. Primorskiy Kray, SE
Ustica, Isola d' *97 B6 island* S Italy
Ust'-Ilimsk *115 E4* Irkutskaya Oblast', C Russian Federation
Ústí nad Labem *98 A4 Ger.* Aussig. Ústecký Kraj, NW Czech Republic
Ustka *98 C2 Ger.* Stolpmünde. Pomorskie, N Poland
Ust'-Kamchatsk *115 H2* Kamchatskaya Oblast', E Russian Federation
Ust'-Kamenogorsk *114 D5 Kaz.* Öskemen. Vostochnyy Kazakhstan, E Kazakhstan
Ust'-Kut *115 E4* Irkutskaya Oblast', C Russian Federation
Ust'-Olenëk *115 E3* Respublika Sakha (Yakutiya), NE Russian Federation
Ustrzyki Dolne *99 E5* Podkarpackie, SE Poland
Ust Urt *see* Ustyurt Plateau
Ustyurt Plateau *122 B1 var.* Ust Urt, *Uzb.* Ustyurt Platosi. *Plateau* Kazakhstan/Uzbekistan
Ustyurt Platosi *see* Ustyurt Plateau
Usulután *52 C3* Usulután, SE El Salvador
Usumacinta, Río *52 B1 river* Guatemala/Mexico
Utah *48 A1 off.* State of Utah; also known as Beehive State, Mormon State. *State* W USA
Utah Lake *44 B4 lake* Utah, W USA
Utena *106 C4* Utena, E Lithuania
Utica *41 F3* New York, NE USA
Utrecht *86 C4 Lat.* Trajectum ad Rhenum. Utrecht, C Netherlands
Utsunomiya *131 D5 var.* Utunomiya. Tochigi, Honshū, S Japan
Uttar Pradesh *135 E3 prev.* United Provinces, United Provinces of Agra and Oudh. *State* N India
Utunomiya *see* Utsunomiya
Uulu *106 D2* Pärnumaa, SW Estonia
Uummannaq *82 C3 var.* Umanak, Umanaq. C Greenland
Uummannarsuaq *see* Nunap Isua
Uvalde *49 F4* Texas, SW USA
Uvarovichi *107 D7 Rus.* Uvarovichi. Homyel'skaya Voblasts', SE Belarus
Uvea, Île *145 E4 island* N Wallis and Futuna
Uvs Nuur *126 C1 var.* Ozero Ubsu-Nur. *Lake* Mongolia/Russian Federation

'Uwaynāt, Jabal al 88 A3 var. Jebel Uweinat. *Mountain* Libya/Sudan
Uyo 75 G5 Akwa Ibom, S Nigeria
Uyuni 61 F5 Potosí, W Bolivia
Uzbekistan 122 D2 *Country* C Asia

Uzbekistan 122

Official name Republic of Uzbekistan
Formation 1991
Capital Tashkent
Population 24.3 million / 141 people per sq mile (54 people per sq km)
Total area 172,741 sq miles (447,400 sq km)
Languages Uzbek, Russian
Religions Sunni Muslim 88%, Eastern Orthodox 9%, other 3%
Ethnic mix Uzbek 71%, Russian 8%, Tajik 5%, Kazakh 4%, other 12%
Government Multiparty republic
Currency Som = 100 teen
Literacy rate 99%
Calorie consumption not available

Uzhhorod 108 B2 *Rus.* Uzhgorod; *prev.* Ungvár. Zakarpats'ka Oblast', W Ukraine
Užice 100 D4 *prev.* Titovo Užice. Serbia, W Yugoslavia

V

Vaal 78 D4 *river* C South Africa
Vaals 87 D6 Limburg, SE Netherlands
Vaasa 85 D5 *Swe.* Vasa; *prev.* Nikolainkaupunki. Länsi-Suomi, W Finland
Vaassen 86 D3 Gelderland, E Netherlands
Vác 99 C6 *Ger.* Waitzen. Pest, N Hungary
Vadodara 134 C4 *prev.* Baroda. Gujarāt, W India
Vaduz 94 E2 *country capital* (Liechtenstein) W Liechtenstein
Váh 99 C5 *Ger.* Waag, *Hung.* Vág. *River* W Slovakia
Väinameri 106 C2 *prev.* Muhu Väin, *Ger.* Moon-Sund. *Sea* E Baltic Sea
Valachia *see* Wallachia
Valday 110 B4 Novgorodskaya Oblast', W Russian Federation
Valdecañas, Embalse de 92 D3 *reservoir* W Spain
Valdepeñas 93 E4 Castilla-La Mancha, C Spain
Valdés, Península 65 C6 *peninsula* SE Argentina
Valdez 36 C3 Alaska, USA
Valdia *see* Weldiya
Valdivia 65 B5 Los Lagos, C Chile
Val-d'Or 38 D4 Québec, SE Canada
Valdosta 43 E3 Georgia, SE USA
Valence 91 D5 *anc.* Valentia, Valentia Julia, Ventia. Drôme, E France
Valencia 46 D1 California, W USA
Valencia 58 D1 Carabobo, N Venezuela
Valencia 93 F3 País Valenciano, E Spain
Valencia, Golfo de 93 F3 *var.* Gulf of Valencia. *Gulf* E Spain
Valencia, Gulf of *see* Valencia, Golfo de
Valenciennes 90 D2 Nord, N France
Valera 58 C2 Trujillo, NW Venezuela
Valga 106 D3 *Ger.* Walk, *Latv.* Valka. Valgamaa, S Estonia
Valira 91 A8 *river* Andorra/Spain
Valjevo 100 C4 Serbia, W Yugoslavia
Valjok *see* Válljohka
Valka 106 D3 *Ger.* Walk. Valka, N Latvia

Valkenswaard 87 D5 Noord-Brabant, S Netherlands
Valladolid 92 D2 Castilla-León, NW Spain
Valladolid 51 H3 Yucatán, SE Mexico
Vall d'Uxó 93 F3 País Valenciano, E Spain
Valle de La Pascua 58 D2 Guárico, N Venezuela
Valledupar 58 B1 Cesar, N Colombia
Vallejo 47 B6 California, W USA
Vallenar 64 B3 Atacama, N Chile
Valletta 97 C8 *prev.* Valetta. *Country capital* (Malta) E Malta
Valley City 45 E2 North Dakota, N USA
Válljohka 84 D2 *var.* Valjok. Finnmark, N Norway
Valls 93 G2 Cataluña, NE Spain
Valmiera 106 D3 *Est.* Volmari, *Ger.* Wolmar. Valmiera, N Latvia
Valozhyn 107 C5 *Pol.* Wołożyn, *Rus.* Volozhin. Minskaya Voblasts', C Belarus
Valverde del Camino 92 C4 Andalucía, S Spain
Van 117 F3 Van, E Turkey
Vanadzor 117 F2 *prev.* Kirovakan. N Armenia
Vancouver 36 D5 British Columbia, SW Canada
Vancouver 46 B3 Washington, NW USA
Vancouver Island 36 D5 *island* British Columbia, SW Canada
Van Diemen Gulf 146 D2 *gulf* Northern Territory, N Australia
Vänern 85 B6 *Eng.* Lake Vaner; *prev.* Lake Vener. *Lake* S Sweden
Vangaindrano 79 G4 Fianarantsoa, SE Madagascar
Van Gölü 117 F3 *Eng.* Lake Van; *anc.* Thospitis. *Salt lake* E Turkey
Van Horn 48 D3 Texas, SW USA
Van, Lake *see* Van Gölü
Vannes 90 A3 *anc.* Dariorigum. Morbihan, NW France
Vantaa 85 D6 *Swe.* Vanda. Etelä-Suomi, S Finland
Vanua Levu 145 E4 *island* N Fiji
Vanuatu 144 C4 *prev.* New Hebrides. *Country* SW Pacific Ocean

Vanuatu 144

Official name Republic of Vanuatu
Formation 1980
Capital Port-Vila
Population 200,000 / 42 people per sq mile (16 people per sq km)
Total area 4,706 sq miles (12,190 sq km)
Languages Bislama, English, French
Religions Presbyterian 37%, other Protestant 21%, Roman Catholic 15%, Traditional beliefs 8%, other 19%
Ethnic mix Melanesian 94%, French 4%, other 2%
Government Multiparty republic
Currency Vatu = 100 centimes
Literacy rate 64%
Calorie consumption 2,739 kilocalories

Van Wert 40 C4 Ohio, N USA
Varakļani 106 D4 Madona, C Latvia
Vārānasi 135 E3 *prev.* Banaras, Benares, *hist.* Kasi. Uttar Pradesh, N India
Varangerfjorden 84 E2 *fjord* N Norway
Varangerhalvøya 84 D2 *peninsula* N Norway
Varannó *see* Vranov nad Topl'ou

Varaždin 100 B2 *Ger.* Warasdin, *Hung.* Varasd. Varaždin, N Croatia
Varberg 85 B7 Halland, S Sweden
Vardar 101 E6 *Gk.* Axiós. *River* FYR Macedonia/Greece *see also* Axiós
Varde 85 A7 Ribe, W Denmark
Varéna 107 B5 *Pol.* Orany. Varéna, S Lithuania
Varese 96 B2 Lombardia, N Italy
Vârful Moldoveanu 108 B4 *var.* Moldoveanul; *prev.* Vîrful Moldoveanu. *Mountain* C Romania
Varkaus 85 E5 Itä-Suomi, C Finland
Varna 104 E2 *prev.* Stalin, *anc.* Odessus. Varna, E Bulgaria
Varnenski Zaliv 104 E2 *prev.* Stalinski Zaliv. *Bay* E Bulgaria
Vasilikí 105 A5 Lefkáda, Iónioi Nísoi, Greece, C Mediterranean Sea
Vasilishki 107 B5 *Pol.* Wasiliszki, *Rus.* Vasilishki. Hrodzyenskaya Voblasts', W Belarus
Vaslui 108 D4 Vaslui, C Romania
Västerås 85 C6 Västmanland, C Sweden
Vasyl'kiv 109 E2 *Rus.* Vasil'kov. Kyyivs'ka Oblast', N Ukraine
Vaté *see* Éfate
Vatican City 97 A7 *Country* S Europe

Vatican City 97

Official name State of the Vatican City
Formation 1929
Capital Vatican City
Population 1,000 / 5,886 people per sq mile (2,273 people per sq km)
Total area 0.17 sq miles (0.44 sq km)
Languages Italian, Latin
Religions Roman Catholic 100%
Ethnic mix Italian 90%, Swiss 10% (including the Swiss Guard which is responsible for papal security)
Government Papal Commission
Currency Lira and Italian lira = 100 centesimi
Literacy rate 99%
Calorie consumption 3,561 kilocalories

Vatnajökull 83 E5 *glacier* SE Iceland
Vättern 85 B6 *Eng.* Lake Vatter; *prev.* Lake Vetter. *Lake* S Sweden
Vaughn 48 D2 New Mexico, SW USA
Vaupés, Río 58 C4 *var.* Rio Uaupés. *River* Brazil/Colombia *see also* Uaupés, Rio
Vava'u Group 145 E4 *island group* N Tonga
Vavuniya 132 D3 Northern Province, N Sri Lanka
Vawkavysk 107 B6 *Pol.* Wołkowysk, *Rus.* Volkovysk. Hrodzyenskaya Voblasts', W Belarus
Växjö 85 C7 *var.* Vexiö. Kronoberg, S Sweden
Vaygach, Ostrov 110 E2 *island* NW Russian Federation
Veendam 86 E2 Groningen, NE Netherlands
Veenendaal 86 D4 Utrecht, C Netherlands
Vega 84 B4 *island* C Norway
Veisiejai 107 B5 Lazdijai, S Lithuania
Vejer de la Frontera 92 C5 Andalucía, S Spain
Veldhoven 87 D5 Noord-Brabant, S Netherlands
Velebit 100 A3 *mountain range* C Croatia
Velenje 95 E7 *Ger.* Wöllan. N Slovenia

Veles 101 E6 *Turk.* Köprülü. C FYR Macedonia
Velho *see* Porto Velho
Velika Morava 100 D4 *var.* Glavn'a Morava, Morava, *Ger.* Grosse Morava. *River* C Yugoslavia
Velikaya 113 G2 *river* NE Russian Federation
Velikiye Luki 110 A4 Pskovskaya Oblast', W Russian Federation
Veliko Tŭrnovo 104 D2 *prev.* Tirnovo, Trnovo, Tŭrnovo. Veliko Tŭrnovo, N Bulgaria
Velingrad 104 C3 Pazardzhik, C Bulgaria
Vel'ký Krtíš 99 D6 Banskobystrický Kraj, C Slovakia
Vellore 132 C2 Tamil Nādu, SE India
Velobriga *see* Viana do Castelo
Velsen *see* Velsen-Noord
Velsen-Noord 86 C3 *var.* Velsen. Noord-Holland, W Netherlands
Vel'sk 110 C4 *var.* Velsk. Arkhangel'skaya Oblast', NW Russian Federation
Velsk *see* Vel'sk
Velvendos *see* Velvendós
Velvendós 104 B4 *var.* Velvendos. Dytikí Makedonía, N Greece
Velykyy Tokmak *see* Tokmak
Vendôme 90 C4 Loir-et-Cher, C France
Venezia 96 C2 *Eng.* Venice, *Fr.* Venise, *Ger.* Venedig; *anc.* Venetia. Veneto, NE Italy
Venezuela 58 D2 *prev.* Estados Unidos de Venezuela, United States of Venezuela. *Country* N South America

Venezuela 58

Official name Bolivarian Republic of Venezuela
Formation 1821
Capital Caracas
Population 24.2 million / 71 people per sq mile (27 people per sq km)
Total area 340,559 sq miles (882,050 sq km)
Languages Spanish, Amerindian languages
Religions Roman Catholic 89%, Protestant and other 11%
Ethnic mix Mestizo 69%, other 31%
Government Multiparty republic
Currency Bolivar = 100 centimos
Literacy rate 92%
Calorie consumption 2,618 kilocalories

Venezuela, Golfo de 58 C1 *Eng.* Gulf of Maracaibo, Gulf of Venezuela. *Gulf* NW Venezuela
Venezuelan Basin 56 B1 *undersea feature* E Caribbean Sea
Venice *see* Venezia
Venice 42 C4 Louisiana, S USA
Venice, Gulf of 96 C2 *It.* Golfo di Venezia, *Slvn.* Beneški Zaliv. *Gulf* N Adriatic Sea
Venlo 87 D5 *prev.* Venloo. Limburg, SE Netherlands
Venta 106 B3 *Ger.* Windau. *River* Latvia/Lithuania
Ventimiglia 96 A3 Liguria, NW Italy
Ventspils 106 B2 *Ger.* Windau. Ventspils, NW Latvia
Vera 64 D3 Santa Fe, C Argentina
Veracruz 51 F4 *var.* Veracruz Llave. Veracruz-Llave, E Mexico
Veracruz Llave *see* Veracruz
Vercelli 96 A2 *anc.* Vercellae. Piemonte, NW Italy
Verdalsøra 84 B4 Nord-Trøndelag, C Norway
Verde, Costa 92 D1 *coastal region* N Spain

Verden *94 B3* Niedersachsen, NW Germany
Veria *see* Véroia
Verkhoyanskiy Khrebet *115 F3 mountain range* NE Russian Federation
Vermillion *45 F3* South Dakota, N USA
Vermont *41 F2 off.* State of Vermont; also known as The Green Mountain State. *State* NE USA
Vernal *44 B4* Utah, W USA
Vernon *49 F2* Texas, SW USA
Véroia *104 B4 var.* Veria, Vérroia, *Turk.* Karaferiye. Kentrikí Makedonía, N Greece
Verona *96 C2* Veneto, NE Italy
Vérroia *see* Véroia
Versailles *90 D1* Yvelines, N France
Verviers *87 D6* Liège, E Belgium
Vesdre *87 D6 river* E Belgium
Veselinovo *104 D2* Shumen, NE Bulgaria
Vesoul *90 D4 anc.* Vesulium, Vesulum. Haute-Saône, E France
Vesterålen *84 B2 island group* N Norway
Vestfjorden *84 C3 fjord* C Norway
Vestmannaeyjar *83 E5* Sudhurland, S Iceland
Vesuvio *97 D5 Eng.* Vesuvius. *Volcano* S Italy
Veszprém *99 C7 Ger.* Veszprim. Veszprém, W Hungary
Vetrino *104 E2* Varna, E Bulgaria
Veurne *87 A5 var.* Furnes. West-Vlaanderen, W Belgium
Vexiö *see* Växjö
Viacha *61 F4* La Paz, W Bolivia
Viana de Castelo *see* Viana do Castelo
Viana do Castelo *92 B2 var.* Viana de Castelo; *anc.* Velobriga. Viana do Castelo, NW Portugal
Vianen *86 C4* Zuid-Holland, C Netherlands
Viangchan *136 C4 Eng./Fr.* Vientiane. *Country capital* (Laos) C Laos
Viangphoukha *136 C3 var.* Vieng Pou Kha. Louang Namtha, N Laos
Viareggio *96 B3* Toscana, C Italy
Viborg *85 A7* Viborg, NW Denmark
Vic *93 G2 var.* Vich; *anc.* Ausa, Vicus Ausonensis. Cataluña, NE Spain
Vicenza *96 C2 anc.* Vicentia. Veneto, NE Italy
Vich *see* Vic
Vichy *91 C5* Allier, C France
Vicksburg *42 B2* Mississippi, S USA
Victoria *102 A5 var.* Rabat. Gozo, NW Malta
Victoria *79 H1 country capital* (Seychelles). Mahé, SW Seychelles
Victoria *49 G4* Texas, SW USA
Victoria *36 D5* Vancouver Island, British Columbia, SW Canada
Victoria *149 C7 state* SE Australia
Victoria Bank *see* Vitória Seamount
Victoria de Durango *see* Durango
Victoria de las Tunas *see* Las Tunas
Victoria Falls *78 C2 waterfall* Zambia/Zimbabwe
Victoria Falls *78 C3* Matabeleland North, W Zimbabwe
Victoria Island *37 F3 island* Northwest Territories/Nunavut, NW Canada
Victoria, Lake *73 B6 var.* Victoria Nyanza. *Lake* E Africa
Victoria Land *154 C4 physical region* Antarctica
Victoria Nyanza *see* Victoria, Lake
Victoria River *146 D3 river* Northern Territory, N Australia
Victorville *47 C7* California, W USA
Vicus Ausonensis *see* Vic
Vidalia *43 E2* Georgia, SE USA

Vidin *104 B1 anc.* Bononia. Vidin, NW Bulgaria
Vidzy *107 C5 Rus.* Vidzy. Vitsyebskaya Voblasts', NW Belarus
Viedma *65 C5* Río Negro, E Argentina
Vieng Pou Kha *see* Viangphoukha
Vienna *see* Wien
Vienne *91 D5 anc.* Vienna. Isère, E France
Vienne *90 B4 river* W France
Vientiane *see* Viangchan
Vierzon *90 C4* Cher, C France
Viesīte *106 C4 Ger.* Eckengraf. Jēkabpils, S Latvia
Vietnam *136 D4 Vtn.* Công Hoa Xa Hôi Chu Nghia Viêt Nam. *Country* SE Asia

Vietnam 136

Official name Socialist Republic of Vietnam
Formation 1976
Capital Hanoi
Population 79.8 million / 635 people per sq mile (245 people per sq km)
Total area 125,621 sq miles (325,360 sq km)
Languages Vietnamese, Chinese, Thai, Khmer, Muong, Nung, Miao, Yao
Religions Buddhist 55%, Christian 7%, other 38%
Ethnic mix Vietnamese 88%, Chinese 4%, Thai 2%, other 6%
Government Single-party republic
Currency Dông = 10 hao = 100 xu
Literacy rate 92%
Calorie consumption 2,250 kilocalories

Vietri *see* Viêt Tri
Viêt Tri *136 D3 var.* Vietri. Vinh Phu, N Vietnam
Vieux Fort *55 F2* S Saint Lucia
Vigo *92 B2* Galicia, NW Spain
Vijayawāda *132 D1 prev.* Bezwada. Andhra Pradesh, SE India
Vijosa *see* Vjosës, Lumi i
Vijosë *see* Vjosës, Lumi i
Vila *see* Port-Vila
Vila Artur de Paiva *see* Cubango
Vila da Ponte *see* Cubango
Vila de Mocímboa da Praia *see* Mocímboa da Praia
Vila do Conde *92 B2* Porto, NW Portugal
Vila do Zumbo *78 D2 prev.* Vila do Zumbu, Zumbo. Tete, NW Mozambique
Vilafranca del Penedès *93 G2 var.* Villafranca del Panadés. Cataluña, NE Spain
Vila General Machado *see* Camacupa
Viljaka *106 D4 Ger.* Marienhausen. Balvi, NE Latvia
Vilalba *92 C1* Galicia, NW Spain
Vila Nova de Gaia *92 B2* Porto, NW Portugal
Vila Nova de Portimão *see* Portimão
Vila Pereira de Eça *see* N'Giva
Vila Real *92 C2 var.* Vila Rial. Vila Real, N Portugal
Vila Rial *see* Vila Real
Vila Robert Williams *see* Caála
Vila Serpa Pinto *see* Menongue
Vilhelmina *84 C4* Västerbotten, N Sweden
Vilhena *62 D3* Rondônia, W Brazil
Vília *105 C5* Attikí, C Greece
Viliya *107 C5 Lith.* Neris, *Rus.* Viliya. *River* W Belarus
Viljandi *106 D2 Ger.* Fellin. Viljandimaa, S Estonia
Vilkaviškis *106 B4 Pol.* Wyłkowyszki. Vilkaviškis, SW Lithuania

Villa Acuña *50 D2 var.* Cuidad Acuña. Coahuila de Zaragoza, NE Mexico
Villa Bella *61 F2* Beni, N Bolivia
Villacarrillo *93 E4* Andalucía, S Spain
Villa Cecilia *see* Ciudad Madero
Villach *95 D7 Slvn.* Beljak. Kärnten, S Austria
Villacidro *97 A5* Sardegna, Italy, C Mediterranean Sea
Villa Concepción *see* Concepción
Villa del Pilar *see* Pilar
Villafranca de los Barros *92 C4* Extremadura, W Spain
Villafranca del Panadés *see* Vilafranca del Penedès
Villahermosa *51 G4 prev.* San Juan Bautista. Tabasco, SE Mexico
Villajoyosa *93 F4 var.* La Vila Jojosa. País Valenciano, E Spain
Villa María *64 C4* Córdoba, C Argentina
Villa Martín *61 F5* Potosí, SW Bolivia
Villa Mercedes *64 C4 prev.* Mercedes. San Luis, C Argentina
Villanueva *50 D3* Zacatecas, C Mexico
Villanueva de la Serena *92 C3* Extremadura, W Spain
Villanueva de los Infantes *93 E4* Castilla-La Mancha, C Spain
Villarrica *64 D2* Guairá, SE Paraguay
Villavicencio *58 B3* Meta, C Colombia
Villaviciosa *92 D1* Asturias, N Spain
Villazón *61 G5* Potosí, S Bolivia
Villena *93 F4* País Valenciano, E Spain
Villeurbanne *91 D5* Rhône, E France
Villingen-Schwenningen *95 B6* Baden-Württemberg, S Germany
Vilnius *107 C5 Pol.* Wilno, *Ger.* Wilna; *prev.* Rus. Vilna. *Country capital* (Lithuania) Vilnius, SE Lithuania
Vil'shanka *109 E3 Rus.* Olshanka. Kirovohrads'ka Oblast', C Ukraine
Vilvoorde *87 C6 Fr.* Vilvorde. Vlaams Brabant, C Belgium
Vilyeyka *107 C5 Pol.* Wilejka, *Rus.* Vileyka. Minskaya Voblasts', NW Belarus
Vilyuy *115 F3 river* NE Russian Federation
Viña del Mar *64 B4* Valparaíso, C Chile
Vinaròs *93 F3* País Valenciano, E Spain
Vincennes *40 B4* Indiana, N USA
Vindhya Mountains *see* Vindhya Range
Vindhya Range *134 D4 var.* Vindhya Mountains. *Mountain range* N India
Vineland *41 F4* New Jersey, NE USA
Vinh *136 D4* Nghê An, N Vietnam
Vinh Loi *see* Bac Liêu
Vinh Thai Lan *see* Thailand, Gulf of
Vinishte *104 C2* Montana, NW Bulgaria
Vinita *49 G1* Oklahoma, C USA
Vinkovci *100 C3 Ger.* Winkowitz, *Hung.* Vinkovcze. Vukovar-Srijem, E Croatia
Vinnytsya *108 D2 Rus.* Vinnitsa. Vinnyts'ka Oblast', C Ukraine
Vinson Massif *154 A3 mountain* Antarctica
Viranşehir *117 E4* Şanlıurfa, SE Turkey
Vîrful Moldoveanu *see* Vârful Moldoveanu

Virginia *41 E5 off.* Commonwealth of Virginia; also known as Mother of Presidents, Mother of States, Old Dominion. *State* NE USA
Virginia *45 G1* Minnesota, N USA
Virginia Beach *41 F5* Virginia, NE USA
Virgin Islands *see* British Virgin Islands
Virgin Islands (US) *55 F3 var.* Virgin Islands of the United States; *prev.* Danish West Indies. *US unincorporated territory* E West Indies
Virgin Islands of the United States *see* Virgin Islands (US)
Virôchey *137 E5* Rôtânôkiri, NE Cambodia
Virovitica *100 C2 Ger.* Virovititz, *Hung.* Verôcze; *prev. Ger.* Werowitz. Virovitica-Podravina, NE Croatia
Virton *87 D8* Luxembourg, SE Belgium
Virtsu *106 D2 Ger.* Werder. Läänemaa, W Estonia
Vis *100 B4 It.* Lissa; *anc.* Issa. *Island* S Croatia
Vis *see* Fish
Visaginas *106 C4 prev.* Sniečkus. Ignalina, E Lithuania
Visākhapatnam *135 E5* Andhra Pradesh, SE India
Visalia *47 C6* California, W USA
Visby *85 C7 Ger.* Wisby. Gotland, SE Sweden
Viscount Melville Sound *37 F2 prev.* Melville Sound. *Sound* Northwest Territories/Nunavut, N Canada
Visé *87 D6* Liège, E Belgium
Viseu *92 C2 prev.* Vizeu. Viseu, N Portugal
Visoko *100 C4* Federacija Bosna I Hercegovina, C Bosnia and Herzegovina
Vistula *see* Wisła
Vistula Lagoon *98 C2 Ger.* Frisches Haff, *Pol.* Zalew Wiślany, *Rus.* Vislinskiy Zaliv. *Lagoon* Poland/Russian Federation
Viterbo *96 C4 anc.* Vicus Elbii. Lazio, C Italy
Viti Levu *145 E4 island* W Fiji
Vitim *115 F4 river* C Russian Federation
Vitoria *see* Vitoria-Gasteiz
Vitória *63 F4* Espírito Santo, SE Brazil
Vitória Bank *see* Vitória Seamount
Vitória da Conquista *63 F3* Bahia, E Brazil
Vitoria-Gasteiz *93 E1 var.* Vitoria, *Eng.* Vittoria. País Vasco, N Spain
Vitória Seamount *67 B5 var.* Victoria Bank, Vitoria Bank. *Undersea feature* C Atlantic Ocean
Vitré *90 B3* Ille-et-Vilaine, NW France
Vitsyebsk *107 E5 Rus.* Vitebsk. Vitsyebskaya Voblasts', NE Belarus
Vittoria *see* Vitoria-Gasteiz
Vittoria *97 C7* Sicilia, Italy, C Mediterranean Sea
Vizianagaram *135 E5 var.* Vizianagram. Andhra Pradesh, E India
Vizianagram *see* Vizianagaram
Vjosës, Lumi i *101 C7 var.* Vijosa, Vijosë, *Gk.* Aóos. *River* Albania/Greece *see also* Aóos
Vlaardingen *86 B4* Zuid-Holland, SW Netherlands
Vladikavkaz *111 B8 prev.* Dzaudzhikau, Ordzhonikidze. Severnaya Osetiya-Alaniya, SW Russian Federation
Vladimir *111 B5* Vladimirskaya Oblast', W Russian Federation
Vladivostok *115 G5* Primorskiy Kray, SE Russian Federation

Vlagtwedde *86 E2* Groningen, NE Netherlands
Vlasotince *101 E5* Serbia, SE Yugoslavia
Vlieland *86 C1 Fris.* Flylân. *Island* Waddeneilanden, N Netherlands
Vlijmen *86 C4* Noord-Brabant, S Netherlands
Vlissingen *87 B5 Eng.* Flushing, *Fr.* Flessingue. Zeeland, SW Netherlands
Vlorë *101 C7 prev.* Vlonë, *It.* Valona, Vlora. Vlorë, SW Albania
Vöcklabruck *95 D6* Oberösterreich, NW Austria
Vohimena, Tanjona *79 F4 Fr.* Cap Sainte Marie. *Headland* S Madagascar
Voiron *91 D5* Isère, E France
Vojvodina *100 D3 Ger.* Wojwodina. *Region* N Yugoslavia
Volcán de Chiriquí *see* Barú, Volcán
Volga *111 B7 river* NW Russian Federation
Volga Uplands *81 G3 Russ.* Privolzhskaya Vozvyshennost' *mountain range* W Russian Federation
Volgodonsk *111 B7* Rostovskaya Oblast', SW Russian Federation
Volgograd *111 B7 prev.* Stalingrad, Tsaritsyn. Volgogradskaya Oblast', SW Russian Federation
Volkhov *110 B4* Leningradskaya Oblast', NW Russian Federation
Volnovakha *109 G3* Donets'ka Oblast', SE Ukraine
Volodymyr-Volyns'kyy *108 C1 Pol.* Włodzimierz, *Rus.* Vladimir-Volynskiy. Volyns'ka Oblast', NW Ukraine
Vologda *110 B4* Vologodskaya Oblast', W Russian Federation
Vólos *105 B5* Thessalía, C Greece
Vol'sk *111 C6* Saratovskaya Oblast', W Russian Federation
Volta *75 E5 river* SE Ghana
Volta Blanche *see* White Volta
Volta, Lake *75 E5 reservoir* SE Ghana
Volta Noire *see* Black Volta
Volturno *97 D5 river* S Italy
Volzhskiy *111 B6* Volgogradskaya Oblast', SW Russian Federation
Võnnu *106 E3 Ger.* Wendau. Tartumaa, SE Estonia
Voorst *86 D3* Gelderland, E Netherlands
Voranava *107 C5 Pol.* Werenów, *Rus.* Voronovo. Hrodzyenskaya Voblasts', W Belarus
Vorderrhein *95 B7 river* SE Switzerland
Vóreioi Sporádes *105 C5 var.* Vórioi Sporádhes, *Eng.* Northern Sporades. *Island group* E Greece
Vórioi Sporádhes *see* Vóreioi Sporádes
Vorkuta *114 C2* Respublika Komi, NW Russian Federation
Vormsi *106 C2 var.* Vormsi Saar, *Ger.* Worms, Swed. Ormsö. *Island* W Estonia
Vormsi Saar *see* Vormsi
Voronezh *111 B6* Voronezhskaya Oblast', W Russian Federation
Võru *106 D3 Ger.* Werro. Võrumaa, SE Estonia
Vosges *90 E4 mountain range* NE France
Vostochno-Sibirskoye More *115 F1 Eng.* East Siberian Sea. *Sea* Arctic Ocean
Vostok Island *see* Vostok Island
Vostok *154 C3 Russian research station* Antarctica
Vostok Island *145 G3 var.* Vostok Island; *prev.* Stavers Island. *Island* Line Islands, SE Kiribati
Voznesens'k *109 E3 Rus.* Voznesensk. Mykolayivs'ka Oblast', S Ukraine

Vrangelya, Ostrov *115 F1 Eng.* Wrangel Island. *Island* NE Russian Federation
Vranje *101 E5* Serbia, SE Yugoslavia
Vranov *see* Vranov nad Topl'ou
Vranov nad Topl'ou *99 D5 var.* Vranov, *Hung.* Varannó. Prešovský Kraj, E Slovakia
Vratsa *104 C2* Vratsa, NW Bulgaria
Vrbas *100 C3 river* N Bosnia and Herzegovina
Vrbas *100 C3* Serbia, NW Yugoslavia
Vsetín *99 C5 Ger.* Wsetin. Zlínský Kraj, E Czech Republic
Vučitrn *101 D5* Serbia, S Yugoslavia
Vukovar *100 C3 Hung.* Vukovár. Vukovar-Srijem, E Croatia
Vulcano, Isola *97 C7 island* Isole Eolie, S Italy
Vung Tau *137 E6 prev. Fr.* Cape Saint Jacques, Cap Saint-Jacques. Ba Ria-Vung Tau, S Vietnam
Vyatka *111 C5 river* NW Russian Federation
Vyborg *110 B3 Fin.* Viipuri. Leningradskaya Oblast', NW Russian Federation
Vyerkhnyadzvinsk *107 D5 Rus.* Verkhnedvinsk. Vitsyebskaya Voblasts', N Belarus
Vyetryna *107 D5 Rus.* Vetrino. Vitsyebskaya Voblasts', N Belarus
Vynohradiv *108 B3 Cz.* Sevluš, *Hung.* Nagyszöllös, *Rus.* Vinogradov; *prev.* Sevlyush. Zakarpats'ka Oblast', W Ukraine

W

Wa *75 E4* NW Ghana
Waal *86 C4 river* S Netherlands
Wabash *40 C4* Indiana, N USA
Wabash River *40 B5 river* N USA
Waco *49 G3* Texas, SW USA
Waddān *71 F3* NW Libya
Waddeneilanden *86 C1 Eng.* West Frisian Islands. *Island group* N Netherlands
Waddenzee *86 C1 var.* Wadden Zee. *Sea* SE North Sea
Waddington, Mount *36 D5 mountain* British Columbia, SW Canada
Wādī as Sīr *119 B6 var.* Wadi es Sir. 'Ammān, NW Jordan
Wadi es Sir *see* Wādī as Sīr
Wadi Halfa *72 B3 var.* Wādī Ḥalfā'. Northern, N Sudan
Wādī Mūsā *119 B7 var.* Petra. Ma'ān, S Jordan
Wad Madanī *see* Wad Medani
Wad Medani *72 C4 var.* Wad Madanī. Gezira, C Sudan
Waflia *139 F4* Pulau Buru, E Indonesia
Wagadugu *see* Ouagadougou
Wagga Wagga *149 C7* New South Wales, SE Australia
Wagin *147 B7* Western Australia
Wāh *134 C1* Punjab, NE Pakistan
Wahai *139 F4* Pulau Seram, E Indonesia
Wahiawa *47 A8 Haw.* Wahiawā. Oahu, Hawaii, USA, C Pacific Ocean
Wahībah, Ramlat Āl *121 E5 var.* Ramlat Ahl Wahībah, Ramlat Al Wahaybah, *Eng.* Wahibah Sands. *Desert* N Oman
Wahibah Sands *see* Wahībah, Ramlat Āl
Wahpeton *45 F2* North Dakota, N USA
Wahran *see* Oran
Waiau *151 A7 river* South Island, NZ
Waigeo, Pulau *139 G4 island* Maluku, E Indonesia
Waikaremoana, Lake *150 E4 lake* North Island, NZ
Wailuku *47 B8* Maui, Hawaii, USA, C Pacific Ocean

Waimate *151 B6* Canterbury, South Island, NZ
Waiouru *150 D4* Manawatu-Wanganui, North Island, NZ
Waipara *151 C6* Canterbury, South Island, NZ
Waipawa *150 E4* Hawke's Bay, North Island, NZ
Waipukurau *150 D4* Hawke's Bay, North Island, NZ
Wairau *151 C5 river* South Island, NZ
Wairoa *150 D2 river* North Island, NZ
Wairoa *150 E4* Hawke's Bay, North Island, NZ
Waitaki *151 B6 river* South Island, NZ
Waitara *150 D4* Taranaki, North Island, NZ
Waiuku *150 D3* Auckland, North Island, NZ
Wakasa-wan *131 C6 bay* C Japan
Wakatipu, Lake *151 A7 lake* South Island, NZ
Wakayama *131 C6* Wakayama, Honshū, SW Japan
Wake Island *142 D1 atoll* NW Pacific Ocean
Wake Island *152 C2 US unincorporated territory* NW Pacific Ocean
Wakkanai *130 C1* Hokkaidō, NE Japan
Walachei *see* Wallachia
Walachia *see* Wallachia
Wałbrzych *98 B4 Ger.* Waldenburg, Waldenburg in Schlesien. Dolnośląskie, SW Poland
Walcourt *87 C7* Namur, S Belgium
Wałcz *98 B3 Ger.* Deutsch Krone. Zachodniopomorskie, NW Poland
Waldia *see* Weldiya
Wales *89 C6 Wel.* Cymru. *National region* UK
Wales *36 C2* Alaska, USA
Wales Island, Prince of *see* Pinang, Pulau
Walgett *149 D5* New South Wales, SE Australia
Walker Lake *47 C5 lake* Nevada, W USA
Wallachia *108 B5 var.* Walachia, *Ger.* Walachei, *Rom.* Valachia. *Cultural region* S Romania
Walla Walla *46 C2* Washington, NW USA
Wallis and Futuna *145 E4 Fr.* Territoire de Wallis et Futuna. *French overseas territory* C Pacific Ocean
Walnut Ridge *42 B1* Arkansas, C USA
Walthamstow *89 B7* SE England, UK
Walvis Bay *78 A4 Afr.* Walvisbaai. Erongo, NW Namibia
Walvish Ridge *see* Walvis Ridge
Walvis Ridge *69 B7 var.* Walvish Ridge. *Undersea feature* E Atlantic Ocean
Wan *see* Anhui
Wanaka *151 B6* Otago, South Island, NZ
Wanaka, Lake *151 A6 lake* South Island, NZ
Wanchuan *see* Zhangjiakou
Wandel Sea *83 E1 sea* Arctic Ocean
Wandsworth *89 A8* SE England, UK
Wanganui *150 D4* Manawatu-Wanganui, North Island, NZ
Wangaratta *149 C7* Victoria, SE Australia
Wanki, Río *see* Coco, Río
Wanlaweyn *73 D6 var.* Wanle Weyn, *It.* Uanle Uen. Shabeellaha Hoose, SW Somalia
Wanle Weyn *see* Wanlaweyn
Wanxian *128 B5* Chongqing, C China

Warangal *135 E5* Andhra Pradesh, C India
Warburg *94 B4* Nordrhein-Westfalen, W Germany
Ware *37 E4* British Columbia, W Canada
Waremme *87 C6* Liège, E Belgium
Waren *94 C3* Mecklenburg-Vorpommern, NE Germany
Wargla *see* Ouargla
Warkworth *150 D2* Auckland, North Island, NZ
Warnemünde *94 C2* Mecklenburg-Vorpommern, NE Germany
Warner *49 G1* Oklahoma, C USA
Warnes *61 G4* Santa Cruz, C Bolivia
Warrego River *149 C5 seasonal river* New South Wales/Queensland, E Australia
Warren *40 D3* Michigan, N USA
Warren *40 D3* Ohio, N USA
Warren *41 E3* Pennsylvania, NE USA
Warri *75 F5* Delta, S Nigeria
Warrnambool *149 B7* Victoria, SE Australia
Warsaw *see* Mazowieckie
Warszawa *98 D3 Eng.* Warsaw, *Ger.* Warschau, *Rus.* Varshava. *Country capital* (Poland) Mazowieckie, C Poland
Warta *98 B3 Ger.* Warthe. *River* W Poland
Warwick *149 E5* Queensland, E Australia
Washington *44 A2 off.* State of Washington; also known as Chinook State, Evergreen State. *State* NW USA
Washington DC *41 E4 country capital* (USA) District of Columbia, NE USA
Washington, Mount *41 G2 mountain* New Hampshire, NE USA
Wash, The *89 E6 inlet* E England, UK
Waspam *53 E2 var.* Waspán. Región Autónoma Atlántico Norte, NE Nicaragua
Waspán *see* Waspam
Watampone *139 E4 var.* Bone. Sulawesi, C Indonesia
Waterbury *41 F3* Connecticut, NE USA
Waterford *89 B6 Ir.* Port Láirge. S Ireland
Waterloo *45 G3* Iowa, C USA
Watertown *41 F2* New York, NE USA
Watertown *45 F2* South Dakota, N USA
Waterville *41 G2* Maine, NE USA
Watford *89 A7* SE England, UK
Watsa *77 E5* Orientale, NE Dem. Rep. Congo (Zaire)
Watts Bar Lake *reservoir* Tennessee, S USA
Wau *73 B5 var.* Wāw. Western Bahr el Ghazal, S Sudan
Waukegan *40 B3* Illinois, N USA
Waukesha *40 B3* Wisconsin, N USA
Wausau *40 B2* Wisconsin, N USA
Waverly *45 G3* Iowa, C USA
Wavre *87 C6* Wallon Brabant, C Belgium
Wāw *see* Wau
Wawa *38 C4* Ontario, S Canada
Waycross *43 E3* Georgia, SE USA
Wearmouth *see* Sunderland
Webster City *45 F3* Iowa, C USA
Weddell Plain *154 A2 undersea feature* SW Atlantic Ocean
Weddell Sea *154 A2 sea* SW Atlantic Ocean
Weener *94 A3* Niedersachsen, NW Germany
Weert *87 D5* Limburg, SE Netherlands
Weesp *86 C3* Noord-Holland, C Netherlands
Węgorzewo *98 D2 Ger.* Angerburg. Warmińsko-Mazurskie, NE Poland

Weimar *94 C4* Thüringen,
C Germany
Weissenburg *95 C6* Bayern,
SE Germany
Weiswampach *87 D7* Diekirch,
N Luxembourg
Wejherowo *98 C2* Pomorskie,
NW Poland
Welchman Hall *55 G1* C Barbados
Weldiya *72 C4 var.* Waldia, *It.*
Valdia. N Ethiopia
Welkom *78 D4* Free State, C South
Africa
Welle *see* Uele
Wellesley Islands *148 B2 island
group* Queensland, N Australia
Wellington *151 D5 country capital*
(NZ) Wellington, North Island,
NZ
Wellington *see* Wellington, Isla
Wellington *45 F5* Kansas, C USA
Wellington, Isla *65 A7 var.*
Wellington. Island S Chile
Wells *46 D4* Nevada, W USA
Wellsford *150 D2* Auckland, North
Island, NZ
Wells, Lake *147 C5 lake* Western
Australia
Wels *95 D6 anc.* Ovilava.
Oberösterreich, N Austria
Wembley *89 A8* SE England, UK
Wemmel *87 B6* Vlaams Brabant,
C Belgium
Wenatchee *46 B2* Washington,
NW USA
Wenchi *75 E4* W Ghana
Wen-chou *see* Wenzhou
Wenchow *see* Wenzhou
Wenmen Island *see* Wolf, Isla
Wenzhou *128 D5 var.* Wen-chou,
Wenchow. Zhejiang, SE China
Werda *78 C4* Kgalagadi, S Botswana
Werkendam *86 C4* Noord-Brabant,
S Netherlands
Weser *94 B3 river* NW Germany
Wessel Islands *148 B1 island group*
Northern Territory, N Australia
West Antarctica *see* Lesser
Antarctica
West Bank *119 A6 disputed region*
SW Asia
West Bend *40 B3* Wisconsin, N USA
West Bengal *135 F4 state*
NE India
West Cape *151 A7 headland* South
Island, NZ
West Des Moines *45 F3* Iowa,
C USA
Westerland *94 B2* Schleswig-
Holstein, N Germany
Western Australia *146 B4 state*
W Australia
Western Desert *see* Sahara
el Gharbîya
Western Dvina *85 E7 Bel.* Dzvina,
Ger. Düna, *Latv.* Daugava, *Rus.*
Zapadnaya Dvina. *River*
W Europe
Western Ghats *134 C5 mountain
range* SW India
Western Isles *see* Outer
Hebrides
Western Sahara *70 B3 UK disputed
territory* N Africa
Western Samoa *see* Samoa
Westerschelde *87 B5 Eng.* Western
Scheldt; *prev.* Honte. Inlet S North
Sea
West Falkland *65 C7 var.* Isla Gran
Malvina. *Island* W Falkland
Islands
West Fargo *45 F2* North Dakota,
N USA
West Irian *see* Irian Jaya
West Mariana Basin *142 B1 var.*
Perece Vela Basin. *Undersea feature*
W Pacific Ocean
West Memphis *42 B1* Arkansas,
C USA
West New Guinea *see* Irian Jaya
West Papua *see* Irian Jaya
Weston-super-Mare *89 D7*
SW England, UK

West Palm Beach *43 F4* Florida,
SE USA
Westport *151 C5* West Coast, South
Island, NZ
West River *see* Xi Jiang
West Siberian Plain *see* Zapadno-
Sibirskaya Ravnina
West Virginia *40 D4 off.* State of
West Virginia; *also known as* The
Mountain State. *State* NE USA
Wetar, Pulau *139 F5 island*
Kepulauan Damar, E Indonesia
Wetzlar *95 B5* Hessen, W Germany
Wevok *36 C2 var.* Wewuk. Alaska,
USA
Wewuk *see* Wevok
Wexford *89 B6 Ir.* Loch Garman.
SE Ireland
Weyburn *37 F5* Saskatchewan,
S Canada
Weymouth *89 D7* S England, UK
Wezep *86 D3* Gelderland,
E Netherlands
Whakatane *150 E3* Bay of Plenty,
North Island, NZ
Whale Cove *37 G3* Nunavut,
C Canada
Whangarei *150 D2* Northland,
North Island, NZ
Wharton Basin *141 D5 var.* West
Australian Basin. *Undersea feature*
E Indian Ocean
Whataroa *151 B6* West Coast, South
Island, NZ
Wheatland *44 D3* Wyoming, C USA
Wheeler Peak *48 D1 mountain* New
Mexico, SW USA
Wheeling *40 D4* West Virginia,
NE USA
Whitby *89 D5* N England, UK
Whitefish *44 B1* Montana,
NW USA
Whitehaven *89 C5* NW England,
UK
Whitehorse *36 D4 territory capital*
Yukon Territory, W Canada
White Nile *72 B4 Ar.* Al Baḥr
al Abyaḍ, An Nīl al Abyaḍ, Bahr
el Jebel. *River* SE Sudan
White Nile *72 B4 var.* Bahr el Jebel.
River S Sudan
White River *44 D3 river* South
Dakota, N USA
White Sea *see* Beloye More
White Volta *75 E4 var.* Nakambé, *Fr.*
Volta Blanche. *River* Burkina
faso/Ghana
Whitianga *150 D2* Waikato, North
Island, NZ
Whitney, Mount *47 C6 mountain*
California, W USA
Whitsunday Group *148 D3 island
group* Queensland, E Australia
Whyalla *149 B6* South Australia
Wichita *45 F5* Kansas, C USA
Wichita Falls *49 F2* Texas, SW
USA
Wichita River *49 F2 river* Texas,
SW USA
Wickenburg *48 B2* Arizona,
SW USA
Wicklow *89 B6 Ir.* Cill Mhantáin.
Cultural region E Ireland
Wicklow Mountains *89 B6 Ir.*
Sléibhte Chill Mhantáin. *Mountain
range* E Ireland
Wieliczka *99 D5* Małopolskie,
S Poland
Wieluń *98 C4* Łódzkie, C Poland
Wien *95 E6 Eng.* Vienna, *Hung.*
Bécs, *Slvk.* Vídeň, *Slvn.* Dunaj; *anc.*
Vindobona. *Country capital*
(Austria) Wien, NE Austria
Wiener Neustadt *95 E6*
Niederösterreich, E Austria
Wierden *86 E3* Overijssel,
E Netherlands
Wiesbaden *95 B5* Hessen,
W Germany
Wight, Isle of *89 D7 island*
S England, UK
Wijchen *86 D4* Gelderland,
SE Netherlands

Wijk bij Duurstede *86 D4* Utrecht,
C Netherlands
Wilcannia *149 C6* New South
Wales, SE Australia
Wilhelm, Mount *144 B3 mountain*
C PNG
Wilhelm-Pieck-Stadt *see* Guben
Wilhelmshaven *94 B3*
Niedersachsen, NW Germany
Wilkes Barre *41 F3* Pennsylvania,
NE USA
Wilkes Land *154 C4 physical region*
Antarctica
Willard *48 D2* New Mexico,
SW USA
Willcox *48 C3* Arizona, SW USA
Willebroek *87 B5* Antwerpen,
C Belgium
Willemstad *55 E5 dependent territory
capital* (Netherlands Antilles)
Curaçao, Netherlands Antilles
Williston *44 D1* North Dakota,
N USA
Wilmington *41 F4* Delaware,
NE USA
Wilmington *43 F2* North Carolina,
SE USA
Wilmington *40 C4* Ohio, N USA
Wilrijk *87 C5* Antwerpen,
N Belgium
Winchester *89 D7 hist.*
Wintanceaster, *Lat.* Venta
Belgarum. S England, UK
Winchester *41 E4* Virginia, NE USA
Windhoek *78 B3 Ger.* Windhuk.
Country capital (Namibia)
Khomas, C Namibia
Windorah *148 C4* Queensland,
C Australia
Windsor *41 G3* Connecticut,
NE USA
Windsor *148 D1* New South Wales,
SE Australia
Windsor *38 C5* Ontario, S Canada
Windsor *89 D7* S England, UK
Windward Islands *55 H4 island
group* E West Indies
Windward Islands *see* Barlavento,
Ilhas de
Windward Passage *54 D3 Sp.* Paso
de los Vientos. *Channel*
Cuba/Haiti
Winisk *38 C2 river* Ontario,
S Canada
Winisk *38 C2* Ontario, C Canada
Winnebago, Lake *40 B2 lake*
Wisconsin, N USA
Winnemucca *47 C5* Nevada,
W USA
Winnipeg *37 G5* Manitoba,
S Canada
Winnipeg, Lake *37 G5 lake*
Manitoba, C Canada
Winnipegosis, Lake *38 A3 lake*
Manitoba, C Canada
Winona *45 G3* Minnesota, N USA
Winschoten *86 E2* Groningen,
NE Netherlands
Winsen *94 B3* Niedersachsen,
N Germany
Winston Salem *43 E1* North
Carolina, SE USA
Winsum *86 D1* Groningen,
NE Netherlands
Winterswijk *86 E4* Gelderland,
E Netherlands
Winterthur *95 B7* Zürich,
NE Switzerland
Winton *148 C4* Queensland,
E Australia
Winton *151 A7* Southland, South
Island, NZ
Wisconsin *40 A2 off.* State of
Wisconsin; *also known as* The
Badger State. *State* N USA
Wisconsin Rapids *40 B2* Wisconsin,
N USA
Wisconsin River *40 B3 river*
Wisconsin, N USA
Wisła *98 C2 Eng.* Vistula, *Ger.*
Weichsel. *River* Śląskie, S Poland
Wismar *94 C2* Mecklenburg-
Vorpommern, N Germany

Wittenberge *94 C3* Brandenburg,
N Germany
Wittlich *95 A5* Rheinland-Pfalz,
SW Germany
Wittstock *94 C3* Brandenburg,
NE Germany
W.J. van Blommesteinmeer *59 G3
reservoir* E Suriname
Władysławowo *98 C2* Pomorskie,
N Poland
Włocławek *98 C3 Ger./Rus.*
Vlotslavsk. Kujawsko-pomorskie,
C Poland
Włodawa *98 E4 Rus.* Vlodava.
Lubelskie, E Poland
Wlotzkasbaken *78 B3* Erongo,
W Namibia
Wodonga *149 C7* Victoria,
SE Australia
Wodzisław Śląski *99 C5 Ger.*
Loslau. Śląskie, S Poland
Wōjjā *see* Wotje Atoll
Woking *89 D7* SE England, UK
Wolf, Isla *60 A4 var.* Wenmen
Island. *Island* W Ecuador
Wolfsberg *95 D7* Kärnten,
SE Austria
Wolfsburg *94 C3* Niedersachsen,
N Germany
Wolgast *94 D2* Mecklenburg-
Vorpommern, NE Germany
Wollaston Lake *37 F4*
Saskatchewan, C Canada
Wollongong *149 D6* New South
Wales, SE Australia
Wolvega *86 D2 Fris.* Wolvegea.
Friesland, N Netherlands
Wolverhampton *89 D6* C England,
UK
Wŏnsan *129 E3* SE North Korea
Woodburn *46 B3* Oregon, NW USA
Woodland *47 B5* California, W USA
Woodruff *40 B2* Wisconsin, N USA
Woods, Lake of the *38 A3 Fr.* Lac
des Bois. *Lake* Canada/USA
Woodville *150 D4* Manawatu-
Wanganui, North Island, NZ
Woodward *49 F1* Oklahoma, C USA
Worcester *89 D6 hist.* Wigorna
Ceaster. W England, UK
Worcester *41 G3* Massachusetts,
NE USA
Worcester *78 C5* Western Cape,
SW South Africa
Workington *89 C5* NW England,
UK
Worland *44 C3* Wyoming,
C USA
Worms *95 B5 anc.* Augusta
Vangionum, Borbetomagus,
Wormatia. Rheinland-Pfalz,
SW Germany
Worms *see* Vormsi
Worthington *45 F3* Minnesota,
N USA
Wotje Atoll *144 D1 var.* Wōjjā.
Atoll Ratak Chain, E Marshall
Islands
Woudrichem *86 C4* Noord-Brabant,
S Netherlands
Wrangel Island *see* Vrangelya,
Ostrov
Wrangel Plain *155 B2 undersea
feature* Arctic Ocean
Wrocław *98 C4 Eng./Ger.* Breslau.
Dolnośląskie, SW Poland
Września *98 C3* Wielkopolskie,
C Poland
Wuchang *see* Wuhan
Wuday 'ah *121 C6* Najrān, S Saudi
Arabia
Wuhai *127 E3* Nei Mongol Zizhiqu,
N China
Wuhan *128 C5 var.* Han-kou,
Han-k'ou, Hanyang, Wuchang,
Wu-han; *prev.* Hankow. Hubei,
C China
Wuhsi *see* Wuxi
Wuhsien *see* Suzhou
Wuhu *128 D5 var.* Wu-na-mu.
Anhui, E China
Wujlān *see* Ujelang Atoll
Wukari *75 G4* Taraba, E Nigeria

Wuliang Shan 128 A6 *mountain range* SW China
Wu-lu-k'o-mu-shi *see* Ürümqi
Wu-lu-mu-ch'i *see* Ürümqi
Wu-na-mu *see* Wuhu
Wuppertal 94 A4 *prev.* Barmen-Elberfeld. Nordrhein-Westfalen, W Germany
Würzburg 95 B5 Bayern, SW Germany
Wusih *see* Wuxi
Wuxi 128 D5 *var.* Wuhsi, Wu-hsi, Wusih. Jiangsu, E China
Wuyi Shan 125 E3 *mountain range* SE China
Wye 89 C6 *Wel. Gwy. River* England/Wales, UK
Wyndham 146 D3 Western Australia
Wyoming 44 B3 *off.* State of Wyoming; also known as The Equality State. *State* C USA
Wyoming 40 C3 Michigan, N USA
Wyszków 98 D3 *Ger.* Probstberg. Mazowieckie, C Poland

X

Xaafuun, Raas 72 E4 *var.* Ras Hafun. *Headland* NE Somalia
Xaçmaz 117 H2 *Rus.* Khachmas. N Azerbaijan
Xaignabouli 136 C4 *prev.* Muang Xaignabouri, *Fr.* Sayaboury. Xaignabouli, N Laos
Xai-Xai 79 E4 *prev.* João Belo, Vila de João *Bel.* Gaza, S Mozambique
Xalapa 51 F4 *var.* Jalapa, Jalapa Enríquez. Veracruz-Llave, SE Mexico
Xam Nua 136 D3 *var.* Sam Neua. Houaphan, N Laos
Xankändi 117 G3 *Rus.* Khankendi; *prev.* Stepanakert. SW Azerbaijan
Xánthi 104 C3 Anatolikí Makedonía kai Thráki, NE Greece
Xàtiva 93 F3 *var.* Jativa;*anc.* Setabis. País Valenciano, E Spain
Xauen *see* Chefchaouen
Xeres *see* Jeréz de la Frontera
Xiaguan *see* Dali
Xiamen 128 D6 *var.* Hsia-men; *prev.* Amoy. Fujian, SE China
Xi'an 128 C4 *var.* Changan, Sian, Signan, Siking, Singan, Xian. Shaanxi, C China
Xian *see* Xi'an
Xiangkhoang *see* Pèk
Xiangtan 128 C5 *var.* Hsiang-t'an, Siangtan. Hunan, S China
Xiao Hinggan Ling 128 D2 *Eng.* Lesser Khingan Range. *Mountain range* NE China
Xichang 128 B5 Sichuan, C China
Xieng Khouang *see* Pèk
Xieng Ngeun *see* Muong Xiang Ngeun
Xigaze *see* Xigazê
Xigazê 126 C5 *var.* Jih-k'a-tse, Shigatse, Xigaze. Xizang Zizhiqu, W China
Xi Jiang 124 D3 *var.* Hsi Chiang, *Eng.* West River. *River* S China
Xilinhot 127 F2 *var.* Silinhot. Nei Mongol Zizhiqu, N China
Xilokastro *see* Xylókastro
Xin *see* Xinjiang Uygur Zizhiqu
Xingkai Hu *see* Khanka, Lake
Xingu, Rio 63 E2 *river* C Brazil
Xingxingxia 126 D3 Xinjiang Uygur Zizhiqu, NW China
Xining 127 E4 *var.* Hsining, Hsi-ning, Sining. *Province capital* Qinghai, C China
Xinjiang *see* Xinjiang Uygur Zizhiqu
Xinjiang Uygur Zizhiqu 126 B3 *var.* Sinkiang, Sinkiang Uighur Autonomous Region, Xin, Xinjiang. Admin. region *autonomous region* NW China
Xinpu *see* Lianyungang

Xinxiang 128 C4 Henan, C China
Xinyang 128 C5 *var.* Hsin-yang, Sinyang. Henan, C China
Xinzo de Limia 92 C2 Galicia, NW Spain
Xiqing Shan 124 D2 *mountain range* C China
Xixón *see* Gijón
Xizang *see* Xizang Zizhiqu
Xizang Gaoyuan *see* Qingzang Gaoyuan
Xizang Zizhiqu 126 B4 *var.* Thibet, Tibetan Autonomous Region, Xizang, *Eng.* Tibet. Admin. region *autonomous region* W China
Xolotlán *see* Managua, Lago de
Xuddur 73 D5 *var.* Hudur, *It.* Oddur. Bakool, SW Somalia
Xuwen 128 C7 Guangdong, S China
Xuzhou 128 D4 *var.* Hsu-chou, Suchow, Tongshan; *prev.* T'ung-shan. Jiangsu, E China
Xylókastro 105 B5 *var.* Xilokastro. Pelopónnisos, S Greece

Y

Ya'an 128 B5 *var.* Yaan. Sichuan, C China
Yabēlo 73 C5 C Ethiopia
Yablis 53 E2 Región Autónoma Atlántico Norte, NE Nicaragua
Yablonovyy Khrebet 115 F4 *mountain range* S Russian Federation
Yabrai Shan 127 E3 *mountain range* NE China
Yafran 71 F2 NW Libya
Yaghan Basin 67 B7 *undersea feature* SE Pacific Ocean
Yahotyn 109 E2 *Rus.* Yagotin. Kyyivs'ka Oblast', N Ukraine
Yahualica 50 D4 Jalisco, SW Mexico
Yakima 46 B2 Washington, NW USA
Yakima River 46 B2 *river* Washington, NW USA
Yakoruda 104 C3 Blagoevgrad, SW Bulgaria
Yaku-shima 131 B8 *island* Nansei-shotō, SW Japan
Yakutat 36 D4 Alaska, USA
Yakutsk 115 F3 Respublika Sakha (Yakutiya), NE Russian Federation
Yala 137 C7 Yala, SW Thailand
Yalizava 107 D6 *Rus.* Yelizovo. Mahilyowskaya Voblasts', E Belarus
Yalong Jiang 128 A5 *river* C China
Yalova 116 B3 Yalova, NW Turkey
Yalpuh, Ozero 108 D4 *Rus.* Ozero Yalpug. *Lake* SW Ukraine
Yalta 109 F5 Respublika Krym, S Ukraine
Yalu 125 E2 *Chin.* Yalu Jiang, *Jap.* Oryokko, *Kor.* Amnok-kang. *River* China/North Korea
Yamaguchi 131 B7 *var.* Yamaguti. Yamaguchi, Honshū, SW Japan
Yamaguti *see* Yamaguchi
Yamal, Poluostrov 114 D2 *peninsula* N Russian Federation
Yambio 73 B5 *var.* Yambiyo. Western Equatoria, S Sudan
Yambiyo *see* Yambio
Yambol 104 D2 *Turk.* Yanboli. Yambol, E Bulgaria
Yamdena, Pulau 139 G5 *prev.* Jamdena. *Island* Kepulauan Tanimbar, E Indonesia
Yam HaMelah *see* Dead Sea
Yam Kinneret *see* Tiberias, Lake
Yamoussoukro 74 D5 *country capital* (Côte d'Ivoire) C Côte d'Ivoire
Yamuna 134 D3 *prev.* Jumna. *River* N India
Yana 115 F2 *river* NE Russian Federation
Yanbu 'al Baḥr 121 A5 Al Madīnah, W Saudi Arabia
Yangambi 77 D5 Orientale, N Dem. Rep. Congo (Zaire)

Yangchow *see* Yangzhou
Yangiyŭl 123 E2 *Rus.* Yangiyul'. Toshkent Wiloyati, E Uzbekistan
Yangon 136 B4 *Eng.* Rangoon. *Country capital* (Myanmar) Yangon, S Myanmar
Yangtze *see* Chang Jiang
Yangtze Kiang *see* Chang Jiang
Yangzhou 128 D5 *var.* Yangchow. Jiangsu, E China
Yankton 45 E3 South Dakota, N USA
Yannina *see* Ioánnina
Yanskiy Zaliv 113 F2 *bay* N Russian Federation
Yantai 128 D4 *var.* Yan-t'ai; *prev.* Chefoo, Chih-fu. Shandong, E China
Yan-t'ai *see* Yantai
Yaoundé 77 B5 *var.* Yaunde. *Country capital* (Cameroon) Centre, S Cameroon
Yap 144 A1 *island* Caroline Islands, W Micronesia
Yapanskoye More *see* Japan, Sea of
Yapen, Pulau 139 G4 *prev.* Japen. *Island* E Indonesia
Yap Trench 142 B2 *var.* Yap Trough. *Undersea feature* SE Philippine Sea
Yap Trough *see* Yap Trench
Yapurá *see* Caquetá, Río
Yapurá *see* Japurá, Rio
Yaqui, Río 50 C2 *river* NW Mexico
Yaransk 111 C5 Kirovskaya Oblast', NW Russian Federation
Yarega 110 D4 Respublika Komi, NW Russian Federation
Yarkant *see* Shache
Yarlung Zangbo Jiang *see* Brahmaputra
Yarmouth *see* Great Yarmouth
Yarmouth 39 F5 Nova Scotia, SE Canada
Yaroslavl' 110 B4 Yaroslavskaya Oblast', W Russian Federation
Yarumal 58 B2 Antioquia, NW Colombia
Yasyel'da 107 B7 *river* SW Belarus
Yatsushiro 131 A7 *var.* Yatusiro. Kumamoto, Kyūshū, SW Japan
Yatusiro *see* Yatsushiro
Yaunde *see* Yaoundé
Yavarí *see* Javari, Rio
Yaviza 53 H5 Darién, SE Panama
Yavoriv 108 B2 *Pol.* Jaworów, *Rus.* Yavorov. L'vivs'ka Oblast', NW Ukraine
Yazd 120 D3 *var.* Yezd. Yazd, C Iran
Yazoo City 42 B2 Mississippi, S USA
Yding Skovhoj 85 A7 *hill* C Denmark
Ýdra 105 C6 *var.* Ídhra. *Island* S Greece
Ye 137 B5 Mon State, S Myanmar
Yecheng 126 A3 *var.* Kargilik. Xinjiang Uygur Zizhiqu, NW China
Yefremov 111 B5 Tul'skaya Oblast', W Russian Federation
Yekaterinburg 114 C3 *prev.* Sverdlovsk. Sverdlovskaya Oblast', C Russian Federation
Yelets 111 B5 Lipetskaya Oblast', W Russian Federation
Yell 88 D1 *island* NE Scotland, UK
Yellowknife 37 E4 *territory capital* Northwest Territories, W Canada
Yellow River *see* Huang He
Yellow Sea 128 D4 *Chin.* Huang Hai, *Kor.* Hwang-Hae. *Sea* E Asia
Yellowstone River 44 C2 *river* Montana/Wyoming, NW USA
Yel'sk 107 C7 *Rus.* Yel'sk. Homyel'skaya Voblasts', SE Belarus
Yelwa 75 F4 Kebbi, W Nigeria
Yemen 121 C7 *Ar.* Al Jumhūrīyah al Yamanīyah, Al Yaman. *Country* SW Asia

Yemva 110 D4 *prev.* Zheleznodorozhnyy. Respublika Komi, NW Russian Federation
Yenakiyeve 109 G3 *Rus.* Yenakiyevo; *prev.* Ordzhonikidze, Rykovo. Donets'ka Oblast', E Ukraine
Yenangyaung 136 A3 Magwe, W Myanmar
Yendi 75 E4 NE Ghana
Yengisar 126 A3 Xinjiang Uygur Zizhiqu, NW China
Yenierenköy *see* Agialoúsa
Yenisey 114 D3 *river* Mongolia/Russian Federation
Yenping *see* Nanping
Yeovil 89 D7 SW England, UK
Yeppoon 148 D4 Queensland, E Australia
Yerevan 117 F3 *var.* Erevan, *Eng.* Erivan. *Country capital* (Armenia) C Armenia
Yeriho *see* Jericho
Yerushalayim *see* Jerusalem
Yeu, Île d' 90 A4 *island* NW France
Yevlax 117 G2 *Rus.* Yevlakh. C Azerbaijan
Yevpatoriya 109 F5 Respublika Krym, S Ukraine
Yeya 109 H4 *river* SW Russian Federation
Yezd *see* Yazd
Yezyaryshcha 107 E5 *Rus.* Yezerishche. Vitsyebskaya Voblasts', NE Belarus
Yiannitsá *see* Giannitsá
Yichang 128 C5 Hubei, C China
Yıldızeli 116 D3 Sivas, N Turkey
Yinchuan 128 B4 *var.* Yinch'uan, Yin-ch'uan, Yinchwan. Ningxia, N China
Yinchwan *see* Yinchuan
Yin-hsien *see* Ningbo
Yining 126 B2 *var.* I-ning, *Uigh.* Gulja, Kuldja. Xinjiang Uygur Zizhiqu, NW China
Yíthion *see* Gýtheio
Yogyakarta 138 C5 *prev.* Djokjakarta, Jogjakarta, Jokyakarta. Jawa, C Indonesia
Yokohama 131 D5 Aomori, Honshū, C Japan
Yokohama 130 A2 Kanagawa, Honshū, S Japan
Yokote 130 D4 Akita, Honshū, C Japan
Yola 75 H4 Adamawa, E Nigeria
Yonago 131 B6 Tottori, Honshū, SW Japan
Yong'an 128 D6 *var.* Yongan. Fujian, SE China
Yonkers 41 F3 New York, NE USA
Yonne 90 C4 *river* C France
Yopal 58 C3 *var.* El Yopal. Casanare, C Colombia
York 89 D5 *anc.* Eboracum, Eburacum. N England, UK
York 45 E4 Nebraska, C USA
York, Cape 148 C1 *headland* Queensland, NE Australia

Yemen 121

Official name Republic of Yemen
Formation 1990
Capital Sana'a
Population 18 million / 89 people per sq mile (34 people per sq km)
Total area 203,849 sq miles (527,970 sq km)
Languages Arabic
Religions Shi'a Muslim 55%, Sunni Muslim 42%, Christian, Hindu and Jewish 3%
Ethnic mix Arab 95%, Afro-Arab 3%, Indian, Somali and European 2%
Government Multiparty republic
Currency Rial and Dinar
Literacy rate 42.5%
Calorie consumption 2,203 kilocalories

Yorkton 37 F5 Saskatchewan, S Canada
Yoro 52 C2 Yoro, C Honduras
Yoshkar-Ola 111 C5 Respublika Mariy El, W Russian Federation
Youngstown 40 D4 Ohio, N USA
Youth, Isle of see Juventud, Isla de la
Yreka 46 B4 California, W USA
Yssel see IJssel
Ysyk-Köl see Issyk-Kul', Ozero
Yu see Henan
Yuan see Red River
Yuan Jiang see Red River
Yuba City 47 B5 California, W USA
Yucatan Channel 51 H3 Sp. Canal de Yucatán. Channel Cuba/Mexico
Yucatan Peninsula 35 C7 peninsula Guatemala/Mexico
Yuci 128 C4 Shanxi, C China
Yue see Guangdong
Yueyang 128 C5 Hunan, S China
Yugoslavia 100 D4 SCr. Jugoslavija, Savezna Republika Jugoslavija. Country SE Europe

Yugoslavia 100

Official name Federal Republic of Yugoslavia
Formation 1992
Capital Belgrade
Population 10.6 million / 269 people per sq mile (104 people per sq km)
Total area 39,449 sq miles (102,173 sq km)
Languages Serbian, Croatian, Albanian
Religions Eastern Orthodox 65%, Muslim 19%, other 16%
Ethnic mix Serb 62%, Albanian 17%, Montenegrin 5%, other 16%
Government Multiparty republic
Currency Yugoslav dinar = 100 para
Literacy rate 93.3%
Calorie consumption not available

Yukhavichy 107 D5 Rus. Yukhovichi. Vitsyebskaya Voblasts', N Belarus
Yukon 36 C2 river Canada/USA
Yukon see Yukon Territory
Yukon Territory 36 D3 var. Yukon, Fr. Territoire du Yukon. Admin. region territory NW Canada
Yulin 128 C6 Guangxi Zhuangzu Zizhiqu, S China
Yuma 48 A2 Arizona, SW USA
Yumen 128 A3 var. Laojunmiao, Yümen. Gansu, N China
Yun see Yunnan
Yungki see Jilin
Yung-ning see Nanning
Yunjinghong see Jinghong
Yunki see Jilin
Yunnan 128 A6 var. Yun, Yunnan Sheng, Yünnan, Yun-nan. Admin. region province SW China
Yunnan see Kunming
Yunnan Sheng see Yunnan
Yuruá, Río see Juruá, Rio
Yushu 126 D4 Qinghai, C China
Yuty 64 D3 Caazapá, S Paraguay
Yuzhno-Sakhalinsk 115 H4 Jap. Toyohara; prev. Vladimirovka. Ostrov Sakhalin, Sakhalinskaya Oblast', SE Russian Federation
Yuzhou see Chongqing
Yylanly see Il'yaly

Z

Zaanstad 86 C3 prev. Zaandam. Noord-Holland, C Netherlands
Zabaykal'sk 115 Ie var. Chitinskaya Oblast', S Russian Federation
Zabern see Saverne
Zabīd 121 B7 W Yemen

Ząbkowice see Ząbkowice Śląskie
Ząbkowice Śląskie 98 B4 var. Ząbkowice, Ger. Frankenstein, Frankenstein in Schlesien. Wałbrzych, SW Poland
Zábřeh 99 C5 Ger. Hohenstadt. Olomoucký Kraj, E Czech Republic
Zacapa 52 B2 Zacapa, E Guatemala
Zacatecas 50 D3 Zacatecas, C Mexico
Zacatepec 51 E4 Morelos, S Mexico
Zacháro 105 B6 var. Zaharo, Zakháro. Dytikí Ellás, S Greece
Zadar 100 A3 It. Zara; anc. Iader. Zadar, SW Croatia
Zadetkyi Kyun 137 B6 var. St. Matthew's Island. Island Mergui Archipelago, S Myanmar
Zafra 92 C4 Extremadura, W Spain
Żagań 98 B4 var. Zagań, Żegań; Ger. Sagan. Lubuskie, W Poland
Zagazig 72 B1 var. Az Zaqāzīq. N Egypt
Zágráb see Zagreb
Zagreb 100 B2 Ger. Agram, Hung. Zágráb. Country capital (Croatia) Zagreb, N Croatia
Zāgros, Kūhhā-ye 120 C3 Eng. Zagros Mountains. Mountain range W Iran
Zāgros Mountains see Zāgros, Kūhhā-ye
Zaharo see Zacháro
Zāhedān 120 E4 var. Zahidan; prev. Duzdab. Sīstān va Balūchestān, SE Iran
Zahidan see Zāhedān
Zahlah see Zahlé
Zahlé 118 B4 var. Zahlah. C Lebanon
Záhony 99 E6 Szabolcs-Szatmár-Bereg, NE Hungary
Zaire see Congo
Zaječar 100 E4 Serbia, E Yugoslavia
Zakháro see Zacháro
Zākhō 120 B2 var. Zākhū. N Iraq
Zākhū see Zākhō
Zákinthos see Zákynthos
Zakopane 99 D5 Małopolskie, S Poland
Zakota Pomorskiea see Danzig, Gulf of
Zákynthos 105 A6 var. Zákinthos, It. Zante. Island Iónioi Nísoi, Greece, C Mediterranean Sea
Zalaegerszeg 99 B7 Zala, W Hungary
Zalău 108 B3 Ger. Waltenberg, Hung. Zilah; prev. Ger. Zillenmarkt. Sălaj, NW Romania
Zalim 121 B5 Makkah, W Saudi Arabia
Zambesi see Zambezi
Zambeze see Zambezi
Zambezi 78 D2 var. Zambesi, Port. Zambeze. River S Africa
Zambezi 78 C2 North Western, W Zambia
Zambia 78 C2 off. Republic of Zambia; prev. Northern Rhodesia. Country S Africa

Zambia 78

Official name Republic of Zambia
Formation 1964
Capital Lusaka
Population 9.2 million / 32 people per sq mile (12 people per sq km)
Total area 285,992 sq miles (740,720 sq km)
Languages English, Bemba, Nyanja, Tonga, Kaonde, Lunda, Luvale, Lozi
Religions Christian 63%, Traditional beliefs 36%, other 1%
Ethnic mix Bemba 36%, Maravi 18%, Tonga 15%, other 31%
Government Multiparty republic
Currency Zambian kwacha = 100 ngwee
Literacy rate 75%
Calorie consumption 1,931 kilocalories

Zamboanga 139 E3 off. Zamboanga City. Mindanao, S Philippines
Zambrów 98 E3 Podlaskie, E Poland
Zamora 92 D2 Castilla-León, NW Spain
Zamora de Hidalgo 50 D4 Michoacán de Ocampo, SW Mexico
Zamość 98 E4 Rus. Zamoste. Lubelskie, E Poland
Zancle see Messina
Zanda 126 A4 Xizang Zizhiqu, W China
Zanesville 40 D4 Ohio, N USA
Zanjān 120 C2 var. Zenjan, Zinjan. Zanjān, NW Iran
Zante see Zákynthos
Zanthus 147 C6 Western Australia
Zanzibar 73 C7 Swa. Unguja. Island E Tanzania
Zanzibar 73 D7 Zanzibar, E Tanzania
Zaozhuang 128 D4 Shandong, E China
Zapadna Morava 100 D4 Ger. Westliche Morava. River C Yugoslavia
Zapadnaya Dvina 110 A4 Tverskaya Oblast', W Russian Federation
Zapadno-Sibirskaya Ravnina 114 C3 Eng. West Siberian Plain. Plain C Russian Federation
Zapadnyy Sayan 114 D4 Eng. Western Sayans. Mountain range S Russian Federation
Zapala 65 B5 Neuquén, W Argentina
Zapiola Ridge 67 B6 undersea feature SW Atlantic Ocean
Zapolyarnyy 110 C2 Murmanskaya Oblast', NW Russian Federation
Zaporizhzhya 109 F3 Rus. Zaporozh'ye; prev. Aleksandrovsk. Zaporiz'ka Oblast', SE Ukraine
Zapotiltic 50 D4 Jalisco, SW Mexico
Zaqatala 117 G2 Rus. Zakataly. NW Azerbaijan
Zara 116 D3 Sivas, C Turkey
Zarafshon 122 D2 Rus. Zarafshan. Nawoiy Wiloyati, N Uzbekistan
Zaragoza 93 F2 Eng. Saragossa; anc. Caesaraugusta, Salduba. Aragón, NE Spain
Zarand 120 D3 Kermān, C Iran
Zaranj 122 D5 Nīmrūz, SW Afghanistan
Zarasai 106 C4 Zarasai, E Lithuania
Zárate 64 D4 prev. General José F.Uriburu. Buenos Aires, E Argentina
Zarautz 93 E1 var. Zarauz. País Vasco, N Spain
Zarauz see Zarautz
Zaraza 59 E2 Guárico, N Venezuela
Zarghūn Shahr 123 E4 var. Katawaz. Paktīkā, SE Afghanistan
Zaria 75 G4 Kaduna, C Nigeria
Zarós 105 D8 Kríti, Greece, E Mediterranean Sea
Zarqa see Az Zarqā'
Żary 98 B4 Ger. Sorau, Sorau in der Niederlausitz. Lubelskie, W Poland
Zaunguzskiye Garagumy 122 C2 Turkm. Üngüz Angyrsyndaky Garagum. Desert N Turkmenistan
Zavet 104 D1 Razgrad, N Bulgaria
Zavidovići 100 C3 Federacija Bosna I Hercegovina, N Bosnia and Herzegovina
Zawia see Az Zāwiyah
Zawiercie 98 D4 Rus. Zavertse. Śląskie, S Poland
Zawilah 71 F3 var. Zuwaylah, It. Zueila. C Libya
Zaysan, Ozero 114 D5 Kaz. Zaysan Köl. Lake E Kazakhstan

Zbarazh 108 C2 Ternopil's'ka Oblast', W Ukraine
Zduńska Wola 98 C4 Łódzkie, C Poland
Zeebrugge 87 A5 West-Vlaanderen, NW Belgium
Zeewolde 86 D3 Flevoland, C Netherlands
Żegań see Żagań
Zefat 119 B5 var. Safed, Tsefat, Ar. Safad. Northern, N Israel
Zeist 86 C4 Utrecht, C Netherlands
Zele 87 B5 Oost-Vlaanderen, NW Belgium
Zelenoborskiy 110 B2 Murmanskaya Oblast', NW Russian Federation
Zelenograd 111 B5 Moskovskaya Oblast', W Russian Federation
Zelenogradsk 106 A4 Ger. Cranz, Kranz. Kaliningradskaya Oblast', W Russian Federation
Zelle see Celle
Zel'va 107 B6 Pol. Zelwa. Hrodzyenskaya Voblasts', W Belarus
Zelzate 87 B5 var. Selzaete. Oost-Vlaanderen, NW Belgium
Žemaičių Aukštumas 106 B4 physical region W Lithuania
Zemst 87 C5 Vlaams Brabant, C Belgium
Zemun 100 D3 Serbia, N Yugoslavia
Zenica 100 C4 Federacija Bosna I Herzegovina, C Bosnia and Herzegovina
Zenjan see Zanjān
Zeravshan 123 E3 Taj./Uzb. Zarafshon. River Tajikistan/Uzbekistan
Zevenaar 86 D4 Gelderland, SE Netherlands
Zevenbergen 86 C4 Noord-Brabant, S Netherlands
Zeya 113 F3 river SE Russian Federation
Zgierz 98 C4 Ger. Neuhof, Rus. Zgerzh. Łódź, C Poland
Zgorzelec 98 B4 Ger. Görlitz. Dolnośląskie, SW Poland
Zhabinka 107 A6 Pol. Żabinka, Rus. Zhabinka. Brestskaya Voblasts', SW Belarus
Zhambyl see Taraz
Zhanaozen 114 A4 Kaz. Zhangaözen; prev. Novyy Uzen'. Mangistau, W Kazakhstan
Zhangaözen see Zhanaozen
Zhangaqazaly see Ayteke Bi
Zhang-chia-k'ou see Zhangjiakou
Zhangdian see Zibo
Zhangjiakou 128 C3 var. Changkiakow, Zhang-chia-k'ou, Eng. Kalgan; prev. Wanchuan. Hebei, E China
Zhangzhou 128 D6 Fujian, SE China
Zhanjiang 128 C7 var. Chanchiang, Chan-chiang, Cant. Tsamkong, Fr. Fort-Bayard. Guangdong, S China
Zhaoqing 128 C6 Guangdong, S China
Zhe see Zhejiang
Zhejiang 128 D5 var. Che-chiang, Chekiang, Zhe, Zhejiang Sheng. Admin. region province SE China
Zhejiang Sheng see Zhejiang
Zhelezndoroznyy 106 A4 Ger. Gerdauen. Kaliningradskaya Oblast', W Russian Federation
Zheleznogorsk 111 A5 Kurskaya Oblast', W Russian Federation
Zhengzhou 128 C4 var. Ch'eng-chou, Chengchow; prev. Chenghsien. Henan, C China
Zhezkazgan 114 C4 Kaz. Zhezqazghan; prev. Dzhezkazgan. Karaganda, C Kazakhstan
Zhlobin 107 D7 Homyel'skaya Voblasts', SE Belarus

Zhmerynka *108 D2 Rus.*
Zhmerinka. Vinnyts'ka Oblast',
C Ukraine
Zhodzina *107 D6 Rus.* Zhodino.
Minskaya Voblasts', C Belarus
Zhovkva *108 B2 Pol.* Żółkiew, *Rus.*
Zholkev, Zholkva; *prev.* Nesterov.
L'vivs'ka Oblast', NW Ukraine
Zhovti Vody *109 F3 Rus.* Zhëltyye
Vody. Dnipropetrovs'ka Oblast',
E Ukraine
Zhovtneve *109 E4 Rus.*
Zhovtnevoye. Mykolayivs'ka
Oblast', S Ukraine
Zhydachiv *108 B2 Pol.* Żydaczów,
Rus. Zhidachov. L'vivs'ka Oblast',
NW Ukraine
Zhytkavichy *107 C7 Rus.*
Zhitkovichi. Homyel'skaya
Voblasts', SE Belarus
Zhytomyr *108 D2 Rus.* Zhitomir.
Zhytomyrs'ka Oblast',
NW Ukraine
Zibo *128 D4 var.* Zhangdian.
Shandong, E China
Zielona Góra *98 B4 Ger.* Grünberg,
Grünberg in Schlesien,
Grüneberg. Lubuskie, W Poland
Zierikzee *86 B4* Zeeland,
SW Netherlands
Zigong *128 B5 var.* Tzekung.
Sichuan, C China
Ziguinchor *74 B3* SW Senegal
Žilina *99 C5 Ger.* Sillein, *Hung.*
Zsolna. Žilinský Kraj, N Slovakia
Zimbabwe *78 D3 prev.* Rhodesia.
Country S Africa

Zimbabwe 78

Official name Republic of
Zimbabwe
Formation 1980
Capital Harare
Population 11.7 million /
78 people per sq mile
(30 people per sq km)
Total area 149,293 sq miles
(386,670 sq km)
Languages English, Shona,
Ndebele
Religions Syncretic (Christian
and traditional beliefs) 50%,
Christian 25%, Traditional beliefs
24%, other 1%
Ethnic mix Shona 71%, Ndebele
16%, other African 11%, Asian 1%,
White 1%
Government Multiparty republic
Currency Zimbabwe dollar
= 100 cents
Literacy rate 91%
Calorie consumption 1,985
kilocalories

Zimnicea *108 C5* Teleorman,
S Romania
Zimovniki *111 B7* Rostovskaya
Oblast', SW Russian Federation
Zinder *75 G3* Zinder, S Niger
Zinjan *see* Zanjän
Zipaquirá *58 B3* Cundinamarca,
C Colombia
Zittau *94 D4* Sachsen, E
Germany
Zlatni Pyasŭtsi *104 E2* Dobrich,
NE Bulgaria
Zlín *99 C5 prev.* Gottwaldov.
Zlínský Kraj, E Czech
Republic
Złotów *98 C3* Wielkopolskie,
C Poland
Znam"yanka *109 F3 Rus.*
Znamenka. Kirovohrads'ka
Oblast', C Ukraine
Żnin *98 C3* Kujawski-pomorskie,
C Poland

Znojmo *99 B5 Ger.* Znaim.
Brněnský Kraj, SE Czech Republic
Zoetermeer *86 C4* Zuid-Holland,
W Netherlands
Zolochiv *108 C2 Pol.* Złoczów, *Rus.*
Zolochev. L'vivs'ka Oblast',
W Ukraine
Zolochiv *109 G2 Rus.* Zolochev.
Kharkivs'ka Oblast', E Ukraine
Zolote *109 H3 Rus.* Zolotoye.
Luhans'ka Oblast', E Ukraine
Zolotonosha *109 E2* Cherkas'ka
Oblast', C Ukraine
Zomba *79 E2* Southern, S Malawi
Zongo *77 C5* Equateur, N Dem.
Rep. Congo (Zaire)
Zonguldak *116 C2* Zonguldak,
NW Turkey
Zonhoven *87 D6* Limburg,
NE Belgium
Żory *99 C5 var.* Zory, *Ger.* Sohrau.
Śląskie, S Poland
Zouar *76 C2* Borkou-Ennedi-Tibesti,
N Chad
Zouérat *74 C2 var.* Zouérate,
Zouîrât. Tiris Zemmour,
N Mauritania
Zouérate *see* Zouérat
Zouîrât *see* Zouérat
Zrenjanin *100 D3 prev.* Petrovgrad,
Veliki Bečkerek, *Ger.*
Grossbetschkerek, *Hung.*
Nagybecskerek. Serbia,
N Yugoslavia
Zubov Seamount *67 D5 undersea*
feature E Atlantic Ocean
Zueila *see* Zawïlah
Zug *95 B7 Fr.* Zoug. Zug,
C Switzerland
Zugspitze *95 C7 mountain*
S Germany
Zuid-Beveland *87 B5 var.* South
Beveland. *Island* SW Netherlands
Zuidhorn *86 E1* Groningen,
NE Netherlands
Zuidlaren *86 E2* Drenthe,
NE Netherlands
Zula *72 C4* E Eritrea
Züllichau *see* Sulechów
Zundert *87 C5* Noord-Brabant,
S Netherlands
Zunyi *128 B5* Guizhou, S China
Županja *100 C3 Hung.* Zsupanya.
Vukovar-Srijem, E Croatia
Zürich *95 B7 Eng./Fr.* Zurich, *It.*
Zurigo. Zürich, N Switzerland
Zürichsee *95 B7 Eng.* Lake Zurich.
Lake NE Switzerland
Zutphen *86 D3* Gelderland,
E Netherlands
Zuwārah *71 F2* NW Libya
Zuwaylah *see* Zawïlah
Zuyevka *111 D5* Kirovskaya
Oblast', NW Russian Federation
Zvenyhorodka *109 E2 Rus.*
Zvenigorodka. Cherkas'ka
Oblast', C Ukraine
Zvishavane *78 D3 prev.* Shabani.
Matabeleland South, S Zimbabwe
Zvolen *99 C6 Ger.* Altsohl, *Hung.*
Zólyom. Banskobystricky Kraj,
C Slovakia
Zvornik *100 C4* E Bosnia and
Herzegovina
Zwedru *74 D5 var.* Tchien. E Liberia
Zwettl *95 E6* Wien, NE Austria
Zwevegem *87 A6* West-Vlaanderen,
W Belgium
Zwickau *95 C5* Sachsen, E Germany
Zwolle *86 D3* Overijssel,
E Netherlands
Zyôetsu *see* Jōetsu
Żyardów *98 D3* Mazowieckie, C
Poland
Zyryanovsk *114 D5* Vostochnyy
Kazakhstan, E Kazakhstan

KEY TO MAP PAGES

NORTH & WEST ASIA 112-113

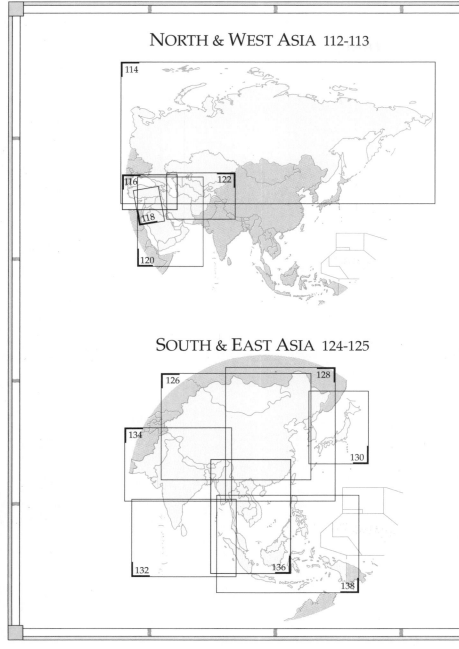

SOUTH & EAST ASIA 124-125